THE AMERICAN IRISH REVIVAL
A Decade of *The Recorder* — 1974-1983

Edited By

Kevin M. Cahill, M.D.

ASSOCIATED FACULTY PRESS, INC.
Port Washington, N.Y. • New York City • London

Manufactured in the United States of America

Published by
Associated Faculty Press
Port Washington, New York

Library of Congress Cataloging in Publication Data

Main entry under title:

The American Irish revival.

(National university publications)
Includes index.
1. Irish Americans—Addresses, essays, lectures.
2. Ireland—Addresses, essays, lectures. 3. Irish
American—Literary collections. 4. Ireland—Literary
collections. I. Cahill, Kevin M. II. Recorder (New
York, N.Y.) III. Series.
E184.I6A64 1984   941.50824   84-2899
ISBN 0-8046-9359-5

In Memory of

TERENCE CARDINAL COOKE

My dear friend, a wise and saintly leader,
who loved America and Ireland
with every fiber of his great heart.

CONTENTS

Section 2 — Historical

Section 3 — Politics

Section 4 — Personal

FOREWORD

Even an ancient Celtic sage, skilled in creating history from myths and in embroidering meager facts with pleasing marginalia, would have found it difficult to produce a narrative of the current events and activities of The American Irish Historical Society fifteen years ago. The rich traditions and the public and literary contributions of the Founders had become vague memories and dusty archives. The Society had an aging—and declining—membership, an ominously barren financial statement, and a home near collapse. Activities were non-existent and its once admired annual publication, *The Recorder,* had deteriorated to a series of obituaries, banal book reviews and an interminable flow of meaningless lists of Irish names associated with every conceivable discipline.

Today the Society is once again recognized as the leading organization linking America and Ireland. Our home has been refurbished (with particular thanks to James G. Kennedy and Joseph T. Sullivan), and now offers a gracious setting for readings, concerts, academic meetings, and general discussions of Irish issues including the seeming endless tragedy in the North of Ireland.

The Recorders of the past decade are a good measure of the remarkable revival of the Society. They have become a primary vehicle in fashioning an American-Irish conscience for our time. I hope that the reader of this collected volume will appreciate—and enjoy—the diverse talents of a new generation of writers maintaining our ethnic love affair with the power, meaning and music of words. In creative essays, original poems, scholarly articles and personal reflections, my fellow authors and I offer an introduction to the history—present and past— of the American Irish dream.

This collection will always fill me with joy, recalling the pleasure of seducing early contributors to participate in the Society's rejuvenation, of editing the prose of politicians and prelates, artists and academicians, of watching *The Recorder* grow from a forgetable throwaway to a collector's item distributed to several thousand libraries per year.

I have separated this collection into four sections and have tried to construct an internal logic that will offer the reader a sense of our rich, if sometimes chaotic, heritage. There is, inevitably, a range of quality in any anthology; part of that fault lies in this book with the Editor whose own evolving definition of the American Irish is reflected in these pages.

I am grateful to Tom Flanagan for his thoughtful Introduction, to Ken Brown of Associated Faculty Press for his interest and encouragement, to my dear friends, Louis LeBrocquy for his memorable cover design, and Bill Hanlon for his subtle humor, generous help and wise judgment during a decade of helping me edit many of these manuscripts. Finally, as always, I gratefully acknowledge my wife who made the whole effort both possible and pleasant.

Kevin M. Cahill, M.D.

INTRODUCTION

In the Nineteen Fifties, I was an instructor of English at Columbia College. Three mornings a week, I would walk west from my Third Avenue walk-up, and wait on Fifth for a bus which would take me to Morningside Heights. Across the busy avenue rose the vast, turn-of-the-century Beaux-Arts facade of the Metropolitan Museum. And behind me stood a building worthy to confront it, a five-storied mansion of about the same period, dark, warm brick and weathered stone, windows gracefully bowed. Behind those tall, balconied windows might once have moved Henry James's gentlemen, tentative and discriminating, and the impulsive, high-strung ladies of his friend Edith Wharton. A brass plaque, unostentatious, scrupulously polished, announced it as "The American Irish Historical Society."

A complex reluctance held me back in those years from walking up the steps to press the bell. What lay visible within was the dark, forbidding coolness of a stern and mysterious foyer. But there was more to my reluctance than this. "American Irish" was a term which I associated not with Fifth Avenue but with my local Third, in those days miles of brick tenements, deep-shadowed even in noonday by the pillars and overhead tracks of the Elevated. American Irish lived in the tenements, and many of them worked as motormen on the Elevated—perhaps, thanks to Mike Quill, in disproportionate numbers. Every fourth front, it almost seemed, was a bar called "Clancy's" or "Sheerin's" or "The Emerald" or "The Shamrock." On hot summer nights, in those days before air-conditioning, the door of "The Shamrock" stood open upon a dark coolness which was welcoming rather than forbidding.

On those Fifth Avenue mornings, I was poised between two worlds. One was the American Irish world which I had walked away from, perhaps in more ways than one, the world of "Clancy's" and the Elevated. The other was the world of Morningside Heights, brick walls, small lawns hedged with flowers, well-proportioned brick lecture halls, a turn-of-the-century campus designed by the same architects who designed the wings of the Metropolitan Museum. McKim, Mead and White gave to New York City its distinguishing appearance in the Age of Theodore Roosevelt, half-patrician and half-opulent. Their bricks and mansard roofs gave visual shape to a Columbia student song of the period, which asked, "Who owns New York?" to which the answer was, "We own New York." And across the Columbia Library, of more recent vintage, ran a long freize of names—Homer, Sophocles, Virgil, Dante—as though the very culture of the world was included in the deed of ownership. By painful contrast, the blocks of tenements along Third seemed to be populated by a people—my own people—who had left behind them their culture, even as they had left their own farms.

Had I possessed in those days the necessary subtlety of wit, I might have situated myself with respect to this architectual geography by thinking about bricks. My family had been brickmakers up the Hudson, and had sent downriver on their barges some of the blocks by which turn-of-the-century New York was built. But in those days, my railroad flat on Irish Third Avenue seemed a deplorable accident, a consequence of the pittances which Ivy League colleges then paid to their instructors. In due course, no doubt, I would be moving to my spiritual home on Morningside Heights, perhaps to Riverside Drive, with a window fronting on the barge-heavy Hudson.

All this, I suspect, lurked beneath the complex musing with which I surveyed that elegant Theodore Roosevelt-era mansion on Fifth Avenue, with its air of Henry James novels and its plaque, "The American Irish Historical Society." I should perhaps have recalled that Henry James, like myself, was the grandson of an immigrant from Northern Ireland. And it would then have surprised me to learn that a member of the founding Executive Committee, in 1897, was the Professor of English Literature at Columbia. And that the first name on the list of that committee is that of Theodore Roosevelt himself, in whose veins (as they would then have said) the blood of the Barnwells of Dublin was mixed with that of his Dutch and English forebears.

Thirty years have passed since my Fifth Avenue mornings, and one of my great present prides is my own membership on the Executive Council of the Society. I have frequent occasion now to climb those steps and ring the bell. Occasionally for meetings of the committee, but far more often, like members of the interested public, in late afternoon or evening, for the lectures, the seminars, the readings of poetry and fiction and drama, the seminars and scholarly presentations which are the heart of the Society's enterprise and purpose. Under the Presidency-General of Kevin Cahill, the Society has in the past decade displayed a strength and an imaginative energy unmatched, it is likely, since those founding turn-of-the-century years. It is my present task to introduce the volume which he has edited from the contributions made, over the course of the decade, to the Society's annual *Recorder*. He has given it, as title, *The American Irish Revival*. To explain the appropriateness of this, I must go back to the foundation of the Society in 1897, and to what was then the position of the Irish in American life.

What is most immediately striking and significant about the letter which brought the Society into being is the defensiveness of its tone. It reminds its addressees that the American of English stock, of Dutch, Huguenot and Spanish stock, has each his historical association, but not the Irish. And in consequence, the facts of Irish history and of the history of the Irish in America are being submerged beneath "the mass of legend and fiction flooding the country under various designations." The "primal object" of the proposed society would be to ascertain those facts, "weigh them in relation to contemporary events, and estimate their historical value, avoiding in this process the exaggeration and extravagance of poorly informed writers on one hand, and the prejudice and misrepresentation of hostile writers on the other. . . . "

Taste and decorum, I suspect, persuaded the writers away from the specifics of the cultural situation, but these would have been well-known to every member of the new Society. The English and the Dutch, those other historical societies to which Theodore Roosevelt could claim membership (and on far stronger grounds), would have felt no need for such defensiveness. These were the ethnic stocks which composed the patriciate of his native New York, and the prejudice which the new Society sought to counter had been roused in them by the arrival upon the shores of great hordes of Irish catholics, along with great hordes of Italian Catholics and East European Jews. These "huddled masses," to use the well-intentioned but condescending words which had ten years earlier been inscribed on the base of the Statue of Liberty, offered a challenge to the earlier American notion of itself as a society welcoming all (or almost all) ethnic stocks, although only on the tacit assumption that they could, and would want to, accommodate themselves to a culture which had been laid out along English and predominantly Protestant lines.

With each of these ethnic waves, there came a specific kind of nativist reaction, and with respect to the Irish, it was especially virulent in the years of the famine immigration and the decades which followed, on into the new century. Eighteenth-century Irish emigration to America had drawn heavily upon the Protestants and Presbyterians of Ulster—as witness, Henry James's County Cavan grandfather—and there had been no need even to draw them within the dominant culture. They contributed splendidly to its very shaping; the signatories of the Declaration of Independence and the list of our early Presidents bear testimony to this. But the famine immigrants and those of the generations which followed, were Catholic, were characteristically Munster or Connaught, and were therefore of a culture strikingly and dangerously different.

The reference in the founding letter of our Society to "hostile writers" doubtless refers to the flood of lurid anti-Irish (or anti-Catholic, or both) tracts and printed sermons and sensational novels of the mid-century. But in fact, in polite and even in serious literature the portraits of urban American Irish Catholics were far from flattering. In stereotype, the men were hod-carriers, the women servant-girls, and the children raised up into a slum world of lawlessness, fighting, saloons, and corrupt political machines. In a word, they were a people without a culture, in the honorific rather than the neutrally anthropological meaning of that term. And in defensive reaction, there had emerged among the more literate of the immigrants what the founding letter I think has in mind when it speaks of "the exaggeration and extravagance of poorly informed writers." That is, a consoling counter-literature which boasted that at some time in the remote and unspecified past, Ireland had possessed not merely a culture but one which surpassed that of Periclean Athens or Florence of the Medicis, with bards loftier than Homer and heroes braver than Ajax.

The "primal object" of the Society was based upon a proper assumption that Ireland, and Irishmen in America, could more justly and more certainly be vindicated by ascertaining the actual facts and placing them in an accurate historical perspective. "That the world may know," the motto which it adopted, accurately states not only the purpose of the society, but the

xviii

emotions by which that purpose was informed. It was a purpose nobly fulfilled. For many years, the *Journal* of the Society, with Thomas Hamilton Murray and Thomas B. Lawler as its first editors, was a primary source of research into the contributions to American life of men of Irish ancestry. The present *Recorder* is its successor. Its most powerful accomplishment, however, was I think the roll-call of its members, men distinguished in the political, the religious, and the cultural life of this country, and proud, all of them, to claim Irish ancestry.

What seems to me however the fact of greatest significance was the evenness with which the lists of early members may be divided between those of the Protestant and those of the Catholic strands in the Irish fabric. The rector of the Catholic University was a signatory to the founding letter, but so too was the rector of St. James Protestant Episcopal Church and the minister of the Park Methodist Church. Beyond such evident marks of identification, there are ways by which the alert and worldy student of Irish-America can safely hazard a guess that Samuel Sweet Green and Admiral Richard Worsham Meade were Protestants, as were also the president of Tufts College and that professor of English Literature at Columbia. When President Roosevelt welcomed the officers of the Society at the White House in 1909, he was hinting at such matters when he praised it for "bringing to light the history of the Irish people in this country, particularly the achievements of those early immigrants who came from Ireland long before the outbreak of the Revolution and planted themselves as the advance guard of a conquering civilization on the borders of the Indian-haunted wilderness."

That faintly chilling reference to the "Indian-haunted wilderness" with its touch of innocent turn-of-the-century racism, brings us, however, to a central and unavoidable issue. American civilization, as Theodore Roosevelt conceived of it, and to a greater extent, probably, than he himself realized, was essentially an Anglo-Saxon Protestant affair, to which the contributions of such groups as the Irish Catholics were welcome, provided that they spoke and thought and acted, and so far as possible, looked, like Anglo-Saxon Protestants. Many upwardly mobile Irish Catholics were happy to accept the stipulation, but it did not meet the issue.

The Irish Catholics of the great cities of the east, New York and Boston and Philadelphia, were, like other immigrant groups, a stigmatized people precisely because they dwelt within cultures which fell somewhat athwart the prevailing ethos. In recent years, we have come to welcome such evidences of cultural diversity and vitality. Perhaps it would be more exact to say that we have developed social pieties which teach us that we are supposed to welcome them. But such was far indeed from the case at the time, let us say, of the First World War.

Theodore Roosevelt (to whom I seem to keep recurring, perhaps because he has been the most illustrious of our active members, perhaps because he was an endlessly fascinating representative American) was more merely than proud of his Irish blood. He was genuinely interested in Irish history and culture, the friend of Yeats and Lady Gregory, the defender of the Abbey Theatre. But he was also a vociferous critic of what he called "hyphenated Americans," a term which may have been of his coinage. After the outbreak of the war, but before we entered it, many Irish-Americans tended not to support the English cause, which seemed to him a sinister evidence of their hyphenization. Many Americans of British ancestry did support England, but this did not prove that *they* were hyphenated. England and America, after all, shared a common Anglo-Saxon civilization. This lurking suspicion within the American social establishment that many American Irish were disloyal lasted until the Irish of the New York regiments drowned it in their blood at Belleau Wood and Chateau Thierry.

Such days seem, and indeed are, so far behind us as to seem remote, antedeluvian. But an historical society should be mindful, above all else, of history. And if the accomplishments of the Society in the past decade, under Dr. Cahill's presidency, are properly to be understood, they must be placed within the perspectives offered not only by the Society's history, but by that of the American Irish. The cultural circumstances of that community have changed dramatically since the Eighteen Nineties, and it has only been within the decade, I think, that the Society has re-defined its mission so as to respond to those changes.

In earlier paragraphs, I have been suggesting that in this country we have had, until recent decades, not one but two cultures—an "official" or "establishment" culture, with a full panoply of powerful cultural institutions to which others were admitted, as it were, upon sufferance. And an "unofficial" culture composed of all those ethnic groups which retained a sense of their quirky, uncomfortable, disturbing individualities —Irish, Jewish, black, and many others. It was a situation ripe with the possibilities of ironies, ambiguities, resentments, suspicions, misunderstandings, and all of these came to flower. "Ghettoization" bred "self-ghettoization." Thus, for example, as any Bostonian of middle years can testify, until a very recent time indeed, the Irish of that city thought of Harvard as "their" —as opposed to "our"—university.

The change which has come about can be given its most vivid illustration by continuing with that example. When America at last chose an Irish Catholic president, he was not merely Irish, but Boston Irish of the Boston Irish. And he was also Harvard, as Harvard in his way as Theodore Roosevelt had been in his, unselfconsciously proud both of his ancestry and of his *alma mater.* In the half-century between the presidencies of these two Americans of Irish descent, the nature of American culture has greatly modified itself, and nowhere more so than in the ways in which Americans think and feel about their ethnic origins.

Although the Society in the intervening decades has maintained its splendid claims, numbering among its Gold Medallists cardinals, generals, ambassadors, labor leaders, governors, judges, and even a president of the United States (not, it must be admitted, from Harvard), it perhaps maintained for longer than it need have that posture which I have described as essentially a defensive one. For some time now, there has no longer been a need to let the world know the Irish descent of Revolutionary War generals and nineteenth-century inventors and governors of Rocky Mountain states. What the world now should know are the ways in which the public and intellectual life of America is being enriched by men and women because of their sharp and vivid awareness of their relationship to the American Irish community, and, beyond it, to the rich culture of Ireland.

Dr. Cahill has titled this volume *The American Irish Revival,* and the title has been calculated to raise an echo. "The Irish Revival" was the name chosen in the Eighteen Nineties by Yeats and Lady Gregory and those who worked with them when they began those labors which in time brought out the rich flowering of modern Irish literature and culture. It was an assertion which had in it at the outset more of hope than of actuality, but a hope based upon first evidences. And there are abundant evidences in the present volume of a new quickening, a new energy and vitality, among the American Irish.

And for this, Dr. Cahill himself deserves more credit, in my judgment than do the contributors whose selections he had chosen to publish. Some of these were written for publication, and others were given first as readings or lectures at meetings of the Society or on special occasions. The works of American Irish writers are included, but included also are the verses of Irish poets, including Seamus Heaney, of County Derry and Harvard University, and the literary criticism of Dennis Donoghue, of County Down and New York University. I have singled out these two less for reasons of their eminence than to suggest, in the names of counties and institutions that the distinction between our "official" and our "unofficial" cultures has become less sharp, or at least more various.

If, in the Nineteen Fifties, the foyer of the Society's mansion on Fifth Avenue seemed to me a shade austere and forbidding, it blazes now with lights on many evenings, and its rooms blaze with poetry, with art, and on accasion with music. *The American Irish Revival* takes us through the door, and escorts us to our seats.

Thomas Flanagan

Section 1 — Literary

The Complex Fate of Being American-Irish

JOHN MONTAGUE

For the title of this brief essay I have borrowed from Henry James, that famous grandson of South Ulster, who having defined the complex fate of being American, spent a large part of his life trying to escape the problem, in France and England. I think I know a little of his dilemma, as a Brooklyn-born Ulsterman with an Irish domicile, but I would be more inclined to stress the potential richness, even the comedy, of such contradictions, as well as the creative anguish.

For instance, was Henry James not also an Irish man, if not an Irish writer? Under the most recent rulings for Irish citizenship he would pass, because of his grandfather. William James left about 1789, an emigrant from the now disputed Border area of Ulster. Had political events anything to do with his emigration? Tom Flanagan might know, as part of his heritage is from the same area. But certainly the wind of history was blowing around his Calvinist coattails, as they would be again for his family, if they had stayed.

But to be more literary, is his grandson's intense sense of evil in any way to be attributed to his Northern Irish heritage? That is the kind of speculation which is beautifully endless, perhaps ultimately useless, the kind of debate one might hope to have in some celestial barroom. But I have a few more puzzling imponderables to add. The family of Poe were neighbors, as the crow flies, over in Ballyconnell. And if there is any area of Ireland with a haunted reputation it is the nearby Moy Slacht, the plain

1

of slaughter, where blood sacrifice may have been practised.

> Here was raised
> a tall idol of savage fights:
> the Cromm Cruaich—
> the King Idol of Erin.
>
> —from the *Book of Leinster*

So do the maelstrom of Poe and *The Turn of the Screw* owe anything to those dark, small hills? There is also the fascinating fact that one of the most powerful traditions of supernatural writing is Anglo-Irish, from Sheridan le Fanu to Bram Stoker. So could we inscribe Poe and the darker side of Henry James in the long line of guilt-ridden Protestants, afraid of the face at the window?

But to return to my own case history. I have known in my own life and work the complex fate of being American-Irish, or Irish-American, whichever way you wish to lay the emphasis. Thomas Wolfe wrote that only the dead know Brooklyn but I was born there, in Bushwick Avenue Hospital in 1929, a combination of time and place that will need no explanation to this audience.

So I played on a tenement roof, put nickels under the subway trains, gaped at the cigarstore Indian in front of the local cinema, spread the Funnies across the floor on Sunday, knew Dick Tracy and Orphan Annie before I saw the Beano. I went to the pictures to see Mickey Mouse and Buck Rogers with my brothers and was pulled through the snow on a curved sleigh by my father. What would have been my future if I had stayed? Again there is that desperate story of Henry James, 'The Jolly Corner,' about the man who returns. Somewhere in New York my *alter ego,* my *doppelganger,* sits brooding over his destiny; would I have become a distinguished American professor, Kevin Flanagan, Tom Sullivan, David Casey, Tom Greene?

2

Or a different kind of Doctor, lynchpin of this society? How would I have woven together my two worlds, the New World and the lost Ireland?

Or to raise the ante, what would Dev have become, if he had stayed: Cardinal or Chief of Police? Of such accidents is a destiny made. Instead, de Valera and I endured emigration in reverse; we were returned to the old sod, the mother country, or, in my case, the lost green field, that truncated part of Ulster known as the Six Counties. In both cases it was simple poverty: there was no way that my parents could bring up their children in what seemed, certainly to my mother, "a wild and threatening world of Prohibition and Depression, cops and robbers, cigarstore Indians and coal-black niggers, bathtub gin and Wop neighbors."

So at the age of four I found myself back on a decaying farm in Tyrone, the heartland of Ulster, unwittingly the heritor of three nationalities, for the post office van that came to our door in the mornings was bright red, Royal Mail. How did I cope? My aunt Freda tells of how I used to speak of visiting my Protestant neighbors as "going to the next block." What the Clarkes thought of that little boy in knickerbockers I don't know but one day I came back late and declared that I had "been kepping the cows."

That day the language of Ulster poetry took a minute step forward. My early poems were attempts to do justice to that world I had returned to, its Scotch, Irish speech patterns, its long history. I had moved back from the twentieth century to at least two thousand years before Christ, the strange signs on the stones of Seskilgreen and Knockmany, or Cnoc Aine, the hill of the Mother Goddess whose saddle shape dominated our little valley where old-style farming still lingered on, and would linger until the tractor drove out the horse, and hens were put into concentration camps.

And yet I have kept a double vision, a part of me still

3

profoundly moved by my American *patria,* my American heritage. In *The Rough Field* there is a section called "The Fault," which seeks to explain the pain of my father, a dispossessed Ulster Republican whose only secure job was as a nickel-pusher on the I.R.T.:

> Often as I descend
> into subway or underground
> I see his bald head behind
> the bars of the small booth;
> the mark of an old car
> accident beating on his
> ghostly forehead.

But there was also my mother who loathed Brooklyn and would not, could not stay. Her main criticism of *The Rough Field* was that it said nothing about her family. It is an irony that the closest relatives I have left in New York, the Carneys, are from what we would call in the North, her side of the house. I have a poem called "A Graveyard in Queens" about the grave where my godfather and name-sake, John Montague, rests beside her brother, Thomas Carney. My uncle John was a musician and as I stood there I seemed to

> hear the creak
> of a ghostly fiddle
> filter through
> American earth
> the slow price
> of a lament.

And in my next long poem, *The Dead Kingdom,* I describe her marriage, part of which was lived under the shadow of the Brooklyn Bridge, that splendid dream in steel whose centenary we celebrate this year. Someday I

4

will put all my American poems together, to suggest the complex fate of being an Irish-American. One I am especially proud of is "All Legendary Obstacles," a love poem set against the background of western America.

All legendary obstactles lay between
Us, the long imaginary plain,
The monstrous ruck of mountains
And, swinging across the night,
Flooding the Sacramento, San Joaquin,
The hissing drift of winter rain.

Why, I demand grumpily, is this not to be found in any American anthology? Is it because I am supposed to be only Irish? Modern poetry used to be a common adventure, above national prejudice; Joyce and Yeats appear in the *Pisan Cantos* of Ezra Pound. And here I must stress another line of exchange between our two countries. Some American artists still feel a specific pull towards Ireland, in particular two of the best poets of recent times. When I brought Ted Roethke to meet Mrs. Yeats it was clearly a major event in his life although it was hardly fair of him to demand that his wife Beatrice should immediately become a medium. And John Berryman chose to end his *Dream Songs* in Dublin, declaring of Yeats, "I have come to have it out with you Majestic shade." I deal with these two strange pilgrims in another forthcoming book but I would like to end with a final comic touch about being American-Irish. If the borough of Brooklyn ever decides to recognise me as a lost poetic son they will not have to go to any trouble to honor me, for there is already a Montague Street. Whatever about their royalties neither Norman Mailer nor William Styron can claim as much!

John Montague, the American-born Irish poet, has written previously for The Recorder about Ireland, America, and Brooklyn.

Leaves of Pain

JIMMY BRESLIN

At first, it seemed to be nothing. It was a curled up dark brown leaf of about the size of a good lock of hair and it was preserved in glass in a room in the Fairlow Herbarium in Cambridge, in Massachusetts. A typewritten card alongside the leaf said that it was taken from an infected potato plant in Ireland during the famines of 1845-50. I looked at the leaf, read the card and began to walk away and, of course, did not leave. Here in this glass case was the weapon used by the earth when it turned against man and nearly ended a nation, the leaf which determined the character of its people, wherever they were, for generations at the least.

Behind the glass case, on long shelves, was an impressive line of books. There also was in the room a man who could help me decipher some of the written matter. I decided to forget about taking one of the morning shuttles to New York. I sat at a table. Usually, when you are around relics of things Irish, you hear in your mind a song or have the feel of a smile. This time, the hand went for a book.

At the time of the famine, the man in charge of the room observed, mycology, the study of fungi, was only beginning. People from a couple of places in the world went to Ireland to collect blighted plants and then took them back to their laboratories to study. But they could give Ireland no help. By the time the famine was ending, the potato fungus only was being given a name: *phytophthora infestans.* One of the things most vile about the use of a dead language is the manner in which the message of horror becomes lost in the struggle to absorb the habitual syllables.

The man in the Fairlow Herbarium suggested one of the books, "The Advance of the Fungi" by E.C. Large. The author noted that in good weather the potato fungus reproduced sexually. However, when conditions were constantly wet and chilly, the fungus reproduced asexually, and at great rapidity. On two occasions during the famine years, there was a chill rain that did not seem to end. Fungus appeared wherever the land was wet. Potato leaves became brown and started to curl up and the potato underneath became purple and mushy. With no food, over a million died and millions fled.

The book says that experiments over the years appeared to show that the blighted potato was edible. Because of the fungus causing the inside of the potato to break down, much of the starch turned to sugar, thereby giving the potato a strange, sweet taste. This is something which can be said in the safety of a laboratory. But while a million were dying, people tried to eat the potatoes and found they could not.

The potato originates in the Andes Mountains of Peru, where it grows in many varieties. However, the English, who introduced it to Ireland in the 16th century, planted only one variety, the clone, and it is susceptible to the wet fingers of fungus. With no second variety of potato plant to withstand the disease, the blight became total. The Irish, ignorant of all this, planted any eyes which seemed even vaguely uninfected and prayed that the next crop would be clean, and the new plants were as infected as the ones from which they came.

As I was reading this, I began to think of the crumbling stone building on Bantry Bay, in Cork. The ruin stands right on the bay, at a point where the rocky shore builds up to great cliffs that go along flat, deep water until the water begins to rise and fall in great swells and suddenly the land ends and now it is ocean, not bay, slapping against the bottom of the cliff and sending spray high into the air, up to the top of the cliff.

The ruins sit in a tangle of rough brush and are difficult to reach. In 1845, at the height of the famine, the place was a granary. Each day, while Irishmen died with their mouths stained green from eating grass, the British worked this granary and filled sacks that were placed on ships and sent to England. Near the end, when there were no people able to work in the fields and supply the granary, the British announced that the granary would be donated to the people. It could be used as a Children's Home, which is a twisted way of saying what it actually became: a morgue for children who died of not having food. The bodies of children were stacked floor to ceiling in the granary.

And now, in this room in Cambridge, with the time passing and the man in charge finding you still more to read about fungus and famine, the line in the English language I always think of first walked through my mind in all its stateliness and wisdom: "Too long a sacrifice can make a stone of the heart."

The sons of this famine burned an orphanage in New York City. It was the Colored Orphan Asylum, of course; when the maimed poor anywhere lash out, they seek not the blood of Dukes and Earls, but rather of victims such as they. The Colored Orphan Asylum was on Fifth Avenue, between 43rd and 44th Streets. At three p.m. on Sunday, July 12, 1863, a crowd of nearly 4,000 Irish broke through the front gate of the orphanage, rushed across the lawns and broke inside. The orphanage officials managed to sneak 400 terrified black orphans out the back door and take them to the safety of a police station. The mob of Irish meanwhile ransacked and burned the orphanage. And throughout the city, mobs of Irish, their hearts shale, their souls dead, rioted and killed blacks.

I always thought it was important to know what happens to men when their insides become stone. The violence, the illegal acts are not to be condoned. But I always want to know why it is that all people, even those of your own, lose control of the devils inside them. Perhaps something can be learned.

The riots in New York are called in history books "The Draft Riots," but at the time the newspapers referred to them as the "Irish Riots." The government in 1863 set up a military draft for New York, a lottery, but one from which any citizen could buy himself out for $300. Which excluded the Irish, who barely had money for dinner. The first drawing was held on Saturday, July 11. When the names were published in the Sunday morning newspapers, growls ran through the tenements where the Irish lived. Soon, people were out in the streets, carrying anything that would hurt, and with their first violence, their first beatings, their first fires, the word struck them, as similar words have sunk into any thrashing crowds throughout history. In Odessa, the crew of the Potamkin mutinied and the people were fighting the troops on the steps rising from the harbor and then somebody screamed the word: "Jews!" It became not a fight against authority anymore; it was a pogrom. And in Manhattan, in 1863, here were the Irish, the sons of famine, out in the streets against the injustice of a system that would allow the rich to buy out of a danger in which the poor must perish. And suddenly, inevitably, as the water of a wave turns to white, the word races through the crowd: "Niggers!"

On 32nd Street between Fifth and Sixth Avenues, a black was hung from a tree and his house burned. An army officer who had tried to stop the mobs was trapped on 33rd Street, between 2nd and 1st Avenues. He was beaten to death and the mob played with his body for hours, as a kitten does with a spool. At 6 p.m., on the second night of the rioting, a mob of 600 Irish attacked a house on the corner of Baxter and Leonard Streets in which 20 black families lived.

The police arrived at this point, two platoons of them, led by three sergeants, listed in the records as Walsh, Quinn and Kennedy. The patrolmen under them all were Irish. At this time, ninety per cent of the police force was Irish: Irish with their trait of loyalty. And loyalty was stronger than stone. There was no question what the police would do: protect the black families and then attack the mob, this mob of Irish. Attack them and beat them and club them and force them to break and run and then chase them down the streets and beat them so they would have no stomach to return for more.

During the three-day riot, the rioters killed 18 blacks. There could have been thousands killed without the police intervention. The police and army units killed 1,200 rioters. Seven thousand were injured. General Harvey Brown, in charge of the army troops, said of New York's Irish police deparment: "Never in our civil or military life have I ever seen such untiring devotion or such efficient service."

In the history of the Police Department of the City of New York, it was the act which first caused people to call them "The Finest." That it came as the result of having to put down savage assaults by Irish is something which should neither be hidden or explained away. Remember it. It happened 114 years ago, which is a short time as the history of the earth is measured. Remember it, and do not condone it. But at the same time know about it. Know by being told what Yeats knew by instinct: the effect of something like this leaf in the glass in the room in Cambridge.

I gave the man back his books, said thank you and left the Herbarium and went to the airport in Boston for the shuttle to New York. I had to be at a wake in Brooklyn, in the Bedford Stuyvesant neighborhood. My friend Mabel Mabry's nephew, Allen Burnett, had been murdered. He was walking along Bedford Avenue and somebody shot him in the back because Allen would not give up his new coat. After the wake, I rode in the cab past the place where Allen was murdered. The one who did the murder had been arrested. He was 24 and the illegitimate son of a woman on welfare who had moved to Brooklyn from South Carolina where her grandparents had been slaves. The kid who did the shooting could not read or write and was jobless. He had prior arrests for heroin and burglaries. He would go to prison for 25 years.

After the wake, I rode in the cab past the place where Allen was murdered. Bedford Avenue at this part, Kosciusko Street, is empty. The buildings have been burned and the sidewalks are covered with glass. In an empty lot alongside a boarded-up building, a pack of dogs rooted through garbage that had been thrown there during the day. Weeds grew in the lot. The weeds made me think of the curled up dark brown leaf I had seen earlier that day.

Jimmy Breslin, author and columnist,
is a member of the Society.

A Happy Collision

BENEDICT KIELY

The nineteenth Autumn had come upon me, as the poet more-or-less put it, when he was writing about the swans, before I read "The King of Ireland's Son." So that I read it as a work of literature, which it is, and with all the wide knowledge of what used to be called comparative literature that nineteen years can give a man. But since I was, even if I say it for myself, one of those young fellows inclined to respect the work of my elders, from Coriolanus down to the Cremation of Sam Magee, I was at the age of nineteen much impressed by the book that was at the core of Padraic Colum's feeling for folklore, Irish and international: and of his gift for storytelling.

As to how he became a folklorist, Padraic spoke with modesty and humour to Zack Bowen:

One day I was down at Mrs. Steloffs, (The Gotham Book Mart in New York.) There was a party for someone, and all sorts of ancient people came in, and amongst them was a queer hunchbacked woman, and they said: "This is Betsy Brewer." Betsy Brewer was the person who launched me into folklore. I said to myself, "Now I'll go home and tell Molly I met Betsy Brewer." I had some books in Irish I was translating just to keep my hand in. Then Willy Pogany, (the artist), said he would like to illustrate an Irish book, but I hadn't any Irish book written. I had these translations and I suddenly thought that I could put them together. And I did and I made the first part of, "The

King of Ireland's Son." Miss Brewer paid me eight dollars a week for it. . . . they had a column in the *Daily Tribune.* . . . That was the first money I got for literature in the States. . . . and then I became an authority on folklore without ever telling anybody I was one.

From such an odd beginning came a beautiful book: and although, when I was reading it first, forty-four years ago, I regarded myself as a young literary gent, I was also in a good position to see how the book affected the young for whom it was primarily intended. For I read portions of it out loud to some of my younger fellow-patients on the balcony in St. Joseph's ward in Cappagh Orthopaedic Hospital outside Dublin—those of my fellows, that is, who were up and walking about. As for myself at the time I was reposing on what was then known as a Whitman frame. Even the name of my couch or rack was literary.

My audience never failed to rise to the story of how Gilly of the Goatskin robbed the robbers. Rereading the book now I can still seem to see their faces as I flick, for the sheer joy of it, from page to page.

Piaras O hUigin, then a Jesuit scholastic and the son of Brian na Banban, a notable old warhorse of an Irish patriot, had brought the book to my bedside and had been astounded that such a scholar as myself had not already read it. The O'Higgins family had been reared on it nor can I think of a better rearing.

Here and now I am on the first page of this wonderful world of stories:

Now after the King and the King's Counsellor left him, (The King of Ireland's Son), to his own way, the youth

13

I'm telling you about did nothing but ride and hunt all day. Well one morning he rode abroad:

> His hound at his heel,
> His hawk on his wrist,
> A brave steed to carry him whither he list,
> And the blue sky over him.

And he rode on until he came to a turn in the road. Then he saw a grey old man seated on a heap of stones, playing a game of cards with himself. First he had one hand winning and then he had the other. Now he would say, 'That's my good right.' and then he would say, 'Play and beat that, my gallant left'. The King of Ireland's son sat on his horse to watch the strange old man.

Now the young and the middle-aged, and even the aged, would be well advised to act cautious with a man like that and, above all, not to play cards with him. The King of Ireland's son was not so cautious and the complications that arise on that page can only be solved by another three hundred pages. Yet there are compensations for the young man: he finds his true love, Fedelma, the beautiful daughter of the strange enchanter of the Black Backlands; he finds his lost brother in that other adventurous young man, Gilly of the Goatskin; and, in between, he has the whale of a time of excitement.

For the reader also there are many compensations: the leaping imagination and invention, the sheer skill of the intricate storytelling, the ability of Padraic Colum, the poet, to set his people moving in all directions and never to be at a loss about what to do next.

Years later another poet, Patrick Kavanagh, and myself were working in Dublin on the old weekly

Standard, under the editorship of Peter O'Curry. Paddy, at the time, was struggling with what was later to be the novel, "Tarry Flynn" and one day he said most mournfully: "I wish to God somebody would teach me how to write a novel. I have this gentleman in a field for a fortnight and I can't get him out of it." Gentleman was not the exact word he used but he had drawn attention to one of the great obstacles to the writing of credible fiction. You might put it this way: Anyone can write the high moments, but to get the fellow out of the field, or out of the chair and out of the room, or across the street, without the writing becoming flat or prosy: *hoc opus, hic labor est.*

Almost certainly Padraic the poet had his mechanical and organisational problems in piling tale upon tale in this book but they certainly do not show. On it goes like the living river that Gilly of the Goatskin so much loved, until the high moment when Padraic, like Prospero, dismisses his multitude of characters and, with particular reference to his two heroes, says cunningly:

> And the deeds of one are in the histories the shanachies have written in the language of the learned, and the deeds of the other are in the stories the people tell to you and me:
>
>> When I crossed the Ford
>> They were turning the Mountain Pass.
>> When I stood on the Stepping Stones
>> They were travelling the Road of Glass.

But seven pages earlier he had described in a way that I can only accept as an ironic comment on the state or plight of the Irish writer, the presents that the storyteller brought back from the double royal wedding:

There were seven hundred guests at the short table, eight hundred at the long table, nine hundred at the round table, and one thousand in the great hall. I was there and I heard the whole story. But I got no present save shoes of paper and stockings of buttermilk, and these a herdsman stole from me as I crossed the mountains.

That first reading of, "The King of Ireland's Son," was, you might say, my second encounter with Padraic Colum. My first was one that most young students in this country are privileged to experience: the reading and the learning by heart of those much anthologised pieces about the drover, and the old woman of the roads, and the men from the fields coming softly in, and about the wandering poor scholar of the 1840's, and that most exquisite song, (sung best by the late Michael O'Higgins), about the maiden who moved through the fair and into shadows and sadness. Then there was the reading of his poetry and prose to which, I may say, I gave a great deal of attention right up even to those valuable documents, "My Irish Year" and "The Road Round Ireland" and that considerable novel, "The Flying Swans." He wrote as many introductions as did G. K. Chesterton: and for his centenary year his play, "The Fiddler's House," was bright as a new penny on the stage of the Peacock Theatre.

My first encounter with the man himself was in University College, Dublin, in Earlsfort Terrace, when we were both lecturing on the same seminar. We met, in fact, head-on, he coming out of the door of the lecture hall, I going in, a happy collision that was the beginning of a long friendship out of which I treasure many bright memories.

16

In Newport, Rhode Island, where we are lecturing together again and living in one of those monstrous mansions, and Padraic coming down the stairs in the morning singing blithely: "I dreamt that I dwelt in marble halls."

In Suffield, Conn., where he was so content with his friends, the Krochalis family and Padraic and a young woman-student and myself walking in the evening along that lovely tree-lined village street. The young woman leaves us to go her own way and walks west, one star in the sky, a scene set for my quoting:

> And then she went homeward, with one star awake,
> As the swan in the evening moves over the lake.

A pub in Ranelagh in Dublin and the barman reciting "The Drover," word-perfect: and an old man putting his hand on Padraic's shoulder and saying: "You're the best from here to Ballyhaunis." Which, as Padraic later commented with no small pride, was what the people used to say about Raftery.

Then an epic journey in Ireland, and Padraic and Sean J. White and myself going west to a prize-giving day at St. Angela's College of domestic economy at Cloghereeva on Lough Gill. On the way and when we were climbing up from the Boyle River and above Lough Key and Lough Arrow, he said: "Where are we now?" When we told him that we were on the Curlew mountains, he said with a smile that they didn't look like much in the way of mountains and we knew that, in the course of his travels, he had seen wilder and loftier peaks.

After Cloghereevagh we went on to Bundoran where there was a marvellous meeting between

17

my mother and himself; and in Bundoran we left him sitting on a bench and waiting for a bus to take him on to John Hyland in Donegal town who was to show him the road round county Donegal. Worried I was at leaving a man of his age to travel on alone, but Sean laughed at me and compared my own poor travelling abilities to the wanderlust of the poet.

That was a moment I was comically reminded of several years later when from Atlanta, Ga., I rang Padraic in Suffield to wish him a happy birthday, and to suggest that he might come South to give a reading in Emory. He said that nothing would please him better, but that on the following day he was flying to give a reading in San Francisco and that, while he was there, he might as well fly on to Australia to see his brother. He said that he might not be so close to him again for some time.

The road round Ireland had so easily become the road round the world and the poet had extended his circuits to circle the great globe itself.

Benedict Kiely is a well known Irish novelist and short story writer.

The Poetry of the Gael

PADRAIC COLUM

Padraic Colum, a Medalist of the Society, delivered this talk to the Society 60 years ago.

Ladies and gentlemen, when I was invited to be amongst you this evening, I felt tremendously— stupendously—flattered that I was asked to be the guest of a society of historians. Then after a while I began to think to myself: "Now, why should I feel so flattered at historians asking me to join them in eating a dinner." Then, coming down on the train this evening, I decided that I would not be flattered by any such attention any more,—I would assert myself and remind the historians that when a poet is amongst them, the poet is their elder brother and the historian is very much the younger brother of the poet. No matter how much gravity the historians may put on, it is the poet, as I say, that has been his elder brother. All history begins with poetry first. It is the poets who write the first history, and it remains for the poet to write the most moving history. Before the historians have come on the scene the poets have already established a tradition—a living tradition in history—that it takes the historians the next thousand years to pick to pieces.

And let me remind you of a few things that the poets have done to baffle the historians. The greatest scholars who are now writing about that great piece of poetry "The Iliad" have said that there is one thing certain about the war against Troy—it is that Agamemnon's men did not take the town; that they went home beaten; and that when they went home beaten they wrote out how it should have been done, and they created a victory that will live forever and will inspire the human race.

And again, surely the king that is seated most strongly on the throne is King Arthur—a mythical king who never reigned and who never lived, but whom the poets created and in creating whom, gave England its first great fame. And in our own country, too—in Ireland, that unity which the strong and ambitious Milesian kings were never able to achieve was achieved for them by the poets who wrote about Tara as the center of Ireland and wrote about the monarchs of Tara as being rulers of Ireland, and created in all minds a great, a magnificent unity, which historians will not acknowledge ever existed.

And so I decline to be patronized by the distinguished historians who are here this evening.

Now, the topic that has been given me to speak on is a very noble one, and I wish I could rise to the occasion and speak of it adequately.

"The Poetry of the Gael"! What is it comes into my mind when I think of that phrase, of that topic, that title? First of all, it comes over me how much poetry has meant to Ireland. I suppose poetry has meant more to Ireland than it has meant to any modern European country; and the first thing recorded in Irish history is a poem. If we open the oldest of the Irish books, the Book of Conquest, the Book of Invasions, that tells about the invasions of Ireland by different races, on the very first

20

pages we have a poem. It is the poem that Amergin, the son of Miledh made, as the ships of the Milesian invaders hailed the island—the Invocation to the Land—in which he begins:

"I invoke the land of Ireland,"

and then invokes the rivers and hills and cataracts and plains, and by his invocation, weds the race to the land they are coming to, dedicates the race to the land they are coming to; and that dedication that is pronounced in the first days of Irish history has bound the poets to dedicate themselves to the land ever since.

And that is the great thing that the poets of Ireland have done for us. They have brought in that spirit of dedication. If we think of Ireland as broken and shattered, as Ireland was broken and shattered in the long wars of the Tudors, the great thing that comes out of it all is a song. There is no great Irish victory but there is a great song, a great praise by a poet that makes victory again. Doctor Thomas in his speech just now said that men do not live by bread alone; but I say that men do not live with victory alone—I mean not by material victory alone—but by spiritual victories; and they are the great victories that are expressed by the poets. And when, at the end of a disastrous war, that Gaelic poet made the poem of Dark Rosaleen that Mangan has translated so beautifully, that was a great victory for Ireland. Though that victory never came in the night of disaster, it became a noble epic of history. The poet is able to inspire generations with the feeling that Ireland would not die, and give that vision of beauty and splendor and something to dedicate one's self to that is in the Dark Rosaleen. And then

21

again when Ireland was even more broken and more crushed, in the Penal Days, the poets that were able to sing of Kathleen Ni Houlihan, the poets were able to say, in the midst of all that poverty and ruin around them, "Young she is and fair she is and she would be a queen were the king's men at home here with Kathleen Ni Houlihan!" That, too, was another great victory for Ireland—a victory that could never be lost; could never be spent.

Now, I say so much for that rapture of dedication that the Irish poets were able to put into their songs; rededicating the people of the country to the cause, or Ireland as we know it today would not exist any more. Ireland without the poets would have been West Britain—a province of the Kingdom, without any history, without any aspiration, without any scope for a separate culture that men may add to the humane civilization of the world.

But we must say this, too. Though I claim that the poets are prior to the historians, there is something else that our poets have done. We have not merely made victory in very flaming and burning words, as Geofrey Keating made a victory in just one line of his,

"Muscail Do Mhisneach, A Bhanba,"

"Lift up thy courage, O, Erin!"
Naked I give thee,
O beauty of beauty!
And I blinded my eyes
For fear I should flinch.

I set my face
To the wind here before me,

22

To the work that I see,
To the death that
I shall meet.

That single verse itself is a single and burning poem; but not only do the poets do this in the language and verses that live and burn and flare; but, as Doctor Thomas said, in this revival of the heroic age in Ireland we have seen poets who have made history as well—who have made it in fact and in deed, as well as making it in the words and in verses.

We have had the first President of the Irish Republic, Padraig Pearse, who is able to tell of his dedication in his beautiful poem written in Irish and translated, in which he talks about all the beauty and splendor of the world that might have come to him and Thomas MacDonagh and Joseph Plunkett, who made history not only in words—and it is a great history and victory in words, too—but they made it in their deeds.

No one ever had a greater faith than Padraig Pearse, when he knew that one man devoting himself to the cause could make that cause live forever. Pearse claimed he could work a miracle, and we now see that he was able to work that miracle.

Let us remember, too, that although the great and beautiful traditions of Kathleen Ni Houlihan and Dark Rosaleen may be passing away, yet remember that the poets themselves have prepared us for their passing; and the poets themselves have told us what is the next phase in Irish history.

You remember that noble poem of Lionel Johnson's, which was written at the time when an Irish insurrection might have broken out ill-prepared and so on, and the poem Innisfail—"a purple and

23

a splendid thrust heartens the host of Innisfail"
. . . Then Lionel Johnson goes on to say that such
a victory may be, after all, only a dream; but he
says:

> "A dream, a dream, an ancient dream!
>   "Yet ere peace come to Innisfail
> "Some weapon on some field must gleam;
> "Some burning glory fire the Gael!"

And then he tells us what is really to be the victory. That victory, he says, may be on some field
won "far from the treading of the hosts;" that victory "may upon some plain be won, where armed
minds do their uttermost." And that is the next
thing that takes place in Irish history; but remember, the victory is of the spirit and of the mind
solely.

Another poet looked into the future—the poet
AE, another poet who intervenes in public affairs
and makes history:

> "We hold that Ireland in our hearts
>   "More than the land that we have seen
> "And love the goal for which we start
>   "More than the tale of what has been."

Ireland has a great history in her poetry, in her
epics and in her sagas—a great and an heroic history; and it is for us to relive that history and that
heroism that has been shown to us by the poets.

Remember that no other people have an epic as
noble as ours. When, in the great Greek "Iliad,"
Achilles and Hector fight, when Achilles slays his
enemy, he ties him to his chariot wheels in the
bitter triumph and drags him around the wall of
the city that this great hero Hector had so nobly
defended. But that is not the way in the Irish epic

when Cuchulain slays Ferdiadh; he weeps over him, he weeps for the friend whom he slew, and he approaches him and his heart is broken because of the bitterness of his own victory.

And remember another passage, too, in that great story of ours, when the great queen Maeve looked at the heroes who were coming against her and as man after man comes forward, instead of saying bitter things about them, to enrage them, and as each of her great enemies comes forward she says: "Now, he is a kingly man indeed! No greater man than he is in this land." That is the spirit of generosity and nobility that we have recently shown in our history, and it is the spirit that we must never allow to lapse.

I remember I believe the first signs of the revival of that great heroic spirit. I remember I was present at, I think, one night, a little hall in Dublin, where the first plays of the Irish Theatre were performed, and amongst those plays was AE's "Deirdre," a dramatization of the most tragic and beautiful of our stories, and suddenly a thrill went through the whole audience—an audience of Dublin working people and with a few intellectuals amongst them. And that thrill went through them at the pronunciation of one single name. When "Deirdre," or "Naesi," perhaps, says: "And there was another in Eman Macha, a boy who was called Cuchulain, a dark, proud boy that was gay in council," and when that heroic name of Cuchulain was pronounced in Dublin I felt a thrill go through the audience gathered together in that theatre and I knew that Ireland would again respond to the most heroic thing in the heroic Irish traditions; and I remember when the author of that play, AE, George Russell, went on to speak. He spoke about the tragic end of his play and how Deirdre and Naesi are killed because they will not take steps—because they trust too much to the generosity and to the pledges of the king; and AE made a speech to the Dublin audience and he said that they knew, as he knew, that it was better to perish in an excess of noble trust than to live in ignoble suspicion of other's motives.

Now, all this, I may say, is just something to remind you of that tradition; to remind you that the historians cannot always be permitted to flatter the poets, but that the poets, especially in Ireland, have a place.

Now, in the old days in Ireland, when any one spoke of poetry he was asked to prove his poetry and he was asked to prove it by making a poem of his own. He could not even join the military companions, the Fianna, if he was not able to prove his poetry by making a poem then and there in a very difficult metre, delivered before somebody who, I am sure, was able to judge the poem. And so I feel, having spoken at such length about poetry, that I have to prove my poetry and say some verses for you of my own. And the poem that I am going to recite to you now is not really my own; it is a translation of a very famous Eighteenth Century poem,—BAN CNUIC, EIRE OIGH, The Fair Hills of Ireland,—a poem of exaltation. Here it is:

Bear the love of my heart to my land far away,
　　And the Fair Hills of Eire O,
And to all of Eivir's race that in her valleys stay,
　　And the Fair Hills of Eire O,

That land of mine beloved, where the brown thrush's song,

26

From hazel glen and ivied close fills the Summer
    twilight long,
O how woeful sounds his music for the downfall of
    the Strong!
    On the Fair Hills of Eire O.

'Tis my lone soul's long sorrow that I must still be
    far,
    From the Fair Hills of Eire O,
Nor watch a maiden coming as through the mist a
    star,
    On the Fair Hills of Eire O.

O the honey in her tree-tops where her oak-woods
    darkly grow,
O the freshness of her cresses where her clear well-
    waters flow,
And the lushness of her meadows where her soft-
    eyed cattle low,
    On the Fair Hills of Eire O!

Now and in Ireland:
The Poetry of Trouble

DENIS DONOGHUE

In January 1919 when Yeats was writing 'The Second Coming,' his mind was recalling a passage from Shelley's *Prometheus Unbound* and turning it into a series of cultural generalizations:

> Things fall apart; the centre cannot hold;
> Mere anarchy is loosed upon the world,
> The blood-dimmed tide is loosed, and everywhere
> The ceremony of innocence is drowned;
> The best lack all conviction, while the worst
> Are full of passionate intensity.

Those lines were in Donald Davie's mind when he made a trip to Belfast, perhaps in 1952 or 1953, and, a few weeks or months later, wrote a poem called 'Belfast on a Sunday Afternoon.' A reader unfamiliar with Belfast would have to know that the Orange Order is a fellowship of Unionists or, as they are now called, Loyalists; men who celebrate, every year on July 12, the victory of King William III over James II at the Battle of the Boyne in 1690. On a Sunday afternoon in Belfast, it would be normal to see and hear the Orange bands practising for the big day, marching up and down the Shankill Road, or going further afield if they felt inclined to taunt the Catholics. Here is Davie's poem:

> Visiting Belfast at the end of June,
> We found the Orange Lodge behind a band:
> Sashes and bearskins in the afternoon,
> White cotton gloves upon a crippled hand.

Pastmasters pale, elaborately grim,
Marched each alone, beneath a bowler hat:
And, catapulted on a crumpled limb,
A lame man leapt the tram-lines like a bat.

And first of all we tried to laugh it off,
Acting bemusement in the grimy sun;
But stayed to worry where we came to scoff,
As loud contingents followed, one by one.

Pipe bands, flute bands, brass bands and silver bands,
Presbyter's pibroch and the deacon's serge,
Came stamping where the iron Maenad stands,
Victoria, glum upon a grassy verge.

Some brawny striplings sprawled upon the lawn,
No man is really crippled by his hates.
Yet I remembered with a sudden scorn
Those 'passionate intensities' of Yeats.

Fair comment, indeed; but if Davie were to go to Belfast now, he could not register a feeling as secure and distanced as scorn. It is a generation too late for that sentiment.

* * * * *

On February 17, 1978, a bomb which exploded in the LaMon Hotel near Comber, County Down, killed twelve people and injured many more. The bomb was set by members of the Provisional Irish Republican Army. There were about 500 people in the hotel at the time, many of them attending the annual dinner of the Northern Ireland Junior Motor-Cycle Club; including several boys who attended to receive their prizes. Other people in the hotel were members of the Irish Collie Dog Club. A warning was

29

telephoned to the hotel just as the bomb was ready to explode, and too late to enable anyone to prevent it. This episode is one of many such; the bombers have sometimes been the paramilitary branch or branches of the Loyalists, but more often the Provisional I.R.A.

My theme is the poetry of such violence; the literature which has been provoked by passionate intensities in the North of Ireland since 1968, when violence again became nearly commonplace. But I must begin further back. I assume that it is not necessary to say much about the English presence in Ireland for the past 700 years, except to remind you of two facts — that the English and Scots who colonized the country established themselves most firmly in the northeast counties; and that the history of Ireland since the Plantation of Ulster in the first years of the 17th century has been taught, in Catholic schools North and South, as a story of national sentiment expressing itself in virtually every generation since the 18th century as a revolutionary act to drive the British out of Ireland. In the past few years, as a reaction to the violence in the North, we have seen a waning of this practice in many schools. There is now a revisionist spirit at large which would persuade our children to turn their minds toward social and cultural factors rather than toward the revolutionary tradition as the historical truth of Ireland. Children are now told that Irish history is plural rather than singular; that many of our revolutionary heroes were Protestants; and that, in any case, there was a local life to be lived between one act of revolution and the next. This revisionist spirit, in its extreme form, would have us bring a certain irony to bear upon the revolutionary tradition. The Easter Rising of 1916 did indeed take place, we are told, but it erupted from a dubious rhetoric of violence and blood-sacrifice, most typically from Padraic Pearse's vision of Ireland as a new Calvary, with Pearse himself as crucified Christ.

The attempt to bring retrospective irony to bear upon the revolutionary tradition seems to me naive. History may be servitude, history may be freedom, but it cannot be wished away or transcended as easily as revisionists think. It may be an embarrassment that the Easter Rising took place; that our modern Irish Free State arose from the violence of rebellion and spent its first year in civil war. Our surviving elders are in a weak position when they preach peace to their children. The I.R.A. maintains that the revolutionary task was not completed by the Easter Rising. So long as the Border is preserved between North and South, with a native government in Dublin and a British Government administering the North, the task remains to be taken up and completed. It is the cogency of this argument which offers the real embarrassment. Attempts to distinguish between the Old I.R.A. and the New have not been convincing. The technology of violence is far more advanced now than it was sixty or seventy years ago: it is ingenuous to claim that the Old I.R.A. would not have resorted to the appalling devices of violence, if they had been available.

Those who repudiate the present violence are ready to maintain any or all of such arguments as these. One: it would be splendid to see Ireland united in a spirit of reconciliation, but the unity of Ireland is acceptable only on peaceful terms and without the shedding of a drop of anyone's blood. (This describes my own sentiment.) Two: the Unionists in the North are entitled to have their loyalty to the British Queen respected. They and their fathers have lived in the North for more than 300 years and are entitled to maintain the institutions which recognize their fealty. Three: in any event, it is impossible to bomb a million people into the unity of Ireland. Four: the Unionists are, after all, different from *us,* the Catholics; let us respect that difference. Five: our future depends not upon ancestral nationalism but upon larger fellowship.

31

We are Europeans. Six: it is a disgrace to find Christians killing one another and, every Sunday, proclaiming our devotion to the same God.

* * * * *

It is not surprising, in this context, that modern Irish literature has been provoked by violence. Our tradition is predominantly histrionic and oratorical. The tone to which our literature regularly aspires is that of the heroic gesture, all the richer if its heroism is predicated upon loss and defeat.

Padraic Fiacc's anthology *The Wearing of the Black* contains many poems, most of them bad, which testify to the thrill of blood and sacrifice. It also contains a few better poems in which the glamor of violence is recognized, its way of turning boredom into drama. In one such poem, John Hewett sees how understandably a young man wants to become a dramatic figure, a personage, in an otherwise wearisome time. The poem is 'Bogside, Derry, 1971':

> Shielded, vague soldiers, visored, crouch
>   alert;
> between tall houses down the blackened
>   street;
> the hurled stones pour, hurt-instinct aims to
>   hurt,
> frustration spurts in flame about their feet.
>
> Lads who at ease had tossed a laughing ball,
> or, ganged in teams, pursued some shouting
>   game,
> beat angry fists against that stubborn wall
> of faceless fears which now at last they
>   name.

> Night after night this city yields a stage
> with peak of drama for the pointless day,
> where shadows offer stature, roles to play,
> urging the gestures which might purge in rage
> the slights, the wrongs, the long indignities
> the stubborn core within each heart defies.

The truth is not as simple or as noble as Hewett's poem implies. Those "lads" have shown themselves ready to knee-cap one of their own, or—a recent exploit—to drop a concrete block upon the hands of a man already wounded. What they do is not always derring-do. But it is well to be reminded by Hewett's poem that when we give our children the idiom of action, gesture, and role-playing, we can't expect to control the drama they will compose for themselves, or manage its theatre.

It is hard to deny a poet the freedom to rant and rage and cry when a deed strikes him as peculiarly outrageous; as the events of the notorious 'Bloody Sunday' in Derry struck Thomas Kinsella and Brian Friel. The very fact that a poet lives in the prison of language makes it inevitable that he should want his words to be, on high occasions, indistinguishable from deeds. It is a scandal, to such a poet, that poetry makes nothing happen; or that there is always a shadow between words and their consequence. Even a quieter poet, like Seamus Heaney, has impatient moments. 'Whatever you say, say nothing,' one of his satires, adverts to the habit, in the North, of keeping one's counsel, reciting the clichés of communication for safety's sake. Heaney rehearses the prudence of such conversation, till he breaks through its conventions into his own direct speech:

> Christ, it's near time that some small leak was sprung
> in the great dykes the Dutchman made
> to dam the dangerous tide that followed
>   Seamus.

33

> Yet for all this art and sedentary trade
> I am incapable.

"This sedentary trade" is a phrase from Yeats's 'The Tower.' Heaney's allusion to it brings his poem under Yeats's shadow for the moment, the theme being poetry's predicament, the gap between words and deeds. It's nearly time, Heaney says, to see the Unionist structure undermined, and he goes back to King William and James and to the Orange Ascendancy in place from that day to this. But his allusion goes further; to Yeats's own sense, rueful, self-mocking, of the quietism of poetry. Words alone may be certain good, as Yeats thought for a time, but he always knew that in other contexts they are good for nothing. I have argued from time to time that conflict and the vocabulary of violence were dear to Yeats because they ensured the force of his energy; he thought himself more in need of conflict, for its drama and vigor, than for the peace that brings it to an end. The grappling of opposites kept his art in force. This motive is still active in Irish poetry, as Fiacc's anthology shows, but some poets have been turning their verses toward some form of transcendence, as if history were too dismal to be contemplated for long. Heaney is the most telling poet in this regard, and the success of his *North* makes the case exemplary. The readers of that book do not see themselves as lords of counterpositions, commanding a perspective in which conflicting forces are held in poise. They find comfort, I believe, in forms of feeling which are in place far beneath the field of violence and ideology; or in a form of time prior to the moment of action.

The governing analogy for *North* is not history but archaeology. Heaney's sense of time accords with his sense of place, the siting of feeling, the slow accretion of cultural life. In 'Belderg' he writes of quernstones, mill-stones discovered in a bog, the hole in the middle of the stone like an eye, a pupil:

> To lift the lid of the peat
> And find this pupil dreaming
> Of neolithic wheat!
> When he stripped off blanket bog
> The soft-piled centuries
> Fell open like a glib.

A glib is a thick mass of matted hair, "formerly worn by the Irish," as the O.E.D. reports. It is typical of Heaney to represent the archaeologist's experience as a human discovery, not merely a discovery of earth. Archaeology is for him the dream of full presence, time at once historical and perennial, in which the dichotomy between self and other is dissolved. The reconciliation which some poets present as a vision of landscape, at once many and one, is available to Heaney as meaning and value lying under the skin of earth, waiting to be discovered. His desire is predicated upon the depth of earth, and its silence; the levels and sites of being, like the eye of the quernstone.

One of the strengths of this analogy is that the feeling it holds can go both ways. In 'The Digging Skeleton' pictures in a medical text are called

> Mysterious candid studies
> Of red slobland around the bones

presumably because the tissue seems alluvial. Generally, Heaney's imagination turns toward the bogland which preserves the human past in silence and patience. He has pointed out that 'bog' is one of the few words the English language has borrowed from Irish. In Irish, it means soft and wet — "a soft day, thank God." He has also remarked that in Derry, his town, they call a bog a 'moss,' a word of Norse origin probably brought to the North by planters in the early 17th century. So he finds in 'bog' and 'moss' a record of colonization and shift of language, and in 'Kinship' he weighs these affinities. The pondering might

35

go further. Bogland, for Heaney, is the meeting-place of vegetable and mineral life, a state of nature which is soft, yielding, maternal, full of occult lore. He has referred to "images drawn from Anglo-Saxon kennings, Icelandic sagas, Viking excavations, and Danish and Irish bogs." In 'Viking Dublin' he writes:

> a worm of thought
> I follow into the mud.

In 'Belderg,' talking to an archaeologist:

> So I talked of Mossbawn,
> A bogland name. But *"moss?"*
> He crossed my old home's music
> With older strains of Norse.
> I'd told how its foundation
>
> Was mutable as sound
> And how I could derive
> A forked root from that ground
> And make *bawn* an English fort,
> A planter's walled-in mound,
> Or else find sanctuary
> And think of it as Irish,
> Persistent if outworn.

Bawn can indeed mean a fort, if you take its meaning from the English or Scots planter; or a place for milking cows, if you take it from Ireland, especially the South. Heaney takes pleasure, and a kind of comfort, from these affinities.

He also likes to think of words as issuing from the accretion of centuries. In 'Bone Dreams' he writes:

> Elizabethan canopies.
> Norman devices,
>
> the erotic mayflowers
> of Provence
> and the ivied latins
> of churchmen

to the scop's
twang, the iron
flash of consonants
cleaving the line.

'Scop' means, in Old English, a poet, minstrel, or satirist;
so Heaney is invoking the two main traditions in the
forked tongue of English, the Anglo-Saxon and the Latin.
He puts them side by side in 'Kinship':

This is the vowel of earth
dreaming its root
in flowers and snow,

mutation of weathers
and seasons,
a windfall composing
the floor it rots into.

I grew out of all this
like a weeping willow
inclined to
the appetites of gravity.

It is common to think of vowels as the 'pleasure
principle' of language, and of consonants as the 'reality
principle'; a notion congenial to Heaney who writes in
'Aisling':

He courted her
With a decadent sweet art
Like the wind's vowel
Blowing through the hazels.

But Heaney likes to play off vowel against consonant,
Latin pleasure against Anglo-Saxon reality, within the large
concession of English, a permeable medium.

I think this goes some way to account for the appeal of
Heaney's poetry: the reader has the satisfaction of finding

that nature and culture are not, as he feared, split apart once for all, or that culture has obliterated its partner. Make a short list of Heaney's themes: salmon-fishing, the blacksmith's craft, the journey of eels, the thatcher's art, threshing corn, pumping water, digging potatoes, water-divining. Think of water-divining, an ancient skill, beneath or beyond explanation, requiring a forked stick, two hands, and the gift of divination. As a parable of the still vivid relation between man and nature, it is nearly complete. It is hardly necessary to write a poem about it, it is already a form of poetry, at once gift and craft. Heaney turns to such parables as readily as Yeats turned from civil war to the honey-bees of generation.

The welcome given to *North* has been remarkably profuse. Part of the explanation is the consolation of hearing that there is a deeper life, richer and far more patient, than the life of bombings and tortures; there are levels of being and action deeper than the divisions of Protestant and Catholic, the Falls Road and the Shankill; archaic processes still alive despite bad times and omnivorous technologies. Heaney is the most eloquent of those Irish poets who are trying to lift the burden of history; finding their analogies in space, depth, archives, levels and sites, field-works and earth-works. We will still have to come back to politics and history, but meanwhile it is a relief to hear again a 'song of the earth,' a poetry of such largesse.

Denis Donoghue—a renowned teacher, author, and literary critic—addressed these reflections to the Society's members in one of the regularly-scheduled lectures.

Poems

SEAMUS HEANEY

A Cart for Edward Gallagher

I
The nineteen-twenties
in west Donegal:
between dry stone ditches,
past turf stacks at gables
and dank fuchsia bushes,
the grocery cart
of Gallagher and Son,
Merchant, Publican,
Retail and Import,
rattles back and forward.
But the son's mind's far away.
Grain-ships locked in ice
on the far St. Lawrence,
dark skies, flurried snow—
each pent-up cargo
of Canadian wheat
falls golden and slow
through a daydream of chutes
along Derry Quay
into bags of flour, bins
of yellow meal and bran . . .
I gaze into a bucket,
smell a near horse's sweat
and hear him mashing corn
on my uncle's street.
It is nineteen forty-seven.

II

Edward, you return me
to that archaic yard,
a grocery cart, a horse
loosed out and watered,
nose-deep in his nose-bag,
the legend on the cart
already legendary:
Teady McErlean,
The Oldest Firm
in the Bann Valley.
It is a covered waggon,
four-wheeled, wooden-spoked,
painted green, each wheel
fat-hubbed and still.
I am taking it all in.

III

And why do I tell you?
It is all a paradigm
of dream and watchfulness,
the music of what happens,
the exact gaze of silence.
Like that morning years ago
I came upon you, stilled
and oblivious,
staring into a field
of blossoming potatoes,
your trouser bottoms wet
and flecked with grass-seed.
On a farm street somewhere
or at the end of a lane
your early-rising son
had parked his mobile shop.
Back in your silent bar
last night's glasses soured
in a pure sea light.

If I could have rode up
like Oisin on a horse
and made the morning ring
with heroic Irish,
hoof-beats, bird-song,
the dazzle and wet blaze
of sand and ocean,
you would not have been drawn
from the covert of your gaze.

Poems

SEAMUS HEANEY

Ulster Quatrains

1. *Sectarian Water*
   I loved soft water, rain water,
   Water from the barrel, from the spouts.
   It sudded like the vowels in *liturgy*.
   It was a soft church-latin *c*.

   But ours was a hard water country.
   Sprung from untainted limestone, cold as glass,
   It made the soap scum and ringed the basin.
   It was a stiff-necked *k* in the meeting house.

2. *Sectarian Latin*
   Weni, widi, wiki—the black gown
   And wide mouth were pure Holbein.
   He was pale fingers in a paved text
   And spoke black-letter exegesis.

   We watched him, cute as foxes, and construed
   With the best of them. But when we read
   Our *veni, vidi, vici* was outlandish
   And hedge-schooled as a hunted brush.

3. *Sectarian Alphabet*
   Here is a sectarian alphabet.
   R is *or* in Dublin, *ar* in Belfast.
   If you *haitch* for *H*, you're Catholic.
   Protestant surnames with an *O* prefix

   Descend from soup and turncoat Catholics.
   Enough? Enough. But while we're on to names:
   Seamus—which I got instead of James—
   Our Registrar of Births entered as *Shames*.

Remembering Malibu

for Brian Moore

The Pacific at your door was wilder and colder
than my notions of the Pacific

and that was perfect, for I would have rotted
beside the luke-warm ocean I imagined.

Yet no way was its cold ascetic
as your monk-fished, snowed-into Atlantic;

no beehive hut for you
on the abstract sands of Malibu—

it was early Mondrian and his dunes
misting towards the ideal forms

though the wind and the sea neighed loud
as wind and sea-noise amplified.

I was there in the flesh
where I had imagined I might be

and underwent the bluster of the day:
but why would it not come home to me?

Atlantic storms have flensed the cells
on Skellig Michael, the steps cut in the rock

I never climbed
between the graveyard and the boatslip

are welted solid to our insteps.
But to rear and kick and cast that shoe!

Beside that other western sea
far from the Skelligs and far, far

from the suck of puddled, wintry ground
our footsteps filled with blowing sand.

Seamus Heaney is one of Ireland's leading poets.

A Christmas Card

JOHN MONTAGUE

Christmas in Brooklyn,
the old el flashes by,
a man plods along pulling
his three sons on a sleigh;
soon his whole family
will vanish away.

My long lost father
trudging home through
this strange, cold city,
its whirling snows,
unemployed and angry,
living off charity.

Finding a home only
in brother John's speakeasy.
Beneath the stoop
a flare of revelry.
And yet you found time
to croon to your last son.

Dear father, a gracenote.
That Christmas, you did
find a job, guarding a
hole in the navy yard.
Elated, you celebrated
so well, you fell in.

Not a model father.·
I was only happy
when I was drunk
you said, years later,
laying a fire in
a room I was working in.

Still you soldiered on
all those years alone
in a Brooklyn boardinghouse
without your family
until the job was done:
then limped home.

John Montague, an Irish poet, currently serves as Professor of Anglo-Irish Literature at the Sorbonne.

Poet of the People

JAMES T. FARRELL

"The world of childhood," William Dean Howells said, "the childhood of that vanished West, which lay between the Ohio and the Mississippi, was, unless memory abuses my fondness, the happiest land there ever was under the sun."

James Whitcomb Riley held sentiments about pre-Civil War Midwestern childhood similar to those of Howells. He was born in 1849 in Greenfield, Indiana. All during his life, he looked backward with nostalgic and sentimental eyes upon his own childhood days in Indiana. He referred to this time of his life again and again in his verse. He turned the yearnings of childhood, the unfulfilled dreams of boyhood into cliché after cliché. In one poem, he wrote:

> Dreaming again, in anticipation,
> The same old dreams of our boyhood days
> That never came true . . .

This quotation is illustrative of what Riley later felt about his childhood. Personal statements of his, made to his biographer, Marcus Dickey, match what he said in his verse.

When Riley was a boy, there was still an enormous frontier. Metaphorically speaking, it was just beyond the horizon of Greenfield, Indiana. As a lad, Riley could see the

48

new pioneers passing along the National Road. He could watch the new waves sweep on, and as he did, his eye would be held, most especially, by those who seemed eccentric, and who might be wearing raggedy clothes.

Many have observed that the migration into the American wilderness was not like the migrations of barbarians in the past. It was a movement from civilization into wilderness. This can be seen more concretely, perhaps, if we try to think of Riley gazing out of his schoolroom window in Greenfield and seeing the wagons going by, watching all kinds and types of human beings as they moved on to penetrate farther into the American West. Those who had come earlier, those who were of the same generation as Riley's father and grandfather, had built schoolhouses similar to the one from which the boy, James Whitcomb Riley, looked out. And this great migration of human beings from civilization into the wilderness, beginning long before Riley's birth and continuing during his boyhood days, was practically unprecedented in history.

The settlers brought with them not only the tools of civilization, but also their ideas of civilization; and in some of their wagons there were books. They came from a background of democratic political experiences. They desired to be free. They were going forth, individually, to find their fortunes, and, socially, to conquer and build a continent. As they moved on, they passed the schoolhouses and courthouses that their pioneer predecessors had already built. Culturally as well as economically, they were to have a part in the shaping of new destinies. Frederick Jackson Turner, commenting on just such matters in *The Frontier in Ameriican History*, wrote: "The conception was firmly fixed in the thirties and forties that the West was the coming power in the Union, that the fate of civilization was in its hands . . ."

The Mississippi valley, during the Jacksonian days, and immediately after them, was not a new Athens. But it was an area in which a vigorous new society lived. And there were books in this area. Marcus Dickey, in *The Youth of James Whitcomb Riley*, remarked on this fact. He pointed out that Scott, Dickens, and other writers were known and read on the frontier. One frequently comes on letters of the pioneers that suggest a level of culture as well as idealism and dreams of an American future. In fact, there is pathos in some of these letters when we read them with the advantages of hindsight. For we are still so far from reaching even an approximation of some of the early dreams and promise of American life.

The role of books in this transplanted culture is most dramatically personified in the career of Abraham Lincoln. And especially for those so-called practical men who scoff and sneer at books, it is pertinent to emphasize the fact that, without books, Lincoln could not have risen and developed to become the great and humane man whose memory is so honored. Lincoln's ambitions were stimulated by the world of books, not by that of crass Philistines: Lincoln's ideas and his emotional and intellectual development were intimately bound up with books.

A later era turned the image of American promise into the Horatio Alger figure, who is thrifty and provident but not intellectually curious. However, the real personification of the promise of American life at its best is Abraham Lincoln. And the story of Lincoln includes the picture of Lincoln reading and studying by candlelight in a log cabin. This image has been sentimentalized, and the significance of the book in this Lincoln picture has been reduced. However, in this image of Lincoln, the book is central. The picture loses all meaning if the book is lost sight of. Abraham Lincoln developed because there were pioneers who brought ideas, democratic hopes and books, as well as tools and arms, with them into the American wilderness. James Whitcomb Riley wrote of Lincoln in this connection:

"Lincoln was a rich man. He lived in the American woods. . . . How rich he was with that handful of seven books by the cabin fire. What value he attached to his visit to this world: every day a day of discovery, a new survey of facts and principles, every day reaching out like widespreading trees around him for soil and water. I would rather see what he saw and loved than see the skyline of a great city."

Mark Twain's career is also bound up with the frontier. The story of Riley's own life indicates that he identified himself with both Lincoln and Twain, but especially with the latter. He often cited Tom Sawyer and Huckleberry Finn and tried to read something of their fictional lives into his own memories of boyhood. And he commented on the fact that he, like Mark Twain, had opposed his father.

Such critics as Van Wyck Brooks and Lewis Mumford, and even Parrington to some extent, have misunderstood what I believe is the most healthy and important element in Mark Twain's work—the influence of the frontier, and the manner in which he reflected its attitudes. Mark Twain was, essentially, a product of frontier culture. Pioneer America possessed the elements of a democratic civilization tha made it possible for both a Lincoln and a Mark Twain to develop. It afforded opportunities for expression, as well as many chances for material advancement.

Looking back on these times in pioneer America, we can see a dawn of intellectual and artistic ambition. Standing behind Twain, there were scores of local humorists. Twain's style—which has permanently influenced American prose—was a relative perfecting of the mutations which many others had introduced into English as it was spoken and written in pioneer America. And as Bernard De Voto has indicated, we can note as traits in earlier American writing, improvisation, inventiveness, a daring and a willingness to launch out in a new use of words and of syntax.

One of the sources of this development is to be found in the local and the country papers. "The country editor," wrote Turner, "was the leader of his people, not a patent insides-recorder of social function, but a vigorous independent thinker and writer." There were energetic men in this period, and many of them contributed towards laying the groundwork of a vigorous culture. Something was happening to rouse the imagination. And a sense of this development did find expression in the great poetry of Walt Whitman.

Granted that we can see what was best, culturally and intellectually, in the lives of figures such as Lincoln and Mark Twain, men like these cannot grow out of an intellectual soil that is totally barren. They must develop in a social and mental climate that can contribute to their perspective and ambitions. We know that such a climate did exist. And in this connection, a descriptive statement of Turner's is illuminating. "Farmer boys walked behind the plow with their book in hand, and sometimes forgot to turn at the end of the furrow; even rare boys, who, like young Howells 'limped barefoot by his father's side with his eyes on the cow and his mind on Cervantes and Shakespeare.' "

America has properly been described as a new world. This simple description can either be a banality, or a meaningful statement in accordance with the way in which we develop and concretize it. What kind of life has been permitted to develop in this new world? How has the individual fitted into it? The meaning of a society is revealed in its most concentrated form in the culture of a society. What kind of a culture did this new world produce? These are only some of the questions we could ask in order to analyze, in answering them, what this new world has meant, or what it might have meant. Here, we cannot even attempt to answer these questions.

However, a few comments and observation are in order. Referring to the literature of the Midwest, Turner observed: "But for the most part, the literature of the region and the period was imitative or reflective of the common things in a not uncommon way. It is to its children that the Middle West had to look for the expression of its life and its ideals, rather than to the busy pioneer who was breaking a prairie farm or building up a new community." The conditions of life in pioneer America were not obviously promising for the development of a high level of humane culture in the European sense. Energies were applied to more practical affairs than those of culture. And material opportunities were too great for most to neglect these for cultural pursuits. In addition, the meaning of life in America was being lived out. The contrast of a new world and an old world existed in the inner world of men as well as in the external sphere.

This contrast can be seen as a contradiction, an antithesis, a split, a dissociation which has often been reflected in American writing. Many illustrations of this could be offered. It is bound up in typical Eastern or Atlantic seaboard attitudes towards writers from the Midwest. The genteel tradition, as it were, opposed itself to those who, while using an old tradition which they inherited, were molding and beginning a new tradition.

Much has been made of the experience of Howells and of Mark Twain when they went East. Other and later writers from the Midwest met with similar experiences. They ran into a snobbery similar to that which Mark Twain and William Dean Howells encountered. One of the essential features of this snobbery is of a repressive character. This repressiveness is to be seen in criticism and objection to Midwestern writers' finding and evolving their own style, their own patterns and ways of presenting characters and events, and their own expressions of what they feel and think and of what their created characters also feel and think.

By and large, this bespeaks a deficiency in understanding. And it has often been parochial. Much parochialism has come out of Midwestern America: James Whitcomb Riley, was, himself, parochial. But many of the exponents of the genteel tradition had their own parochialism. In our own century, we can see this exhibited by the late Dr. Irving Babbitt of Harvard, who, in effect, tried to confine the culture of mankind to a small village church and a small village church cemetery of the spirit.

Critics of Midwestern writing have often borrowed the achievements of English and Continental culture, and used this borrowing—with which they had nothing to do—as a means of attacking and slurring Midwestern writers. This is irrelevant, and it is often lacking in sincerity. And it is a revelation of dissociation in American culture. "The English language," declared Thomas Bailey Aldrich, "is too rich and sacred a thing to be mutilated and vulgarized." On the basis of such a view, he preferred the more formal verse of Riley to the latter's dialect verse. And this same attitude has been revealed again and again by exponents of the genteel tradition, and, also, by bifurcated exponents and appreciators of the great traditions of Continental culture.

Aspects of this same contrast and dissociation can be perceived in *The Adventures of Tom Sawyer*. Mark Twain's parody of romantic literature, for instance, is related to what was expressed about kings and royalty in *The Adventures of Huckleberry Finn*, and to the view of feudal culture, satirized in the tale of his Connecticut Yankee. We can see his attitude focused in the contrasting characterizations of Tom Sawyer and Huckleberry Finn, a contrast which is even revealed in differences in the language which he put into the mouths of these two boys.

Huck Finn spoke the language of his environment. Tom spoke this language, but he also talked the language of the romantic novels which he had read. Huck's language is, on the whole, recognizably more expressive and more poetic. Tom ritualizes the play of the boys. They must play pirates according to "style." Style is what is described as having been done by pirates in the books. Tom is inventive and his ability to improvise in play suggests that he well could have grown up to become the Connecticut Yankee.

But in this ritualization of play as "style," Mark Twain was satirizing romantic falseness. It is akin to his satire of the methods of teaching also to be found in *The Adventures of Tom Sawyer*. It was a means of poking fun at sentimentality. Huck Finn, as Bernard De Voto has aptly suggested, is a kind of a boy squatter. Whereas Tom's mental universe is partly formed out of the romantic books he has read, Huck's grows out of his direct experiences. In this sense, we can assert that as a literary characterization,

Huck Finn reveals himself as an American boy who is *feeling* his own environment. It is not too exaggerated to describe him as an imagined American cultural personification.

Huck is confused by what Tom calls style. It is beyond Huck's range of experience. And this is the precise point which I wish to stress here. These were elements of old world culture which were either beyond the range of experience of many in pioneer America, or else, these were not especially useful and helpful in the process of coming to feel and see the meanings of life in this new world. And when "vulgarity" and "mutations" in language and in literary themes were, in reality, an effort to grasp something of the emotional and intellectual significance of the evolving life of pioneer America, they were not vulgarity.

Frank Norris declared: "A literature that cannot be vulgarized is no literature at all and will perish." Here, of course, we know what was called vulgarity. It included the work of Mark Twain and of Walt Whitman. Later, it included many others writers. We are not discussing principles in a vacuum, or in general terms. We are, likewise, not dealing with taste on a merely formal level. We have, rather, problems and developments which related to a full and rich historic content.

Vulgarity, in this context, was used to include sincerity, simplicity, frankness, humor, expressiveness, responsiveness to immediate experience. Vulgarity, in fact, meant much of life as it is lived: it also meant the expansion and adaptation of language as this language was being changed in a New World.

We could further explore the issues which I have raised. As a matter of fact, this entire field still remains quite open, and we have much to learn from it. We understand it only superficially. And this field is that of our own origins.

II

One of the problems of cultural history and analysis which is all too infrequently dealt with in America is this—

how does the consciousness of writers evolve, develop, take shape in this country? Here, however, I can only suggest that such a problem should be posed and dealt with, and that it is also pertinent to the works of James Whitcomb Riley.

The analysis presented above should suggest the kind of cultural climate in which Riley grew up. Riley spoke at length of his boyhood, and his remarks are copiously quoted in Marcus Dickey's, *The Youth of James Whitcomb Riley*. Riley loved nature. He loved the streams, the fields. He hated and resented school. In after years, he spoke of school with contempt, because of the discipline of the three R's, the whippings, the floggings, and the boresomeness of the appeal to pure verbal authority.

"Omit the schoolmarm from my history entirely," he said to Marcus Dickey, "and the record of my career would not be seriously affected." Reading this and other and longer statements which he made to Marcus Dickey, I am inclined to suspect that he was overstating his resentment, and that there is in his words something of the affected note of a man consciously speaking to impress an audience by an appeal to stereotyped attitudes.

However, I do believe that there was no such affectation in another of his remarks to Mr. Dickey when he said of himself that he "was a timid boy as I have been a bashful man." To me, the over-crystallized nostalgia for his own boyhood at a time when dreams and anticipations never came true strongly suggests timidity. Likewise, his stereotyped poems sentimentally dismissing the attractions of fame, suggest the desire for fame on the part of one who, while bashful and timid, is also highly self-centered and ambitious.

However, these remarks can lead us into psychological speculation. Let it suffice for our purposes here that we accept his own statement about his timidity.

Marcus Dickey remarked of Riley that "The pioneer past was a rich landscape for him. At the time Riley attended school—school that was pretty much of a closed and narrowed universe for him—there was that continuing flow of new pioneers, roustabouts, itinerants, nondescripts and others, past the schoolhouse. School and knowledge signified a discipline of the three R's imposed by adults. But outside the wagons flowed on to the West."

Besides, there was that world of nature he loved. Here was a rich and open world of material to feed the senses of boys. The world of pioneer America was a rich one for boys because there was so much upon which the senses could feed, so much upon which the imagination could fasten. There was the awesome beauty of nature, there was a sense of space, there was the animal world, and there was the opportunity for free and wide-ranging play.

Along with this, there was a social world of building, of motion, which embodied a genuine confidence in the future. Careers were open. To the West there was free land. Many who were dissatisfied could pick up and move on. These boys were the sons or the grandsons of those who had left their homes to forge ahead through the Cumberland Gap and over the Alleghenies to this new world.

We see then that there was a social basis for the kind and quality of dreams and experiences of many boys in the American Midwest, prior to the Civil War. All of us are, more or less, nostalgic for our childhood. This note of nostalgia for childhood, which was expressed by Howells, by Mark Twain, and which was one of the major, if stereotyped, themes of James Whitcomb Riley, can, in the light of these remarks, become doubly understandable to us.

I have mentioned James Whitcomb Riley's resentment of school. This seems to be part of a commonplace and possibly affected resentment of authority which we can find in his life, but not in his work. The Rileys were poor in the post-Civil War days. Riley's father, a village lawyer, never recouped what he lost by serving in the Union Army.

One night in his youth, Riley dressed up to go out: he was dressed very shabbily. His father, noticing this, told him that he could come into the garden and hoe. Riley obeyed. But suddenly, he threw his hoe over the fence and into the garden of a neighbor. This was his declaration of independence.

At a later date, when speaking of this incident in his life, he said: "I used language that would sear the walls of a synagogue. I resolved never to work with a hoe again—and I never did." After throwing the hoe over the fence, Riley marched off, resolute and angry. From this time on, his relationships with his father were strained.

During this youthful period, he worked at various jobs, and then he became an itinerant. When he first began to write verse, his father believed that this was not a proper career for a young man. But while Riley avowed that he had no objection, per se, to working with a hoe, he did not want this kind of work for himself.

We cannot attempt to analyze this action of Riley's fully, but we can note that involved in it was the dawning of cultural aspiration. And this dawning of cultural aspiration in American youth is something much more common than many may be aware of. There have been American youths throwing away their hoes, literally or symbolically, for many decades. This is a natural, normal, and fairly characteristic aspect of American experiences. Riley's action here forms the pattern for the actions of many American writers of widely varying degrees of talent and achievement.

Since others have discussed Riley's verse in detail, I shall confine myself to a few rather general and characterizing observations.

Riley's verse emphasizes a feeling for security. It gives almost endless expression to received sentiments. It tends to ritualize human emotions in terms of accepted sentimentalities. I have already spoken of the awesomeness of the open world of pioneer America. Life was, as it were, very new and very young and it was changing and full of motion. But there is, also, much evidence to suggest that many hungered for security. The history of the building of the American continent shows how many went so far, emigrated, set up their stakes in a new place and there settled down, wanting, for themselves, no more change and uncertainty.

This desire for security has permeated small town life. The sentimentality of Riley—at times his verse became like a fog of sentimentality—seems to me to be but one of many expressions of this feeling for security. The emotions which he expressed are usually safe. They are lost in nostalgia, quilted in formalized reveries, and they are rarely spontaneous.

Insecurity, adventure, freedom is expressed, largely, in the image of the ragged and shabby itinerant who is a stage or typed character. Riley's verses are highly self-centered, and again and again, satisfaction is expressed in terms of cliché. In particular, love is rendered into a cozy cliché. Thus, these concluding stanzas from *An Old Sweetheart of Mine:*

> When we should live together in a cozy little cot
> Hid in a nest of roses, with a fairy garden spot,
> Where the vines were ever fruited, and the
>   weather ever fine,
> And the birds were ever singing for that old
>   sweetheart of mine.
>
> When I should be her lover forever and a day
> And she my faithful sweetheart till the golden
>   hair was gray;
> And we should be so happy that when either's
>   lip were dumb
> They would not smile in Heaven till the other's
>   kiss had come.

Many favor Riley's dialect poems and value them more highly than his formal verse. These offended such an Easterner as Thomas Bailey Aldrich, whom I have quoted above. In these, something of the life and interests of the farmers and of small town life creeps into the lines, but these are also usually stereotyped. They contain lines which are also fresh or perceptive, but as a whole, this dialect poetry is contrived and artificial. However, it does reveal something of the life, the character, the social relationships and interests of the farmers and small town people of his time. It gives a mirror—often distorted by sentimentality, however—of the times.

Donald Culross Peattie, in his preface, "Riley as a Nature Poet," to *The Complete Poetical Works of James Whitcomb Riley*, divided nature poets into two schools: ". . . those who find in Nature, a reflection of their own moods or a sermon for human betterment, like Wordsworth, and that rarer sort that tries to echo Nature with her own voice. It is a comparatively easy and pleasant thing to talk about one's self; apparently it is harder, as the naturalists already know, to report Nature." Peattie was setting up a misleading contrast here, for he used this contrast in order to establish Riley's reputation as a nature poet.

This is unnecessary, and like most such comparisons and contrasts, when used to hail a writer, it lacks validity. It is open to question as to whether or not we can say that nature has moods. The major illustration from Riley's poems which Peattie cited, was a descriptive one, delineating a blue jay. Peattie's inconsistency here suggests the misleading character of his unnecessary comparison with Wordsworth. I should agree with Peattie that Riley was a nature poet. His observation of phases of nature, of birds, of trees, fields, streams and sky was often very clear. And he, at times, registered seasonal changes with high suggestive power. I would here especially cite his poem, "August."

But Riley talked about himself in his nature poetry, as much as, if not more than, did Wordsworth. And usually he talked about himself less interestingly. He often used nature as a means of alluding to banal reveries which he allegedly had. He marred his nature poetry with accounts of his ever-recurrent and weak nostalgia for the boyhood and the boyhood dreams and visions, which "never came true."

Riley's poetry is part of the regional literature of the Midwest, generally characterized by Frederick Jackson Turner in the quotation which I have cited above. It was largely "imitative and reflective of common things in a not uncommon way." It contained, in some of the dialect poetry, especially "Little Orphan Annie," elements of a new expression, and of native humor. And it contained passages of true nature poetry, revealing feeling for the barnyards, fields, trees, streams, and skies of Indiana. This contrasted with his many crystallized sentimentalities.

Furthermore, he was, at times, bumptious and bucolic. His feeling of individualism at times approaches a rigid self-centeredness, as well as a confidence about the community in which he lived. This spilled over into parochialism. His work can be related to that of such writers as George Ade and Booth Tarkington, but this is a task that must be left for another occassion.

Riley can also be seen as a Midwestern phenomenon at a time of change. There is, in my mind, a sociological significance in his sentimentality, in his demonstration of a will for security in a world of change. He reveals an inner world at great variance with a changing outer world. He drew on the sources of culture brought into the West with the pioneers, and added to these touches of the new and evolving life which was being created all about him.

But he closed out of his verse more of this new world than he let into it. Again and again he tamed this world, and locked it up safely in his clichés of emotion, as Whitman and as Mark Twain did not do. We can here note how he reveals the dissociation which I have commented on above. He drew on resources from without, from English literature in particular, but only to make of these an imputation which was not individualized, not used as a cultural heritage to be assimilated as part of the cultural background from which the New World culture would be created.

After all, he wrote very many poems like "A Life-Lesson," which I quote in full:

> There! little girl; don't cry!
>   They have broken your doll, I know;
>   And your tea-set blue,
>   And your play-house too,

Are things of the long-ago;
  But childish troubles will soon pass by—
  There! little girl; don't cry!

There! little girl; don't cry!
  They have broken your slate, I know;
    And the glad, wild ways
    Of your schoolgirl days
  Are things of the long-ago;
    But life and love will soon come by—
    There! little girl; don't cry!

There! little girl; don't cry!
  They have broken your heart, I know;
    And the rainbow gleams
    Of your youthful dreams
  Are things of the long ago;
    But Heaven holds all for which you sigh—
    There! little girl; don't cry!

The "long ago" of Riley was usually the dreamed-of "never was," which walled out the spontaneous welling up of dream and feeling and emotion and aspiration which is, or should be, part of every human life. The "long ago" was a dream of false inner security.

III

Writing about "An American Literature" in *Democratic Vistas*, Walt Whitman stated: "What is the reason our time, our lands, that we see no fresh local courage, sanity, of our own. . . . But always, instead, a parcel of dandies and en-nuyees, dapper little gentlemen from abroad, who flood us with their thin sentiment of parlors, parasols, piano-songs, tinkling rhymes, the five-hundredth importation—or whimpering and crying about something, chasing one aborted conceit after another, and forever occupied in dyspeptic amours with dyspeptic women."
And in contrast to this, Whitman spoke of the possi-

bilities of a great new poetry in this country. "America," he asserted, in this same essay, "demands a poetry that is bold, modern, and all-surrounding and kosmical, as she is herself. It must in no respect ignore science or the modern, but inspire itself with science and the modern. It must bend its vision toward the future, more than the past. Like America, it must extricate itself from even the greatest models of the past, and, while courteous to them, must have entire faith in itself, and the products of its own democratic spirit only." And he also declared that this prophetic poetry which he called "the divine pride of man in himself" should be placed "in the van."

What Whitman called for, in such lines as those I have quoted, should be regarded as a perspective, and not as a rigidly accepted program. And the most important emphasis in Whitman's perspective is on the meaningfulness of the experiences of Americans in their new world. Whitman was profoundly aware that a new world was in the making. He hailed science and technology. But more than anything else, he emphasized the importance, the dignity of each and every human being.

In another portion of *Democratic Vistas*, he wrote: "As I perceive, the tendencies of our day, in the States (and I entirely respect them) are toward those vast and sweeping movements, influences, moral and physical, of humanity . . . on the scale of the impulses of the elements. Even for the treatment of the universal, in politics, in metaphysics, or anything, sooner or later, we come down to one single, solitary soul."

Many others beside Whitman have stressed the need for a new culture in America. I have chosen to cite and quote Whitman here because he perceived, so clearly, that men must be seen as ends, not as means or instruments, and that a new culture must celebrate the dignity of men and women. Thus truism is at the roots of all great cultural traditions.

However, I think it necessary to add that dignity is not

to be seen in an honorific sense. One does not attribute dignity to men and women by flattering them, by falsifying the nature of their emotions, or by neglecting to try and understand more than we now do of the nature of their experience. It is not by mere elegance of language, by hymns of virtue and purity, by an ostrich-like attitude toward what is weak in men that we see their real, or their potential dignity. In substance, we can state that Whitman called for a poetry, a literature that would honestly explore the nature of experience in America.

We are familiar enough with the general nature of the changes which have come about, not only in America but in the entire world, during the hundred and twenty-five years since James Whitcomb Riley was born. These have come "on a scale of the impulses of the elements." Thus, the beginnings of the discovery concerning the use of atomic energy.

We seem more than a century and a quarter away from our forbears of who were alive at Riley's birth. Our inner world seems to us to be different from theirs. Collectively, we possess much more power than they possessed: individually, we feel much less confident, much less secure than they felt. Collectively, we live in a world of greater danger and menace than they did: individually and in a temporary social sense, we seem to be more secure from visible dangers. We face no dangers of the wilderness. Our wilderness is ourselves, our emotions, our fears, our anxieties, our despairs, our individual and lonely fears, in the face of the collective power of man to utilize the very "impulses of the elements" in a way that can destroy us all.

Materially, we have seen the day when many of the promises of American life have been fulfilled. Socially, and in a human sense, we are far, very far from achieving even an approximation of these promises. Some of the best of our modern American literature, for instance the work of Theodore Dreiser and of Sherwood Anderson, has dramatized this fact. It has dramatized something of the story of what the development of American civilization has cost in terms of the quality of ideals in America, and in terms, also, of what this has meant emotionally and psychologically.

The type of security which was reflected in Riley's writings—and about which I have commented above—is non-existent. His verse here might be described as an unreal little dream village in a world of social and psychological wilderness. And this social and psychological wilderness might also be described as the new American frontier of our day.

When Riley was born, there was a great physical and material unknown not far beyond the Indiana horizon. Today, we can say that there is a great psychological and social unknown and that it is in ourselves, and in each and every "single, solitary soul." America was discovered by Columbus. It was conquered and built up to its present state of power and greatness by the pioneers and by many of the sons and daughters of the pioneers. The new discovery of America, the re-discovery of America, awaits us and our children. And this re-discovery must involve the winning of a greater sense of what all of this has meant, and what all of this felt like, not only to masses, but again, to the single, solitary soul, to many single solitary souls. And literature is one of the most powerful of human inventions which permit us to make such revelations.

We are still linked with our pioneer and our frontier past. It is our social and cultural womb. Its democratic hopes, its independence, its courage, all of this has been passed on to us. And this legacy has been personified for us most admirably in such great figures as Abraham Lincoln, Walt Whitman, and Mark Twain.

The American past, the American present, the American future are all part of an undiscovered cultural world. The "long ago" of our history was a world of human beings as complex, as fallible, as psychologically complicated as we are, or as we may deem ourselves to be. What they did needs to be understood.

That increased understanding can amount to an enlargement and to a re-discovery of the past. The past, coming down to us in traditions, should not be a dead and rigid system of formal wisdom, of sentiments hallowed by honorific words, of merely received opinions and received sentiments. Rather, it should be part of a living tradition that transmits what has been done, what has been thought, what has been experienced and felt. In our culture, in our literature, we can strive to carry this on, and we can strive to transmit something of what we have done, what we have thought, what we have experienced and felt.

But to try and achieve this, we need to stimulate new and sincere cultural impulses all over this country. Some inspiration—much inspiration—can be drawn from the frontier and pioneer past. But this should be an inspiration to encourage us in using our own eyes and in seeing with them. We can continue the best of this tradition by trying to clear and to conquer our own social and psychological wilderness. To do this, we need to understand more, and to feel more deeply. And a frank and fearless contemporary literature can help us to try and do this.

Writing of "The West and American Ideals," Frederick Jackson Turner took Tennyson's Ulysses as a symbol. These lines of Tennyson which he quoted are so appropriate that I shall re-quote them here.

> . . . I am become a name
> For always roaming with an hungry heart,
> Much have I seen and known . . .
> I am a part of all that I have met;
> Yet all experience is an arch, where thro'
> Gleams that untravelled world, whose margin
>   fades
> Forever and forever when I move.
> How dull it is to pause, to make an end.
> To rust unburnished, not to shine in use!
> . . .
> And this gray spirit yearning in desire
> To follow knowledge like a shining star
> Beyond the utmost bound of human thought.

. . . Come my friends.
'Tis not too late to seek a newer world.
Push off, and sitting well in order smite
The sounding furrows; for my purpose holds
To sail beyond the sunset, and the baths
Of all the Western stars until I die
. . .
To strive, to seek, to find and not to yield.

American literature, can seek, like Ulysses, to become
that name for the experiences of the men and women who
live as citizens of the nation that has been built out of a
wilderness.

Mr. Farrell has written extensively of the American Irish in the
STUDS LONIGAN *trilogy and other works.*

The Irish Physician as a Poet

KEVIN M. CAHILL, M.D.

No one knew the Irish peasant, his customs and problems, as well as the Irish physician. Although many of us are aware of medicine's debt to Irish clinicians, few realize that they are remembered as well for songs and poems contributed over the centuries to the Celtic heritage.

The history of Eire has often been sad, and the Irish poets have mirrored her moods. The joy of the green hills and salmon-filled lakes is captured in lilting rhyme as are the anguish of famine, the hopes of emigrants, and the anger and hatred of the oppressed. When her conquerors forbade the very word "Ireland," the Irish sang lovingly of Eileen Aroon. When her schools were closed down, the Irish hedge masters passed on the Celtic legends in epics and ballads to the young in the fields. The opportunities of higher education were often limited for the Irish, however, and writing was a talent too few possessed. It was the intellectual leaders of Irish communities, frequently the physician or priest, who were often called upon to express or translate, and thereby preserve, the poetic heritage of the land. The renowed contributions of Irish medicine have been reviewed already, but the debt owed to Irish physician-poets has not been appreciated.

Examples of physician-poets can be found in every era of Irish history—the Gaelic, the eighteenth-nineteenth centuries and the twentieth century. The men selected in this study all were born and trained in Ireland so that even those who emigrated did so with the formative impressions of Eire upon them. The examples of poetry included have not been chosen primarily for their literary quality but rather as representative selections of the emotions of a particular era in Irish history or as evidence of the influence of medicine on the poet's composition.

It is often impossible to dissociate myth from reality in studying the lives of early Gaelic personalities. The poet is often regarded (if only by himself) as seer, priest, healer and judge as well as a scholar, entertainer and poet. In reviewing manuscripts of the Royal Irish Academy, Dublin, one finds, nevertheless, at least a half dozen examples of poets who practiced medicine as a profession and who were regarded by contemporaries as physicians.

Besides transcribing an early (1139 A.D.) Materia Medica of Ireland, Eoin O'Callanain, a seventeenth century Dublin physician, wrote at least nine poems still extant in various Celtic manuscripts. A long ballad by his contemporaries in praise of O'Callanain's medical knowledge is in the Gaelic collection of the Royal Irish Academy. Another physician-poet of whom we know little is Eamonn O'Cassaide, one of the scribes of a long medical treatise written in 1676. Nothing remains of his biography, and the sole poem known to have been composed by him is partly illegible. A long medical poem of the late seventeenth century is ascribed to "Diarmuid O'Siadhail, an eminent doctor of physic." The epic is divided into thirty-one chapters, each dealing with a distinct aspect of diagnosis and therapy. The poem opens with a consideration of the problems of the skull:

A headache to the tip of the head—
It is fitting to cure it with the efforts
Of crosses, as you formerly said,
And with planks and herbs.

The Aisling or Vision poem in Irish literature represents a poignant lament in a Gaelic parable of the state of Ireland under foreign domination. In one of the most exquisite examples of this type of poem, Donnchadh O'Calanain, a seventeenth century physician, writes of a maiden bemoaning the loss of her green cloak—i.e., the land of Ireland. In classic Aisling form he begins:

On a bright morning with a gentle mist
I went into the wilderness.
I saw a regal woman, and she
    standing on a bright hillock.
The sound of her voice was more beautiful
    than the music of faeries or cuckoos.
The beginning and end of her role
    concerned a little green cloak . . .

Another Irish manuscript is prefaced by a scribe with, "Seadhan O'Dubhthigh is cuimhin liom doctuir leighis agus priomascollaire"—I remember Sean O'Duffy, a doctor of medicine and an eminent scholar. The long ballad tells of his experiences "when he travell'd abroad to discover the Longitude." Dr. Seamus Woods (1758-1828) was a Gaelic speaking physician, antiquarian, and poet. He is remembered in Irish

70

literary history as the sponsor of a large Iomarbhaigh or bardic festival in 1825. In a contemporary manuscript he is described as "a prominent physician beloved and highly respected by all." A ballad, which was written in honor of Daniel O'Connell's return from London, may be translated:

> We welcome you, O gracious guiding star.
> Your coming from the noble mansions of Breachtan—
> Full of vice and unwarlike gloom—
> Through the guile of every fool in that tricky family.
> O distinguished star who shall save us
> From the fearful Penal Laws,
> Our strong affection will be with you
> To the eternal limit of the world.

Medical licensing was not vigorously enforced in eighteenth century Ireland, and great doubt surrounds the validity of the qualifications of some of our physician-poets. Oliver Goldsmith (1728-1774), one of Dublin's most famous sons, is known to have studied anatomy in Edinburgh but was found "not qualified" as a surgeon in London in 1758. After 1763, however, he referred to himself as "Doctor" intimating that he had received his medical degree during his travels to Padua, Louvain and Paris. There is no record that he ever qualified at these universities, but he did practice medicine briefly in Ireland before devoting his full time to literature. To select any one passage from his numerous works as reflecting the sensitivity or insight from his medical leanings is impossible for, as Dr. Johnson said, "There was almost no kind of writing that he did not touch, none that he did not adorn."

Doubt surrounds the qualification of Paul Hiffernan (1719-1777), a friend of Goldsmith, who returned to Dublin as an

M.D. after seventeen years of "unhappy notoriety for imprudence" in France. He claimed to have been trained at Montepellier, but there is no record of his having studied medicine there. In addition to his lucrative private medical practice he also served the local English gentry by composing satirical poems about Irish nationalists. He finally fled to London where he paid for his debauches by lecturing on anatomy and writing political tracts and magazine articles; nothing of literary value remains.

Michael Clancy (1704-1761) also supplied his own M.D. without benefit of University conferral. He, at least, had apprenticed himself to several physicians and on the death of one wrote to Dean Swift:

> My faithful friend is gone, and you
> The worth of Helsham's friendship knew.
> Alas, weak mimic of his skill
> I learned to guide the healing pill.

Medical practice was cut short by blindness and he devoted himself entirely to literature, producing one comedy that flourished on both the Dublin and London stages for several seasons.

Several of the Irish physician-poets of the eighteenth century are remembered more as political figures than as either medical or literary men. John Brenan's (1768-1830) medical reputation in Dublin was due largely to his use of turpentine for the treatment of puerperal fever. Even this controversial custom, however, waned before the scurrillous poems he published in his *Milesian Magazine*. One epic of satirical rhyme, exceeding 1000 lines of libel, was entitled a "Poetical Review of the Dublin Doctors".

Jeremiah John Callanan (1795-1829) was characterized in

an English obituary as "indolent, irresolute and unpractical"; his decision to forsake medical practice and become a wandering bard in the wild mountain areas of Southwest Ireland was not calculated to win English understanding or admiration. He collected and preserved in verse many of the popular traditions of Kerry and Cork and his poem, "Gougane Barra" not only captures the rugged beauty of that lovely spot but pictures the resentment and dreams of a captive people and the prophesies of an idealist:

> Still, still in those wilds might young liberty rally,
> And send her strong shout over mountain and valley,
> The Star of the West might yet rise in its glory,
> And the land that was darkest be brightest in story.
> I too shall be gone; but my name shall be spoken
> When Erin awakes and her fetters are broken.

The Drennan family provided several generations of physician-poets. The elder William Drennan (1754-1820) obtained his medical degree in Edinburgh and practised in Belfast and Dublin. Apart from his large medical practice he became a leader in the movement for Catholic Emancipation and Gaelic renaissance; he was a co-founder—with Theobold Wolfe Tone—of the United Irishmen. These interests culminated in his arrest for "seditious treason" and he was quietly retired in Belfast. His literary endeavors included translation from Latin, Greek, French and Gaelic, and in one of his delicate lyrics he first coined the phrase, "The Emerald Isle." His noble efforts for Ireland's freedom are obvious in the proud refrain:

> In her sun, in her soil, in her station, thrice-blest
> With her back turned to Britain, her face to the West,
> Erin stands proudly insular, on her steep shore,
> And strikes her high harp to the ocean's deep roar.

Both his sons followed the medical and poetic footsteps of their father. William Jr. (1781-1847) translated ballads of Irish history and popularized many German songs. His brother John (1784-1859) evidenced their medical background more clearly:

> By a patient too fair sate a doctor too young
> With eyes more intent on her lips, than her tongue;
> He tested her heart, as its pulse's recorder
> But alas! in his own was the latent disorder;
> And soon from the region in which it was bred,
> That sad "tremor cordis" so muddled his head
> That instead of some physic to mend her condition
> He urged, as a recipe, take your physician.

A poet who emigrated to the United States after also being accused of "sedition" was Robert Dwyer Joyce (1830-1883). After graduating from Queens College Medical School in Dublin he developed a reputation for his nationalistic verse as "Poet of the Fenian Movement." He served briefly as Professor of English at Catholic University of Dublin before political pressures forced him to flee. After many years of successful medical practice in Boston he returned to Dublin where he died. Richard R. Madden (1798-1886) studied medicine in Paris, Naples and London, obtaining an F.R.C.S. and establishing a large surgical practice on Harley Street. His political ambitions were nurtured by appointments as Justice in Jamaica and Colonial Secretary in Australia. Returning to Ireland as a government official in 1848 he was overwhelmed by the misery associated with the Potato Famine and forsook his diplomatic posts to aid in the fight for Irish freedom. His poetic contributions include a presentation of a Jamaican slave's prayer, a collection of literary works of the United

Irishmen, and several autobiographical volumes containing light verse.

Richard D'Alton Williams (1822-1862) incorporated in his life and work many of the features peculiar to Irish physician-poets. During his medical training at St. Vincent's and Steevens' Hospitals in Dublin he became involved in Ireland's struggle for independence. Writing under the pseudonym "Shamrock" he edited and contributed to nationalist magazines and papers. After being arrested for treason he fled to the United States. A selection of his early humorous poems were collected as "The Misadventures of a Medical Student," but the impact of his hospital experience is even more clearly manifest in the opening stanza of his poem, "The Dying Consumptive":

> From a Munster vale they brought her,
> From the pure and balmy air;
> An Ormond peasant's daughter,
> With blue eyes and golden hair.
> They brought her to the city
> And she faded slowly there—
> Consumption has no pity
> For blue eyes and golden hair.

One final political figure of the eighteenth century physician-poet group was Robert Adair (1711-1789) who, as a young surgeon, departed from Dublin after an illicit love affair. He settled in London, married into nobility and retired many years later as Surgeon-General of the English Army. His own verse is not nearly as well known as his wife's lonely lament:

> What's this dull town to me?
> Robin's not near

He whom I wish to see,
Wish for to hear,
Where's all the joy and mirth
Made life Heaven on Earth?
O! they've all fled with thee,
Robin Adair.

William Henry Drummond (1854-1907) was born in Co. Leitrim but emigrated to Canada at an early age. He obtained his M.D. from McGill University and later became Professor of Medical Jurisprudence there. In spite of his limited association with Eire many of his poems mirror the dreams of Irish immigrants in the New World.

His eyes may never see the blue
Of Ireland's April sky
His ear may never listen to
The song of lark on high,
But deep within his Irish heart
Are cloisters, dark and dim,
No human hand can wrench apart
And the lark still sings for him.

Charles Lever (1806-1872) wrote a half-dozen popular novels during a productive life in medicine and diplomacy. Schooled in Dublin, he traveled to Louvain for his M.D. and returned then to practice in Ireland. Because of an outstanding performance as medical superintendent during a cholera epidemic in Ulster, he was offered a position as a physician to the British Diplomatic Corps. He gradually retired from medicine and served in Consular posts in Spezzia and Trieste. Throughout his novels are many stanzas of light verse and pleasant lyrics.

In an era of Irish history when opportunities for professional training were curtailed it is not surprising that the educated served simultaneously as clergy and as physicians. Charles P. Mulvaney (1835-1885) graduated from Trinity College and served as a British Naval Surgeon for several years before emigrating to Canada as a minister of the Church of England. His parodies and lyrics were familiar in the Irish magazines during the mid-nineteenth century. William Reeves (1815-1892) obtained a medical degree in order to serve his parishioners more fully. A scholar and renowned linguist he was rapidly elevated from local minister-physician duties to academic positions in the Church. His monumental history of Irish ecclesiastical counties and his original contributions in archeology were recognized by his election as President of the Royal Irish Academy. Although his practice of medicine lasted but a brief time he was elected a Fellow of the College of Physicians of Dublin. In his tenure as Librarian of Armagh and as Bishop of Down he created and translated many Gaelic poems including the bouyant welcome of Columcille to Dublin:

> Delightful to be on the Hill of Howth
> After coming over the white-bosomed sea
> To be rowing one's little coracle
> Ochone! on the wild-waved shore.

John Todhunter (1839-1916) is yet another example of the Irish physician, well-trained and successful in medicine, who found his greatest fulfillment in poetry. During his early years he was a clinical clerk to the great Dublin cardiologist, William Stokes, and later pursued specialty training in Paris and Vienna. He loved literature more, however, and after only a year of medical practice he retired to accept a Professorship of English Literature in Dublin. His writings were

77

concerned with the Celtic legends, Irish tales and the people he knew so well; they can be found in most anthologies of Irish poetry. An early little known effort, "The Daughter of Hippocrates—A Legend of Cos," more clearly indicates his medical heritage:

> Long did they live, and long from every land
> Thronged to them annually, a pallid band
> Of sick folk, by their hands to be made whole
> For, as was blazed abroad, they had control
> Of all diseases—skilled in secret lore
> And occult arts; and ever more and more
> Their fame grew loud, and of their wondrous cures
> And wealth and charities, the noise endures
> Even to this day in Cos, their island home.

George Sigerson (1836-1925) attained eminence in science, literature and politics during a long life. A medical graduate of Cork, he studied neurology in Paris and made the first translation of Charcot's *Diseases of the Nervous System* into English. He was professor of biology at the National University of Ireland and represented that body as a Senator of the Free State. His Dublin home served as a focal place in the literary as well as revolutionary life of early twentieth century Ireland. Although his ballads (often published under the pseudonym "Erionnach") appear contrived to the modern ear his translation of the early Gaelic epic of Sedulus and his history of Ireland were major contributions to Irish literature. A more simple, but no less important, contribution was his rendition of a twelfth century Norse poem expressing the attraction Dublin still has today for the traveler:

> Why should I home depart?
> Dublin now holds my heart.

Autumn comes—but we cross
Not then to Nidaros.

William M. Crofton (1879-1974), a descendant of the "pipe-water Croftons" who built the Dublin canals, received his medical degree at University College, Dublin and lectured there for over thirty years on bacteriology and special pathology. This latter field included controversial work on therapeutic immunization for cancer. His literary efforts have included the composition of an eleven-act opera on Gaelic mythology, *The Cuchulain Trilogy*. Another recent Irish physician-poet is Dr. John H. Pollock (1882-1964), a Dublin pathologist. Best known for his novels written under the pseudonym of "An Philibin", he has also published several volumes of literary criticism, plays and poems. Many of his lyrics can be found interspersed throughout his novels.

The final, and perhaps the finest example of the Irish physician-poet is Oliver St. John Gogarty (1878-1957). He lived an almost charmed life, excelling as a surgeon, scholar, wit, writer, poet, politician and aviator. Intimate with Yeats, A.E. and other leaders of the Irish literary revival in the first quarter of the twentieth century he was immortalized by his former roommate, James Joyce, as the bulky Buck Mulligan of *Ulysses*. In his political entanglements he survived an assassination attempt by diving into the dark water of the Liffey, and then proceeded to serve as a Senator of the Irish Free State for fourteen years. An outstanding otolaryngologist, he maintained busy offices in London as well as Dublin. In one of his biographical works, *Tumbling in the Hay*, he has left a flamboyant portrait of the life of a medical student, and his knowledge of human disease and suffering permeates all his writing. With the insight of a medical mind, the warmth of an Irish heart and the Celtic ability to focus on the brighter

79

aspects he wrote the delicate lyric of a physician-poet:

Death may be very gentle after all:
He turns his face away from arrogant knights
Who fling themselves against him in their fights;
But to the loveliest he loves to call.
And he has with him those whose ways were mild
And beautiful; and many a little child.

Dr. Cahill is President-General of the Society

James Joyce and Anglo-Ireland

KEVIN SULLIVAN

This talk was delivered at the Joyce centennial celebration at the Society.

When Joyce was a young man in Dublin there was talk among his literary elders—George Moore, AE, W. B. Yeats—of a Sacred Book, a book not then in existence but, presumably, about to be written by one or the other of them, no one was quite sure who. Nor were they at all sure about the contents of that book or its purpose—whether it was to restore Ireland to a place among the nations of the world, or simply to redeem the country from cultural apathy, or—more ambitiously still—to carry some sort of messianic message to the world at large that the world might be redeemed from the hells of materialism by the grace of Celtic imagination. Despite a certain dimness of purpose there was an obvious analogy in all this with the Bible, more especially with the Old Testament, a book that had once plucked from the wasteland of history a wandering tribe of Semites and given them definition as the children of Abraham, the people of God. And implicit in the analogy was the belief that one of the prime functions of a great literature was to bring a people to a knowledge of themselves by imbuing them with a heroic sense of their own value and destiny.

So it had been, these writers knew, from the beginnings of Western culture to the present day. If Hebrew literature had revealed God to man, Greek literature had revealed man to himself, and when their time came the Romans, confirming and solidifying the work of Greece, celebrated in their literature the rule of law which, rising out of a profound sense of Virgilian *pietas*, made possible that order among men which we call civilization. Subsequent vernacular literatures, when they arose more than a thousand years later, were all to measure themselves against the high standards set by these forebears. Yeats, Moore, Russell, most of the writers active in the Irish literary movement at the start of the century accepted all this as an article of literary faith. But it was for James Joyce, who had early dissociated himself from that movement, actually to accomplish what these writers had been talking about so ardently and so vaguely. For it was Joyce who faced up to the reality of modern Ireland and, in a rhetorical flourish at the end of his first novel, has his surrogate, Stephen Dedalus, declare that he was setting out to forge in the smithy of his soul the uncreated conscience of his race.

Why it should be Joyce and not another who would provide Ireland in our century with a profane and secular scripture will now involve us in a brief skirmish with Irish literary history—a field, it should be said, pockmarked with pitfalls for the unwary. But here too Joyce can serve as guide and strategist, for it is his view of that history that determined his response to it.

During his self-imposed exile in Trieste, an Italian city then under Austrian rule, Joyce was occasionally asked to speak on matters of Irish interest at the local Universita del Popolo. On one such occasion in early May 1907 his subject was James Clarence Mangan, a poet of his own people, whose name was not however a household word even in Ireland. Knowing his audience would have small acquaintance with Giacomo Clarenzio Mangan, Joyce began by sketching in a general background against which his central figure might be seen in some sort of perspective.

"Ireland's contribution to European literature," he told them, "can be divided into five periods and into two large parts, that is, literature written in the Irish language and literature written in the English language." With a schoolmaster's neatness, a role he was much at home in, Joyce then divided Gaelic literature into two periods, one preceding and the other following the Norman invasion of the twelfth century. Ireland's literature in English he divided into three equally distinct periods: the first encompassed the whole of the eighteenth century (Swift, Goldsmith, Sheridan, Burke), the second culminated in the Young Ireland movement of the 1840's (Moore, Davis, J. C. Mangan), and the third beginning in the last years of the nineteenth had continued into the twentieth century (Yeats, Synge, Lady Gregory) as the Irish literary revival. At this point a page is missing in the manuscript of Joyce's lecture so that there is no way of knowing how he might have developed this simple historical outline. Even so it will serve our purpose if we bear in mind that the year is 1907 and all of Joyce's major work was still before him, work that radically altered the kind of contribution Ireland would make to European literature in the years that followed.

What is immediately apparent from Joyce's sketch is that the native literary tradition behind him is broken and fragmented. A thousand years of it were lost to him on the other side of a language which was for him irretrievable. What remained was two hundred years in which a handful of strangers—alien in blood and belief, in speech and sensibility—had taken over not only a country but the conscience of a country. "A Protestant Ireland," one of them had boasted, "is really the proper name for the Ireland conceived of by the intellectuals. It was in Irish Protestantism that Ireland, dumb through the ages, had found a voice." But this was not the voice of Joyce's Ireland, and Joyce knew it. When he sends his surrogate Stephen Dedalus walking through the streets of his native city, that young man passing the grey block of Trinity College, then one of the citadels of the Protestant ascendancy, finds himself "striving this way and that to free his feet from the fetters of the reformed conscience." And later when Stephen stands in Kildare Street staring angrily into a softly lit dining room where he imagines the patricians of Ireland are housed in calm he reflects bitterly on "how he could hit their conscience or how cast his shadow over the imaginations of their daughters, before their squires begat upon them, that they might breed a race less ignoble than their own."

It is not of course some residually Catholic conscience, presumably unreformed, that is the source of resentment here. Joyce is, and Stephen fancies himself to be, an artist, and the conscience of the artist is more complex than that of the devout, more scrupulous according to its lights, and more alienated in the encircling gloom of those orthodoxies—racial, religious, social, or aesthetic—from which it strives to release itself.

84

Because he was scrupulous, because he was alienated, cut off by the vicissitudes of language and the nightmare of history from Ireland's old literary tradition, Joyce could not accommodate himself to the Anglo-Irish writers' desire to revive that literature in its own, Anglo-Ireland's, image and idiom. Looking around him he saw that the best of these writers—Yeats, Lady Gregory, John Synge—were motivated by precisely this passion, however finely modulated. Yeats, the foremost of them, remembering forgotten beauty, believed (or would have liked to believe) that "when his arms wrap her round, he presses in his arms the loveliness which has long faded from the world." To which Joyce replied, "Not this. Not at all. I desire to press in my arms the loveliness that has not yet come into the world." That was Yeats in middle age, Joyce in his youth. In his old age Yeats was to boast:

> John Synge, I and Augusta Gregory, thought
> All that we did, all that we said or sang
> Must come from contact with the soil, from that
> Contact everything Antaeus-like grew strong. . . .
> . . . .
> Dream of the noble and the beggar man.

At about the same time a mature Joyce, who had once had a more intimate knowledge of beggary and who had always had an innate suspicion of *soi-disant* nobility, was setting down in *Finnegans Wake* another kind of dream, that of an Irish Everyman, a man of the people, and not of the Irish people alone, but of all those generations that had crowded into the world since Adam first knew Eve.

And as with Yeats, so with Lady Gregory. That

85

lady, moving from cottage to cabin in the barony of Kiltartan, gathering story and folklore from among the peasantry, would afterward set them down in a pretty Anglo-Irish dialect formed by superimposing English as she spoke it upon the idiosyncratic syntax and vocabulary of her Irish peasantry. This may be thought an activity less reprehensible than that of some of her family who, it was said, had earlier, in the famine times, moved among their peasantry with a bible in one hand and a bowl of soup in the other. But Joyce did not think so. Not that he cared much about proselytizing, but that he cared passionately about language and the shaping power of language. There is a famous passage in *A Portrait of the Artist as a Young Man* in which a mutual misunderstanding arises between Stephen Dedalus and his English-born dean of studies about the meaning of a word, and Stephen reflects: "The language in which we are speaking is his before it is mine. How different are the words *home, Christ, ale, master,* on his lips and on mine! I cannot speak or write these words without unrest of spirit. His language, so familiar and so foreign, will always be for me an acquired speech. I have not made or accepted its words. My voice holds them at bay. My soul frets in the shadow of his language."

Since all language is acquired speech Stephen would seem here to be leaving himself little choice but to go off and invent a new language of his own (which some think is pretty much what Joyce did in *Finnegans Wake*). But beneath the surface of Stephen's fretfulness is another more somber concern. If to Stephen the native English of the dean of studies sounded foreign, to Joyce the contrived Anglo-Irish idiom of Lady Gregory and company was not only foreign but freakish, as artificial and perishable as the society in which it had been devised. He could have no more to do with it—except to parody it as he did later in *Ulysses*—than he would have to do with the neo- or pseudo-Celtic aesthetic which Yeats had been formulating in support of it.

There remains John Synge. Yeats, finding him in Paris morosely contemplating a career as literary critic, directed him to the Aran Islands where he might discover among an unspoiled people fresh material for that literary revival which Yeats had already set in motion. Synge went, and if he went at first like an amateur anthropologist to observe the tribal mores of a little known people, it must be said to his credit that he returned through his plays as an artist, second only to Yeats among Anglo-Irish writers in creating a permanent body of work. Joyce admired Synge and may even have envied him a little, though he was not ordinarily much given to that most Irish of the deadly sins. But grounds for envy were there in the sense that Synge, unlike Joyce, had a choice in the matter, and exercising that option which is part of every Anglo-Irishman's cultural heritage he had *chosen* Ireland. He might, like George Bernard Shaw or Oscar Wilde, have gone off to England where Shaw prospered by quite preposterous demonstrations of the Irishness of the English and the Englishness of the Irish and the beguiling foibles of both; and where poor Oscar, after a brilliant debut, became in the end more English than the English themselves and had later to pay the price for that English peculiarity. But James Joyce had no such option. "This race and this country and this life produced me. . . . I shall express myself as I am," Stephen Dedalus declared. And Joyce himself, in conversation with his English friend Frank Budgeon, asked the unanswerable question: "Tell me why you think I ought to wish to change the conditions that gave Ireland and me a shape and destiny?" It is as simple and complex as that: Ireland was Joyce's destiny, a condition of his being with which he could come to terms, it seems, only in a characteristically Irish way— through rebellion.

But before he could mount his rebellion against Ireland proper (so to speak) he had first to dispose explicitly of Anglo-Ireland and its alternate literary tradition which for him, as we have seen, was no valid alternative. He does so in a number of ways, only one of which, and that the most amusing, may be mentioned in passing: a set of satirical verses, composed in the manner of Jonathan Swift, and entitled *The Holy Office*.

In an early poem ("To Ireland in the Coming Times") Yeats had written:

> Know that I would accounted be
> True brother of that company
> That sang to sweeten Ireland's wrong. . . .

Joyce echoes those lines in parody:

> But I must not accounted be
> One of that mumming company
> With him who hies him to appease
> His giddy dames' frivolities
> While they console him when he whinges
> With gold-embroidered Celtic fringes. . . .

After ticking off Yeats and a long roster of his literary friends and disciples (including George Russell, the mystic, who, he says, "once when

88

snug abed/Saw Jesus Christ without his head")
Joyce concludes:

> So distantly I turn to view
> The shamblings of that motley crew
> Those souls that hate the strength that mine has
> Steeled in the school of old Aquinas.

The reference to Aquinas need not be taken any more seriously than the rest of the satire, but at the same time it is not entirely frivolous. Here and elsewhere it is a clue, albeit a minor one, to the direction Joyce's own work would take, a direction which at every step multiplied the distances between himself and Anglo-Ireland. Where those writers were, in his view, provincial, he would be perennial; while they were fabricating a Celtic past, he would rediscover Europe—that of Aristotle and Aquinas no less that that of Ibsen and Hegel—and, paradoxically, by becoming European he would become at the same time more Irish still. In place of their vague romantic aspirations, he would construct a system, detailed and particular in its intellectual clarity, and capacious enough to accommodate the whole of the human family. This construct took the shape in literature of a modern city, specifically Dublin, but a Dublin that in *Ulysses* is more than itself, transformed now into the city of mankind.

So far did Joyce come from the Anglo-Ireland of Synge's rustics, Gregory's peasants, and the heroic and nostalgic dreams of W. B. Yeats.

But there is another distance, more difficult to measure, one that cannot be travelled far in the time at our disposal, which must at least be mentioned. This is the distance that lies between diverse kinds, different qualities of imagination.

89

Let us call them for convenience, but without invidiousness, the Protestant and Catholic imagination. As we have seen, it is imagination which shapes the conscience and modulates the characteristic voice of a people. Joyce had rejected one of these out of hand—that which had boasted, an idle boast, that Ireland, dumb through the ages, had found its voice in Protestantism. When late in life a woman asked Joyce if, having left Catholicism, he had become any kind of Protestant, Joyce replied: "Madame, I have lost my faith, I have not lost my mind." In this he was plagiarizing himself when in *Portrait*, to the same question put by his friend Cranly, Stephen answers: "What kind of liberation would that be to forsake an absurdity which is logical and coherent and embrace one that is illogical and incoherent?" Stephen, among other things, is distinguishing here between intellect and imagination. For when Cranly persists that his mind is supersaturated with the religion in which he does not believe, Stephen acquiesces. The distinction is critical for Joyce himself. For one whose imagination has been nurtured by belief in a supernatural order and sustained by the life, real or illusory, of sacrament and ritual, knows—even after that order and that life have been replaced by the life and order of rational intellect—that intellect cannot be made to do the work of imagination. And in this W. B. Yeats would have agreed: "The abstract," Yeats wrote a few weeks before he died, "is not life. . . . You can refute Hegel but not the Saint or the Song of Sixpence." In this at least Yeats and Joyce are at one, in their insistence as artists on the autonomy and the power of the imagination.

In exercising this freedom and power Joyce, we

90

can see now, accomplished three things of major importance. He restored the broken and fragmented tradition he had inherited by placing it in a new perspective. "Even a superficial consideration will show us," he wrote, "that the Irish nation's insistence on developing its own culture by itself is not so much the demand of a young nation that wants to make good in the European concert as the demand of a very old nation to renew under new forms the glories of a past civilisation." Secondly, he liberated Irish writers who came after him from the constraints of the Anglo-Irish tradition by providing them with another kind of literary conscience and with a new kind of technique, as well, should any of them find it useful in articulating that conscience. In this respect it is not, I think, too much to claim that Joyce is in fact the founding father of *modern* Irish literature, a kind of secular scripture in which Ireland has been and is continuing to be re-defined. Finally, his accomplishment is such that no artist anywhere in the last fifty years has sat down to write without the example of James Joyce in mind. Without him, writing as we know it today is, as one critic remarked, unthinkable—as unimaginable as modern physics without Einstein, modern psychology without Freud. It is for these reasons, among others, that we remember Joyce today, and for these same reasons he will continue to be remembered wherever language is honored and the gifts of language held dear.

Professor Kevin Sullivan is Director of Irish Studies at Queens College.

Gaelic Verse Translations

THOMAS KINSELLA

MISE RAIFTEIRÍ

Mise Raifteirí, an file, lán dóchais is grá
le súile gan solas, ciúineas gan crá,
ag dul síos ar m'aistear le solas mo chroí,
fann agus tuirseach go deireadh mo shlí;
tá mé anois lem aghaidh ar Bhalla
ag seinm cheoil do phócaí falamh'.

I AM RAIFTEIRÍ

I am Raifteirí, the poet, full of courage and love,
my eyes without light, in calmness serene,
taking my way by the light of my heart,
feeble and tired to the end of my road:
look at me now, my face toward Balla,
performing music to empty pockets!

BEATHA AN SCOLÁIRE

Aoibhinn beatha an scoláire
   bhíos ag déanamh a léighinn;
is follas díbh, a dhaoine,
   gurab dó is aoibhne in Éirinn.

Gan smacht ríogh ná rófhlatha
   ná tighearna dá threise
gan chuid cíosa ag caibidil,
   gan moichéirghe, gan meirse.

Moichéirghe ná aodhaireacht
   ní thabhair uadha choidhche,
's ní mó do-bheir dá aire
   fear na faire san oidhche.

Do-bheir sé greas ar tháiplis,
   is ar chláirsigh go mbinne,
nó fós greas eile ar shuirghe
   is ar chumann mná finne.

Maith biseach a sheisrighe
   ag teacht tosaigh an earraigh;
is é is crannghail dá sheisrigh
   lán a ghlaice de pheannaibh.

THE SCHOLAR'S LIFE

Sweet is the scholar's life,
   busy about his studies,
the sweetest lot in Ireland
   as all of you know well.

No king or prince to rule him
   nor lord however mighty,
no rent to the chapterhouse,
   no drudging, no dawn-rising.

Dawn-rising or shepherding
   never required of him,
no need to take his turn
   as watchman in the night.

He spends a while at chess,
   and a while with the pleasant harp
and a further while wooing
   and winning lovely women.

His horse-team hale and hearty
   at the first coming of Spring;
the harrow for his team
   is a fistful of pens.

Thomas Kinsella is one of Ireland's leading poets, and read his new work at the Society.

*In our effort to leaven this journal with poetry we are for-
tunate to present a Gaelic composition with translation by
the distinguished diplomat-writer, Gearoid O'Clerigh.*

—K.M.C.

Foighne

(Ar iris áirithe achasán do chaitheamh ar aigne na
ndaoine faoina ndúil a bheith aonta)

Sula dtáinig Liam Buí go Baile an Fhaoitigh
is Pádraig Sáirséal d'fhágaint slán againn
nó Cromall sular shuigh faoina hata iarainn
ar muin capaill i nDroichead Átha
nó fuireann Dóvair lena ngunnaí 's a bpící,
sular bhris ar dhá fhórsa i lúb Chionn tSáile,
Strongbó na saíodóirí—gí gur bheag an líon díobh—
in Uibh Bhairrche sula raibh nó timpeall Carman
is cine Gael féin, óna áirmhítear ríthe
Fir Bolg, Laighin agus Cruithin ársa,
bhí seilbh Éireann ag a pobal dílis:
torc óir faoin chré caillte is táilcheann báite
i loch an dearmhaid le bliain is ceithre míle,
aigne ghrean gréas gaoiseach roimh Pádraig
do theacht is tobar fós í go doimhneacht,
súil fuarchúise ag eo feasa de shíor ag snámh ann.

Patience

(Upon a publication called *Inside Ireland* terming the Irish people "primitive" and "atavistic" in their desire for unity)

Before the Williamite train reached Ballyneety
and the Jacobites got off the boat in France
or Cromwell called whoa! to his horse when seated
in Drogheda under a hard hat
or the guns and pikes of the Elizabethan
drove Spaniard and Ulsterman down and back,
before Norman marksmen came to Wexford's beaches
for the hunting season—no numerous pack—
or the Gaels, whose royal blood most of us chiefly
claim, or previous half-remembered immigrants,
already "Your Ordinary Irishman" was the people:
torque and adzehead though lost beneath earth
or lake these thousands of years past
alive today the mind's matrix of their cunning makers,
dark source whose depths since before Saint Patrick
have housed coldeyed shadows, subtle salmon of knowl-
      edge.

Mr. O'Clerigh is the Consul General of Ireland in New York.

One of the great treasures of Ireland is her language.
We are delighted to present this beautiful Irish poem
inspired by the birth of a child. The author is a physician from Waterford now working on Staten Island.
On the facing page is a prose translation.

—K.M.C.

Bíonn

Bíonn réamhrá trí ráithe ar gach éinne
I dtimpeallacht dorcha, chiúin, socair, aonarach
Ar crochadh sa mhéan cian-ársa bunaidh.
Go bpléascann isteach sa tranglam daonna
le smacht a chur ar an saol nua-dhéanta.
Is aoibhinn do má cuirtear fáilte beag roimhe.

Glacann sé chuige i ndiaidh a chéile
balcaisí a thurais, giúirléidí a chinniúna,
Réalt Íudach, dian-creideamh Muslamach, uabhar Francach
Tríd an saol ag déanamh aithris ar dhaoine eile
Ag iompar lasta na nglún tá thart.
Ní beag an deor, má siltear ina dhiaidh.

I rith a thréimhse beo borrann an fuinneamh ann
Ar neart a thola tógtar mion-eachtraí a shaoil.
Bolgáin a ghníomhartha ag leathnú uaidh amach
Go sútar isteach iad ag amhal-ábhar na cruinne.
Bailíonn sé leis ó dhromchla na beatha.
Filleann suaimhneas dorcha, ciúin, síoraí.

—Rísteard Ó hÉalaidhe
Mi na Lunasa 1980

Is

Every one has a three-season prelude / In a dark,
quiet, secure, solitary place / Suspended in the
aeon-old original abyss / Until he bursts into the
human bustle / To master the newly-fashioned world.
How lucky if he gets a little welcome.

He gathers around him by and by / Rags for his
journey, the bric-a-brac of his fate / A Jewish
star, Muslim devotion, French pride / Mimicking
others on the way through life / Carrying the load
of past generations / The tear is not small, if shed
after him.

During his time, life surges within him / Minor
events are built on the strength of his will /
Bubbles of action blowing away from him / Until they
are sucked in by the vastness of the universe.
He departs from life's plain / Returns to the dark, quiet,
eternal tranquillity.

—translated by Micheál Kennedy

Dr. Healy is the founder and editor of the Irish journal, Nua Eabhrach.

Genesis of an Historical Novel

THOMAS FLANAGAN

The Year of the French takes as the center of its narrative the weeks of late August and early September, 1798, when a small French force landed on the Mayo coast, was joined by a few thousand rebels, fought its way into the midlands—the Leitrim-Longford border—and was then crushed.

It is, of course, an historical novel, and certain challenges to a writer are inherent in the genre itself. They were problems inherent from the first, and we encounter them in Scott and Hugo and Balzac and Tolstoy and Stendhal. How does an historical novel differ from other kinds of novel, on the one hand, and, on the other, from a formal history. There are many proper, and some less than proper, ways of responding to each of these questions, but in my own case, I found the two converging. That is, my imagination was quickened by the events of those distant weeks, and I found them forming shapes, patterns of significance, relationships of characters to one another, and patterns which were, ultimately, tragic. But I also took it as a principle, not merely an historical, but an esthetic, an artistic principle, that my book should be as faithful as it could be to our knowledge of what actually did happen, and how and why it happened.

Now as it happens, I had command of a fairly

good knowledge of the social history of eighteenth century Mayo, and the research which I had yet to do was into the actual bones and tissues and blood of those few weeks of rebellion, battle, and defeat. Both the British and the French forces sent detailed despatches to their governments, and these are preserved in the two ministries of war. They must be read with some reserve, for in neither case is the commander entirely disinterested, but on the whole they agree. And there are proclamations, records of trials, lists of suspected rebels, petitions of indemnification, and other materials. There are also letters, a few chronicles, and at least one substantial memoir—that of Joseph Stock, the Protestant Bishop of Killala. This gave me the germ out of which I created the character of one of my own fictional narrators, the Rev. Arthur Vincent Broome. And here I may pause over one instance of the ways in which a novelist manipulates fact.

In 1798, and indeed until the 1830's, Killala was an episcopal see, but I abolished it, and made Broome a simple clergyman. And, again, Stock was an Anglo-Irishman, Broome an Englishman. I made these transpositions for what might be called tactical reasons. I wanted, for the narrator of these portions of my story, someone who would not be involved in the centuries-old Irish labyrinth of loyalties, passions, and prejudices, but, rather, someone who would be viewing them from fresh eyes. And a simple clergyman seemed better for my purposes than a bishop. But I made also a more drastic change. Stock, as his personality emerges from his pages, was a dry, irascible fellow, decent enough and surprisingly balanced, but with rather a narrow range of human sympathies. But for Broome I created a quite different character, or rather it created itself for me, a fussy, kindly, puzzled man, and, as a friend has remarked, a natural Christian. And he grows in the course of the novel—in his capacity to feel, in his sense of the tragic, above all in his increasingly complex understanding of the Irish. And all this is I think permissible, because, until almost the end, he is a witness and a reporter only, taking no part in the historical events. Though in the end, his is one of the voices of judgment in the novel, one of those through whom the action is weighed and judged and given a moral evaluation.

But the written and printed sources are, almost entirely either English or French, and there was a third side, for me the most important one—the Irish had no ministries of war to which to send despatches, and here one was compelled to turn to folk tradition, to song, to legend, to memories which have clung to a stretch of road, a townland, the foundation stones of a vanished cabin.

For the historian, this is difficult material, for the oral tradition of a people—any people—is perishable, and as elusive as quicksilver, with the magical capacity of turning ordinary people into heroes or ogres, working upon their human flesh the alchemy of the imagination. Shortly after the novel was published, I began to discover, through letters, that with the possible exceptions of parts of Siberia and the Nile Delta, everyone on the globe has at least one Mayo grandmother. Some of the letters, though, were both precise and accurate, and one was from a fellow in the Mid-West, who had been told by his grandmother that she came from a place near Ballina called Barneysop, and he had never been able to find it on a map.

That is because it is not a name, but a nickname, and it still lingers in the Mayo air. Humbert, the French commander, landed at Kilcummin, then marched upon Killala. And from Killala he moved upon Ballina, which was garrisoned by yeomen and elements of the regular army. Ballina lies to the south, on Moy, but the rebels did not take the coach road. Humbert moved them by night, through the demesne of Lord Lucan (the "Big Lord" of the novel), past Rosserk Abbey. It was a difficult road at night, not much more than a path, and so the peasants came from their cabins and lighted torches of straw for them. In the 1930's, Richard Hayes met an old woman there who remembered a grandfather's story: "There was one Myles Ford lived here then, and he brought the straw mattress he had for a bed and lighted it to a great blaze to show them the way. And up to the day he died, and he lived to be an old man, he was known by no other name than Mylie French." And the road itself became known as *boher na sop,* the road of straw. Barneysop, the road of straw.

But when one has gathered up all that can be known, in records, maps, despatches, memoirs, legal papers, there comes a time when one realizes that all that can now be recovered is at best a fragmentary record of what *was.* The historian stops here, and upon this evidence shapes his narrative and his structure of explanation and interpretation. But the novelist has the dangerous and risky privilege of bringing to bear his imagination and his instincts, his sense of "what *must* have happened, what it *must* have been like." Thus, in *The Year of the French,* many of the characters are actual people—Ferdy O'Donnell the peasant captain at Killala, John Moore who became president of the short-lived Republic of Connaught, Lord Cornwallis, Dennis Browne the Sheriff of Mayo, and so on. We know a fair amount concerning some of these, but others I had to re-create upon the basis of no more, perhaps, than a stray phrase in a memoir. But this is a fairly conventional problem for the novelist, and is really not what I have in mind when I speak about the imaginative process.

One of my first decisions with respect to *The Year of the French* was to employ not one but a number of narrators—the Rev. Mr. Broome; Malcolm Elliott, a Protestant solicitor and small landowner, and a committed United Irishman, whose account is given in retrospect as he awaits execution in Dublin; Sean MacKenna, a schoolmaster and draper in Castlebar, whose diary I have modelled somewhat upon that of the actual Humphrey Sullivan's diary; Judith Elliott, Malcolm's wife, and a sentimental, romantic patriot; Harold Wyndham, a young officer, attached to the staff of Lord Cornwallis; George Moore of Moore Hall, a liberal Catholic intellectual. And another, anonymous narrator, fiction's conventional third person, speaking in various kinds of situations, but, in particular, when the book moves close to one of its central figures, the Gaelic poet and hedge-schoolmaster Owen MacCarthy, who drifts reluctantly into the rebellion, deserts from it, and then, for reasons which he himself does not fully understand, rejoins it, is present at the final defeat, and is brought back to Mayo and hanged. The narrative method implies an attitude, an assumption, and an intention.

Ireland of the eighteenth century was a fragmented culture, a fragmented society, rich and various in its fragments, but incoherent. Each of my narrators perceives one, perhaps several of the fragments, but not the shattered mosaic. My assumption was that if I gave to each of these fragments its voice, and its colors and textures, the novel itself might serve as that mosaic, its design not far to seek beneath the surface.

But I also saw the novel's shape in terms of an action, and, specifically a tragic action. The main action is of course a tragic one—a doomed rebellion. But I intended something larger than this, of which the rebellion would serve as emblem and image. With the rebellion, what remained of one Ireland, the surviving fragments of the old Gaelic order, shattered, and a new Ireland came into being: Ireland of the nineteenth century, and stretching forward into our own time. Now in strictly historical terms, this is at best a partial truth. That is to say, this new Ireland was shaped in part by the 1800 Act of Union between Britain and Ireland, and the rebellion was, in fact, used as a justification of the Union. But I believed for a number of reasons which seem to me valid that the rebellion could be made to symbolize the close of that world, and the death of a culture seems to me an inherently tragic event.

And, above all, that seemed to me crystallized in the mind and feelings and fate of Owen Mac-Carthy. MacCarthy I have created as one of the last in the series of eighteenth-century Gaelic poets of Munster, the line that stretches from O'Rahilly and O'Brudair to Owen Sullivan. It was a line which, quite literally, died away, because the social order by which it had been sustained perished, and because its language almost perished, supplanted, in the nineteenth century, by English. (In literal fact, incidentally, none of these actual poets was involved in rebellion; they were on the whole a quite conservative, indeed snobbish group, and quite unlikely to involve themselves with United Irishmen, let alone whiteboys). MacCarthy is drawn into the rebellion by a complexity of feelings, among them a loyalty toward his father, who had died in poverty, but one is a sense of the relationship between poetry and history. Like the others, he had written of the French ships which would one day sail into an Irish harbor, and now, unexpectedly, and in an unexpected form, they were here.

MacCarthy, as I have created him here, is a complex fellow, intelligent and quick-witted, though not, like George Moore, an intellectual, and with a sense of his people, with a sense of the countrysides in which he has written and taught school and got himself in mischief of various kinds. And, above all, he has pride in his art, and in that tradition of poetry of which he knows himself a part. And before his race is done, he knows, more fully than any of the others, that the world of which he has been party is coming to an end.

Thomas Flanagan whose novel, The Year of the French, *received the 1979 National Book Award, is a Professor of English at SUNY, Stony Brook.*

Flanagan's Crowded
Field of Folk

BENEDICT KIELY

Thomas Flanagan has George Moore of Moore Hall in the County Mayo writing a letter in the year of 1798 to the Rt. Hon. Edward Barrett, member of Parliament at Westminster. This is not, as the date might indicate, George Moore, the novelist, but his grandfather: a man in his youth noted for duelling and gallantries in the great world of London. But, being also of a philosophical cast of mind, he returned to his native Mayo and devoted his time to writing the history of the Girondins, a work never to be published.

The novelist, Flanagan, reasonably assumes that George Moore, the novelist, who is very close to us, was not totally unlike George Moore, the philosophic historian. He even attributes to the historian a few of what have, here in Dublin, come to be known as Flanaganisms. But then, as Flaubert would have been the first to admit, it might be difficult to write a novel of five-and-a-half-hundred close pages, to paint a canvas as crowded as Maclise's great rampage around the wedding of Eva and Strongbow, and not allow yourself an occasional, sly, ironical, Hitchcock appearance.

Moore is writing to London on behalf of his younger brother, John, who, following on the landing of General Humbert and his handful of French at Killala, has got himself involved in rebellion against the British Crown to the absurd extent of allowing himself to be appointed as the first president of the Republic of Connacht. Very conscious that he is writing from the wilds of Mayo to what was then the world's most powerful city, or one of the four of them, Moore allows himself a little meditation on the history of his benighted and misgoverned country:

How many dramas of modern history have chosen for setting this God-forsaken bog, and always without any recompense for my unfortunate countrymen save further misery? What were the rebellions of Desmond and Tyrone but chapters in the struggle between Elizabeth and Spain, and thus of Reformation and Counterreformation? What were the wars of Cromwell here but a sideshow to the English Civil War, in which the divine right of Kings was challenged and overthrown? When James and William, the two kings, faced each other at the Boyne, the game was Europe, and Ireland but the board upon which the wagers were placed. The history of Ireland, as written by any of our local savants, reminds me of a learned and bespectacled ant, climbing laboriously across a graven tablet and discovering there deep valleys, towering mountains, broad avenues, which to a grown man contemplating the scene are but the incised names of England, Spain, France. Now the name of France appears a second time upon the table.

An elegant if cynical point-of-view. Yet from what we know of George Moore, the historian, it seems certain that he would have thought and written exactly like that. And his is only one of the many points-of-view that Flanagan uses in a novel elaborately and brilliantly constructed. He calls to his aid five narrators who, along with about fifty other characters, make up a considerable cast: a large crowd to handle as the Russian high command might have said at the battle of Stalingrad. There are also the French, the Irish rebels, and the army of Cornwallis. Yet nowhere is there any fault in logic or coherence.

* * * *

Four men in a tavern by Kilcummin strand, there in all its innocence waiting for the French, or three men and a bullock with brains, talk of the Whiteboys, and of Cooper,

108

a squire of Cromwellian origin, of the Big Lord who is as faraway in London as the Lord Almighty in the high heavens, of rumors of thousands of men out on the road of Wexford, of the fabled army of the Gael marching at last, of militia and yeomanry beaten, and redcoats dead on the thick-grassed fields, and of the French upon the sea.

The four men are Connacht peasants, down as low as they were when Caesar Otway saw them living in holes in the ground in Erris and Tyrawley. Among them a Munster poet (his original is not far to seek) conscious of their pitiful plight and of his own: he will, in a mood of contempt and cynicism, write their Whiteboy proclamation and go, almost like a sleepwalker, to Ballinamuck, and back again to the gallows. His head filled with poetry he is very conscious that in Mayo he is Ovid: "banished to wild Tomi."

With the Protestant clergyman, Arthur Vincent Broome, M.A. (Oxon.), he has a most ironic conversation about the exact meaning of the Irish verse that tells of Troy and Rome and Caesar and Alexander and their passing, and prophetically holds out the hope that the power of England might go the way they went: and Tara itself is grass. Broome is conscious of the irony, and writing about it afterwards in a self-mocking effort to be the Edward Gibbon of the events that happened at Killala, he says: "How little we will ever know these people locked as we are in our separate rooms. . . . He (the poet) dwells deep within the world of his people, and theirs is an unpredictable and violent world."

But Hegel said that we learn from history that men never learn anything from history: and that ironic reflection allows Flanagan to allow Broome some of the profoundest paragraphs in the book. For Broome had once asked a learned and sagacious friend if man learned anything from history and was told that he did not, but that it was possible to learn from historians. To this matter, while reading the capacious works of Hume and Gibbon, he had given much thought. Then follows, in relation to Gibbon, a meditation on history as striking as anything I have ever read:

Gibbon gives to us the breadth of the classical world, from the Hellespont to the pillars of Hercules, a vast temple with colonnades and recesses, glowing white marble beneath a blazing Mediterranean sun, and displays to us then its hideous and shameful destruction. How firm a sense do we derive of all its constituent parts, of their intricate relationships! How certain is its destruction, with alien creeds subverting its powers and alien races wearing away its far-flung frontiers. Each cause and reason is locked securely into place. And over all the mighty drama presides the awesome authority of Gibbon's splendid language, his unimpassioned rationality. Here, we think, is the chief civil drama of human history, in which tens and hundreds of thousands played their parts, but a drama compelled by the human mind to yield up its uttermost secrets. Great was Rome and catastrophic was its fall, but great too is the energy of the historian's mind, the cool deliberation of his judgement.

But then afterthoughts come to the Rev. Mr. Broome, the Gibbon of Killala.

Perhaps it had not been at all as Edward Gibbon had described it. Perhaps everything had been chaos, chance, ill-luck, or simply the judgement of God, as had, in more pious ages, been believed. Perhaps everything that he had read had been only Gibbon's imagination:

And the past remains therefore unknowable, shrouded in shadow, an appalling sprawl of buildings, dead men, battles, unconnected, mute, half-recorded. Perhaps we learn nothing from history, and the historian teaches us only that we are ignorant.

Broome sees himself (his poor self, as he put it: for he is a genuinely humble man) as a confused clergyman with an indifferent education, a lover of comfort and civility and buttered toast: and so he is made to seem to the reader. But also, nor is he allowed to know it himself, he is a man of gentleness, sensitivity and humanity. In electing to play Gibbon to the events that happened around him, he finds that he has written only about a squabble in a remote providence, a ragbag army of peasants, files of yeomen and militia, ploughboys hanged from crossroads gallows.

* * * * * *

The doomed, drunken poet, the dryasdust clergyman who would be an historian, are but two in Flanagan's crowded field of folk. His people range from Humbert in the bogs to Boney in the desert; from Tone and Teeling in Paris and on the sea with the French to a half-crazed prophecy-man hanged for shouting out about the Place of the Pig, or just for existing; from Cornwallis in the field to the Big Lord in London concerned about the condition of chimney-sweeps and the abolition of negro-slavery, but with his scrawny withers unwrung by the woes of the tenants on his land in Mayo.

For some of the throng Flanagan had copious historical material to work on. For others, less: and some had birth only in his brain.

All are alive and forever memorable.

Benedict Kiely, one of Ireland's leading writers, is a former contributor to The Recorder.

111

Some Notes on the Flanagan

KEVIN SULLIVAN

Un écrivain Americain existenlialist —so runs the catch-phrase of a French critic writing some years ago about Thomas Flanagan. The man was not of course thinking of *The Irish Novelists* (1960) nor of *The Year of the French* (1979), the two books that, years apart, secure the foundation of their author's reputation as scholar and novelist. What the critic did have in mind was a handful of short stories, uncommonly good stories, published between 1948 and 1957 in *Ellery Queen's Mystery Magazine*. One of these, "The Cold Winds of Adesta," won that magazine's award for the best story of the year (1957), all have been republished in one or another anthology of "best" stories in subsequent years, but there is no single collection, at least in English, of all eight stories. The Japanese are said to have brought out one such collection, but I have never seen a copy (nor, it appears, has the author) so that, lost to us in the far reaches of oriental translation, there is no way of knowing what sea-changes they may have undergone—miniaturization perhaps?—in their passage from America to Japan.

Despite early success and frequent republication, their author seems to have dismissed these stories as literary trifles—less out of modesty, I have sometimes thought, than in nagging recollection of their provenance. And this not simply because EQMM was a far remove from prestigious publications like those at, say, Yale or Antioch, but because in their origin the stories were for him bread-and-butter work, the kind of thing that in less talented hands might easily have been considered hackwork. A word then about their particular provenance.

All of them were written while Tom Flanagan was a graduate student at Columbia, and in that time and that place the life of a graduate student, however gratifying intellectually, was not conspicuously affluent. Even those of us with a University stipend (never munificent) had need occasionally to grub about *extra muros* to flesh out the economic man that the inner man might be decently sustained. True, one or two of our more fortunate, or more prudential, fellows may have circumvented this need by expeditious marriage to a rich, or at least a working, wife. But the more common experience for many of us during those years was to provide a part-time corps of highly educated, often erudite and (I'm afraid) unspeakably articulate bartenders, sidemen, saxophonists, cab-drivers, copy-writers, life-guards, proof-readers, photographers, even at times the odd pornographer—in short, a body of apprentice-scholars who in their resourceful evasion of near poverty contributed their side-talents to the cultural diversity of a great city. Though his need may have been no less than ours, Flanagan's side-talent was, let us say, more condign—considering the careers we all then contemplated. His early stories may have been bread-and-butter work, but they were not trifles.

Mark Van Doren, then teaching at Columbia, once observed that the controlling image implicit in these stories was that of an enclosed garden, a place secluded but one taut with the possibilities of intrusion from without and betrayal from within. This is one of those images that seem part of racial memory, and its presence in fiction may serve to elevate the ordinary matter of that art—a crime, a quarrel, a conspiracy—to other levels of meaning or implication. It is an image, too, that in terms of action effects little or nothing, but in terms of atmosphere affects everything—modulating the tone and texture of a story until it

113

seems perhaps something other or more than it had first appeared. This perception of Van Doren's is worth bearing in mind and we will return to it again near the end of these notes.

Other members of the English department at Columbia, then one of the most prestigious in the country, also showed an interest, not perhaps as perceptive as that of Van Doren, in Flanagan's stories. Individually and as a group they were an impressive lot these teachers, scholars, critics, so impressive that even their names tended to be overpowering. Sometimes, as if to support the weight of its owner's reputation, the name came in three parts, the whole constituting a balanced metrical resonance: Joseph Wood Krutch (spondaic), William York Tindall (trochaic), Marjorie Hope Nicolson (dactylic); and where else in academe was there to be found a name equal in euphonic elegance to the Adonic perfection of Lionel Trilling? The interest of these exceptional people in Flanagan's stories was not so much in the texture of his prose as in the identity of some of his characters, in one or two of whom they were tempted to see a sly resemblance to one or other of their distinguished colleagues.

This kind of speculation was not implausible, for Flanagan sometimes located his stories on or near Morningside Heights and he was not above planting a fictional professor on the scene as foil or victim. Though he would still deny it, I had myself no difficulty in identifying the heavy body, and heavier irony, of Professor Randall in "Suppose You Were on the Jury," as one of our more ponderous instructors—an identification which, since the man is still among the living, will not be disclosed even at this late hour. But it was the identify of a professorial corpse, the aptly named Professor Grendel (whose specialty was, of course, Anglo-Saxon) in "This Will Do Nicely," that stimulated the most avid speculation. Grendel had been done in by his wife—one may suppose in self-defense if fear of her own death out of sheer boredom may be so considered. Innocent malice, even among some Columbia wives, could provide no end of candidates for the role of poor Grendel. All of which proves little perhaps except that Flanagan's short stories, in addition to having sustained the inner man, were also highly satisfying entertainments and that they had for those of us around Columbia at the time an extra intramural dimension more entertaining still.

A future graduate student at Columbia or elsewhere may one day decide to write his thesis on Thomas Flanagan, in which event a question he will eventually ask is what, if any, connection exists between these stories and the late work, *The Irish Novelists* and *The Year of the French*. A reasonable question to which a bright student may be expected to find one or more reasonable answers—none of which, however, will be anticipated here. Here it will be enough simply to indicate the general direction in which such answers may lie—a description, so to speak, of the general lay of the land rather than a detailed map of any particular terrain.

The detective story, the work of literary history, and the historical novel would seem at first to have little in common except the medium of language. In conception, the intent and emphasis of the first is on ratiocination, that of the second on interpretation, that of the third on (for want of a better word, if there is one) illumination. In execution, the reward for the reader, if the writer has done his work well, is in the first instance the satisfaction a man takes in the solution of a puzzle, in the second the pleasure of the mind in the resolution of a problem, and in the third the gratification of the spirit in the presence of some human mystery which has, if only for a time, absorbed him. Between conception and execution there are of course any number of ways in which things may go wrong in, for example, the choice of theme or method of

115

treatment, so that it must be understood that what is said here applies only to an ideal detective story, an ideal work of literary history, an ideal historical novel.

With that Platonic caveat in mind, consider now the ways in which these literary forms may be interconnected. Like the detective, the literary historian is a kind of private eye, research being a most solitary occupation, and as the special business of the criminal investigator is to detect clues and establish a relationship of cause and effect between them, the scholar's task is to decipher codes, the body of material turned up by his research, and to determine the relative significance of one to the other. One demands, or seems to demand, analytic intelligence; the other, no less demanding, a talent for synthesis. Both are concerned with order, one with imposing it on the sprawling disorder of human experience and event, the other with exposing patterns of meaning from among the sprawling records left behind by the human imagniation in its passage through time. But there is a difference. The writer of a detective story knows the solution before he constructs his puzzle, he knows from the beginning where he's going. The literary historian has no such advantage. His first problem is to define the problem itself, and that is not possible until he has mastered—not *invented*—all the relevant facts. He does not know where he's going until he gets there.

Tom Flanagan did not get to Ireland until two years after the publication of *The Irish Novelists*. That summer of 1962 his flight from San Francisco to Dublin touched down briefly in New York and I went out to what was then Idlewild Airport to see him on his way. Over a drink he seemed apprehensive—not about his flight, but about his destination. "Suppose," he said, "suppose after all I don't like the bloody place?" I laughed. He was like a young man going off on a blind date not knowing that he was already half in love. And, as I had anticipated, since

116

that summer the attachment has been continuous and un-wavering. Flanagan has put down deep Irish roots, many of his closest friends are there, and to this day the country still absorbs much of his attention and affection. Anyone familiar with his study of the Irish novel, which remains the standard work on the subject, could have predicted this. For as the ideal detective is a man of cold, almost inhuman, analytic intelligence, the ideal scholar is a man whose comprehensive and disciplined knowledge of his subject is permeated by a sympathy that is at the same time perfectly impartial and deeply human.

Sympathy when cultivated may develop into a passion, and just such a development can be observed in the trans-position of the scholar who wrote *The Irish Novelists* into the novelist who wrote *The Year of the French*. The scholar, whatever his sympathy for his subject, may not exceed in claim or judgment the bounds imposed by his material. The novelist is not so constrained. But however large the novelist's canvas, however original his "story-line" or faithful to experience his delineation of character, his narrative is a house of straw inhabited by paper men if the whole is not also informed by passion, the spirit that gives life. History may indeed be a body of accepted lies, but these lies seem, for better or worse, fixed forever, like eternal truths, in the one place. The novelist may tinker with certain details, but he cannot alter the essential con-figuration of the past. (He may, for example, let George Washington lose his wooden teeth, but he cannot allow him to win the battle of Long Island.) Finally, the serious historical novelist (not the lad in fancy dress or lady in unbuttoned blouse) is, like the scholar, concerned not only with the events of the past and the men and women who took part in them, but with the interpretation of those events, the nature of the past in relation to the present, the meaning of history.

A combination of skills—the story-teller's art, the

117

scholar's precision, the philosopher's judgment—is required for an undertaking of this magnitude. In *The Year of the French* each of these skills is on display from moment to moment, and in the final movement of the novel, the Epilogue, all are quietly orchestrated in falling cadences that reflect ironically on all that has gone before. One example must suffice.

The Reverend Mr. Broome who, as Protestant vicar at Killala, has witnessed, after the arrival there of a small French army, the savage insurrection and more savage suppression of the Irish peasantry in surrounding Mayo, has returned to his native Derbyshire and there meditates upon the cruel events in which he has been casually caught up in that late summer of 1798. "Does man learn from History?" he asks, and answers sadly, "No, I believe we do not. But it's possible to learn from historians." Then, troubled by the thought that even as great an historian as Gibbon may have done no more than interpose a capacious and capricious imagination between the past and present, he adds more sadly still, "And the historian teaches us only that we are ignorant." A bitter kind of lesson indeed, though not unsalutary. But history is not quite done as yet with the Reverend Mr. Broome.

On his way back to Killala he stops in London to visit Lord Glenthorne, a little monkey of a man who is also a grandee, the absolute and absentee proprietor of vast estates in Mayo populated by a swarm of peasants to whom Glenthorne is known (in Gaelic) only as the "Big Lord," a figure as remote, invisible, unimaginable as one of the mysterious old gods of Irish myth. Broome describes him as "the absent center of our Mayo world and the estate is his tarnished Eden. Like the Lord of Creation, he is everywhere and nowhere, center and circumference." (There are few more telling descriptions, even by one of those Irish novelists in Flanagan's earlier study, of the pervasive power of the great Irish absentee landlords of the

118

eighteenth and nineteenth centuries.) Reflect now that the world Broome is talking about is a world that has been re-created in the experience of the novel. Mayo as microcosm, a model of the larger world scaled down to size. And observe that at the center of this world is a "tarnished Eden," the governing Presence of which is in fact an Absence, a lord with hardly even a remote interest in what is going on in or around it. This controlling image, this tarnished Eden, is, we now see, none other than that enclosed garden which Mark Van Doren had detected in Flanagan's early stories, no more than implicit then, now made quite explicit—a secluded place that has been, it would seem inevitably, both betrayed from within and ravaged from without.

So much for the human face of history. And what of the God of History? In a recent novel by Umberto Eco, *The Name of the Rose,* an aged Benedictine monk, a medieval counterpart to the Rev. Mr. Broome, reflects much as Broome does on the tragic events in which he had been caught up and, like Broome again, gives himself over to religious meditation on the meaning of his personal history and the history of his times. In croaking German but with Benedictine clarity he gives voice to the thought that, though present, can find no voice in Broome's quiet Protestant reverie: "Gott ist ein lauter Nichts, ihn rührt kein Nun noch Hier." And this thought that God may be the pure form of a Nothingness not to be encountered in space or time has, I think, sufficient existential resonance to satisfy even Flanagan's French critic.

Kevin Sullivan, professor of English and director of Irish Studies at Queens College, CUNY, is a member of the Society's archives advisory group.

119

A Night Piece for Tom Flanagan
SEAMUS HEANEY

The dark has blotted out Howth Head,
The family have gone to bed,
The traffic eases on Strand Road,
　　The cork is drawn —
The kind of night, Tom, when we could
　　Talk until dawn.

But since you cannot share the glass
Familiars will take your place,
Those famous shades you've raised for us
　　From our own dream;
They're gathering around the house
　　Like moths round flame.

I sense the nimble step of Tone,
Our subtlest, mocking Jacobin.
He asks about this Flanagan
　　Who seems to know
The roll-call of United Men
　　From Down to Mayo.

Maria Edgeworth rustles in,
Ripe blackberries piled in her tin,
(She sucks one as she sips the wine)
　　She curtsies
To thank you, that you could condone
　　Her class neurosis.

Next John Mitchel downs a mouthful,
Struts a bit, salutes your style
As different but still equal
　　To bear the brunt.
You smile, he stares: the ironical
　　Embalms the violent.

120

And here's an ironist you like.
A Mr. Moore. But which? No pike-
man he, though he can wound and strike
    From his divan.
It is the author of *The Lake*,
    "More mob than man."

What next? The accents of Tyrone!
The robust stagger of Carleton
(We recognize him, thanks to Ben)
    Has cleared the room
And will demand the poitin soon
    By the look of him.

So I get up, walk to the door,
Hear seabirds on the darkened shore
And think of one out walking there
    With his ash-plant,
Headed from Night-town to the Tower,
    By Sandymount.

Our *genius loci,* fount of inwit,
Our conscience-forger lifts his hat
And tips you an old world salute
    As if to say
"Yes, yes," to you and all you write,
    Your mastery.

And now a bat flits from the trees
To grow a form I recognize,
The silent flap of W.B.'s
    Great soul in flight
He circles thrice to greet you, flies
    Into the night.

Seven sages! They speak for me
Who, this side idolatry,
(A quote speaks volumes for the shy)
    Year after year
Take delight in your artistry,
    Arch-raconteur.

I know you too recall with pleasure
At P. J. Clarke's, the steak tartare;
The night you read, in Terenure
   Road East,
The first draft of the first chapter;
   Many a feast

On Bret Harte Road; Sonny Dalton
In the rain; and in the sun,
Corned beef hash on Highway One.
   And Baggot Street —
Doheny's snug! Ochone, ochone!
   When can we meet

Again in that half-lit, musty lair,
That confessional atmosphere
Where red herrings are *plat du jour*
   And reticences
Are brewed up in the smoky air
   To confidences?

The tide is on the turn, though dawn
Still wears black velvet gloves upon
Her rosy fingers. But here's the moon
   As clouds unblock it.
In your time zone, it will rise soon
   On East Setauket.

So love to Jean. To Ellen. Kate.
To Drew. To Hope. And though it's late
I'm going in to wet my throat
   And drink a toast
To you, my friend, the out and out
   Gold medallist.

Seamus Heaney, a poet well-known and much-respected both here and in Ireland, has read his work on several occasions for the Society's members.

Arson

DENNIS SMITH

Jerry slammed the sedan door, pinned his gold shield to his lapel, and began to push through the crowd which had backed up to the spraying Delacorte Fountain. The small street before him was a circus of flashing red lights, arriving and departing ambulances, police cars, fire apparatus, all with sirens crashing through the still, spring evening. Carriage horses lined before their victorias at the edge of Central Park were prancing nervously, distraught, and unnoticed by their drivers who had fled into the crowd, mingling with still shaking people dressed in silk evening clothes, dresses and tuxedos. A doorman stood below the distinctive copper canopy of the Plaza Hotel, dressed in red and gold. There were tears in his aged eyes. "I knew them all," he was saying, again and again, to no one in particular.

Still pushing, Jerry passed scores of cops and ambulance attendants who stood idly, waiting for instructions. Jose Gillespie, as always, was limping just a little behind.

Two firefighters were lying on the rug-covered steps of the hotel, mask cannisters dropped at their feet, sucking noisily at the city washed air, as machines in need of oil. The crowd looked at them silently, sympathetically, as they listened to the gaspings, until their attention was drawn to a stretcher being carried up the stairs from the Sophia Club. On it was a young woman, dressed, it seemed, only in glossy underwear. Her eyes were closed, and her legs were blackened. She looked famous. Even with closed eyes, and grime covered, she was recognizable. "That's Desdemona," a man in a tuxedo said to the fur-wrapped woman next to him. "That's the twelfth stretcher," someone said. "It's the fourteenth," another replied.

The crowd was again silent as the ambulance drove by, and they could then hear the horse hoofs banging intemperately on the blacktop of Central Park South.

Jerry and Jose stopped in the middle of the street and let the ambulance pass, and then continued to the polished brass railing that separated the entrance to the Plaza from the entrance to the basement discotheque, Sophia. Standing there, with his hand on the railing, was an assistant chief of the department. Jerry was about to report to him, but then thought better of it. "He looks like he's thinking of what he'll say to the fire commissioner when he shows," Jerry said.

"Gotcha," Jose replied, "and the mayor. They'll all be here."

They passed the chief, and walked to the Sophia entrance, which was faced with a tile mosaic that ran around an alcove that was cut into the side of the building. In the middle of the mosaic was the word *Sophia*, ornate in the Byzantine style, and below it was the entrance stairwell. The stairs were wide, and made of small tiles, colored orange, blue, and yellow. From the top of the stairs, Jerry could see a group of firefighters sitting on a table below, waiting, Jerry thought, to pack up their hose. Small wisps of smoke were floating up the stairwell. The smoke had a strange smell, curiously sweet. Perfume, he thought.

They walked past a police officer on guard duty and down the stairs to the tiled entry foyer, stepping carefully over the two lengths of two-and-a-half inch hose that ran into the basement. Jerry looked closely at the frescoed walls on either side of the entrance to the interior discotheque, and made a note on a scratch pad. The black charring started three inches above the gold plated baseboards. There was no doubt in his mind then just where the fire originated. How it had originated was still a question. Jose would answer that one.

Jerry walked into the large inner room. The indirect lighting running beneath a copper frieze, around the sidewalls, a foot or so from the ceiling, was still working. The fire had not been sustained long enough to burst the bulbs. There were two badly burned bodies at his feet. He stepped over them, and walked across the ruined, partially burned and soot stained gold carpeting to the edge of the dance floor. The rug was water soaked, and made an eerie, squishing noise. He stood at the edge of the oval dance floor. It was a mosaic, a scene of a naked Eve feeding an apple to a naked Adam, done in small green and brown and white tiles. The figures, wide eyed and expressionless, seemed to Jerry to be in shock. Lying just above the mosaic scene, on the far end of the dance floor, were two bodies, joined as if they might have died dancing. Their skin was crisp, and steaming, the water from the hose not yet evaporated by the heat lifting from within them. The woman was in shoes, and she was wearing a small diamond tiara around her darkened forehead. The rest of her clothes had been burned away. The man was partially clothed, his shoes and the upper part of his tuxedo jacket not having burned completely. His arm was around the woman's neck, and his arm and the woman's neck were one, fused together unalterably.

There were six columns placed around the dance floor, each rising up to a vaulted ceiling. The ceiling was black, but Jerry could see that it was made of plaster, and unevenly painted. The blistering gave a hint to the design that had been painted on it. The capitals at the head of the columns were also made of plaster, carved into small scrolls and intricate foliage. Jerry reached up with a pen knife and dug a triangular piece out of one of the charred capitals. The charring was less than one sixteenth of an inch deep into the plaster. More like one thirty-secondth. He made a note, and put the piece of plaster into a plastic baggie. He would measure it another time.

He could see the rest rooms in a far corner, and before them he counted four bodies. In the opposite far corner, in front of the swinging kitchen doors, there was a larger group, fifteen at least, some lying one on another, all steaming, peeling, disfigured horribly. Jerry was transfixed by the sight, his mind impaled by the thought of being in the presence of so many who had suffered so much so needlessly. "My dear God," he thought, "I can feel the pain in the air. The room shakes with the pain, and with the suffering."

Jose had limped up behind him, but Jerry did not hear the squishing of his soles on the rug. He started as he heard his partner's voice. "It's awful," Jose said, "the battalion chief counted thirty-five dead." Before he finished the sentence Jerry turned quickly, his face ashen gray, and he put his hands up, as if in defense.

"Hey man," Jose said, "are you okay?"

126

Regaining a sense of place, Jerry turned again to the dance floor, saying, "Yeah, I'm all right. It's just that I suddenly realized that I have to be here, that I can't run up those stairs and out of here forever, like I would like to, that's all."

Jose put his hand on Jerry's arm, and tapped it slightly, saying, "I gotcha, partner, me too, but we got work to do."

Two companies of firefighters were in the room, standing at rest, waiting for a chief to direct them to pull another piece of the ceiling down, or pry up another piece of carpeting, or move another table or chair. The men did not say much. There was no small talk as there would be in other clean-up operations. Jerry looked into their faces, and he could see that they were moved, as he was, by the awesome, tragic waste about them, and that they felt the gloom that was thick in the air. He let his eyes wander again to the kitchen doors and to the crowd of dead life that was lying there. Human beings, he thought. No matter who they are, or what they stood for, they were still part of us, and Christ, it's a horrible end to come to.

"Jerry," Jose called, again interrupting the reverie. "Let's go, pal."

"Yeah," Jerry replied, "coming."

They walked back towards the entrance, and Jerry noticed a man lying on the floor in front of a coat check counter that ran along the front wall. Jerry looked over the counter and saw a woman lying in the rubble, still grasping the remains of what looked to be a fur coat. He made a note on the pad, and said to Jose, "They had some time, enough for a man to run for his wife's coat."

"Maybe he was checking it," Jose said.

Jerry pointed to two grime covered quarters on the counter top. "He wouldn't have left this," he said.

A battalion chief joined them, saying, "Some job, huh?"

"Awful," Jose replied.

"We told the men not to touch any of the roasts until you guys got here. How long will you be?"

"The department photographers ought to be here soon," Jerry replied. "When they get finished you can ship them to the morgue."

"I think they're going to set up a temporary morgue in the hotel lobby. The only problem is that we don't have enough body bags."

"I guess you could use blankets from the hotel," Jose said, "and they must have a few rolls of masking tape. It won't be as good as a body bag, but it will stay closed anyway if you wrap the tape tight enough."

"Yeah," the chief said, "that's an idea. Listen, you know how it started yet?"

"Not yet," Jerry said. "How many people got out?"

"About a hundred sixty, seventy maybe, all through the kitchen exit. Most of them are up in the bar, the Oak Room, or outside."

"We know that the fire came in through the front," Jose said. "Some of the survivors will tell us more."

"Okay," the chief said, "I'll be around. Ahh, one other thing though, how are you going to I.D. the roasts?"

"The Police Department Homicide Squad will be here," Jerry replied. "They have all the equipment. They'll just tag and number them."

The chief walked off, and the two fire marshals

stood at the coat check counter. Jose began to draw a schematic of the room, but he looked up and said, "You know, Jerry, there's a funny smell in here that reminds me of something, like the smell of shoe polish reminds me of the army."

"I know," Jerry replied, walking to the entrance door frame. "It's more prominent over here. It's not gasoline."

Jose joined him, walking around the two bodies that were lying before the entrance. "Yeah, it's stronger here," he said. "I'll think of it."

Jerry stared down at the bodies before him, a man and a woman. Most of the man's tuxedo had been burned away, but parts of it seemed to be melted into his skin. He was lying face down. The woman was lying on her back, the front of her long dress was missing, and most of her underwear had been eaten by the fire. She was large breasted, and her breasts were hanging to her sides. Her hair seemed to be a coil of burnt wire, brittle and flaking, and her skin was blotched, black and crisp in parts, with splashes that were pink and moist. She was wearing a four-tiered emerald necklace, but one side of the necklace had fallen strangely over one blistered ear, and the ear seemed to be breaking apart with the weight of the jewels.

God, Jerry thought, is there no order, even in death?

He knelt beside the woman, gently lifted the necklace from her ear, and placed it on the side of her neck. As he drew his hand away he brushed it against the side of her face, not deliberately, but carelessly. His hand was trembling slightly, and he felt the back of it sweep across the crisp, rough skin. The skin crumbled. But then, oddly, he felt a hard, smooth surface. He pulled his hand away quickly, and looked closely at the woman's cheek. It was totally burned, but he saw, embedded like a phenocryst into her skin, a small piece of glass. It was less than an inch wide and U-shaped, covered with the black grime of carbon. Jerry picked the glass gingerly from the woman's face, stood, and placed it into the plastic bag along with the cut of plaster. He again looked down at the woman, at the small patch of unburned skin which the glass had covered, and which stood out like a birthmark against the surrounding ash.

Jose's head was also down. He was looking at the necklace. "A lot of glitter here," he said.

"Yeah," Jerry replied, looking first at the charred woman, and then at the heavy emerald necklace, at the pile of dead strewn before the kitchen doors, and at the ornate capitals rising in irreverent majesty into the ceiling, at the steaming woman lying on the Byzantine dance floor, and at the diamond tiara that seemed to be penetrated into her fire blackened forehead. His eyes swept the room from end to end. It was a room of riches, but the riches had burned away, and all but the stones had become rubble. It was a black room now, dank and grotesque, and the sense of death was overwhelming. Jerry breathed in heavily, held his breath a moment, and repeated, "Yeah, glitter. Glitter and ash."

Dennis Smith is a fireman and author.

An Irish Coffee

JIMMY BRESLIN

It is when things are best that those who are brave enough to draw our love also are able to return it by teaching.

The two walked on this day in their work boots along one piece of pipe, with the sky around them and the street covered with bricks and glass below. Louis Carroll went first, with rope looped about his legs and chest. Bill Stewart was behind him. At the end of the pipe, Louis Carroll sat down, legs dangling in the air. Then one leg stepped out into the air and now the other one did, too, and now Louis Carroll was swinging on a rope in the air, swinging at a point 15 feet from the edge of the building. He was being lowered 15 feet through the air. He was dangling more than 450 feet from the ground. Stewart, balancing himself on one piece of pipe, leaned into the air as he held the rope attached to Louis Carroll.

This was on an afternoon at the top of a building on Madison Avenue in Manhattan. A crane had collapsed, the boom snapping and leaving the tip, weighing perhaps a ton, hanging by one piece of bent metal and pointing directly at the street. One man walking on the street already had been killed by falling debris. If the heavy piece of boom fell to the street, carnage was assured.

Out in the air, Carroll spun and went onto his back, turning the sky into a bed, his legs working like scissors, just cutting the air until one foot

131

touched metal and now his arm came out and he grabbed the broken section of boom and began to loop cable about it that would prevent it from falling.

On the street below, businessmen standing behind police barricades looked up at Carroll, who swung on a rope in the sky, and Stewart, who leaned into the sky and held the rope.

A businessman on 53rd Street, arms folded, looked up at them until his eyes hurt, then he turned to the one with him and said, "I wonder if they get anything extra for doing this?"

As the businessmen around him nodded and said they hoped the workers in the sky would be paid handsomely, they were validating the notion that the values of this country have changed: once, the ability to assist was treasured and now it has been discarded and the new standard is greed.

And then it was over in the sky, and Carroll and Stewart appeared on the ground, both Irish, and both noting that they had been working at other sites when the crane collapsed and they ran to this building because it was their job, taking down a derrick, and when somebody mentioned money, they both seemed annoyed.

"You don't do this for money," Carroll said.

Stewart said that he assumed that what he had just done would cost him money, for he had left his own job and probably would be docked.

"Somebody will make good," he was told.

"I don't want anything for this," Stewart said.

As they both were Irish, it was assumed that their reward would come at the bar. As Louis Carroll started to disappear into the crowd at the sidewalk, somebody called to him.

"Will you have a drink?"

"Not today," Carroll said.

"You need one to calm down."

"Not today or tomorrow."

"Come on. You deserve one."

"I want to go home and sleep. I just got back from Ireland yesterday."

"Then you must have had a good go at it."

"Not a drink. Actually, I was working on this house my father owns in Wexford. He's property there and in Wicklow town."

"And he worked you so hard you didn't have time to tend to thirst?"

"I've been on the dry the last few years. My father hasn't had a drink in 37 years."

"Stop it."

"You stop it. I don't like the hangovers. When you grow up and learn that, you're better off."

"They got that bad for you."

Carroll shook his head. "I couldn't have done it today with a drink in me. That's why I feel so good right now, except I'm tired and I'm going home."

He was gone in the crowd. Now, Bill Stewart stepped out of the building. A hand grabbed his thick arm.

"Have a drink?"

Stewart shrugged. He looked at his hands, which were coated with grease. "I can't go in any place looking like this," he said.

"You can go in anyplace you want," he was told.

He thought for a moment. "To tell you the truth, if you don't mind, I'd rather have a cup of coffee.

"You best have at least one drink for your nerves," he was told.

He shook his head. "I'd rather not. I haven't

133

had a drink in a couple of years. The hangovers ruined me."

"You don't drink during the week?" he was asked.

"I don't drink anytime. I would've been a dead man if I tried going out there today with a hangover. And there's no sense in spoiling a whole weekend because of some cheap whisky on a Friday night."

Stewart had a second cup of coffee. He is 50 and has a strong body and soft blue eyes. His family is from Galway and settled in the Bronx. Stewart on this day was a great hero in the largest city on earth, and he drank coffee. By now, the other hero, Louis Carroll, was somewhere on the subway to the Bronx, where he lives with his father, and the son had risked his life because it was his way, and the father was quite proud of him, and when the son arrived home neither of them had a drink and they are quite Irish.

Jimmy Breslin, novelist and journalist, is a previous contributor to The Recorder

Affirmative Action

MICHAEL DALY

The woman at the employment agency on Court St. ran her finger down James P. Minehan's resume and clucked her tongue.

"Brooklyn College, one year with OTB, six months with the Health and Hospitals, then laid off," the woman said. "This all looks very good. Unfortunately, I can't see anything we have at the moment that would be suitable for you."

"What if I was an Eskimo woman?" Minehan asked.

"No problem," the woman said.

"I see," Minehan said.

On the way down in the elevator, Minehan pulled an envelope out of his jacket pocket and crossed out the last of the 26 employment agencies, business firms, and city departments scrawled on the back. Turning off Court St., Minehan ducked into a saloon called Minsky's. When he arrived at his apartment on Seventh Ave. four hours later, he looked and smelled something like a week-old bar rag.

"I didn't want any of those jobs, anyway," Minehan said to his wife. "There's only one thing I want."

"I know," the wife said. Since he was old enough to read a badge number, the wife knew, Minehan has wanted one thing. Like his father, both his grandfathers, and all five of his uncles,

Minehan's sole goal has been to wear the blue uniform of the New York City Police Department.

"But they aren't hiring Irish guys," Minehan said. "My family has been cops in Brooklyn for 50 years, and now it's my turn and they say they have to hire minority people."

"We've been through this a thousand times," the wife said. "Accept it. Maybe you could go back to California and try it again."

"Never," Minehan said.

Seven months before, Minehan had flown to the west coast to take the exam for the Santa Monica Police Department.

"You can use my address to establish residency," Minehan's cousin, Sean, said when he met Minehan at the Los Angeles airport. "But you got to get some new clothes. You can't walk around here in wool pants."

The following morning, Minehan was in a clothing store on Ventura Blvd., selecting a new wardrobe.

"Can I pay with a check?" Minehan asked the cashier.

"Of course," the cashier said. "Your driver's license, please."

"I don't have a license, yet," Minehan said.

"Everybody has a driver's license," the cashier said.

"Not where I come from," Minehan said.

"How did you get to the store?" the cashier asked.

"I took the bus," Minehan said.

"Then take the bus home in your old clothes," the cashier said.

That evening, the cousin took Minehan on an automotive tour of the Los Angeles area. Towards midnight, the whoop of a siren announced Minehan's first encounter with California law enforcement.

"Get out of your car and keep your hands where I can see them," an officer named Monday said to Minehan and his cousin after informing them they had exceeded the speed limit by 10 mph. While her partner rummaged the car, Monday circled the suspects, her hand clasping the butt of her .357 Magnum revolver.

"Now," Monday said to the cousin, "stretch out your arms. Touch the end of your nose with your right index finger."

"I haven't been drinking," the cousin said.

"Shut up," Monday said. "Now touch the end of your nose with your left index finger."

"What is this?" Minehan asked. "Simon says?"

"You are under arrest," Monday said, throwing Minehan over the hood of the car.

Charged with disorderly conduct, Minehan was whisked to the Wilshire stationhouse. After confiscating his belt and shoelaces, a guard threw Minehan into a padded cell already occupied by a disturbed gentleman from Hong Kong.

"How am I supposed to hang myself with shoelaces?" Minehan demanded.

"You never know," the guard said. Four hours later, the cousin posted $300 bail and Minehan was released.

"I'm leaving," Minehan told his cousin later that morning. "This place isn't worth living in."

"I'm beginning to suspect you're right," the cousin said. The cousin had just learned that his neighbor was suing him because the noise of his power saw had caused her "emotional trauma."

And now, seven months after his trip to Cali-

fornia, Minehan sat in his living room and repeated his conviction that those sprawling territories outside the city limits called the United
States is no place for an Irish boy from Brooklyn.
Unemployment had driven his best friend, an
ironworker named Timmy Carey, to Houston.
The Barry family downstairs had left for Phoenix
to find work. The Breens across the street had
moved to Atlanta. But this was one emigration
James P. Minehan was not going to join.

"It's bad enough my people had to leave Ireland," Minehan said. "I don't even speak the language out there. Anyway, there's only one real
police department, and that's the NYPD."

"Well," the wife said. "There's no way you're
going to wake up black or Puerto Rican. And, if
you're not black or Puerto Rican, you could be
John Wayne and you won't get on."

"John Wayne, John Wayne," Minehan repeated
to himself. Falling silent, Minehan walked to the
window and looked down onto Seventh Ave. An
idea slowly bubbled up from the core of his brain.

"John Wayne's real name was Marion Morrison," Minehan said. "How'd he change his
name?"

"I suppose he went to a lawyer," the wife said.
"Why?"

"I just figured out how Irish guys can become
minorities," Minehan said.

The next morning, Minehan was on the phone
to a friend who is a lawyer in downtown Brooklyn.

"Rubin Hernandez," Minehan said. "I want to
change my name to Rubin Hernandez."

"Where'd you get that name?" the friend asked.

"The phone book," Minehan said.

"But you got red hair," the friend said.

"Never mind," Minehan said. "What do I have to do?"

"It's very simple," the friend said. "You just file a petition with the clerk at the Civil Court on Livingston St. saying you want to change your name. You also file an affidavit saying why you want to change your name and saying you're not doing it to escape any debts or obligations."

"Fine," Minehan said. "I'll be right down."

"Wait," the friend said. "Why do you want to do it, anyway?"

"I like the ring of it," Minehan said. "All my life people have been calling me the same thing. I'm tired of it."

That afternoon, Minehan dropped the documents off at the Brooklyn Civil Court clerk's office. Hopping the IRT home, he spotted a Police Department recruiting ad bearing the legend "We Made It." Minehan studied the advertisement and noted that none of the faces looked even remotely Irish.

Three weeks later, the friend who is a lawyer called Minehan's home.

"Mr. Henandez," the friend said. "The judge has approved the petition. Now send me the $100."

"Si," Minehan said.

At the end of the month, Minehan registered for the police examination.

"I refuse to answer any questions concerning my Hispanic background," Minehan wrote on the application. "I am tired of prejudice."

The day after he registered, Minehan's wife showed him a newspaper clipping reporting that "the Police Department is pressing its minority recruiting drive."

"We recognize the problems of the past," a police spokesman was quoted as saying. "We are confident that, in the future, the department will be in balance with the makeup of the city."

"That's wonderful," Minehan said. "Racism is a terrible thing."

On June 30th, Minehan passed the police exam. By all indications, Officer Rubin Hernandez will soon be pounding a beat, keeping up the great tradition of the Irish policeman.

Michael Daly is a writer with the New York Daily News.

Intimations of Political Mortality

ROGER McHUGH

"When the Irish party met," said my grand-father, "Tim Healy spoke in support of Parnell. Healy told them not to question Parnell's leadership. 'Don't speak to the man at the wheel,' he told them. 'He's more an institution than a man.'"

My grandfather paused, as if focussing his anger.

"And after the split," he continued, "Tim Healy said 'I'll drive him to his grave or to a lunatic asylum.'"

That was my earliest recollection of politics. And it was inextricably connected with dissension. When in later years I read about the ruined Christmas dinner of Stephen Dedalus I would remember my grandfather and say to myself in exasperation, "why didn't I ask him more?"

For he remembered far back. He remembered right back to the Famine, when he would have been a lad like me. His mother used to send him sometimes to leave food near a hedge where the famine victims lay. He was not to go near them because of the fever, only to leave the food there for them, his mother said. That was on their small bit of land at Gorteen, on the shores of Lough Gara.

Sometimes he talked about the local hedge-school to which he had to bring two sods of turf for the teacher. He came back home from school one day and there was a souper reading the bible at his mother. That time there was a fine dish of potatoes on the table. He picked it up and flung the potatoes over the souper. So then at sixteen he had to go on his keeping for some time.

And he remembered the years after the Famine, the years of the Great Silence, when you could travel mile after mile on the countryside and feel a deathly stillness over everything. Not a sound of animal, bird, human.

He did not read a lot but would occasionally ask somebody to go to the Carnegie Library round the corner to get him a book. He sometimes wanted Lever's novels—*Charles O'Malley* or *Jack Hinton* or *The Martins of Cro' Martin*—but the book he would ask most frequently for over the years was Carleton's *Traits and Stories of the Irish Peasantry*, which would content him for a long time. When he told us stories they were usually tales of wonder about Finn MacCool, or about the pike in Lough Gara who would clap their tails in their mouths and whistle shrilly when a stranger approached.

My grandfather was strongly Parnellite. For him the test of political figures in the period between the death of Parnell and the Easter Rising was whether they had stood by Parnell or not. John Redmond was good because he had stood by Parnell. Tim Healy was bad because he didn't. I suspect that my grandfather revised his opinion of Redmond after he pledged the Volunteers to side with England in the war, but I cannot remember anything definite about this. I remember the Easter Monday of the rising because we boys were to go walking with him in the country. On our way to Harcourt Street to get a train to Bray we found knots of people standing near Portobello bridge looking anxiously towards the city. A red-faced man rushed up, shouting "the Shinners is in the G.P.O.!" and after a while we were taken home decidedly puzzled. Who were the Shinners and what was the G.P.O. and why couldn't they be there some other time? To add to our puzzlement, adults seemed to speak in hushed voices after that although some names were clear: Sheehy-Skeffington, Pearse, MacBride, Casement, MacSwiney.

After the Easter holidays we went back to the convent school. It was run by a French Order but most of the nuns were Irish. They taught us new songs which were different from *Ave Maria* and *Hail, Glorious Saint Patrick*. Now it was *Wrap the Green Flag Round Me, Boys* and *Whack Fol the Diddle*. There was a puzzle about the second of these. When we came to the line 'but old Britannia loves us still,' we sang it with enthusiasm. We didn't know who Britannia was. Telling us that she was the figure on the coins didn't help much.

"No, no," said the nun, "sing it sarcastically."

Sing it sarcastically. What did that mean?

"Sing it as if you didn't mean it," she said.

We didn't see the sense of that. What was the point of singing anything if you didn't mean it?

But somehow the songs helped to crystallize the political problem so that by the time the Black and Tans arrived on the scene, we recognized a situation of Them (the British) and Us (the Irish). The continuation of our schooling at Synge Street had something to do with it, for the brothers were not notably pro-British.

Our boyhood heroes were Michael Collins and

143

Cathal Brugha. We saw Collins at the funeral of Arthur Griffith. Then in a few days (it seemed) we saw the funeral of Collins himself, shot by the Republicans. And Brugha was shot by the Free Staters. A slogan appeared on the wall of General Dick Mulcahy's house nearby—"move over, Mick, make room for Dick." It seems now to sum up the malevolent jocose ferocity of the Civil War, though at that time we were completely bewildered. Our grandfather's allegiance seems to have been decided on the simple argument that any government that had Tim Healy as Governor-General couldn't be good. He bought *An Phoblacht* every week and would read out the speeches of Mary and Annie MacSweeney.

"Those are the girls," he'd say, "those are the girls!" And he would laugh heartily at any dissent.

But by that time we had begun to enter our own teens and to conform to the pattern described by Cap'n Boyle in *Juno and the Paycock*: "Take the real Dublin people; they know more about Charlie Chaplin and Tommy Mix than they do about SS. Peter and Paul." O'Casey's plays seemed to stamp that period on our memory as being exciting and, in a way, comic, and I think that people were only too willing to laugh at it afterwards so that they could forget its suffering.

Roger McHugh is an almost legendary figure in modern Irish literary teaching. He virtually founded the discipline of Anglo-Irish Studies, training a generation of Professors and contributing extensively to our appreciation of current Irish writers.

Yeats, India and Long Island

NARAYAN HEGDE

To those who may not readily appreciate the notion that knowledge and scholarship transcend cultural and national limits, a man from India, at an American university, entrusted with the care of the invaluable papers of one of Ireland's greatest poets, is apt to seem incongruous. History, that enormous storehouse of the improbable, would, however, point out that, after all, the Irish and the Indian have had a common legacy—that of British dominance. Among the earliest leaders of India's struggle for political freedom from the British rule were Annie Besant, C. F. Andrews, and J. H. Cousins—all Irish. George Russell (A. E.) immersed himself in the spiritual lore of India and could rightly have been called a yogi. The Irish have been dear to the Indian intellectual, for they have the gift of the English language and literature and yet happily lack the rigid reserve of the English.

During my undergraduate days in India, I often heard Yeats and Eliot hailed as the prophets of modernity in literature. The professors were persuaded not so much by the reputation which Eliot and Yeats enjoyed in the West as by the central place that Indian subject matters occupied in the works of the two poets. Their praise of Eliot's and Yeats's use of Indian subject matter was often a

145

means of chastising us for our scepticism about our own Indian tradition.

I hope I may be pardoned for the luxury of my belief that in my research into the enormous legacy of Yeats, Yeats's own search in the Indian subject matter has come a full circle—a subliminal thought not too disagreeable to Yeats's soul, I suppose.

Yeats's lifelong preoccupation with India is by now commonplace knowledge among the students of Yeats. While Yeats was not alone among the Western poets to be drawn to India, there is some reason to suppose that his affinity with Indian thought and Indian outlook on life has somehow been closer than that of any other comparable Western poet who came under that spell.

Yeats's early interest in India, however, is a direct outcome of his interest in such matters as mysticism, magic, and the occult. As a reaction against the rationalism of Huxley, Spencer, and Mill whom his father admired, young W. B. Yeats turned to the exploration of the supernatural and the mystical forces. In his quest he was aided by his fellow-student, George Russell who had an extraordinary knowledge of the Upanishads and the Vedas.

Yeats's Indian connection has deeper roots because it is also partly his Irish connection. For he had come to see primitive Ireland and India as complementary to each other. "To turn to the East is like turning to the ancient West or North. The one fragment of pagan Irish philosophy, 'The Song of Amergin'," says Yeats, "seems Asiatic." In a note on some later poems, Yeats says, "I associated early Christian Ireland with India." The early Christian Ireland and India—the India

146

where "all popular literature is religion"—shared some common qualities such as their dependence on legends, their belief in the supernatural and their emotional appeal for the believers.

Yeats's interest in Indian thought was sustained through many contacts—Mohini Chatterjee, Madam Blavatsky, Rabindranath Tagore, and Shri Purohit Swami with whom he translated the ten principal Upanishads and Patanjali's Yoga Aphorisms. Nor was this a question of personal encounters; it is clear that his Indian interest was a persistent bent of mind and lasted till the very end.

This would also explain his enthusiastic sponsoring of Rabindranath Tagore whom he, in a manner of speaking, helped to discover for the Western world. Yeats found him interesting because, as he himself said, Tagore represented a tradition where poetry and religion have been the same thing.

Perhaps the most lucid expression of Yeats's Indian experience is to be found in those lyrics Yeats calls 'supernatural songs' woven around a hermit called Ribh who has had mystic experiences. Ribh is an Irish hermit but the philosophy he is accorded is distinctively Indian. There is a joyous note audible in these hermitic songs which is recognizably Indian or Eastern. It is a note of peace that must come from a quiet conviction of Divine participation in everything human.

To Yeats, even till his last years, India remained the Byzantium he wished to sail to. But he never visited India. His plans to go to India with Shri Purohit Swami had to be dropped because of his deteriorating health. Instead, Yeats and the Swami went to Majorca where they translated the

Upanishads together. India seemed to Yeats the logical destination of his spiritual journey. So, in May 1937, at the time of the publication of *A Vision*, Yeats wrote to Purohit Swami who had then returned to India: "Before the end of the summer 'A Vision' will be out and only in India can I find anybody who can light up on certain of its problems."

Today, W. B. Yeats's standing as one of the most distinguished poets of this century is generally unchallenged. His reputation has continually risen since he won the Nobel Prize in 1923. In 1940, just after his death, T. S. Eliot called him "the greatest poet of our time—certainly the greatest in this language, and so far as I am able to judge, in any language." The realisation of the significance of Yeats's poetry to the history of our time prompted Eliot to say:

> There are some poets whose poems can be considered more or less in isolation, for experience and delight. There are others whose poetry, though giving equally experience and delight, has a larger historical importance. Yeats was one of the latter. He was one of the few whose history was the history of our own time, who are part of the consciousness of our age, which cannot be understood without them.

In 1976 the William Butler Yeats Archives—the most complete and largest collection of manuscripts, documents and memorabilia of the Irish poet and playwright—was established at the State University of New York at Stony Brook. It was then, as part of my training for the doctoral candidacy in English, that my association with the Yeats Archives began. Plunging headlong into the jumbled maze of notebooks, correspondence, and other memorabilia, I prepared a working inventory. The official opening of the Archives was marked by a Yeats Festival on May 1, 1976 with Senator Michael Butler Yeats, Mrs. Yeats, Miss Caitriona Yeats, and Dr. Patrick Henchey, Director of the National Library of Ireland as distinguished guests. The day-long event featured lectures by noted Yeats scholars as well as poetry readings and drama performance.

The circumstances that led to the establishment of the W. B. Yeats Archives at Stony Brook are, however, less dramatic than one would imagine them to be in the context of such a significant literary event.

Following a lecture-visit to the Stony Brook campus by Senator Michael Yeats—the only son and literary executor of the celebrated poet, negotiations had begun for creating a repository for the Yeats papers in Stony Brook. An active member and the Vice President of the European Parliament, Senator Yeats was often away from his Dublin home and so could not always be on hand for the visiting scholars, a large number of them from North America, who wanted to study the Yeats papers in his possession. Creating a repository in the U.S. would not only free Senator Yeats from his involuntary role of the curator of his father's papers, but also would spare many an American and Canadian Yeats scholar his or her annual pilgrimage to Dublin.

Senator Yeats later said that the selection of Stony Brook as the home of the William Butler Yeats Archives was based upon the quality of the university's arts and humanities programs and its special resources in the field of computerization for modern scholarly research.

"In recent years," Senator Yeats said, "the National Library in Dublin has received more requests for copies of Yeats's papers from the United States than from the rest of the world combined. Stony Brook is singularly qualified by reputation, academic resources and location to respond to scholarly inquiries in the future."

The archival collection at Stony Brook now duplicates all Yeats materials held by the National Library of Ireland in Dublin and also contains previously uncataloged Yeats family correspondence, important manuscript notebooks, juvenalia as well as other scholarly materials that have been in the possession of Michael Yeats.

In addition to essays, poems and original manuscripts detailing Yeats's interest in the occult and native Irish legends, the Archives contains much of the prolific correspondence between the poet and the other members of the Yeats family. Included are family letters from the poet's father, artist John Butler Yeats, to William and to brother Jack Butler Yeats, also a well-known painter.

No other great poet of our time demands the readers's familiarity with the poet's life and times for a fuller appreciation of his work as much as Yeats does. The movement of the present time is to understand Yeats in terms of his Irishness and his interest in many literary, philosophical and religious traditions.

Never before has so complete a record existed of the creative life of a great poet. Vision and revision were the poles between which Yeats's genius alternated. "It is myself that I remake," he wrote of his perpetual revision of earlier work. Revision was regeneration for him. A manuscript poem reached final form "with a click like the closing of a box" and then was published, only to be revised again in a later edition.

Yeats's habit was to keep (often dated) journals of thoughts, diaries in which he recorded events, drafts of plays, stories, poems, literary essays, letters, occult schemata, and speculative thought. These he preserved. In addition, the vigilance of Mrs. Yeats and of earlier associates rescued from the waste basket thousands of loose-leaf pages. The result is an accumulation of materials, most of them in the home of Senator Michael Yeats, the National Library and the Abbey Theatre in Dublin.

As critical studies on the published work continue, knowledge of the manuscript materials is now a requirement for competent Yeats scholarship: the writing of an official biography, the editions of the letters, poems, plays, stories, essays, his occult diaries, and of his "public philosophy," *A Vision*. From graduate students writing their doctoral theses to writers of books on Yeats, an increasing number of scholars are discovering the importance of the Yeats papers as key to a fuller understanding of the published works of Yeats. There is also research into the Yeats family and publication of manuscripts of J. B. Yeats, the poet's painter father who spent the last fourteen years of his life in New York, of Jack Yeats, the poet's brother and Ireland's great painter, of his sisters, Lily and Lolly Yeats who operated the Cuala Press and Cuala Industries. There is also research into the lives, works and correspondences of Yeats's friends and associates. Scholars doing research in these areas use the archival material either through correspondence with the staff of the

Yeats Archives or by actually visiting the Archives.

Located in the Melville Library as part of Stony Brook's Center for Contemporary Arts and Letters, the W. B. Yeats Archives consists of nearly 80,000 microfilm frames that reproduce the original papers of Ireland's greatest lyric poet. A detailed catalog of these manuscript materials is in preparation with a view to eventually computerizing the information. When the project is completed, the W. B. Yeats Archives at Stony Brook is expected to become the nation's first computerization of a major literary archival collection and the hub of research activities which Senator Yeats lightheartedly calls "the Yeats industry."

Narayan Hegde is the acting curator of the W. B. Yeats Archives at Stony Brook.

Poems

PETER A. QUINN

The Emerald Isle

Your green eyes in that lovely
face: The map of Ireland, they say
(they who've never been there),
yet those of us who shivered
in dank streets and waited
stone drunk in a soot-rich fog
for a tram that never came,
who spent our nights in a wet
cold bed and woke to cold
insipid tea, who watched
a sunken wreck of an old woman
sing for her next drink,
we know your face is no copy of
rain-logged, peat-bog earth
but a moment of pure sunlight
in a damp and bitter day.

On Seeing Your Likeness in a Crowd of Faces on Fifth Avenue

The ancestor of a friend,
a decayed Irishman of quiet ferocity,
once told me he shot a Hun in 1917,
one neat hole in the heart,
dead.

"At such near range," he said,
"I held his stare,
and thought, or remembered thinking,
My God, I know this man.
O'Leary's son.
Seamus from Killybegs."

Those who penetrate so deep
discover, I suppose, only what
they hoped they wouldn't find:
images of home, a common dread,
an aching to connect,
a commotion in their heads.

The eyes I mistook for yours,
scumbled and amazed,
stared back at me and said,
I still think of you;
your soft voice;
your long, skinny legs.

154

Deirdre

You seemed, I thought,
wise beyond your years.

Then I remembered Deirdre.

The hard-edged knowledge
of those who learn early
loss is the other half of
love and can scatter your
head like a stone.

Peter Quinn attempts—in prose and poetry—to un-
ravel the mysteries of the American-Irish scene for
numerous journals.

Irish Sonnets

ANDREW M. GREELEY

Ballendrehid

Grandpa walked down this winding track,
Left the white stone house where his life began;
His family knew he never could come back,
The second son, no one would see again.
The first born stayed here, lucky, on the farm,
Wrestled life from this stern and soggy ground,
Enjoyed the stone fences and home's familiar charm,
Mourned for early death, all his brother found.

His quiet gentle offspring still work the land,
A hard task but healthy folk and strong,
Their life prospects, I fear, not exactly grand,
Unneurotic, they know where they belong.
Sorry, cousins, I'm from beyond the sea.
Poor sad grandpa; affluent, lucky me.

Achill Island

Blue surf gently climbs up the clear white sand,
Purple waters glisten in the noonday air,
Whitewashed houses dot the sun drenched land,
Fresh winds rumple the handsome young folks' hair.
It's Italy, maybe the Amalfi Drive,
Capri, Ischia; but, waiting for our car,
Why there's Crogh Patrick, it's not Naples I've
Left behind but the "town called Castlebar"!

Someone has lied, lovely island, the poets perhaps,
How come rocky Ireland dares look so nice?
Confront, bring suit, demand they change the maps,
Insist that you're a tropic paradise;
Still, when I come back next year, if you please
Warm the ocean waters just a few degrees.

Fr. Greeley is an internationally known sociologist
and ethnologist.

Brendan Behan and the Gaelic Tradition

COLBERT KEARNEY

The social position of the poet in Gaelic Ireland was so different from that of his modern counterpart as to invite special attention. He was descended from the druid, that mysterious pre-Christian figure who combined the functions of priest, professor and poet. The Gaelic poet played a distinct and distinguished role in society—being historian, panegyrist, academic and artist. So much greater was the emphasis on craft rather than on individual inspiration that the art of poetry was handed on within families just as membership in craft unions is passed from father to son today. The practice of poetry survived the loss of the Gaelic patrons: the poets who would once have been members of a powerful and affluent elite were now to share the general decline and to earn their livings as vagrants, laborers, schoolmasters, farmers or innkeepers. They were, nonetheless, accepted as essential witnesses to the glories of the past and carriers of the national lore which sustained the people through decades of oppression.

At no stage in the Gaelic tradition was the artist anything like the individual outsider who has become familiar in Europe since the Romantic era. His place was always fixed *within* the community. In recent centuries Gaelic poetry—even of the most

158

sophisticated or learned varieties—was popular in a way in which the poetry of Milton, Keats or even Tennyson was not. Again because of the accepted public role of the poet, there has always been a strong tradition of public or political poetry in Gaelic. The work of such poets as Ó Rathaille, Ó Súilleabháin and Rafteri—individuals so very different from one another in inspiration and expression—has always been the public property of the Irish-speaking people. By contrast, English poetry for the past few centuries has tended to be the preserve of an educated minority. In Gaelic Ireland—before and after the fall—the poet was the educator. When the Penal Laws denied formal education to Catholics, the poets and storytellers were the principal educators because so much of what constituted a liberal education in Gaelic Ireland was contained in oral literature.

The Gaelic literary tradition was always predominantly oral. The poet and the storyteller confronted their audiences face to face; they did not communicate through the medium of print to a distant reader. In that sense they were performers. After the fall of the Gaelic order they had no special facilities. They performed in houses and taverns, generally before an audience that was a cross-section rather than a selection of the local community. The storyteller was an ordinary member of the community, ordinary, that is, apart from his ability to recite hundreds of stories, some of them the length of novels, word-perfect and with such skill as made his audience long to hear them again and again. He could also listen to a new story—lasting, perhaps, several hours—and repeat it word for word immediately afterwards. The storyteller was respected by his audience but by no means immune from criticism; he had to be careful lest he lose his audience even for a moment and this demanded a phenomenal memory and a dramatic style in which the vitality of the material was communicated by a process of enactment rather than one of description.

This inherited sense of the literary profession is not the least of the influences which the Gaelic tradition has had on Anglo-Irish literature. The traditional storyteller functioned in a society which was largely illiterate: his work would never have been recorded if outsiders had not come along with paper or tape. When in the 18th century the bourgeois novel, mass produced and mass circulated, began to dominate European literature, the Gaelic communities, deprived of formal education, printing, libraries and reviews, had no option but to cling to their oral tradition.

There are three hallmarks of the Gaelic literary tradition: it is dramatic; it is comic rather than tragic, grotesque rather than deferential, surrealistic rather than rational; it combines extremely daring imagination with a stubbornly concrete language by which the furthest flights of fancy are always made dramatically vivid by being described in terms of everyday material.

Brendan Behan is an example of a modern Irish writer drawn towards the Gaelic language and tradition. In this he is not exceptional: the journey westward was the norm among Irish writers from the late nineteenth century onwards.

Born in 1923, the year of the foundation of the Irish Free State, Behan was one of the first Irish writers to be entitled to a free primary school instruction in the Gaelic language and literature. Neither of Behan's parents spoke Irish but they were, like many others then and now, in favor of others learning it. Republicans, they would have seen the English language as a remnant of the English conquest which had yet to be dismantled and would have considered the restoration of the Gaelic language as an aspect of Irish freedom which had yet to be achieved.

Young Brendan, fascinated by words and politically conditioned, delighted in this other language and those who knew him at school recall him "roaring out the Irish." He did not embrace the Christian Brothers who taught him with the same enthusiasm but was grateful for the grounding they gave him in Gaelic—if for nothing else. The Brothers did not always approve of Behan's extra-curricular reading but made no objection when they found him reading Daniel Corkery's *The Hidden Ireland*. Behan, like many others then and since, was stirred by Corkery's account of those Gaelic poets who had preserved the ideal of a future Ireland in which the Gael would triumph over the Gall. Corkery's book helped Behan to hope that he could integrate his two ambitions— to become a writer and to play his part in the achievement of a full free Irish republic. Other books did much the same thing but perhaps *The Hidden Ireland*, more than the others, led him to believe that it was only by means of the Gaelic language that Gaelic Ireland had managed to withstand poverty and oppression and that it was only by means of the Gaelic language that a genuinely free Ireland could be achieved. It is important to distinguish between the influence of the Gaelic tradition on Behan's career and the influence on his individual works. His career, an attempt to dedicate his individual literary talent to

161

the communal political struggle, shaped almost everything he wrote and it is arguable that he would not have persevered in such a career had he not found sanction for it in the lives of the poets of the Gaelic tradition.

Behan's formal schooling ended when he was fourteen but his higher education was only beginning. His involvement with the IRA brought him into contact with all sorts of people, many of them studious and well-read, some of whom came from the Gaeltacht, native speakers of Gaelic who knew the songs and stories of the Gaelic literary tradition. Although not all members of the IRA were Gaelic-speakers, they were almost all committed to the restoration of the language as a long-term objective. Young Behan shared this hope and rejoiced in learning as much of the language and culture as he could.

His studies were interrupted by his imprisonment in England from 1939 to 1941 but were resumed in 1942 when he was imprisoned in Ireland. Between 1942 and 1946 he was among prisoners and internees who were very different from Borstal boys. Many of them were educated men who organized classes in a number of subjects, including, of course, Gaelic. During these years, while learning a considerable amount of the Gaelic language and literature, Behan was also trying to write. Initially it was mostly in English, a play, an unknown number of stories and sketches and some preliminary work on a book about Borstal, but under the influence of the current Gaelic revival, he translated his play into Gaelic and began writing a play about an execution which would eventually emerge in English as *The Quare Fellow*.

Towards the end of this period of imprisonment Behan contributed a poem in Gaelic to the magazine *Comhar*. This was the beginning of a short but important phase in which he emerged as one of the leading contemporary Gaelic poets, a status which was confirmed by the inclusion of two of his poems in *Nuabhéarsaíocht*, an anthology which appeared in 1950. It was a remarkable achievement in the circumstances. The reader of his Gaelic verse is taken by the author's ability to handle such traditional forms as the *amhrán* with its demanding vowel-pattern and the poem of repentance. With other forms, such as the apparition poem and the social satire, he goes far beyond imitation: he parodies the apparition form to great effect and his satire on the bourgeois prudes and clodhoppers of the language revival movement has all the verve and dexterity of his predecessor, Brian Merriman. He also tried to widen the scope of current Gaelic verse by writing of his life among the bohemians of Paris and of his meditation on the house in which Oscar Wilde died.

Despite his success in this medium he wrote little. His abandonment of Gaelic is anticipated in two of the better poems: *A Jackeen Cries at the Loss of the Blaskets*, in which he laments the decay of the Gaeltacht, and *The Rimer's Prayer*, in which he lacerates the puritanism of the revivalists. He recognizes that a great poet, a *file*, is needed to create a work sufficiently great to stir up Irish society; he himself is a mere rimer, a run-of-the-mill poet, not up to such a task. Soon after facing these facts he turned from Gaelic poetry and towards the composition of his masterpiece, *Borstal Boy*.

There is a great deal of emotional pressure behind his lament for the community which once lived on the Blasket Islands; that the quintessential Dubliner should be so moved is at first surprising but the reduction of the Gaeltacht meant for Behan the further disappearance of the ideal Gaelic community which epitomized his aspirations, social and literary. He felt at home in the Gaeltacht as he did in the working-class areas of Dublin city. One of the attractions of the Gaeltacht was its apparent classlessness and the absence of a system of accents denoting social status—so different from the literary circles of Dublin where Behan encountered much condescension and prejudice. In the Gaeltacht he found an integrated community which was proud of the traditions it had preserved against the odds and which accepted as part of that tradition the role of the literary artist. There was here no self-conscious awkwardness between the poet and his audience—no more than between the shopkeeper and his customers. Nor was Gaeltacht life depressed by the puritanism then rampant in the rest of Ireland: the Gaeltacht had never been unduly influenced by Victorian prudery. The way of life was earthy, direct and cultured: the people accepted spiritual abnegation and Rabelaisian gusto with equal ease. They took Behan for what he was—hardliving, generous, hard drinking, sympathetic, serious, exuberant and entertaining. He took them for what they were, without wishing to change them or make them what they were not.

For such reasons Behan loved the life of the Gaeltacht. When the social structure of the Gaeltacht is compared with that in which Behan was reared and formed, it is possible to understand why he felt so much at home in the Gaeltacht. The community around Russell Street into which Behan was born was also a tightknit society, conscious and proud of its identity and culture. Though their dialect and their life-style was influenced by such colonial features as the army and the music hall, they were basically Gaelic in structure. Like their Gaeltacht counterparts, the people around Russell Street were given to rich conversation, to the pleasures of language, and they relished the songs and the stories and the turns of phrase which identified them. Among them the ability to use the spoken word with skill and precision was the equivalent of a university degree; the ability to sing a good song or tell a good story was a passport to social success; to have a tongue like a hachet was a useful means of self-defense. At its best their dialect shows that combination of imagination and concrete detail which is the hallmark of the Gaelic style and which was made known to the world by writers such as Joyce, O'Casey and, later, Behan himself.

Behan's parents may usefully be compared to the *seanchaí* and the *scéalaí* of the Gaeltacht. His mother was (and is) a celebrated store of genealogy, history, music and local lore—traditionally in the Gaelic tradition the preserve of the woman. His father was a superb *scéalaí*, a storyteller, as well as being a wit and raconteur, dominating any company with narratives delivered with fluency and spiced with his iconoclastic sallies and Rabelaisian humor. In later years, many members of the international media who came to interview Brendan remained to observe his father. He was not abashed in the company of NBC or Evelyn Waugh for he was a professional performer with a lifetime of practice behind him. To an intensely serious lady reporter who asked him how a Dublin working man could have produced such a talented family, Behan's father replied that it was a simple matter of biology. From the time he mesmerized a house full of children to the day he died, Stephen Behan was the typical *scéalaí*, or storyteller.

Behan inherited his father's talent for entertainment, delighting an audience with a parade of learning, licentious wit, parody, mimicry, song and gesture. Ironcially it was this facility which so often hindered his efforts at the less convivial art of writing. In the beginning, writing was for him an attempt to emulate the thin bare style associated with the early Joyce and Hemingway. How well he succeeded in this line may be seen in a story like *After the Wake* but, consciously or unconsciously, he must have known that this meditative, even morbid medium could not sustain the essentially comic exuberance of his experiences in England as they were being shaped and colored by his creative imagination. Style is the attitude of an artist to his experience. Behan had already discovered his attitude and had regaled his friends with live performances of his experience. What he needed was a literary style which would communicate to the reader what he could almost naturally communicate to an audience. Eventually, helped by his work on his play and his efforts at journalism, he glimpsed the way forward: a literary transcription of oral techniques.

In *Borstal Boy* his task was to describe the experiences of a young boy—intelligent but adolescent and emotionally confused—and to show how these experiences had changed his whole life. The changes had been intuitive rather than intellectual; his story was not a rational chronology but a drama. He set out to relive the events and take the reader into the mind of the prisoner. Behan was a gifted oral performer but it would be a mistake to think that the translation to the printed page was an easy one. Behind the apparent spontaneity there is a considerable literary technique but one which is basically similar to that of the live storyteller.

The high points of *Borstal Boy* are the hilarious orchestrations of comic description such as the Easter ceremonies in the second part. The most memorable aspect of the work is the language. It would be wrong to assume that the language of *Borstal Boy* is the everyday language of Dubliners. It is not: it is the style of a great storyteller. It involves a repertoire of Dublin-accented formulae—oaths, obscenities, similies, proverbs, stock-expressions—and it is based on the rhythms of Dublin speech but it has been arranged and orchestrated by a great storyteller. Behan's greatest gift was a comic imagination which extended the resources of the language he inherited.

Consider the fall of the Chief Officer. It happened in Christmas Week. Behan, excommunicated, remained in his cell as the other Catholics went to confession. The monotonous rhythms underline the alienation of the prisoner and the penal boredom.

> It was too dark to read and, anyway, I wanted to save all the reading I could for these four days, and there was a bit of white light in the sky and the snow coming, and I decided the screws might be a bit easy on us even if they caught us, it being the day before Christmas Eve, so I pulled over my table and got up to look out the window.

167

The six words of the next paragraph—'And as well that I did'—introduce one of those musical transformations which Behan manages so well. The quickening of the pulse is due to the introduction of the present tense, compound images and emphatic syntax.

> Our Chief Officer, the stocky cruel-faced turkey-toed bastard, walks out with his glare and his strut, looking round and down at the snow, and up at the windows, five tiers of them in the square round the yard, in dead silence, and he knowing we were looking at him, and he glaring up at the barred windows, and some near me, though they must have known that he could not have seen them at that distance, got down in fear. But I did not, thank God that I did not, and those that got down must have been cutting their throats a minute later, for the next thing is, the Chief Officer, with his red-faced glare and his strut, walks clean off the steps and into six feet of snow.

The Officer is described as 'turkey-toed' and this fantastic attribute is realized in the dactyls and anapaests, *cru*-el-faced, *tur*-key-toed, with-his-*glare*, and-his-*strut*, which suggest the rhythms of a turkey's gait. It is amplified by the movements of the head, looking down and round and up. The Hiberno-English syntax implies the smouldering anger of this Walton Chaunticleer: "and he *know*ing . . . and he *glar*ing" is much more emphatic than the standard 'knowing . . . and glaring' for the extra words merely accentuate the active root of the participles. On the cue of 'the next thing is' we zoom in on the Officer, now a compressed variation of his original self, his red-faced glare emphasized before his total loss of identity in the white snow. The surrealism is balanced by concrete details: those who missed this fall were not merely disappointed, they cut their throats; nor was it an ordinary fall, but a walk *clean* off the steps and into *six feet* of snow—exceptionally heavy for the latitude but perfect for the occasion.

> He floundered and was lost in it, there was even hope he'd smother in it, and oh, Jesus, what a shout went up from all the windows. What delight, what joy, and as a bonus on it, didn't the old bastard, when he struggled up a step, shake his fist in anger and fall down again . . .

The second fall induces an ecstasy as palpable as a pay-packet. The religious invocation is not entirely blasphemous: through the barrier of ex-communication young Brendan sees the hand of the Almighty.

> I sat down again at my table, and was thankful to God and His Blessed Mother for this. If I had gone to confession, I'd have missed it, and I was consoled. God never closes one door but He opens another, and if He takes away with His right hand, He gives it back with His left, and more besides.

The concrete imagery of the Irish proverbs lends utter conviction to this declaration of faith.

Although this passage is one of the highlights, the narrative mode is typical of the book as a whole. What seems at first sight a transcription of colloquial delivery begins, under analysis, to show signs of consummate skill in arrangement. The storyteller has made good the disadvantages of print by varying the tempo and dynamics of his telling. This is done chiefly by means of syntax which pays little attention to rules of standard written English and which makes great use of the plasticity of spoken Hiberno-English. Paragraphs which would normally—in a book—be divided into sentences are allowed to rush on without pausing for breath, while sentences which would normally—again, in a book—be integrated by a complex of clauses are left in an unresolved catalogue.

I think it can be seen that the relationship between *Borstal Boy* and the Gaelic oral tradition is striking. I do not wish to suggest that it was because of his sojourns in the Gaeltacht that Behan wrote like this: the work owes as much to Russell Street as to the Aran Islands. But I suspect that it was his awareness of the modern Gaelic literary tradition—the classics of which, such as *Peig* and *An tOileánach* and others, are based on the speech of gifted storytellers who knew no written tradition—which showed Behan the possibilities of using his inherited talents for literary purposes.

There are other relevant features related to the Gaelic tradition not only in *Borstal Boy* but in his other works as well. The experience of brutality and deprivation does not automatically generate a comic form but for Behan it did. Part of the comedy of *Borstal Boy* lies in the fact that it is a parody—a favorite Gaelic form—of previous accounts by Irish prisoners of their sufferings for Mother Ireland.

The modern urban *scéalaí* is likely to see the theatre as his natural medium and it was as the author of *The Quare Fellow* that Behan first achieved fame. The manner in which Behan insists on the involvement of the audience at this play has led some to compare it with the experiments of Beckett and Ionesco—and rightly so. I would also relate it to its Gaelic context. We in Ireland are indeed shocked at the grotesque black humor of the play but we recognize it as the tra-

170

ditional communal response to the terrors of death. *The Quare Fellow* is an attempt at exorcism, an effort to effect a ritual banishment of death by means of laughter: it is a theatrical version of what happens at that most terrifyingly funny of all Irish institutions, the wake.

To sum up. The fact that Behan was born in an English-speaking area two centuries after the fall of Gaelic Ireland did not mean that he was cut off from the Gaelic tradition. Much of what was typically Gaelic survived in the dialect and cultural forms which he inherited. However, his conscious study of the Gaelic tradition was crucial in his literary career. Firstly, his reading of the Gaelic poets encouraged him to combine both his political and his literary aspirations. Secondly, his reading of modern Irish prose—some of the best of which is based on *caint na ndaoine*, the spoken language of the people, and written down by celebrated storytellers—made him aware of the literary potential of his own storytelling talents. Finally his efforts to write in Gaelic, to address a tiny audience in an acquired language, forced him to dedicate himself to the craft of writing and helped him overcome—to some extent—that desire for instant reaction which his performing talents led him to expect.

Colbert Kearney teaches in the Department of English, University College, Cork.

The Sage of Saratoga

JOHN J. CASSIDY

"Kindly spend the enclosed on some fripperies, and oblige."

So began the first letter I remember receiving from Frank Sullivan, the humorist; it reached me—then an impecunious undergraduate at Union College in Schenectady, N.Y.— a few days before prom week in 1953.

It was the first of many wonderfully funny and engaging letters I was to receive from Frank up until he died five years ago (1976), at age 83, in his beloved home town of Saratoga Springs, N.Y.

At the time of his death, Frank was the doyen of American newspaper humorists, the last surviving example of an age of American journalism that, regrettably, has passed.

His heyday was a time when New York newspaper readers could choose from a dozen or more daily papers, when they could look forward to reading the light-hearted expression and prankish humor of Sullivan and his friends Robert Benchley, Alexander Woollcott, Franklin P. Adams, Heywood Broun, and Dorothy Parker, and many other keen wits of the day. Is it possible that *The New York World*, journalistic haven to Sullivan and many of his friends, has been gone for fifty years? Sadly, the answer is yes.

Frank Sullivan made his mark on American humor through hundreds of short essays published in newspapers and magazines over a period of fifty years, beginning in the 1920s. Gentle, cerebral humor was his trademark. His objective was to produce chuckles, not belly-laughs. His metier was whimsy and spoof. He poked fun, not egos or issues.

And he poked fun at such unlikely subjects as overuse of footnotes (in "A Garland of Ibids for Van Wyck Brooks"), the too-numerous composers Bach ("The Forgotten Bach"), run-on sentences ("Proust and the Life Sentence"), and unusual names of people, through the so-called Novel Nomenclature Club, to which he contributed such peerless real-life examples as Friend Hoar, Hyacinthe Ringrose and Cloud Wampler ("He wamples clouds, I suppose.").

The cliché was the butt of much of his humor. Through his fictional creation, Mr. Arbuthnot, the cliché expert, Sullivan laid bare and impaled the inanities and hackneyed phrases of writing and conversation. In question-and-answer interviews, Mr. Arbuthnot proved himself a never-ending source of timeworn clichés in subjects ranging from baseball to splitting the atom, as witness this exchange from "The Busy Cliché Expert":

Q. What else do you do, Mr. Arbuthnot?
A. Well, let me see. I take into account, I go far enough, I look for support, I deem it a privilege. I put in an appearance, I get the upper hand of, I bring the matter up, and I let the matter drop.
Q. Mr. Arb—
A. No, hear me out, Mr. Todd. You asked for it. I take to task, I knuckle down, I buck up, I level criticism, I venture to predict, I inject a serious note—that reminds me, do you realize why I am not wearing any pearls?

Q. Why not?
A. Swine got 'em.

After *The World* folded in 1931, Sullivan found plentiful other outlets for his humor, including *The New Yorker*, *Harper's Magazine*, *The Saturday Evening Post*, *Good Housekeeping*, *Town & Country*, *Atlantic Monthly*, and the munificent if little-known *Detroit Athletic Club News*. In the 1940s he wrote a humor column for Marshall Field's short-lived New York tabloid, *PM*.

Frank wrote the popular Christmas poem in *The New Yorker*, from the poem's inception, in 1932, until 1974. Entitled "Greetings, Friends" it expressed rhymed benisons to famous people and, occasionally, to hometown friends, as in the 1974 version, which read in part:

> May Christmas Day be fair and merry
> For the first Ms. and President Jerry!
> Many happy returns of the Day
> To Marsha Mason and Gordon Ray.
> Peace to Peter Lisagor,
> Stevie Wonder, and Dinah Shore!
> Our fond regards to Miguel Piñero
> Marybeth Hurt, José Quintero,
> Lewis Thomas, the peerless physician,
> And Pierre Boulez, the ditto musician.

My student days at Union were brightened by this passage in Sullivan's 1952 Christmas poem:

> John Cassidy, Good King Wences'
> Best to you and Concordiensis.

(I was then the editor of the student newspaper at Union, *Concordiensis*.)
The best of Frank's pieces were published in

174

book form, including *In One Ear . . .* (1933), *A Pearl in Every Oyster* (1938), *A Rock in Every Snowball* (1946), and *The Night the Old Nostalgia Burned Down* (1953).

Frank Sullivan was born in Saratoga Springs on September 22, 1892, the son of Dennis (born 1845, County Kerry) and Kate (born 1851, County Limerick) Sullivan. The family lived on a street that is now incorporated into the grounds of Saratoga Race Track.

As a boy of 10, Frank remembered working as a water pump boy in the betting ring of the race track, and serving tin cups of water to such illustrious patrons as Lillian Russell and her flamboyant companion, Diamond Jim Brady. To one of his biographers, Frank said, "It was a swell job, easy hours, plenty to see, little to do, 10 to 15 bucks a day in tips, and no income tax."

Frank graduated from Saratoga High School in 1910, his classmates including lifelong friends Dr. John E. Heslin, who rose to be President of the American Urological Association (Dr. Heslin is 90 and still lives in Saratoga), and Charles Brackett, who won fame as a producer and director of Hollywood comedies, usually in collaboration with Billy Wilder.

After graduating from Cornell in 1914, Frank got a job as a reporter for the local daily, *The Saratogian*, at the princely starting wage of $7 a week. His career in journalism was briefly interrupted by military service during World War I, after which he soon headed for New York, where he landed a job on *The Herald* and, later, on *The Evening Sun*.

In 1922, Frank joined the writing staff of *The World*, a much-sought-after opportunity that brought him under the tutelage and supervision of Herbert Bayard Swope, the paper's colorful and autocratic editor. Frank started out as a rewrite man on the copy desk, but soon was churning out two or three humor columns a week.

According to one account, Swope assigned Frank to write humor after Frank messed up an obituary on a prominent socialite, a story he had taken over the phone and which appeared on page one of the bulldog edition of *The World*. "It was correct in every detail save one," Frank used to say. "She wasn't dead."

In an interview with Alden Whitman of *The New York Times* about five years before Frank died, Frank said he was so embarrassed by the obituary mistake that he tried to resign, but that Swope told him: "You're too emotional for the news columns, Sullivan. From now on you're writing funny stuff exclusively." Thus are humorists made, not born.

Armed with his newly won fame as a newspaper columnist, and a hefty salary increase, Sullivan soon became a dashing man-about-town, frequenting the speakeasies until, as he put it, "the wee 'sma hours." Short, cherubic, rotund and jolly, Frank was great fun to be with in a bar.

He was welcomed as a member of the Algonquin Round Table, a collection of writers and wits who met at the Algonquin Hotel for luncheon and sparkling conversation. Benchley, Broun and Parker also were members, as were playwrights Marc Connelly, Russel Crouse and Robert E. Sherwood. Frequently, some of his Round Table friends accompanied him on his speakeasy rounds.

Frank lived in Manhattan for over 20 years. During much of that time, he shared bachelor's quarters with Corey Ford, a freelance magazine writer. Sullivan referred to himself as Ford's "ugly roomer" and commonly crawled into bed, after a night on the tiles, only a few hours before Ford arose, around dawn. When Ford left for work in the morning, he customarily threw open the door of Frank's bedroom and shouted at the sleeping Sullivan, "Get up, lazybones, I've been up for hours."

This matutinal scenario went on for several years until one Easter Sunday morning when it was Sullivan who rose early, in order to get to Penn Station in time for a train taking him to a dinner date on Long Island, and Ford who slept in. When Ford awoke later that morning, he found a note pinned to his door. It read, "Get up, lazybones, I've been up for hours." It was signed, "Jesus Christ."

After *The World* folded in February of 1931, Frank wrote, "When I die, I want to go where *The World* has gone and work on it again." However, he soon transferred his journalistic loyalties to the upstart new magazine, *The New Yorker*, and its crusty editor, Harold Ross. Frank became a regular contributor to *The New Yorker* and its blossoming role in American literature.

I first met Frank Sullivan in 1942, after he returned from New York to live with his older sister, Kate, in the family home on Lincoln Avenue in Saratoga Springs. I was then a sixth grader, and I remember Frank loaning me a copy of *Nicholas Nickleby*. Thereafter, I was to be a more or less regular visitor to his home and borrowed almost all of his Dickens collection.

In those days, newspaper delivery boys used to sell war bonds and stamps, and Frank became my best customer—even though his home was not on my delivery route.

After I achieved majority, I frequently saw and talked with Frank in his favorite Saratoga taverns: The Colonial and the Worden Inn. His usual drinking companion was Monty Woolley, a Saratogian and former English professor who achieved stage and screen stardom in the role of the irascible Sheridan Whiteside in the Kaufman-Hart comedy, "The Man Who Came to Dinner."

I recall Sullivan introducing me to Monty and telling him, "He's been reading Trollope in college, and actually likes him." On that unlikely basis, Monty deigned to let me prepare his martinis when I tended bar at the Colonial my last two summers home from college.

Frank's spontaneous wit earned him the title "Sage of Saratoga" and placed him in great demand as a guest at cocktail parties and dinners, particularly during the racing season. He visited the track as often as his writing schedule and, later, his health, permitted. He was strictly a two-dollar bettor, and when track officials named a race in his honor in 1969, he wagered on every horse in the race in order to be sure to have the winner.

Frank's tree-cloaked, modest home was located, as he liked to recall, less than a furlong from the race track. He did most of his writing in a small office on the second floor. There were books everywhere in the house, along with autographed photos of famous friends and contemporaries. As to his work schedule, he confessed to Alden Whitman, "I dislike it—working—and sometimes I don't do any."

The last fifteen or so years of Frank's life were

not entirely happy ones. His sister died, leaving him alone at home. His diverticulitis, a health problem from which he suffered for many years, worsened and became more painful. Worst of all, the market for his humor dried up. Aside from *The New Yorker* poem and an occasional piece for *The New York Times*, his public pen was stilled.

But he did not stop writing humor. If anything, he increased his output, in the form of hundreds of marvelously humorous and entertaining letters to his friends. As his friend Marc Connelly observed, "Getting a letter from Sullivan makes any morning a sunny one."

I was fortunate to be one to whom Frank wrote with some frequency, and offer these examples to prove his is a form of humor that will endure:

On his boyhood in Saratoga:

"At Christmas time Ruth's (an orphan) grandmother would give me a couple of bucks and I would go down to the 5 & 10 and stock up with enough tree ornaments to decorate three trees, and then I would go out to Yaddo (a private estate) and chop down the tree myself. One Christmas I gave Yaddo a rest and took my sled out to the end of Jefferson Street where there was an evergreen wood, to see what I could find (steal). There wasn't any small tree that pleased my eye but I thought that the top of a fine-looking twenty-foot or so spruce would make a dandy. So I climbed the spruce and lopped off the top six feet. That was Ruth's tree that Christmas. And if the farmer who owned that woodlot had caught me I'll bet my ass would have tingled all the way home, right past Frankie Hamilton's 'inn' and other similar establishments which enlivened Jefferson Street. Those places don't exist any more, because sex has been abolished, you know."

On being a reporter during Prohibition:

"Your favor received and in reply beg to state will take two of each. Those Bawl Street Journals (parody of The Wall Street Journal) I know of old. Long ago in my 'career' back in the days when reporters wore powdered wigs and satin smallclothes—Ben Franklin was my city editor—I used to cover the annual picnics of the Bond Club which got out the Bawl Street Journal. They were held at some country club in Westchester and were magnificent brawls. I seldom came back to the office sober enough to write my story."

On giving up coffee (on doctor's orders):

"I tried two coffee-less mornings and began to have withdrawal symptoms, picking at the coverlet and mistaking your father for Elizabeth Taylor when he came in. Coffee may be an irritant but as I said in my sermon last Epiphany, life is an irritant, too. This remark was widely quoted and made the "Quote for Today" box in the Times two days in succession."

On getting a new typewriter:

"The big test will come when I have to change the ribbon for the first time. Werner Von Braun will be in charge of the countdown. Straw will be placed on Lincoln Avenue to deaden any noise that might throw me off. The press will be allowed to come but will have to stay downstairs and keep very quiet. Doctors will be at hand in case I need oxygen or in case I blow my top in rage at the damn contraption and have to have strong sedatives to prevent my dashing the machine against the wall. Three of the top public relations men from the Smith Corona people will be on hand and Truman Capote has consented to ghost my first-hand account of the ordeal. After the ribbon is fixed a waiting ambulance will speed me to the Mosher Clinic for a month's rest."

On receiving an honorary doctorate
from Skidmore College in 1967:

"Why there was even some trepidation when word got about that I was to be made an honorary member of the Class as statistics proved that I would lower the beauty standard of the Class by 17.09 per cent. Everything went off beautifully at my consecration except that the tassel of my mortar board kept tickling my nose, causing me to sneeze at inopportune moments. In all respects I conducted myself with dignity and decorum and every time a friend came up and said, 'Congratulations, you deserve the honor,' I would say modestly, 'Oh no I don't really.' Until I said it once too often and a fellow replied, 'I know damn well you don't but can't I be polite.' "

On living alone:

"Got almost through the winter without a sniffle and then two weeks ago I got a good one. I have been trying to cure it without the aid of a doctor, possibly a mistake. I think that being alone in this house for two weeks has been worse than the aches and pains of the grippe. I yield to no man in admiration for the matchless charm of that saint in human form, F. Sullivan, but I have to testity that two weeks alone in his company comes under the head of cruel and unusual punishment."

On failing memory:

"I read an interesting item in the NY Times two days ago about Dr. (Ewen) Cameron of your Medical Center, who has discovered a medicine which will help the memory of aged people. It interested me because, though I hate to admit it, I have been having some trouble lately remembering names. They don't come trippingly on the tongue as they always have done. I'm not kidding about this, Hennessey, I really have trouble."

On longevity:

"Just because I've happened to survive longer than most of my contemporaries except Marc Connelly, I get these imperious requests every so often from dusty little pedants trying to write their theses for a PhD and too goddam lazy to do the work themselves, so they sponge on senile old men. Nowadays the requests go into the waste basket.

I am now 80 or will be in 2 weeks. Hardly a man is now alive.

Love to all, from the man you adore."

The universality and civility of Frank's humor guarantee him a permanent place in the annals of American humorists. One hopes his place will be as lofty as that projected by Lewis Nichols in the *New York Times Book Review* in 1970: "A case can be made by any working sentimentalist that only one true humorist remains . . . Frank Sullivan. He belongs to the Mark Twain, George Ade, Booth Tarkington line."

John Cassidy, bred and reared in Saratoga Springs, now resides in Slingerlands, New York.

Brian O'Doherty/Patrick Ireland

DOROTHY WALKER

Brian O'Doherty first came to the United States in 1957 on a postgraduate fellowship to Harvard for studies in visual perception. He had already qualified in medicine at the National University of Ireland, coming from a medical family in which all four brothers were doctors. He was born in the west of Ireland at Ballaghadereen, County Roscommon, in 1935.

O'Doherty's earliest foray into art criticism was a television series for a Boston station in which he took viewers through the Boston Museum of Fine Art, giving his own insights and perceptions of the great treasures of that prestigious collection. In 1960, he married the art historian Barbara Novak whom he had met at Harvard, and they moved to New York. He rapidly became known as an incisive and perceptive art critic, writing first in *The New York Times.* In 1968, he published *Object and Idea,* a collection of his art criticism.

An artist himself, he also at this time worked closely with a group of American artists, then little known but subsequently world-famous: Sol Lewitt, Robert Smithson, Eva Hesse, Dan Graham and Mel Bochner. O'Doherty used the Old Irish ogham alphabet as a visual tool to make highly interesting serial drawings, which later were transposed into very beautiful stainless steel sculpture incorporating the ogham incisions on angled surfaces reflecting into each other.

In 1969, Brian O'Doherty was appointed Director of the Visual Arts Program of the National Endowment for the Arts (NEA) in Washington, D.C. This appointment had a major effect on the art of the ensuing decade in the United States. The brilliant, sometimes flippant, but always successful art scene of the sixties—successful in critical and commercial terms and in public acceptability—began to yield to entirely different concerns.

Artists began to produce work that could not be sold, in protest against the increasing manipulation of their careers by the overriding preoccupation with saleability on the part of gallery owners. Conceptual art in its manifold forms began to replace saleable, paintings and pieces of sculpture. Special projects out in the landscape, or special installations in museum spaces, were carried out by artists all over the United States, thus also breaking the monopoly of the New York-based commercial galleries. This most un-American revolt by leading artists against the market system led to the development of forms of art that brought about an unprecedented broadening of the range and public impact of art. Still, the works required funding, and the National Endowment for the Arts gave the crucial support to specific art projects that were outside the scope of the normal market. Other sponsors followed suit, and the decade of the seventies became one of the most interesting and creative, in which works of art of a breathtaking and hitherto unimaginable scale took form across America.

An inspired bureaucracy is critical to the activity of even large, well-endowed museums, but more so to the smaller, less independent institutions where more creative work might well originate. Brian O'Doherty built up the credibility of the National Endowment at a time when accurate understanding of the work in progress was essential, but rare among art bureaucracies anywhere in the world.

At the beginning of the seventies, O'Doherty was also editor of *Art in America,* a publication he saved from

184

almost total failure and, in three years, turned into a thriving enterprise under a new publisher. He rescued the magazine by the same blend of administrative intelligence and understanding of the new art that distinguished his work at the NEA.

Meanwhile, he was also developing his own art, but events in Ireland were becoming increasingly distressing. On 31 January 1972, later known as Bloody Sunday, British army paratroopers shot dead thirteen civilians during a peaceful demonstration in Derry. Later that year, Brian O'Doherty—writer, art administrator and medical doctor—added the name Patrick Ireland to his identity in a formal, legal act in Dublin at the Irish Exhibition of Living Art. The legal document reads as follows:

November 29th 1972

From this date artworks by Brian O'Doherty will be signed

PATRICK IRELAND

until such time as the British military presence is removed from Northern Ireland and all citizens are granted their civil rights.

The name-change was accompanied by a performance in which the artist was carried in on a stretcher, dressed entirely in white with a white stocking mask over his face. Two fellow-artists, Brian King and Robert Ballagh, began to paint him at either end, one with green paint and one with orange, in the colors of the Irish flag. As the two colors drew near to confrontation and the white peace area diminished, a certain tension built up in the audience, but when the logical conclusion materialized wherein the green and the orange merged and continued on to either end, the positive intention of the action became apparent and was applauded.

185

From that time until the present, Brian O'Doherty has continued to show his work under the name Patrick Ireland. Himself very much a practitioner of what he preached in the seventies in an influential and widely noted series of articles ("Inside the White Cube" in *Artforum,* 1975–76), he makes in situ rope-drawings: subtle, linear, spatial constructions of rope-lines in space acting in confluence with painted areas on the surrounding walls.

His work has become increasingly well-known and for this reason he relinquished his directorship of the Visual Arts Program of the NEA, lest his own art career conflict with the interests of other artists. He became Director of the Media Arts Program, a post he still holds, and where he pursues a similar pioneering role in fostering creative work in video and film, work which might not necessarily attract the support of business corporations. Thus he has been able to assist the work of creative people in the cinema who are anxious to help young film-makers to make a start in that most competitive art. He himself has also maintained his early involvement with television, in an early-morning art program on one of the national networks, and also in making high-quality documentaries such as "The Treasures of Ireland" which accompanied the travelling exhibition of Irish antiquities in the United States in 1978–79. His first film, an innovative, highly original documentary on the American artist, Edward Hooper, called "Hooper's Silence," was included in the New York Film Festival in 1981. He is now seeking the necessary backing for an equally original film on the pioneer of American Abstract Expressionism, Jackson Pollock.

Brian O'Doherty is a brilliant writer, artist, critic, and art administrator, and a profound admirer of Irish writers such as Flann O'Brien. In his double persona, O'Doherty/

Ireland embodies the often-split Irish personality, the double identity like Flann O'Brien/Myles na gCopaleen, E.C. Earwicker/Perse O'Reilly, the Irish Renaissance man of many names, many parts. We begrudge him to America, but then we were always a race of begrudgers.

Dorothy Walker is President of the International Association of Art Critics.

O'Casey and the Labor Movement

MAUREEN MURPHY

The major Irish television event of 1979 was
Radio Telefís Eireann's serialization of James
Plunkett's novel *Strumpet City*. Aside from its interest as a period piece, *Strumpet City* dramatizes
Ireland's less well-known rising of the second decade of the twentieth century, the Dublin general
strike and lockout which began August 26, 1913.
The history of that event has yet to be written,
but such a history might argue that the general
strike was, in fact, The Rising. It occurred three
years earlier than the Easter Rising; it involved
more people over a longer period of time; it was
responsible for the first workers' army, the Irish
Citizen Army; it developed a social conscience
and it produced its own Promethean hero in Jim
Larkin. As we honor the memory of Sean O'Casey
in his centenary year, let us consider him in the
context of the 1913 strike, a major shaping force in
his life and work.

One of Michael and Susan Casey's thirteen children (eight of whom died in infancy), John Casey
was born at 85 Upper Dorset Street, Dublin, on
March 30, 1880. Dublin in that year had the highest death rate for any major city in the world:
higher proportionally than Calcutta, for example,
or Alexandria.

The years intervening between Casey's birth

and the general strike brought little improvement in living standards for the Dublin workingman. The Governmental Housing Commission's report of 1913 paints a grim picture. Fully one-third of the city's population lived in squalid tenement houses where, in most cases, a single room flat accommodated the entire family. There was rampant disease. High unemployment kept wages low; the average workingman took home fourteen shillings for a seventy-hour week; women made between five and ten shillings for up to ninety hours of work. (A simple gauge of the buying power of these salaries is to say that a pound of good butter cost a shilling at the beginning of World War I.)

After short jobs as stock boy and van boy, O'Casey entered that work force as a pick and shovel man on the Great Northern Railway of Ireland in 1903. Three years later, he joined the Drumcondra Branch of the Gaelic League and adopted the Irish form of his name Seán O'Cathasaigh. The Irish language and the labor movement were to be two life-long commitments. He became Secretary of the Drumcondra Branch of the Gaelic League in 1908. Like many Irishmen, it was a short step for O'Casey from the language movement into a nationalist organization. He joined the Irish Republican Brotherhood in the same year; however, when he joined Jim Larkin's Irish Transport and General Workers' Union in 1911, he began a course that would take him away from Irish nationalist politics to international socialism.

O'Casey's firing in December, 1911, as a consequence of his union membership, was a measure of the kind of employer attitude toward organized

189

labor that resulted in the 1913 strike and lockout. O'Casey's belief that the workingman had no hope unless he organized informed his activities in Larkin's union. In June, 1912, he began writing features for the union paper, *The Irish Worker*, including a series on working conditions on the Great Northern Railway. A year later, in 1913, O'Casey was to play a major role writing, organizing relief and working on behalf of striking workers.

James Larkin (1876–1947), who came to Dublin from Belfast in 1907 as a strike organizer in the Dock Labourer's Union, tried to organize the Dublin tram workers in 1913. William Martin Murphy responded by requiring a nonunion pledge of employees; the alternative was a lockout. Larkin called a strike on August 26, 1913, and by the end of the month there were 25,000 men out of work. Dublin Castle and the Catholic Church sided with the employers, and the nonunion workers who kept the trams running were protected by the Royal Irish Constabulary. Within a week there were riots.

The *London Times* for September 2, 1913, reported one killed, 460 injured (including 60 R.I.C.) and 210 arrested during riots the previous day and predicted "it will appear like a playful skirmish compared with what may be expected." A consequence of these riots was the formation, in October, of the Irish Citizen Army, an army of laborers organized to protect striking workers. O'Casey served as the first secretary of the Citizen Army and later wrote its history, *The Story of the Irish Citizen Army*, a pamphlet listing its author as P. O'Cathasaigh published by Maunsel and sold for a shilling (1919).

When the nationalist Irish Volunteers were founded by Eoin MacNeill in 1913, O'Casey wrote an "Open Letter to Workers in the Irish Volunteers" urging them to resign from the Volunteers and to join the Citizen Army. O'Casey's argument was that the largely middle class Volunteers did not serve the workingman's interest. O'Casey's earlier letters reveal his hope to unite labor and nationalism but he was disappointed in the clearly apolitical nature of the Gaelic League as an organization and the lack of support of individual Gaelic Leaguers like Padric Pearse whom O'Casey criticized for riding the trams during the strike.

Aside from the Irish Citizen Army, O'Casey devoted extraordinary energy and effort as Secretary of the Women and Children's Relief Fund to raising money through direct appeals to Dubliners and through a letter-writing campaign to friends of Irish labor. The response to Dublin strikers from British workers convinced O'Casey that Irish workers had more in common with British workers than with Irish employers.

The strike collapsed after six months when the union capitulated. O'Casey's hero Larkin went to America leaving James Connolly in charge of Liberty Hall. Though Connolly was the most original social thinker in the Ireland of his time, O'Casey was skeptical of Connolly's rapprochement with the nationalists. He resigned from the Citizen Army in 1914 in protest. He later wrote that under Connolly the Irish Citizen Army became the "militant left wing of the Irish Volunteers." When Connolly committed the Citizen Army to the Easter Rising, O'Casey believed he sacrificed socialism for an Irish nationalism that was unresponsive to Irish social issues.

O'Casey gave up active involvement in the labor movement when he left the Citizen Army; however, his interest in labor and in the welfare of the workingman was life-long and is reflected in much of his work. Although the theme of the three Dublin plays is Irish nationalism at various stages during the Irish War of Independence, the relationship between labor and nationalism is directly or indirectly central to all three plays.

The plough and the stars, the banner of the Irish Citizen Army, not only provided the title for the play of that name, but it fired O'Casey's imagination. Commenting in the *New York Times* in December, 1960, O'Casey said ". . . the events that swirled around the banner and that of the Irish Volunteers, the tricolor of green, white and orange—gave me all the humor, pathos and dialogue that fill the play." In characterization, Jack Clitheroe and The Covey represent one contrast between the ideal and the real. Clitheroe, a bricklayer, dies vaingloriously in the Easter Rising. O'Casey suggests he was betrayed by personal vanity. Early in the play a neighbor, Mrs. Gogan, and later his wife reveal that Clitheroe had left the Citizen Army when he was not made captain of his unit. He rejoins the Army for the Rising when he learns he has been appointed a Commandant by Connolly in a letter that his wife destroyed. Mrs. Gogan's recollection of Clitheroe's pride in his Sam Browne belt is a reference to O'Casey argument, made while Secretary of the Council of the Citizen Army, that the Army not adopt uniforms. He contended that guerilla warfare was the mode for the urban rebellion and he was skeptical that a Citizen Army uniform would be recognized by international law.

It is The Young Covey who expresses O'Casey's views about the relationship between labor and nationalism. When Clitheroe complains about Captain Brennan "swanking" as he carries the plough and the stars, The Covey snaps that the real disgrace is that a labor flag is used for politics. "It's a flag that should only be used when we're buildin' th' barricade to fight for a Workers' Republic." He repeats his claim that the goals of labor are different from the goals of nationalism in the Pub scene with Rosie Redmond. When Rosie says, "They're not going to get Rosie Redmond to fight for freedom that wouldn't be worth winnin' in a raffle," The Covey responds, "There's only one freedom for th' workin' man: conthrol o' th' means o' production, rates of exchange, an' th' means of disthribution."

In *Juno and the Paycock*, O'Casey's play set during the Irish Civil War, the heroine Juno Boyle puts it more simply. Her son Johnny who was wounded in Easter Week says, "I'd do it agen, Ma, I'd do it agen, for a principle's a principle." Juno replies, "Ah, you lost your best principle, me boy, when you lost your arm; them's the only sort o' principles that's any good to a workin' man."

Even *The Shadow of a Gunman* was influenced by O'Casey's Citizen Army experience. The play is partly based on O'Casey's experience when the Black and Tans raided his house in Mountjoy Square. In the play Seumas Shields and Donal Davoren are made uneasy by what they feel is an incriminating letter. The incident is probably based on the fact that when the Tans raided the Mountjoy house, O'Casey had in his possession the minutes of the Irish Citizen Army given to him by Delia Larkin, minutes that became the basis for *The Story of the Irish Citizen Army*.

In spite of the great success of the Dublin plays, the directors of the Abbey Theatre rejected O'Casey's next play, *The Silver Tassie*, a departure in theme (World War I) and in technique (experimental not realistic) from his earlier work. The rejection caused a break with the Abbey and further convinced him that his decision to move to England, as he did in 1926, was the right one.

O'Casey turned back to the 1913 strike in two later plays, *The Star Turns Red* (1940) and *Red Roses for Me* (1943). *The Star Turns Red*, dedicated "To the men and women who fought through the Great Dublin Lockout in 1913," was O'Casey's opportunity to rewrite history. Larkin was, of course, "Big Jim" and Brannigan was based on Barney Conway of Liberty Hall. The forces of socialism represented by Big Jim are set against the forces of fascism represented by the Catholic Church, the ally of employers in 1913. Even Tomas MacAnna's imaginative 1978 Abbey production of *The Star Turns Red* could not make it a good play; it is polemic not dramatic and its characterization—usually an O'Casey strength—is weak. His worship of Larkin dominates the play shifting its theme finally from the class struggle to a celebration of Red Jim, the controlling presence in the play.

The apocalyptic last act is O'Casey's Armageddon between the communists and the fascists, but the army refuses to fire on the workers and their cause is joined. At the curtain, the Star of Bethlehem becomes the workers' star and turns a fiery red, an appropriate symbol for O'Casey's Promethean Larkin. O'Casey held to the view he espoused in *The Star Turns Red*. Writing in a letter in 1960, he said about *The Star*, "No, my views have not changed. Indeed that play was prophetic, as one of four drama critics foresaw."

O'Casey's later strike play *Red Roses for Me* was not about the future or the 1913 strike as it might have been; it is set in the past and meant to dramatize not the reality of the strike but the idealism of the cause of labor. As *The Star Turns Red* focused on the ideal labor leader, so the character of Ayamonn Breydon, the hero of *Red Roses for Me*, is O'Casey's ideal worker. Breydon, like O'Casey, is a self-educated railroad laborer; like O'Casey he can be a bit selfish, but he shares O'Casey's vision for the workingman and he embodies O'Casey's belief about the transforming quality of sacrifice. When the Dublin railway workers strike for a shilling raise, Ayamonn joins them. When he dies in a police charge, the Inspector dismisses his death for a single shilling raise as unworthy. Sheila, Ayamonn's girl friend, who recognizes the significance of his death says, "Perhaps he saw the shilling as the shining emblem of a larger life."

The "larger life," in dramatic terms, has made O'Casey's later plays difficult to stage and contributed to the critical opinion that only the Dublin plays are worthwhile. Themes of the later plays frequently lend themselves to self-indulgence; dramatic tension is sacrificed for social comment, and the plays become pageants. For many, O'Casey's reputation will rest on the early plays and on the later six-volumes of autobiography that he wrote between 1939 and 1954.

Part autobiography, part fiction, part social comment and part criticism, the portraiture is to the autobiographies what characterization is to the best of O'Casey's plays. The power of the portrait of Larkin in "Prometheus Hibernica," a chapter in *Drums Under the Window*, the most turbulent volume in the autobiographies, is one of a number of cameos of historical and literary figures in the Dublin of his time.

As Larkin was O'Casey's Promethean hero kindling hope in the Dublin laborer with his fiery speeches, O'Casey's life and work created its own fire, a comet's burst of color, language and music illuminating a world of social idealism that in his eighty-four year celebration of life, he never stopped believing was possible.

Maureen Murphy is Professor of Irish Studies at Hofstra University.

196

The Irish Mind

RICHARD KEARNEY

Is there an Irish mind? In recent centuries the existence of such a mind was frequently contested. This contestation took the form of both a negative and an affirmative discrimination. The negative discrimination against the very existence of an Irish mind was vividly epitomized by the colonial portrayals of the Irish as brainless savages. Disraeli, the Prime Minister of England, wrote as follows in 1836:

> The Irish hate our order, our civilization, our enterprising industry, our pure religion. This wild, reckless, indolent, uncertain, and superstitious race have no sympathy with the English character. Their ideal of human felicity is an alternation of clannish broils and coarse idolatry. Their history describes an unbroken circle of bigotry and blood.

The British historian Charles Kingsley provided further justification for the colonial suppression of his neighbors when he composed this racist portrait of the Irish in 1860:

> I am daunted by the human chimpanzees I saw along that hundred miles of horrible country. I believe that there are not only many more of them than of old, but that they are happier, better and more comfortably fed and lodged under our rule than they ever were. But to see white chimpanzees is dreadful; if they were black, one would not feel it so much, but their skins, except where tanned by exposure, are as white as ours.

So much for negative discrimination.

The positive discrimination against the Irish mind was more subtle, more benevolent, and for those very reasons, more effective. This discrimination stemmed from the conviction, perhaps best summed up by Matthew Arnold and his Victorian peers, that the Irish were great fantasizers, great peddlers of myths, dreams and mysteries, but ultimately incompetent and irresponsible when it came to translating dream into decision, when it came to ordering or organizing their boundless fancies. Accordingly, Arnold could enthusiastically commend the "Celtic *soul*" with its readiness to revolt against the despotism of fact; but he never recognized the existence of the Celtic mind as such. And this quaintly Victorian version of Platonic dualism was unambiguously evidenced in Arnold's vigorous opposition to the Home Rule for Ireland Bill of 1886.

The Irish Revival, when it finally flowered in the early decades of this century, operated on a number of fronts—linguistic, political and literary—to counteract the colonial prejudice against, among other things, the Irish mind. The Revival's attempt to liberate the Irish from their incarcerating colonial self-image was pursued with the idea of reconquest, but reconquest—as Seamus Heaney has observed—not only of territory but more fundamentally of mind and imagination.

If it is true that there is an Irish mind, what *is* this mind? What are its essential and distinguishing characteristics?

The Irish mind does not reveal itself as a continuous or homogenous identity; it is at least twofold (to take the most obvious example, Gaelic and Anglo) and in fact, when one takes a closer look,

198

manifold. From the earliest times, the Irish mind refused to conform to the linear, centralizing logic of Graeco-Roman culture. This dominant and often domineering culture, based as it is on the Platonic logic of non-contradiction, operates on the assumption that order and organization result from the dualistic separation of opposite or contradictory terms. Hence the mainstream of Western thought rests upon a series of fundamental oppositions between being and non-being, reason and imagination, the soul and the body, the transcendently divine and the innocently temporal etc. . . . the list could go on.

The Irish intellectual tradition constitutes a counter-tradition to this mainstream of hegemonic rationalism—what Jacques Derrida has aptly termed "logocentrism." The Irish mind challenges such logocentrism by showing that truth is not one but many, that meaning is not a logic which centralizes but a logos which disseminates: a nomadic dispersal (or diaspora) forever desiring what is *other*, what is irreducibly diverse.

In contradistinction to the orthodox dualist logic of either/or, the Irish mind promotes a logos of both/and: an intellectual ability to hold the traditional oppositions of classical reason together in creative confluence. This does not mean, as the colonial prejudice presumed, that the Irish abandoned order for disorder, reneged on conceptual rigour to embrace formless chaos. The complex ideology of life and death articulated by the symbols of Irish mythology or the neolithic Newgrange, for example, does not bespeak primitivistic unrule. As the recent research of such anthropologists as Dumézil, Levi-Strauss and Eliade have enabled us to recognize, the symbolic struc-

199

tures to be found in Newgrange and Irish mythology testify to an alternative form of order and organization. We have here not formlessness but another kind of form, not meaninglessness but another kind of meaning, not confusion but another kind of coherence.

Similarly, one can argue that Joyce's *Finnegans Wake* is not a surrender to a capricious anarchy of sounds, but a challenge to the reader to discover another and possibly higher order of articulation. Joyce thereby endorsed Jung's belief that there exists an alternative logos of order (what he calls non-causal or synchronic orderedness) in those depth regions of the psyche suppressed by logocentric reason. Thus Joyce gaily subverted the established modes of linear or narrative thinking in order to sponsor a more profound mode of experience: a mode of experience which welcomes rather than revokes heterogenous meanings. Accordingly, to cite some obvious examples, Joyce could refer to Dublin as "lugly" communicating his ambiguous perception of his native city as both "lovely" and "ugly." In similar fashion, Yeats referred to his art as a "beauty born out of its own despair" or to the Easter Rising of 1916 as a "terrible beauty" and so on. The Irish painter, Louis Le Brocquy confirmed this aspect of the Irish mind when he declared recently that his art operates according to a "secret logic of ambivalence." And I quote:

It would appear that this ambivalent attitude . . . was especially linked to the prehistoric Celtic world, and there is further evidence that it persists to some extent in the Celtic mind today. . . . I myself have learned from the canvas that emergence and immergence—twin phenomena of time—are ambivalent; that one implies the other and that the matrix in which they exist dissolves the normal sense of time producing a characteristic stillness.

Le Brocquy concludes:

Is this the underlying ambivalence which we in Ireland tend to stress; the continued presence of the historic past, the indivisibility of birth and funeral, spanning the apparent chasm between past and present, between consciousness and fact . . . day consciousness/night consciousness, like (Joyce's) Ulysses and Finnegan . . . the old synecdochism of the Celt.

The Irish poet, Tom Kinsella, has described this essential ambivalence (or polyvalence) of the Irish mind as a *divided* or *double* vision. This double vision frequently expressed itself as a *comic* vision (for what is laughter but a response to the simultaneous juxtaposition of two or more opposing elements). And this comic vision extends from the ancient mythic sagas and medieval bards up to Swift, Shaw, Wilde, Joyce and Beckett.

A parallel can also be found in Irish philosophy. It is a curious if often neglected fact that our two greatest thinkers, John Scotus Eriugena in the ninth century and Berkeley in the eighteenth century, reacted against the mainstream logocentric philosophies of their time in an effort to embrace heterodox or marginal streams of thought. In Eriugena this decentralizing scruple was evinced in his spirited resistance to the prevailing orthodoxy of Aristotelian metaphysics. Eriugena turned instead to the peripheral Eastern spirituality of thinkers like Maximus the Confessor and the

201

Pseudo-Dionysius. For his pains he was branded as a heretic. Berkeley was equally iconoclastic in his refutation of the established mechanist philosophy of British empiricism (spawned by Hobbes, Locke and Hume who, as Yeats put it, "took away our universe and left us excrement instead"). Looking beyond the colonial curtain to the outlawed thought of the Continent, Berkeley bravely championed an Irish version of Cartesian Idealism. In short, both Irish philosophers found themselves as outsiders to the intellectual mainstream of their time and responded by espousing what they considered to be alien or alternative modes of thought.

This pattern of intellectual decentralization also expresses itself in a recurring pattern of intellectual dissemination. The Irish experience of residing on the margin of logocentric traditions is almost invariably accompanied by a dialectical movement of exodus towards the *other*. In the case of the Irish Saints and Scholars (including Eriugena who left Ireland to teach in France) this exodus took the form of a "navigatio" to foreign lands. In the case of many Irish emigrants and writers (notably Joyce and Beckett) this exodus took the form of voluntary or involuntary "exile."

Joyce's experience of exile, to take the most germane example in this centenary year, was not only geographical but also cultural and linguistic. Even though he wrote in English, Joyce was perpetually mindful of the fact that he was never quite at home in its vocabulary; he knew full well, and often exulted in the knowledge, that his writing was a Trojan horse in the city of the Anglo-Saxon tongue.

The ambivalent counterposition of the familiar and the foreign, which I have suggested is perhaps the most singular watermark of the Irish mind, is also witnessed in the work of one of Ireland's foremost contemporary poets, Seamus Heaney. A northern Irish poet now living in southern Ireland, at once in exile and at home, exposed to the double vision of colonizer and colonized, Catholic and Protestant, Celt and Anglo-Saxon, Gaelic resonances and English sentences, Seamus Heaney has eloquently embraced the rich ambivalence of the Irish mind. I would like to conclude by quoting a statement of Heaney's in the first issue of *The Crane Bag* journal:

I am convinced that one can be faithful to the nature of the English language and at the same time to one's own non-English origin. This is a proper aspiration for our poetry. In the Sweeney Story (which I translated from the Irish) we have a northern sacral king, Sweeney, who is driven out of his home in Country Antrim. There is a sort of schizophrenia in him. On the one hand he is always whinging for (home), but on the other he is celebrating his free creative imagination. Maybe here there was a fable which could cast a dream or myth across the swirl of private feelings in me. But one must not forget the other side of the poetic enterprize, which is precisely the arbitrariness and the innocence of the day to day poetic impulse. . . . This inner impulse has to be preserved, however essential the outward (mythic) structures may be for communication, community and universal significance. . . . Yeats and Kavanagh point up these contradictions: (Yeats) with his search for myths and sagas, the need for a structure and a sustaining landscape; (Kavanagh) with his need to be liberated and distanced from it, the need to be open, unpredictably susceptible, lyrically opportunistic. . . . You need both.

Richard Kearney is a Professor of Philosophy at University College, Dublin.

Section 2 — Historical

Landfall

TIMOTHY SEVERIN

During the night of June 25 we were able to distinguish faint pinpricks of shore lights to the
south of us; and when a dull grey morning broke,
our noses confirmed the sighting. Across the
water came the definite smell of pine trees wafted
by a gentle off-shore breeze from the great forests
of Newfoundland.

To our delight the numbers of whales actually
increased as we made our approach to journey's
end. It was as if the companions of our odyssey
were coming to see *Brendan* complete her mission,
for on that last morning we were accompanied by
large numbers of humpback whales from a great
whale colony which spends the summer in Sir
Charles Hamilton Sound on the Newfoundland
coast. We followed the surging movements of the
humpbacks on all sides of *Brendan*, surfacing and
blowing, diving with the unmistakable slow arch-
ing of their backs which gives them their name,
followed by the graceful skyward wave of the tail
before the animal slips below the surface. Then
we could trace the huge white patch beneath the
water as the whale swam over toward *Brendan*
and passed close beneath the hull to inspect it. In
the distance other whales were leaping clear out
of the water and toppling back with great
splashes, or sometimes thrusting their tails from
the water and repeatedly slapping down their
flukes on the sea with mighty bursts of spray as if
in farewell.

Gradually, we began to accept the fact that we were certain to make landfall. The coast drew closer. It was low and featureless, and protected by a string of small islands. The radio began to chatter with messages from Coast Guard radio stations. A helicopter loaded with photographers clattered out and circled around us, its pilot careful not to capsize *Brendan* with the downdraught from his rotor blades. Another, larger helicopter appeared from the airport at Gander. It too was loaded with cameras, wielded by servicemen from the airbase. Suddenly, from behind one of the islands a pair of small Coast Guard boats came skimming over the water toward us. "There's a small fishing port three miles or so up the coast called Musgrave Harbor," shouted one of the coxwains as he roared up. "We can tow you in there if you like."

"No. Thank you. First we want to land by ourselves," I called back, and checked the chart once again. Downwind of *Brendan* lay the small island chain of the Outer Wadham Group, uninhabited except for lighthouse-keepers. The islands were an ideal spot for a quiet landfall. The nearest was called Peckford Island. "There's nowhere to land on that island. It's all rocks on the beach," warned a voice from the Coast Guard boat as *Brendan* changed course. But it did not matter. There had been no port in Saint Brendan's day either, and I reckoned that if *Brendan* had come through the Labrador ice, she was tough enough to stand a final landing on a rocky beach.

"Trondur, stand by to drop over an anchor. Boots, pull out an oar and get ready. We're going to make our touchdown."

George went forward to lower and stow *Bren-*

dan's little foresail for the last time. Under mainsail alone, she crept toward the rock-ribbed shore. The swell heaved and sucked on ledges of bare, grey rock. Boulders dotted the shore, and grass and scrub covered the inner dunes. "Let go the anchor!" There was a splash as Trondur dropped the anchor overboard, paid out line, and gave a great tug to make sure that it had set firmly. We might need the anchor to pull *Brendan* off the rocks once a man had been put ashore.

"George, can you take a line onto land?" He looked doubtfully at the slippery rock ledges and the foam of the undertow. "Yes, if I don't break a leg," he muttered. "There's no point in getting wet at this stage." Pulling on his immersion suit, he climbed out on the bow with his legs dangling on each side.

Brendan eased forward. Not with style or speed, but in the same matter-of-fact manner that she had crossed three and a half thousand miles of sea. The red ring cross on her mainsail began to sag as I eased the halliard a few feet to slow the boat even more. Trondur took up the slack on the anchor rope and handed it gently over the gunwale. Arthur made a couple of dips at the water with his blade to keep the boat straight. *Brendan* nosed quietly onto the rocks. George leaped. His feet splashed, and touched ground . . . and I thought, "We've made it!"

* * *

Brendan touched the New World at 8:00 P.M. on June 26 on the shore of Peckford Island in the Outer Wadham Group some 150 miles northwest of St. Johns, Newfoundland. She had been at sea for fifty days. The exact spot of her landfall has no particular significance to the story of the early Irish voyages into the Atlantic. It was merely the place where the wind and current had brought a twentieth-century replica of the original Irish skin vessels. Earlier navigators could have made their landfalls almost anywhere along the coast of hundreds of miles in either direction. What mattered was that *Brendan* had demonstrated without a shadow of a doubt that the voyage could be done.

A leather boat that some had feared would disintegrate in the first gale off the Irish coast had successfully crossed the Atlantic.

When *Brendan* nuzzled her bow onto Peckford Island, she may have looked more like a floating bird's nest than an ocean-going vessel, an untidy muddle of ropes and flax, leather and wood. But she was strong and sound; and the four of us who sailed her knew that she was still seaworthy to our highest expectations. She had brought us safely through gales and pack ice and through two seasons across some of the most unforgiving waters in the Atlantic. We had put our trust in her, and she had repaid that confidence. She was a true ocean-going vessel, and there was no longer any practical objection to the idea that Irish monks might have sailed their leather boats to North America before the Norsemen, and long before Columbus.

Brendan had demonstrated that the voyage *could* be done with medieval material and medieval technology. But in the final analysis the only conclusive proof that it *had* been done will be if an authentic relic from an early Irish visit is found one day on North American soil. Perhaps it will be a rock scratched with an early Irish inscription, or the foundation of an Irish beehive hut that can be dated accurately to the days of the extraordinary Irish voyages. Admittedly the chances of such a discovery are slim. Irish relics have not yet been found in Iceland, where it is known the Irish did touch; on North America, they would have left only the lightest fingerprint. It would be singularly fortunate if such a faint trace is located on a very long coastline which is either desolate and little known, or in well-favored areas covered over by more recent development.

This being so, it was all the more vital that *Brendan*'s successful voyage should have rescued the early Irish seafaring achievement from the category of speculation and doubt, and returned it to its proper arena of serious historical debate. At best, land archaeologists should now be encouraged to search for Irish traces in the New World, and at very least, it is difficult any longer to bury the early Christian Irish sailors into a footnote in the history books of exploration on the excuse that too little is known about them and their claims are physically impossible.

What sort of men, then, were these monks who deliberately launched out into the Atlantic in small open boats? Many must never have returned, but perished at sea. Aboard *Brendan* we had the advantages of being in touch with the outside world by radio, and we knew that if they could reach us fast enough, the Coast Guard or the deep-sea fishermen of the North Atlantic would have tried to rescue us in an emergency. But the Irish monks and their curraghs had none of these advantages. A dozen or more men would have been packed into a boat the size of *Brendan* and would have endured far greater discomfort. They would have been colder, wetter, and—in one sense—more isolated than we were aboard *Brendan*. Such men must have been special people, even by the exacting standards of their own day. They were directed by a sense of dedication which had to have been the single most important factor in their success. Out of this dedication came much of their suitability as open-boat sailors on long northern voyages. As monks they were inured to hardship. Life in a medieval monastery with its meager food, seasonal shortages, stone cells, abstinence, long hours of tedium, obedience, self-mortification and discipline, was an ideal training for a long journey in an open boat. Equally, their mental preparation must have matched their physical readiness. The outlook of their leaders, if not of the rank and file, was a bold combination of intellectual curiosity and a fearless trust in God. This trust encouraged them to launch their voyages and, once at sea, to sustain their efforts through adversity. The journey itself was regarded as important in its proper execution as reaching a landfall. To venture out in a boat was by its very nature an act of faith in a God Whose divine providence would show them wondrous sights and, if He so wished, bring them safely to journey's end. Should adverse winds or currents beat them back, that too was His will. If their craft foundered underneath them and the crew perished, then they reached their divine reward doubly blessed because they had died in God's service.

God's service on these voyages did not have its modern sense of an overseas mission to go to convert heathen lands. On the contrary, the terri-

tories that the Irish monks sought were the unknown and uninhabited lands beyond the
horizon, the special places, the wondrous lands to
be revealed by God. In the apt phrase of the time,
they were the Promised Lands. To reach these farthest territories was a heavenly gift; to be able to
live in them, isolated from the evils of the world,
was an even greater prize. There can seldom have
been a stronger drive to probe the unknown in
the entire story of human exploration. It was the
quintessential motive for exploration at almost
any price, and there is no reason why it should
not have brought them across the Atlantic.

Timothy Severin is the author of The Brendan
Voyage.

More Than Barren Sympathy: Daniel Mannix on Ireland

WILLIAM HANLON

The Prime Minister notified the Admiralty and the signal was flashed to the British fleet. Destroyers changed course and steamed towards the Irish coast with orders to patrol in battle formation. Search and destroy missions were nothing new to these men, seasoned veterans of a conflict that had sent too many of their mates to an early grave. But these orders were different and must have seemed queer to sailors who, one presumes, were denied the luxury of daily newspapers.

It was 1920. The war, of course, was over. The world had been made safe for democracy. The object of these naval maneuvers was not a German warship but a British ocean liner and, in particular, one of her passengers. They were looking for the *S.S. Baltic* of the White Star line—and for Daniel Mannix: Archbishop of Melbourne, Australia; former president of Maynooth College; native son of Charleville (Ráth Luirc), County Cork. Mannix was on his way to Rome for the mandatory *ad limina* visit during which he would give an accounting of his stewardship to the Pope. His itinerary had taken him through the United States. He had sailed from New York and intended to visit his aging mother in Charleville before going on to Italy. Why, then, all the fuss?

It's a long story. Literally. Daniel Mannix was born in 1864 and died just months short of his 100th birthday, in November, 1963. Although the deadly acid of assassination has etched that month deeply and painfully into the memories of most Americans, few, at least of my generation, can recall the passing of the venerable prelate from Australia. And yet, during a life that was filled with controversy, his largest and most ardent audiences were probably those in New York City where he championed the cause of Irish independence and the principle of self-determination enunciated by an American president, Woodrow Wilson. In fact, for several months in 1920, he was a frontpage item in American newspapers and magazines.

There is not much remarkable about his early life except that he was an exceptionally bright boy who was growing up during very turbulent years in Ireland. His father was a farmer, a no-nonsense man who managed to keep his family's life stable. That was no easy task for an Irishman in those days and young Daniel surely saw less fortunate families fall victim to avaricious landlords, rack-renting, and eviction. He attended the Christian Brothers school in Charleville, then went to St. Colman's junior seminary at Fermoy and from there to Maynooth.

During this time Parnell was at the peak of his career. Michael Davitt had founded the Land League which promised to improve the lot of Irishmen through such tactics as non-cooperation and boycott. But with crop failures increasing and the memory of the famine still fresh in the minds

215

of the poor, more violent tactics became common. The British responded typically. An Act of Parliament suppressed the Land League and suspended legal rights in Ireland so that soon the jails were crammed. Among the prisoners were Irish members of Parliament, including Parnell.

In time, Gladstone realized the futility of wholesale imprisonment and negotiated a settlement with Parnell. Gladstone would agree to release Parnell and other Irish leaders if they would return home and convince their followers to desist from acts of violence. In return, he promised land relief legislation. The promise of this "new departure" was shattered when, in 1882, Lord Cavendish, Chief Secretary of Ireland and the Under Secretary, T. H. Burke, two newly appointed officials more sympathetic to Irish grievances than their predecessors had been, were stabbed to death in Phoenix Park. In retaliation Parliament imposed on Ireland the most stringent laws since the Penal days. Niall Brennen, a biographer of Mannix, describes what happened:

> "Unlawful assemblies" were forbidden. A curious crime called "intimidation," designed to cover the protest of the Catholic Irish, was put on the statute books. Trial by jury was abolished in many places. Curfews were imposed on all Catholics; newspapers could be suppressed at will; suspects could again be imprisoned. In cases where juries were retained, Catholics were excluded from jury service, and when the editor of the Dublin *Freeman's Journal* called attention to this fact, he was convicted of contempt, imprisoned for four months, and fined £500.

Mannix left no record of his thoughts during these days. But we should remember that he was a teenager when all this was happening. Even for a seminarian, that is a time of life when there is no more cardinal sin than injustice, when compromise is seen as the equivalent of treason, when even benign authority is viewed with suspicion.

Without question, these were decisive years for young Mannix. Surely, the character was being formed which would make him a hero to his people and a pest of unspeakable annoyance to his enemies. But it would be some time before this man of scholarly disposition and rigidly ascetic habits emerged in that role.

He was a brilliant student at Maynooth. Ordained in 1890, he was appointed a year later to the Junior Chair of Philosophy and three years after that became Professor of Theology. His reputation as one of the great academics of Ireland grew and he became President of Maynooth in 1903. Under his leadership, the College became part of the National University of Ireland in 1909.

In 1912 his name appeared on a list. He was among the nominees, submitted by the Australian bishops to the Pope, for the post of Coadjutor Archbishop of Melbourne. His appointment was confirmed. Having spent some 35 years in seminaries—as student, teacher, and administrator—he was now to pass the rest of his life, more than half a century, down under.

The political climate in Ireland at this time was uncertain. Some form of Home Rule seemed inevitable. For a man from Maynooth, traditionally conservative in politics, this solution to the "Irish question" may have seemed reasonable. But just about the time that Mannix was sailing for Australia a group of Protestants led by Sir Edward Carson gathered in Belfast and put their names to a document called the Ulster Covenant. The intent of the document was bold—and treasonous. It said that Home Rule would not be tolerated in Ulster and the signatories were confident enough in the strength of their ties to Britain to defy Parliament without fear of reprisal. But still no comment from Mannix.

He left Ireland and arrived to a warm-hearted reception in Melbourne. Most of the Catholics there had come from Ireland, either as "convicts" or refugees. Few at that time had acquired wealth, most were poor laborers. But Australia was not Ireland. It was a young country far distant from Ireland and England, pluralistic, more tolerant, with greater opportunities for all. The culture shock was too much for Mannix and his first year there was a disaster.

Mistaking a small group of bigots for the traditional persecutors of the church in Ireland, he railed out at the entire Protestant community and thereby alienated many who had welcomed him openly and had hoped that his talents would be used to benefit all Australians. "He saw," says his biographer, "only the church and its enemies. And it seems that he could not comprehend the notion of a sincere Protestant."

Mannix was now almost fifty years old. The post of Coadjutor carried with it the right of succession. Had the rest of his career followed the pattern established in this first year at Melbourne, there would have been little in it to interest anybody except, perhaps, ecclesiastical scholars or students of Australian politics.

But while he made no public statements about Ireland, events there did not escape his notice. The fire lit during his teens had smouldered these many years and was about to burst into a white hot heat of superb rhetoric and impeccable logic.

England was now at war. In Ireland there were those who calculated that there was no better time to win independence from British rule. There is no need to recount here the series of plans gone awry that thwarted the Easter Rebellion in 1916.

Mannix made a cautious statement on the failed rebellion saying that he was "grieved at the loss of life," in Ireland. But he did not leave the matter there. "I am," he said, "quite clear in my mind that the British Government, by its failure to deal with the treason of the Carsonites, by its shifty policy in regard to Home Rule, had unwittingly led up to the result that all must deplore."

The rebellion had been small, disorganized, and far from enjoying universal popular support. It was easily crushed and would have been soon forgotten had not the British done an incredibly stupid thing. They sent Brigadier-General Sir John Maxwell to Ireland with powers to deal with the situation as he saw fit. His actions guaranteed that no one would ever forget Easter 1916. Despite pleas from all over the world for clemency for the rebels, Maxwell began executing the leaders of the rebellion beginning with Padraic Pearse, founder of St. Enda's School. Mannix, as former president of Maynooth, must have been familiar with Pearse and his work in Gaelic studies. One incident is illustrative of his feelings at this time:

> There was an old Irishman who used to work at the West Melbourne presbytery where Dr. Mannix lived, and one evening after the rising, Daniel Mannix went into the old man's room. He threw the evening paper on to the old man's bed. "Michael," he said, with tears in his eyes, "they've shot some of them."

219

Mannix was fifty-two years old. His public statements from now on would make him the most controversial prelate of his day.

First came the issue of military conscription in Australia. Mannix had become more and more closely identified with the Labor Party which drew much of its support from Irish Catholic workers whose experience had made them wary of militarism. On the other side was William Morris Hughes, Prime Minister of Australia since 1915 and leader of the right wing of the Labor Party which supported the war and military conscription. Hughes went all about the country on a speaking tour to stir up support for conscription. Mannix, true to what had become his favored approach, would let remarks slip out at groundbreakings, dedications, and ribbon-cuttings. At one such affair he said that he had been told that the war was being waged to protect small nations. If that were the case, he said, they could start with Ireland. "I will not favor the sending of troops overseas as long as the causes and purpose of the war are suspect." Amid charges that Mannix was "disloyal to the empire," pro-German, and a security risk, the issue of conscription for overseas military service was put to a referendum. In October 1916, conscription was narrowly defeated and Mannix had won his first political contest. The following year, on the death of Archibishop Carr, Mannix became full Archbishop of Melbourne.

By now he had become "good press." He issued no formal political statements, but reporters listened to his sermons and followed him as he went about his routine episcopal duties throughout the Archdiocese, waiting for him to inject

220

some "treasonable" remark into one of his speeches. They were not disappointed.

Consider some examples:

Trade is an important matter to a nation and everything should be done to foster it. We have heard a great deal about the cause of the war and the rights of smaller nations, but as a matter of fact it is simply an ordinary trade war. Those who are now our enemies, before the war had been capturing our trade. I say deliberately that in spite of all the things we say about the war, it is an ordinary trade war.

Or:

Murder is murder whether it is committed in Belgium or in Dublin and you cannot blot out the bloody stain simply by covering it with the Union Jack.

Or:

I am proud of being an Irishman and every night I thank God that I am not an Englishman, a Welshman, or a German.

Prime Minister Hughes, it should be noted, had been born in Wales. The rift between the two men widened. In 1918, the issue of conscription was again put before Australian voters and again failed. Mannix commented on the outcome:

I have no antipathy at all for the British Empire, or for any other Empire. . . . Some people are fond of calling England the mother land. It is not my mother land . . . indeed England is my stepsister.

Calls to intern Mannix or to deport him increased. The speaker of the Legislative Assembly, Sir Frank Madden, called him "an enemy to the country" and suggested that the Federal Government send him back to Ireland "where he could do no harm."

221

Such suggestions were by now futile. Mannix had incurred the wrath of many powerful people through his utter refusal to court the favor of the ascendency group in Australia but in doing so had won broad popular support among the large Irish Catholic working class. He was untouchable.

In 1920, Mannix made plans for his *ad limina* visit to Rome. Lloyd George was the British Prime Minister. Woodrow Wilson was in the White House. Ireland was under martial law with the Black and Tans menancing the people. Late in 1918, parliamentary elections had been held in England and Ireland. Of the 105 Irish seats, 73 had gone to Sinn Feiners, most of whom at the time were in prison, all of whom had pledged, if elected, not to sit at Westminster. In 1919, the Sinn Feiners assembled secretly in Dublin, to open the first Irish Parliament. Reaffirming the republic proclaimed in 1916, they chose as its first president a former professor of mathematics at Maynooth and a participant in the Easter Rebellion, Eamon DeValera. Just about the time Mannix was sailing for the United States, DeValera was being smuggled out of Ireland. He, too, was headed for the United States—to raise funds for the cause of Irish independence.

As Mannix prepared to leave Melbourne, charges against him of disloyalty and sedition were still common. Some feared that the St. Patrick's Day parade in March, 1920, with the Archbishop at its head, would be a boisterous, emotional display of anti-British feeling. Once again Mannix confounded his critics. He indeed led the procession. But surrounding his car was a mounted honor guard of fourteen men—all Catholics and all wearing the Victoria Crosses they had won in the war for valor in defense of the Crown.

The Archbishop's tour of America was triumphal. Landing in San Francisco, he traveled across the country, enthusiastically received everywhere but nowhere more warmly than in New York City. He was granted the freedom of the City of New York by Mayor Hylan in accordance with a resolution adopted by the Board of Aldermen. In speech after speech he hammered away unrelentingly at the British, always justifying his argument with references to Woodrow Wilson's Fourteen Points.

He was generally careful to praise Wilson but at one point seems to have come very close to publicly scolding even him. "I have no welcome from the President of the United States," he said, "but I have got a welcome from those who made him President."

Indeed he had. At the rally to welcome him on July 18, Madison Square Garden was jammed. On the platform with Mannix were Archbishop Hayes of New York and Eamon DeValera. Everything Mannix said at this rally and at other appearances was quoted in the press—usually on page one. A few quotes, gathered from the pages of the *New York Times*, the *Gaelic American*, and the Jesuit journal, *America*, will give the reader some feel for Mannix's style:

At the Madison Square Garden rally:

> We are here because we are not hypocrites who say one thing and mean another. We are here because you and I believe in the principles so nobly enunciated by the President of the United States, because we sincerely hold those principles, and are consistent. We have no favorites among the tyrants of the world and,

223

as a consequence, we want to apply President Wilson's principles to England and Ireland as well as to Germany and Belgium.

Or arguing against the British contention that the strategic defense of England would be endangered by granting Ireland independence:

They say that Ireland could be free, if it were only a thousand miles away. That is what is called the strategic reason. The meaning of it is that Ireland is so near that they require it in order to protect their own coasts, and that because they require it, they are going to hold it, whether they have a right to it or not. I can understand that argument; it is a splendid British argument. In fact, it is a good downright British argument, and the only argument they have. But what does it come to? It comes to the naked fact that might is right when the might is in British bayonets, and the right is in Ireland, or in Ireland's cause. Then might is right, and as long as they are able, they will hold Ireland, even though they have no right whatever to it.

But if the proximity to England gives them the right to hold Ireland, there is as much right, in fact, a greater right, to hold France, because France is nearer to them than Ireland. If they were able to hold France, they would be glad to do so. As a matter of fact, they did take France and they did hold France as long as they could, and they gave it up only when they could no longer hold it. They took Ireland also, and they held it, and they will hold it as long as they are able. But they will give it up only when they cannot hold it, and that will be very soon.

What followed in July, 1920, indicated that Mannix's barbs had hit their intended targets. First his archrival in Australia, William Morris Hughes, announced that he would appoint a High Commissioner in America "to speak author-

224

itatively when a man like Mannix is responsible for utterances repugnant to Australians." "Australia repudiates him," Hughes said.

Mannix responded almost, it seems, with glee. Recalling the two conscription votes and noting Hughes' desertion of the Labor Party, Mannix called him a "renegade, a Britisher and an imperialist of the worst type."

> Premier Hughes seems to think that I have stated in this country that Australia desires to separate from the British Empire. I have made no such statement, but if Australia ever comes to feel that separation from the Empire can best serve her interests, the opinion of Mr. Hughes will count for very little.

> He has said that the people of Australia repudiate me. There is nothing new in that. He said the same on two former occasions and when he went before the people on the issues on which I opposed him, although he had in some manner secured all of the newspapers and all other capitalistic agencies, he found that he was mistaken. When the votes were counted it was the Prime Minister of Australia and not the Archbishop of Melbourne whom they had repudiated. But I will deal with Hughes when I return to Australia.

But first he would have to deal with a more formidable opponent, Lloyd George. The Premier announced in Commons that Mannix would not be allowed to land in the British Isles because of his utterances in the United States. There was some initial confusion in the reporting of the order and it was later amended. Mannix would be allowed to visit England but not Ireland. He had already booked passage on the *Baltic* and had no intention of changing his plans:

> I shall sail on Saturday at noon. And I shall sail with regret that the British Government, which is so un-

willing that I land, had not the courage to begin the battle here in New York. But they have already retreated to the Old World, and nobody can foretell what will happen there. They seem to have some difficulty in deciding what they will do with me. But I know what I am going to do, and that is the difference between me and Lloyd George.

My speeches in America, so we are informed by the press, have been reported verbatim over the cables to the British Government. Mr. George thinks that they are "most mischievous utterances," and therefore that I must not land in Ireland lest I speak there also the same unvarnished truths.

I have spoken of things that I know to be true. I have done the things I believe to be right and I am unafraid of the consequences. I am represented in certain quarters as a promoter of strife. In fact I am working for peace in Ireland, in the British Empire and outside that Empire.

I go further and say that if the Irish people are rightly struggling to be free, they have a claim to look to me for something more than tolerant and barren sympathy, for, like them, I am an Irishman, bone of their bone and flesh of their flesh.

A dispute between two unions of the *Baltic's* crew threatened to delay the Archbishop's departure. Some members of the Cooks' and Stewards' Union believed that he should not be permitted to sail on a British vessel. But those in the Seamen's and Firemen's Union, predominantly Irish by birth or descent, felt that the Archbishop should cross the Atlantic as an honored guest of the ship. The *Times* reported that some of the firemen had sworn "that if the Archbishop came to the pier and any of the other unionists attempted to bar him from the ship, they would send a delegation composed of the huskiest men in the engine room and carry him on board on their shoulders." Might makes right can work both ways.

The dispute was resolved and Mannix sailed, as planned, on July 31, 1920. A huge crowd gathered at the pier to see him off. Mannix had to help police calm the crowd when a melee broke out. Somebody—whom the *Gaelic American* delicately labelled "an unmannerly Englishman who showed his bad breeding by hissing the Archbishop"—had started a wild fistfight but it was soon quelled and the *Baltic* sailed out of New York harbor bound for Liverpool with a stop at Queenstown, Ireland, en route.

Several weeks before his departure from New York, Mannix had written to a friend, the Bishop of Cloyne in Cork, expressing his intention to land at Queenstown and adding "I wish, for many excellent reasons, that my arrival should not be heralded in any way. I therefore count on your cooperation in enabling me to reach Charleville in peace."

He must have known that this was a wish now impossible to grant. Newspapers on both sides of the Atlantic were following closely the battle of wills that had developed between him and Lloyd George. While Mannix was enjoying a calm voyage at sea, predictions on where he would be landed multiplied daily.

It was first reported that the *Baltic* would be diverted from Queenstown and taken under destroyer escort to Liverpool. Then dispatches came from Fishguard, Wales, stating that preparations were being made for the arrival of a "mystery passenger." The harbor master at Fishguard had received instructions from London to keep in touch with the Admiralty and to hold a harbor launch in readiness to proceed to sea. One report even suggested that Mannix would be taken to Cherbourg, France.

In the meantime, a spokesman for the Sinn Fein announced that his men stood ready to run any British blockade and take Mannix to Ireland soon after he landed in England. But he went on to predict that "the Archbishop will show his contempt for England by refusing to get off the ship and will return to New York without setting foot on English soil."

By August 8th, Queenstown had still received no wireless messages from the *Baltic* about her position or time of arrival. Few now believed that the ship would call at the Irish port. But, if Mannix could not land in Ireland, he would be greeted, nonetheless. Plans were laid to light bonfires all along the coast of Cork as the *Baltic* sailed into St. George's Channel. These plans were reportedly dampened by a pervasive Irish rain and none of the predictions about where he would land came to pass.

What did happen surpassed, in melodrama, absurdity, and extremity, any scenario that could have been imagined.

As the *Baltic* sailed into the Irish Sea, a convoy of British destroyers closed on her. Two destroyers followed the ocean liner until darkness fell, then signalled her to stop and prepare to receive a boarding party. Two naval officers and two Scotland Yard detectives went aboard the *Baltic* carrying official documents to present to Mannix: a prohibition by the British Commander-in-Chief in Ireland, Sir Neville Macready, against his landing in Ireland; and a prohibition by the Chief of the Imperial General Staff, Sir Henry Wilson,

228

against his visiting Liverpool, Manchester and Glasgow.

When Mannix refused to leave the *Baltic* willingly, one of the military officers placed him under formal arrest by laying a hand upon his shoulder. The arrest, it was later disclosed, had been made under provisions of the Defense of the Realm Act, a wartime security measure still officially on the statute books.

Mannix was taken by launch to the destroyer, *Wivern;* the *Baltic* proceeded on to Liverpool. The *Wivern* made for Penzance. Penzance! Not some port on the Welsh coast with a consonant-jammed, unpronounceable name, but Penzance— a name forever associated in the English-speaking world with pirates.

The following day Mannix made a statement:

> I think the government is making it worse for themselves than for me. They are putting me to a little inconvenience, but they are making themselves very silly. I think the people of Ireland know their business as well as the people over here. I was not going there to tell the people my views at all, because they have made up their own minds without any reference to me.

There are many who agreed with this evaluation even if they did not full-heartedly support Mannix. G. K. Chesterton asked, "what harm is the man going to do in Ireland? Denounce the British Government to a million Irishmen? Why those million Irishmen are spending all their time denouncing the British Government to the rest of the world." And reflecting on the American dimension, he added: "It will take time to make America believe that England is not a tyrant, but

229

it can be done, though history has nasty things against England and history is strengthened by the tyrannical treatment of Archbishop Mannix."

Within a week of Mannix's arrest, there were mass protest meetings in New York, Philadelphia, Montreal, Melbourne, and London. A more unusual protest soon followed, which showed Mannix had struck a chord that found resonance in even the most conservative of Irish hearts. All the Catholic bishops of Ireland signed a statement which read, in part: "we assure him that the efforts of the British Government to heap, so undeservedly, indignities upon him will only increase our respect and esteem for his exalted character as a great Archbishop and champion of Irish freedom based on justice."

But the government did not relent. Although Mannix was free to speak whenever he could find an audience, he was kept under surveillance and prohibited from visiting Ireland or those cities with large Irish populations—Liverpool, Manchester and Glasgow. He stayed in London but traveled frequently, speaking against the government's Irish policy and against the brutality of the Blacks and Tans.

Finally, in March 1921, he traveled to Rome and had his visit with Benedict XV. He was not censured as some had predicted he would be. In fact, the meeting was quite cordial. In April he returned to London and sailed in May for Australia to resume his daily duties as Archbishop of Melbourne.

Later that month, the North of Ireland was partitioned and within a year Ireland was engaged in a bitter civil war.

Mannix was allowed to visit Ireland in 1925 but

his mother had died the previous year. Over the ensuing years, Ireland was never far from his thoughts. Nor did Ireland forget him. In 1939, when the Cathedral at Melbourne was completed with the addition of spires, the cross on top was a gift from the DeValera government.

Mannix died at Melbourne in his 99th year. There are, certainly, some prerogatives and joys that come with advanced age. There must also be sadness in watching new generations endure suffering and pain from evils that one had sought long ago to eradicate. This thought came to me recently as I read the headlines in the newspapers:

BELFAST DEAD 17—RIOTS IN THREE TOWNS

DARKEST TIME IN 60 YEARS

OUTBREAKS DISTURB MANY IRISH TOWNS

PRISONER BEGINS HUNGER STRIKE

These headlines were the more poignant because they were not recent. I was looking for information on Daniel Mannix and was seeing them on the screen of a microfilm viewer in a library and the datelines read 1920.

It was unsettling that the news from Ireland sixty years ago was so similar to today's. Unsettling, like the sense of déjà vu. But it was different. For that phenomenon is nothing more, they say, than a sensory disorder which creates an illusion to trick us. We think some event is happening exactly as it happened before when, in fact, it is being experienced for the first time. It is certainly one of the tragedies of modern Irish history that this sense of unnerving repetition is no illusion at all but an undeniable, verfiable fact.

Few knew this as Daniel Mannix did. As boy and man, he saw his people subjected to injustices of the basest sort. He was, to be sure, no diplomat. Nevertheless, he had a personal magnetism and a quiet, though stinging, oratorical style and he used these strengths to call attention to the suffering imposed upon his people. For this he was roundly criticized.

I imagine him as a very old man wondering to himself whether he should have remained silent and whether his utterances had accomplished anything at all. I hope his answers to himself were No on the first count, Yes on the second.

Bill Hanlon writes from Castleton-on-Hudson, New York.

232

John Devoy: Recollection of an Irish Rebel

PETER A. QUINN

I first met John Devoy in an old photograph, the third from the left, two down from my grandfather, the steamfitter with the crooked bow-tie. May, 1904, it reads on the back. A Clan-Na-Gael dinner held somewhere in Brooklyn with rows of serious looking Irishmen, all appearing ill at ease in gentlemen's evening wear. Amid the postured solemnity of these would-be revolutionaries, Devoy alone glowers back at you, still looking as if he were ready to pounce, to take hold of your lapels, and force you to see his side of the argument.

Devoy was like a character out of Celtic mythology, a modern day Conchobhar, fearless, implacable, forever engaged in controversy. His long career as an Irish revolutionary began in the 1860's when he joined the Fenians in their abortive conspiracy to overthrow British rule in Ireland, and lasted through the Anglo-Irish War of 1919–1922, a struggle he helped start and finance. The British Intelligence Service, encountering his name in the aftermath of the Easter Rebellion, was incredulous that it was dealing with the same man their files showed had been arrested as a revolutionary in 1866. "All departed," wrote P. S. Hagerty, "Devoy remained."

He was born on a small Kildare farm in 1842, a

child of the famine generation, and was raised in Dublin after his family joined the exodus from the countryside. He grew up at a crucial time in Irish history. O'Connell, the Repeal Movement, the Young Irelanders—the whole agitation of the 1840's—was a fast fading memory; the mass of landless laborers and marginal farmers had been swept away by the famine; Gaelic Ireland survived only in remote areas. Her Majesty's Government hoped somewhat optimistically that Ireland, with a radically reduced population, increasingly anglified in language and culture, was ready at last to assume a quiet place in the United Kingdom.

From his earliest days, Devoy was determined not to let that happen. He began his career as an Irish revolutionary in 1852 when, at the age of ten, he was expelled from school for fighting with a teacher who had struck him for refusing to sing "God Save the Queen." Nine years later, already a committed Fenian, he left to join the French Foreign Legion to gain the military experience he thought he would need as a revolutionary.

He returned in 1862 and began work as an organizer for the rapidly growing Fenian movement. The Fenians were the brain-child of James Stephens, a veteran of 1848, who had returned to Ireland after exile in France, and decided the country was ready for a true revolutionary movement based on the model of the continental radicals: a secret network of self-contained cells each responsible to a "centre" who, in turn, reported to a "Head Centre."

Stephens' organization, formed in conjunction with Irish revolutionaries in New York, signalled the arrival of Irish-Americans and their financial

234

resources as a potent force in Irish politics. Fueled by American money and the bitter memories of the famine years, especially among the emigrants in America, the Fenians threatened to bring about an insurrection that would prove bloody and costly to British rule in Ireland. The American Civil War provided Stephens with an invaluable pool of Irish veterans and it offered the further hope that the U.S.A. would go to war with Britain or, at least, maintain a policy of non-interference toward Fenian conspiracies.

In 1865 Devoy was appointed by Stephens as "Chief Organizer of the British Troops in Ireland," a position that made him responsible for subverting the loyalty of Irish troops serving in the regiments stationed in Ireland. Although still in his early twenties, Devoy did a remarkable job, making himself the master of a reliable system of spies and collaborators, both in and out of uniform, and effecting the rescue of Stephens, the Fenian Chief himself, from Richmond Prison.

As Devoy put it, this was to be "the one proud day of the Fenian movement." Stephens proved to be less than the decisive leader he made himself out to be; he frittered away crucial time trying to decide on a suitable course of action while a thoroughly alarmed Dublin Castle moved swiftly through informers and a Coercion Act to break up the Fenian organization. A split in the American organization merely added the finishing touches to an already desperate situation.

Devoy was spared involvement in the final debacle of March, 1867, when the remnants of the Fenians made a feeble attempt at national revolution. Betrayed to the authorities the year before, he was kept in Mountjoy Prison until a military tribunal condemned him to twenty years hard labor. He was then sent to serve out his sentence in a London jail where Irish prisoners could not count on the favors of Irish jailers.

Prison conditions in Victorian jails were designed for punishment rather than rehabilitation and the convicted Fenians, denied status as political prisoners, were set to the hard labor, long hours and meager rations that were the rule for dangerous felons. After four years, Devoy was pardoned along with other Fenians on condition of not returning to the British Isles "during the balance of their existence." In January, 1871, he arrived in New York with his fellow exiles to a tumultuous welcome from the city's Irish community.

Once in America he took up the struggle that had been interrupted by his imprisonment; New York was only another base of operations for directing the campaign for an Irish republic. Devoy would never understand those among the Irish in America who were primarily interested in assimilation, in using their political power to advance themselves instead of the Irish cause. For the balance of his existence—longer than Mr. Gladstone's government could have possibly imagined—he worked out of New York to create a movement that put the growing strength of the American Irish behind the separatists at home.

Devoy had little formal education, but he was a quick-witted, sharp tongued Irishman who could write as forcefully as he spoke. Apparently, James Gordon Bennett, editor of the *New York Herald*, recognized a natural born newspaperman when he saw one, and gave him a job as a reporter on his paper. Devoy thrived on printers' ink, spending the rest of his life as a reporter, an editor and a publisher.

By 1878 he headed the foreign desk at the *Herald* and was the director of the Clan-Na-Gael, the reorganized American branch of the Fenians. In Ireland Parnell had begun to make the Home Rule Party a major political force and Devoy saw in him the kind of personality able to unite the disparate elements within Irish nationalism.

Although the head of a revolutionary organization, Devoy refused to confine his activities to planning for some far-off military confrontation with Great Britain or directing a campaign of assassination and dynamite that did nothing to create the broad national coalition required by a party seeking support from a significant part of the Irish people. "We must come out of the rat-holes of conspiracy," was his advice to the revolutionary party on both sides of the Atlantic.

In the summer of that year he was introduced to a recently pardoned Fenian, Michael Davitt, who had just arrived in New York. The two of them developed the idea of proposing a policy of cooperation among the constitutional home-rulers behind Parnell, the Clan-Na-Gael in America, and the I.R.B. that would derive its strength from a common campaign to overthrow the landlord system in Ireland.

The "New Departure" as it came to be called, marked a turning point in Irish history. For the first time the fundamental issue in Irish society, the ownership of the land, became the basis for a political movement; and for the first and last time, constitutionalists, revolutionaries and land reformers formed a common front that made some fulfillment of Irish separatist hopes seem inevitable.

Devoy travelled back to Europe for secret meetings with Parnell and the leadership of the I.R.B. He battled with the revolutionary purists, like Charles Kickham and John O'Leary, who thought such compromises were immoral and looked on the Land League as undignified. In June of 1879, risking rearrest, he met with Parnell in Morrison's Hotel, Dublin, and reached agreement on a common program aimed at eventual separation from Britain.

Throughout the 1880's Devoy fought a continual struggle to keep the Irish-American factions behind Parnell. Whether or not he felt that Parnell was using him, mouthing revolutionary phrases while moving further and further from his position, Devoy recognized that the end they sought was the same. If the union between Ireland and Britain were broken, no matter how incompletely, then the desired result would be achieved. The extremist wing of the American Clan-Na-Gael, dominated by Alexander Sullivan, had little patience with Parnell's tactics and several times threatened to undertake extensive terrorist operations in England; it did, in fact, finance the dynamiting campaign of 1883–85.

To Devoy, Sullivan and his party represented the very worst elements in the Irish-American community. Besides their advocacy of terrorism and their mismanagement, if not embezzlement, of funds, Sullivan and friends used their organization in Chicago to advance their own political fortunes. J. J. O'Kelly, a former colleague on the *Herald*, a member of the Parliamentary Party and

Parnell's liaison with Devoy, wrote to him in 1885 to ask his help in restraining this "Opera-bouffe element" in America, but Devoy needed little encouragement in this.

The murder in 1889 of one of Devoy's associates in Chicago, Dr. P. H. Cronin, led to an open schism in the Clan. Devoy had no doubt that Sullivan and his party had carried out the murder and he moved to Chicago to direct the campaign to crush the Sullivanites. It was a long and divisive struggle, embittering men on both sides of the controversy. In England a youthful W. B. Yeats, perhaps attracted by Sullivan's extremism, wrote an article defending the Sullivanites and commented on Dr. Cronin's murder, "A spy has no rights."

The factionalized Clan pursued its own vendettas while the Home Rule Party collapsed around Parnell and Mrs. O'Shea. After Parnell's death in 1891, a deep disillusionment with politics settled over Ireland. The energies of Ireland were channeled into a cultural reawakening that, for the moment, showed no interest in politics. Land reform did what the battering ram and the Royal Irish Constabulary had failed to do, bringing a measure of peace to the Irish countryside.

It was a discouraging time for those who had spent their lives in the cause of Irish nationalism. Devoy was now over fifty, and had survived years of prison, exile and controversy only to see his work fall to ruin. Yet a description of him written at this time conveys a sense of the self-discipline and determination that marked his whole career. Like Nietzsche, what did not kill him, made him stronger:

Loose limbed, yet sturdy, long of arm, of medium stature and with a thundercloud cast of face, dark complexioned, dark-eyed, dark-browed, dark thick beard left to grow its own way, and with locks of black hair tumbling in thick confusion over a lofty forehead—he bore the stamp of character.

Devoy was speaking before a poorly attended meeting in Harlem, with the fortunes of Irish separation at a low point, but if he was discouraged, he gave no outward sign of it:

He spoke that evening to the people about Ireland. He stood before them unconsciously defiant of all the arts of oratory, and said the things that were on his mind. He swayed his body to and fro, sawed the air, nearly swept the floor at times with his supple-jointed fingers and waved his arms widely, while he poured out concentrated common sense, or condensed scorn, or rolling massive periods hot with passionate love or passionate hatred. He stood before that audience in the unaffected simplicity of his manhood, unconventional, uncompromising, combative . . . He strikes you as being a man who would run that butting forehead of his against stone walls and batter them down.

Devoy has been called the "Lenin of the Irish revolution," and in their imprisonment and exile, their single-mindedness, their skills as propagandists and rigid dedication to a cause they bear a resemblance. Devoy may have had as little use for the orthodoxies of international socialism as Lenin had for those of Irish nationalism, but with the outbreak of World War One, they came to share space in the file cabinets of the German High Command, each one noted as a potential disrupter of the Allied cause.

Devoy was certainly no stranger to conspiracies with Britain's foreign enemies. He always felt the

Irish cause could only succeed if Britain were involved in a major war elsewhere. In 1914 he had quickly established contact with Count von Bernstorff, the German Ambassador, but nearly forty years before, during the "Bulgarian agitation" when Britain and Russia seemed close to renewing the Crimean War over the fate of the Turkish empire in Europe, Devoy had approached the Russian Ambassador in Washington to seek arms and money for the Irish separatists. The Ambassador had refused to help because, he said, the Irish question involved social reform not national revolution. This reply stung Devoy into realizing how far Ireland's case for a distinct identity had fallen in international eyes; from it had come his commitment to the New Departure.

Now Britain's massive involvement in the war on the continent offered the opportunity he had waited so patiently for. The election of a Liberal Government in England in 1906 had revivified the Irish demand for Home Rule and in the ensuing decade a rising tide of nationalist agitation had swept across Ireland. The return to Dublin in 1907 of a diminutive, bespectacled ex-convict went almost unnoticed by the police, but Tom Clarke breathed new life in the I.R.B. and brought young men into the organization who were capable and dedicated.

From New York Devoy spun the web of conspiracy that led to the Easter Rebellion. He was a constant source of money and advice, and with the start of the war in Europe he became the liaison between the Germans and Irish revolutionaries. After years of disappointment and waiting, he was convinced that a show of arms was necessary, sharing the conviction of Pearse and

Clarke that it would trigger a nation-wide insurrection.

He was at the center of the struggle that followed, a seventy year old man with the energies and passion of his youth intact. He spoke at rallies, raised money and poured out a constant stream of propaganda in his paper *The Gaelic American*; he excoriated President Wilson for ignoring the Irish cause and pounded the Democrats and Republicans with the demand they uphold self-determination for Ireland; he was abrasive, demanding and tireless, quarreling with those who questioned his authority, attacking anyone who stood in the way of severing the connection with Britain.

In 1924, then over eighty, he had the supreme satisfaction of returning to the Free State he helped to create. In view of his moderate position in the 1880's—his ability to settle for measures that led in the right direction—it is not surprising he supported the Treaty, but he was considered by some to have "sold out." At last, however, he acted as though he was above controversy. Taken around Ireland, he visited the places he had not seen in half a century. In Dublin, he was toasted at a dinner in his honor by W. B. Yeats, one of the few enemies he ever seems to have forgiven.

But he did not stay. The Ireland of his youth was dead and gone and he was too old to be of service to the new government. In any case, they were probably not anxious to have the services of a man of such ferocious reputation, who was never far from controversy except when he helped to found the American Irish Historical Society.

The old revolutionary died peacefully in Atlantic City in the fall of 1928 while putting the finish-

ing touches to his *Recollections of an Irish Rebel,*
unwilling to leave his opponents with the last
word.

*Peter Quinn is writing a doctoral thesis on John
Devoy for Fordham University's History Department.*

A Fenian Physician

Kevin M. Cahill, M.D.

The path of Patrick McCartan's life seems unpredictable, unless one accepts the theses that titles need not be restraints, and that the person with multiple interests can occasionally weave a cohesive pattern from diverse endeavors.

Patrick McCartan was, among other things, a physician, a writer, an editor, a revolutionary, politician, diplomat, friend and confidante of artists, sailor, candidate for President of Ireland, and one of the strongest continual American-Irish links in the first half of this century. He was not a dilettante, merely diffusing a limited talent in a random arc and leaving no impression anywhere. He was one of those remarkable figures who played an equally significant role in the careers of Yeats the Poet and DeValera the Politician. His name is as prominent in the history of the Irish Republican Army, the IRA, as it is in the Irish Academy of Letters. 1978 is the centenary of McCartan's birth.

There is a romance about McCartan's life—and a rare courage and optimism—that was present even in his youth. As a poor farm boy from Tyrone he funded his immigration to the States by trading two bullocks in the Derry market for a steerage ticket to Philadelphia. There he worked as a bartender for one of the powerful Fenians of the period, Joseph McGarrity. From McGarrity he not only drew his salary but found the channel

244

through which he could funnel his enormous energies, his love of Ireland and his obsession with freeing his native land from the intellectual and political slavery he had known as a child.

While working in Philadelphia McCartan became involved with the *Clan-na-Gael*, the American arm of the Irish rebel movement, and began to contribute articles to John Devoy's, *Gaelic American*.

When he had saved enough money for tuition he returned to Ireland in 1905 to study to become a doctor. Although young McCartan started his medical education at University College Dublin his political activities quickly brought him to the attention of the government authorities directing that state supported school and he was fortunate to be able to transfer to the independent Royal College of Surgeons in Ireland. While still a medical student he not only wrote articles on Sinn Fein and the Irish Republican Brotherhood (IRB) for his former colleagues on the *Gaelic American*, but founded and edited a new radical periodical, *Irish Freedom*. In 1908, still as a medical student, he was elected Sinn Fein member of the Dublin Corporation, and appointed to the Supreme Council of the Irish Republican Brotherhood. It was this latter group that planned the Easter Rising.

After graduation Dr. McCartan became a Dispensary Physician in his native Tyrone, and his practice—and income—grew till the point he could personally fund and train a volunteer rebel force capable of participating in the coming fight for Irish freedom. His own movements, however, became the subject of such attention that the British secret service filled several large dossiers on his contacts and frequent journeys to Dublin.

Under the guise of a young physician taking a holiday he traveled back to America in 1914. There he met Roger Casement, helped to coordinate the efforts of the IRB to obtain foreign arms, and smuggled thousands of dollars in gold back to his colleagues, Padric Pearse, Tom Clarke, John McBride, James Connolly—those who became the heroes of modern Ireland when they were executed by the English after the abortive Easter Rising in 1916.

Dr. McCartan, who organized the Rising in Tyrone, was not captured and managed to evade the British for six months "on the run", living in barns, and moving through his home town in elaborate disguises. His letters of the period provide one of the only records of a leading planner of the Rising, for all the others were killed or jailed. Dr. McCartan would send his notes by messengers to supporters in the United States, particularly to McGarrity in Philadelphia and Devoy in New York. These notes, scrawled on scraps of paper and on the backs of boxes, have been lovingly edited in the *Clogher Record* (1966). Years later, as the last survivor of the IRB leadership, Dr. McCartan recorded his memories of the period for the historian, F. X. Martin, and these too have been documented in the *Clogher Record* (1964). At the end of 1916 he came out of hiding but was almost immediately arrested and sent to a detention center in England.

In 1917, following the general release of Irish prisoners, Dr. McCartan was smuggled into America disguised as a common seaman. There he bore the credentials of Envoy Plenipotentiary of the Provisional Government of Ireland to the United States, thus becoming independent

Ireland's first diplomat. Traveling throughout the United States he rallied public and financial support, insisting always on full recognition for the outlawed government led by DeValera. The formalities of diplomacy, however, were dull duties for a man of McCartan's energies. He founded and edited the Philadelphia weekly, *New Irish Press*, during his stay and, while still in America, ran unopposed as the Sinn Fein M.P. candidate of Offally County. Trying to purchase military equipment he attempted, in 1917, to travel to Germany but was caught again in the disguise of a sailor by the British secret service and briefly jailed. William Butler Yeats wrote a poem about this episode entitled, "McCartan Before the Mast".

After his release from prison McCartan was briefly appointed as Ireland's first Ambassador to Russia, but his efforts to secure the recognition of the Bolshevik regime that had just toppled the Czar failed, and he returned to his post in the United States. Dr. McCartan recorded the details of those critical years in American-Irish relations in his book, *With DeValera in America*, (Devin Adair, 1932).

By the early twenties McCartan's pure concept of Irish freedom was clouded by the growing civil war between Free State and Republican elements. He broke with DeValera over the Treaty. He was sickened by the death of his dear friend, Michael Collins, by the destruction of the homes of his friends, Oliver St. John Gogarty and Lady Gregory, and became so disenchanted with the policies of DeValera that he resigned his political posts and returned to the practice of medicine.

Never a man to rest idly on past laurels or exhaust himself in a single pursuit, McCartan not only built a large clinical practice in Dublin, but helped his friend, Joseph McGrath, set up the Irish Sweepstakes for the Hospital Trust, probably the most successful lottery in history. Dr. McCartan's critical role was to unify the physicians and hospital administrators of Ireland behind this unconventional method of funding health care. For anyone familiar with the machinations of medical politics and the fierce independence of Irish physicians, this accomplishment of Dr. McCartan must rank him high on the all time list of doctor-diplomats. His old friend McGarrity became the American representative for the Sweepstakes, a lucrative, if slightly illegal, position.

By 1927 McCartan began to feel he had no more worlds to conquer; in the words of Charles T. Rice, his friend and the President-General Emeritus of this Society, "he had a loose foot, was not married and wanted to stretch out from the narrowness of Dublin to the full breadth of New York." Between 1927 and 1938 Dr. McCartan practiced medicine in New York City, taught Gaelic, Latin and Greek to youngsters on Saturday mornings in his townhouse on East 59th Street, and became a major factor in the cultural life of our city. He arranged for the first American tour of Jack Yeats' paintings, raised funds and found new plays for the Abbey Theater, and befriended an almost endless stream of American and Irish literary figures. For several years he almost single-handedly supported Joseph Campbell in New York; when that Irish poet's muse began to fail in the loneliness of a city apartment, McCartan paid for this trip home and helped to re-establish him in rural Ireland. His generosity to Sean O'Casey during his American tour is acknowledged in the playwright's autobiography.

Dr. McCartan believed that the strength of the Irish literary revival in the first 25 years of the twentieth century had to be leavened by the realism of the new world. He obtained the rights, for example, to Eugene O'Neill's plays and promoted their production at the Abbey Theater. He also organized elaborate tours of Ireland for O'Neill and his confreres from America, tours that were personally directed by Yeats, Gogarty and Lady Gregory, tours that cemented the bonds between the cultural elements of the old and new worlds. He was equally intent on making certain that Americans appreciated the contributions of Irish writers, and that those writers received the necessary support to remain creative, a none too easy task in a society recovering from civil war, in the throes of the worldwide economic depression that followed the stock market collapse of 1929, and in a nation with a sad tradition of repressive censorship. With two American friends Judge Richard Campbell and Eugene F. Kinkead, McCartan joined with some literary figures in Ireland to establish a formal structure for fostering the best in modern Irish arts.

Dr. McCartan became the chief American fundraiser and was certainly the main stimulus behind the founding of the Irish Academy of Letters. Based on the concept of the French Academy, the new organization was designed to recognize and honor outstanding living Irish literary figures, and also to support young writers. To provide the financial foundation for the latter aim Dr. McCartan provided the annual O'Growney Award for Gaelic writing; the first two winners were Maurice

O'Sullivan for *Twenty Years a Growing* and Peig Sawyers for her tales of life in the Blasket Islands. The writers selected as founding members included William Butler Yeats, George Bernard Shaw, Frank O'Connor, A.E., Oliver St. J. Gogarty, Sean O'Faolain, Austin Clarke, Liam O'Flaherty, Padraic Colum—an incredible anthology of the great writers of the twentieth century. Sean O'Casey and James Joyce were invited to join but the bitter feelings that had caused them to leave Ireland were still too fresh, and they both refused.

McCartan's overriding interest in promoting the Academy was to provide William Butler Yeats the financial security necessary for him to continue creating poetry. McCartan believed that Yeats was the greatest living poet in the English language; although that view was supported by numerous awards and honors, including the Nobel Prize for Literature, it was difficult to survive on medals. Till the 1930s Yeats had never made more than a few hundred pounds per year from his writings. McCartan arranged for Yeats' first reading tours of America, and later guaranteed an annual income to the poet.

The highest award of the Academy was the Lady Gregory Medal, offered only once every three years. In 1937 Yeats presented the award to Dr. McCartan stating that "but for him the Academy would not exist". The remarkable relationship between the poet and the physician flourished, with each contributing essential support for the growth of the other and for the common goal of elevating the level of Irish art. John Unterecker has captured their symbolic relationship in his book, *Yeats and Patrick McCartan,*

A Fenian Friendship, (Dolmon Press, 1965). Much of the doctor's financial support came through James A. Farrell, the Chairman of the American Steel Trust; McCartan, not incidentally, served as chief medical advisor for the 65,000 American steel employees. At the dinner following the presentation of the Gregory Medal, Yeats read a Dedication Poem which acknowledged both:

> *"First I greet McCartan, revolutionary leader,*
> *He, disguised as a sailor before the mast,*
> *Travelled to and fro across the Atlantic;*
> *He, though but a landsman, went to the masthead*
> *Then Farrell, steel king, master of men . . ."*

Dr. McCartan married a young Irish girl, Betty Kearney, in New York in 1937 and shortly thereafter returned to Ireland. Though he maintained a clinical practice in Dublin his main medical activities were with his old friend McGrath and the Hospital Trust of the Irish Sweepstakes. He also dabbled in business and watched a gypsum mining company he had purchased rise and fail several times. He worked vigorously to maintain Irish neutrality during World War II, and poured his enormous energies into associations promoting Gaelic culture and land reform. His love of politics persisted, and his base of support and respect steadily widened throughout Ireland.

In 1945 Dr. McCartan ran against his comrade in arms from the Easter Rising, Sean T. O'Kelley, for the Presidency of Ireland. His platform drew upon his record of service to Ireland, a lifetime that had included the contributions of doctor and diplomat, rebel and writer, politician and poetmaker. His candidacy won the support of *The Irish Times* and of independents around the country but he lost to the overwhelming strength of the established party candidate. During the next few years Dr. McCartan remained a conscience in Irish political life, founding a new party, *Clann na Poblachta*, with Sean McBride. When McBride became Foreign Minister of Ireland in the late 1940s Dr. McCartan was again recognized officially by his native land, and they acknowledged their debt to this remarkable physician-citizen, appointing him an At-Large Senator in the Coalition Government.

He spent his declining years on a lovely Wicklow estate, Mount John, with a famous portrait of Roger Casement in the foyer, and his books, family and friends around him.

Dr. Patrick McCartan died in 1963 and is survived by his widow, daughter, Dierdre, and son, Padraig, whom it has been my honor to know.

Dr. Cahill is the President-General of the Society.

Eamon de Valera
Informal Reflections

JOHN A. MURPHY

During the centenary year of 1982, much was written about Eamon de Valera's role in modern Irish history. I should like to consider him here on a more personal level, to set down my own memories and impressions of him and to reflect on the conflicting emotions he aroused.

Two years before he died, he was made a Freeman of the City of Cork. He travelled south to receive the distinction at the hands of the then Lord Mayor and to say predictable things about the imperishable memory of Terence MacSwiney and Tomas MacCurtain. He was led from his car to the door of the City Hall, shuffling and blind and heavily dependent on his *aide-de-camp,* but still dignified and striking, his eagle's face graven and impassive. (The macabre but complimentary joke being retailed during those years of apparently endless old age was that de Valera had really died years before and that, by a Fianna Fáil party conspiracy, an animated puppet was trotted out from time to time to be properly venerated and to sustain national morale, rather like a perpendicular and mobile Lenin.) A ragged cheer went up as he moved through the small crowd and, self-consciously performing a historical ritual I lifted up my eight-year-old Eileen to get her first-and-last glimpse of the Chief. That was in March 1973 and he never came to Cork again.

Afterwards it occurred to me that I was about the same age as my small daughter when I first saw Dev, then in his political prime. The connection here was my uncle, Daniel Corkery (not to be confused with his literary

253

namesake), a guerilla hero of the revolution and a member of the First Dáil. His talents did not stretch to extended political peroration and it was a cause for family pride that during the historic Dáil debates on the Treaty he should have made the second shortest speech on either side. The laconic brevity of his contribution stands in salutary contrast to the theatrical verbiage filling most of those 388 columns. He and the people of mid-Cork, he said, had no intention of going in as "a prop to hold up a rotten Empire." Whether you were pro- or anti-Treaty, you could only applaud the simple magnificance of the sentiment.

My native town of Macroom, thus splendidly seceding from the crumbling Raj, is the gateway to West Cork, as the tourist literature puts it. To the east, the Lee winds its placid way towards Cork City through a pleasant and fertile valley. Immediately west of Macroom, the rocks and rugged hills beckon and beyond them the 'county bounds' rise to the blue-green magic of Kerry. Macroom had something of the history of a frontier town and it was an active area of conflict in both the "Tan" war and the Civil War. It was from Macroom that the Auxies "sped to their doom" a short distance away at Kilmichael, and Michael Collins was to be seen in the town before the fateful tour of his beloved and trusted West Cork tragically ended at nearby Béal na Bláth.

Political feelings in the town were still very bitter as de Valera and Fianna Fáil surged inexorably to power in 1932. My first conscious political memory is of the uproar caused by a Blueshirt march, which included a contingent of formidable females from the locality, a veritable "monstrous regiment of women." The general elections of the 1930s took place in tumultuous excitement as Dev successfully played the green card. His presence in Macroom during a campaign meant that he was lending the inestimable asset of his own personality to his party's tough fight in a marginal constituency. I remember vividly the marching band and the horses, the blazing tar-barrels and, in the town square, the upturned sea of dark, hungry (some literally so), passionate faces beneath the Town Hall balcony from which Dev spoke after an interminable succession of local un-notables. Later, he rested at the Corkery house, taking counsel with the chosen few and it was there I was ushered into the Presence. My mother led me upstairs into a sitting-room where the Long Fellow sat on an armchair by the fire. I think I did something like a double genuflection (as at an exposition of the Blessed Sacrament) as he murmured a greeting in Irish.

That was my political initiation cermony and although later on I was to lapse from the Fianna Fáil faith I always had some of the guilty feelings of the once ardent believer. My parents were life-long followers of de Valera though they became increasingly disenchanted with some of his lieutenants. My father in particular was typical of those plain people on whom the Fianna Fáil party was built and prospered. The only newspaper he took was the *Irish Press,* the daily gospel in our house from its first issue in 1931. He used to plank down his hard-earned half-crown on the table outside the chapel gate on national collection Sunday for Fianna Fáil, being sent in due course a receipt from party headquarters bearing the franked de Valera signature which we children believed to be the real thing. We gazed at it admiringly, before the piece of paper was carefully folded and reverentially placed under the Sacred Heart lamp. Thus did we honor the twin and sanguine pieties of Faith and Fatherland. God was in his Irish Catholic heaven and de Valera would surely put things right one day with our part of the world.

Of de Valera's greatness my father, who was five or six years younger, never entertained any doubt until the day he died, some months before Dev's own death in 1975.

On occasion, he would confidently proclaim his faith in song:

> De Valera lead you
> Soldiers of the Legion of the Rearguard.

As we moved into the late 1940s, and the once crusading party grew stale and inept (if not worse) during long years in office, my father once again exemplified that steadfast voting allegiance which kept Fianna Fáil in office by making the vital distinction between party and leader. Whatever about the deterioration of the party and even the whiff of corruption, Dev himself was above suspicion, my father stoutly maintained, and it would be unthinkable to abandon him in favor of a newer god.

For a time, that newer god seemed to be on hand in the person of Seán MacBride. I was briefly starry-eyed about Clann na Poblachta and MacBride, but my father scoffed at the 'Man of Destiny' feature in *Life* magazine and remained loyal to de Valera. He would brook no criticism of the ageing Chief. Indeed, though a devoutly religious man he would only mildly demur at a skeptical or irreligious comment but was much less tolerant when the fatherland was under attack, and Dev was the fatherland personified. To insult him was to be guilt all at once of blasphemy, *lèse-majesté*, and high treason.

One of my close relatives was a civil servant whose opinions were usually highly respected by the family. He shared the disenchanted view which many of his colleagues took of an administration too long in office and which moreover was niggardly in the matter of civil service pay. More than that, he belonged like me to a generation that realized the futility of the de Valera *aisling* in the face of emigration, unemployment and grey poverty. For us, Dev was becoming the embodiment of a stale and faded dream.

I didn't realize then that Dev's greatness was something quite other, existing independently of his failure in the socio-economic area.

My father was serving his customers in our pub in Macroom one night in the mid-1950s when the relative happened to be home on holidays. The talk turned to Dev who was then undergoing an eye-operation in Utrecht or Geneva. (Joyce and de Valera were the same age, both were afflicted with eye trouble, and had little else in common, but did not Joyce once recommend, through a third party, the name of a specialist to his fellow-sufferer?) As befitted the serious topic, the conversation was conducted in a low respectful tone. "Ah, yes," my father observed sadly, "they say he's almost blind now, poor man, God help us." A brief silence ensued. The close relative, that night in a particularly acerbic mood, took a large swallow from his pint and made a loud and provocative pronouncement. "A great pity the hoor wasn't blind twenty years ago," he said. All hell, as they say, broke loose. "No one," shouted my normally mild-mannered da, his blue eyes flashing, "no one will ever again talk like that about Dev in this house." And so it proved. The relative was suitably chastened, I also found it a sobering experience and although affectionate family relations were soon restored and flourished thereafter, I never forgot the episode and its significance.

De Valera, like all personalities of stature, fiercely polarized emotions in a way that hasn't been true of any of his successors. People might respect or dislike Lemass, regard Jack Lynch with affection as "one of our own," admire Haughey's powers of survival or distrust his political skills. But only Dev could inspire such passionate devotion and such apparently unreasoning hatred. After he had spoken at an election meeting in Cork, a waitress at our table in a Patrick Street cafe shook with red rage at the very idea of his being present in the town she loved.

257

I have kept several letters from a Limerick man, now deceased, who from time to time helpfully offered me various suggestions on the interpretation of modern Irish history. They all really pointed to the same interpretation which was that most of our complex problems had one simple root — the malign influence of Eamon de Valera, or, as he was obviously pleased to call him, "the Butcher from Bruree."

On the other side of the coin, there is the true story of the old man in County Galway who was being teased by a reporter I know. The latter showed him a press report on a de Valera scion who was sowing some moderately wild oats at the time. The old man, however, would believe no ill of any of the family. "Ah." he said doggedly, "they must be some other de Valeras." But it was Clare that was the great center of the living de Valera cult, the microcosm of the rural Ireland which never wavered in its allegiance despite the sore sacrifices it was compelled to make, the historic constituency (in both a territorial and cultural sense) which massively endorsed him from 1917 to his last hurrah in 1957, and which then bade him an emotional farewell as he came to say goodbye before leaving the party political arena in 1959.

I happened to be in Clare when he died and I took part in a television program which attempted an assessment there and then of de Valera in a Clare context and which was shown on the night of the funeral. It was meant to be a judiciously critical appraisal but perhaps the timing was inappropriate. It raised a storm of protest at the next meeting of Clare County Council which expressed the furious and dismissive view that the program was the work of drunken intellectuals. Indeed, I was informed that I would not be welcome in future in one of my very favorite counties but I purged my contempt in other ways and the incident was soon forgotten. Senator Tras Honan, the Chief's most devoted adherent in Clare, regarded me for a time with profound distrust which finally evaporated when we both served together in the Senate (a body de Valera once abolished because it was like "a hobble skirt," he complained, impeding legislative and constitutional progress).

But, if Clare was the citadel of faith in de Valera (and his grand-daughter believes it still is, since she has set her sights on a Dail seat there) there was always the occasional intransigent infidel within the walls. I know an otherwise happy and contented man from the Banner County, now living in Cork, who is a fanatical Fine Gaeler, principally because of his unshakeable belief that de Valera's economic policies in the 1930s brought ruin to the poor deluded farmers of his native county, including his own family. Once I told Jimmy the story of the Dublin reporter who was covering de Valera's participation in the Anglo-Irish talks of 1938, and who, far gone in his cups, wired his editor a sensational stop-press headline: "De Valera arrested on serious charge in London: alleged interference with little boys." Jimmy was not amused by the story of the drunken prank. "Interfere?" he snorted, "sure that old bollocks couldn't even interfere with himself."

My recollections of de Valera included a picture of him reviewing a great army march-past in Cork towards the end of World War II. The bicycle was the most popular, indeed the only reliable, mode of transport in 'Emergency' Ireland and, though not a very athletic teenager, I thought nothing of pedalling the twenty-four miles along the Lee Valley from Macroom to Cork, to attend a concert or a game. On this occasion the attraction was the spick-and-span turn out of the defence forces, complete with military bands, and I wanted to be a living element of that great and unifying consensus of Irish neutrality which is central to the history of the Irish state and the maintenance of which was spiritedly symbolized by the marching troops. But the star attraction of the parade was de Valera himself, unmistakeably civilian (he was never much of a soldier at the best of times) and yet undeniably the unique personification of the nation's determination to defend its hard-won sovereignty.

In later years, I went to watch and listen during various election campaigns, as Dev made his regal and ritualistic entry into the sturdily nationalists area of Blackpool (Jack Lynch's heartland) on the outskirts of Cork City. After the enthusiastic march into the city center, and the inevitable contributions by lesser luminaries, the crowd would listen with respectful patience to a frequently long and invariably rambling speech from Eamon de Valera. It mattered not that the topic was often boring, the syntax convoluted, the flat Limerick monotone unmusical. (There are some classic de Valera texts, but as a deliverer of speeches he was rarely memorable.) Once a political hero of Dev's rare stature is accepted as such by the people, what he has to say on any given occasion is immaterial, and a reading from the telephone directory would draw reverential applause.

One regrettable consequence of beatifying a great historical personality (an exercise frequently indulged in by relatives and party hacks during the centenary year of 1982) is an inevitable dehumanization and a shrinking of credible dimensions. A false sense of reverence robs the idol of his full humanity. So it is that the human and humorous side of de Valera flashes out only now and then, usually reflected to us informally by his biographers and by others who directly experienced his personality for themselves. On a recent radio program, Michael Mulvihill recalled how as a Dublin schoolboy he was given the awesome task of welcoming Dev on a visit to the school, and how he immediately sensed the presence not only of greatness but of warm graciousness and humor. Mulvihill told the Chief that a class had been set a de Valera speech as an exercise in translation into Irish and that considerable difficulties had been experienced because of the labyrinthine structure of the original. Thereupon, Dev laughed heartily, not to say uproariously.

He must have grinned at his own witticism on the day Nelson's Pillar was blown up. "I thought," he remarked to one of his official biographers, "that the newspapers missed the chance of a good headline this morning."

"What was that, sir?"

"British admiral leaves Dublin by air," said the Chief.

The other biographer relates a homely incident which afforded Dev much amusement. He was campaigning in a remote rural area and called to a cottage where a very old woman, something of a character, lived alone. She welcomed her famous guest warmly but she was far from being overawed. When he accepted her offer of a 'drop' of tea, she threw out the dregs of the cup from which she had been drinking, refilled it and handed it to the head of the Irish government. Combining fastidiousness with diplomacy, he transferred the cup to his left hand so that he could drink from the other side. The stratagem, though not its purpose, was immediately noted by his host who crowed delightedly: "Ah, you're a *ciotóg* [left-handed person] like myself—you can be sure of my No. I!"

De Valera, unwittingly or otherwise, projected an austere, if not puritancial, image of himself. The general opinion was that he disapproved, *inter alia,* of strong drink (advocating, however, at one stage that a homemade light beer should replace tea in the national diet). It would seem that he mellowed considerably in this respect in his years in Arus an Uachtaráin. The late Seamus Murphy, the Cork-based sculptor, spent several sessions in the Arus where the President sat for the second of two fine Murphy heads, the first being in 1944. It seems that there was no shortage of hospitality in the Arus and the President was a congenial host at leisurely luncheons. That was in 1959. Later still, Dev provided draught Guinness for the favored

261

few who might be invited to the Park after an all-Ireland final. Guinness was a far cry from the light beer he had advocated in one of his more paternalistic moods, but what could be more Irish than a draught dispenser in the house?

I don't know if Dev ever heard Myles na Gopaleen's most celebrated story in the Keats-and-Chapman *genre,* but it is certain that he would have enjoyed it hugely, particularly because the punchline is in the Irish language he so deeply loved. It should be explained that on the rare occasions when he was unsuccessful in elections, he was given to quoting philosophically the traditional saying 'Beidh lá eile ag an bPaorach' (Power—an individual signifying everyman—will have another day), thus giving the phrase a wide popularity among a politically-conscious populace. According to this particular Keats-and-Chapman story, the famous literary pair were invited to Arus an Uachtaráin by President de Valera after he had met them at a hurling game. Both were eager connoisseurs of whiskey and were delighted when Dev opened a bottle of 15-year-old Power's. They finished the first measure with relish and held out their glasses for the second with lip-smacking anticipation at which point the President re-corked the bottle and put it back in the liquor cabinet, remarking with a wicked grin as he did so: 'Beidh lá eile ag an bPaorach'.

He might have enjoyed that joke right enough but we cannot say what his reaction would have been to the story of the anti-Fianna Fáil cab-driver who was asked by a foreign fare why de Valera was not commemorated in street names. "Because," came the tart reply, "there is no street in Ireland long enough or crooked enough to call after that bugger."

Stories about de Valera, favorable and otherwise, are legion. He was part of the social and political folklore, rather as Daniel O'Connell had been over a century before, though the community which produced O'Connell was still largely traditional and Gaelic and it wove him as hero and *gaiscíoch* and superman into the fabric and framework of the folklore in a way which was no longer possible in the middle of the twentieth century. Yet de Valera, whatever his shortcomings, shares a place in the Irish pantheon with O'Connoll and Parnell, a place which cannot be offered to any other figure in modern Irish history, no matter how worthy his credentials. All three to some extent left the material expectations of their followers unfulfilled but all three nonetheless stood up for a people scarred by history and therefore athirst not only for political independence but for a dignity and self-respect denied them by a contemptuously arrogant neighbor. In his time, Dev supplied and maintained that dignity: was he not, in the popular phrase, "the man who gave Churchill his answer?" That kind of leader and the filling of that kind of role are rare phenomena. It is unlikely that Ireland will see a repeat performance in this century. Caesar may have had his flaws but he was still Caesar. "Here was a Caesar," de Valera's devotees might well have exclaimed when he died, as they contemplated a seemingly bleak future for Fianna Fáil bereft of the holy founder, "here was a Caesar, when comes there such another?"

John Murphy is Professor of Irish History at University College, Cork.

Irish Neutrality in
World War II

KEVIN McAULIFFE

A British occupation of Eire would present enormous difficulties, not so much from the point of view of the debarkation as from that of maintaining order thereafter. An American occupation would be far preferable, for the people could really be convinced that it was intended to be but a temporary measure. Whatever resistance might be opposed to an American landing would be merely pro forma.

. . . The people of . . . Eire . . . have bonds of interest, sentiment, affection, and blood with those of the U.S. which might enable Americans to perform actions without offense which would be bitterly resented if performed by the British.

Those cables were sent from Washington to Dublin in early 1942. They advocated a military gamble the United States never took—the invasion and occupation of Ireland.

Ireland, although neutral in World War II, was not uninvolved. Taoiseach Eamon De Valera's intractable policy of neutrality cost him and Ireland the affection of many on the American side of the Atlantic. In Ireland, it was his finest hour and the peak of his popularity.

In 1935, when he had seen war coming, De-Valera had sworn that Ireland "would never be permitted to be used as a base for attack upon Britain." But his message to Britain was charac-

264

teristically bittersweet. He simultaneously abrogated the 1921 peace-and-partition treaty, promulgated a new Constitution, and engaged in economic war with Britain over unpaid land annuities. Despite the treaty abrogation, the Chamberlain Government—loath perhaps to fight another Irish rearguard action in the event of war—returned the last four Royal Navy bases (Cork, Queenstown, Berehaven and Lough Swilly) to the Free State on schedule in 1938.

With the declaration of war in September 1939, DeValera reiterated his position but the I.R.A., having fallen out with him before his accession to power, began a terror bombing campaign in Ulster, Britain and the Republic, capped by a spectacular Christmas Eve 1940 raid on the Government's Phoenix Park arms magazine. DeValera's response was tough: trial by special court, five executions, 1,000 internments, and censorship. "Even an opinion on Ireland's neutrality expressed in a private letter directed outside the country may be an offense under the Emergency Powers, punishable with imprisonment," a United States Embassy dispatch reported home in August 1940.

The necessity for the policy was quickly evident to the Irish people. During the Battle of Britain, bombs were dropped in Ireland—not just Belfast, hit twice in the spring of 1941 (DeValera, typically, protested Germany's attack on *Irish* soil), but Dublin (Germany apologized for the "accidental" raid) and Wexford as well (two raids, news of both suppressed by DeValera). That year, DeValera called for 25,000 volunteer coast watchers to supplement the regular army and "local defense forces." Cork and other vital harbors were mined.

Meanwhile, German agents were parachuting into Ireland, going underground and escaping with I.R.A. help. Nonetheless, Irish public opinion, especially after the fate of the small, neutral Low Countries, was beginning to be "passively pro-British," reported one U.S. intelligence estimate. A letter opened and shown to American intelligence agents portrayed the mood in Ireland. "Mr. DeValera has again warned us to get ready and to be making preparations for the attack each day, because he says that unless by God's great providence we won't escape war."

But with only 54 planes, mostly trainers, in its air force and memories of the Dublin raid still fresh the Irish people "are in terror of their ports and cities being bombed," Col. Frank Sharp told Washington, "for they know how vulnerable and defenseless they are." German propaganda "has been highly successful," he wrote.

Of course, fear of attack was only part of the reason for the policy of neutrality. "Sympathy has remained consistently anti-Hitler," one dispatch on the eve of Pearl Harbor reported, "even if the confusion still persists in some Irish minds that to say a good word for England is to abandon one's love of Ireland." Ireland maintained diplomatic relations with Germany and Italy, recognized Pétain's regime in Vichy, and did not resort to a blackout during the blitz. Not totally unconvincingly, the Irish position was that the RAF would be stretched too thin trying to defend Irish as well as British targets, and the best turn it could do Britain was its unprovocative lights-on policy.

One week after Pearl Harbor, DeValera served notice the situation had changed—but not enough. The war's "extension to the United States of

America brings a source of anxiety and sorrow to every part of this land," he said in a Cork speech.

> There is scarcely a family here which has not a member or near relative in that country. In addition to the ties of blood there has been between our two nations a long association of friendship and regard, continuing uninterruptedly from America's own struggle for independence down to our own. The part that American friendship played in helping us to win the freedom that we enjoy in this part of Ireland has been gratefully recognized and acknowledged by our people. It would be unnatural then if we did not sympathize in a special manner with the people of the United States and if we did not feel with them in all the anxieties and trials which this war must bring upon them. For this reason strangers who do not understand our conditions have begun to ask how America's entry into the war will affect our State policy here. We answered that question in advance: the policy of the State remains unchanged. We can only be a friendly neutral.

That stance vexed no one more than America's Ambassador to Dublin, David Gray. Gray was a successful newspaper publisher who had visited Ireland on several hunting trips. His wife was an aunt of First Lady Eleanor Roosevelt. Despite the barb printed about him in the *London Daily Express*—"a pillow which bore the impress of the last person who sat on it"—Gray was such an extreme anglophile that he and his military attachés now set about to practically force U. S. military action against the Irish.

In a flurry of wires, cables, letters, dispatches and memoranda to Washington, they elaborated their rationale. "To defeat Britain, it is unnecessary for Germany to invade Britain, but only to occupy Ireland," they wrote. So doing, Hitler could use Irish harbors and airfields to strangle Britain's Atlantic lifeline. They predicted that the Germans would replicate the strategy used in taking Crete, with German gliders landing 200,000 soldiers who could live off the land, over the heads of the Royal Navy.

> The distance between Cork and Cherbourg is only 316 miles. . . . Landing by air could be made at almost any point in southern and southwestern Ireland without serious opposition. . . . Bravely as it will resist, the Eire Army would be brushed aside by the sort of invasion that fell on Crete.

Gray and his staff estimated that there were 150,000 I.R.A sympathizers to act as a German fifth column and predicted that "by the time the Allies could put into effect their plans of defense, the airfields, ports and beaches and the key positions in Eire might be in German hands." To prevent that and "in anticipation of attack" they urged that "we should have an adequate secret force of persons of unquestioned trustworthiness . . . in other words, an effective fifth column of our own . . . (and) obtain possession of all desirable strategic ports in Eire at the earliest possible moment by the most practicable means."

There was little doubt what that meant, as the accompanying maps of Ireland detailing transit routes and possible interdiction points made clear. But, despite Gray's hard lobbying, his plan was not accepted. For one thing, he had sounded out Lt. Gen. McKenna, the Irish Army Chief of Staff, about the probability of a German invasion without detailing his plan to prevent it. McKenna's rebuttal letter, "Denmark will not be repeated here," was duly forwarded. Another rebuttal came from

Col. Dan Bryan, head of Irish Intelligence. Bryan alertly noted to his Anglo-American counterparts that Luftwaffe fighters could not make it to Ireland and back to base without refueling and would, therefore, be unable to provide the kind of air cover that had allowed the invasion of Crete to succeed.

More decisive was the apprehension in Washington that the Irish would shoot back, even at Irish-American troops—and the opposition of British Prime Minister Winston Churchill.

Churchill was, of course, as wily a British nationalist as DeValera was an Irish one. He had been a supporter of Irish Home Rule-with-Ulster back in 1912 and a signatory member of Lloyd George's treaty delegation in 1921. Possibly because he knew first-hand the kind of pressure exerted on Ireland to accept partition, his understanding of Irish sensitivities throughout the war on a variety of subjects comes across as much deeper than that shown by many American Protestants in the State Department and the military. In 1944, he wrote President Roosevelt about Ireland, "we should let fear work its healthy process." Churchill saw that the Allies' *ability* to invade Eire carried with it a political advantage which outweighed the military advantage of actual invading and inviting another Easter Week. And so Roosevelt personally assured DeValera the U. S. had not the "slightest thought or intention of invading the territory of Ireland or of threatening the security of the Irish."

The Irish fears had not been unfounded. On January 10, 1942, as part of Operation Magnet, 105,000 American troops of the 5th Army Corps landed in Ulster on a double mission: "in cooperation with British Ulster Defense Forces, to defend Northern Ireland against attack by the Axis powers and to be prepared to move into Southern Ireland for the defense thereof." The I.R.A. immediately declared war on the United States and Cardinal MacRory of Belfast made public reference to "my own corner of our country overrun by British and United States soldiers against the will of the Nation."

Gray took offense. In a letter to MacRory, he wrote:

> Regardless of religious views, regardless of party lines, the American people for nearly a century have thought of themselves as the special friends of Ireland. Eminent Irishmen have stated publicly that without this powerful friendship, Irish Nationalism would not have succeeded as it has. We have asked nothing from Ireland. We have always given, but we have always believed that we could rely on Irish friendship and that in an hour of need we should have Irish help. Now in our life and death struggle you warn us off the strategic position so necessary to us and to our Allies. This position, however much you and I may wish it might be otherwise, has been, as you know, recognized by the nations of the world, including the then newly established Irish Free State, as under British sovereignty.

Gray warned the cardinal that public statements such as his might lead to "murderous outrages" against U.S. troops by the I.R.A. and that Ireland's attitude could well create "resentment that will last for generations."

> Some Americans understand that Mr. DeValera in protesting the arrival of American troops may have wished to emphasize his claim to sovereignty over the six counties, but they ask why he protested American troops coming as friends for the protection of Ireland

270

> . . . (and) they feel that his attitude has been more friendly to Germany, from whom he obtains nothing but bombs.

The fear that U. S. troops would invade the Republic had abated before the March 1944 order barring all U. S. and U. K. soldiers from crossing the Ulster border but American fears that the I.R.A would kill a U. S. soldier did not. Nor did David Gray's outrage at Irish neutrality stop after his invasion plan was discarded. He protested every sale of military equipment to Ireland and, noting its trade dependence on Britain, advocated economic coercion.

The invasion plan had been replaced with an attempt at persuasion. In the summer of 1943, the U. S. drew up a note to Dublin seeking Irish military bases. In Roosevelt's name, it used many of Gray's favorite arguments.

> . . . Germany has bombed Irish cities and destroyed Irish lives and property with impunity. A German plane has sunk a ship carrying a cargo of American wheat to Ireland and Axis submarines have sunk other ships carrying supplies to Ireland. Both of the ships . . . (were) sailing under the Irish flag. . . .

> Americans of Irish blood and background are loyal American citizens and are making their full contribution to the war in every way. . . . The opportunity to help save the lives of these men and of all those fighting with them must surely strike a sympathetic chord in the hearts of the people of Ireland.

Unmentioned in the note was the ulterior motive—the U. S. hoped to lure the Germans into attacking the bases and wipe out the Luftwaffe's fighters in an air battle over Ireland. Nor was there any mention in the initial approach to the Irish authorities that the bases would have been available for British use. At any rate, this plan, too, was eventually dropped.

In the meantime, Gray kept up a flow of reports to Washington on all real or imagined I.R.A. fifth column activities. He wrote Secretary of State Cordell Hull:

> It is foolish to assume that the Gestapo does not make use of them (I.R.A.) here as it has made of similar Quislings in other countries. . . . They are in the civil service, in the army, and everywhere in civil life. . . . On this coast there are thousands of fishermen, many of them members of the I.R.A., whose business takes them into waters where a rendezvous with a German submarine is a simple matter. With a very moderate expenditure it should be entirely feasible for the German Mission, which has power to move about the country freely and under cover of correct social relations, to make contact with key men in the I.R.A. to establish an efficacious system of espionage without the use of a single German national.

Other reports reaching Washington at the time painted a different picture. In fact, some of the American reports sent back home during this period showed great knowledge of and sympathy toward the Irish situation. For instance, Washington was accurately told that "by and large the vast majority of the population of Eire, while having a certain amount of emotional sympathy with the objectives of the I.R.A., regard them as fanatical zealots who are costing the taxpayers large sums of money for their surveillance, apprehension and internment" and "are on the side of the Allies."

A May 1942 status report by Col. John Reynolds ran a litany of Irish-borne hardships. Peat, for instance, was down to a three-month supply.

All private automobiles are forbidden. . . . Ration books are now being distributed through the mails. . . . There is a marked scarcity of many food items in the shops. . . . There is no kerosine for sale. . . . Even in Dublin the street lights in the suburbs are to be eliminated. . . . So serious is the newsprint situation that the Swedish Consul in Dublin has left for Sweden to try to arrange for shipments of pulp wood. If he is unsuccessful, newspapers will cease being published in Eire.

But most reports routinely drummed the theme, as another by Reynolds did, "that the increasing disqualified element in Eire will pin their faith on Hitler because the Irish . . . have always turned to the enemies of England for help."

Still other confidential estimates of the Irish contained some very hard-core stereotypes. Gray himself once wrote: "the key to the Irish situation is that it is dominated by a pathological neutrality not open to reason as we understand reason. . . ."

And an unsigned OSS report in February 1943 went overboard:

When Britain withdrew from Eire in 1921, it left behind no class trained in the art of Government and hence what has obtained in Eire for the past 20 years is government by a system of trial-and-error—an appallingly wasteful process.

The members of the Government of Eire are also members of the Irish Roman Catholic Church which is the real power governing Ireland today. . . . With the exception of Mr. DeValera . . . all the other members of the Government of Eire are clerical Fascists of varying degrees. . . .

One fact to be kept in mind when describing any aspect of Irish life is the surprising lack of what, to an

273

American mind, passes for logic. The Irish Roman Catholic Church looks upon the United States by and large as an immoral, irreligious, materialistic Protestant country chosen by God to be led along the paths of salvation by the Irish and Irish-American Roman Catholic clergy. . . . The lack of self-enlightenment which obtains in the Irish Church today is little short of appalling. . . . The Irish Roman Catholic Church is in large part responsible for the complete concealment of the real nature of continental Fascism from the mass of the Irish people. ·. . .

By contrast, in the same dispatch the policy of the Ulster Unionist regime toward its Catholic minority was described only as "somewhat repressive."

In 1944–45 the historical low point in American-Irish relations was reached. It began with the American demand that Dublin expel the German and Japanese Ambassadors.

The case for doing so was not wholly implausible. OSS reported to Washington on February 28, 1944, "through a friendly informer," that:

German information pertaining to Allied activities in England comes from the German legation in Ireland. The legation, which is heavily staffed, has succeeded in infiltrating agents into England . . . (and) the OberKomander der Wehrmacht have been supplied by the German intelligence network, operating in Eire, with the most accurate data concerning the concentric massing of Anglo-American air forces and all large dumps of fuel, armament and food.

By that time, the note to Dublin had already been sent. American Intelligence believed Germans were transmitting such information from a wireless radio inside their Embassy. "There is supposed to be a monitor watch on this set," Gray

274

had written Secretary of State Hull in December 1943, "but the monitoring is done by Irish civil servants and cannot be considered as providing reasonable security." And on February 21, 1944 a note signed by Hull was sent. It included a sentence drafted by Gray: "despite the declared desire of the Irish Government that its neutrality should not operate in favor of either of the belligerents, it has in fact operated and continues to operate in favor of the Axis powers and against the United Nations on whom your security and the maintenance of your national economy depend."

DeValera met Gray the same day and said it was "impossible for the Irish Government to comply." Eight days later, the two met again, and, in DeValera's words, he was reassured "that the American Government did not contemplate proceeding to military or other measures because of the reply which had been given."

Reciting various Irish anti-espionage efforts and minimizing the damage caused by German and I.R.A. agents, DeValera asserted that "Should American lives be lost it will not be through any indifference or neglect of its duty on the part of this State" and pointedly concluded:

> . . . . The feelings of the Irish people towards Britain have during the war undergone a considerable change precisely because Britain has not attempted to violate our neutrality. The Irish Government feel sure that the American Government would agree that it would be regrettable if any incidents now should alter that happy result.

The Government-owned Irish *Press* gave the Irish side of the story—in the words of Robert

Brennan, Dublin's Ambassador to the United States:

Is there no limit to the credulity of Americans? I have recently been called to the State Department to explain a report from Ireland that 3,000 Japanese had landed there and were living in disguise.

On hearing the story the first questions an Irishman would have asked are: where did the Japanese come from? how was the influx concealed in a country whose total Japanese population numbers 4?. . . . Nobody on the American side seems to have been gun-up enough to ask these questions.

In the early days of the war we were supplying German submarines with petrol, night, noon and morning—until it was suddenly discovered by the authors of this fiction that submarines did not burn petrol at all. . . . The next story was that our fishermen brought fresh vegetables and fruit far out to sea to supply the submarines which, of course, came to the surface and risked destruction for these succulent Irish cabbages. . . . It was followed by a circumstantial account of how German U-boat officers (gold braid and all) and their crews were being entertained royally at our seaside hotels—no doubt having hitched their submarines in the meantime to the nearest lighthouse!. . . . It was soon replaced by the 'Lights of Dublin.' These, it appears, were guiding the German planes in their raids on British cities and only for them no British city would be bombed.

Germany and the Italian Legation . . . had staffs of 300, no 400, no 500, no, by Jove, 800! These staffs all had radio transmitters and were working day and night. . . . When it was at last accepted that the German Legation staff numbered six, then each of them became a courier who ran from Berlin to Dublin twice daily. . . .

276

Pointing out that all Berlin-Dublin international cable lines had to pass through London and had been wide open to MI5 interception all along, the *Press* concluded:

> The whole thing would be a joke if it did not seem probable that such fictions were taken seriously—so seriously in fact as to have influenced the sending of the American Note. Diplomacy based on misinformation and hostile rumor is anything but a joke.

In the aftermath of the note, Lt. Col. John Hathaway informed Washington, the average Irishman's "confidence in the benevolence of the United States towards Eire has been rudely shaken" and "the majority of the thinking people here . . . feel a strong resentment against the head of this mission." Some of the resentment against Gray was the result of an Associated Press story reporting on the private meeting between De-Valera and Gray about the American Note. De-Valera was quoted as saying "this is an ultimatum." The Irish *Press* picked up the story. "The only deduction which ordinary people will make," it said, "is that Mr. Gray told a Press man what purported to have passed at an interview with the head of our Government." Gray, of course, denied doing so, and Hathaway's report attributed the flap to "Mr. DeValera's policy of keeping alive the animosity caused by" the note—and suggested the U. S. cut off Ireland's tea supply as punishment.

A second note was drawn up, answering De-Valera and reiterating the demand, but was not sent—upon Churchill's advice and receipt at State on March 31 of a message, "informally and confi-

dentially," from OSS "that Ireland has now offered its prompt cooperation in adopting whatever security safeguards we and the British desire
in Ireland."

The ironic undercurrent to the affair was that
Ireland had *secretly* been helping all along. On
December 15, 1942, it "informally" notified the
U.S. that from then on all Allied planes that landed
"by mistake or through necessity" on Irish soil,
even if armed, would be returned and their crews
freed. WE ARE ANXIOUS THAT NO REPEAT NO
PUBLICITY ATTEND ANY OF THESE INCI-
DENTS, the Joint Chiefs memo said.

None did until late November 1945, with the
war safely over, an article appeared in the Irish
Times detailing all the aid Ireland had offered to—
and taken from—the Allies. Its author was Randolph Churchill, journalist son of the by-now former British prime minister. The German Embassy
transmitter, it turned out, had been handed over
on Irish demand on Christmas Eve 1943—two
months before the American note—while the British Ambassador to Dublin, Sir John Maffey, "had
three transmitters throughout the war in constant
use." The German air crews who landed on Irish
soil were immediately interned on the grounds
that they had been "engaged on operational flights"
while "the convenient fiction" obtained for Allied
planes that they were "out on training flights."
Nazi agents had been "at once made available to
the British authorities" and Royal Navy torpedo-
boats had been allowed to rescue torpedoed merchant ships using Irish harbors. A December 5,
1945 dispatch by Lt. Col. George Sprague reported how in the Dail there had been questions
about Ireland's secret help to the Allies. "Mr.

DeValera's replies to the questions were as evasive as he dared to make them."

But damage—perhaps irreversible—had been done, symbolized by riots on the night of V-E Day. It began as Trinity College students unfurled the Allied flags to celebrate. An angry crowd in the street jeered them, one student burned the Irish flag in retaliation, and a riot was on through the streets of Dublin that did not end before American Embassy windows had been smashed. As young Churchill wrote in his article, Ireland's secret help "did not arise from any love of Britain, but from DeValera's recognition (that) Ireland's safety was bound up in Britain's." That opinion was undoubtedly based on information supplied by his father who, in the aftermath of the war, had exchanged barbed national radio addresses with DeValera concerning Ireland's neutrality.

The article questioned whether DeValera's neutrality had served Ireland well. "If DeValera had declared war on Germany in 1942 or '43," Churchill wrote, "he might well today be nearer to his goal of a united Ireland."

That was the rub. In fact, Gray had reported back to Washington in 1942 that Britain in 1940 had tried to get Ireland to enter the war and "the consideration offered was the promise of the British Government to use its best efforts to end partition after the war." Gray further reported that the Irish Secretary for External Affairs "told me he had documentary proof" which Gray could see "after the war" and a British Naval Intelligence officer had confirmed the offer's existence. Similar rumors abounded in Ireland after DeValera's death in 1975.

But, whether it was lack of trust in Britain after

1921 or a sense of Ireland's security first, De-Valera—if the offer was really made—was not moved. And when after the war—with Roosevelt dead, Churchill out of power, and his own stringent wartime repression measures having led to his 1947 electoral defeat—DeValera toured the world to plead Ireland's case for reunification, he found the view articulated by an anonymous American official of his wartime conduct had prevailed:

> . . . . I am sure that Mr. DeValera intends to appear at the postwar Peace Conference and basing his claim on the Atlantic Charter will seek the repeal of partition. . . . To counteract this I should advise that . . . an intensive campaign be carried on in the American Press. . . . The object . . . should . . . be the complete disillusionment of certain Irish and Irish-American elements with Ireland's domestic troubles, so that the American delegation could quite truthfully reply to Mr. DeValera that Ireland's problems, because of Eire's neutrality, had ceased to interest anyone in America.

To a large extent—until 1969 at least—they did.

Kevin McAuliffe teaches in the Department of Communications at Fordham University.

Opening Casement

B. L. REID

I was led into the field of Irish biography by years of work as a student and teacher of modern Irish literature. Reading that writing and talking about it had left me fascinated with the phenomenon of Irish genius. How did it happen that the most brilliant work in English during the twentieth century, in all the major forms, was done by Irishmen?—in verse by W. B. Yeats; in fiction by James Joyce and Frank O'Connor; in drama by Oscar Wilde, George Bernard Shaw, John Millington Synge, and Sean O'Casey. Without them English literature in our day would have been a far less distinguished thing, and a great deal duller. But apart from the mystery of genius, I was caught by the flair of personality in these writers and by the color and energy in their subjects: the sense of a life that was cranky and original and bold, a passionateness at once bitter and gay. I felt a flood of humor and suffering, both brilliant and formidable.

The wish to understand this phenomenon, to get at the life behind the life, was what set me in the direction of Irish biography. I turned first to the Irish-American lawyer John Quinn (1870–1924) because he was available to me, a provincial American, and because I had been puzzled for years by his ubiquitousness—the way he seemed to have known and served virtually everybody who was anybody in the major movements in the arts in the first quarter of this century. My long book on Quinn (*The Man from New York: John Quinn and His Friends*, 1968), based largely on his rich correspondence, occupied the free time of several years of teaching, plus a year of research in England, Ireland, and France and the better part of another year in the writing. At the end of it all I felt more at home with the Irish but by no means bored with them.

Moreover the process of looking into Quinn's associates had left me possessed of a list of seductive subjects for biography, Irishmen of importance whose careers deserved and needed further investigation: John Butler Yeats, the father of the poet and of the painter Jack B. Yeats; George Moore the novelist; George William Russell (AE), post, painter, journalist, mystic, and practical man, perhaps the most complex and significant person in the whole modern movement in Ireland; and Roger Casement, certainly the most ambiguous and perhaps the most striking figure in the Easter Rising of 1916. I ruled out George Moore for the time being, doubting that Joseph Hone's book could be improved upon in the present state of the evidence. By the time I was able to anticipate a bit of freedom from academic duties, I had been forestalled by swifter scholars who had already gone to work on J. B. Yeats and on Russell. And so my choice had been narrowed forcibly and quickly to Roger Casement.

I felt a little disgruntled at the way things had turned out; for whereas I had no doubt that Casement was an authentic subject, I did not feel greatly drawn to him personally from what I could see of him as a man. On the other hand there was an attraction in the very fact that one could see so little of him, clearly, as a man, a credible person. I knew enough about him to know that one needed to learn a good deal more. In trying to understand his part in the story of Quinn, for example, I had been frustrated by the general shoddiness of the printed accounts of Casement and his actions. Nearly all the writing about him was vague and unscholarly, sensational on the one hand and sentimental on the other. Contradictory and unclear, it did not compose a figure that one could know and believe. And yet, like W. B. Yeats who heard the ghost of Roger Casement "beating on the door" twenty years after his execution for high treason, one felt haunted by the impression that Casement was a man who mattered profoundly, and not only to the Irish. Handsome, sad, confused, and imposing, he had the look of one of the symptomatic creatures of our whole divided era.

While working on the Quinn biography I had had some correspondence with Casement's two baffled final legatees, brothers who were both former British army officers, nephews of Casement's beloved cousin Gertrude Bannister. As they saw the matter, all they had inherited was the embarrassment of being helplessly linked with Casement's name: they could take no pleasure in being associated with an Irish rebel and a British traitor who was also said to have been a record-keeping homosexual. One of the brothers had managed, however, to work up a general humane curiosity about Casement; I wrote to him to ask the blessing of the heirs upon my proposed biography, and he wrote back cordially. I felt better, supposing that my way was now cleared to the use of certain primary documents in the story, especially Casement's famous Black Diaries, which the English had used to prove him "a man of infamous life," in the words of the Home Secretary in 1916, and which many Irishmen still believed to be forgeries on the order of the famous Piggott forgeries designed to inculpate Charles Stewart Parnell.

The fact that agitation in the House of Commons had recently forced the English government to open the original diaries to scholarly inspection was one of the conditions that made the time right for a full new biography of Casement. I wrote to the Public Record Office in London and received a clearance to study the diaries. By now I had been given a senior fellowship by the National Endowment for the Humanities and I had a year's sabbatical leave forthcoming from Mount Holyoke College, so all the portents looked favorable. The only really ominous sign was the state of affairs in Ulster, where the brutal new Troubles were well under way. I feared the Troubles would hamper me seriously in moving about and talking to people; but I could at least hope for an early peaceful settlement that might smooth my way. In any case I could only seize the day that was available to me.

In the late summer of 1971 my wife and I flew to London and found a flat in South Kensington with an anglicized Irish landlady. I tucked into the daily nine-to-five job of reading the diaries, aiming to study them more carefully and objectively than I suspected they had been studied in the past by persons who had pronounced upon them confidently, *pro* or *con*, as authentic or forged, generally on the evidence of fragmentary transcriptions. The mass of the diaries was considerable and the circumstances of their handling were complex and annoying—an indication of the continuing liveliness of the controversy they still formed between England and Ireland, and another warning of the sensitiveness of the Ulster issue, on which English people in general felt baffled and edgy. The diaries were kept in a locked steel box that was locked into a vault at night and brought out for me every morning. A clerk of the PRO was required to remain in the room with me at all times. All notes had to be taken in pencil and no photocopying was perimtted. When I began collating the manuscript diaries against the Olympia Press *Black Diaries* (1959), I saw that the printed text was littered with errors, and I deduced that it had been made from a faulty copy, probably the hurried Scotland Yard transcript of 1916. And the important 1911 diary of Casement's return to the Amazon was omitted altogether. I spent many days copying that diary out by hand into a notebook of my own, finding little difficulty with Casement's clear handsome script.

The retired military brothers who were Casement's unwilling heirs invited my wife and me down to Kent for a weekend to confer and make acquaintance. We found them very pukka-sahib but cordial and kind. They possessed no papers or information, however, and so I learned little; but they drove us over to Tenterden to meet Montgomery Hyde, who had done a very good book on Casement's trial and who as an Ulster M.P. had been a prime mover in opening the diaries for study—and that made an informative afternoon. In Kent I also heard rumors that Brian Inglis was at work on a biography of Roger Casement. This was daunting news, for Inglis would be a formidable rival. An Anglo-Irishman from Malahide, he had taken a Ph.D. in history at Trinity College, Dublin, and worked on the *Irish Times* before moving on to a distinguished career in London as a historian, a journalist, and a producer of television documentaries.

Back in London there soon came an awkward morning when I crossed paths not only with Brian Inglis but with a bright young playwright from County Armagh, David Rudkin, who was hard at work on a play about Casement for BBC Radio. The three of us were trying to read the same diary at the same time in the same locked room at the PRO. In the Gents' room I had a few quiet words with Inglis about the difficulty of making one life of a man who seemed to have lived several lives concurrently. My heart sank when Inglis told me he was nearing the end of his own manuscript. What could I do but persevere and do my best to write a better book?

I went on with my analysis of the diaries and with the collation of the manuscript and printed diaries, a process that ultimately filled three solid months. It was a strange and in some ways a disenchanting experience. Primarily of course I was seeking information and clues to the character of the man. But I always had to stay alert for evidence on the vexed questions of homosexuality and the suspicion of forgery. When I found no signs of tampering in the form, the style, or the content of the texts, I concluded that the diaries were all of a piece—all original and all Casement's own: his jotted record of concentrated portions (less than three years) of his life in several parts of the world. Accounts of homosexual episodes were plentiful and unmistakable, though many of them seemed to have proceeded no farther than a wistful voyeurism—looking and longing. At first I found this side of the story baffling and repugnant; but after a few weeks I realized that I had somehow worked through to a sympathetic acceptance in which Casement's alternative sexuality seemed still strange but no longer dirty and certainly not contemptible. When I realized that I was not called upon to make a moral judgment of these matters I was able at last to take them in simply as useful biographical data.

What was harder to make peace with was the sheer dullness of the diaries: the range of triviality to which the diarist's interest and patience extended, and the almost total absence of reflection or ideas. I found myself thinking, if this is Casement, why bother? But again what could one do but record as a fact the diaries' intellectual poverty and move on to check the impression against other kinds of evidence?

By early November I was ready to move on to Dublin. We settled first in Buswell's Hotel in Molesworth Street, depressed to see that the fine big rooms we remembered from an earlier visit had been divided in half, tarted up "modern," and doubled in price. I did not yet realize that Buswell's had been a Dublin headquarters for Casement, where he and others had plotted the July 1914 gun running at Howth, and where he, Bulmer Hobson, Eoin MacNeill, and Colonel Maurice Moore had sullenly capitulated to John Redmond's demand that they admit his men to the Executive of the Irish Volunteers. In a day or two we found a flat at the top of a Georgian house in Merrion Square, across the handsome green from where Yeats had lived and where AE had edited the *Irish Homestead*. Our rooms did not face the Square, however, but looked backward over rooftops toward the Customs House and the ships in the Liffey. It was an easy walk to the National Gallery and the National Library where I would be doing most of my work, and our only serious trial was our neighbor at the front of the house: a retired Irish-American banker who talked loudly to imaginary visitors, threw furniture and kitchen utensils about, and suspected my wife and me, as Americans, of being members of the Mafia. He was quite mad but fundamentally harmless.

One of my first actions on reaching Dublin had been to publish a note in the *Irish Times* and in the English *Times Literary Supplement* announcing that I was on the scene, hoping to write a full and objective life of Casement, and asking for information. The results, useful or useless but always interesting, trickled in all during the winter. Two Englishmen wrote to say that Roger Casement's ghost still inhabited the quarters he had occupied at the turn of the century as a British consul at Old Calabar on the west coast of Africa. The apparition, wrote one, was always said to be of "kindly" aspect. The other man wrote that he had seen the ghost himself. My first actual caller was a disciple of the deceased Dublin doctor, Herbert O. Mackey, one of the leaders of the school devoted to proving the purity of Casement's character and so a proponent of the theory of the forgery of the diaries. Dr. Mackey's disciple wanted to make sure that I did not make the mistake of accepting the diaries as evidence of character. But I had seen Mackey's quack scholarship, based largely on the faulty *printed* texts, and I knew it could not be taken seriously as argument or information.

More helpfully, a middle-aged civil servant called to tell me of the friendship between Casement and his father, a doctor on Tawin Island: the two men drawn together by a common interest in the movement to preserve the Irish language and by common concern for the lot of the poor folk of the west coast. He described his father's rage and his indignant protest, years later, on finding Casement's effigy in Madame Tussaud's Chamber of Horrors in London. The Dublin actor Liam Redmond invited me out to his house in Chapelizod on the Liffey, haunt of that heartbreaking man James Duffy of Joyce's story "A Painful Case." I took a bus to the end of the line and walked on in the rain, eventually losing my way amid green fields. When

I asked directions of a countryman tinkering at his motor-
cycle, he loaded me onto his pilion and we dashed back
two miles through the puddles, my briefcase flapping in the
wind. Liam Redmond proved both impressive and charming, and an unexpected bonus of his house was his wife,
who turned out to be the daughter of Thomas MacDonagh,
one of the martyrs of the Rising. She showed me a big
painting by George Russell of two children cowering in
the shelter of a brown rock amid sand dunes. She had
always associated the image, she told me, with the situation
of herself and her brother, both small children at the time
of her father's execution.

Soon I renewed acquaintance with Michael Yeats, son of
the poet and now leader of his party in the Irish Senate, and
with his wife Grainne, an accomplished concert singer and
performer on the Irish harp. Mrs. Yeat's father, P. S.
O'Hegarty, had been a close friend of Bulmer Hobson and
of Casement. The young Dublin sculptress Nuala Creagh,
a distant relation of Casement's who had carved both his
gravestone in Glasnevin Cemetery and his monument on
Banna Strand in County Kerry, asked us to dinner in her
house in Rathfarnham. And I talked at considerable length
with the fine seafaring scholar John deCourcy Ireland who
had done an excellent little book on "The Sea and the
Easter Rising." On his wall hung the framed chart of the
voyage of the U19, the German submarine that had put
Casement ashore in Kerry on Good Friday 1916. Dr. Ireland had become a friend of Raimund Weisbach, commander of the U19, and learned among other things that it
had been Weisbach's hand that fired the torpedoes that
sank the *Lusitania*.

But all these personal encounters took place about the
edges of my fundamental task, the study of the immense
collection in the National Library of letters, journals, and
documents of many kinds having to do with Casement and
his associates. I pored over those all day every day for
nearly five months, and gradually a picture took form that
restored my interest and my faith in my subject. I began to

see a Casement who was no less complex than I had supposed, and perhaps even more profoundly flawed, but a man who possessed grandeur and nobility, if not absolute greatness: a man of powerful vanity, deeply divided in mind and spirit, yet superb in his courage and his generosity, his suicidal loyalty to his ideals of which Irish freedom came first of all.

When I tired of reading and taking notes I would go down and walk the portico of the Library where Stephen Dedalus had dawdled peevishly in the twilight with his university friends and meditated flight to Europe, "a hawk-like man flying sunward above the sea." Or I would watch the parliamentarians hurrying down the court to sessions of the Dail; or cross the court to the National Museum with its great collection of artefacts out of the deep past of Ireland and its 1916 Room filled with pathetic and impressive relics of the Rising including Roger Casement's heavy overcoat of Irish frieze, drenched in the Atlantic surf on that Good Friday dawn.

The life of the ordinary Dubliner seemed to us a bit harried and a considerable struggle to make ends meet, yet superficially peaceful, eerily insulated from the murderousness that was going on in the North. Yet that tension filled the air one breathed in the Republic; and after Bloody Sunday when thirteen men died in Derry the streets of Dublin were black with people marching to protest in front of the British Embassy, a few doors from us in Merrion Square. That night we heard the doors blown in and in the morning the building was a fire-gutted ruin and stood like a blackened tooth in the visage of the beautiful Georgian square. Our feelings were deeply mixed, sad and sorry, for everyone concerned. One understood the Dubliners' rage and frustration, but that lovely house, a legacy of something solid and fine in the Ireland of Swift and Grattan, seemed to have little to do with the case. One could feel no hope that an independant and united Ireland could rise out of this chaos of sectarian jealousies and hatreds.

By March, when my wife was called home by the illness

of our son, I was pretty well finished with my work at the Library and I resolved to spend a final week in a quick tour of the North and the western perimeter of the island down to Kerry, hoping to get into closer touch with places sacred to Casement and with the few surviving persons who had knowledge of him. I invited our County Wicklow friend, the poet Richard Weber who had seen comparatively little of his own island, to go along with me. Relieved by the news that the IRA Provisionals had suddenly declared a 72-hour truce, we took a train to Belfast and alighted in the station that was blown up a week later. In an agency digging out after its second firebombing we rented an Austin Mini and made our way slowly out of the city, being stopped several times by rifle-carrying soldiers who found my friend's big black camera case on the back seat an especially suspicious looking object.

Our first destination was Crawfordsburn in County Down, where lived Mrs. Florence Patterson, the surviving sister of Bulmer Hobson, one of Casement's closest friends. I had had considerable correspondence with her from Dublin, rather guarded on her part until she decided to trust me. We spent an afternoon and evening with Mrs. Patterson, who turned out to be both winning and imposing, a scholarly old lady of more than ninety, perfectly clear intellectually and full of valuable information and recollections. She was able not only to identify but to give character and life to many persons who had been only names to me. From Crawfordsburn we moved slowly north, past Derry looking like a city at war, through the lovely Antrim Glens, Casement's truest spiritual home, and on to Ballycastle on the northeast shoulder of the island, where the impecunious orphan Casement had grown up a maverick among his Loyalist relations. I had been warned that the present powers in the family preferred to pretend that their embarrassing relation had never existed. But I thought I should at least give them a chance to refuse to talk to me, and I wanted to see the coast and the countryside anyway. In due course I received a chilly rebuff and

Richard Weber and I drove on along the northern coast to the Giant's Causeway, then angled southwest back into the Republic and on to the west coast in Donegal.

Both of us had traveled the Yeats country before, and time was short, so we paid only a quick ritual call at the grave of the poet in Drumcliff Churchyard and proceeded south through Sligo, Connemara and Galway. We turned inland to Corofin in the weird stony landscape of the Burren, where Jack Sweeney of Harvard had built a retirement home. Here again I received a surprise bonus: Maire Sweeney turned out to be a daughter of Eoin MacNeill, a leader of the Gaelic League with Douglas Hyde and the bemused and confused head of the Volunteers when the Easter Rising was called without his knowledge. Mrs. Sweeney well remembered Roger Casement as a guest in her father's house in Dublin before the Great War. We turned back to the coast now and on south to Tralee and the Kerry peninsula.

With the help of maps and local guides we found the bleak shingle beach where Casement, the loyal Robert Monteith, and the renegade nonentity Julian Bailey had struggled through the surf to the shore, leaving a wide trail for casual or systematic pursuers, found the deserted monument in the dunes erected after fifty years, and finally McKenna's Rath, the prehistoric earth fort where the exhausted Casement had waited in hiding while his companions trudged into Tralee seeking help, and where he had been arrested by a Dogberry of the Royal Irish Constabulary and carried off to the Tower of London to stand trial for high treason. As I gloomily forced my way through the bramble growth of generations around the perimeter of the earthwork, I found it easy to picture the whole episode, the tragicomic catastrophe of the tragic story that was the life of Roger Casement.

I dropped Richard Weber in County Wicklow, left our rented car in Dublin, cleared out of the flat in Merrion Square, and flew back to London for a final month's work at the Public Record Office. I was concentrating now on

British official documents, chiefly records of Casement's twenty years as a consular officer in Africa and South America, and as photocopying was allowed with these papers, the work went much faster than before. But I failed to broach two crucial files, a secret Home Office dossier on the last stages of Casement's career, and a Scotland Yard file that I hoped would straighten out the story of the search and seizure of his effects, notably the diaries. Both files were classified as Secret, "closed for 100 years," and so unavailable to me in spite of my best pleading. In any case I had a great heap of material and I felt ready to write a life. Yale University Press had given me a contract, and I thought I would call my book "The Strangest Story," for that was the way it had all seemed to me: the strangest true story I had ever come across.

Professor Reid is a member of the Department of English at Mount Holyoke College.

The Fevers of the Great Famine

WILLIAM O'BRIEN, M.D.

The Great Famine of 1845 to 1850 was but the greatest of a succession of famines which had occurred regularly over the previous 150 years in Ireland. Many died but these deaths were mainly the result of pestilence which accompanied the famine. It has been estimated that ten times the number of people died from "fever" than perished from starvation. Though dysentery, smallpox, severe measles and typhoid contributed, the two principal causes of death were louse-borne typhus and louse-borne relapsing fever. Cholera, which had affected Ireland during the pandemics of 1817 and 1832 and was to do so again in 1848, was not, as is sometimes stated, one of the fevers of the Great Famine.

During the first half of the 19th century the economic state of the Irish poor, a majority of the population, was appalling. The population had almost tripled between 1778 and 1841. The mass of the peasantry rented, often on an annual basis, miserably small plots of land and lived in windowless, chimneyless, single-room mud huts. Furniture was a luxury. Nor was the condition of the poor in towns any better. The cabins of Tralee "down noisome lanes" consisted of two compartments separated by a wooden partition. One compartment without a window was barely large enough to contain a bed on which three or four people slept. The "filth and smell of these bedrooms was such that it needed considerable fortitude to enter."

Often the only sustenance available came from the potato. Unless an Irish laborer could get hold of a patch of land on which to feed himself and his children, the family starved. The potato provided an abundant supply of cheap and nutritious food which compared favorably with the English laborer's diet of bread and cheese. It was produced at a trifling cost from a small plot of land and only a spade was needed.

There were however disadvantages to relying on potatoes as the sole source of food. They could not be stored from one season to another and thus were in short supply during the summer months when the old potatoes had been eaten and the new crop had not yet come in. As a result, a summer ritual developed. Many families would sow their potatoes, shut up their huts, and roam the country looking for work, trusting to the known hospitality of the towns and villages for shelter and subsistence, until the time for digging their potatoes arrived. Thousands of laborers came annually from Connaught to the neighborhood of Dublin, from Clare to Kilkenny, from Kenmare to Cork and from Derry to Antrim in quest of harvest and other work. "The stranger found every man's door open and would walk in without ceremony at meal times, and to partake of the bowl of potatoes was always sure to give pleasure to everyone in the house, so that even those who begged elsewhere were desirous to exercise hospitality in their own homes."

Another and even more serious disadvantage

was that the potato crop failed at fairly regular intervals. Dominic Corrigan one of the greatest Irish physician/statesman of the period, described the result:

> If the crop was unproductive the earnings of the laboring classes were insufficient to purchase alternative food. Corn was altogether outside their reach so they must starve amidst abundance. The potato was the curse of our country. It had reduced the wages of laborers to the very smallest pittance and, when a bad crop occurred, there was no descent for them in the scale of food and the next step was starvation.

In 1845 came the worst of these failures when the fungus *Phytophthora infestans,* accidentally imported from America, devastated the potato crops of 1845, 1846 and 1847. The distress was overwhelming and there was widespread starvation.

The miserable housing and living conditions of the poor in Ireland at that time have already been referred to and it is not surprising that many were infested with lice. As one medical historian commented, those exhausted by hunger and struggling to keep body and soul together were not likely to trouble greatly about personal cleanliness even if they had the strength to fetch water and a fire to heat it. Such of their clothing that had any market value they sold to passing peddlers; the rags that were left they wore night and day, huddled together for warmth.

Louse-borne typhus fever is an infection with an organism intermediate between a bacterium and a virus which circulates in the blood during the 14 day fever. When a louse takes a blood feed from an infected person, the organisms multiply in the louse gut and are passed in its feces. Lice thrive at the normal body temperature and when this changes as in fever or death, they actively seek a new host. The infected feces are deposited on the skin, which the organisms can penetrate, and thus the infection is spread. Alternatively infection may be spread through inhalation of dried lice feces. Epidemics of louse-born typhus depend upon three conditions: a source of infection; a population infested with lice; and susceptible recipients.

Typhus was endemic in the depressed and congested parts of Ireland, and every doctor in the country was familiar with "the fever natural to the climate." Between epidemics the fever was never extinguished but "lay deceitfully buried under its embers, only to blaze out again with a volume proportional to the fuel which its concurring causes afforded." Robert Graves, the renowned Dublin physician, stated that at no period from the earliest records had it been entirely absent, and occasionally from one year to one season, or succession of years or seasons, it would become epidemic. Typhus is a mild disease in childhood and in endemic areas people suffered less severely probably because they had developed some degree of immunity from a mild or even unrecognized attack in childhood. It is now known that following an attack of typhus, the organism may lie dormant in the tissues for at least 20 years before re-emerging to cause Brill Zinsser's disease, a source of infection to others.

Immunity to many infections is greatly impaired by gross malnutrition such as the famine brought. Even those partially protected by previous exposure or harboring organisms in a dormant form, may well have become susceptible to

296

a new attack. Even more important was the great extension of the traditional habit of migration. Crowds of starving and lice-ridden people forsook their homes and took to the roads, carrying disease wherever they went. Families with children on their backs affected with fever, and roving beggars sleeping every night in a different house, swarmed into the poorer parts of the towns and villages so that the householders of the suburbs soon became infected and the disease was propagated "in a most frightful manner." Soup kitchens, relief depots and workhouses might help to relieve hunger but were disastrous sources of infection. Convalescents were particularly dangerous and the route of a tinker from Donegal to Sligo, who had just recovered from typhus, was clearly marked by an outbreak of fever ten to fourteen days after his visit in each house in which he had slept. Another mode of propagation was through attendance at wakes where, for two nights and two days during which the corpse lay unburied, there would be twenty to thirty persons from a radius of five miles present in the cabin.

It was fortunate that at this time Dublin held such physicians as Graves, Stokes and Corrigan. It was Corrigan who gave a classic description of the disease. In the days before microscopy was generally available, he was able through clinical observation to deduce correctly the basic pathological lesion as an inflammation of the smallest blood vessels. "In observing the several signs of capillary abnormality we are not seeing a mere local derangement, for the signs are indicative of the state of the circulatory system as a whole." In a series of lectures he described the clinical features of severe typhus as seen at the Hardwicke Hospital. The fever rose rapidly and remained high for 14–17 days. Patients were prostrate from the start, with headache and intolerance of light or noise. Bleeding from the nose was common and relieved the headache but did not abate the fever. The face was congested, the eyes suffused, and the expression a mixture of anxiety and a certain characteristic dullness. The tongue was dry and covered with a heavy brown coat, and the teeth were covered with sordes. The breath was offensive and there was a pungent mousy smell of the skin. Cough was nearly constant and though most patients were constipated there were no other abdominal disorders. On the fifth day a characteristic rash appeared and this was accompanied by an intensification of all symptoms. Patients lay helplessly on their backs, headache became intense, and a low delerium often supervened. Insomnia was a special feature and some did not sleep for a week. Some patients lapsed into stupor or coma; others, especially the more robust, would develop a state of great agitation with furious delerium and even outright raving, so that they might require physical restraint.

If patients survived until the fourteenth day there was often a sudden improvement though this was sometimes preceded by an aggravation of symptoms. Thus a maniacal patient would suddenly fall into a deep sleep which might last for days and was clearly differentiated from coma by the fact that now, for the first time, the patient was lying on his side. The change was very sudden and Corrigan had learnt never to abandon a case however severe it might seem as long as there was life. One day a patient might appear moribund and yet within 24 hours he was out of danger.

Medical practitioners outside hospitals saw a much milder form of typhus, especially in areas where typhus had been endemic. On the other hand the mortality was very high indeed amongst the better off in whom it varied between 33 and 70 per cent. The mortality rate increased with age while children of all classes generally recovered.

A description of typhus in Ireland would be incomplete without referring to the conditions under which so many suffered. They lay in horribly overcrowded workhouse hospitals, often on the floor or in their dark miserable cabins where a whole family might be stricken, lying side by side on a single bed, the dead remaining for days beside the languishing survivors who were too weak to move them. Yet others were consigned to the so-called fever huts, crude shelters erected on the sides of the roads, fields, or ditches. There on a bundle of straw, without medicine or even water and with scarcely any protection from the weather, the helpless victims lay unattended and "consigned themselves to the mercy of God and the sympathy of man."

The typhus organism alone would have been devastating enough, but the lice carried another menace to the poor. Louse-borne relapsing fever, first recognized by Hippocrates, had been redescribed in 1741 by Rutty from Dublin. Though the organism, a spirochaete, differs from that of typhus, its mode of transmission and the conditions under which it flourishes are so similar to those of typhus that they commonly occur together. Both diseases occur in a relatively mild endemic form but war, famine, poverty and overcrowding are all liable to result in epidemics in which the disease is severe and often fatal.

Especially at the start of the illness, the clinical features were very similar to those of typhus so it was not surprising that it was often mistaken for that infection. Without specific means of treatment doctors in those days were not particularly interested in labelling disease. In fact many felt that "the methodical division of fever into species and varieties had been a serious evil in medicine especially when it was made the foundation of distinct modes of treatment. It was a dangerous practice to treat fevers according to their names which were and ever would be arbitrary." Nevertheless, many practitioners during the famine did make the distinction and the fevers were often divided into those which mainly affected the head (typhus) and those mainly affecting the liver (relapsing fever).

Some fevers, in contrast to the 14 day fever, terminated on the fifth to the seventh day with profuse sweating and in these the tendency to relapse was remarkable. The earlier the crisis, the more liable was the patient to relapse and this type of fever was confined to the poor. At some periods in the epidemic relapses became so frequent that they occurred in almost every case. Other distinguishing features included a great irritability of the stomach which rejected everything, constant thirst, most severe and disabling pains in all the muscles, and jaundice. A fatal complication was suppression of urine.

The crisis was often preceded by a rigor and always occurred between the third and seventh day of the fever, usually between the fifth and seventh days. It was sudden, the patient fell into a most profuse perspiration and it was accompanied by alarming symptoms. Some patients died unexpectedly following it. Patients might relapse two or three times but usually only once, and in these relapses inflammation of the iris occasionally occurred. These features are so typical of relapsing fever that there cannot be the slightest doubt concerning the diagnosis.

When it came to measures to control these epidemics, there was unfortunately little agreement in high places. Corrigan proclaimed "no famine, no fever" and though in this he was largely correct, his insistence on a single "grand cause" was to have disastrous consequences. He considered that time and money spent on containing contagion was wasted and did not believe that the traveling mendicant was a disseminator of the fever. For this attitude he was fiercely attacked by Graves, who believed that the rapid spread and unusual mortality of the fever of 1847 must be ascribed to the prominence which from the first was given to famine as the exciting cause.

> The text put forward so authoritatively "if there is no famine, there will be no fever" prevented proper attention being paid to the real causes which produced and promoted spread of epidemic diseases. The Irish epidemic had its origin in the congregating together of large masses of people at public works, the overcrowded workhouses and relief depots. Eagerness of impulse to apply relief continued with total disregard of mode, and pestilence had followed the footsteps of benevolence and death wakened no suspicion of error. These measures were agencies of slaughter.

It was unfortunate that the report of Barker and Cheyne following the 1818 epidemic had not been given more careful consideration, for they presented a more balanced view. They held that there was no doubt that famine was the original prime cause. Epidemics had occurred in Ireland from time to time and each had followed a failure of the usual source of food. This seemed to have been forgotten and steps should be taken to avoid another catastrophe of the same nature.

Even though fever arose from the many and great needs of the poor, it was maintained by contagion operating on subjects predisposed to hunger and not protected by habits of cleanliness. Those who argued against the contagious nature of typhus were entirely mistaken and were a danger to society. The spread of the epidemic was to a large extent due to movement of infected people from their homes, and their congregation together in masses. Barker and Cheyne also recognized that clothes and bedding were vehicles of infection. Once there was evidence of spread of fever there was much that could be done to contain it.

The measures they advocated were little different from those used today to contain epidemics of these two diseases. Local temporary fever hospitals where the sick could be separated from their families should be established immediately. Clothing and bedding should either be disinfected by exposure to the heat of stoves or destroyed by burning; houses should be purified by cleansing, whitewashing and ventilation; wakes should be prohibited. Relief efforts should concentrate on providing sufficient quantities of nutritious food to homes and villages, thus avoiding the migration to other towns. Such measures if put into operation might well have saved many thousands of lives.

Typhus and relapsing fever are now mainly confined to the tropics. It is often not realized that tropical medicine deals not so much with a number of rather exotic diseases, but is largely concerned with the diseases of poverty and deprivation. Famines are still with us and in their wake stalk louse-borne typhus and louse-born relapsing fever. We may rightly criticize the administration of 19th century Ireland, but perhaps it might be more profitable to examine our own consciences as to what practical aid we ourselves are giving out of our plenty to people in precisely the same plight today.

Dr. William O'Brien is Senior Lecturer in the Department of International Health at the Royal College of Surgeons in Ireland.

Dominic Corrigan and the Great Famine

EOIN O'BRIEN, M.D.

In the autumn of 1845 the Irish peasant was performing the most important task of the year. From his small patch of land he was digging the potato crop that had been planted in the spring. The "Lumpers" as the commonest variety of potato was called would normally provide enough food for him and his family for the next year, and monotonous though the diet might be, it was nutritionally adequate. He could not afford to plant other crops such as corn, and only a small number of enterprising communities had learned to fish the plentiful waters of their land.

In this autumn of 1845 there were some who viewed with trepidation the increasing dependence of the populace on the potato for nourishment. From England had come news of a new and devastating blight that had spread from the Isle of Wight to Kent. Dominic Corrigan, a Dublin doctor, was convinced that if this blight spread to Ireland the results would be catastrophic. He had more reason than most to fear the consequences. As physician to the Sick-poor Institution in Meath Street, he had experienced the terrible misery of the great epidemic fever of 1826, and had warned the authorities then that sooner or later there would occur an even greater pestilence if the people were not provided with an alternative food to the potato. His counsel went largely unnoticed, and little was done to make the peasant less dependent on the potato.

As reports of blight in the Irish potato crop began to reach Dublin in 1846, Corrigan published a pamphlet directed towards the authorities and the wealthy minority of Irish society. Aware that he might be labeled an alarmist, he nonetheless made no apology for anticipating "how helpless on occasions of great panic is the public mind." By analyzing the epidemics of the previous century Corrigan demonstrated that important though contagion, poor sanitation, poverty, and climate were in propagating epidemics of fever, there was one outstanding feature common to all epidemics—famine. Furthermore, he wrote, the commonest cause of famine in Ireland had been failure of the potato crop.

> The people of Ireland are peculiarly liable to become the victims of such a pestilence. The effect of competition among a superabundant unemployed population has been to reduce their wages to the lowest sum on which life can be supported. Potatoes have hence become their staple food. If this crop be unproductive, the earnings of the labouring classes are then quite insufficient to purchase the necessary quantity of any other food. . . . The potato has, I believe, been a curse to our country. . . . When a bad crop occurs there is no descent for them in the scale of food: the next step is starvation.

He deplored the fact that corn was abundant but out of reach of the poor: "they STARVE in the midst of plenty, as literally as if dungeon bars separated them from a grainary. When distress has been at its height, and our poor have been

305

dying of starvation in our streets, our corn has been going to a foreign market. It is, to our own poor, a forbidden fruit." He urged the political economists to study Ireland's needs so that future epidemics might be prevented. The remedy, he claimed, was "to be found, not in medicine, but in employment, not in the lancet, but in FOOD, not in raising lazarettos for the reception of the sick, but in establishing manufactories for the employment of the healthy."

He quoted descriptions from previous famines in an attempt to motivate the charitable instincts of his readers.

> On the road leading from Cork, within a mile of the town, (Kanturk) I visited a woman labouring under typhus: on her left lay a child very ill, at the foot of the bed another child just able to crawl about, and on her right the corpse of a third child who had died two days previously, which the unhappy mother could not get removed.

The mortality from the epidemic fever was often startling but a statistic did not give any real impression of the terrible suffering that was endured by the survivors. To many, Corrigan declared, death would have been a happy release, and he warned that "the offspring will inherit for generations to come, the weakness of body and apathy of mind, which famine and fever engendered."

Corrigan was too astute a judge of human nature to rely solely on a humanitarian appeal to "those who are placed in power, and who possess wealth." Drawing on the statistics from previous epidemics he commented on the surprising fact that fever affected the wealthy far less often than the poor, but that when it did so the mortality among the rich was ten times higher. "It seems, therefore," he wrote, "that while the rich possess constitution and means which enable them to resist the ordinary contagion of fever, the seizure, when it does come, is in itself demonstrative of a greater amount of virulence."

He was critical of the recent Poor Law Act which allowed for the conversion of workhouses into fever hospitals in times of emergency.

> Sickness should not be made a chain to drag a man into a poor house. An hospital should be an institution provided for the decent, the honest, the industrious, who may be suffering from temporary sickness, or accident, to enable them to obtain what is only thus within their reach; the highest professional aid, to restore them as soon as possible to their former station in society, and should never be permitted to be made the medium of degrading its inmate to the level of a pauper.

Hospitals were necessary in epidemics but more important Corrigan believed, was the provision of food to the populace. He advocated a simple method of dispensary relief. As physician to the Sick-poor Institution in Meath Street he had seen the charitable ladies of the city provide both food and medicine to the sick poor. Medical attendants were provided with tickets which they could give to their patients who were then entitled to "so many pints of whey, gruel or broth, as may be ordered, each pint of gruel being accompanied with half a pound of bread, and each quart of broth with one-fourth of a pound cut up in it." Corrigan saw this as "the most perfect and most economical system of out-door relief for the sick poor that could be devised, and would moreover form the most grateful link of union between rich and poor, the link of active charity."

He ends his pamphlet with a plea. "If there be no famine, there will be no fever—and if active and timely exertion be made to afford sufficient employment and wages to our people, I believe there will be neither FAMINE nor FEVER."

How much this pamphlet influenced Government policy is difficult to ascertain. Corrigan's warnings were at least noted, and the Government in anticipation of an epidemic passed the Temporary Fever Act in 1846, which empowered the Lord Lieutenant to appoint commissioners of health to constitute a Central Board of Health. This Board was empowered to establish temporary fever hospitals, to provide medical assistance and to appoint extra medical officers. The Prime Minister, Sir Robert Peel, ratified the appointments of Dr. Dominic Corrigan; Sir Philip Crampton, the Surgeon-General and President of the Royal College of Surgeons; Professor Robert Kane, a distinguished chemist who had studied the potato blight; and Mr. Twistelton, the resident Poor Law Commissioner.

Corrigan was now in a position to effect the reforms which he had so ably stated in his publications, and yet the Board seems to have run into trouble from its earliest moments. To begin with, it completely underestimated the risk of an epidemic, a surprising miscalculation in view of Corrigan's conviction that a major famine must lead inevitably to an epidemic. The Board noted that the fever admissions of 1840 were very much higher than those of 1846 and concluded that because no serious devastation had followed in

1840, there was no need for alarm. The Board's greatest error was in assuming that the next year's potato crop would be normal, as indeed had been the case in previous blights. In fact, the Board seemed in agreement that many circumstances favoured a major epidemic, but surprisingly it assured the government that such would not occur.

By 1847 this optimism proved ill-founded. One and a half million acres of potato had been lost in the blight. Epidemics of the louse-borne typhus and relapsing fevers swept through a starving nation. The populace was prostrated and the next year's crop of potato was not planted. By the end of the decade somewhere around 1½ million perished through starvation and fever, and a million emigrated of which nearly 700,000 went to America. The Great Famine, as it was to be called, and its epidemic fevers, were to bring about the largest population movement of the nineteenth century.

Once the Board of Health appreciated its error in underestimating the danger it did set about establishing temporary fever hospitals throughout the country and appointing extra medical officers. Corrigan became in effect the Board of Health, attending twice as many meetings as any other member and working very long hours. However much his efforts were appreciated by the government (he was later to be created a Baronet of the Empire) the medical profession had never been happy with the Board's constitution as the government had not consulted with the Royal Colleges.

The Royal College of Surgeons was still smarting from a public correspondence it had had some years earlier with Dominic Corrigan on the Medical Charities Bill in which the Lord Lieutenant had supported Corrigan. When the Board announced that the Treasury would pay Medical Officers five shillings a day in addition to any permanent salary for attendance at fever hospitals the profession was furious at what it considered a derisory fee. Their wrath was understandable particularly as many doctors were themselves dying in the epidemic. William Wilde (father of Oscar), editor of the *Dublin Quarterly Journal of Medical Science*, promoted a public meeting at which 1160 practitioners signed a memorial to the Lord Lieutenant. The press overwhelmingly took the side of the profession and the government hid behind the Board of Health.

It was not long before Corrigan was singled out to take the brunt of public and professional opprobrium. The *Nation* excoriated Corrigan pointing out that only a year earlier he had protested against fever hospitals being built in proximity to poor houses.

> He had not, as yet, felt the pulse of an Excellency. However, since he has done so a new light has burst on him and closed his mouth. In every part of Ireland for the last six months, fever hospitals have been erected in connection with—generally speaking, on the ground with—the poor houses; and every frightful consequence predicted by Dr. Corrigan has occurred. . . . Put the man in office himself, change his point of view, immerse his head in a cocked-hat. . . . and he becomes a partner in the insulting offer to the members of his own profession, of five shillings a day as state payment, for constant fever practice, in sinks of contagion whose destructive atmosphere no man knows better than he.

The Board had become the scapegoat for a nation in the throes of an appalling catastrophe, and Corrigan's name was the one most associated with the Board. He was in an invidious situation. On the one hand he was doing all he could to see that the Board's role of providing adequate facilities was achieved, while on the other he was up against an obdurate government which did not wish to put its hand into its pocket for the Irish poor, and when it did so it only threw out a few coppers. Did the profession or the public seriously believe that Corrigan and the other medical members of the Board had not pressed the treasury as far as possible for remuneration for the services of their medical officers? There were in fact a few doctors who considered five shillings a day quite adequate when compared to previous awards.

But the most vitriolic personal attack of all on Corrigan was to come from his senior colleague Robert Graves of the Meath Hospital. To appreciate fully the significance of Graves's censure it is necessary to remind ourselves that he was one of the most respected figures in Dublin medicine. Kings' Professor of the Institutes of Medicine, author of the celebrated and much translated *Clinical Lectures,* and past-president of the Kings and Queen's College of Physicians he was renowned internationally by the eponym "Graves's Disease" for his account of exopthalmic goitre. He was, moreover, held in high regard as a man of personal integrity and a doctor whose devotion to his patients was absolute.

In a thirty-page letter to the *Dublin Quarterly Journal of Medical Science* Graves expressed his indignation at the way in which the government had constituted the Board without consultation with the profession, and in particular he resented the fact that for many weeks when Corrigan was the only active member of the Board, neither of the Royal Colleges were represented. He accused Corrigan of seeking personal aggrandizement through his involvement with the Board. "But Dr. Corrigan may be excused from becoming a little giddy when he ventures into the same car with Sir Philip, and, to the amazement of all, suddenly finds himself at an altitude so elevated, that his companion, although a veteran aeronaut, betrays distinct evidence of alarm." Many of the points raised by Graves were valid, but his personal rejoinders on Corrigan were unkind, excessive and bearing in mind the difficulties under which Corrigan was labouring to make the Board function at all, the attack was misdirected, and should have concentrated more on the other members and on the government.

Corrigan chose to remain silent, and resisted suggestions from the journals and the press that he should resign from the Board. He continued to work toward the relief of fever, and with a cholera epidemic following immediately on the great famine there was plenty for him to do. He would have done well to let the storm clouds pass but unwisely chose this time to seek election to Honorary Fellowship of the Kings and Queen's College of Physicians in Ireland, and was ignominiously black-beaned by his colleagues. The government watched in silence, and showed its appreciation of Corrigan's untiring work by appointing him Physician-in-Ordinary to Queen Victoria in Ireland, a decoration never before given to a Catholic.

Let us close this sorry chapter in Irish history by looking more closely at the enigmatic *persona dramatis* of this piece—Dominic Corrigan. Born in 1802 in his father's hardware shop in Thomas Street, he was brought up in a middle-class Catholic home, and sent for schooling to the Catholic Lay College at Maynooth. He studied medicine initially in Dublin, and later at Edinburgh where he graduated in 1825. Returning to Dublin he practiced among the sick-poor of the City and was Medical Assistant in the parish of St. Catherine.

Corrigan was determined to overcome the obstacles that lay in the way of a Catholic achieving a staff appointment to a Dublin hospital. He equipped a small laboratory in his rooms in Upper Ormond Quay in which he studied the physiology of the heart and circulation in animals, and he observed and recorded carefully the manifestations of heart disease in his poor patients. A series of brilliant papers in the medical journals assured him an appointment as physician to the Charitable Infirmary, the oldest voluntary hospital in the United Kingdom. Here with only a few beds at his disposal he published a paper on incompetence of the aortic valve of the heart and achieved for himself eponymous immortality; the disease is still known as "Corrigan's Disease" and its peculiar pulse as "Corrigan's Pulse." It was not the only disease to be named after him; a fibrosing condition of the lungs was for many years known as "Maladie de Corrigan." In 1840 he was appointed physician to the House of Industry Hospitals, better known today as The Richmond or St. Laurence's Hospital.

He published frequently on medical advances

and was renowned as a teacher and lecturer. Always interested in education both general and medical he was a member of the General Medical Council and of the Senate of the Queens University of which he became Vice-Chancellor in 1871. As we have seen he was black-beaned from the College of Physicians when he sought honorary fellowship, but he then sat humbly for the Licentiate examination of the College after which he was eligible for full fellowship. He then went on to become President on five successive occasions, a feat not since equalled. Furthermore, during his presidency he instigated and saw to completion that which the College had lacked for the previous two hundred years of its existence—the college hall at Kildare Street. In 1866 at the age of 60 the government in recognition for public services created him Baronet of the Empire. For most men this would have seemed a fitting climax to a remarkable career as doctor and humanitarian, but Sir Dominic Corrigan remembered the difficulties he had had to overcome and in 1870 he sought election to Westminster and was returned in the Liberal cause for the City of Dublin.

Corrigan's parliamentary career was to last less than four years and in this time he tried to temper Britain's reaction to disturbances in Ireland and was probably successful on a few occasions in pouring oil on troubled waters. His reputation with the Catholics of Ireland reached its zenith at this time, but he was viewed with some apprehension by the Protestant stock.

> For the people of Ireland he had a character of which, perhaps, he was not himself altogether conscious. They regarded his career with peculiar interest, and

314

his success with gratified pride; because they saw in him evidence of a Catholic rising against all opposition to the highest position possible for him to acquire. This feeling was nowise sectarian, it was rather racial and national; they felt that intellectual triumph was their best and noblest vindication against the contumely which had fallen on them, in consequence of the ignorance enforced upon the nation by the penal laws.

Indeed Corrigan was very aware of the disability under which Catholics laboured by virtue of not having adequate educational facilities and was a staunch supporter of equal rights in education. When the University Education (Ireland) Bill came before the House he made his position quite clear. "The State," he said, "should be equally impartial to all denominations, giving equal aid to all—to those who desire to have denominational education and to those who do not." While supporting certain aspects of the Bill he was vehemently opposed to the proposal that the Lord Lieutenant of Ireland should be Chancellor of the University. "I consider it an indignity little short of .insult to do it," he told Parliament, "and that, if done, it will destroy the independence of science; and the Conviction will be that the only way to University distinctions and emoluments under such Chancellorship, will be up the back stairs of the Castle." The Castle, of course, was the seat of officialdom in Victorian Dublin. He deplored the method of educational endowment whereby "Trinity College is left in possession of at least £50,000 a year wrung by oppression and confiscation from the Catholics; while Royal and endowed schools are scattered through the length and breadth of the land all devoted exclusively to

Protestants, Catholic Colleges and Catholic Schools derive nothing from the State." He begged Parliament to give the Catholic a fair chance, and if he could not avail of it, he then had only himself to blame.

> Let them have a fair start in this educational competition. If they then fail in the competition for degrees, emoluments, and honour, they will not be able to say that they have not had fair play; but if they fail under the proposed Bill, which leaves thousands on thousands with Protestant and Presbyterian Colleges, and gives nothing to them, they will attribute their failure to injustice; and every rejection of a Catholic candidate that will occur will be a never failing repetition of heart-burning, sectarian discord, and disaffection in Ireland.

Corrigan had pleaded his case strongly and sincerely. Like Daniel O'Connell with whom he had been acquainted he believed that Parliament could be persuaded by reasoned rhetoric. However well his performance may have appeared to Catholic Ireland, there were many to whom "his strictures gave deep offence." He decided not to contest his seat in the election of 1874 and retired to his seaside home at Coliemore in Dalkey. He died on February 1st, one hundred years ago, in his 79th year.

Dr. O'Brien is a physician at The Charitable Infirmary, Jervis Street, Dublin.

Ireland's First Ambassador to the United States

HARRY O'FLANAGAN, M.D.

Ireland's birth as a free nation was hardly smooth, and remarkable men were required to guide a divided land and a troubled people through the first decades. The complex history of the Easter Rising in 1916, the Home Rule struggle, the period of Black and Tan guerrilla warfare, the civil war between Free State and Republican forces, and the efforts to win popular support in the United States for an independent Ireland have been detailed in previous volumes of *The Recorder*. Even those remotely familiar with Irish history know of Eamon DeValera and Michael Collins, Pearse and Connolly, Childers and Cosgrave, and a long list of other men and women who contributed to the making of modern Ireland. Without American support, however, the struggle for Irish freedom could not have succeeded, and, in this context, it is of a gentle, self-effacing scholar who served as Ireland's first representative to the United States that I write.

Timothy Smiddy was born in Cork in 1875 and received his education at the Queens College in that city. When University College Cork was founded in 1912, Smiddy was appointed Professor of Economics and Dean of the Faculty of Commerce. He later served as Economic Advisor to Michael Collins during the treaty negotiations in London in 1921. This treaty established the Irish Free State as part of the British Commonwealth; the Dominions, however, were not permitted to accredit envoys or ambassadors to other nations.

To skirt this restriction and to promote Ireland's interests in the United States, Smiddy was sent by the Irish Parliament, the Dail Eireann, as Economic Envoy and Fiscal Agent to Washington. Although there was no formal recognition of his position as Ambassador, Smiddy proceeded around the United States explaining Ireland, her problems and potential, to political leaders, university audiences, and those committed to a better Ireland.

In the files of James McGurrin, long-time President-General of our Society is a description of the difficult path Smiddy had to tread in those early years: "Smiddy's achievements were many but to my mind the most notable is that he took over the diplomatic office in 1922 when it was a bone of contention between two Irish parties in this country and when our prestige amongst the ordinary Americans had fallen low owing to internecine strife; he held on in the most difficult circumstances."

Professor Smiddy's equanimity and persuasion prevailed. On October 7, 1924, Smiddy was received by President Coolidge as Minister Plenipotentiary of Ireland. The United States was the first sovereign country to accept a diplomatic representative from a Commonwealth country. Not only from the Irish point of view but also from the Commonwealth's, this was a major breakthrough. Smiddy's acceptance by the Americans represented the culmination of a struggle which the Irish and the Canadians had been carrying on for separate diplomatic recognition of the individual members of the Commonwealth. The accomplishment had a very great significance in world history and Smiddy was one of those most responsible for it.

The new Ambassador continued to teach America about Ireland, concentrating on economic development. He travelled widely, speaking to University gatherings, civic receptions and a multitudinous number of clubs. He avoided

318

alluding to individuals, speaking collectively of Ireland and the people of Ireland. Reading his speeches, one notes that his approach was always positive, optimistic, and free from any taint of bitterness despite the constant personal attacks he endured from die-hard Republicans.

He stressed the new independence of Ireland within the Commonwealth. He extended the hope that a prosperous Free State would attract the North into a voluntary union. When dealing with the 1921 treaty, he always stressed that the Free State retained the hope of the ultimate re-union of Ireland under one government. He pointed out that Ireland supported the League of Nations and desired to play a full part in its work for peace. Regularly he reported the economic progress being made by the young state in terms of its expanding agriculture, its growing industries, its introduction of the City Manager system, and that great act of faith, the harnessing of the River Shannon for hydro-electric power. He spoke often of the lack of religious bigotry in the South. How timely so many of his speeches are today!

As a university teacher, Smiddy had acquired an unflappable presence and a unique manner of delivery that served him well as he travelled the lecture circuit of America. A colleague in Cork recalled: "Smiddy invested his subject with an air of mystery. He scarcely ever made a humourous remark although there were situations when humour would be used to cover up some obscure parts of a subject. He rarely lectured without a gown, firmly believing in Belloc's dictum that a man never teaches so well as when dressed up in a teaching fashion. His ordinary dress was so varied and artistic as to constitute a distraction to some."

Smiddy remained as Ambassador in Washington until 1929, having cemented firmly a diplomatic relationship between the new Ireland and America. A local newspaper article about his departure captured some of the qualities that had been missed by many: "The Professor is a great favorite in administrative circles in Washington and his urbanity of manner and intellectual attainments have won him a host of friends.

He represents a side of Irish life with which the people of the United States have scarce been familiar. He is broad-minded and conservative in outlook, and his sympathies have been very pronounced on the side of law and order. No better representative could have been secured than Timothy Smiddy —a scholar and economic expert, a calm, patient, persistent man, with no ambition for personal glorification. He avoided pitfalls of every kind, conciliated all shades of public opinion and made possible the successful visit of President Cosgrave to the United States. To the irreconciliables who envisaged England solely as the enemy of Ireland, Mr. Smiddy brought home the economic fact that 96 percent of the exports of the Free State found their only possible outlet in the London market.

"The hard social grind that goes with a diplomatic position at Washington has not been without its effect upon the retiring minister. He appears less scholastic, more the man of the world. Probably he has had more to overcome than any other ambassador, and has really accomplished more for his country."

Amongst the many posts subsequently held by Smiddy in a long career of public service were High Commissioner to England; Member of the Tariff Commission; Economic Adviser to Mr. DeValera; Director of the Central Bank; Chairman of the Agricultural Commission; and Chairman and later Managing Director of Arklow Pottery.

In the summer of 1952, Smiddy received the honorary degree of Doctor of Economic Science from his alma mater, University College Cork.

He died a decade later.

Historically, Smiddy was one of the critical figures in American-Irish relations, his name and contributions, unfortunately, being too little known because of his innate modesty and professional sense of diplomacy.

Doctor O'Flanagan is the Dean and Registrar of the Royal College of Surgeons in Ireland.

AMERICA'S *Lonely Stance:*

Irish Independence, 1916 - 1921

JOSEPH P. PARKES, S. J.

In 1909 the Jesuits of the United States and Canada launched an ambitious project: the publication of a weekly magazine that would, as the lead editorial of the first issue proclaimed, strive "to broaden the scope of Catholic journalism and enable it to exert a wholesome influence on public opinion, and thus become a bond of union among Catholics and a factor in civic and social life." The new periodical nearly foundered during its first few years of existence, as the financial and personnel problems faced by any such new undertaking did not escape the pioneering Jesuit Fathers. But with the appointment of Fr. Richard H. Tierney, S. J., as Editor-in-Chief in May, 1914, AMERICA soon became a lively, influential and controversial review.

Richard Tierney was born in New York on September 2, 1870. His father's ancestors were from Tipperary and his mother, Bridget Shea, hailed from County Clare. The Tierneys lived in the Spuyten Duyvil section of the city. Mr. Tierney, the superintendent at Johnson's Iron Foundry, was active in parish missions in the area that were served first by Jesuits from Fordham, and later by the newly-founded parish of St. Elizabeth's in Fort Washington. Richard attended St. Francis Xavier College on Sixteenth Street, and entered the Jesuits after graduation in 1892. Upon completion of the long period of Jesuit training, Fr. Tierney taught philosophy to Jesuit students at Woodstock College in Maryland from 1909 until he joined the staff of AMERICA in early 1914.

Fr. Tierney can best be characterized as a crusading editor who wielded a scathing pen and seemed to thrive on controversy, especially when championing the justice of Catholic causes and attacking anti-Catholic prejudice. Tierney sought to make AMERICA's readers more aware of international issues, and the burning issue of Irish freedom fired his imagination and zeal. Throughout the period from the Easter Rising of 1916 up to the signing of the Irish Peace Treaty in December, 1921, the pages of AMERICA bristled with outrage at English policies toward Ireland (especially the conscription of 1918) and the failure of President Woodrow Wilson to apply his principle of self-determination to Ireland. News coverage of Ireland in the "Chronicle" section was designed to counter what Tierney felt was the all too Anglophile attitude of most of the American press. Several dozen articles during this period examined the historical background of the English occupation, the Irish resistance to that occupation, the moral and legal justification of such resistance and the debate over possible forms of government that would best suit Ireland. These latter articles inspired many a "Letter to the Editor," and that section of the magazine during this period is filled with lively correspondence.

* * *

The editorial reaction to the Easter Rising at first glance seems schizophrenic. The opening paragraph states: "An act of rebellion is an act against God. . . No ebullition of patriotism can take from rebellion its true character as an act derogatory to the majesty of the God of men and nations. Such is the prescription of the natural

322

law, reenforced by the law of Revelation and the teaching of the Catholic Church. From it there neither is nor can be an appeal that is justified in Heaven." The rest of the editorial, however, sings of the glory of the patriots. "With all this said, who shall undertake to judge the motives of any man who gives his life that his country may live? . . . But who will say that an attempt to free one's country, prompted by present wrong and the recollection of centuries of dishonoring oppression, implies in those who make it, the moral iniquity of rebellion? . . . For the history of conquered Ireland and oppressing England is ever the same; a narrative of savagery and blood, met by intrepid patriotism and unswerving fidelity to the teachings of Jesus Christ."

AMERICA's position on Irish independence was based on the distinction made in this editorial between rebellion against legitimate authority and rebellion against an unjust oppressor. This point would be driven home again and again in the following years.

In 1917, and especially as a consequence of America's entrance into World War I, the refrain "What About Ireland" rang through the pages of AMERICA. An editorial under that headline placed the question of Irish freedom in the context of the Allied struggle to protect democracy.

> For some time past England has been proclaiming that the Allies are at war in the cause of democracy. At every opportunity British statesmen have lifted their voices to say that their nation is sacrificing itself in the cause of freedom, especially for the liberty of weak and abused peoples. Quite naturally this protestation has been met by the query: What of Ireland? and England has been silent or evasive. . . True, this is a question with many complex ramifications. But at least two features of it are perfectly clear. Fundamentally it is a purely ethical problem that has been given an acute international emphasis

323

by the entrance of the United States into the war in behalf of liberty. . . However much Americans may have deplored Casement's exploit, they cannot, if they are true to the ethical sense and to the traditions of freedom, repudiate his last words: "Self-government is our right. It is no more a thing to be withheld from us or doled out to us than the right to life or light, to sunshine or spring flowers."

In 1917 AMERICA published a series of articles by advocates of the various forms of government that an Irish nation might adopt. "What Does Ireland Want" by Shane Leslie argued for Home Rule within the framework of the English empire. Other authors, including Mrs. Hanna Sheehy-Skeffington, widow of Francis, argued for complete independence and separation from England. In response to Mr. Leslie's article, a reader fired off a letter to the editor in which he quoted from Cardinal Newman's response to the Jesuit poet Gerard Manley Hopkins regarding the latter's dismal view of the Irish.

> Your letter is an appalling one, but not on that account untrustworthy. There is one consideration, however, which you omit. The Irish Patriots hold that they never have yielded themselves to the sway of England, and, therefore have never been under her laws, and never have been rebels.
>
> This does not diminish the force of your picture, but it suggests that there is no help, no remedy. If I were an Irishman, I should be (in heart) a rebel. . .

This correspondent goes on to note that in politics the Cardinal was considered a Tory, and that no man was prouder than he of being an Englishman.

In an editorial on March 30, 1918 the connection between American participation in the war and Irish freedom was argued again.

324

The war is ours for freedom's sake, that small nations as well as large may enjoy the right of self determination, and thus work out their destiny according to high purposes. From this it follows that the welfare of every nation under arms has become an American issue, the welfare of Siberia no less than that of France, of Ireland no less than that of Belgium. America is pouring out blood and gold for a principle of universal application, and our people are not in a mood to suffer restriction of freedom according to the whim or fancy of any particular people.

In April of 1918, the English government voted to extend conscription to Ireland. The uproar over this measure, and the Irish Bishops condemnation of it, were duly reported on each week. On May 11, an article by John F. Fogarty, "The Genius of Sinn Feinism," traced the reason for the rise of Sinn Feinism, "from academical insignificance to a position of mighty prominence" back to the English mishandling of the 1916 Easter Week Rising. He argued that the attempt at conscription was the last straw in a series of foolhardy English policy decisions that had driven the ordinary Irish people to embrace Sinn Feinism.

The editors took the occasion of the Armistice in November to raise the question, "Again. What About Ireland?"

The war is over and the age long Irish problem has come into the open once again, this time in a form so simple even an Orangeman can understand it. Many nations, England included, have been at death grips with a powerful enemy, for one only cause, to make the world safe for democracy. . .

Nor should it be thought that this is only England and Ireland's problem. Before the war it may have been theirs alone; it is the world's now, and ours in a special way.

325

A post-Armistice article by William J.M. Maloney, "The Irish Issue in its English Aspect," charged that English propaganda was exerted to cause American opinion to go against Ireland after the war. "Britain asserted that Ireland was an enemy both of England and America, was, moreover, a friend of Germany and was, therefore, a menace, and should be outlawed and debarred from justice." Fr. Tierney aggressively exposed such propaganda ruses and pointed out that the Ulster Volunteer Force had received a shipment of 50,000 rifles from Hamburg in March of 1914. AMERICA argued that this purchase of weaponry by the Unionists had exposed the weakness of Great Britain's Empire and encouraged the German plan to wage war against her imperial rival.

Attacks on Great Britain became stronger as the question of Ireland appeared to get lost in post-war peace negotiations. An editorial on June 21, 1919 observed that "So does the whole world think Ireland should be free, except the British Government, morons and a few cads. . ." President Wilson was time and again excoriated for failing to press the issue of Irish freedom with Lloyd George.

On February 7, 1920 Fr. Paul Blakely, S.J., an associate editor, published an article, "Ireland in Bonds," in which he stated: "Free Ireland is no longer the sole issue. Justice and the possibility of peace among the nations of the world are now weighed in the balance. If the nations look on, unmoved, as a people are crushed, they will know that with England's sanction brute force may be made the fundamental principle of political philosophy. . ."

An editorial on March 13, 1920 proclaimed: *"Ireland is a nation once again,* as a popular slogan, is consistently rejected by the thoughtful friends of Erin. For they well maintain that from at least the time of St. Patrick down to today that country never ceased to be a nation."

This line of reasoning led directly to the magazine's call for official recognition of the self-proclaimed Irish Republic. When Congress voted to do so and Wilson refused, he was accused of having entered into a secret agreement with Lloyd George to compromise Ireland's claim to complete sovereignty.

AMERICA supported Terence McSwiney's hunger strike and eulogized his death in rhapsodic terms. A letter to the editor questioning this position asked: "If Mayor McSwiney's hunger strike can be justified why cannot the hunger-strike of the suffragists also be justified?" Fr. Tierney's reply deserves to be quoted, both for his reasoning in defense of McSwiney and his lack of sympathy for the suffragists.

> There is no parity between the hunger-strike of Mayor McSwiney and that of the suffragists. 1) The Mayor abstained from food to *vindicate a natural right* violated by an alien aggressor; the suffragists abstained from food *to obtain a privilege; 2) the Mayor abstained from food to vindicate justice and liberty;* the suffragists abstained from food *to frustrate justice;* 3) the Mayor acted as a duly accredited, unjustly imprisoned official of an oppressed nation in a *state of war* with a foreign nation; the suffragists acted as private citizens imprisoned for the violation of the law of their country.

Throughout 1920-1921 AMERICA continued to praise and justify Eamon de Valera and the aspirations of the Irish people. The editorial on December 17, 1921 marking the creation of the Irish Free State seems almost anticlimactic in comparison with the hard-hitting stance of the previous years. It remarks that not everyone will be happy with the articles of agreement, but reminds readers that the issue must be settled by the Irish people themselves. The editorial concludes: "It is not perfect.

327

But that it will be rejected by the Irish people is well-nigh unthinkable, if for no other reason because there is no alternative."

* * *

The volumes of AMERICA from 1916-1921 reveal that the magazine was a forceful ally of the movement for Irish independence. The style and tone of the arguments, the zealous and intrepid efforts to defend the Irish cause show that the magazine had begun to fulfil its goals of broadening the scope of Catholic journalism and becoming a factor in civic and social life. Fr. Richard Tierney, S.J., had wielded a pen and an imagination as powerful as any in support of Ireland. And you could look it up.

Father Parkes is an Associate Editor of America.

Louis Henry Sullivan

ADOLF K. PLACZEK

He was born the younger son of an Irish dancing master, Patrick Sullivan, and a Swiss mother, Andrienne List. He was named Louis Henry Sullivan, and he became one of the great architects this country has produced. He was also a splendid writer—a poet of architecture—a fighter for the new ideas, a preacher, a teacher and a dreamer; and to quote a well-known saying, he had his heart broken in the end.

Sullivan's father, the dancing master, came to America in 1847. He settled in Boston where he opened a music and dancing academy with moderate success. There he married Andrienne, the beautiful strong-willed girl of French and German stock who with her parents had recently arrived from Geneva. Louis Henry Sullivan was thus, as he put it, of "mongrel origin." In fact, as has often been said, he was the most Celtic of Celts—if there is such a thing and if verbal brilliance, mercurial temperament and poetic passion are some of its hallmarks. He was fond of his mother, but obviously disliked his father on whose "excessive Irish face and small repulsive eyes—the eyes of a pig" he remarked in his autobiography. In this love-hate conflict and his uncertainties about his heritage may lie much of the cause for his later tragic difficulties.

Louis Henry Sullivan was born in Boston in 1856. He was "neither christened nor baptized," his father "being a free-mason and not even sure whether he was a Catholic or an Orangeman." About Patrick Sullivan's Irishness, however, there was no doubt. Louis Henry has a charming recollection about the name Sullivan which deserves quotation in full:

> . . . So his father told him this tale: Long ago in Ireland, in the good fighting days, there were four tribes or clans of the O'Sullivans: The O'Sullivan-Moors, the O'Sullivan Macs, and two others. That *We* were descended from the O'Sullivan-Moors, and that all four tribes were descended from a Spanish marauder, who ravished the west Irish coast and settled there. His name it appears was O'Soulyevoyne or something like that, which, translated, meant, The Prince with One Eye. Now, however great was the glory of this pirate chief, his descendant, Louis Henri Sullivan O'Sullivan-Moore-O'Soulyevoyne, had this specific advantage over him of the high-seas. The prince had but one eye that must have seen much; the youngster of six had two eyes that saw everything, without desire to plunder.

Louis Henry spent much of his youth on the farm his maternal grandparents had acquired in Massachusetts. His love of nature, natural forms and nature imagery remained with him all his life and was a decisive element of his architecture and his architectural theory. Already at the age of 13 he decided to become an architect. It was this unwavering lifelong sense of purpose and inspiration which was to carry him to greatness—and to collision. In 1872 he entered the Massachusetts Institute of Technology. He worked briefly in the office of Frank Furness, a highly original architect in Philadelphia, then went to Chicago, where he worked for William L. B. Jenney, who was one of the pioneers of steel frame construction. In 1874 he went to Paris to study at the École des Beaux Arts, but after a year returned to Chicago, where modern American architecture—the architecture of great office and commercial buildings, the architecture of the skyscraper—was beginning to take shape.

Among Sullivan's many extraordinary talents, his magic draftsmanship stands out. He could conjure up the vision of a building with a few faint pencil lines or design a sequence of the most elaborate ornaments with hardly a superfluous or erroneous stroke. The drawings now preserved at the Avery Library of Columbia University are among the most evocative architectural sketches in existence. (They have been recently published by the Princeton University Press.) Having this skill, he started his great career as a draftsman; he rose rapidly to become a full partner in a firm called Adler and Sullivan (1881). It was to be a spectacular if short-lived association. Dankmar Adler was the engineer and the practical man, Sullivan the designer. Together they built (1886–89) the Chicago Auditorium, a combined hotel-office building-opera house, a superb structure of dramatic space, ornamented in Sullivan's subtle and rich decorative style. The building now houses a University (Roosevelt) and is again a musical theater. Next came the Wainwright building at St. Louis, Mo. (1890–91), one of the first of the "pure" skyscrapers not hidden in eclectic or imitative forms, square, with the strong verticality of powerful piers, ending in a massive cornic cap. It is still a landmark of modern functional design. Many commissions followed. Outstanding among them is the other great skyscraper-office building, the Guaranty building in Buffalo, N.Y. (1894–95). Sullivan's greatest contribution is in fact the development of the high-rise building.

For the Chicago World's Columbian Exposition of 1893 Adler and Sullivan built the Transportation building, a great arcaded hall with a famous golden doorway of concentric arches in the middle. The Chicago World's Columbian Exposition was a highpoint of American architectural grandiosity: but it also ushered in a great upsurge of classical and eclectic building which to Sullivan and his new "Chicago School" meant a decisive setback. Sullivan, in spite of the great success of the Transportation building, felt the Exposition was a disaster akin to a deadly disease that would last for generations (it didn't). In Sullivan's eloquent words:

> . . . We have Tudor for colleges and residences; Roman for banks, and railway stations and libraries,— or Greek if you like—some customers prefer the Ionic to the Doric. We have French, English and Italian Gothic, Classic and Renaissance for churches. In fact we are prepared to satisfy, in any manner of taste.

In 1895 Sullivan and Adler parted company. The loss of his sturdy partner was a blow for the sensitive undiplomatic and unrealistic man. In 1893 he had also dismissed his best draftsman, Frank Lloyd Wright. Henceforth he was alone. Among the great work of his late years is the famous Carson Pirie Scott department store in Chicago (originally Schlesinger and Mayer, 1903–04), a masterpiece of commercial building. In New York City he built only one building, the Bayard-Condict building on Bleecker Street

332

(1898), an office building with a facade of powerfully clear, but intricately interwoven rectangular elements achieving an almost perfect vertical-horizontal balance. His commissions, however, began to dwindle. His preaching of functionalism and truth in architecture was largely ignored. He quarreled with his clients, began to drink heavily, separated from his wife, lost his pupils and finally died, penniless and alone, in a small hotel room in Chicago on April 14, 1924. But even in his declining years, he maintained his creativity. It was in the last years of his life that he wrote the moving and passionate *Autobiography of an Idea*, which was published in book form only a few days before his death. It contains the story of his growth, of his philosophy and of his hopes.

Sullivan's most famous dictum is: "form follows function." It is one of the basic tenets of contemporary architecture, always quoted when modernism is discussed. It is also frequently misquoted and even misinterpreted. Sullivan very definitely did not believe in architectural forms as machinery, nor in functionalism as a form of technology. He did not even believe in the equation of structure and function, namely that every part of a building should functionally reveal or express its structure. For him, forms and their function were derived from nature and should express the poetry of creation—and if this is the voice of the Celt and the mystic, so be it!

> Whether it be the sweeping eagle in his flight or the open apple-blossom, the toiling work-horse, the blithe swan, the branching oak, the winding stream at its base, the drifting clouds, over all the coursing sun, form ever follows function, and this is the law. Where function does not change form does not change.

Among the people he admired most was Walt Whitman. And it is also Whitman's voice we can hear in these words, not the voice of scientific functionalism or even rationalism. "With me," Sullivan said to his pupil Claude Bragdon, "architecture is not an art, but a religion, and that religion but a part of democracy." It was from him that Frank Lloyd Wright took much of his early inspiration in his search for an "organic" architecture. While Sullivan's architecture is often highly individualistic and his ornament "Sullivanesque"—unmistakably his own and nobody else's—his message of form and function, of nature and idea has become a basic source of truth in architecture. He was, in the phrase of his biographer, Hugh Morrison, the Prophet of Modern Architecture.

Adolf Placzek is the Librarian at Columbia University's Avery Architectural Library.

George Washington
Parke Custis

MICHAEL J. O'NEILL

It may come as a blow to the more militant
Irishmen in our midst but one of the greatest
champions Ireland ever had in this country was a
rollicking old Virginia Gentleman in a Kelly green
frock coat who wasn't Irish at all.

He was George Washington Parke Custis, the
adopted son of our first president, father-in-law
of Robert E. Lee, a wealthy landowner and confirmed Episcopalian. And for 30 years before the
Civil War, no man in the United States raised a
louder voice—or more glasses, for that matter—in
support of Ireland's causes.

Custis, a playwright, songsmith and painter as
well as the original master of the Custis-Lee Mansion in Arlington, campaigned to get the English
out of Ireland long before Congress ever heard of
the late John E. Fogarty and his anti-partition resolutions. In a time of intolerance, he urged fair
play for the Irish Catholics streaming into this
country from the potato famine and British oppression. And almost every year, until his death
in 1857, he was the principal speaker at the big St.
Patrick's Day celebrations in Washington.

Apparently the only time he failed to appear
was in 1841 when, sad to relate, a Catholic Tem-
perance Society seized temporary control and the
annual banquet was dry. Custis, a man of stub-

335

born principle, refused to honor the breach in tradition and, together with other statesmen, lobbied successfully to have drinking restored the following year.

In return for his considerable services, Custis made only one request. During his address to the St. Patrick's Day Fleadh of 1844, when he was 62, he expressed the wistful hope:

"It may not be in my day, but I trust in God that when it shall be, though years after my mortal body shall have been laid in the bosom of our common mother, some Irish heart may come and, dropping a shamrock on my grave, cry, 'God bless him!' "

His comrades were apparently so overcome with emotion at the time that they never remembered the old man's wish and, for nearly a century, no shamrock ever graced the Custis grave, on the gentle hill overlooking the Potomac, and no Irish heart ever cried "God bless him." His speeches and his songs, his "Ode to Young Ireland," were forgotten. And new generations of Irish-Americans grew up without hearing his name.

Finally, in 1956, a National Park Service historian, Murray H. Nelligan, reminded the Irish of their long-neglected duty and now, every St. Patrick's Day, Friendly Sons and Hibernians gather at the mansion, sing the Old Orator's songs, and place a shamrock on his grave. The memory of a man who fought for Irish rights when that was unpopular in the United States is continually refreshed.

Custis was born in 1781, the son of John Parke Custis who was Martha Washington's only son by her first marriage. When he was only six months old, his father died of swamp fever and he was taken in by the childless Washingtons who raised him with all of the love and personal attention they would have given a son of their own.

At Mt. Vernon, and later in the presidential mansions in New York and Philadelphia, the impressionable boy found himself in a constant whirl of revolutionary excitement, meeting famous men, listening to great issues being debated, and sitting raptly for hours while the general and his comrades recounted their stories of the war. Stories, for example, of Irishmen who were heroes in the American Revolution, like John Barry, John Sullivan, John Fitzgerald, and John Byrne, the soldier who was tortured in a British prison ship at Charlestown.

"Dive into the depths of centuries," Custis said in a speech years later, "and you can find no more brilliant example of courage in the midst of despair, of zeal and fidelity to the cause of human liberty, than is shown in the story of John Byrne, the Irish soldier of the Revolution."

To Custis, these were Washington's friends, men who had risked their lives to help the colonies win their freedom from England. They were the sons of a land still oppressed by the British, still denied the liberty America had won, a nation without nationhood, full of human suffering. And all his life he would take the side of the Irish against tyranny, speaking out against political and religious persecution even when American prejudices were rising against Catholic immigrants.

Washington died in 1799 and Martha followed less than three years later. At the time, Custis was 21, medium height, slightly built and rather

337

good-looking. Although his foster father had closely supervised his education at Princeton and Annapolis and had tried to prepare him for public life, he was more interested in agriculture. After Martha's death, he moved to a 1,100-acre tract of land that his father had left him on the banks of the Potomac across from Washington. And he quickly established himself as a very skillful, innovative, and successful farmer.

Almost as soon as he took over his estate, Custis began building the mansion that is now so familiar a landmark in Arlington National Cemetery and in 1804, when the North Wing had been completed, he married Mary Lee Fitzhugh of Chatham, Va. Four years later, the couple had a daughter, Mary, who became the childhood friend, sweetheart and, eventually, the wife of Robert E. Lee.

During those early years at Arlington, Custis pursued an incredibly wide range of interests. He filled the mansion with Washington memorabilia and invited countless visitors, unknown old revolutionary war veterans as well as the most famous people of the time, like Sam Houston, Daniel Webster, Andrew Jackson and the Marquis de Lafayette.

He fostered scientific farming. He published his own "Recollections and Memoirs of Washington." He composed songs and poetry, contributed regularly to the Washington Intelligencer, and wrote a number of plays that were rather amateurish but played professionally from Boston to Charleston and helped stimulate a new native trend in American drama. He even tried his hand at painting.

Most of all, however, Custis was an orator in the grand tradition of the early 19th century and, over the years, he delivered innumerable speeches in support of innumerable causes—for political and religious liberties, for freedom for Poland, Greece, and the countries of South America, for equal rights for all men. He opposed slavery and, even though he was a son of Virginia, he argued against secession when nullification threatened to break up the union in 1833.

But beginning in 1826, when he was 45, and already balding, Custis developed a consuming interest in the cause of Irish Freedom and this stayed with him the rest of his life. For it was in 1826, when the drive for Catholic emancipation was at its height in Ireland, that Custis and a few similarly inspired friends called on all the "friends of civil and religious liberty" to rally at City Hall in Washington in order "to express their sympathy for the people of Ireland and an earnest desire and hope of a speedy amelioration of their condition."

Custis, of course, presided at the meeting and delivered the main oration, an uncharacteristically short speech but powerful, a ringing demand that Americans forget their political and religious scruples and rise to the defense of the Irish as the Irish had so freely done in America's own cause.

Some Americans refused to speak out for Ireland, he said, because they were afraid to interfere in another country's political affairs but he insisted there was no reason to fear Britain. Some other Americans, he continued, were reluctant to get involved in a religious controversy, but he denounced this, too.

During the Revolutionary War, he said, when Irishmen were welcome comrades in the fight for freedom, "Americans were not sticklers in doctrinal matters . . . we were glad to receive the religionists of any creeds and found to our comfort, and to our independence too, that a Catholic arm could drive a bayonet on the foe, and a Catholic heart beat high for the liberties of our country. . . . When our friendless standard was first unfurled for resistance, who were the strangers that first mustered round its staff? And when it reeled in the fight, who more bravely sustained it than Erin's generous sons. . . ?"

If the Irish needed any more proof of their worth, it was that "Washington loved them, for they were the comrades of his toils, his perils, and his glories, in the deliverance of his country." And if Washington himself loved these sons of Ireland, Americans could do no less.

As the friends of liberty cheered, the lord of Arlington laid down his final challenge:

"Can you . . . will you . . . dare you, Americans, talk of interference—and withhold your voice from a general acclaim which should thunder in this land 'till its echoes reach the Emerald Isle in a prayer for deliverance. If there is an American who does not feel for the wrongs of that country, which so nobly contributed to the establishment of our rights, I pronounce him recreant to the feelings of virtue, honor, and gratitude!"

Strong words from the adopted son of the first president, words that struck like a stiletto at the anti-Catholic feelings which even in those early days, before the mass migrations, prevented many Americans from defending the Irish or their causes. But Custis, with his imposing credentials and historic lineage, could not be attacked easily. And under his spell the friends of civil and re-

340

ligious liberty issued a formal declaration of support for Irish liberty:

"We consider the cause of the Catholics of Ireland, contending for inalienable rights, as the cause not only of Catholics, and of Ireland but of all Ireland and of the whole human family. For if it be once conceded that conscience can be enslaved, where is the neck which may not be made to feel the yoke?"

Custis and his friends spoke out at a time of rising hope in Ireland. In that same summer of 1826, Daniel O'Connell and his Catholic Association won a stunning victory in the parliamentary elections and, within three years, the long-sought Catholic Emancipation Act was passed. This act was a turning point in Ireland's struggle against England. O'Connell was swept to new heights of power and popularity. And no one was more enthusiastic than the Old Orator of Arlington. At a testimonial dinner in Washington in 1832, he showered praise on O'Connell, calling him a great leader who made progress by gentle means, without war and bloodshed.

Custis voiced the hope that O'Connell would quickly complete the task of freeing Ireland from English occupation so that it could stand as an independent nation and an equal member of the British empire. Although this sounds surprising now, O'Connell also had this same view that a free Ireland would still remain in the British empire.

But O'Connell's peaceful methods failed. Although he won many reforms in the 12 years after the Emancipation Act was passed, all progress ended when Robert Peel returned to power as prime minister in 1841. And O'Connell's final desperate effort to repeal the Act of Union between Ireland and England was crushed in 1843.

As the years passed without victory. Custis became more and more disillusioned with O'Connell and his non-violent ways. He began calling for stronger measures and, in speech after speech, cited the heroic acts of America's revolution as examples for Ireland to follow. By the time of his St. Patrick's Day address in 1842, he had become harshly critical. "Let Ireland take warning from the history of America's days of trial," he cried. "Let Ireland cease to bend at the footstool of power, with her honor, her dignity, and her manhood trailing in the dust, or we shall, by and by, hear of the cowardly Ireland."

In his frustration, Custis turned away from O'Connell to the idea of a "Young Ireland" led by young Irishmen who would fight to liberate old Ireland from its misery and replace it with a new Ireland of freedom and hope. And for the St. Patrick's Day celebration of 1842, he wrote an "Ode to Young Ireland" that ended with the lines:

"Appeal to the Being to whom there belongs,
*   Power, justice and mercy combined;*
Remember, Young Ireland, thy centuries of wrongs,
*   And strike for the rights of mankind."*

Custis claimed that he had coined the phrase "Young Ireland." But there is a hint in one early speech that he actually had been inspired by the "Young Ireland" movement which was just gaining momentum in Ireland in the 1840s. The "Young Irelanders" were followers of O'Connell who became disillusioned and broke away to take action on their own. In keeping with Custis' call to arms, they launched a revolt in 1848 but, like so many others earlier and later, it ended in disaster.

Despite the endless setbacks, Custis' enthusiasm for Ireland's causes never flagged. The great halls of Arlington House rang with his Irish songs and poems and the spirited talk of Irish defenders who were always welcome guests. Even the Robert E. Lees, who spent many years at Arlington after their marriage in 1831, were infected with the Irish sympathies that engulfed them.

And every year on St. Patrick's Day, the Son of Mt. Vernon and the Irish of Northern Virginia boarded a boat in Alexandria. With the flag of Free Ireland flying from the yard and Custis standing in the bow, wearing his green frock coat and knee breeches that were even then out of fashion, they sailed up the Potomac to the wharf at the foot of 14th Street in Washington.

While the U.S. Marine Band played Irish tunes, the party disembarked with full ceremony and passed through elaborately positioned ranks of Washington Irish who had just arrived from the mass at St. Patrick's. The Virginian and Washington contingents then marched together up 14th Street to Carusi's Saloon, or some other appropriate place of assembly. And with unchanging ritual, the long afternoon and night were filled with speeches, songs, and toasts—mostly toasts.

In his last years, when he was in his 70s, Custis' voice still rose and his bright eyes still sparkled at the mention of Ireland. But his dream that another Washington would emerge to win its freedom had begun to fade. And it had all but disappeared when he died in 1857.

Four years later, General Lee left the Custis Mansion to take command of the Army of

Virginia. In another month, his wife fled when she learned that union forces were planning to move into Virginia. And later still, federal troops occupied the mansion.

The Irish echoes died away. The songs and poems and the revolutionary talk were forgotten. Forgotten for nearly 100 years, until an Irish heart finally remembered the old man's wish and Hibernians and Friendly Sons marched to the gray obelisk behind the Custis-Lee Mansion and placed a shamrock on his grave, and someone at last cried: "God bless him!"

Michael J. O'Neill is a Medalist of the Society.

Facets of the Mexican War

WALTER POWER

¡Vuela, mi canto, vuela!
en alas de cenzontle de los bosques
   de México
en alas de quetzal guatemalteco, en
   alas
de colibrí nicaraguense
y pechirrojo de Sonora, a Erin
la isla verde que el rocio amamanta,
y dile que la amamos —

The war fought in the late 1840's between the United States and Mexico has been virtually ignored by most historians, even though practically the entire southwest United States was annexed as a result of the conflict. Professor Justin H. Smith, in his *The War with Mexico*, cited two reasons for this peculiar indifference; the conflict was overshadowed by the Civil War and succeeding wars of much greater magnitude and duration; and, secondly, it was highly unpopular with a large segment of Americans while being fought. And yet, this almost forgotten war holds a particular Irish interest. It was one in which thousands of Irish fought, many distinguished themselves, and a small number played a highly dramatic but controversial part. In addition, it occurred at a time when The Great Famine was raging in Ireland and the effects

345

of the potato blight were to reach, in a particularly poignant way, into the Mexican theatre of war. Ironically, it was the outbreak of the famine in Ireland in 1845 that was one of the major factors which allowed the United States economy to sustain a strong war effort. As Professor Smith described it: "In 1846 came the great Irish Famine. British provision laws were suspended. Faced with starvation, people cared little what they paid if they could obtain food. [In the United States] agricultural products which had fallen heavily in market value since October 1845, rose with astonishing buoyancy. Grain that had been scarcely worth transporting became precious. A ship could earn thirty percent of her cost in one round trip, yet hardly enough vessels could be found."

Space does not allow a detailed discussion of the origins of the war, suffice to reiterate that it was unpopular with many in the United States, particularly in the North. While this anti-war attitude was widespread, it was virtually absent among the Irish Americans who, as Sister Blanche Marie McEniry has pointed out in *American Catholics in the War with Mexico*, were wholehearted in supporting the war, almost to the man. This enthusiasm was not merely vocal. Although accurate numbers are not available, there is no doubt that thousands of Irish flocked to the colours. Referring to this contribution, General Winfield Scott, commander in chief of the United States armies in Mexico, wrote that, of his 3,500 regulars, more than 2,000 were Irish, and, about their dedication, remarked, "It is hazardous and may be invidious but truth obliges me to say that, of our Irish soldiers, save for a few who deserted from General Taylor and who had never taken the Nuturalisation Oath, not one ever turned his back on the enemy or faltered in advancing to the charge." The few referred to by Scott comprised what has been referred to as the "Battalion of Saint Patrick," "The Legion of Strangers," "The Company of San Patricio," "The Colorados," or, more familiarly, as "The San Patricios." This group, in the main soldiers who defected from the American army, has tended to overshadow, by their courage, gallantry and sacrifice in the Mexican cause, the total Irish contribution to the war, which was important, and arguably vital, in serving the United States' interests. Therefore, it is necessary to regard the role of "the San Patricios" not in isolation, but in the context of the entire span of the war.

Military operations against Mexico commenced when General Taylor was ordered to lead his army to the Rio Grande, which he reached on March 28, 1846. From that moment until the end of the war two years later, the Mexican authorities tried constantly to persuade the American troops to desert. These efforts were directed in the main at the foreign-born soldiers, and most particularly at the very large Irish contingent. The inducements were varied and were both of a material and psychological nature. They included offers of free land in Mexico; attractive opportunities in the Mexican army; free transportation to Europe after the war; fomenting concern that a United States victory would result in the extension of slavery (which would place free labor at a competitive disadvantage); and highlighting the fact that the war was being waged by the Protestant United States against Catholic Mexico. It cannot be denied that this propaganda was, at least partially, successful.

Groups of American deserters fought in a number of engagements, but on only two occasions do they appear to have fought as a recognizable military unit—at Buena Vista in February 1847, and at Churubusco outside Mexico City in August of the same year. In both battles, the Irish distinguished themselves, but their stand at the Convent of Churubusco was memorable. There they were described as "fighting like tigers," "fighting until their ammunition was exhausted," and "their flag was the last left flying." The sequel can only be described as dramatic. After the battle, seventy of the captured survivors were tried by court martial. They were tried fairly. General Scott wrote that he "would rather have his whole army put to the sword than do an injustice in the matter," and he issued instructions that the number of death sentences be kept to a minimum. Four survivors were released, sixteen were lashed, branded, and imprisoned for the duration of the war. Of the rest, sixteen were hanged at San Angel on September 9, 1847, four more were hanged at Mixcoatl on the following day, and the remaining thirty were hanged at Tacubaya four days later.

The execution of those last was carried out with a touch of brutality by a Colonel Harney, an outstanding officer, who ironically was of Irish descent. The day designated for the executions coincided with the American army's attack on Chapultepec Castle—the last Mexican bastion before Mexico City. The prisoners were placed on carts in sight of the assault with nooses around their necks and were hanged at the moment the Stars and Stripes was hoisted over the castle. Chapultepec witnessed a great deal of courage that day—the *élan* of the American storming parties; the valiant Mexican cadets who defended the castle so fiercely; and, not the least, the San Patricios—many horribly wounded—who awaited their end on the gallows, stoic and unrepentent.

By the next spring, the battalion was reformed and refitted, only to be finally disbanded later in the summer of the same year.

The first mention of the Irish in Mexican records was made in late 1846 during Santa Anna's advance on Buena Vista. Their unit was referred to as a company of Irish volunteers. It was after the battle of Buena Vista that the first reference by the Mexicans to the "Company of San Patricio" was made. Three months later the unit became known as the "Foreign Legion" or "Legion of Strangers." Thereafter, a decree issued on July 1, 1847 by the Mexican authorities, stating, "Two infantry companies of territorial militia are to be formed from the unit known as the Legion of Strangers. They are to be known as the 1st and 2nd Territorial Militia Companies of the Battalion of San Patricio. Each company will consist of a captain, a 1st lieutenant, two 2nd lieutenants, one sergeant 1st class, four sergeants 2nd class, nine corporals, four buglers and 81 privates." Their uniform was to be the uniform prescribed for the Territorial Militia.

Following the battle of Churubusco, a Mexican report dispatch reported the losses suffered by the battalion as being "killed in action, two 2nd lieutenants, four sergeants, six corporals and twenty-three privates." The report concluded by stating, "the rest are either prisoners or dispersed."

However, by March 1848, another San Patricio Battalion of two companies was formed. Its exact composition is unknown. Presumably it consisted of the survivors of the original battalion and of more recent deserters from the American ranks. In June 1848, while the unit was stationed at Guadalupe, its commander became involved in a conspiracy against the Mexican President Herrera. His arrest aroused the San Patricios, and they threatened to gain his release by force. They were appeased without bloodshed, but the battalion was disbanded later that summer, presumably to avoid future disturbances.

What types of men comprised the battalion? Judging from the only list of names available (namely, those who were court-martialed) only a minority appeared to have been definitely Irish, although it must be conceded that Irish influence was paramount in the battalion. Certainly, other nationalities were represented because, in at least two cases, German-speaking interpreters had to attend the court martials. Additionally, a number of references were also made to a John Wilden, who was described as an Englishman in the Mexican service.

By themselves the court martial records reveal little. They follow a set pattern. The prisoner is charged. Evidence of desertion is given. Further evidence is provided of his being taken prisoner in Mexican uniform. The accused in most cases asks for character references to be taken into account. Thereafter, the verdict of the court is decreed.

Usually, the character references were favorable. In the trial of Abraham Fitzpatrick, for example, Lieutenant Longstreet (later the Confederate hero) wrote to the court on his behalf and, after giving details of Fitzpatrick's bravery against the Mexicans early in the war, concluded by saying, "he always, prior to his desertion, behaved as a most faithful and energetic soldier, prompt and willing to obey and execute." (The service record of Fitzpatrick was recently located in the United States Government's archives. His birthplace is given as Kingscourt, County Cavan. Previous occupation is stated as being a wheelwright. It shows that he was twenty-six when he enlisted in 1844 and that he surrendered to the United States forces on August 30, 1847.) Thanks to his previous good record and the intervention of Longstreet, Fitzpatrick was sentenced to be shot rather than hanged. However, the sentence was later remitted by Scott.

One exception to the generally favorable character references dealt with a Lachlin McLaglin. The court received the following appraisal from his former commander, "he had no character at all, he was almost always in the guard house, and a few days earlier to his desertion, charges for mutiny had been withdrawn."

The excuse offered to the court in virtually every trial for desertion was drink, in that the accused had allegedly been captured by the Mexicans while drunk and forced, while in that state, to join their army.

The best-documented court martial of all was that of the most colorful of the San Patricios, John Reilly, their commander. His service record shows he was Irish by birth and twenty-eight when he enlisted in the American army. His height was over six feet, and he had blue eyes, dark hair, and a sandy complexion. His previous occupation is given as being a labourer. He is supposed to have deserted the British army in Canada, and to have worked for some time in Mackinac, Michigan. He enlisted in the American army at Fort Mackinac on September 4, 1845, and deserted on April 12, 1846, on the Rio Grande. In the course of his trial, Abraham Fitzpatrick claimed he had been forced to join the Mexican army when Reilly raised his Legion. On the other hand, Reilly claimed he had been dragooned into the Mexican ranks and had later demanded to see the British Consul in Mexico to get himself released. Nonetheless, while awaiting the visit of that official, Reilly had been working his way up through the commissioned ranks of the Mexican army. Originally sentenced to death, he was later reprieved by Scott on the basis that he deserted before war was declared.

During his subsequent imprisonment, he wrote to his old employer in Mackinac. "I have taken the liberty of writing to you hoping that you are in good health as I am at present, thank God for it. I have had the honour of fighting in all the battles Mexico has had with the United States and by my good conduct and hard fighting, I have obtained the rank of Major, a rank which no other foreigner who has fought for the Mexican Government has ever attained. I suppose from the accounts you have seen in the United States papers you have formed a very poor opinion of Mexico and its Government, but do not be deceived by the prejudice of a nation which is at war with Mexico, for a more hospitable and friendly people than the Mexicans there exists not on the face of the earth. As a foreigner, and especially as an Irishman and a Catholic, it grieves me to have to inform you of the deaths of 51 of my best and bravest men who have been hung by the Americans for no other reason than fighting manfully against them. Especially my First Lieutenant, Patrick Dalton, whose loss I deeply regret. He belonged to Ballina Tirnally in the Country of Mayo. ***In all my letter I forgot to tell you under what banner we fought so bravely. It was a glorious emblem of nations' rights, that banner which should have floated over our native soil many years ago, it was Saint Patrick, the Harp of Erin, the Shamrock upon a green field."

Reilly's former employer, upon receiving the letter, forwarded it to General Scott with the following comments: "I do herewith enclose you the letter of the deserter, John Reilly, written to me from the City of Mexico. The said Reilly was in my employ off and on for the span of two years, with whom I had more trouble than all the other men who worked for me, more particularly as a Justice of the Peace, for he was always in variance with anyone he had anything to do with. Such was my opinion of him that I said

351

(when I heard of the desertions) that Reilly was one of their number. In duty to my country I feel myself bound to let his superiors know of his dissatisfaction and intentions towards them."

Meanwhile, Scott had received another letter signed by sixteen "foreigners resident in Mexico City," which reflects a different aspect of Reilly's character, "We, the undersigned citizens of the United States and Foreigners of different nations in the City of Mexico, humbly pray that his Excellency, the General in Chief of the American forces, may be graciously pleased to extend a pardon to Captain John Reilly of the Legion of Saint Patrick and, generally speaking, to all deserters from the American service. We speak to your Excellency, particularly of Reilly as we understand his life to be most in danger. His conduct might be pardoned by your Excellency in consideration of the protection he extended in the City to the persecuted and banished American citizens whilst in concealment, by nullifying an order he held to apprehend them and not acting on it. We believe him to have a generous heart, admitting all his errors."

* * *

Traditionally, the San Patricios have been annually honoured over the years on each September 12 in Mexico City by a simple commemorative ceremony sponsored by the municipality at a memorial erected some twenty years ago in the Plaza San Jacinto in San Angel. The inscription on the memorial reads: "In memory of the Irish soldiers of the heroic Battalion of Saint Patrick, Martyrs, who gave their lives for Mexico during the unjust North American invasion of 1847," being followed by the names of those court-martialed and later executed.

It is surprising, when one considers the thousands of Irishmen who, over the centuries, fought in the armies of the United States, Britain, France, Spain, and many other countries, that only in Mexico are Irish soldiers publically commemorated today as Irishmen. Nor is this a recent practice, for the San Patricios have been honoured in that land from the day the women of San Angel cut down their bodies from the gallows in its plaza.

> *Fly, my song, fly!*
> *Fly on the wings of the cenzontle from*
>   *the woods of Mexico*
> *On the wings of the Guatemalan quetzal,*
>   *on the wings*
> *Of the Nicaraguan humming bird,*
> *And of the red breast of Sonoro, to*
>   *Erin*
> *The green isle of the suckling dew*
> *And tell her we love her —*

Mr. Power, an executive of Aer Lingus, has lectured and written widely on this topic. The lines he quoted are from "Evocación de Píndaro", a poem of Salomón de la Selva, in commemoration of the San Patricios.

Hugh Gallagher,
Indian Agent

WILLIAM HANLON

In 1968, caught up in the surge of interest that
Robert Kennedy had inspired through his efforts
on behalf of the American Indian, I arranged to
work on a reservation. I went to a travel agent in
the Bronx—somewhere on Webster Avenue, I
think—to plan the trip. I always remember how
that man's absolute confidence in his ability to get
me within walking distance of any point in the
world turned into frustration when, after consult-
ing his air, rail, and bus charts, he admitted that
he couldn't get me any closer than 60 miles to my
destination.

At any rate, I boarded a plane at La Guardia on
a sweltering July morning and landed fourteen
hours later in Chadron, Nebraska, which that
night was registering a temperature of 32°. I have
never since consulted a travel agent.

These memories came back to me recently as I
was reading a letter dated October 1, 1886 from
one Hugh Gallagher to his wife informing her
that he had arrived at 3:03 am in Rushville, Nebraska. I don't know how long it took Gallagher
to get there from his home in Indiana. But,
strangely, he was able to get, by public convey-
ance, 30 miles closer to the same destination than
I was some 80 years later. For we were both
headed to the Pine Ridge Indian Reservation.

354

The reservation lies in the southwest corner of South Dakota and stretches north and east to cover 5000 square miles. Parts of this territory are a moonscape of eerily eroded bad-lands; the rest is gently rolling plains suitable for little else but grazing cattle. Just about the only bountiful natural resource of this region is the ring-necked pheasant. It is said that there are more pheasants than people in South Dakota.

Although the summers here are bearable, the winters can be unbelievably cruel. And the two seasons often abut without benefit of spring or autumn.

This is the home of the Oglala Sioux. Not surprisingly, it was not their home of choice. In better days, before the coming of the white man they preferred the deep green beauty of the country to the north. Paha Sapa they called it, "the Black Hills." It was a land teeming with wildlife, covered with scrub pine, and crossed by lucid streams. Of no interest to the Oglalas was the gold beneath that earth.

It was the gold, though, that attracted the white miners. It also brought detachments of cavalry under Generals Crook and Custer with orders to chase the miners from the hills. They all came in violation of the Treaty of 1868 which stated in part: "No white person or persons shall be permitted to settle upon or occupy any portion of the territory, or without the consent of the Indians, to pass through the same."

It was the gold, eventually, that would lead to Custer's defeat at the Little Big Horn in 1876, to the final subjugation of all "hostiles" and to their confinement within federal reservations such as Pine Ridge.

And so it was the gold, ultimately, that brought Hugh Gallagher to Pine Ridge as the new Indian agent in 1886.

As schoolchildren we learned about this era of our country's history and were fascinated by the pioneers. They were immigrants who came to America seeking a better life and, not content with what they found in the cities of the East, undertook a second journey fraught with as many perils and uncertainties as their voyage across the ocean. They were men and women of daring spirit who risked everything for the promise of land and riches in the West.

In school we did not learn much about the native Americans who were displaced by this wave of settlers and who had fought desperately to defend their homeland. While "savage" was the adjective most frequently used to describe Indians, it more aptly could have been employed to depict the treatment they received at the hands of the white man. Americans of Irish descent acted as badly as anyone in this regard. But the career of Hugh Gallagher provides at least one proud page in this often neglected chapter of American-Irish history.

While gathering my thoughts for this article, I wrote to a friend, an expert on Western history. His reply was bittersweet:

> I have always noticed a strong similitude—or at least thought I did—between the Indians and the Irish: their mysticism, their seemingly similar attitudes towards life and spirituality, their ability to roll with the punches, to relax in life, and yet, at the same time, to be quite aggressive when necessary. And even their humor. One might also include their tradition of oratory and storytelling. By and large, however, my im-

pression is that the Irish in this country were extremely hard on the Indians. Irish army officers, for instance, were unmercifully cruel. Hugh Gallagher was a notable exception.

When Gallagher arrived as the new agent for the Pine Ridge Reservation in 1886, the shooting wars were pretty much over. Some of the great chiefs of the Sioux such as Crazy Horse were dead. Sitting Bull had returned from exile in Canada and was living on a reservation. Red Cloud was weary of battle. He had been a great warrior but, like all men close to the earth, was a realist. He saw the white men advancing from the East like a prairie fire burning out of control. His people did not understand this other people's strange thirst for owning land. But they knew now that they could not beat the newcomers and were neither inclined nor invited to join them in full partnership. It was Red Cloud's task to seek, by his wits, the best compromise he could for his people. And the Indian agent was the link between the chief and the government.

Indian agents were political appointees. Robert Utley points out in his *Last Days of the Sioux Nation* that "when Grover Cleveland led the Democrats to power in 1885, after twenty-four lean years on the outside, more than 50 of the 58 Indian agents surrendered their jobs to Democrats." Hugh Gallagher, a Civil War veteran and politician from Indiana, was one of the beneficiaries of that purge. He was devoutly Democratic and Catholic—or is that redundant?

Red Cloud had been trying for years to get permission from Washington to have the "Blackrobes" open a school for the children of his tribe. Since the days of the great Jesuit missionary, De

357

Smet, the Sioux had come to know the blackrobes as their friends. But by government edict each reservation was assigned to a single Christian denomination which had an exclusive franchise, as it were, to civilize that particular tribe. As it turned out, no member of the Catholic clergy was allowed on The Pine Ridge. And so any of these Sioux who had already become Catholics were denied, by government decree, the freedom of attending services of their adopted religion. A Father Meinrad McCarthy had attempted to break this barrier in 1879. He arrived at Pine Ridge, presented letters of introduction to the government offices, and requested permission to start a mission. Gallagher's predecessor wired Washington for instructions and subsequently sent Fr. McCarthy a note stating: "I have the honor to inform you that your presence on the reservation cannot be allowed ecclesiastically or otherwise."

In 1886, during Gallagher's first year as agent, the Commissioner of Indian Affairs granted the authority necessary for the Jesuits to establish a school—18 years after the Sioux were restricted to reservation life. Gallagher wrote to his wife, Mary, on July 27, 1887: "Fr. Jutz is here with a lay-brother to determine upon a site for the school. They are trying to secure a place I showed them, distant some six miles from the agency. Red Cloud went out with them today to assist in negotiations for the place."

The negotiations were successful for the Sisters of Saint Francis who worked together with the Jesuits at the new school, recorded in their diary of 1888:

Before the close of the opening day of school, there were 20 pupils, and before the end of the year, that

358

number had risen to 100. This was largely owing to the broadmindedness of Colonel Gallagher, the Agent, who from the first allowed the parents to send their children to the Catholic school if they so desired, even though they had previously attended a Government school. This is, of course, only as it should be, but later Agents were far from imitating Colonel Gallagher in his just policy; indeed the history of Holy Rosary Mission has many a page on which narrow-minded bigotry left its mark.

In the unlikely event that Hugh Gallagher's cause for beatification should ever arise, the Sisters' diary would be a goldmine for any Postulator. They record that Gallagher was "a devout Catholic, and one who was ever unfailing in courtesy toward both Fathers and Sisters." The praise gets a bit over-lyrical when the Sisters record the arrival in Rushville of a statue of Our Lady which they had purchased for the Mission: "Colonel Gallagher and his wife followed in their carriage to act as an escort: surely a chivalrous act, worthy of a Celtic name!"

But praise came from other quarters, too. The Board of Indian Commissioners—less prone to pious exaggeration—noted in its *Annual Report* for 1887 that "Agent Gallagher seems to enjoy the reputation of being a fair and honorable officer."

If Gallagher's piety was impeccable, his credentials and connections as a Democrat seem to have been in equally good order. Despite his geographical isolation he continued to do whatever he could for the party. On November 2, 1886, one month after his arrival in the Dakotas—which, incidentally, were not granted statehood until 1889—he wrote back to his wife, Mary, in Indiana:

I can imagine this was a pretty stirring day in the States when hot election contests were coming off. It was quite different here. I did not hear a person mention the election all day. Yesterday I let one of our school teachers go down to Rushville as he claimed to have gained a residence there and wanted to put in a democratic vote. Our Agency foreman wanted to go with him but knowing him to be a Republican I couldn't spare him.

And in January 1887 Mary wrote him expressing a very domestic concern. She wondered—since he had not yet been officially confirmed as Agent by the Senate—whether she should go ahead with the packing necessary before she and the children could join him in Pine Ridge. Without a glimmer of timidity he wrote back immediately:

There is scarcely a doubt of the Senate's action being favorable, and should they refuse to confirm the appointment the President would simply recommission me after the adjournment of Congress and then the matter would come before them again at the next session. So let it be understood that you will come back with me in the latter part of next month.

And that October Mrs. Gallagher wrote to her mother that Hugh had been in Omaha. "He saw President Cleveland and Wife there Thursday," she writes, "and brought several photographs of them home."

The documents show Gallagher as a conscientious administrator tending to his fiscal reports, supervising beef-issue days, and accompanying Indians off the reservation for court trials. Certainly, he got along better with Red Cloud than any other agent had. He was capable of meting out stern justice but was always willing to speak out when he saw the Indians subjected to injustice.

The letters also record his complaints about the bitter Dakota cold and even about such petty inconveniences as the lack of good calendars, the kind "that tear off by months." But despite everything he seems to have been enchanted by the rough beauty of the Great Plains and by its native people. During a visit back to Indiana late in 1888, he wrote to Mary in Pine Ridge. "I have seen all my old friends and am therefore about ready to go back. Give me the West, Pet."

But all was not well. Despite Gallagher's repeated protests to Washington, bread rations for the reservation had been cut in half between 1886 and 1889. And during this same period, a cult was developing among the Indians. It was called the Ghost Dance religion. Its devotees believed that by chanting the right prayers and dancing in the prescribed ceremonies, they could achieve the miraculous. They believed that the shirts they wore would be impenetrable by the soldiers' bullets, that the white man would disappear and the buffalo return.

I think it is fair to say that few white men of the time understood the significance of the Ghost Dance cult. In hindsight we can see it as the last desperate, visionary hope of a proud people who had been defeated by impossible numerical odds and humiliated by their victors.

At any rate, on October 9, 1890 Hugh Gallagher was relieved of duty by the new Republican agent, Mr. Royer, whom the Sisters, with an uncharacteristically harsh comment, described in their diary as "destitute of the necessary qualifi-

361

cations: experience, courage, and sound judge-ment." And Young-Man-Afraid-of-His-Horses asked in bewilderment: "Why are the agents always being changed? Why was Agent Gallagher discharged when he wrote that our crops had failed, and our rations must not be cut down?"

The Indians apparently did not understand a political patronage system any more than the white men understood their growing discontent.

Ghost Dance activity increased and culminated on a bitter December day in 1890 with the massacre of several hundred unarmed men, women, and children of Big Foot's band at Wounded Knee on the Pine Ridge Reservation. Some students of the period see it as a retaliatory raid by the Seventh Cavalry in retribution for Custer's defeat more than a decade earlier. And some think that, had Hugh Gallagher still been the Agent, there would have been no massacre.

That is a conjecture, of course, but judging from what I have been able to learn of Gallagher, it is a sound one.

I left Pine Ridge in 1973 having booked—without the services of a travel agent—a five hour flight back to New York. Shortly before I left, sitting outside the dormitory of the school that Red Cloud had dreamed of and Hugh Gallagher had helped make possible, I could hear distantly the sound of automatic gunfire. The majority of tourists that year were Federal marshals and FBI agents who had converged on the Pine Ridge Reservation to contain the takeover, by militant Indians, of Wounded Knee.

I left, as I'm sure Gallagher had, enriched by my contact with the Oglala Sioux. And I left with the realization which he must also have shared, that things hadn't gotten much better for our having been there. But maybe a little better. We hope.

Bill Hanlon was a teacher at Red Cloud Indian School for five years.

Pedro O'Crouley, One of Ireland's Wild Geese

SEAN GALVIN

The flight of the armies of Hugh O'Neill and Rory O'Donnell six years after their defeat at the Battle of Kinsale in 1601 marked the beginning of Irish migration for the centuries to come.

Throughout most of the seventeenth century a glimmer of hope could be seen as these Irish leaders and their descendants tried to assemble armies in the hope of returning to Ireland and releasing it from the English stranglehold. However, the defeat of James II and the Catholic forces at the Battle of the Boyne in 1690 and the signing of the Treaty of Limerick in the following year by another great Irish general, Patrick Sarsfield, largely dissolved this military impetus. To keep the unruly Irish under control, the English Government drew up a set of laws known as the Penal Laws. These Laws in essence made it impossible for any ambitious Irish man to remain a Catholic and stay in Ireland. Fortunately for them they did have somewhere to go. As fighters they were without equal and the countries of France, Austria and Italy were always eager to employ them in their armies. Yet of all the countries in Europe it was in Spain that they achieved the most recognition. There they found themselves Catholics in a Catholic country. Their situation was further enhanced by the very correct belief that Ireland had been settled by the people of the Iberian culture about three thousand years before Christ. Thus the 'Wild Geese' as they were called settled themselves in Spain as Spaniards and were treated as such.

Pedro Alonso O'Crouley was one such man whose parents had left Ireland to escape this dominance of English rule. Though born in Cádiz in 1740, his father was a native of Limerick and his mother was an O'Donnell from County Clare. At the age of nine he was sent to France to be educated and upon the completion of his education he chose the career of merchant. This must not have been simply by chance for Cádiz, a seaport town in the south western part of Spain, was at the time the gateway to Spain's rich and unknowingly large colonies. It is of no surprise then that at the age of twenty-four the young O'Crouley made his first trip to what we now call Mexico but was then the Kingdom of New Spain. No doubt he was first lured to this New Spain by the promise of riches for which that land was fabled. He did well as a merchant yet he also found time to observe and record his impressions of that land of contrasts.

In 1774 he set down these observations in book form though it was never published in his life time. Called *A Description of the Kingdom of New Spain*, the original manuscript in Spanish lies in the Biblioteca Nacional in Madrid.

As O'Crouley was interested in both the past and the present of the land that he was visiting he gathered for his book information from whatever sources were available to him. During his visits to New Spain he was fortunate enough to be witnessing a complete change of the political, economic and military policies that were formerly adhered to. Also Carlos III, King of Spain, in an effort to raise revenues to the crown had completely restructured the trade situation between Spain and its Colonies. O'Crouley's history mirrors much of the crisis of the missions and northern frontiers in the years that

365

he was in Mexico. The presidios, inherited from earlier decades as a system of frontier defence, were unable to protect the northern settlements from the fierce Apaches. In 1772 the 'New Regulations of the Presidios' directed that a cordon of presidios from the Gulf of California to the Gulf of Mexico be organized and another Irishman, Hugo O'Conor, was the man selected for this task. O'Conor who at one time had been the Governor of Texas waged a vigorous campaign against the hostile Indians and by 1777 he had established an effective boundary.

Though O'Crouley tells us nothing of himself in his manuscript his own character quite clearly emerges from his observations. In repeating the oft-told tale of Cortes' victory over Montezuma's subjects, he remarks that "it was a happy day for Spain and much more so for the Indians, who with the loss of their earthly empire were on the threshold of the Heavenly Kingdom." Reviewing the hard conditions of the life of the Indians in his own time, O'Crouley exclaims indignantly that he has been "amazed to hear people say the comfort and mild treatment are bad for the Indians, that in order to get them to work one must drive them like animals and that considerations and kindness spoil them and are detrimental to their health." Moreover, that "many wealthy citizens live with the sole aim of hoarding when they should live and spend in proportion to their means, thereby giving occupation and benefits to the poor, whose protectors they are by law and custom and by God's teaching too." Clearly O'Crouley was a social moralist of a kind coming to the fore in the eighteenth century. Perhaps he was also aware of the plight under which his own forebears had been and were being subjected to in Ireland? Consider the following: "The strongest considerations cry out on behalf of these people. I wish it were nothing more than that these are the only ones employed in the agriculture of so vast a land; but with harsh treatment and want they are going to be destroyed: it is painfully obvious that with each passing year this useful class of inhabitants is of fewer numbers." And again: "On large farms where they are not kept in barracks they live in small palm-leaf huts like pigsties, and the owners make sure that they are continually in debt to them by advances of pay to keep them always in the same condition, which means a slavery of sorts though it seems voluntary. The fact is that, although the little they receive in advance is not much, it is difficult to discharge the debt."

On a lighter note there did seem to be an attempt by the Indians to preserve some remnants of their once proud civilization when O'Crouley says the following: 'These people have a strange attachment to their own language and although many have a knowledge of Castilian they do not speak it unless from dire necessity.'

As was usual in the eighteenth century the strange and the unusual was discussed and presented with great fervour and even greater imagination. Consequently in his manuscript he devotes a chapter on what he calls the 'Remarkable Curiosities' of the Kingdom of New Spain. One can nearly feel his own incredulity as he writes: "In Puebla I have seen a white woman who with one man alone had forty-eight children, twins at each of twenty-four births; many trustworthy people of the town have testified to this. In the same city there was a brother in the convent of C_____ who had not slept for many years; not since, he being then a novice, they awakened him by giving him a fright and a scolding!" And he continues: "Amongst Indians, idlers and poor people, one finds a number of rare accomplishments. I have actually seen in Mexico City a flea leashed with a gold chain composed of links so thin and light that it does not keep the creature from leaping, pricking and running as if it had been loose. The same skill produced little gold boxes as watch-charms that were no bigger than a large bean and had a lock and hidden key and, within, a needle-case with needles, scissors with steel blades, and other exquisite objects."

However not all the Indians were as subjected as the Spanish would have liked to think and one tribe in particular that was most feared and difficult to control were the dreaded Apache. A scattered people living in the northern areas of New Spain, O'Crouley describes their habits and lifestyle with a mixture of awe and no doubt some little fear that every traveller throughout that land must have felt. Not for the Apaches the treatment meted out to the majority of the native Indians. For as O'Crouley tells us: "The Apaches occupy the highest lookout points in order to watch for carelessness on the part of Spaniards and fall upon them, and beat a retreat if pursued by superior numbers. It is their custom to use smoke signals to let each other know when soldiers enter their territory. By the time the soldiers see the first smoke it is useless to undertake pursuit, for by the time they arrive the Apaches are already in territory bordering on that of the Moquis, where it is impossible for the soldiers to penetrate because the mountainous districts are so rough and far extending. They are a bold tribe and artful in the way they handle their arms, which are the bow and arrow and the lance. They admire ironwork of all sorts and they like things that are bright red. They wear the pelts of pumas and deer and wander from one to another part of the sierrra. They set up huts on small encampments and if anyone dies they consider it bad luck and break camp. They are very fond of the flesh of horses and mules, which they consider the sweetest and tastiest of meats. To get it they make their raids. They elect a chief to lead them in war; otherwise each family is ruled by its head. The many runaway Indians, deserters from the Faith, who live amongst them are the greatest cause of harm to us."

O'Crouley's was an age of societies and academies for the enlargement of knowledge about everything and anything, whether in the arts, sciences, agriculture, commerce or antiquities. He belonged to the Real Sociedad Vascongada, founded in the Basque provinces in 1763 and by 1776 numbering a thousand members, not only throughout Spain but also in England and as far away as America. He was a member also of the Real Sociedad Económica Matritense, which applied itself to the study of industry, with a special interest in the latest machines for improving agriculture. He was a corresponding member of the Society of Antiquaries of Edinburgh. He did his duty as a defender of the public safety, being a 'teniente quadrillo mayor' of the Santa y Real Hermandad Vieja de Toledo, which in effect was a kind of civil police force to act against robbers, highwaymen, murderers and other perpetrators of the "continuas atrocidades" that plagued the land, Spanish Kings being too often occupied with wars and unable to safeguard their own subjects. He also had the distinction of receiving a Papal decoration of Honour, a Flor de Lis.

After concluding his business ventures in New Spain, O'Crouley remained in Cádiz and pursued his interests in antiquities and history. In 1784 at the age of forty-four he married Maria Power who was also of Irish ancestry and together they produced nine children.

That he was a successful businessman can be seen from his publication in 1794 of *Musaei O-croulanei*, a catalogue of his own private collections. It lists more than five thousand Greek and Roman coins and about two hundred paintings including works by Van Dyck, Rubens, Murillo, Velazquez, Zurbaran and Ribera. Also catalogued are many geological specimens that he had

369

gathered in New Spain. In qualifying for membership in the Real Academia de Historia, in 1795, he submitted a translation of Joseph Addison's *Dialogues upon the Usefulness of Ancient Medals especially in relation to the Greek and Latin Poets*.

The house where he lived in Cádiz still stands and above the main doorway can be seen the O'Crouley coat of arms. In 1855 the municipal authorities, to honour this 'renowned antiquary' of their city, hung a portrait of him in the Museo Histórico Municipal, where it can be seen today. A street in Cádiz is also named after him.

Had O'Crouley's father not left Ireland it is doubtful if his son would have ever had the slightest possibility of achieving the same success as he did in Spain. As many Irishmen left Ireland for America and in doing so grasped the opportunities that awaited them so too did O'Crouley look to and find through his own efforts the riches that abounded in New Spain. Despite his success he does not seem to have lost a basic understanding of mankind. Not only in regard to his fellow man but also to himself. Perhaps the final paragraph of his *Description of New Spain* describes his own attitude to life: "He who applies himself seriously to the subject will find some measure of enlightenment. As for me, I shall always have the satisfaction of having amused myself."

Sean Galvin is an authority on the Spanish and Irish influence in the western United States.

Irish Colonists on the Plains

ROBERT SAVAGE

Out on the high, treeless plains of northern Nebraska, where a man can look from horizon to horizon and see little but a vast sea of grass, there is, along the banks of the Elkhorn River, which twists its way through these prairies, a thriving community, known as "The Irish Capital of Nebraska." It's the child of an Irishman's grandiose dream—one that never quite came true.

It was but part of a noble scheme, if you please, for a new and imaginative strategy to free Ireland from English domination. This prairie village, a tiny spot in the great American West, was to be the first of a far-flung chain of Celtic colonies forming "a New Ireland, radiating political influence around the globe and commanding the complete respect of the British crown."

The story of this Nebraska town cannot properly be told without first a bit about its founder, one General John O'Neill. If, perchance, you've heard his tale before, don't stop me. It bears repeating, if only briefly. For no matter what one may think of his impracticality, his imprudence, or his soaring flights of fancy, one cannot impugn his dedication and his boundless love for Ireland and the Irish. And surely the memory of that is worth more than half an ear.

He was but a stripling of 14 years when he

371

came to America in 1848, living first in Elizabeth, New Jersey. When he was 21 he was the proprietor of a Catholic bookstore in Richmond, Virginia. Two years of that and he sold out for a more adventuresome life, joining the First Dragoons which was setting out to help quell the Mormon Rebellion in Utah. It has been said that because this affair involved no fighting, he deserted, joined a party of emigrants, and went on to California. In San Francisco he joined the First Cavalry, and when the Civil War broke out he was a sergeant. He distinguished himself in several actions, was wounded at Cumberland Gap, and ended his military career in 1864 as a captain.

But while he fought the good fight for his adopted country, he never forgot the agonies and ordeals of his native land. He had been appointed government pension agent at Nashville, Tennessee, but resigned that post in 1866 to join a Fenian army, said to be made up of 35,000 Civil War veterans, who were going to attack Canada, and hold her hostage until England freed Ireland.

Three times O'Neill invaded Canada, and three times he and his madcap followers were thrown back across the border. Even after the second attempt, when O'Neill was arrested by United States authorities and sentenced to two years imprisonment, he didn't give up. After serving three months he was given a presidential pardon. That was in 1870. In October of 1871, he tried to join his now meager forces with Riel's Rebellion of French Métis in Manitoba; but no sooner had he and his men crossed the border from North Dakota than U.S. troops, with Canada's permission, brought them back. O'Neill stood trial, but immediately was released.

If it's true you can't keep a good man down, John O'Neill was all of that. If he hadn't the means to win militarily he would do it politically. Thus was born the idea of the globe-girdling Celtic colonies which, through their international influence, would be able to bring moral and, possibly, economic pressure on England.

But there was more to it than that. All along the Eastern seaboard, in the cities and in the mines of Pennsylvania, O'Neill's countrymen were caught in an oppressive web of poverty, prejudice and degradation. Many were little better off, if even that, than if they'd never left Ireland. For hundreds of thousands it was a tragic and disgraceful existence.

And yet, all over Western America there were millions of acres of good land, almost for the asking. The Homestead Act had been passed in 1862, and the first homestead, located in Nebraska, was now already ten years in existence. Here was the perfect opportunity for O'Neill to begin the grand scheme for his "New Ireland" and, at the same time, to alleviate the suffering of the Irish immigrants.

"I have always believed," he wrote, "that the next best thing to giving the Irish people their freedom at home is to encourage such of them as come to this country, either from choice or from necessity, to take up lands and build homes in America."

It was a gratuitous ambition, yet he made no secret of the fact that he had not abandoned his illusion of one day conquering Canada. "I had a double object," he said, "first that they might better their families and, second, that they might be in a position from their improved circumstances and their nearness to the contemplated field of future operations to assist in the cause of Irish liberty."

In 1872 and '73 he travelled Illinois, Missouri, Wisconsin, Minnesota, Iowa and Nebraska, making himself familiar with the lands and the opportunities each seemed to offer.

At Lincoln, Nebraska, he met one Patrick Fahy, a land agent, who interested him in establishing a townsite in Holt County, in north-central Nebraska. On condition that he would bring immigrants to the area, O'Neill was paid $600 and some lots in the townsite. News of this arrangement brought unjustified, niggling criticism of his motives. Since leaving his position as military pension agent in Nashville, he hadn't had a paying job in seven years. And while he had passed on many pensions for others, he refused one for himself.

The Nebraska location had special advantages. In this state railroad lands as well as government lands were available for little or no money, an item of no small importance for the impoverished people who were to begin this new life. Furthermore, at a future date the railroad was to be extended through northern Nebraska. Its construction would mean good-paying jobs for many new settlers.

During the first three months of 1874 he sought out Irish communities in the cities and mining districts of Pennsylvania, bringing them a glowing message of a better life awaiting them in this "Promised Land." And, like a 19th century "Irish-Moses" he excoriated them for not taking advantage of the rich opportunities America offered—the very essentials for the kind of life they had

374

been denied in their history. "Why are you content to work on the public projects and at coal mining," he questioned, "when you might, in a few years, own farms of your own and become wealthy and influential people?"

With sharp and vivid colors he painted for them a verbal portrait of the typical Irish immigrant and his often-misdirected efforts. Of course, they had fought courageously for the victorious armies of the North. Indeed, they had worked hard for material benefits and provided much needed labor for the enormous expansion of industry, transportation and commerce which followed the wake of the war. "But," he asked, "what have you done for yourselves?"

While the Irish were allowing themselves to be trapped in the role of providers of brawn, he told them, other nationalities were already enjoying the prestige, influence, respectability and material blessings that accrue from the ownership of land.

All along those railroads where land was given away a few years back, now beautiful cities and towns and magnificent farms are seen. But you are not the owners.

In those beautiful cities raised by your patient skill and industry, you are not the owners. You pay a landlord for the privilege of occupying some flatroofed attic or unhealthy basement.

You work for a master. You sleep under a master's roof. You trade at a master's store, and are expected to vote at a master's bidding.

Is this independence?

You fled from beneath the shadow of the British flag to seek independence in this land of the free but, alas, you have not gained it. You have but changed masters.

He distributed pamphlets telling them what they would need to make the trek West, and how much money they should have to make their start in the "New Ireland." He estimated initial costs for the first year: "temporary house, $50 to $75; team of oxen, $80 to $125; breaking plow, $24 to $30; corn planter, $2 to $3; other tools, $10 to $15; stove, $24 to $30; cooking utensils, $10 to $20; cheap furniture, $20 to $30; cash for expenses, $50 to $100; total, $270 to $428."

On May 12, 1874, the first contingent of the Irish colonists arrived—thirteen men, two women and five children. The railway took them to Omaha where they had to change to a different line. After Omaha they had to change railroads two more times, and when they got to the end of the line they were still 110 miles from their destination. For the next 35 miles they went by stage-coach, but no records are available to tell us how they negotiated the last 75 miles. Undoubtedly at the last stage-stop they procured wagons, horses or oxen, tools and other equipment.

When they arrived at the future site of O'Neill there was not a building to be seen. Not even the surveying and platting of the townsite had been completed. Only the ceaseless, monotonous prairie stretched across the landscape in every direction. Surely it was a scene none of them had ever experienced or envisioned. They had been led into a wilderness, awesome and frightening, with not even the rudiments of any kind of primitive shelter.

The men immediately set about cutting the prairie sod into strips, laying them up like bricks to form a sod house measuring thirty-six by eighteen feet—but no roof, for the only timber to be had for that was some miles away on Red Bird Creek. Six of the men headed out across the plains, marking their trail at regular intervals by poking willow sticks into the ground, to make sure they could find their way back in this always-the-same-wherever-you-looked land of never-ending waves of grass. One week from the day they arrived, the roof was on and they were settling into their new home. They named it "Grand Central Hotel."

Now came the formidable task of conquering this wild prairie and taming it to produce corn and potatoes and beans. The top of the land had to be split open, turned over and sliced into bits to make a seed-bed. And already it was late in the season.

Once the crops were in they set about constructing individual homes. Grand Central Hotel was proving to be no Waldorf. These first homes were dugouts, carved into the earth, about four feet deep, ten feet wide and sixteen feet long, covered with limbs hauled from Red Bird Creek. They were crossed to form a gable, then all plastered over with mud, grass and sod. These crude shelters provided privacy, protection from searing summer winds and the arctic blasts of winter that came howling down over this vast and open land.

Eventually the dugouts were replaced with the traditional sod houses of the Western prairies, and some cabins were built of cottonwood logs, which had to be hauled 18 miles to the building sites.

Their first year's harvest was meager, and little wonder. The colonists were inexperienced at this kind of farming, and the land itself, bordering on Nebraska's famed Sandhills, was not meant for cultivation.

By autumn about half the original settlers remained. In November three new colonists arrived, and as these settled down for a long, hard winter, General O'Neill returned East to lure more Irish to the land of opportunity. But word of the hardships preceded him, and he ran into strong resistance until he received the following letter from Fahy, dated January 1, 1875:

> The country for several miles around the town is now thickly settled, and my brother, James, who has just returned from there, informs me that settlers are coming in rapidly, even at this season of the year, and undoubtedly by spring there will not be a claim untaken within eight miles of the town. When you return in the spring we will have the county organized with O'Neill City as the county seat, and as there will be a large hotel, business houses and other buildings put up in the spring and summer, lots will become valuable and command a ready sale.

This was all the General needed to convince a second group to make the move. They arrived in late April, appalled to find there were no buildings, no businesses and no thickly settled countryside. Fahy had lied, and the General, like his followers, had been taken in. Furthermore, much to the surprise of the settlers, bonds had been issued for O'Neill City and Holt County, and were now being offered for sale by Eastern bankers!

In a letter, which appeared in *The Irish World*, O'Neill blasted Fahy and severed all connections with him. The following August the Holt County settlers passed resolutions for publication in *The*

Irish World declaring their support for the General and urged their countrymen to seize this opportunity to secure homes for themselves—"an opportunity which will be irretrievably lost in the near future. . . . no part of the West offers so many advantages. . . . splendid land, pure water, healthy climate. . . . we will extend a helping hand to those who come here to settle, etc.," ending with "warmest thanks to General O'Neill."

Now came a stroke of Irish luck. General George Armstrong Custer had let out the word that the Black Hills, about 250 miles northwest, were rich in gold. The rush was on, and O'Neill, the last place where gold seekers could buy provisions, was right in its path. Hagerty's General Store, occupying the first building to be erected in the town, was employing ten to twenty clerks and netting over a thousand dollars a day.

By the spring of 1876 more buildings were erected and O'Neill began to take on the appearance of a town. The next group of settlers numbered 102 men, women and children.

In 1877 extension of the long-awaited railroad was about to become a reality. The General lost no time in extolling the opportunities this offered:

> With a certainty of getting work on the railroad I have no hesitation in saying to a single man of sober, industrious, economical habits, who can have $75 or more . . . come out . . . take up a homestead of 160 acres, which will cost you $14; have ten acres broken . . . cost $25; plant the whole of it to corn and potatoes, seed cost not over $5. Leave your crop in charge of a neighbor. Go off and work on the railroad all summer. In the fall return, secure your crop, put up a cabin. With plenty of fish in the river and an abundance of game all around . . . and money you made

during the summer . . . you will get along nicely all winter. You may have to go off to work for three seasons, but after the third you will be in a position to remain at home, a free man on your own farm, the balance of your days, instead of being a slave, working for others.

He further assured them there would be "a number of good-looking girls" from which to select a wife.

Such were the promises of this prairie paradise. But for many it was often a hell on earth. For three years running, 1874, '75 and '76, grasshoppers came in sky-darkening swarms, so thick they shut out the sun, and when they left, not a leaf remained on the corn or the beans or the potatoes. In years when the grasshoppers failed to arrive, prairie fires sometimes took their place. Walls of flame, ten feet high raced across the countryside, chased by the wind. And always, or so it seemed, there was the wind, insistent, wearisome, wailing through the tall grass, sandpapering the nerves of the tired women in their hovels and their men in the fields.

Yet, they survived and more colonists continued to arrive and settle the land. By 1894 two railroads served the community, and the town had its own electric light plant and water works.

The General's knowledge of what constitutes good farming land may have left much to be desired. And yet, as luck would have it, the whole of the countryside sits above one of the world's greatest supplies of underground water, the Ogallala Aquifer. Today giant irrigation rigs, operating like Brobdingnagian lawn sprinklers, tap this rich source of crystal clear water, keeping miles-long fields of corn and vast hay meadows emerald-green, summer after summer. Today's farms in this "New Ireland" range from the traditional family farms of 160 acres to 500, plus many spreads of two thousand and more acres.

The once tiny village now has about five thousand inhabitants, served by 300 businesses. And the fact that there are 12 Christian churches reveals that, over the years, many other nationalities, in addition to the Irish, were attracted to what is still known, however, as "The Irish Capital of Nebraska."

The General never saw this flowering of the seed he had planted. Early in November, 1877, he suffered a slight stroke. The following day his wife took him to St. Joseph's Hospital in Omaha. About six weeks later he died and was buried in Omaha's Holy Sepulcher Cemetery. His impressive monument, a granite shaft fifteen feet high, is incised with Irish and American symbols—the Harp on one side, and the American Eagle, entwined with garlands of shamrocks on the other. The inscription reads, "General John O'Neill, Hero of Ridgeway, Born in Ireland, March 9, 1834, Died in Omaha, January 8, 1878. By nature a brave man."

Robert Savage, a life-long student of the American West, lives in Omaha.

Irish Movers and Managers: Montana, 1875–1900

JOSEPH F. X. McCARTHY

We eastern Americans of Irish descent seldom think about the role of our kinsmen in the development of the western states. We may know about the role of Irishmen in the Gold Rush to California, or their part in the great mining bonanzas of Virginia City on the Comstock Lode; seldom do we even advert to so remote a state as Montana.

Yet, Montana, from its early development to the present, has been enriched by Americans of Irish descent who played prominent state and even national roles. The name of Ambassador, former Senator, Mike Mansfield draws quick recognition today, as did the name of Senator Thomas Walsh in the 1920's and 1930's. Walsh, who had led the investigation into Teapot Dome scandals, was for a short time a possible "compromise" candidate for the Democratic nomination for President in 1928.

Many New Yorkers recall the romantic heroic posture of General Thomas Francis Meagher, transplanted from Waterford to New York by way of a British jail and exile in Tasmania. Meagher was dispatched to Montana Territory as Territorial

Secretary in 1865, served as Acting Governor in the turbulent months that followed, and died under quite mysterious circumstances in 1867. Today, the Montana State Capitol is adorned with an equestrian statue of Meagher, a reminder of his services and spirit.

There were other Irishmen, dozens of them, who helped fashion the course of history in the wild and remote land of Montana. But one man, Marcus Daly, had perhaps the most dramatic and lasting impact through his role in the development of the Montana copper mining industry during the late nineteenth century.

Ever since the 1849 Gold Rush, men were almost irresistably drawn to the deserted mountain streams of the west, to dig and pan for gold, and perhaps to return to civilization fabulously wealthy. One of the chief figures of our western folklore is the prospector, the sourdough, on a burro headed for a "dig." His tools were few—a pick and shovel, a pan in which to wash out gravel in the search for grains or flecks of gold. As in most folklore, there is an easy mingling of fact and fancy in this picture of the lone prospector. Some men indeed did go off on their own, a fortunate few survived, and some of these made discoveries that paid off—either for themselves or for others better equipped and organized. Such an early prospector was one Francois Finley, a shadowy figure who appears to have made a gold strike in 1852 in southwestern Montana, but who passed off the scene without any substantial impact on later developments.

A much more common form of prospecting involved a team of men, who would pool their resources and seek gold as a group. That way, they might be able to divert the water from a promising stream bed, and dig deeper into the gravel to bedrock where the heavy particles of gold lay. Teams were responsible for most of the major gold strikes in Montana—the strikes that lured numbers of people into the territory. Irishmen were among the teams of prospectors in Montana as they had been in California and Colorado: Bill Sweeney, for example, was one of the six prospectors who found gold at Alder Gulch in 1863—a discovery that led its founders to name the area "Virginia City" after the fabulously successful Nevada town of that name. Sweeney and his friends amassed considerable fortunes in the gold diggings.

Once a site was found which promised to yield gold or silver, the pick and shovel prospector was not really in a position to exploit his findings. Mining law permitted claims to be filed, including one hundred feet of land on both sides of a stream. To hold such claims a certain amount of work had to be done each year, but in fact a desirable area had to be worked rapidly, before competitors picked it clean, jumping claims if necessary. A serious effort to extract gold from a river bed called for a good deal of labor and equipment: coffer dams to make excavation of the river bed possible, crushing equipment to get at gold locked within rock formations, and mills to process the ore.

All this called for capital, and for a larger labor force than the one-man prospector could think of organizing. As exploration and mining proceeded, the goal was to find the "Mother Lode," the source of the gold flakes found in a stream. This generally required underground mining, the use of explosives to break loose the ore and the surrounding rock, and of timbers to support mine galleries and shafts. Clearly, that sort of investment required proof that the gold or silver was in sufficient supply to return a profit after shipping the equipment, timber, and men to the mines from the nearest railhead, and getting the ore out and to market.

During the 1860's, a good many Irish miners lived and worked in California, Colorado and Nevada. Following the 1867 discoveries at Alder Gulch and Bannack, Montana, many of these men moved to the new mining frontiers in Montana.

It would be misleading to picture a vast population on the move: miners were often fairly isolated, and the numbers of men who built the mining frontier were never very large by modern standards. In 1870, for example, there were only about 20,000 people in Montana—men, women, and children (relatively few of either women or children, incidentally). Of that number, almost 7,000 were listed as "miners," leaving the rest of the population in the territory to handle trade, banking, transportation, railroad building, and whatever farming and ranching could be found. There were enough Irishmen in the western mines to lend at least some feasibility to the rumor that Fenians among them planned to seize British Columbia.

The talk of gold and silver may seem a bit aside from copper, but in fact the three metals are closely related in the history of American mining. The area around Butte, Montana, was originally a gold and silver mining prospect, one that attracted a fair number of miners, but was never quite the wealthy center its residents hoped it

385

would become—until the 1880's. The story of Butte's skyrocketing development a hundred years ago is largely the story of the career of the Irish immigrant, Marcus Daly, and his friend turned rival and political foe, William Clark, of Scots-Irish descent.

Marcus Daly, born to a County Cavan farm family in 1841, left to seek his fortune in America as a teenager. He landed in New York, worked on the Brooklyn docks for a time, then, in 1861, made his way by ship and Panama railroad to San Francisco, where a married sister was living. The young man joined a kinsman and moved to the minefields of California and Nevada: he took work where he could find it, but he brought to his mining work an active intelligence and the kind of powerful ambition that moved him first from Ireland to Brooklyn, then from Brooklyn to California.

Daly had no formal education, so his experience working in the mines became his laboratory exercises in minerology and engineering. He moved from California to the Comstock Lode area of Virginia City, Nevada, where he had an opportunity to see extensive underground mining under way; there, the timbering system that supported underground mines was very well demonstrated; there, too, he won his first supervisory job: a mine worker named John W. Mackay gave him the chance to prove that he could manage men and get results.

The Comstock didn't hold Daly very long. In 1869 he was hired by Walker Brothers, a very successful firm of Salt Lake City businessmen, and managed a series of mining claims for them. These claims included one particularly large mine, the Emma, which led to a mild international crisis when shares in it were sold for high prices to British investors—just before the lode it was working ran into a fault line and disappeared. While working for the Walkers, Daly had met George Hearst, founder of the Hearst family dynasty in California, who was scouting out suitable mining properties. Daly recommended one mine to Hearst after the Walkers had turned it down. Hearst bought the mine and soon realized enormous profit from it. He naturally held Daly in high regard thereafter.

By 1876, Daly was a much trusted employee of the Walker Brothers, and had already made some investments in mining properties himself. That year, Daly was sent to Butte, Montana, following the discovery of some gold and silver properties in that area. He was to evaluate them, and invest Walker Brothers money in suitable claims or actual mines. By this point in his career, he had better than fifteen years of mining experience, ranging from underground manual labor to management, from sweat equity to cash investment. His income had allowed him to have a relatively small stake in some properties, and his ambition was clearly to be an owner-manager on his own.

Silver and gold were still the major minerals in the Butte scene, and Daly's first Montana activity was in a silver mine, the "Alice," which he managed for the Walkers, and in which he had a part ownership. For a brief time he remained as manager of the Alice mine, a very profitable operation (capitalized at $10 million). However, opportunity began to open for him in quite a different direction. Mixed with the silver, Daly found significant amounts of copper. Unlike his competitors in Montana, Daly decided that the copper would be worth mining in and for itself, and he set out to develop such a venture. His opportunity came with the offer of an operating, but not particularly successful, silver mining property on Butte hill, named "Anaconda," owned and operated by another Irishman, Michael A. Hickey. Daly bought a share in the Anaconda, became convinced that it lay on top of a very valuable lode of high grade copper ore, and in June 1880 turned to his friend George Hearst for direct financing.

As a result, a partnership was formed consisting of Daly, Hearst and two San Francisco lawyers and mine investors, Lloyd Tevis and J. B. Haggin. While the funds for expansion were guaranteed by the three investors, the on-the-scene management and direction were in Daly's hands, and the vision to bring about a copper revolution in Montana was in his mind. A long series of business coups ensued, during which Daly acquired other claims on the mountain, consolidated them into Anaconda, and began the development of a major industrial enterprise.

The work involved not only developing mills and smelters, it meant in effect building a new city in a location with the ample water supplies essential for smelting and treating ore. Daly selected a site some miles northwest of Butte for his company town and named it Copperopolis. When the postmaster discovered another town of the same name, the new city was renamed Anaconda, after the original mine. Prepared to go to any lengths to ensure the success of his dream, Daly imported the best smelting equipment available, from Wales, along with Welshmen to operate it, and had a large body of employees both in Butte itself (largely the residents of "Dublin Gulch") and in Anaconda.

Vertical organization was introduced into the business: timber was secured from the Bitterroot mountains (some claimed it was taken from public land without permit), water and ore from Butte and Anaconda, and financing from as far away as France. Soon the Anaconda output came into direct competition with the copper produced by Lake Superior mines. The superior quality of the copper ore from "the richest mountain in the world," plus the latest techniques for extracting, concentrating, and processing the metal in huge quantities, gave Daly's company a dominant position in the world market. When one considers that this precise period coincided with the development of the electrical industry and the demand for ever more copper wiring for the transcontinental and local telegraph and telephone lines, it is easy to see that an organizational genius—for such Daly undoubtedly was—with access to this remarkably rich ore, would turn himself into one of America's most successful entrepreneurs.

Butte, in the late 1880's and 1890's, could boast of the largest concentration of millionaires in proportion to total population of any city in the United States. Two of these were Marcus Daly and William Clark, whose early business careers had brought them together, and whose political views brought about one of the most remarkable confrontations in American party history. Clark, who was American born and early on the scene, began his mining interests in Butte through banking: he loaned money to prospectors in exchange for shares in their diggings, and on occasion he took over mines in exchange for debts. Clark and Daly were both interested in many of the things that great wealth made possible and that made an intellectual and cultural life feasible in the mountains. Clark, for example, introduced a theatrical company, headed by John Maguire, to Butte: its theater was located at the end of the trolley line, which, conveniently enough, was also owned by Clark. Daly, on the other hand, built a theater of his own in Anaconda, and named it for his wife, Margaret. Daly's contributions to Montana popular culture included the Montana Hotel, one of the most lavish in the west.

Journalism, too, profited from the Clark-Daly rivalry. Clark owned and operated the *Butte Miner*, and Daly responded by founding *The Anaconda Standard*. This became one of the best managed and best written papers in the west, indeed in the country. Based in Anaconda, rather than Butte, it qualified for an A. P. franchise, which enabled it to compete, quite effectively, for circulation in Butte as well as Anaconda itself. One minor touch that showed the Daly approach was his introduction of the first four-color press in the west, which enabled him to provide colored comics as a feature of his paper.

American railroading was influenced greatly by the copper industry, which Daly dominated and in which Clark had a prominent competing role. The massive shipments of ore and equipment called for better transportation than was available by wagons or by narrow-gauge railroad from Ogden, Utah. The Northern Pacific and the Great Northern railway systems competed for the freight business to the mining area of Butte, both systems reaching it in the 1880's. Meanwhile, a third railway provided connections between the Butte mines and the Anaconda smelters. When, in 1891, this connection was threatened by a railroad industry battle over rates, Daly solved the problem for his company by building his own line, the Butte, Anaconda & Pacific—the first completely electrified railroad in America.

The political rivalry between Clark and Daly surfaced first in 1888, when Montana was electing a Territorial Representative to serve in Washington until statehood could be attained. Clark had the Democratic nomination, while a man named Carter was the Republican candidate. Daly, who was a Democrat by instinct and connection, switched his support to Carter in a surprise move. He reasoned, it seems, that Carter was likely to have more influence in Republican-dominated Washington where decisions were pending concerning the harvesting of timber from publicly owned forests. Successful mining, of course, demanded enormous amounts of timber both to support mine shafts and to fuel smelters. Carter won the election.

The first Senatorial contests in the new State of Montana continued the Clark-Daly split. Clark had the Democratic endorsement for one of the new State's two seats, but an unending dispute in the state legislature ended with four candidates (two Democrats and two Republicans) going to Washington with disputed credentials. When the Democrats organized a State convention in 1890, Daly's friends placed an Anaconda attorney, William W. Dixon, on the ballot as the senatorial candidate, and Daly is said to have contributed over $50,000 to the election campaign, in which Clark's forces were again defeated.

The Clark faction won one major issue: a fight over the site for Montana's permanent capital. Daly wanted this plum for Anaconda, and Clark was willing to see it anywhere else in the State. The runoff election between Helena and Anaconda gave Daly his worst political defeat, and established Helena as the capital by a margin of 27,028 to 25,118.

Political issues continued to interest both men, and Daly in particular took a prominent role in national Democratic politics. He was reputedly the largest single contributor to William Jennings Bryan's campaign in 1896 and even brought Bryan to Anaconda for a mass meeting at which thousands cheered the Free Silver doctrine. From a business point of view, free silver was obviously good for Montana copper miners, for silver was then, as it is today, an important by-product of the copper industry.

The two men continued their rivalry down to the end of Daly's life. Clark succeeded in winning a senatorial election (then, of course, conducted in the State Legislature) in 1899, after a singularly complicated series of charges and counter-charges involving bribery of state legislators. Daly followed the case to Washington, D.C., where he testified at the Senate investigation into the seating of Clark. After much investigation and confusion, Clark's campaign manager was disbarred, and Clark himself was forced to offer his resignation from the Senate. With Daly on his deathbed in New York, Clark's seat in the Senate was granted to him after still another Montana legislative election.

Marcus Daly was known as the Copper King of Montana, a title more fitting than the somewhat less reverential ones of White Czar or Irish Shy-lock which were assigned him during his long feud with Clark. His work was sensational, and it was solid: the Anaconda Company, when Daly died in 1900, employed almost three-fourths of all the wage earners in Montana. The Irish-born, self-educated miner enjoyed good relations with his employees at a time when few capitalists could make such a claim. He had worked in the mines himself, and had a "common touch" that stood him in good stead with his workers.

No evaluation of Daly would be complete without at least a word or two about another of his absorbing interests. After his fortune was secure in Anaconda, Daly bought himself a great estate in the Bitterroot mountains, where he ran a stock farm: there, among others, he had a great racer whom he named Tammany, and with whom he won several major events. As one might suppose, his racing silks were copper and green, the colors of his business and his birthplace.

Marcus Daly had accomplished much in the time since he left that birthplace. But the strenuous years spent building his copper empire had taken their toll. In his final years he travelled to European spas in an attempt to restore his failing health. Returning from one of these trips, he fell ill again and died in New York on November 12, 1900. At the same time his funeral was being conducted at St. Patrick's Cathedral, church bells all across his beloved Montana tolled in his memory.

The twentieth century history of Anaconda and the copper industry in Montana is a complicated and illuminating study of a major American industry. The company moved into, then out of, the Standard Oil empire, but there was an unmistakable Irish-American tone to the top management of the firm through three generations: Cornelius Kelley and John D. Ryan succeeded to the great mantle of Marcus Daly as the guiding hands of this international firm.

Few men have left such an impact on American industry as Daly did on the copper industry and the development of Montana. He stands in Butte yet, in a monument commissioned by his friends and followers in the years just after his death. The bronze statue showing him standing, hat in hand, was executed by Augustus Saint-Gaudens, the Irish-born sculptor. It stands today at a prominent site on the campus of the Montana School of Mines, overlooking the city of Butte and the "richest hill on earth."

Daly had led hundreds of his countrymen to Montana, their "new country." He was a leader whose vision and skill showed what could be done, in the yeasty days of the 1870's and 1880's, by an unschooled Irish immigrant whose capital assets were physical strength and intellectual curiosity. His is an Irish American success story, the story of a manager who moved mountains, and who left an industry as his monument.

Joseph McCarthy is Vice President for Academic Affairs at Fordham University.

Owen J. Goldrick:
The Career
of a Denver Irishman

PATRICIA McGIVERN

All hail then to the pioneers who, with no smooth roads
to follow, nor beaten trails to guide reached and redeemed from the sway of the savage, made a garden of
this "American Desert," built a big city in the wilderness
and opened the vaults where the gold dust shines, and
gave us the key of the silver mines.

These words from Owen Goldrick's celebratory address of July 4, 1876 on the admission to the Union of the
State of Colorado, aptly summarize the proud spirit and
accomplishments of those first Denverites, the "Fif-
tyniners," who crossed the plains to Colorado in search
of gold and fortune. What could be more appropriate
than to have O.J. himself deliver the salutation? In the 17
odd years since he had come to Denver, as the legend
goes, wearing a glossy plug hat, white gloves (or laven-
der, as some observers reported), striped trousers and a
Prince Albert hat, driving an ox cart and swearing at
them in Latin or Greek, Owen Goldrick had made his
mark as a schoolteacher, superintendent of schools, reporter, editor and publisher of the *Rocky Mountain Herald*
from 1868 to 1882, in which capacity he was also a poet
and a man of letters. While there is a great deal of research to be done on Goldrick and his times, it is possible
to put together at least a sketchy portrait of Denver's
most colorful character, a portrait gleaned from spotty
evidence handed down to us from family and friends,

but mostly from the lively pages of the *Herald*, which served as an optimum organ for Goldrick's wit, sarcasm and verbosity.

It is not surprising that Goldrick had a talent for oratory and writing. Born in Ireland anywhere from 1829 to 1832, and emigrating at an early age, Goldrick brought with him the traditional Irish interest in learning, appreciation of oral tradition, and love for the music of language. His speeches and high flown, extravagant writings suggest the stylistic influence of the Irish dramatists, Macklin and O'Malley; the Gallic poet, Merriman; and the Anglo-Irish poet, Moore.

An investigation of his early days in Ireland might throw light on the events of his later life. However, not much is known. Even his first name is a puzzle. The only biography published on Goldrick gives his first name as Oscar. Although he used "O.J.," family letters on file at the Colorado History Society refer to him as Owen. While his place of birth is often given as Sligo, the county presumably, the *Fiftyniner's Directory*, lists it as the City of Sligo. We know that he sailed from Sligo with his brother, James, on the bark, *Adario* and arrived in New York on September 16, 1847.

Fascinated by New York, Owen wrote to James from a hovel on Grand Street in the city's Irish ghetto on November 7, 1847, exulting in its wonders, "This is the greatest place in the world." Nonetheless, he complained of his poor cot and the rotten coffee. Mindful of his continuing family obligations, he also wrote that he planned to send a draft of $50 on a Sligo bank.

By 1850, Owen was teaching in Reynoldsburg, Ohio, where his brother, William, practiced as a physician, and James, though dissatisfied, was also a teacher. As a condition to teaching, Owen agreed to be certified or examined, for the job. "I will submit myself to egotism and say that I am fully prepared to be examined for and teach any of your Borough or City schools." In spite of this confidence, Owen's qualifications are unknown. He claimed to have degrees from Trinity College, Dublin, and Columbia University. However, his relative, Mrs. Joan Goldrick Johnson, confirmed in 1964 that Owen had not attended either institution.

Owen was not without academic talent. A letter dated March 6, 1850, from James to the parents presaged Owen's latent talents as an educational administrator and a writer.

> Owen will be a successful and popular teacher. He will . . . distinguish himself, I think . . . . He has learned some useful practice personal lessons since I last wrote that benefitted him some; he studies mine and other good books more also and has either no other society or much better; and from his desire for teachers' associations, periodicals and their acquaintance, he may become an essayist.

It would seem that life in Reynoldsburg was comfortable, serene and, maybe, a bit static. Before long, Owen had moved on to St. Louis lured by an inherited streak of independence, which had caused Owen, Sr., many years earlier, to renounce his Roman Catholic background and all forms of popish trappings.

In St. Louis, Owen was hired by J. B. Doyle, a wealthy merchant, to tutor his children. Later, Doyle took Owen back to his home in New Mexico where we may surmise that he became bored because a friend of Doyle's lured Goldrick to Denver by sending him a small vial of gold dust. Arriving in Denver with fifty cents in his pocket, half of which he invested in a cigar and the rest in Taos lightning, and dressed in his Beau Brummel duds, he is reputed to have exclaimed in Latin or Greek, "Do I go to Rome or do I remain here?" Remain he did and soon hung out his "shingle" by advertising his school and listing his qualifications in the *Rocky Mountain News* of August 27, 1859.

From many years' experience as Principal and Superintendent of schools and academies in the East, and a familiarity with the latest approved modes of teaching and successful governing, he trusts to be able to secure the speedy and substantial improvement of all grades of pupils . . . .

As there is no evidence to suggest that he had been a superintendent, O.J. was clearly stretching the truth. The word travelled around Denver that he had been educated at a leading Irish University. Who would disbelieve him? In those early days in Denver, when all varieties of people from every walk of life, some of whom had pushed wheelbarrows across the plains, came to dig for gold and pitch tents along the South Platte River, no one was presumptuous enough to question his credentials.

In opening the first school, in October, 1859, Goldrick registered "sixteen students, three or four Mexican half breeds, three or four Indians, the rest being strange to say, from Missouri." That Goldrick was a success as a schoolmaster is attested to by an article in the *Rocky Mountain News* of October 20, 1859:

The discipline is just what it ought to be; not too harsh, nor yet too indulgent; and Professor Goldrick's mode of instruction is simple enough for the smallest, while it is scientific enough for the largest, who may avail themselves of its benefits.

A few months later, O.J. opened a larger school and a Sunday school serving all denominations. In 1861, he was elected superintendent of schools in Arapahoe County and later served in that capacity in Boulder County. Although Goldrick is remembered by Denverites as "the Professor," founder of the first school and teacher of trigonometry, chemistry, physiology, astronomy, grammar and composition, he is best remem-

398

bered as a flamboyant, enigmatic and sometimes egotistical Irish journalist.

Why William Byers, empire railroad builder and owner of the *Rocky Mountain News*, ever hired O.J. as a reporter is a mystery to some, who claim that Goldrick was to write the dullest column in the history of the *Rocky Mountain News*. In spite of this opinion, Goldrick's writings were popular and, by 1864, he had a byline. One of his most famous pieces was his lengthy article on the Cherry Creek flood of 1864, which was published in the May 19 issue of the *Daily Commonwealth* since the *News* offices had floated away. In this article in which one sentence contained 132 words without ever mentioning the flood, O.J. concluded bombastically that, "men are mere ciphers in creation: at least chattels of the elements and creatures of circumstance and caprice." Impressing the readership with his learning, Goldrick proclaimed that, "the inundation of the Nile, the Noahian deluge and that of Prometheus' son Deucalian, the Noah of the Greeks, are now in danger of being outdeluged by this great phenomenon of '64."

During the sixties and seventies, the stories citing Goldrick as the "character" began. He became a legend in his own time. Like the Irish stereotypes in Macklin's and O'Malley's plays, Goldrick came to personify Teague, the Irish figure in 18th and 19th century drama, who is consumed with drinking, brawling, and making speeches. Moreover, he maintained for a long time his bachelor status escorting local ladies to balls and other social affairs; finally, however, he relented and married a Chicago widow, Mrs. O'Driscoll, in May, 1873. Reported the Rocky Mountain Herald on May 7, 1873, "that the well known and worthy Goldrick has finally gone and done it like the gallant gentlemen he is and ever has been since Colorado was settled."

While Goldrick enjoyed his whiskey (especially a variety known as Taos lightning), he was a model of sobriety after the wedding and during his married life, but went back to the bottle after his wife's death in 1877. A newspaper colleague, S. T. Sopris, recalls that, "While working on the *Rocky Mountain News*, Goldrick became dissipated, and seldom went to bed sober, known by everyone, he could find shelter any time of night. When he failed to show up on the *News*, people would say "who will go and find Goldrick?"

An account of his sometimes pugnacious tendencies relates to a dueling incident in 1863. On his way to a party, dressed in his famous formal attire of striped trousers, swallow tail coat and plug hat, O.J. stopped in the Iambian Saloon on Larimer Street. There a certain Ameil Berraud passed a remark about the professor's clothes and was immediately challenged to a duel. The duel took place and Berraud feigned injuries by having bitters poured on his shirt. Later, it developed that blank cartridges had been substituted for the real ones by the seconds.

When he assumed the editorship and publication of the *Rocky Mountain Herald*, O.J. continued to write lively, zesty pieces, essays, and poems on every subject from ladies' fashions to the Fenian Movement. Goldrick's pieces include the poems: "Kourting in the Seasons," "Fashion on the Brain," and "Wheel of Fortune"; the essays: "Prairie Pepper," and "Tit Bits"; the stories: "A Woman's *No*" and "My First Flirtation." While his writing on pioneers and the West's history is generally known and reprinted to this day, O.J. Goldrick's interest in the political future of his native Ireland, as reflected in his paper, was intense.

An ardent Fenian, elected to the Denver Chapter of the Irish National League, Goldrick wrote, in an editorial on St. Patrick's Day, 1864, a glowing tribute to the land of his forefathers. It also demonstrates his alliterative style

400

and vitality. "[Ireland's] lovely lakes and charming coves, its capes and causeways, crowded towns and shady solitude diversify its surfaces . . . ." Living on the hot, dry and dusty slope of eastern Colorado, O.J. must have been thinking of his native Sligo when he wrote this. Continuing the editorial, he reflects on the past. "That little isle, weak for lack of franchise, but famous in song and story as long as freedom is a notary, or eloquence an admirer, exists at present only as a crumbling ruin of once a great independent nation. . . ." Recalling the glorious past of Ireland's pre-Christian and early Christian period, he quotes from Moore's "The Harp That Once Through Tara's Halls." Finally, the editorial lashes out at imperialist England's dominating poor, old Ireland which "has been basely hurled into thralldom by the selfish sceptre of monarchic England, whose bloodhounds have been lapping the gore of her liberties for nearly a century. . . ."

To paraphrase, O.J. cites the renowned patriots of the past, Emmet, Burke, and Grattan, and hopes to see Ireland righted of her wrongs and brought back to former glory. For Denver's Irishmen, the editorial would keep alive the sacredness of that annual anniversary of vanished glories. Like the leaders of the minority groups today, Goldrick felt it necessary to reinforce the accomplishments of his people in the hope that the Irish American eventually would find respectability and acceptance on these shores.

Along with praise of Ireland, the traditional dislike and mistrust of Britain runs through the pages of the *Herald*. On February 1, 1868, he wrote, "The *London Times* allows in plain language, that an Irishman and an Englishman have nothing in common, but that the former, was made to be led by demagogues." How Goldrick loved to deliver jibes at Britain by reporting

Fenian news and victories. On March 21, 1868, the *Herald* mentioned that the Fenians had a new method of twitting the English. When the agents of the British absentee landlords came to collect rent from the impoverished Irish farmers, the Fenians were often there to receive them. "Bailiffs are hunted like wolves, and their offenders when arrested are promptly acquitted by Fenian juries." On February 14, March 21 and May 30, 1868, the Herald reported on the Fenian uprising in the United States and Canada. On April 1, 1870, the *Herald* reported that O'Neill's army planned to invade Canada at three points. Eventually, the uprising collapsed, and Fenianism endured as a vivid memory.

Besides Irish political news, Goldrick's paper also reported Irish social news. Fenian events were always covered. The February 8, 1877 edition of the *Herald* reported at length Goldrick's election to the Fenians. There was, in addition to recitations and literary exercises, a grand ball of the Mitchel Guards, the local Fenian society, presumably, named for John Mitchel, the young Ireland activist. A huge *Cead Mille Failte*, translated as "100,000 welcomes," hung over the dais.

Goldrick was interested in an offshoot of the Irish political problem, namely, religious coexistence. Although his own affiliations seem to suggest Protestant connections, such as attendance at Trinity Collge and the apostasy of his father, he was neutral in his view of the religious conflict in Ireland. In an editorial in the Herald on July 15, 1871, Goldrick wrote, "Papacy and Protestantism will have to accord each other's rights ere the reign of any Utopia on Irish soil."

In a lighter vein, Goldrick's *Herald* offered a wealth of scintillating reading on life in small western United States during the latter half of the 19th century. In the *Herald* of September 9, 1868, his essay entitled *A Bachelor's Defense* was printed.

These fellows [married men] are always talking about the
loneliness of bachelors. Loneliness indeed. Who is pelted
to death by ladies with marriageable daughters, invited
to tea and evening parties and told to drop in just when it
is convenient. The bachelor. St. Paul says that he that
marries not does better.

O.J. was speaking from experience. Recall Sopri's
comment about Goldrick's having a welcome bed anywhere in Denver. O.J. must have been Denver's most
eligible bachelor and a prime target for the attention of
the ladies at balls when he wrote his stinging *Essay on Old
Flirts* in the February 22, 1868 *Herald*. Disparaging the old
flirt, especially the spinster between 38 and 48 who
wears low cut dresses and cannot get anyone to dance
with her, Goldrick lets loose his venom on the hostess
who solicits available men as dance partners. In spite of
his prized freedom, Goldrick went off to Chicago on a
business trip, met, and married a middle-aged widow of
whom little is recorded. When the former Mrs.
O'Driscoll died in 1877, O.J. wrote a moving obituary to
her.

There exists more evidence of a good natured cynicism
toward women and their preoccupation with fashion. In
the February 22, 1868 edition, he penned,

> *Here's to the maids with borrowed braids*
> *And here's to the girls with curls, sir,*
> *Here's to lass of every class,*
> *Unjeweled or in pearls, sir.*
> . . .
> *Upon your hair bestow less care*
> *And more upon your soul, Miss.*

On March 7, 1868, the *Herald* carried an article which
objected to women who practiced law in Kansas. Such
women were suspect in Goldrick's eyes, since
". . .crusty old chaps might get confused by the pleading

of some fascinating advocate." Goldrick continues on the subject on women in the March 21, 1868 edition, by distinguishing boys from girls, "Boys tend naturally toward fun out-of-doors life, leaky boots and shoes and torn trousers. Girls tend toward the sober proprieties, pensive poetry, hemming handkerchiefs and a few calls on their neighbours." If Goldrick thought that poetry writing was a feminine activity, he had no qualms about his own verse. In the twenty years or so that he left his imprint on early Denver, his florid poetry tirelessly celebrated his beloved Colorado.

> *All hail to Colorado!*
> *The Rocky Mountain Gem!*
> *That glistens on the summit*
> *Of Columbia's diadem!*

With his Celtic love of words and wit, Goldrick bequeathed to Western history a newspaper legacy of daily doings in the "Boss City" between St. Louis and San Francisco. While the *Herald* was cosmopolitan in its coverage of news, Goldrick, as its editor, created an atmosphere of tremendous civic pride in Denver. Moreover, although he had travelled thousands of miles from his native Ireland, he kept alive the values, traditions and uniqueness of his countrymen. For the citizens of Colorado, while Goldrick himself at times was the stereotype of the exaggerating and drinking Irishman, he projected a positive image of the immigrant Irishman, especially in terms of intellect. On his death, the Reverend Reuben Jeffreys remarked in his eulogy, "Professor Goldrick was a forcible, trenchant writer, fearless and outspoken in his manner, had little regard for the conventionalities of society and heartily detested sham and hypocrisy in all its forms."

Ms. McGivern is a school teacher.

Irish Pioneers in Northern New York

JAMES H. TULLY, JR.

IN THE EARLY DECADES OF THE EIGHTEENTH CENTURY, NEW York was far behind the other colonies in population and development. In 1750, it had a population of 80,000, while Virginia had 275,000 inhabitants, Massachusetts 180,000, Pennsylvania 150,000, Maryland 137,000 and Connecticut 100,000. If it were not for New Yory City, it would have been further behind; although New York was the sixth largest colony, its principal city was the third largest in the colonies. There are two major reasons for this. The first was the manner in which New York was settled. The Hudson Valley was divided into manors, containing many acres of land owned by a family but worked by tenant farmers. These manors were vast. For instance, the holdings of the Rensselaers around Albany encompassed all of present day Rensselaer County and much of present Albany County. Thus, fee title to property could not readily be obtained by a migrant in much of the Hudson Valley. Secondly, west of Albany was found the powerful Iroquois nation, consisting of six Indian tribes (namely, the Mohawks, Oneidas, Onondagas, Cayugas, Senecas and Tuscaroras), which stood together in a strong confederation and controlled the Mohawk Valley. Accordingly, there were no White settlements from Schenectady to present day Buffalo.

A consequence of these facts was that the main industry in New York in the eighteenth century was the fur trade. The

405

Indians, acting both as original suppliers and middlemen, brought pelts to Albany. The furs were traded there, brought down the Hudson, and shipped all over the world.

To this setting came an extraordinary Irish immigrant, William Johnson, in 1738. One reason that Irish Americans do not know more about him is that that great conservator of our cultural heritage, the parochial school system, largely ignores him. He is ignored, I believe, because he is in some ways a bit of an embarrassment. Firstly, he and his family remained loyal to the Crown through the Revolutionary War, and, secondly, he renounced the Church when he recognized it was an impediment to his advance. Moreover, I fear there was something even worse. Johnson was an avid admirer of womankind, and left much evidence of it—a stretch of illegitimate children from Albany to the dusty longhouses of the great Seneca Nation in the far western reaches of New York.

Johnson was born in 1715, the child of an unacceptable marriage between Ann Warren, the daughter of Protestant landowners in County Meath, Ireland, and Christopher Johnson, a Catholic tenant on the Warren property. Because of his connection with the landowning family, Christopher Johnson was allowed to be a tenant miller. But, as a Catholic, he was forbidden by law to purchase land, or rent it for more than thirty-one years.

William Johnson realized early that he was not being treated as well as his Warren cousins in the family's manor; it took no unusual power to discern that the only people who could remain Catholic in the British Empire were peasants, priests and martyrs. He, accordingly, abandoned his Catholic faith, retained a vague belief in God, and outwardly adopted the precepts of the Church of England.

Johnson's life changed dramatically in June 1737 when he received a letter which read:

My Dear Nephew William—

Although we have never met, I have heard from my beloved sister Anne—your mother—that you have grown to be a fine, strong, intelligent young man with great imagination and distinct qualities of leadership. I am pleased to learn this, for it has become my lot to seek the services of just such an individual, to manage for me a bountiful section of land I have become possessor of in the valley of the River Mohawk here in America. This title encompasses an area of 14,000 acres of fine ground.

Should you care to accept the offer I am about to make, I should like you to recruit a goodly number of peasants in your neighborhood (or elsewhere in Ireland), men of no more than twoscore years of age, married, honest and hale of health, and both fit and willing to work as tenant farmers on the said land in New York Colony in return for their passage to America, such passage to include wife and not more than two children. You may offer them tenant parcels of 200 acres each and an indenture of five years, after which time, should they so desire, they may stay on and draw wages and also receive, at nominal cost, up to ten acres of their own, or, if they desire it, to leave and go where they will as free-men. You, in turn, would manage them on this land, which in fairness I must add, is essentially wilderness. You would see to the management of all affairs there as my agent. This would include the establishment of a plantation which would be yours to operate, accountable to none but me.

I would imagine you should have little difficulty in finding such men as are required, and I urge that you recruit with selection and make such offer only to those who are good men and able to sign their indenture bills in their own hand. I would not care to see among this number that you may re-cruit, any men in whose background there is evidence of mutinous nature, or men who have, for any reason whatso-ever, served a period of time in prison. From such come the seeds of discontent.

Provision will be made for your passage first and their's later. I would be on hand to greet you on your arrival in Boston, at which time we could, in greater detail, discuss what must be done.

I look forward to your quick reply and trust that it shall be in the affirmative.

> With affection and sincere
> good wishes for your continued
> health, I am,
> Your Uncle,
> Peter Warren

New York
April 29, 1737

On March 16, 1739, William Johnson arrived with twelve County Meath families in Boston. He was described by contemporaries as being tall and well built, a swarthy complexion and dark hair. He cared little about dress and, at the time he arrived, was hardly literate.

His uncle, who later became Admiral Peter Warren, told him where he was to go and what he was to do. He was to travel to New York City, and then up the Hudson to the Dutch city of Albany, thereafter to another Dutch city of Schenectady, and then go twenty miles beyond Schenectady to what Sir Peter called Warrensburg—twenty-two square miles at the point where the Schoharie Creek meets the Mohawk on its west bank. His duty was to establish a plantation with the Irish families and eight German families, who were waiting for him in New York. He was to give each family 200 acre plots, and to do the same for any other tenant families who would arrive.

When Johnson arrived, he found not open fields and farms, but wilderness. There was a fort where the Schoharie met the Mohawk, Fort Hunter, with a garrison of twenty soldiers. At the neighboring village of Teantontalogo, there were 360 Mohawks. He soon established a trading post where liquor, knives, calico, rifles and bullet molds were sold to the Indians with considerable success. Perhaps recalling his own exposure to discrimination in Ireland, he insisted that the natives be treated fairly and decently, thereby establishing strong bonds of friendship.

In a few years, William left his uncle's interests behind him when he invested his trading profits in land across the river, where he built first Fort Johnson, then Johnson Hall, and then Guy Park for a married daughter, all of which still stand, becoming in the process the greatest landowner in the Mohawk Valley. Needless to write, his friendship with the Indians enabled him to purchase property on very favorable terms.

Allen Eckert, in *Wilderness Empire*, remarked:

The Indians could scarcely believe what happened when William dealt with them. As was usual in trading deals, liquor flowed in abundance, but it was there that common custom ended. It was normal, after imbibing to excess, for the braves to fall into drunken stupor and then awaken to find their pelts mostly gone as payment for the rum that had been drunk, and not enough skins left with which to buy clothes and blankets and ammunition for them and their families in the months ahead.

Not so when William Johnson dealt with them.

This is what astounded them: when they came groggily erect the next morning, they found that the rum they had drunk was not charged against them, that their pelt bundles were intact, and that an excellent deal awaited them in the trade. And when the pleasant trading was finished, Johnson presented each man with a jew's-harp, showing them how to play it and then joined them in the gales of laughter which swept them all as they attempted to play.

One man in the valley penned this opinion of Johnson in his diary:

Something in his natural temper responds to Indian ways. The man holding up a spear he has just thrown, upon which a fish is now impaled; the man who runs, with his toes turned safely inward, through a forest where a greenhorn could not walk; the man sitting silent, gun on knee, in a towering black glade, watching by candle flame for the movement of antlers toward a tree whose bark has already been streaked by the tongues of deer; the man who can read a bent twig like an historical volume—this man is William Johnson, and he has learned all these skills from the Mohawks.

Because of his relationship with the Indians, whom he allied with the British against the French on many occasions, he became the Crown's agent in its dealings with the Mohawk Nation. However, more importantly, before he received that appointment, he had become, in 1742, a blood brother of the Mohawks, receiving the name Warraghiyagey (meaning "one who undertakes great things")—the only white man who could speak at the longhouse council of the Iroquois Nation.

After observing Johnson's treatment of the Mohawks and his awkward effort to learn the Mohawk tongue so that he could "more fairly deal with them and help them," the chief of the Mohawks, Tiyanoga, pointed out to a meeting of the six nations of the Iroquois at Onondaga in October 1742 that they desperately needed a White champion who could candidly and wisely advise them in their dealings with other Whites. Tiyanoga told the chief such a man was William Johnson and recommended that he be adopted as a full member into the Mohawk tribe as well as in the Iroquois league. After the proposal was adopted, a day was set for the ceremony at the principal Mohawk village of Canajoharie. For three days prior to the ceremony braves arrived from throughout the six nations—from the Cayugas, Onondagas, Oneidas, Tuscaroras and Senecas, as well as the Mohawks. No White other than Johnson was permitted to attend. He was stripped and painted. He was instructed in the ways of the league and made a brother of the Mohawks.

Until his death, Sir William led the Iroquois, time and again, against the French. His greatest triumph was at Lake George, in September 1755, where he and his Indians, with a few British soldiers, defeated the French army under Baron Diskeau, which had been sent to capture Albany. As a result of this victory, he was made a Baronet on December 31, 1755. His last dealings with the Indians occurred in July 1774 at Johnson Hall when he successfully persuaded them to remain loyal to the Crown, rather than side with the Revolutionists. During these exertions, he suffered a fatal stroke.

Johnson's son, Sir John Johnson, by a liaison with Catherine Weisenberg, a German servant with a Dutch family in Schenectady, led the Tories in New York after Sir William's death, and, in alliance with the renowned Indian leader, Joseph Brant, led the Indians on savage forays in the Mohawk and Hudson Valleys—forays which are still remembered, particularly in the Cherry and Schoharie Valleys. (Brant was either Sir William's brother-in-law or his son. In his later years, Sir William had formed a liaison with Molly Brant, a full-blooded Mohawk, and Joseph was raised in their home as her brother. He left his name to Brant Lake in the Adirondacks.)

After the Revolution, Sir John and the remaining members of the Johnson family fled to Canada.

It is to state the obvious to say that Sir William failed to back the winning side in the Revolution; accentuating the positive, however, I suggest that he should be commemorated in our State's history as an empire builder who converted a vast wilderness into productive land, who transplanted immigrants from a barren existence to a gainful life, and who stood up for Indian rights when that stance was unpopular.

* * * * *

Another interesting Irish immigrant was William Prendergast, an unsung hero who was the first to lead the tenants of the Hudson River manors in rebellion against the patroon system. He was unsuccessful, however, and a century passed before the tenant system was finally broken.

Prendergast was born in Kilkenny, Ireland, where he doubtlessly learned something about tenant associations. After emigrating to America, he became a tenant on the estate of a Philipse family, who lived in a manorhouse overlooking the Hudson at Yonkers. Prendergast aroused the farmers of the Hudson Valley and of Dutchess and Westchester Counties with the rallying cry, "Pay your honest debts as honest men should—but not a shilling for rent." With his sympathizers, he

411

led a raid on Justice Peters' home, whose decisions had thrown many a tenant into jail, and proceeded to give that magistrate a ducking, dragged him through the mud, and beat him with a whip. When Peters objected, pointing out that he was a representative of the King, Prendergast retorted: "If the King were here, I would serve him the same way."

On April 15, 1754, he led a thousand farmers, each carrying six days' provisions, arms and ammunition, through the valley in a march on New York City. In their trek, they invaded the manors of the Hudson Highlands, dispossessed tenants who had taken over the acres of farmers ejected for debt, and returned the land to the original holders. Throughout the lower Hudson Valley, the farmers left their Spring plowing, took their guns, and rode out to join their neighbors.

While New York City waited, the army reached Cortlandt Manor and pronounced all Westchester manor rents invalid. General Gage ordered the militia to be ready. The Governor issued a proclamation offering a reward of 100 pounds for apprehending "William Pendergass [sic], the head and leader of said Rioters." The troops landed at Poughkeepsie and Prendergast was driven back to Quaker Hill, and finally captured and taken to New York City and imprisoned. His trial, however, was held in Poughkeepsie. The judges were the Honorable Horsmanden, Chief Justice of the Supreme Court of the province, and Judge Livingston of the same court, who was also a member of his Majesty's Council and a landowner. When it came time for his defense, William's wife stood behind him and as an old chronicle stated, "reminded him of and suggested to him everything that could be mentioned to his advantage." When the prosecutor berated him with fiery rhetoric as a dangerous criminal, she gently interposed that, before the recent disturbances, he had been "esteemed a sober, honest and industrious farmer, much beloved by his neighbors." The prosecutor wanted her removed from the courtroom "lest she too much influence the jury." "She does not disturb the court," replied the Chief Justice, "nor does she speak unseasonably." "Your Lordship, I do not think that she should speak at all, and I fear her very looks may too much influence the jury." "For the same reason you might as well move the Prisoner himself be covered with a veil," said Justice Horsmanden.

The old journal continued by remarking that Mrs. Prendergast's "affectionate assiduity filled every observer with a tender concern." Nonetheless, the prisoner was found guilty and sentenced to be hanged. Mrs. Prendergast, though, was not to lose her Billy so easily and, in an appeal to the Governor, persuaded him that he defer the execution. There was another practical problem: Sheriff Livingston of Dutchess County was having difficulty finding a hangman. The king later pardoned Prendergast.

Prendergast and his wife thereafter moved to Pittstown in Rensselaer County, and finally left the State entirely. In the Spring of 1805, when William was seventy-eight, and his wife sixty-seven, they set out with four sons, five daughters, several sons-in-law, some grandchildren, and a Negro slave for Tennessee. Their son, James Prendergast, returned to New York in the autumn of 1810, and founded Jamestown.

* * * * *

We now turn from a couple of Irish immigrants whose lives were dramatic to the great mass of immigrants who were driven from their birthplace by poverty and discrimination to the canals, foundries, and cement mines of northern New York. The start of the large migration was prompted by the construction of the Erie Canal. (The English, in building their canal system in Britain, had used Irish labor to get the job done as economically as possible.) A man named Canvass White led the campaign to recruit Irish laborers as a work force on the canal. White, while in England on a canal inspection tour in late 1817 and early 1818, had become acquainted with an experienced canal construction engineer, J. J. McShane, an Irishman from Tipperary. White persuaded McShane and his

413

crew of canal maintenance men to come to America, and take jobs on the Erie Construction Project. Then, he set about the task of recruiting a force of Irish laborers to work under McShane's direction.

The principal source of Irish labor was in the cities, and when the call went out, hundreds of brawny young men responded willingly and were shipped to America in 1818—a time when that part of the canal which had been under construction since the previous July looked, in the words of one historian, "like a dotted line of poorly dug, unfinished ditches."

A canal expert, Lionel Wyld of the University of Buffalo, put it this way in his *Low Bridge:*

> The Irish have come in for perhaps more than their share of the ribbing as foofoos (non-native workers on the canal) on the canal as well as off it, but they were, by and large, well respected as the backbone of canal construction. Imported largely to serve as laborers, the Irish proved to be the greatest of boons to the digging of the Ditch. They turned "Clinton's Folly" in the Grand Western Canal. Few people could stand the conditions which the Irish laborers tolerated. Local inhabitants, Pennsylvania Dutch, and Negroes from the South were all tried, but the Irish bogtrotters proved always the best of the lot. They had stamina and they had grit. Some of the Irish, like Paddy Ryan of prizefighting fame, made names for themselves after they left the canal behind; but the bulk of the Irish made their contribution as diggers and construction help. And, among their other qualities, they had a sense of humor . . .

Hiring agents for the contractors were at the ship docks in New York in the spring of 1818 and many of the incoming Irish hardly had put foot on American soil before they found themselves on their way up the Hudson by sloop toward the interior and their jobs on the canal.

"The country at the end of the voyage was rougher than anything the men had known in Ireland," wrote Samuel

414

Hopkins Adams. "Owl and wildcat music in the woods kept them awake and scared at night. The first time a snake came into camp, the whole lot nearly deserted. There are no snakes in Ireland. They thought this one was the devil.

" 'Wild Irish,' the upstate folk called them. They looked it, and the language they spoke was strange to American ears. Frightened farmers got out their 'scatterguns' and stood nightly guard over their homes.

" 'Mohawks and Senecas we have survived,' an Oneida County housewife wrote, 'but these strange folk look fitter for crime than for honest work. I misdoubt that we shall find ourselves murdered in our beds one fine morning.'

"She was wrong. The Irish proved to be a law-biding lot so far as their neighbors were concerned. If they fought among themselves on a Saturday night, that was their business. When it came to digging, they set a pace that made the Americans blink."

The truth was that the Irish diggers were mostly trying to make the best of things in the new land. The rôle of laborer actually was a strange one to most of them. The Irish at home had been farmers and field workers. Their roots were in agriculture as they still are to this day on their island home. But in the New World, fighting for a survival that no longer was possible at home, they had to adapt to a new rôle.

The laborers received only about fifty cents a day but it was better than Ireland. In 1818 there were over 3,000 Irishmen working on the canal and more and more came. They left their ballads and the memory of their loneliness.

George Potter says in his great work, *To The Golden Door:*

> The canal produced a class of Irish contractors and sub-contractors. The canal commissioners early concluded that the most politic mode of proceeding with the work was to parcel out contracts for small sections to responsible bidders rather than concentrate it in the hands of a monopoly or a few large contractors. Ambitious Irishmen bid for sections,

varying from forty rods to three miles, and since the state of New York advanced sums for a contractor to set up with teams, implements, provisions and other essentials and covered monthly payrolls, the Irish canal contractor was born along the route of the Erie. When the main canal was finished in 1825, Irish contractors kept together cores of fellow countrymen and bid for sections on new canals which the Erie had inspired. Later, these same contractors and other Irishmen, who had moved upward from laborers, turned into railroad contractors. They were a numerous and, generally, a respected class.

The Erie and the branch canals it spawned in New York required great numbers of men for maintenance and operation, and the Irishman settled along the routes where his shanty was a familiar sight. The booming cities which the Erie had raised from villages gave work to Irish canal laborers. They were saltmakers around Syracuse. They found employment in quarries; the Irishmen were particularly skilled in all branches of stonework. They went into the forests as choppers and they hired out as farmhands. They added to the populations of Albany, Troy, Utica, Syracuse, Rome, Auburn, Rochester, Lockport, and Buffalo, in the last place loading and unloading the lake ships and rearing up a tough, hard-fighting, hard-drinking breed of lake sailors.

The roaming Irish mission priests made the line of the works their parishes while the canal was under construction, saying Mass in the shanties of the workers. The dollars of the canal workers helped build the parish churches that grew with the congregations along the waterway. Out of the parish churches and the mission activities of the priests rose the sees of Albany, Buffalo, and Rochester. As Thomas D'Arcy McGee, the Irish-American journalist, expressed it, these poor, rude Irishmen were not only building a canal, they "were working on the foundations of three episcopal sees [and] opening the interior of the State to the empire of religion, as well as of commerce."

We can be assured that many of these men led lonely lives, trying to save enough money to bring their families out of the barrenness of Ireland to join them, as reflected in the following letter from a railroad worker:

Peekskill
March 8, 1848

My Dear Wife and Children:

I received yours of January 20, 1848 which gave me to understand that you were attacked by a severe fever but thanks be to God that you are recovered and well as I am at present. Thanks be to his kind mercy to us all. Be on the watch at the post office day after day. I won't delay in relieving yours as it is a duty encumbered on me by the laws of church and I hope God will relieve me.

I work on a railway at 8 shillings per day and pay 18 shillings per week for my board. This is a good country for them that is able to work and no other. I will be able to pay your passage with the help of God on the first of August next. The sending of this sum of money to you compels me to let it be back til then and I long to see that long wished for hour that I will embrace you in my arms. There is nothing in this world gives me trouble but you and my dear children whom I love as my life.

Please let me know how my sons, Patrick and Francis, are, not forgetting my dear father and mother, friends and neighbors and your sister, Bridgette, thanking God she was with you in your sickness and sorrows, which I will never forget.

I expect to go to New York on the 17th of March to send you this bill of 6 pounds which you will get cash for in the Provincial Bank of Ireland. I will send it in the Reverend Patrick O'Gara's care for you.

I feel very sorry for my brother Francis that lived in St. John. I fear he is dead.

Don't answer this letter until you receive the next in which the money will be for you. Keep your heart as God spared you so long you will be shortly in the lands of Promise and live happy with me and our children. No more at present.

> Your faithful husband to death,
> Thomas Garry

P.S. I was ready to go to New York to pay passage for you and the children but I consider you would not stand the wracking sea till you be nourished for a time.

Mr. Tully is Commissioner of Taxation and Finance of New York State.

Governor Thomas Dongan

RICHARD J. CONNERS

It is fitting, perhaps, that a Member of Assembly write about Thomas Dongan who convened the first popular Assembly in the Colony of New York on October 14, 1683. That Assembly framed the Charter of Liberties and Privileges which proclaimed the people's right to participate in government, religious freedom for all, trial by jury, immunity from arbitrary arrest, and freedom from martial law. The "Charter of Liberties" served as the foundation for New York State's subsequent constitution and contained many of the provisions incorporated 104 years later in the Constitution of the United States.

Dongan was born in the Manor House of Castletown, County Kildare, in 1634. He was the product of a marriage that united two distinguished Anglo-Irish families who played significant roles in the political upheavals of 17th century Ireland. His father, Sir John Dongan, was a member of the Irish Parliament. His mother was a Talbot and a sister of the Archbishop of Dublin and of Richard, Earl of Tyrconnell, Lord Deputy of Ireland under James II.

His two older brothers, Walter and William, were active in the Confederation of Kilkenny. When that cause collapsed in defeat, Thomas, then only 15 years old, fled to France with his surviving brother, William. In this flight they became two of the earliest "wild geese" presaging the journey of thousands of Irish soldiers to fight in the armies of the continent.

For the next 29 years, Thomas Dongan served in the armies of France until 1678 when he returned to Britain at the request of Charles II. Dongan had won valuable military experience in the French campaigns in the Low Countries and had made the friendship of James, Duke of York, who had also spent part of his exile in the French army.

Now, trained in the premier military force of his day, fluent in French and Dutch, a proven friend of the Stuarts, Thomas was regarded by Charles and James as a man of practical intelligence and ability who could be trusted to fulfill whatever responsibility they assigned him.

Thomas was first named as Lieutenant-Governor of Tangiers and then, in 1682, James named Dongan Vice-Admiral in the British navy and Governor of the colony of New York which his brother had granted him after its seizure from the Dutch in 1664. The colony then included what is now known as New York State as well as that portion of Massachusetts comprising Martha's Vineyard, Nantucket and Elizabeth Islands and, in Maine, Pemaquid—land lying between the Penobscot and St. Croix Rivers.

Dongan arrived in the former settlement of New Amsterdam the following summer. It had some 4,000 residents at that time. He came there through Long Island Sound on whose eastern end he met delegations from the Indian tribes en route to New York.

Even in 1683 New Yorkers spoke in 18 different languages. Its northern boundary was today's Wall Street. The settlement (which he was to make a City with Charter in April, 1686) had both wild animals and Indians in its domain. In fact, Dongan attended a bear hunt in an orchard located between today's Maiden Lane and Cedar Street. He was also entertained by the corporation (as both Dutch and English called their settlement government) at a banquet whose master of ceremonies was the Mayor.

Then, with the receptions and social events behind him, Governor Dongan swore in his council and faced the considerable tasks ahead. He was aided by the fact that his reputation for fairness had preceded him. Even the Dutch Reformed congregation on its Thanksgiving day offered up prayers which included:

> Whereas, the consistory of the Congregation have resolved to appoint the coming day of rest—as a special day of Thanksgiving, Fasting and Prayer, for the purpose of thanking God for his undeserved compassion and, at the same time, to entreat Him with loyal and earnest prayers, to preserve his Royal Majesty of Great Britain (Charles Second) to bless the Duke of York (James) and his Governor (Dongan) and to spare His Church.

Shortly after his arrival in New York, Governor Dongan, bearing in mind the Duke of York's intention to reform the government, issued writs of election. He used the British term of "ridings" in his call for an Assembly, having three ridings of Yorkshire, four from the settlement of New York and Haerlem, two from Esopus, two from Albany and Rensselaerwyck, one from Schenectady, and one each from other groups of settlements.

The recent history of the colony had been marred by question of taxes, land-ownership and the residual ill-will between Dutch and English

421

settlers. The Stuart propensity for ruling without the advice of their subjects had not been weakened by the voyage across the Atlantic and James may have imagined his new possession would quietly produce revenues.

He was quickly disabused of this expectation, however. English merchants residing in New York demanded a voice in the affairs of the colony and, imitating the tactics of the men who had made life so difficult for James' father, Charles I, they withheld custom monies. When James' Collector of Customs attempted to seize their merchandise in payment of their debts, he was shipped back to England along with the demand of New Yorkers for a regularized system of government that would give them a voice through an elected Assembly of Freeholders. By 1681, Anthony Brockholls, military commander in the colony, wrote James to inform him that it was becoming next to impossible to maintain order.

Thomas Dongan was by profession a military man but he displayed a wider understanding of men and affairs than this might imply. He had neither the temperament nor the means for forcing a despotic rule on the colony and in calling for an assembly he hoped to create the civil and political compromises necessary for the future of the colony.

The Dongan general assembly was held October 17, 1683, at Fort James, the center of officialdom in colonial New York; its most memorable accomplishment was the Charter of Liberties and Privileges which divided the colony of New York into counties—Kings, Queens, Suffolk, Orange, etc.—and established a system of county and local courts as well as granting the "rights of English-

422

men" to the colonists. "Every freeholder," said the Charter, "and freeman shall vote without restraint. No freeman shall suffer but by judgement of his peers and all trials shall be by a jury of 12 men. No tax, tillage, assessment, custom, loan, benevolence or imposition whatever shall be laid, assessed, imposed or levied on any of his Majesty's subjects within this province, or their estates, upon any manner of color or pretense, but by the act of the Governor, Council and Representatives of the People in General Assembly met and assembled."

More importantly, it included a provision that established religious toleration, a pioneering declaration in the atmosphere of intolerance that prevailed in the 17th century. Dongan had experienced the effects of religious intolerance as a youth in Ireland and he was determined to protect the rights of religious minorities within a constitutional framework. His commitment to this principle led him to recommend that Jews be included in this provision, and when the council refused to follow his lead, he drew New York's small Jewish community under the protection of his prerogative powers, allowing them to found a synagogue and worship in public.

After granting civil and religious freedom and setting up local courts through the Charter of Liberties, he granted New York a City Charter on April 26, 1686, with a municipal corporation headed by a Mayor, Recorder, City Clerk, six Aldermen (in territorial sections) and six Assistant Aldermen. Under the New York Charter the Mayor and Sheriff were to be appointed by the Governor and Council (forerunner of the State Senate) while the Aldermen, their assistants and the petty constables were elected by freeholders of each ward. All New York City installations were made on October 14, 1686, on King James' birthday.

Meanwhile Albany petitioned for and was granted incorporation as a City on July 22, 1686. Dongan's Albany Charter was virtually intact until late in the 19th century (first two sizable amendments in 1870 and a major set of changes in 1883). The Charter, when strengthened by the State Legislature, provided Albany with a strong Mayor form of government which it has to this day.

But Dongan's Charter of Liberties, the keystone of his plan for governing the colony of New York, did not last. James, still Duke of York and preoccupied with ensuring that his Catholicism did not exclude him from the royal succession, gave tentative approval, but when he became King in 1685 the document fell under consideration of the Committee of Trade and Plantations. This body—jealously guarding the economic and political controls of the mother country—bristled at the central role given to the colonial assembly and secured the King's veto.

In any case, Dongan was increasingly preoccupied with the very immediate threat of the French and Indians, an issue more basic to the colony's survival. Although England and France were technically at peace—indeed Charles and James both received secret subsidies from the French king—the monumental struggle between the two empires for control of North America was beginning.

The French relied on their Algonquin and Huron allies to exclude the English from the profitable fur trade of the North but incurred the enmity of the Iroquois with this alliance. Dongan recognized that no colony could survive without Indian allies and he knew that the superb fighting abilities of the Iroquois could counterbalance the French superiority in numbers. Accordingly, Dongan met with Mohawk chieftains, leaders in the Five Nation Iroquois Confederation, in October, 1683 and received a promise of allegiance to the English King inscribed on deerskins. Thus began a hundred-year alliance that would prove invaluable to the British in their eventual victory over the French.

At the same time, Dongan was vexed with the problem of warding off attempted infringements on New York land by neighboring colonies.

William Penn had been granted his colony in 1681. When Dongan arrived in New York two years later he heard that Penn was in Albany negotiating with the Iroquois to purchase the upper Susquehanna Valley in New York State. Hastening to Albany, Dongan told Penn that sale of the land would be against the King's interests. He proposed, instead, that the King have a line "from 41 degrees and 40 minutes in the Delaware River to the falls upon the Susquehanna and for Mr. Penn to keep all below." The Cayugas listened to Dongan and, with the approval of the Mohawks, conveyed the tract to the New York government.

A year later, Penn resumed the argument and again Dongan refused, stating that Penn had more land than he could furnish people to till for the foreseeable future. Dongan thus made an enemy of Penn who thereafter used his own friendship with James to the Irishman's disadvantage.

Dongan also fended off Connecticut's grasp and pointed out that the King's Commissioners had placed the Connecticut province line 20 miles east of the Hudson River—not 10! New Jersey and Massachusetts also re-opened old claims (which would deprive Albany and the New York government of its fur traffic) but Dongan was adamant in his refusal. Dongan's boundary decisions took years to finalize (1834) but the courts did uphold his viewpoint.

In another field, Dongan followed his patron's instructions to follow quit-rents and manorial privileges. All titles were ordered produced and valid titles reissued—avoiding future trouble when titles passed. Manorial patents were also reviewed, such as the Rensselaerwyck domain— 700,000 acres which today would comprise all of Albany, Rensselaer and Schenectady Counties plus parts of Greene, most of Columbia and some of Dutchess.

Besides these improvements in the administration of the colony, Dongan proposed the establishment of a mint and post offices in the Northeastern part of the country, and an update on immigration and naturalization laws.

He also established a Latin School where Trinity Church stands today. Father Thomas Harvey, a Jesuit who had accompanied Dongan to America as his chaplain, was its first head and taught there with other Jesuits.

But as time went by Dongan's efforts were more and more diverted from the administration of the colony to its defense. It became apparent to him that the French planned another expedition against the Iroquois. Though the English King insisted on remaining close to Louis XIV, Dongan, on the scene, knew how valuable the Indians were to the English cause and was still using the Five Nations as a buttress against French inroads. His last summit with the Five Nations was in 1697. He even sent Indian runners to Canada to get the Christian Indians to return, promising them English priests and a piece of land (Saratoga) where they could live and build a church.

Suspecting war was at hand, Dongan got the Indians to send their wives, children and old people out of harm's way, finding them hostels at Catskill and along the Hudson. With 400 soldiers and more than 800 Indians he stayed in Albany over the winter of 1687 to be able to go to the Iroquois defense if need be. This time the French flanked Dongan by signing a peace pact with the Indians.

At any rate his career as governor was soon to be cut short. For all Dongan's services to James, there was little gratitude in return. James' tottering fortunes in England made him extremely sensitive to French support and he was unnerved by Dongan's skirmishings in New York. Likewise, he was trying to win Protestant support for his rule and when he at last consolidated the provinces of New York and New England, he removed Dongan and appointed a Protestant as the new governor.

Dongan did not accept the King's offer "to proceed to England to receive the thanks and rewards of the King." Instead he retired to his farm on the shores of Lake Success where he hoped to spend his days away from the turmoil and intrigues of the City.

He was to have no peace, however. Anti-Catholic sentiment had never been very far below the surface in colonial New York. When William of Orange assumed the throne in England, that sentiment broke in its full fury, not only in England and Ireland but also in New York. Rumors of Papist plots were everywhere.

Jacob Leissler, a captain of the militia, seized Fort James, called a Committee of Safety and had himself designated Commander-in-Chief of the fort. He issued warrants for the arrest of Dongan who, as the most well-known Catholic in New York, was presumed to be a conspirator in every supposed Papist plot such as the burning of Schenectady by the French and Indians.

Finally, in 1691, Dongan, hunted as a criminal in New York, sailed to London. He arrived there almost penniless. His salary as governor had more often than not gone unpaid. He had used up his own money and even incurred a personal debt of 17,000 pounds to finance his administration of the King's affairs in New York. At the death of his brother, William, in 1698, the title "Earl of Limerick" had devolved to him but he received nothing more than the title. His brother had remained loyal to James and gone into exile with him. And so his estates in Ireland, some 26,000 acres, had been expropriated and conferred upon Baron de Ginkel, a Dutch general loyal to the new King.

Dongan petitioned repeatedly for payment of what was due him in unpaid salary and personal funds advanced for public service in New York. He received only permission to repurchase his patrimony in Ireland—a generous concession to a penniless man—and the promise of a small ship to transport him back to America—where his lands had also been expropriated or sold to pay his debts.

Thomas Dongan died in London in 1715, at the age of 81. Since he had never married, the title "Earl of Limerick" died with him.

In New York State to which he gave so much in religious and civil liberties, in visions of a humane government, and in the creation of an Assembly in which such as I serve today, little remains to mark his path.

On Staten Island, where Dongan had property and a home named after his birthplace, there is still Castleton, and a section called Dongan Hills and Dongan Street.

In Albany, he is remembered annually in ceremonies conducted by the North Albany Limericks, the Kiwanis Club and the Ancient Order of Hibernians. And in 1976 a memorial stone was placed in front of American Legion, North Albany Post 1610. It reads:

GOVERNOR THOMAS DONGAN
CHARTERED ALBANY AND NEW YORK (1686)
DONGAN, EARL OF LIMERICK
DIED DECEMBER 14, 1715
DEDICATED TO HIS MEMORY

In New York City, the Knights of Columbus unveiled a bronze tablet in 1911 affixed to St. Peter's Church, to memorialize Dongan's contributions during his five years as Governor.

So far as official recognition of Dongan is concerned, however, we are reminded that after many years of success, Babe Ruth had a poor year in 1925. Mayor Jimmy Walker as toastmaster of a dinner for him said, "So sad that yesterday's cheers have such short echoes."

Assemblyman Dick Conners represents the 104th District, the City of Albany and part of the City of Rensselaer, in the State Assembly of New York.

The Last of
the Irish Bosses

ROBERT P. WHALEN, M.D.

The modest green and yellow, shingled cottage is reached by a tortuous, narrow road carved into the side of the Helderberg Mountains. Driving past, one is aware of a few non-descript outbuildings and a wooden fence to which a horse is sometimes tethered. Altogether, it's an undistinguished place, except for one thing: the view. Looking east, through a break in the trees, one is awed by the sweeping prospect of the state's capital city, Albany, commanding the alluvial fields of the Hudson River Valley.

The man who made the simple cottage his summer home headed a political machine which ruled that city, paternally but firmly, for a period of 56 years until his death in February of 1977. His was the longest dynasty in American political history—longer by far than that of the Bosses Flynn, Hague, Curley or Daley. Not only did he hold power longer, his style was totally different. No glory seeker, he was a virtual recluse who seldom appeared in public and, until the last few years of his long life, never granted interviews to newsmen, and then only to a select few.

His name was Daniel Peter O'Connell and, together with his brothers, he was the undisputed boss of Albany from 1921 until his death. He was the last of the old-fashioned, czar-like urban po-

431

litical leaders and the most unlikely member of their group. Born November 13, 1885, in Saint Anne's parish in Albany's South End, Dan was one of four sons born to John and Margaret Doyle O'Connell. The O'Connell clan had lived in the South End for two generations, and traced their roots to County Sligo.

Dan's youth was as unpromising as one could imagine. Public school, a one-year commercial course in business college, work as a cook, baker, bartender and saloon keeper, and, at the age of 31, enlistment in the Navy during World War I. Discharged two years later, he returned to an Albany that was in the grip of a ruthless and corrupt Republican machine. The Democratic organization on the other hand was weak, ineffectual and split by internecine struggles.

Perhaps because they were so well-known by the Irish and German residents of Albany's South End, the O'Connell brothers, helped by support and encouragement from the patrician and Protestant Corning family, decided to enter politics and gain control of the County Democratic organization.

As they stealthily went about the process of lining up support, Dan and his brothers—Ed, Packey and Solly—proved to be surprisingly adept at political fence-mending. The first fruits of their efforts came in 1919, when Dan stood for his first and only elective office—assessor—and won. In 1921, the O'Connells and their allies elected the first Democratic citywide ticket to hold office in 22 years.

Thus began Albany's O'Connell Machine. In the years after 1921, it lost a few political battles, but it has continuously controlled Albany's city hall to this day, and the current mayor, Erastus Corning II, is the son of the O'Connells original patron and political ally. He's been the mayor since 1942!

Albany under the O'Connell machine became the benchmark of fiscal and political conservatism, so much so that one New York Times reporter, assigned to cover the Capitol, wrote an article describing Albany as "the most resolutely backward city in the world." Low property taxes, good police protection, "hard on crime" judges, clean drinking water and safe city parks—these were some of the promises the O'Connell machine promised—and delivered—to the voters.

With entrenched power came spoils—alleged links between the Machine and gambling interests, "sweet" real estate deals, control of the liability insurance business, and even a "Democratic" brewery—Hedrick's—and woe be the saloon that did not have that brand on tap. But every investigation to which the machine was subjected—usually by a Republican Governor—came to nought.

Oh, Dan did go to jail once—as did James Michael Curley—but only for a month, for refusing to answer questions in federal court about Albany's baseball gambling pools.

Whatever his transgressions, Dan was forgiven by the voters and for most Albanians he came to be known—either endearingly or with begrudging respect—as "Uncle Dan." He became a political legend, a man of remarkable political acumen and considerable power whose support was sought by Presidential and gubernatorial candidates alike.

But, numerous students of politics have expressed bewilderment at the continued success and dominance of the O'Connell organization over so long a period of time. What was his secret?

I'm not sure that I have the answers, but I did have an opportunity to witness how Dan and various components of his organization functioned during the ten years I served as Albany County Public Welfare and Health Commissioner from 1953 to 1963.

My earliest recollection of Dan O'Connell's organization occurred during my senior year at Albany Medical College when his nephew happened to be a patient on a service to which I was assigned. I cannot recall the reason for his hospitalization, but I do recall that we became friendly and during the course of one of our conversations I told him that I had an urgent need for a copy of my birth certificate. In fact, I needed it the next day in order to attach it to my internship application. I also told him where I was born: Newburgh, a city 80 miles south of Albany.

"Don't worry," John said, "just go down to the County Clerk's office, tell them I sent you, and tell them what you need. They'll take care of you."

That afternoon, I did as directed. When I presented myself at the County Clerk's office, I was referred downstairs to the basement room in which vital records are stored. There I found three men who were playing cards. One of them looked up long enough to inquire what I wanted. He told me to fill out the necessary forms and I would have my birth certificate . . . in about three weeks.

When I told him I needed the document the next day, and that Mr. O'Connell promised me

434

that they could get it for me, they started to pay more attention to me. I explained who I was and how I had come to meet Mr. O'Connell.

With that, one of the men turned to one of his friends and said "Go get it." And that same afternoon, an employee of the Albany County Clerk's office got in his car, drove to Newburgh, and brought back a copy of my birth certificate.

That was my first lesson in the credo of the O'Connell organization: When a guy has a problem, help him.

There is no better example of this than the legion of elderly men, including my father, for whom Dan found city and county jobs. He believed that there was no dignity in handouts, the dignity came from working, so he directed that jobs be found for old men—raking leaves in the city parks, shoveling snow from sidewalks and serving as caretakers at city bathhouses.

In his eyes, no man was too old to work, in consequence of which Albany at one time had an octogenarian school superintendent and a nonagenarian fire chief.

But Dan could be authoritarian as well as kindly.

My predecessor as County Health Commissioner once was asked by a local newspaper reporter if he was in favor of fluoridating Albany's public water supply. He said he was, citing various dental health benefits accruing to people who drank water with fluoride in it.

When Dan saw the story in the next day's paper, he quickly let it be known that "Nobody was going to put anything into Albany's water," the purity of which Dan considered more sacred than vestal virginity.

To the chagrin of my predecessor and all who succeeded him, no one ever did fluoridate Albany's water supply then . . . or since.

As a further example of Dan's doctrinaire authority, I cite the Medical College pathology professor who went to see Dan in an effort to convince him that Albany County needed to replace its outmoded coroner system with a modern medical examiner's office. I like to think that this individual did so not entirely out of desire to have the job for himself.

In any event, the pathologist was granted a rare audience with Dan and for 20 minutes extolled the virtues of trained medical examiners, while at the same time pointing out the drawbacks of the untrained political hacks, as he called them, who served as coroners. After a long and eloquent presentation during which Dan had not said a single word, the pathologist asked him, "Well, what do you think?" And all Dan replied, perhaps recalling that the "hack" coroners were friends and political allies, was: "I don't understand a word you're saying."

To this day, Albany remains one of the most populous counties in the State not to have replaced its coroners with a trained medical examiner.

But, on "bread and butter" health issues, such as clinics for the needy, Dan could be especially generous, and the Albany County Health Department offers an extremely ambitious and well-staffed community health program.

A physician friend of mine once owned a home near Dan's cottage. Wishing to live closer to town, my friend sold his home to a couple who were moving to Albany from Ohio. On the day the couple moved in, the woman and one of her young children walked down to Dan's place to say hello. Spying a number of chickens running about and realizing her larder was bare, she asked Dan if she could buy a few eggs.

"Lady," he said in a gravelly voice produced by lifelong cigarette smoking, "there ain't a hen on the place." Which is how Dan's new neighbors learned that he was a devotee of cock-fighting and raised his own fighting cocks.

He was also a Civil War buff, visited the major battlefields and frequently amazed friends and reporters with his knowledge of that conflict. He even kept a Civil War diorama in his home in Albany.

Dan's sense of humor often had a barb buried in it.

Some years ago when adverse conditions at the County jail made the sheriff expendable, Dan did not hide that fact from the news media. Nonetheless, the lame duck sheriff floated a trial balloon, suggesting that he might run for that post again in the fall. When a reporter called Dan to tell him that the out-of-favor sheriff was thinking of running again, Dan replied, "Oh, yeah, in what county?"

Dan's concern for the elderly was particularly manifest in the interest and philanthropy he lavished on two institutions: The County-operated Ann Lee Home and the privately-endowed Hospital for Incurables. The Ann Lee Home, which I once served as medical director, was the first county infirmary in the state to offer its residents a physical rehabilitation program. The Hospital for Incurables was, until its closing about eight years ago, a remarkably warm and friendly place where physically disabled people played a significant role in their own care. Both institutions flourished under Dan's patronage.

But not all health care institutions in the County fared as well in their relationships with the O'Connell organization. The biggest voluntary hospital in town, Albany Medical Center, was frequently antagonistic in its efforts to get what it considered a fair rate of payment for care of welfare patients. Whenever the hospital pressed its case for higher rates, Dan would announce that the County was studying the possibility of building its own hospital in the city's Washington Park.

Finally, the Medical Center went to court and when a favorable decision was handed down, the County agreed to make a large retroactive payment to the hospital.

To signify there were no hard feelings over this episode, Dan and the hospital director had their pictures taken, shaking hands, by one of the local newspapers. One account has it that one of Dan's confidantes leaned over Dan's shoulder, after the picture-taking, and whispered, "Count your fingers."

Some might question Dan's policies, but none ever doubted his political wisdom and foresight. In 1948, when few Democrats gave Harry Truman a chance for re-election, Dan called them "a bunch of rats deserting a sinking ship." Dan said publicly, "We're for Truman right down the line." Perhaps he did so because he hated Tom Dewey as an old nemesis, but regardless of the reason, Dan proved correct in predicting Truman would win, and thereafter the President told New York

State Democrats, "Whatever the guy in Albany wants, he can have."

If one were to sum up Dan's personal qualities, one would include phrases and words like "fiercely loyal," "charismatic," "stubborn," "abrasive humor," and "captivating." None of these explain the reasons for his political success. Perhaps the best explanation is that he never forgot that he was a man of the people, and he never got so big that he lost his interest in, and concern for, the problems of the little man.

If one were to write his political epitaph, one could do worse than quote the words of one of his most worthy political adversaries, Teresa Cooke, who said, after Dan's death in 1977, "It is the end of a colorful saga, the last Albany Democrat to lead quietly behind the scenes, the last with a personal charisma that made him a beloved folk hero of the 'coal delivering era.' Some might dispute and disagree with him, but he was never to be underestimated."

One thing is certain: There'll never be another like him.

Dr. Whalen is the Commissioner of Health of New York State.

Senator James A. O'Gorman

THOMAS W. RYLEY

The place in history of James A. O'Gorman, United States Senator from New York, 1911 to 1917, is secure if for no other reason than the manner of his selection to that body. O'Gorman, the last person to be selected by the state legislature for the Senate (the 17th Amendment came into effect shortly after) was chosen after a long and bitter fight in 1910 that developed when a number of independent Democrats broke discipline and opposed the original nominee of their party, William Sheehan. Sheehan was the handpicked candidate of the Tammany leader, Charles Murphy; and the man who has become the symbol of the opposition to that selection was Franklin D. Roosevelt. Virtually every historian who has dealt with Roosevelt's early legislative years has pointed to this event as the single most important milestone in his transition from patrician politician to political leader of the first rank. From this point on, his career—now a symbol of opposition to boss rule—was on the rise; within three years he was Under-Secretary of the Navy, a post for which he had to meet the approval of the man he had helped send to the Senate.

Yet overlooked in many of the accounts are some interesting points. The candidate whom the insurgents put up against Sheehan was the choice

440

of the Brooklyn leader, certainly no less a "boss" than was Murphy. Second, and of particular interest to the readers of the *Recorder*, is the fact that when O'Gorman emerged as a compromise choice, a seat on the New York State Supreme Court became vacant and was filled by Daniel Cohalan, one of the founders of the American Irish Historical Society. Finally, there was the person of O'Gorman himself.

O'Gorman was just as much a Tammany man as was Sheehan. In fact, he had once held the title of Grand Sachem of the Hall. Born into a fairly well-to-do family, he had become involved with the organization while still a student at CCNY and had gradually moved through the ranks until he received a series of judgeships, culminating with his place on the New York State Supreme Court. About the only deviation from this well-trod path was a brief excursion into independent politics as a supporter of Henry George. Certainly, O'Gorman's Tammany roots were deep and the fact that the insurgents agreed to him as a compromise choice can only be attributed to political naivete or just plain exhaustion after the long fight.

O'Gorman has one other notable distinction. As Oscar Handlin pointed out in his biography of Al Smith, O'Gorman's selection was one of the first visible signs to the Irish of New York that they had arrived. The United States Senate was then, as now, a club in which the pedigreed qualifications, particularly in the east, were extremely exclusive. O'Gorman was the first genuine product of Irish New York to reach that body, even though he was born into somewhat better economic circumstances than most. He was not, however, the only Irish Catholic in the United States Senate. One of his colleagues for most of his career was the famous Thomas Walsh of Montana. Another, William Hughes of New Jersey, had been born in Ireland.

Throughout his term, the issues with which he would become most closely identified were patronage and the "Irish question." The latter did not surface until later in his career, when the support by the Wilson administration of the British position in World War I caused concern and outright anger on the part of many Irish-Americans. In the early part of his career, O'Gorman supported the presidential candidacy of Woodrow Wilson; indeed, he and Roosevelt were among the few in New York to back the New Jersey Governor in 1912 while the rest of the delegation seemed to swing in the direction of Speaker Champ Clark. But his relationships with the White House began to disintegrate shortly after the election.

Wilson, a prisoner to some extent of his reputation as a reformer, which had helped bring him to office, was determined not to give the Democratic leadership the support they needed in the form of jobs and other emoluments. He preferred to see a more independent leadership develop in the party and looked towards the newly appointed Under Secretary of the Navy for advice. This brought about a rupture between Roosevelt and O'Gorman that never healed; Roosevelt the upstate patrician with the reputation of being a reformer and an independent, pitted against O'Gorman, the Irish Catholic product of Tammany Hall and committed to supporting its interests in the patronage fight. Roosevelt would later remark that he deeply regretted his action in bringing about O'Gorman's selection.

O'Gorman had one weapon on his side, his vote on a number of the crucial issues that Wilson was proposing as part of his "New Freedom" program. He broke with the President and opposed in committee the bill to create a Federal Reserve System. Most historians attribute his opposition largely to the struggle over patronage in New York politics, particularly the dispute over who would get the choice appointment as Collector of the Port of New York.

The post went to John Purroy Mitchel, a nominal Republican of independent leanings, who almost immediately emerged as the insurgent candidate against the Tammany choice in the city mayoral election of 1913. Mitchel's victory, as well as the loss of other posts, hurt Tammany and seems to have chastened O'Gorman somewhat, because he was less belligerent during the next year or so. Some have suggested that he was soothed by the selection of Dudley Field Malone to fill the vacant post of Collector of the Port of New York. Malone, a distinguished trial lawyer, and member of the defense team in the Scopes "Monkey Trial," was O'Gorman's son-in-law.

With the outbreak of the war in Europe, and the increased frustration of the Irish who saw the prospects for Home Rule beginning to fade, the senior senator of New York became increasingly antagonistic to the president. Irish-Americans saw in Wilson's policies a decided pro-British slant and were critical of him for apparently ignoring their desire to see Home Rule in their mother country. The strong Irish American feeling was partially responsible for the unseating of Mayor Mitchel in 1917, who, ironically enough, was the son of an Irish patriot. The Mayor had been a strong supporter of the war and was viewed by German-Americans and many Irish Americans in the city as a symbol of support of the conflict. He was decisively defeated, first in the Republican primary and then, as an independent, in the general election.

In his efforts to demand of the administration a more even-handed policy, and to call attention to British violations of international law, O'Gorman acquired the bitter opposition of the *New York Times*. The spokesman in the east for the allied position, the *Times* delighted in calling attention to O'Gorman's alleged lack of loyalty to the policies of his president. In a bitter and wholly undeserved slap at him as he ended his career in the Senate, the *Times* charged that he had "faithfully served" the Sinn Fein.

The remark was unfair and inaccurate. O'Gorman was only insisting on a more even-handed approach to the war. That he was motivated by his ancestry and by the concern of his constituents cannot be denied, but to some extent, his position on most of the matters with which he took issue with the president has been justified by history. Yet the temper of the time was such that to the pro-ally press, anything such as the stance he took was disloyal, and they took delight in printing President Wilson's famous letter to Jeremiah O'Leary, the Irish-American leader and head of the American Truth Society, in which the president spoke of large numbers of "disloyal Americans."

Even before the war, O'Gorman's support for causes he believed helpful to the Irish and to Irish-Americans was obvious. First was his strong opposition to the Panama Tolls question, a government measure that he believed would be profitable to Great Britain. In addition, there was his strong opposition to a proposed literacy test as a standard for immigration, a measure favored by those who were attempting to curb the flow of immigrants to America's shores.

Early in the war, O'Gorman criticized the British "blacklist" and, by inference, the American position of accepting this while condemning Germany's use of submarines. (At no point did he approve of German methods, simply the apparent double standard employed.) He also opposed the administration's 1914 Ship Purchase Bill, which provided one of the first tests of anti-war sentiment in the national legislature. The bill, which would have provided for the acquisition by the United States of the vessels of belligerents tied up in American harbors, bothered people on both sides of the war issue. O'Gorman was one of several senators who broke party discipline on the matter. The key vote (the major issue was ultimately defeated) was on an amendment to provide for an embargo of munitions. It was a clear-cut challenge to the president's right to make foreign policy and O'Gorman, along with a number of fellow Democrats, supported the amendment, which was also defeated.

In 1915, O'Gorman was one of the few senators who did not join in the call for increased belligerency in light of the *Lusitania* sinking. He called for "coolness" and caution in the matter and later said that he believed that Bryan's resignation as secretary of state over the matter was a serious blow to the country.

O'Gorman also objected to the Wilson administration's insistence that American citizens had the right to travel on the vessels of belligerents, for it had objected vigorously to the sinking by German submarines of such vessels. In 1916, the anti-war forces introduced a motion that would withdraw the protection of the United States from citizens travelling on such ships. O'Gorman supported the resolution which was defeated, but not without considerable manifestation of anti-war sentiment.

By now, the senator from New York was viewed in most circles, particularly by the *New York Times,* as a consistent critic of the government's attitude on the war. O'Gorman, for himself, had decided that he had had enough of Washington. His decision not to seek re-election was due less to his troubles with Wilson than to the fact that he had never really adjusted to life as a senator. At any rate, his decision made him even more independent of the president in the last months of his Senate career. The administration had to be worried, for he sat on two of the most important committees in the Senate, the Foreign Relations Committee and the Judiciary Committee.

The latter was of immediate concern because early in 1916 the president had placed the name of Louis Brandeis before the Senate to be an Associate Justice of the United States Supreme Court. This nomination would occasion virulent anti-semitic utterances from the citadels of the eastern legal establishment. The Senate, which would have to approve the nomination, dragged its feet while lengthy hearings inquired into the character

446

and qualifications of the nominee. O'Gorman was one of those whose position was in doubt, and administration forces feared that his vote might defeat the nomination in committee.

Part of the legend attached to the Brandeis nomination fight is that the senator from New York was "captured" by the Wilson administration as a result of the president's intervention in the case of Jeremiah Lynch, an Irish-American under sentence of death for his part in the Easter Rising. There was considerable agitation among Irish-Americans in New York City over the death sentence, as there was against those carried out against others caught up in the action, and O'Gorman sought the president's intervention. Wilson was away when the request arrived, but his secretary, Joseph Tumulty, reached him and the president dictated a cable to London asking for a delay in the execution. Lynch was ultimately sentenced to ten years. Whether Wilson and Tumulty discussed the implications of this action is not known, but O'Gorman did switch from undecided to a vote for Brandeis in committee and on the floor of the Senate.

Some writers have suggested that O'Gorman was angling for a judgeship during the last days of his Senate career. However, this seems doubtful, since he had ample opportunities to ingratiate himself in Wilson's eyes and seems to have done anything but try to curry favor. If he ever did have his eyes on a judgeship, the last acts of his Senate life would certainly have destroyed this ambition.

Running on a platform of "he kept us out of war," Wilson was re-elected over Charles Evans Hughes in 1916. (Hughes had the support of most

Irish-Americans as New York swung into the Republican column.) Shortly after, the president severed diplomatic relations with Germany after that country resumed unrestricted submarine warfare. O'Gorman supported this action, but when the president leaked to the press the contents of the Zimmerman Telegram, the message by which Germany proposed an alliance with Mexico against the United States, O'Gorman became indignant. His speeches on the floor reflected his view that the telegram was possibly a hoax, that Britain was behind the matter, and that the president should reveal to the country how this nation came into possession of it. He carried this fight to the Senate Foreign Relations Committee but was unsuccessful. While the message is now accepted as being genuine, O'Gorman was correct in suspecting British duplicity; they had been holding it, waiting for a propitious moment to give it to the Americans.

The last week of O'Gorman's term in the Senate saw the famous Armed Ship Bill filibuster. Wilson, with only a few days left in the session asked the legislature to give him the power to arm merchant ships, a power that many believed he already had. Some charged that he was simply trying to capitalize on sentiment whipped up by the Zimmerman note to bring the public around to a more pronounced pro-ally position. In the Foreign Relations Committee, O'Gorman supported an amendment that would deny these arms to vessels carrying munitions, an amendment that the administration would not accept.

Despite the fury caused by the Zimmerman Telegram, the future of the bill was uncertain. The House passed it by a large margin, but a filibuster developed in the Senate. O'Gorman was not part of the filibuster, but because of his position on the amendment and his refusal to sign a "round robin" letter indicating support for the measure, he was lumped with them as the "little group of willful men who . . . had made the country look weak and contemptible." O'Gorman's total contribution to the debate was less than five minutes and no evidence exists that he was ever part of any conscious filibuster planning. But just as he began his Senate career as a footnote in history, he ended it in another one, as one of Wilson's "willful men."

He issued a statement denying his participation in the filibuster, but the firestorm created by the debate made his denials useless. He then faded quietly into history, urging support of the war and continuing his efforts on behalf of Ireland. Subsequently, he retired to the practice of law and became somewhat of an elder statesman of New York politics although he never tried to get back into elective office nor seek a judgeship. He died in 1943. His funeral drew almost every important figure from several generations of New York politics.

Thomas Ryley is Professor and Chairman of the Social Sciences Department at New York City Community College.

Charles O'Conor and
the 1872 Presidential Election

JOSEPH R. PEDEN

IN A PLACE OF HONOR IN THE ENTRANCE HALL OF OUR SOCIETY'S home is a marble bust of one of the truly eminent Americans of Irish descent, Charles O'Conor.

With scarcely any formal schooling, O'Conor rose from poverty to wealth and national fame, becoming, at middle age, one of the most sought-after attorneys of the New York bar. According to Samuel J. Tilden, a close friend and colleague, O'Conor had a knowledge of jurisprudence surpassing that of any other person of his time. As Governor of New York, Tilden constantly turned to him for legal advice, and would have named him as Attorney General if he had become President in the hotly-contested election of 1876. In the latter days of his career, O'Conor's opinions were frequently cited in decisions of the highest federal and state courts. Indeed, another bust of O'Conor stands today in the central foyer of the Appellate Court of the State of New York in New York City in commemoration of his contributions to his profession.

Although he appeared to some to be merely another poverty-stricken Irish urchin peddling newspapers on the streets of New York, young Charles knew he was the scion of one of the most distinguished families of Ireland, in whose ranks were the medieval kings of Connaught. His grandfather,

450

Charles O'Conor of Balanagare, was the greatest Gaelic scholar of the eighteenth century, and a staunch supporter of Wolfe Tone. Because of his political activities, his father, Thomas O'Connor (he used a double N), had been forced to emigrate to the United States after the failure of the rebellion of 1798, and being a sworn member of the revolutionary United Irishmen, was here attracted to the Jeffersonian party and eventually became a sachem of Tammany Hall, as well as a prominent leader in the Irish Catholic community. What scant education Charles received was given by his father, who eked out a precarious existence as a sometime editor and journalist.

While writing of Charles O'Conor's character, his deep attachment to his Catholic faith, his unobtrusive philanthropic work, and his political and legal careers (including his successful prosecution of the notorious Tweed Ring) would doubtlessly provide an engrossing biography, it would also be of interest to focus on a brief, little-known episode in his long career: his nomination and unwilling candidacy for the Presidency of the United States—the first Catholic of Irish ancestry so honored by his fellow citizens.

* * *

The year was 1872 and U. S. Grant was completing his first term as President. In January, the ruling Republican party split apart as a result of the dissatisfaction among the liberal reform wing with the widespread corruption and ineptitude of the Administration. The liberal reformers, acknowledging Grant's control over the regular party organization, called a separate convention to meet in Cincinnati on May 1 to nominate an anti-Grant ticket. Much to the surprise of the men who initiated the party split, the delegates nominated as their candidate, Horace Greeley, the radical and pugnacious editor of *The New York Tribune*.

Meanwhile, the Democratic party, which had been in eclipse since it had been rent by the issues of slavery and secession in 1860, desperately hoped to recover its national

451

prestige and control over the Administration. Many of its leaders hoped that the split among the Republicans would provide an opportunity for them to return to power, and to assure it, they decided to accept the Liberal Republican platform and candidates as their own. Accordingly, when their convention met in Baltimore on July 10, they also nominated Greeley for the Presidency.

To many old time Democrats, Greeley's nomination was an affront. The New York editor had been a consistent and bitter enemy of the Democratic party and its historic principles during his entire life. The nomination for them was tantamount to a sellout of principles in anticipation of the spoils of office. As a result of their disgust with the Greeley candidacy, the traditional Democrats (called the Straights) issued a call for still another national convention to be held in Louisville on September 4, where candidates would be chosen who were true to the principles of the party of Jefferson and Jackson.

Among those enthusiastically endorsing the call for the Louisville convention was O'Conor, who was one of the leaders of the New York Democratic party. He had recently enjoyed national acclaim for his prosecution of the notorious Tweed Ring, whose control over the New York City and State governments symbolized for many the corruption that had infected the country's body politic after the Civil War. O'Conor confessed that he had not paid much attention to the contest for the Presidential nomination; he was too busy with his war against the Tweed Ring. But news of Greeley's nomination by the Democratic party left him outraged. He viewed the possibility of Greeley's election with "inexpressible aversion." To a friend in Virginia he wrote of Greeley:

"The long and disastrous war that filled [the nation] with fratricidal slaughter and involved the whole country in debt and demoralization was due to the unequaled energy and transcendent ability of this one exceedingly able, exceedingly amiable, and exceedingly mischievous man."

452

O'Conor joined other Democrats in preparing for the creation of a second Democratic party, the Straight Democrats. But, despite wide support among the Democratic editors and intellectuals, and the older traditional members, few Democratic office holders or party leaders were willing to repudiate the Baltimore convention and its candidates. Thus, while both the major parties had experienced splits, the dissenters in each were more ideological in their concerns than practical. The loss of liberal reform support for the regular Republican candidate, Grant, was balanced by the loss to the Democratic party of the dissident Straight Democrats. The Straights, unable to endorse Greeley, now sought a candidate whose personal integrity and devotion to Jeffersonian and Jacksonian conceptions of government would symbolize to them a return to true Democratic principles. And they wanted a candidate whose wide public reputation would immediately attract the attention of the electorate. In these circumstances, even before the Louisville convention convened, the delegates were agreed upon nominating Charles O'Conor as their candidate for President.

As soon as O'Conor realized that he was certain to be nominated by the Louisville convention, he prepared a lengthy address to be read to the delegates at the opening session. In it he first outlined his view of what was wrong with the political life of the country and what must be done to correct it. He then pledged his support in every way but one: he refused to accept any nomination to public office.

O'Conor offered a cogent masterful analysis of the American political system as it had developed since 1776. The founding fathers had hoped to preserve the liberties of the people by abolishing both monarchy and aristocracy, creating a representative republic in which abuse of power and the corruption by misrule would be limited by a system of checks and balances and the doctrine of strict interpretation of the Constitution. But this great experiment had failed, and it was now clear that the "only efficient protection against official misrule is in totally prohibiting those powers which cannot

453

be effectually controlled by law." "Governmental intermeddling with those concerns of society which, with judicious laws, might beneficially be left to individual action, is the only real evil actually developed in our system . . . . and it is the fruitful parent of all others existing." The great bulk of governmental intervention in society should be dispensed with. Most especially, said O'Conor, the right of the government, on any level, to finance its activities by the creation of a public debt ought to be prohibited. The public debt was creating a new aristocracy, the bondholders, whose insatiable demand for further indebtedness and higher interest rates was reducing the taxpayers to bond-slavery. To O'Conor, pay as you go was a maxim as sound in public, as in private, affairs. He also insisted that all taxes be direct, simple, and visible levies. The use of such indirect taxes as tariffs, excise, or sales taxes was extremely harmful since their relative invisibility to the tax-paying public made the people less aware of the gross extravagance, waste, and peculation of government. If taxes were exacted directly from the taxpayers, a powerful group of citizens would be enlisted in the duty of guarding public spending.

To O'Conor, "paternal government in a republic" based on universal suffrage was the "sum of all villanies." A government that used some of its powers to put money in some men's pockets must employ other powers to extort money from others, and this necessitated a continuous policy of rapine and favoritism. As for Horace Greeley, he was the "recognized champion" of ever greater governmental control and interference in the lives of the people. While the election of Grant might involve no important consequence, that of Greeley "would consecrate practices . . . which are absolutely incompatible with the permanency of republican institutions."

But O'Conor's powerful exposition of the Straight Democratic philosophy did not include his willingness to be the candidate of the party. "Love of that absolute independence which can hardly be maintained in public office, and a desire to promote your success instead of impeding it, have created

454

an unalterable resolve in my mind to remain in private station."

The eloquence and brilliance of his address confirmed the delegates' opinion that Charles O'Conor was the most worthy candidate for the Presidency. They unanimously proclaimed his address to be the platform of their party and nominated him to be their Presidential candidate by acclamation. Later, to demonstrate to the candidate and the public the extent of their support, a roll of the states' delegates was called and O'Conor received 600 of the 604 votes cast. Later, they nominated John Quincy Adams II, the son of the former President, as their Vice-Presidential candidate. Adams telegraphed his acceptance on the condition that O'Conor would accept the Presidential nomination.

O'Conor, working in New York, was stunned to hear that the convention had ignored his clear refusal to run for office. He immediately sent a telegram rejecting the nomination but pledging his constant support in every other way. A *New York Times* reporter who managed to interview O'Conor, despite his known aversion to the press, reported that O'Conor considered office seeking one of the great mischiefs of the day, that he had made up his mind not to go into that business, and that nothing would ever make him accept any nomination from any quarter for any office. The refusal of a nomination to the highest public office was unprecedented and left the citizenry incredulous. The result was great confusion among the public and politicians. O'Conor was to be besieged by committees, reporters and personal friends for weeks to come, all wanting to know how he could possibly mean what he plainly said: he would not accept any nomination for public office, even the Presidency!

On September 5, the convention was late in reconvening, largely due to confused meetings among the delegates as to how to proceed in the face of O'Conor's second refusal of the nomination to the Presidency, and Mr. Adams' qualified acceptance of the Vice-Presidential nomination. When finally called to order, the Louisiana delegation had lost heart and, pronouncing the cause hopeless, announced its plan to with-draw from the convention. But Judge Goodlett of New York urged the convention to ignore O'Conor's declination, and recommend his candidacy to the voters as if he had accepted. Mr. Moreau of Indiana protested that the delegates owed it to their self-esteem to nominate alternative candidates. But when Colonel Duncan of Kentucky read a letter from Adams flatly refusing to run for any office but that of Vice-President on an O'Conor slate, the delegates realized that they had no viable alternative candidate of national repute. At Mr. Moreau's motion, the convention then reaffirmed its nomination of O'Conor for President and Adams for Vice-President by a vote of 544 to 30. After a few more resolutions were passed, the convention adjourned *sine die*.

On September 10, the convention committee headed by Mr. Moreau called upon O'Conor in his Wall Street law offices. It reviewed the purposes of calling the Louisville convention and appealed to O'Conor to accept the leadership of the Straight Democrats "to rescue the old organization from the hands of its enemies." The convention could find no other person whose "lofty and unsullied purity and integrity, broad and comprehensive statesmanship, large and varied experience in governmental affairs, learning, ability and unquestioned democracy" could give equal assurance to the people that they might see "peace and tranquillity restored" to the nation.

Despite the flattery, O'Conor was adamant. He asked that they return the next day when he would make a formal reply to the effect that he was fully aware of the issues at stake in the election, but that he had principles of his own which made it impossible for him to accept their nomination. As to the political party system, he believed that it was crucial that parties represent consistent political principles, regardless of whether they win or lose particular elections. Otherwise, "they are mere factious combinations to delude the people and divide, as the profits of a trade, such portions of wealth as can be wrung from the [people] under the forms of law." As for the coalition that combined to nominate and elect

Greeley, "its folly is manifest and its failure inevitable . . . The people may be sacrificed by a secret betrayal; they will never consent to an open sale."

At this point O'Conor felt obliged to reveal some of his intimate convictions, and his sincerity is evidenced by the rare glimpse into his mind and heart. First, he acknowledged that, according "to the vile code advocated by the hirelings of misrule," success was "the first and paramount aim in every human effort." But his moral sense "inculcates honorable and manly struggles for the right however slight the prospect of immediate advantage to the actor or even to the cause." While other children selected as their heroes those "whose victorious chariot wheels, stained with the blood of vanquished millions, conducted them to power and renown," his heroes were "Troy's champion at his last stand, Leonidas in the Grecian pass, and the dissenting consul Aemilius at Cannae." These were the ideals "adopted early in youth at the footstool of one who taught that constancy in honest endeavors at right-thinking and well-doing, though in the teeth of resistless antagonism, is the first of human duties. All the cardinal virtues are developed in its performance." (Here we note the faith, determination and teaching of O'Conor's father, whose life was dedicated to the liberation of Ireland, a goal which, to many, seemed hopeless.) Thus, he concluded, it was not fear of ridicule or the hopelessness of the cause that compelled him to refuse the candidacy.

To O'Conor, the "vices of the nomination system" were personally offensive to his sense of morality. The bargaining that precedes nominations and the imposition of a "platform" which seldom conforms to the candidate's own principles, but binds him to pledges not of his own making, repel him. Unless a man adopts the rôle of the most conspicuous beggar in the land, he is deemed unworthy of the highest office. "Faith teaches that the poor in spirit will receive the radiant blessing of the future life; but it is no part of my political creed that poverty of spirit in worldly affairs should be a passport to the respect and confidence of a great people or a qualification for their chief magistracy . . . Self-respect and modesty unite in forbidding me to play, in these days of degeneracy, the part of chief postulant in any such drama."

O'Conor's "great refusal," commented the editor of *The New York Evening Post*, was "incomprehensible to the average American because an honest reluctance to accept high office would not generally be considered as compatible with a sound mind." "The position was so novel, so out of the field of the ordinary philosophy of politics, [that] the public, failing to understand it, assumed that O'Conor considered the cause hopeless." The public generally has no understanding of the ethical imperatives which motivate men like O'Conor. In politics, they want a show. Principles are good if they lead to some immediate gain. Opinions barren of immediate results are well enough in the study, but the man of the world of affairs should have no truck with them. Notwithstanding, the *Post* editor concluded, "It is the man of thought and not the man of action who governs the world, and the O'Conor movement, however small it may prove to be now, will be looked back to at a not distant day as all that was left of that great party which, except at brief and distant intervals, has governed the country ever since the Republic was founded."

The convention committee, having allowed itself time to consider the situation, decided to issue a statement explaining that O'Conor's refusal was based on the idea that the Presidency was an office neither to be sought nor declined, and that to accept a nomination from any convention would be repulsive to his feelings and judgments. Also, to say explicitly that he would serve if elected would be tantamount to saying he was a candidate. Therefore, he chose to refuse the candidacy and remain silent as to whether he would serve if elected. The committee considered his actions "proper and judicious," though at the risk of being misapprehended and, therefore, would proceed with the task of organizing slates of electors pledged to O'Conor and Adams in all the states in accordance with the will of the convention.

While O'Conor concentrated on assuring the political defeat of the remnants of the Tweed Ring, the Straight Democrats throughout the country began to meet in conventions to nominate slates of electors pledged to the O'Conor-Adams ticket. By October, delegates were convening in Michigan, Ohio, Missouri, New York and California. But by mid-October, it was already clear that Greeley could not win, and that O'Conor's only chance was that Greeley would withdraw before election day. *The Chicago Sun Times*, the leading Democratic paper in the region, had endorsed O'Conor in early September, and now hoped that, if Greeley would resign, the Democratic party might still unite and win with O'Conor and Adams. O'Conor himself remained opposed to Greeley, and let it be known that he would not take offense personally if others chose to work for his candidacy. But he did nothing to advance it in any way.

In the end, the O'Conor-Adams ticket appeared on the ballot in 23 of the 37 states, but garnered less than 30,000 votes out of more than 6,400,000 cast. Grant won 56% of the popular vote, the highest recorded for a Republican candidate in the nineteenth century. Conversely, Greeley, running on both the Democratic and Liberal Republican tickets, had the lowest percentage of popular vote—44%—ever given to a Democrat between 1848 and 1904. Thousands of Democrats stayed home rather than vote for a candidate so unrepresentative of their political ideology.

Grant's second administration proved to be a personal and political tragedy marked by corruption that reached into the Cabinet and the very office and family of the President. The Secretary of War was ousted under threat of impeachment and dozens of officials, including the President's personal secretary, were indicted.

Four years later, O'Conor's dim view of Presidential politics was confirmed when his closest political friend, Governor Tilden, was nominated by the Democratic party for the Presidency. A detailed presentation of O'Conor's conception of American democracy was published as one of three official

459

position papers. But despite Tilden's attaining a majority of the popular vote, corrupt influences led to a disputed counting of the electoral votes, which eventually compelled him to capitulate. Acting as his counsel, O'Conor urged him to press his claims. But Tilden declined, recognizing the risk of another Civil War.

* * *

In our days, with the recent trauma of Watergate exactly a century after O'Conor's nomination, and a persistent loss of confidence in public officials evidenced by a continuing decline in the numbers of citizens participating in elections, the ethical ideals which motivated his refusal to seek the Presidency offer us an arresting perspective of the problem of representative democracy. Do the methods of choosing Presidential candidates, and the consequent demands of appealing to a mass electorate, preclude the selection of the worthiest men for public office? There is no doubt about O'Conor's final grim conclusion. In an address to the New York Historical Society in his seventy-third year, he predicted the growing monarchial character of the American Presidency, and, going to the root, urged the systematic reduction of Presidential powers until the office was so unattractive that men could only be persuaded to hold it in monthly terms on rotation. Solution to the danger that O'Conor so clearly perceived is obviously still to be sought.

Mr. Peden is a member of the History Department of Baruch College, City University of New York.

Mary Mallon: Alias Typhoid Mary

MARY C. McLAUGHLIN, M. D.

Typhoid is a world-wide disease caused by the typhoid bacillus of which there are about 50 types. It is transmitted by food or water contaminated by feces or urine of a patient or a carrier. A carrier is a person who has not shown clinical evidence of typhoid fever within 12 months, but who harbors the typhoid bacillus. The incubation period is about one to three weeks. The patient complains of fever, headache, malaise, lack of appetite, spots on the trunk of the body and constipation. Without treatment, the mortality rate is 10%, but with today's antibiotic treatment is reduced to two to three percent or less. Two to five percent of cases become permanent carriers.

But this is the story of a woman—not a disease. Her name is Mary Mallon, born in County Tyrone, Ireland, on September 23, 1869; the daughter of John Mallon and Cathrine Igu. The Mallons or Mellons were indigenous to the territory called Meallanacht, i.e., O'Mellons County, which includes the present area of Cookstown, County Tyrone.

Mary Mallon was the first typhoid carrier recognized in the United States. The fascinating story of her life fills one alternately with amazement, horror, sympathy, disgust, understanding and anger. It is ultimately a sad story but one that fires the imagination. She is a woman who remains shrouded in mystery despite all that has been written about her. She was the living paradox of virtues.

Mary Mallon first became known through the work of Doctor George A. Soper, an epidemiologist and sanitary engineer. His painstaking investigations have given us the most completely validated story available. In the winter of 1906–1907 he was assigned to investigate a typhoid outbreak which had occurred in August, 1906, in Oyster Bay. General Henry Warren, a New York banker, had rented a house there for the summer. He had a family of three and seven servants. Late in August, six of the eleven persons in the house were taken ill with typhoid. Immediately, experts were called in, but they could not ascertain the cause.

Dr. Soper, renowned for his work with typhoid and known as "the epidemic fighter," was asked to look into the case. He painstakingly rechecked all the suggested sources—the well, the overhead tank, the cesspool, the privy, the food, bathing and sanitary conditions of the property and of the house, and those of the adjoining properties. The closest he came to a cause was polluted shellfish brought to the house by an old Indian woman who lived on the beach. However, this theory did not stand up under close examination.

Not much was known about carriers in the United States at that time. Although the carrier state had been postulated in Germany several years earlier, Dr. Soper did not know of these German papers until after his investigation of Mary Mallon was complete. Thus it was only

462

through the painful process of exclusion, that his search focused on a cook who had left soon after the epidemic started six months before. He could find out little about her. She had been employed through a well-known agency on 28th Street. She came to work on August 4, and the first person became ill on August 27. All cases occurred within seven days. Mrs. Warren, her employer, knew little of her since she kept mostly to herself. Mrs. Warren said she was a good, plain cook, not particularly clean.

Dr. Soper went to the employment agency to get her references in order to back-track on other places of employment. A complete listing was not possible because she did not get all of her jobs through agencies. She also replied directly to advertisements in newspapers. George Soper investigated some of her previous places of employment and uncovered seven household epidemics! In all instances, the source of the epidemic had not been found and the cook had never been suspected.

In his back-tracking, the earliest record he could find was in 1900. Mary Mallon was employed in Mamaroneck where a family had rented a house for one month. A young visitor came down with typhoid ten days after his arrival. However, his illness was thought to have been contracted in East Hampton near the Montauk Army camp where there was typhoid.

The next episode was in 1901–2 when Mary had lived with a family in New York City for eleven months. The laundress was taken to Roosevelt Hospital on December 9th with typhoid. The case was not investigated.

In 1902, Mary was taken to Dark Harbor,

Maine, to a new house rented by Coleman Drayton, a New York City lawyer. The first case occurred on June 17, in a footman, two weeks after Mary Mallon arrived. The footman had been blamed for the epidemic. Seven days later the second case occurred, and soon seven out of nine were sick. Mr. Drayton, who had had typhoid, remained well and he and Mary cared for the ill. He was so grateful to her he gave her an extra $50 in addition to her wages.

In 1904 in the household of Henry Gilsey, in Sands Point, Long Island, there were four members in the family and seven servants, including Mary. First the laundress, then the gardener, then the butler's wife and then the wife's sister became ill. Since all the servants lived in a separate house from the family, it was thought that the source was related to factors associated with that house. This outbreak was investigated by the then Superintendent for Communicable Disease in the New York City Department of Health. He thought that the laundress was the source of these infections, but he was not sure.

In the fall of 1906, when Mary left General Warren in Oyster Bay, she was employed as a cook in Tuxedo Park, N.Y., from September 21st to October 27th. Fourteen days after her arrival a laundress was taken to the hospital with typhoid.

All these episodes had a common thread. In nearly every case, the family was wealthy, left the city for the summer and had servants—particularly a cook. Except in the Drayton case most cases of typhoid were in the servants. It is postulated that the food prepared by Mary for members of the various families was mostly cooked and thus the typhoid bacillus killed. The uncooked desserts were probably prepared and served by the butlers or maids. The chances of Mary handling desserts of the servants was greater. In the case of the Drayton's, Mary was known on one occasion to have prepared ice cream with fresh peaches which she cut directly onto the ice cream. It is thought that the ice cream and peaches were well laced with *Salmonella typhosa!*

Several weeks after Dr. Soper began his epidemiologic study, he finally caught up with Mary. At that time she was the cook in an old-fashioned house on Park Avenue and 60th Street, two doors above the church. Here, once again, the laundress had recently been sent to the hospital, and the only daughter of the family was dying. Dr. Soper, speaking to Mary in the kitchen asked as nicely as he could if he could have samples of her blood, feces and urine since she may have been the unknown cause of making people sick. He states: "She seized a carving fork and advanced in my direction." He escaped as quickly as possible.

Soper really did not need the specimens to prove she produced the outbreaks, but he wanted to know how. He looked into Mary's after-work habits and found that she had a friend in a rooming house on Third Avenue, below 33rd Street, where she would go evenings. According to Soper, he was a disreputable looking man who spent his days in the local saloon. Dr. Soper got to know him and arranged to be at his room on an evening that Mary was expected. He brought along Dr. Hoober, later the head of Children's Hospital in Detroit.

When Mary caught sight of the good doctors, she was very angry. Despite Dr. Soper's well-prepared speech that he wanted to help, he was unable to get her to listen. She violently denied any illness or knowledge of typhoid and ranted that there was typhoid everywhere. Furthermore, she was in perfect health. The doctors left with a volley of verbal abuse following them down the stairs. Knowing her usual pattern of behavior, Soper knew that she would be leaving her present employment very soon. He therefore considered it necessary to report her to Commissioner Thomas Darlington and Dr. Hermann Biggs, Medical Officer of the New York City Department of Health. He recommended that she be taken into custody to have her excreta examined at the research laboratory.

A Health Inspector, a gentle woman named Dr. Josephine Baker was sent to see if she could get the required samples from Mary. When she arrived, Mary promptly slammed the door in her face. In her book *Fighting for Life*, Dr. Baker described Mary as a neat, clean and self-respecting Irish woman with a firm mouth and her hair tied in a knot. Undaunted, the next day Dr. Baker went back—this time with three policemen. One was stationed around the corner and one at the front door. One was at Josephine Baker's elbow as she rang the basement door bell. Mary answered and she was ready. Dr. Baker states: "Mary was ready with a long kitchen fork in her hand. As she lunged at me with the fork, I recoiled on the policeman." When they recovered, they set out to find her. But she had literally vanished. For three hours they searched the house and adjoining property, but she could not be found. Exhausted, Dr. Baker called her supervisor, Dr. Bensel, who said: "I expect you to get the specimens or take Mary to the hospital." Dr. Baker corralled two

466

more policemen and continued the search. They noticed that footprints led across the snow in the back yard to a chair against the fence. In the next yard, a bit of calico was seen caught in an outside closet door with ash cans piled against it. Mary was found. In Dr. Baker's words, "She fought and struggled and cursed . . . with appalling vigor and efficiency. The ride down to the hospital was quite a wild one." Dr. Baker rode sitting on Mary Mallon's chest, and likened the experience to being in a cage with an angry lion.

Mary was placed in isolation in Willard Parker Hospital. The study of the stool by Dr. William Park was a "pure culture of *Bacillus typhosus*." Three times a week for eight months her stools were positive except for a few instances. Dr. Soper visited her in her isolation quarters, and explained that the removal of her gall bladder would probably help get rid of the bacillus and offered to help in any way he could. He even offered to write a book about her case, to keep her anonymous and to give her all the royalties. But Mary was convinced they wanted to kill her. As Dr. Soper spoke, she rose, pulled her bathrobe around her and without her eyes leaving his face, went into the toilet, slammed the door, not to return while he was there.

Shortly after, Mary Mallon was sent to Riverside Hospital on North Brother Island. She was given a small bungalow about 20' x 20' with a living room, kitchen and bath. It was on the riverbank next to the church. Her food was brought to her and she cooked it, but ate alone.

In a sympathetic story in *The New Yorker* magazine, Stanley Walker wrote of Mary's "involuntary confinement" or "incarceration." He spoke of the cold dismal spot to which she was confined: "At night the dirty water of the East River laps against the rocks, making a messy, ghastly noise."

After two years, Mary sued the City for her release. Her lawyer, George Francis O'Neil, made an impassioned appeal that she was imprisoned without due process of law, that she had not been properly accused and that she had had neither a hearing nor representation by counsel. Mary stated she was treated like a leper. However, Dr. Park testified that despite all that was said, she was a menace to public health. The judge, Justice Mitchell Erlanger, dismissed the case on July 22, 1909, unwilling to take responsibility for releasing her.

Sometime later, on February 19, 1910, Dr. Ernest Lederle, the Commissioner of Health, feeling she now understood her condition and her risk of infecting others, released her after she pledged not to work as a cook or handle other person's food, to observe sanitary precautions and to report to the Department every three months.

On release, Mary promptly disappeared. She violated every pledge. Under assumed names of Marie Breshoff and Mrs. Brown, she cooked in hotels, restaurants and sanatoria. One time she ran a boarding house. For five years, she traveled New York without being discovered. In 1914, in a sanitarium in Newfoundland, New Jersey, there was a typhoid outbreak and it was found that Mary had worked there as a cook. Once again she had left before she got caught. There was also an attempt to tie her to an epidemic in Ithaca, but this could not be proven.

When I undertook to write this paper, I was fortunate to have my husband recall that a friend,

Mr. Joel Bennett, once said his family had hired Typhoid Mary. In my back-tracking, another unreported outbreak was discovered. Mr. Bennett's grandparents, named Bryant, had hired Mary for service in their home in Marblehead, Massachusetts. A short time after she arrived two members of the family and one servant became ill with typhoid. No one associated Mary with the cases; in fact, a local physician was said to have quelled the investigation lest unfavorable publicity or attention be focused on that fair town. One of the members of the family states that Mary was a wonderful, warm, friendly person who was particularly proficient in baking cookies. She loved sewing and made many rag dolls. Soon after the outbreak she left but remained very close to this family, writing to them often.

Interestingly, the Bryant family source stated that Mary was closely tied into the Irish Movement in America, raising money to support the Irish cause. Everyone including her lawyer was convinced that Mary was being persecuted. In fact, Yeats' friend, Countess Markiewicz, was said to have waged a campaign through the American-Irish press to get signatures for a petition to the authorities to release Mary. Mary was apparently convinced, I am told, that the efforts of the doctor to cure or confine her were all part of an English conspiracy.

Finally one day, a Dr. Edward Cragin, head obstetrician and gynecologist at Sloan Hospital For Women, called Dr. Soper to please come. When he arrived, Soper was told of 20 cases of typhoid fever. Jokingly, the staff there called the cook "Typhoid Mary." The cook was not in the hospital at the time but when Dr. Soper was shown some papers in her handwriting he had no doubt. The cook was indeed Mary Mallon. Once again the Department of Health was notified, and once again Mary was sent to North Brother Island in 1915. Mary was now 48 years of age. She remained there the rest of her life. It is said by Stanley Walker, that for 10 years she was like a "moody, caged, jungle cat." Dr. John Cahill, Superintendent of Riverside Hospital at the time and, incidentally, the father of Dr. Kevin Cahill, stated: "She knew how to throw herself into a state of almost pathological anger."

Finally, as time passed, a peace seemed to come over her. She did not try to escape. She was older. Perhaps, she now realized what must be done. She had a comfortable home, she could cook, read, sew and her livelihood in old age was provided for. The people on the island were kind to her. She announced the past was a "closed incident." She went to work in the laboratory and was paid well. Mary Mallon loved her job and read avidly all possible books relating to her work. As the years passed she finally was granted trips to Manhattan and Corona, Queens, alone, and she always returned. She made friends with some of the doctors, nurses and co-workers. Everyone knew not to mention typhoid. When they visited her, none would eat with her.

Typhoid Mary became the topic for many newspaper and magazine articles. The press alternately told of her persecution and depicted her standing over a caldron stirring typhoid bacillus into the pot.

Mary Mallon is known to have caused at least 53 cases and three deaths from typhoid but there were undoubtedly more.

She still is a woman of some mystery. Much of her time is unaccounted for. She states she was born in Ireland. According to her death certificate, she lived in the U.S. for 55 years which meant she came to the U.S. when she was about 14 years of age. The immigration of very young Irish girls to America in those days is well known. Whether any other family came with her or not is unknown. Physically she is said to have been a big woman, athletic and plump. She was a clear talker, always cheerful, eager and alert. She loved company and was particularly fond of children. In investigating Mary's story I spoke to a Thomas Murray, son of the Coast Guard Lighthouse Keeper on North Brother Island when she was there. He remembers meeting her as he strolled the island and Mary always gave him fruit! Here her generosity really was a fault.

Some references referred to her walk as having a masculine quality to it and simultaneously stated that so did her mind. (I wonder what was meant. Just how does a man think as compared to woman?) Her close friends in early adulthood were few. Only once was there any reference to a possible romance. A Mr. Reuben Gray wrote to the Health Commissioner in 1909 telling him he was a farmer and if they sent Mary to him in Lansing, Michigan, he would marry her. He also said, off-handedly, that he was once adjudged insane.

Only when typhoid was mentioned did Mary become a violent, angry woman, not adverse to taking physical action to prove her point. She was a formidable foe. Dr. Baker states in her book that she often worried what would happen to her if Mary was released.

Mary Mallon lived a good part of her life with families as a servant. She did not make friends easily with other servants, perhaps in order to maintain as much anonymity as possible. Indeed, she knew she would always have to move on. She knew she had to be one jump ahead. What a lonely, fragmented existence it must have been!

Yet, this intelligent woman refused to accept reality. She consciously refused to face the fact that she was a source of illness and death. One must pause and wonder whether her nights were filled with guilt and dread seeing the faces of those who became ill, especially the little girl who died. I think it to be more likely that she, like many, had a blind spot, which prevented her from recognizing her potential for harm to others.

Her only hope of cure was removal of her gall bladder which is about 85% effective in terminating the carrier state. This she refused. She was sure that her pursuers meant to kill her. Many Irish in those days had a "fear of the knife" and the hospital where they were sure one went to die.

Today, we have drugs which will terminate the carrier state in many patients. Maybe today it would be an entirely different story for Mary.

Mary, despite being the first carrier identified in the United States, was listed as Carrier #36 because when registration became mandatory all known carriers were listed in alphabetical order and then assigned numbers.

Once listed as a carrier, there are rigid requirements for removal of the person from the roster. Currently we have about 110 carriers on the New York City roster. But, according to Dr. John Marr of the New York City Department of Health, that number is not accurate since many so listed would by now be over 100 years of age and are probably dead.

In 1907 there were 4426 cases of typhoid and 740 deaths. Now our average number of cases for one year is 20–30. The advances in the treatment of sewage, the purification of water, pasteurization of milk, temperature and quality control of foods and the isolation of cases and control of carriers have contributed to the spectacular decline. In 1978 there were 42 cases reported. The increase was due to a rabbi, nicknamed "Typhoid Mosher" by the Health Department, who was responsible for eleven cases. Forty-three percent of cases are acquired out of the United States.

Mary does not hold the record for causing the most known cases of typhoid. Indeed there is the case of a man in Brooklyn who sold ice cream in a candy store and caused 110 cases and six deaths. There was also a farmer in Camden, New York, in 1909, who is said to have been the cause of 409 cases and 40 deaths from shipments of cream. However, Mary was the first charted carrier and as Dr. Baker said: "For that she paid in life-long imprisonment."

On December 25, 1932, Mary Mallon was found on the floor of her cottage paralyzed by a stroke. She was taken to Riverside Hospital where she remained until her death on November 11, 1938, at the age of 69. Her death certificate, #11377, lists the cause as terminal bronchopneumonia of seven days duration, chronic nephritis and myocarditis for 10 years and lists a contributory cause of typhoid carrier for 24 years. It was signed by Doctor David Cohen. At last Mary was completely free. Her debt was paid.

Mary Mallon, alias Carrier 36, Mrs. Brown, Marie Breshoff, was buried from St. Luke's Church at 138th Street in the Bronx, with nine persons present. No one followed her to the grave. On her tombstone in St. Raymond's Cemetery are the words:

"MY JESUS MERCY"

Dr. McLaughlin is the Chairman of the Department of Community Medicine at Long Island Jewish-Hillside Medical Center.

A Kingly Speculation

WALTER J. P. CURLEY

There are enthroned today in Europe nine hereditary rulers. There are thirteen additional countries on that continent whose thrones are claimed by living Pretenders.

To those whose interest in Ireland is whetted by blood, affection or curiosity, these facts prompt a hypothetical question: If Ireland were a monarchy today (as indeed, she once was), who might we expect to find on her ancient Celtic throne?

The invasions, occupations, struggles, battles and wars that have swept across this island over the centuries have virtually obliteratd the ancient, native Gaelic royal dynasties—at least the expected evidences and trappings. The Irish, from time immemorial, however, have been ardent genealogists bent on preserving the identities and relationships of their tribes, clans, septs, and families in the face of great opposition—particularly during the invasions and occupations of the Danes, Normans, and the English.

This makes it difficult for any but the most intrepid royalty-watcher to find what he seeks in Ireland. He must combine certain characteristics of the archaeologist, anthropologist, librarian, hiker, sportsman, and *bon vivant*. He may find himself in a bog in Mayo, on a sheep farm in Roscommon, in a Regency dining-room in Limerick, or at a hunt ball in a castle in Meath. Anywhere.

There are three Irish families today which represent a royal legitimacy that can challenge any of their continental counterparts on the scores of antiquity and traceability. The leaders of such families are the Reverend Charles Denis Mary Joseph Anthony O'Conor; the Right Honorable Lord Inchiquin, seventeenth Baron of Inchiquin, Sir Phaedrig Lucius Ambrose O'Brien; and Jorge, The O'Neill of Clanaboy.

I

The O'Conor don is a Jesuit priest, an intellectual of the first order, and a gentle man. Charles Denis Mary Joseph Anthony O'Conor teaches at Clongowes, the Jesuit college which lies in green, flat country some twenty miles from Dublin.

The O'Conor don is descended from the first Christian king of Connacht in the fifth century, and King Roderic O'Conor, the last Ard Ri (High King or Supreme Monarch) of Ireland, who died in 1198. He is the only representative in Ireland of the old Royal Gaelic families who still own at least a part of their ancestral lands and is still a Catholic. The *Book of Annalists* claims that the O'Conors are descended from Heremon, one of the sons of Milesius, king of Spain, who invaded Ireland around 300 B.C.

The House of O'Conor reached the crest of its power in the early twelfth century with High King Turlough Mor O'Conor, whose son, Roderic, or Cathal Crovedearg of the Wine Red Hand, was the last High King of Ireland. The Normans arrived during Roderic's reign and ended the High Kingship. The O'Conors, however, remained kings of Connacht until the end of the fourteenth century.

By the end of the seventeenth century only a fraction of their lands was held by members of the O'Conor family in County Roscommon in Connacht. Today, only Clonalis, near Castlerea, survives. It is the only historic house open to the public in Ireland which represents the Irish rather than the Anglo-Irish tradition, and illustrates the survival of this tradition from the coming of Christianity to Ireland in the fifth century up to the present day. The history of Clonalis is, in miniature, the history of Ireland.

II

The Right Honorable Lord Inchiquin, seventeenth Baron of Inchiquin, Sir Phaedrig Lucius Ambrose O'Brien, is the direct male descendant of King Brian Boru, the Ard Ri of Ireland who was slain by the Danes in the eleventh century. Although the O'Briens' High Kingship was subsequently cleaved, they remained the reigning dynasty of Thomond in the province of north Munster until the middle of the sixteenth century.

The O'Briens are also descendants of the Spanish King, Milesius, through his sons Heber and Heremon, who reputedly led the Milesian invasion of Ireland, and settled there about the time of Alexander the Great. The Milesians established the dynasties of the ruling Gaelic families of Ireland, including the O'Briens, O'Neills, and O'Conors.

Lord Inchiquin succeeded his brother, Donough, to the title in 1968. He was born in April, 1900, and was educated at Eton, Magdalen College, Oxford, and Imperial College, London University.

Lord and Lady Inchiquin have family ties to both Ireland and England. Lady Vera is descended from an old Saxon Catholic family, and on her mother's side from the O'Neills.

In spite of more recent English connections, the O'Briens have struggled continuously to maintain their Irish inheritance. In 1582, an earlier Donough O'Brien was executed by order of Queen Elizabeth I for opposing her conquest of Ireland. Less than 150 years ago, William Smith O'Brien, a famous patriot and great-great-great uncle of the current claimant, was found guilty of high treason by the British. Today, although their instinct is no longer physical, the

477

O'Briens' zeal to preserve the Irish tradition is as intense as their forebears'.

III

The O'Neill of Clanaboy, Chief of his ancient and Royal name, and recognized by the Genealogical Office in Dublin as heir male of the last "properly inaugurated Prince of Clanaboy, senior branch of the old Royal House of Ulster" is, paradoxically, a Portuguese nobleman, as his predecessors have been for generations.

Lord O'Neill, however, is the head of the house of O'Neill in Ireland. He succeeded his father, the third Baron, who was killed in action with the British forces in Italy during World War II.

Lord O'Neill went to Eton, the Royal Agricultural College in Cirencester, England, and served as a major in the North Irish Horse Regiment. He is married to the elder daughter of Lord Francis Scott, the brother of the Duchess of Gloucester.

The O'Neills, who live at Shane's Castle in County Antrim about twenty miles from Belfast, are the descendants of King Niall of "The Nine Hostages" who lived 1,500 years ago and asserted at least nominal suzerainty over the whole island of Ireland—a High King. The O'Neills provided High Kings to Ireland from the fifth century until the thirteenth century, and reigned as provincial kings in Northern Ireland from 425 until 1603. The present fourth Baron's family, the Chichesters, married into the O'Neills and took the title by royal license about 150 years ago.

In our topsy-turvy world of today, who can deny that Fate could beckon one of these men to assume the crown of his ancestors?

Mr. Curley is an investment banker and a former Commissioner of Public Events for New York City.

"A Stranger Among Strangers"
John Butler Yeats in New York

HILARY PYLE

"Solitude is I find very good for the intellect, but a terrible drain on the spirits," the painter, John Butler Yeats wrote to Susan Mitchell one year after his arrival in New York.

> Never before did I know solitude—I have been alone for months together in London & in Dublin—but here it is being alone with a vengeance. In the first place there is nothing to distract your attention from your solitide. . . . Except to put your hand into your pocket now & then you can give all your attention to your solitude. I was never intended to be solitary—it is against the nature of artists—*we must have people about us. It is the very meaning of the artist mind.*

Despite the warmth of this affirmation, and despite repeated efforts by his children to bring him home to Ireland, John Butler Yeats (JBY) was to spend the remainder of his life, some fourteen years, in the American solitude that disturbed, and yet attracted him. Many statements in his letters are semi-contradictory: he tended to write in the emotion of the moment, except in the more public epistles to his son, W.B. Yeats; and in the hitherto unpublished letter to Mitchell, a kindred spirit, admitted his yearning for such mundane articles as the potato, the onion, and bacon and ham. Inevitably he was gathering people around him: admirers, at first, and later, a coterie of similar-minded Irish-Americans. Yet solitude was, perhaps, what he required at this stage of life, a detachment from the gigantically-gifted family of two genius

479

sons, and two creative daughters, who were in danger of swallowing up his own reluctant daemon: and, at sixty-eight, this was his last opportunity to break away.

Right at the beginning of his career, as a law student in Dublin, JBY has spoken about the "task of Self-Culture," the working out in "a well-acted life . . . the convictions that have been formed in seclusion." He was referring here to the privileged seclusion of the student. He himself remained a student all his days. Near the end, he told his brother, Isaac Yeats, that he had never settled in New York. "Always I have been a stranger among strangers," he said, but he admitted that in this way only could he reach "the repose of a complete solitude." "What America needs to rescue it from its unrest and delirious collectivism is *poets and solitaries,* men who turn aside and live to themselves and enjoy the luxury of their own feelings and thoughts."

He had spent the greater part of his adult life turning aside. A year after being called to the bar in 1866, he moved to London to attend art school. He had his first commission for portraits in Killarney in 1872, after which he returned to London, to leave it again for seven years in 1880 to paint portraits in Dublin. Back in London once more, he tried his hand as a black-and-white illustrator, as his son Jack was doing more successfully at the same time. He didn't handle a paint brush for some years. When his wife died in 1900, he was easily persuaded, at the age of sixty-one, to go back to Dublin to hold his first one-man show, and to embark on the most successful period of his career, as portrayer of the prominent creators and intellectuals of the Irish Renaissance.

There were still problems and uncertainties, disagreements with Lane, his patron: but what prompted him to leave six years later, in December 1907, he never divulged. He went to New York for a holiday, ostensibly, in the company of his daughter, Lily, who was going on business:

he hoped to find new commissions. But he never returned. With the exception of Willy, who paid him a short visit with his new wife, he never saw his family again. He was to live longer in New York than he had lived in any one place before.

JBY liked the Americans, their frankness and their kindness. "They seem to have no secrets," he told Susan Mitchell in the same letter of 1908. "They all live in the open air & the open daylight." It meant much to him to be for the first time a real success, among people whom he found idealists, full of imaginative desire and longing for perfection in everything including behavior. He observed their practicality. "A man is judged by them as they would judge a wheelbarrow," he commented. "They are very proud of their practicality in automobiles & aeroplanes & cooking & railway trains—but in the world of literature & art they are good children & very submissive." Much of his critical writing from now on was to make direct comparisons between his new country and Europe: and there was no doubt that the new environment, where he was a stranger, was a stimulus to him.

In Dublin, when putting his realizations of the characters he protrayed into paint, it was like a dialogue between compatible personalities. There must be empathy, otherwise the portrait was not a success. He encouraged his sitters to talk: and orated incessantly himself, walking backwards and forwards from sitter to easel, conducting a conversation in pigment. In America, he sought a dialogue with himself. He tried to define himself at last, sketching and painting self-portraits, the major self-portrait taking over eleven years, and still incomplete at his death. He discussed with himself, in ink and print, hoping for achievement as a writer. He still failed to satisfy WB with the short stories he offered him for criticism. But he knew that the letters he wrote to the poet, and his American essays, were going to be published. He had always lived to himself. Now he could at last savour the luxury of his own feelings and thoughts.

His aphorisms are constantly quoted: he intended them for quotation. Less attention has been given to the development of his art in New York, though he sketched continually—often without payment, and never demanding more than fifteen dollars for a drawing—and he has left images in pencil and oil of all the friends and associates of his last years. He found himself being drawn to the artists in New York who were in sympathy with the new movements in Europe.

At the time he arrived there, Luks, Sloan and Glackens, three pupils of the socialist painter, Robert Henri, had recently been turned down for the annual exhibition of the National Academy of Design. All had worked as newspaper artists, and their approach was direct and immediate, dealing with city life in its actuality, rather than looking for pleasing anecdote, as was currently the practice in the Academy.

William Macbeth, who had been acting as agent for JBY's son, Jack, decided to exhibit the work of these rejected artists, with some others, in his gallery. The exhibition was called "Eight American Painters," from which they were nicknamed "The Eight": but they soon earned the further nickname of "The Ashcan School," because critics thought their work was provocatively crude and vulgar. While still representational, and not, from our viewpoint, seeking out the controversial or tragic elements of urban life, they were moving from photographic realism to a looser style of painting, where colors were intensified, and details glossed over. Impact, and social awareness, were what mattered.

These were the men whose company JBY enjoyed at the small French boarding house, to which he was to move permanently, after his initial feted stay in the Grand Union Hotel. In his letter to Susan Mitchell, he jotted down his first impressions of the French restaurant, where he dined regularly, mentioning that he had been invited for supper, at 11 o'clock, on Christmas Eve night.

> Three Breton women keep it. Young & good-looking, & very hard working & probably *avares*—I fancy they are rather *harsh*. Good lips closed tightly. Seldom open or smile. Black eyes. Good figures held erect—quick alert movements—strong sense & sincerity. Nothing about them appeals to you because you feel that they are quite able to take care of themselves—rather everything about them including their youth & good looks does appeal to you only you check the movement to respond because you see that they have as much feeling for you as a crocodile that was going to eat you.

The following year he moved in with the crocodiles—he was to paint a full-length of the youngest one as a marriage present some years later. It was here too that Sloan painted him in the now famous group portrait, "Yeats at Petitpas," in the tradition of Fantin-Latour and Manet, but with a modern robustness: JBY seated like a patriarch among the group to whom he had become so close. Each might have been a son to him as regards age. Van Wyck Brooks, the critic, was his firm supporter. They had met through John Quinn, the collector, who brought JBY to America. John Sloan was of Northern Irish Presbyterian stock, perhaps formed a link with JBY's own boyhood in County Down; and Dolly Sloan, his wife, was the descendant of Irish Catholic immigrants. Robert Henri was sympathetic with the Russian revolutionaries. JBY didn't like revolution, but he was in favor of independent government for Ireland.

JBY exhibited with Henri, Sloan, Prendergast and their group in 1910. All tended to conservatism in their own painting. Ironically, after organizing, a couple of years later, the spectacular Armory Show, which changed the face of American art, opening it up to direct continental influence, the Ashcans themselves fell into obscurity. JBY was not so impressed by the show, having had some experience of modern art in London and Dublin. However, it had its impact on him. "I mean to go to it very often," he said, "& try try try and try again—to understand the Cubists, which at present seem to me largely damnable— for work which I recognize as the very best is by artists who I think are in sympathy with them."

Much greater on him, in this American phase, was the influence of John Sloan. (Sloan, conversely, admitted the influence of Yeats.)

JBY's first portraits, of the 1870s and 1880s, had concentrated on character, rendered with a sensitive academic realism, much hampered by the "imperfect technique" that he lamented. In the late 1890s and early 1900s, his paintings were to benefit from the sketch-like quality of the black-and-white illustrations, which had taken him away from the easel for years: and he aimed to preserve this quality of a sketch, believing that the sketch contained personal comment as well as fact. Apart from the face, details in the portraits were dwelt upon only where they elaborated character. Hands, for example, he frequently ignored: but in the case of George Russell, whom he painted in 1903, and knew as "a long-fingered visionary," the hands are elegant and beautiful. Spectacles in his wife's portrait, of some years earlier, are used as semi-opaque screens, masking her patience and suffering, where, in other instances, the spectacles may be only briefly indicated. Much is made of the wide-brimmed hat and the spade beard of John O'Leary in his more famous portrait of 1904, to convey the image of a traveller and a visionary. What is important to the artist in these mid-period paintings is his interpretation of the inner personality—something that fails altogether in the case of Lady Gregory, whom he reduces to a dazed-looking schoolgirl, but that triumphs with Rosa Butt, for whose father

484

he had devilled. "With all his faults and disasters—the most lovable man who ever breathed," he wrote: "his daughter seems to me to inherit all his qualities." Painting her in 1900, JBY captured her mischievous intelligence in her animated brown eyes and wide mouth, her reserve in the tightly clasped hands.

The sketch-like quality of these portraits is projected in the cobwebby brushwork, the restrained films of paint, the impressions of forms, out of which the faces grow and are highlighted. Through contact with Sloan and the Ashcan painters, his brushwork grew broad and strong, rather than suggestive. Color, which had mattered little to him before, except for interpretative purposes, became rich and defined; often light toned, with a preference for yellow. He was, of course, painting in a nation of extroverts, and so concentrating on the outer, and confident image, rather than on the enigma of introversion, which had obsessed him before.

His drawings, too, changed from the rapid impressionist likenesses in Dublin, with crosshatching and scribble, through an intermediate stage of clear, brilliant realism—for the faces—to the more aggressive attack in the drawings of his final years. In these strong images of Jeanne Foster and of WB's wife, George, thick blurred pencil shading replaces the former scribble fill-in. Interestingly, the energy of these last extrovert portrait drawings seems to refer back to the confidence of his early magnificent chalk portrait of Isaac Butt.

The American paintings differ, also, from the mature Dublin canvases, in that, instead of envisaging an impressionist image, hovering in a neutral ground, that is lit with subdued touches of color for mood, JBY now deliberately creates a setting, an interior or suggestion of an interior, something he must have taken from the Ashcans. Never before had he been interested in background. Even in the early drawings, illustrating Browning's poem, "Pippa

485

Passes," he concentrated on the girl herself, rather than on the landscape through which she was passing.

Yet, in the likenesses of Mrs. Caughey and of Mary Lapsley Guest, of 1916, by highlighting a door, or the detail of a chair, he achieves a sense of immediacy, that links the pictures with Post Impressionism, despite their inherent academicism. The small, half-length self-portrait, of the same year, with its modern choppy brushwork, indicates the vertical of interior, in a Modigliani-like fashion, so dividing the personality into the inner and the outer man. The large masterpiece, on which he worked for so many years, surrounds the artist with his painterly and literary tools, in an interior that has become overcrowded.

Solitude, it seems, had brought him full circle, from the day when he first excitedly referred to the "task of Self-Culture," as a law student in Dublin. In "a well-acted life," he had continued to work out "the convictions that have been formed in seclusion": in this last great self-portrait reaching a completely objective view of himself. It has the fire in it that he felt should be in any true work of art, the fire of the original inspiration—apparently forgotten by the artist—which reemerges as "the personal ego is dropped away."

John Butler Yeats died on the day that Joyce's *Ulysses* was published. Characteristically, he was an admirer, though of a much older generation, of this complex and innovative fellow countryman. His daughter, Lily, who had psychic leanings made the point that JBY had been born in the year of the Big Wind. Like Odysseus, buffeted by experience, eluding fate through the benevolence of ministering spirits, and with as rich a perception of life, he travelled life, to return to himself, and to his professional image, in paint. Still, his interest in others equalled the obsession with his self-portrait. "Give me another chance to save my soul and your face," he requested his friend, the poet, Jeanne Foster, two weeks before he died. "Both are for eternity."

Hilary Pyle, a well-known art historian, writes from Cork.

Nocturne: A Tribute to John Field

EILY O'GRADY PATTERSON

I first came into contact with John Field when, at the age of eleven, I was studying a test-piece for the Dublin Feis Ceoil. The piece was Field's Nocturne in B flat major. The beauty and simplicity of the melodic line and the gentle flowing quavers in the left hand accompaniment immediately captured my imagination. I resolved to find out more about this inspired composer.

To my delight, I discovered that John Field was an Irishman and it came as a great surprise to read that he had, in fact, invented the Nocturne. I had always thought that the great Chopin invented this mode of composition, but Field's first Nocturnes were published in 1814 when Chopin was only four years of age.

John Field was the first composer to free himself from the constraints of pure classical form. He was the forerunner, the pathfinder of lyrical and romantic compositions and greatly influenced many of his famous contemporaries, among them Schumann, Mendelssohn, Liszt and Chopin. The latter was greatly flattered when his own early compositions and style of playing were compared to those of the Irishman. Field's compositions were known and admired throughout the entire musical world, but it was as a concert pianist that he became a legend in his own lifetime. Even today he is regarded by many as one of the greatest pianists of all time.

John Field was born in Dublin on July 26, 1782. It is interesting to note that three years earlier another great musician and poet, Thomas Moore, had been born in Dublin and that the two talented lads lived within a stone's throw of each other, the young Field living in Camden Street and Moore just down the road in Aungier Street.

Field's father was a theatre orchestra violinist and his grandfather an organist in one of the City churches. Young John began piano lessons with his grandfather and immediately showed exceptional talent. He was then sent to Thommaso Giordano, a noted Italian singer, composer and pianist, who had settled in Dublin. Giordano lost no time in showing off his young pupil's extraordinary gifts. On March 2, 1792, he made his debut at a concert in the Rotunda, Dublin. Field was then less than ten years old and his magnificent playing caused a sensation. The press notices of the day described his playing as "really an astonishing performance by such a child." A few more public concerts in Dublin followed before John left his native land forever.

In 1793 the Field family moved to London where his father received an appointment as violinist in the Haymarket Theatre. John became a pupil of Muzio Clementi, the most noted pianist and composer in London. "The young Irishman," as he was called in his early reviews, became very popular among London's music lovers. Haydn attended one of his concerts and predicted a great future for him. And Clementi, in a letter to Pleyel in Paris in 1801, described him as "a very promising genius, who is already a favourite in our

489

Country, both in respect of his compositions and his performances.''

The following year teacher and pupil left London for Paris, later travelling through Europe until they reached St. Petersburg. Here Clementi and Field parted company, Field deciding to settle in Russia, where he remained for the rest of his life save for an extended European tour in the 1830's.

In Russia his unique and extraordinary talent as a pianist was quickly recognized and his genius as a composer began to flourish. He was much sought after as a teacher and Field's pedagogic activity laid the foundation for the great development of piano-forte playing in Russia during the second half of the 19th century. His name is allied with those of Russian pianists who later developed the singing tone and expressive piano-forte playing. He, in essence, was the first musician in Russia to reveal the secrets of real artistic mastery to his students. For this contribution, Field is still much honored as a pianist and pedagogue.

He married Adelaide Victoria Percheron in 1810. They had one child, a son, but their marriage was not a happy one and they parted in 1821. Even before Field and his wife separated, he had a love affair with a singer, Madamoiselle Charpentier, by whom he had another son, Leon. A strong bond of affection emerged between Field and this son. The boy was a very talented pianist and later became an operatic tenor of some merit. Together with his father, he gave many concerts. The composer's legitimate son, Adrian, was likewise a musician but he became addicted to drink and eventually died in obscurity.

In 1831, Field embarked on an extensive European tour. The tour was an artistic triumph. Everywhere he was greeted with rapture and packed concert halls. The critics were wild in their praise. He toured England, France, Belgium and Switzerland making his way to Italy where he became seriously ill. With the help of some Russian friends he started the long journey back to Moscow, stopping off at Vienna. There, despite being dangerously ill and in great pain, Field gave three concerts and composed perhaps the most beautiful of all his Nocturnes, the great C major. Finally, he arrived back in Moscow in a deplorable condition, suffering from intestinal cancer. He died of pneumonia on January 27, 1837.

A tremendous crowd came to accompany the musician on his last journey: pupils, artistes and musicians and all who had loved him as an inspired performer and a kind man. In the Vedensky Cemetery, a tombstone was erected on his grave with the following inscription:

JOHN FIELD
Born in Ireland in 1782
Died in Moscow in 1837
Erected in his memory
by
His grateful friends and scholars

Eily Patterson, Ireland's leading harpist, has performed at many of our Society's Dinners.

John Hughes: A Man of the People

ROBERT P. WHALEN, M. D.

This year was an important one in the history of the Catholic Church in New York City. It marked the centennial of the opening and dedication of what many consider the finest example of gothic cathedral architecture in the United States. Construction of St. Patrick's Cathedral began in 1858 and was interrupted several times, once by fire and once by the economic impact of civil strife; but when the Cathedral was dedicated in May of 1879, it gave the Catholic Church a prominence and prestige it had never before enjoyed in New York City. To this day, Saint Patrick's is the leading symbol of the Church's presence in the City.

The man whose vision it was to build Saint Patrick's Cathedral was an Irishman by birth, an American by chance, a battler by instinct, and a member of the Church hierarchy by only the greatest fortuity. His name was John Hughes, although his bellicosity was to earn him the nickname "Dagger John," and his rise to fame makes Horatio Alger's pale in comparison.

He was born into abject poverty, the son of a Catholic tenant farmer in the north in 1797. He barely survived his childhood; one of his three brothers and one of his three sisters did not. The year 1814 was a ruinous one for Irish farms, and

492

John's family, which had sacrificed to keep up his education, found it necessary to take him from school to join his sisters and brothers on the farm.

In 1816, Patrick Hughes, John's father, sailed with one of his sons to America, where he was to find work in Pennsylvania, near the Maryland border. John sailed to join them the following year, arriving in Baltimore. His mother and sisters and oldest brother had to remain behind to harvest the crops necessary to pay for their passage, and it was several years before the family was to be reunited. In the meantime, John joined his father and brother and worked in various pursuits; farming, gardening, building roads and bridges, and digging stone quarries in and around Chambersburg, Pennsylvania and Emmitsburg, Maryland.

It was in the latter community that John Hughes was to realize his religious destiny, for in that community at the time were two remarkable priests who had come to America to escape the horrors of the French Revolution and Terror. In Emmitsburg, they founded a seminary in 1808 in which they determined to educate a native American Catholic clergy. The two were John DuBois and Simon Brute.

The seminary they founded is today Mount Saint Mary's College. I visited the college recently, on the way back from a meeting at the National Institutes of Health in Bethesda, Maryland. It was a homecoming of sorts for me, because I received my pre-medical training there almost thirty-five years ago.

As I drove through the area, I thought about the great impact that Emmitsburg and its environs have had on American history. It was in Emmitsburg that Mother Elizabeth Ann Seton founded the Sisters of Charity, one of the achievements that was to make her the first American-born saint. Just up the road a few miles is Gettysburg, where the climactic battle of the Civil War was fought. And down the road about five miles from Emmitsburg is Thurmont, the location of Camp David, where contemporary American history has been written by President Carter in domestic and international summits.

It was in 1818, one year after his arrival in America, that John Hughes obtained work as a laborer in Emmitsburg. His biographers described him then as a wiry, rawboned young man. Almost every Irishman, when he is young, is described as wiry. As a physician, I've always felt that the leanness of Irish youth represented a rather uncharitable view of Irish cooking, although most of us seem to flesh out pretty well as we grow older.

Sometime shortly after his arrival in Emmitsburg, John Hughes made up his mind that he wanted to enter the priesthood. He called frequently on DuBois and Brute in an effort to gain admission to Mount Saint Mary's. But the two priests apparently wrote him off as an empty-headed, uncouth dreamer, and he was continually rebuffed.

According to his biographer, Richard Shaw, Mother Elizabeth Seton saw something in Hughes that was not apparent to DuBois and Brute, because she interceded with them on the young man's behalf, and a compromise was struck. Hughes would be hired by the seminary as a gardener, and in lieu of wages, he would receive lodging, food and occasional tutoring. However, the archivist of Mount Saint Mary's College indicates there is no confirmation of Mother Seton's intervention in the records of the College or of the Sisters of Charity.

The ice was broken, but more than a year passed, when Father DuBois happened upon Hughes during dinnertime and found him studying instead of eating, before DuBois began to perceive that John Hughes was far more than a poorly-educated Irish day-laborer. And so, DuBois relented, and, in 1820, at the age of 23, John Hughes became one of the sixty-or-so students enrolled in Mount Saint Mary's seminary.

All this while he remained close to his family and oftentimes on a Saturday he walked the thirty miles to Chambersburg to be with them, walking back the following day after Mass. On one of these trips he brought back his sisters Margaret and Ellen and enrolled them in the Sisters of Charity School.

He advanced academically, and at the end of his first year in school was described by one of his mentors as "equal to the school's best student," despite his lack of scholarly preparation. The day-laborer turned student was being transformed into a cleric.

In due course, in 1825, he was ordained a deacon and assigned to St. Mary's Church in Philadelphia, where over the next several years he was to become deeply embroiled in a controversy over a recalled bishop. It was in Philadelphia that John Hughes began to develop and demonstrate his considerable skills as a preacher, administrator and polemicist. He engaged in a heated, written debate with a leading Presbyterian minister.

Keep in mind that anti-Catholicism and anti-

Popery were rampant at the time, and Hughes' outspoken courage soon won for him a reputation as a Catholic folk hero, one who cherished a good fight, and who seldom lost a battle of words. Soon, he built a new parish and a new church, Saint John's in Philadelphia.

In 1837, at the age of 40, and with only a dozen years of service in the priesthood, John Hughes was elevated to the rank of bishop and made co-adjutor of New York, where he was reunited with his old mentor, Bishop John DuBois, who was then fifty years a priest. New York at the time had 30,000 Catholics, out of a total population of 300,000.

Within two months of his arrival, the old bishop suffered a stroke, incapacitating him to such an extent that from that point forward, John Hughes was effectively in jurisdictional control of the New York Diocese, a see reaching all the way to Buffalo and embracing more than 200,000 faithful. There are some who say that the Catholic Church is not in the least democratic—that's with a small "d"—but in what enterprise could a young, uneducated emigre rise to the top as fast as did Hughes?

Hughes, who was now the head of the Diocese in fact if not in name, soon found himself embroiled in an issue that was to establish his reputation as the spokesman and advocate for the immigrant poor, particularly the Irish, of New York City. The issue was education and centered around the City's so-called public schools which in reality were the exclusive domain of the native-born, the well-to-do, and the Protestant.

The issue was put in perspective by then Governor William H. Seward, who in his 1840 address to the State Legislature, said:

The children of foreigners, found in great numbers in our populous cities and towns, are too often deprived of the advantages of our system of public education in consequence of the prejudices arising from difference of language or religion. It ought never to be forgotten that the public welfare is as deeply concerned in their education as in that of *our* children. I do not hesitate, therefore, to recommend the establishment of schools, in which they may be instructed by teachers speaking the same language with themselves and professing the same faith.

In 1849 the Public School Society, which was under the monopolistic control of a nonelected group of wealthy men, controlled 100, or virtually all, of the schools in New York City. As a consequence, the Common Council, all of whose members served as ex-officio members of the Public School Society, voted the Society the lion's share of the education funds received from the State. Catholic children forced to attend these schools found themselves in an atmosphere hostile to their religion. None of the textbooks except those in mathematics were free of anti-Catholic bias.

In every public school was a book, *The Irish Heart*. A character in the book was Phelim Maghee, portrayed as a model of Catholic conscience. The book related, "When Phelim had laid up a good stock of sins he now and then went over to Killarney of a Sabbath morning, and got releaf by confissing them out o' the way, as he used to express it, and sealed up his soul with a wafer, and returned quite invigorated for the perpetration of new offenses."

The preface of the book declared:

The emigration from Ireland to America, of annually increasing numbers, extremely needy and in many

497

cases drunken and depraved, has become a subject for grave and fearful reflection . . . Should the materials of this oppressive influx continue to be the same, instead of an asylum our country might appropriately be styled the common sewer of Ireland.

Books and teachings like this led immigrant parents to keep their children away from school in droves. The Catholics of New York held meetings and made a formal application for school funds from the Common Council. Shortly afterward, Bishop Hughes told a cheering audience of supporters, ". . . Give us our just proportion of the common school fund and if we do not give as good an education, apart from religious instruction, as given in the public schools, to one-third a larger number of children for the same money, we are willing to renounce our just claim."

Hughes campaigned for school aid as though he were running for office. In a three-and-a-half hour talk before the Common Council, he continually reiterated a central theme: "We are a portion of this people and we merely ask to be placed on an equality with the rest of our fellow citizens." His presentation led one Protestant newspaper of the day to observe, "No one could hear him without painful regret that such powers of the mind, such varied and extensive learning, and such apparent sincerity of purpose were trammelled with a fake system of religion."

But the issue dragged on into 1841, when Governor Seward's annual message to the Legislature again urged school reform, observing, "The evil remains as before, and the question recurs, not merely how or by whom shall education be given, but whether it shall be given at all . . ."

But the Common Council heeded neither

Hughes nor Seward and on February 11, 1841, with but one dissenting vote, it turned down the Catholic petitions for school funds. Hughes told a huge audience gathered for the vote, "We have come here denied of our rights, but not conquered." And he went on to comment, "While it is the Catholics today, it may be the Universalists, or the Jews, or the Baptists, or the Unitarians tomorrow who may suffer." He indicated his next step: "We have an appeal to a higher power than the Common Council—to the Legislature of the State." A petition with 7,000 signatures was sent to Albany.

Soon afterward, the Secretary of State issued a report to the Legislature, reasserting what Seward had said, and observing that more children were unschooled in New York City than in the entire rest of the State. By general agreement of both sides, there were about 32,000 school-age children roaming the streets of New York at this time. He proposed that elected officials from each ward serve as commissioners for the public school system, a proviso that would break the monopoly of the Public School Society in the City.

Two bills were introduced, and one, based on the Secretary of State's report, seemed to have the better chance of passage. It would have extended the statewide district system to New York City, effectively ending the private monopoly of the Public School Society, and establishing elected school boards for each ward of the City. After acrimonious debate and threats of political retribution, the bill was bound over until the next year.

In the intervening months, Hughes and his followers worked feverishly to line up Legislative support, particularly among the Democrats, and proposed candidates to oppose those found wanting. He so exasperated one newspaper editor by his energetic efforts that the editor dubbed him the "Bishop of Blarneopolis."

In the fall elections Democrats were victorious throughout the State. What Hughes had done was fuse together a hitherto amorphous political force—mostly Irish Catholic immigrants—and present them as a unified vote. Attacked in the press for his tactics, Hughes replied in kind. He said: "When several strong denominations attack one that is weaker in a manner that turns religion into politics and politics into religion, the sentinels of our liberties at the press are asleep."

The Maclay Bill, which provided for an elected Board of Education in New York City, passed the next session of the Legislature. John Hughes had won a significant moral victory. After gaining for immigrants the right to control their own schools, he turned his back on the public school system and began to build a fledgling parochial school system. Instead of state aid, he relied upon an army of teachers drawn from the religious orders. His advocacy of the Catholic school system became so strong that he declared: "I think the time has come when it will be necessary to build the schoolhouse first and the church afterwards."

And he built more than churches and schools. He founded what was to become Fordham University. It was originally called St. John's, as were the first church and two orphanages founded by Hughes. In 1841, he brought over from France a colony of Ladies of the Sacred Heart, who opened a girls' academy at Manhattanville. And he started a hospital staffed by the Sisters of Charity. During his reign as Bishop he founded one hundred churches.

From this point forward, he became the most visible and outspoken representative of the Catholic Church in America, appearing, as one of his biographers was to write, in the newspapers as often as in the pulpit. In particular, he was to win widespread notoriety as a consequence of a love-hate relationship he enjoyed with James Gordon Bennett, editor and publisher of *The New York Herald*. It was Bennett who wrote of Hughes that he was "more a Roman gladiator than a devout follower of the meek founder of Christianity."

But, for the Irish immigrant, Hughes was a natural hero. He had arrived, like them, penniless in the new world, and had risen to the pinnacle of the church hierarchy. The greatest social factor in the lives of most Irish was the Roman Catholic Church. And the Irish were arriving in ever greater numbers after the Potato Blight of 1845. In 1847, 53,000 Irish arrived in New York City; the next year the total grew to 91,000, and in 1851, the peak year, 163,000 arrived. Hughes became their defender and their advocate.

The old Bishop, DuBois, had died in 1842, and Hughes had succeeded him in title as well as in fact. Then, on October 3, 1850, came word from Rome that New York was to become a metropolitan see, and that Hughes was to be an Archbishop with supervisory powers over the Dioceses of Boston, Hartford, Albany and Buffalo.

His fame and power grew. He was invited to the White House as a dinner guest of President Fillmore. He made frequent trips to Europe, including his native land in his itinerary.

In the middle 1850's, his health began to fail; he

suffered from rheumatism and several bouts of pneumonia. But, somehow, his energies never diminished. He had one special dream: he wanted to build a cathedral equal to those in Europe. As one of his biographers expressed it, he sought "An expression in stone to confirm for both immigrants and natives that the Roman Catholic Church was a part of the United States." Finally, on the feast of the Assumption, August 15th, 1858, before a crowd of more than 60,000 people, and described by *The New York Herald* as "one of the grandest ceremonies that was ever witnessed on this continent," the cornerstone was laid and a large white wooden cross was placed where the altar would stand.

The Cathedral was to be the grandest the City had ever seen. It was to fill the block bounded by Madison and Fifth Avenues, 50 and 51st Streets. The building was to be 332 feet long, 174 feet wide, and the tallest of the towers was to be 330 feet high. The exterior was to be of white marble from quarries in Pleasantville and Lee, Massachusetts.

In this, the moment of his greatest triumph, Hughes was lionized by even his old foes of the press. *Harper's Weekly* wrote of him, "No individual, perhaps, in this country, in office or out of it, wields a greater influence over a greater number of minds."

But, alas, construction was stopped in 1860 as a consequence of a strike, and the outside wall of the Cathedral, then 35 feet high, was to remain that way until after Hughes' death.

But, despite his failing health, Hughes still had two important tasks ahead of him. During the Civil War, President Lincoln sent him to France as a special emissary. Incidentally, Hughes angered more than a few people by flying the stars and stripes atop the old Cathedral during the war. After his return from France, his last public appearance was in the form of a personal appeal to the Irish of New York to end the bloody draft riots of 1863.

He died peacefully on January 3rd, 1864. On the day of his funeral many businesses closed in the City and more than 100,000 people massed around the Cathedral for the services.

To him we are indebted not only for a great Cathedral; he was also the founder of the Catholic school, college and hospital systems in New York City; the unintentional author of the public school system that still exists here in the City; and the principal animus of the Catholic Church as a political and social force in 19th century America.

An American priest of his day, asked by an Italian Cardinal, how Hughes enjoyed such great popularity, responded, "I think that it is because he is always *game.*"

But, most of all, he will be remembered as a man of the people. In his 25 year career as Bishop, John Hughes reflected the American Dream of the self-made man and of the battle of the poor immigrants to make the United States their own country. He reached the very top of his calling through determination, hard work and an unquestioned ability to lead. And throughout, he earned the love and respect of the little man, for whom he fought so hard.

Dr. Whalen, who has previously contributed to the Recorder, *delivered this speech at one of the Society's monthly lectures.*

Canvas and Lace

KEVIN M. CAHILL, M.D.

Dr. Cahill, President-General of this Society, gave this talk for the St. Patrick's Society of Brooklyn.

It is a pleasure to be here tonight as we celebrate Tom Moore's 200th birthday. Your Society commemorated his centennial in 1879 by donating a statue of him to Prospect Park. It is still there—while many a statue in Dublin has fallen. Its presence must reflect either the wisdom and foresight of the St. Patrick's Society or the unheralded peace of Prospect Park. And it is pleasant— if perhaps too optimistically nostalgic—to imagine that generations of young men have courted their lovers beneath it with Moore's words:

> Believe me, if all those endearing young charms,
> Which I gaze on so fondly today. . . .

Many of you probably know the basic facts of Moore's life and achievements: born in the flat above his father's grocery store on Aungier Street, Dublin; a very happy childhood; a distinguished student at school and at Trinity College; a friend of Robert Emmet. He became the most popular— and, incidentally, the highest paid—lyric poet and songster of his day. His great gift was his ability to discern a spirit struggling to be born among his countrymen and, by fashioning words and adapting ancient melodies, to evoke a roman-

504

tic Ireland of the past that was enormously appealing both to his oppressed countrymen and to the more "polite" societies of London and Paris. He became the unofficial poet laureate of Ireland and is credited by some with "putting Ireland back on the cultural map of Europe."

Yet there are those who see the hero Moore supported by clay feet. Although the speaker in Prospect Park a hundred years ago summarily dismissed these iconoclasts as "carping and ignorant critics. . . .", the truth is that such charges dogged the heels of Moore even in his own time and continue today. Honestly compels us to assess them. Did he have an unmanly sense of accommodation and an overriding penchant for opportunism?

Until the year before Moore entered Trinity, Catholics could not get into the college at all. When the admissions ban was lifted in 1793, there remained some restrictions. Catholics were not eligible for scholarships, fellowships, or various monetary prizes. Moore was a brilliant and ambitious student. The critics point out that someone who stood to benefit from his success must have thought that it would be a shame if the restrictions against Catholics were to hinder his advancement and his rise to fame and therefore decided to list him as a Protestant.

It has been suggested that two people had motive—as they say in the courtroom—for the Protestant designation: Moore's mother, Anastasia, the original stage mother; and his famous and ambitious tutor, Samuel Whyte. In any case, the lapse of conscience was temporary, for when Moore actually entered Trinity it was as a Catholic, excluded from the scholarships reserved for Protestants.

Anastasia's influence continued to dominate Tom's life. She was ever solicitous for Tom to do the "right" thing, to mingle with the "right" people, and the right people very definitely did not include his elder at Trinity College, Robert Emmet. It is unclear whether Moore, at his mother's prompting, deserted Emmet or whether Emmet, sensing that Moore was not the stuff of which rebels are made, excluded him from any confidence about the United Irishmen. Emmet was well aware of the apron strings that reached from Aungier Street to the halls of Trinity.

When the college authorities resolved to purge the university of its rebels, Emmet and others fled. Moore remained and, before the college "Inquisition," refused to answer any questions that would incriminate others. It was a very theatrical gesture but somewhat empty because Moore, in fact, knew nothing of the rebellious activities. He had been kept innocent of them by his mother and by Emmet. The rebellion of 1798 failed but Emmet, unlike Wolfe Tone and Fitzgerald, survived to lead another rising five years later. It too failed; he was tried and condemned to death.

By that time Moore had already found his niche in London. In 1800 he was introduced to His Royal Highness George, Prince of Wales, who thanked Tom for dedicating *Anacreon* to him and who hoped that they would have many opportunities of "enjoying each other's society." Moore was beside himself with that tribute. It was the ultimate coup for Tom who, as one biographer notes, seems to have been on an endless circuit of garden parties.

At the same time Emmet was being executed, Moore was sailing for Bermuda to establish his claim to the patronage post of British Admiralty

Registrar. There is no entry in Moore's diary recording Emmet's execution. It may, however, be inferred from two songs that he was not unmoved by the death of the man he had admired from a safe distance. The one to Emmet has the lovely lines:

> O breathe not his name, let it sleep in the shade
> Where cold and unhonor'd his relics are laid.

The other to Emmet's lover, Sarah Curran, offers the poignant picture:

> She is far from the land where her young hero sleeps,
>   And lovers are round her, sighing:
> But coldly she turns from their gaze, and weeps,
>   For her heart in his grave is lying.

Sarah Curran at the time had married and was living in India. But Tom Moore was never one to let the facts interfere with his romantic imagination.

Another charge is that he plagiarized melodies without acknowledgement and that he distorted them. In my library I have the first and second editions of Bunting's *Ancient Irish Melodies*. It is sad to read the Preface to the later edition where the modest Gaelic music scholar calls attention to the far more famous songster who had become a living legend—and a very wealthy one—by adapting Bunting's melodies without bothering to acknowledge their origin. Ironically, Bunting's main complaint was not even the personal hurt but the fact that traditional Celtic airs had been distorted.

Most of the other products of Moore's very prolific pen have been blessedly forgotten.

So what can we make of our Tom Moore? What

507

sort of man was he? He was the minstrel boy who played his harp in the drawing room rather than on the battlefield. He was brilliant, graceful and gay. His temperament was suited to the society of the elite—with their clever conversations and carefully observed social amenities. He did not have the heart of a rebel. He lacked the courage and passion of an Emmet or a Tone, or a Fitzgerald.

And it probably is unfair to blame him for not being someone else. A butterfly does not soar—an eagle does. We don't, on that account, condemn the butterfly. Its light fancifulness appeals to another part of us.

The pioneer needs canvas—not lace—to protect him from the raw elements. But there are times when the delicate filigree of lace is more suitable.

Tom Moore's gift was more romantic than mystical, more melodious than poetic. But he used his gift fully and was rewarded with as much fame as anyone could expect.

It is worth noting that he also had more sadness in his personal life than most men. He outlived all of his five children. His three daughters died very young and his two sons on the threshold of maturity. Such tragedy must have been devastating for a man who so meticulously tried to avoid first-hand experience of the painful and brutal sides of life.

His critics, James Joyce among them, see in him an ignoble accommodation to the enemy. Stephen Dedalus, gazing on the statue of Moore at Trinity College sees "a sloth of the body and of the soul creep over it like unseen vermin, over the shuffling feet and up the folds of the cloak and around the *servile* head."

508

His admirers portray him as the unflagging patriot and national poet whose "sweet plangent strains woke in his countrymen a living sense of their lost heritage, and, coupled with O'Connell's energy, inspired them to regain it." We will not resolve tonight a question whose answer lies in the minds and hearts of men long dead.

A more relevant question might well be—what did the St. Patrick's Society of Brooklyn represent in 1879 when they spent their scarce dollars for a statue not of Robert Emmet, not of Wolfe Tone, not of the emigrant, but of Thomas Moore?

Did they know that Moore had visited New York in 1805 and had described the town as "depressing" and the inhabitants as "stupid, without taste and feeling"?

It must not have occurred to them that Moore would have been very ill at ease indeed among the Irish immigrants here who, for the most part, were not fancy people. They lived—most of them—in tenements and entered drawing rooms only as servants. They sang Moore's melodies of romantic Ireland believing he was one of them, and not realizing that he had little but disdain for simple people.

Our choices betray our values. Can it be that the choice to honor Moore with a statue reflected a desire in the members of the St. Patrick's Society to wipe from their minds the cruel realities of famine and oppression and poverty and to memorialize instead a Romantic Ireland that they knew in their hearts never was?

I merely suggest that the choice of Moore strikes me as slightly odd. But then, perhaps, it very appropriately reflected the feelings of the Irish immigrants. For as Glazer and Moynihan

509

pointed out in *Beyond the Melting Pot*, they, more quickly than any other ethnic group, loosened their ties and became Americans.

Today, however, when the search for "roots" is so much in vogue, we should take care not to romanticize the past. And that is where a real contribution can be made by societies such as St. Patrick's or the American Irish Historical.

As I see it, the role of these Societies should be to honor the sacrifices of our forebears by making their tremendous contributions to our country known to anyone who seeks to understand how things came to be as they are.

Even our own children are much farther removed than we from a heritage that, whether acknowledged or not, shapes our thinking, our actions, and our view of the world.

Thomas Moore is part of that heritage. How great a part has been debated by honest men. "Time has laid its honor at his feet," certainly. He has his statue in the park.

If I have played the role of the Devil's Advocate tonight, it is not because I wish to denigrate a man's character or accomplishments, but simply because of my conviction that, if we are to draw strength from it, we must attempt to understand our heritage—and its heroes—honestly and intelligently. A simplistic or romanticized approach to Irish history and culture—so common even among those of Irish descent—yields nothing more than a mere caricature of the reality.

And that is precisely the sort of distortion that our societies were founded to dispel.

A Mission Remembered

MAUREEN MURPHY

A sentimental nineteenth century novel of virtue rewarded tells the story of an Irish immigrant girl who came to New York in the 1870's. Subtitled "A Tale Founded on Fact," *Annie Reilly or the Fortunes of an Irish Girl in New York* describes Annie's arrival at Castle Garden: immigrants confused and exhausted, luggage broken or lost, possessions scattered, indifferent officials, "sharks and runners" ready to prey on immigrant ignorance. Fortunately for the fictional Annie, she has the address of a friend in New York and a wise travelling companion, Mrs. Duffy, who shows her safely to the streetcar which will take her there.

The portrayal may, indeed, be founded on fact but it describes one of the luckier Irish immigrant girls who arrived at Castle Garden. As she leaves the scene of utter confusion, escorted by Mrs. Duffy, Annie notices "a few, lonely, dejected creatures remained behind hoping to find employment through the free labor bureau."

What about those real Irish immigrant girls without Annie's resources? They arrived in America jobless, homeless and friendless. What was done to safeguard their arrival in New York?

One of the most significant efforts to provide for the welfare of the Irish immigrant girl was the inspiration of Charlotte Grace O'Brien (1845–1909), the daughter of the Young Irelander William Smith O'Brien who was transported to Van Diemen's

Land for his part in the 1848 Rebellion. In 1881, she wrote two articles: the first, "Eighty Years," published in *The Nineteenth Century*, described the anguish of emigration; the other, "The Emigration and the Waste-Land Clauses," a criticism of assisted emigration, appeared in *Fortnightly*.

While she spoke out against emigration, Charlotte Grace O'Brien was, nonetheless, a realist. Obviously, she could not stop emigration but she could help protect those leaving Ireland for America. Inspired by J. F. McGuire's *The Irish in America* she visited the ships in Queenstown and was appalled at travel conditions for emigrating Irish. She began to visit the ships daily to campaign for better conditions and opened her own lodging house for 105 travellers.

In 1882, eager to learn what lay in store for the young immigrant girls passing through her lodging house in Queenstown, she decided to investigate conditions in New York. She sailed to New York, lived in a tenement house in Washington Street and became convinced that something had to be done to protect the Irish immigrant girl from the moment she arrived in America. Advised to see the progressive Archbishop John Ireland of St. Paul, Charlotte Grace O'Brien presented her plan to him and won his support. A home for Irish immigrant girls was proposed at the 1883 meeting of the Irish Catholic Colonization Society in Chicago.

Cardinal McCloskey of New York took the initiative. He appointed Father John Riordan chaplain of Castle Garden with particular responsibility for safeguarding the interests of Irish immigrant girls. On October 1, 1883 Father Riordan established the Mission of Our Lady of the

Rosary for the Protection of Irish Immigrant Girls. Its objectives were three: to establish a Catholic information bureau at Castle Garden, to provide a temporary home for Catholic immigrants, and to build a chapel for Catholic immigrants.

The Mission began to function in January, 1884. For a few months, immigrant girls were sent to local respectable boarding houses. In May the Mission opened its own temporary home at 7 Broadway with a Mrs. Boyle, recruited from the Labor Bureau, serving as matron. Father Riordan acquired a permanent home for the Mission in December 1885 when he purchased 7 State Street from Isabella Wallace for $70,000. In its first year, the Mission received 3,341 immigrant girls.

By the end of 1885 the Mission had a parish as well as a home. In September of that year, Cardinal McCloskey had directed that St. Peter's parish be divided and that the 1,500 Catholics living at the tip of Manhattan—the area bounded by Wall Street, Broadway, the Battery, the Hudson River and including the harbor islands—make up the new parish of Our Lady of the Rosary. In addition to parish support, the Mission began an active program to raise money to fund services offered free to immigrant girls.

The Mission relied on an annual subscription every October, the month dedicated to the Rosary, as its chief source of revenue. The *Mission Newsletter* for 1900 described its operation:

> Cards of membership are sent to authorized collectors in every State of the union. The Collector's duty is to secure members for the Society. Membership is 25¢. This entitles the membership to a share in the merit of the good works accomplished by the Mission and to the benefit of masses which are offered at the Home every week during the year for the living and the dead.

Other fund raisers included an annual picnic, an annual ball and the very successful Metropolitan Fair. Opened by Cardinal Gibbons on May 5, 1890 at the Old Armory on Broadway and 35th Street, the Fair ran for three weeks and raised $40,000 for the Mission. It was supported by the clergy, by city parishes who manned the booths, by prominent Irish-Americans and even by a former First Lady. Mrs. Grover Cleveland sold roses for an evening. Before his death in 1895, Father Michael Callaghan, the third rector of the Mission, was able to retire the Mission debt of $70,000.

Responsibility for immigration passed from state to federal control during Father Callaghan's time. As a consequence, the immigrant depot moved from Castle Garden to Ellis Island on January 1, 1892. The first immigrant station on the Island was destroyed by fire in 1897 and with it the records of the Mission's first years. Immigrants returned to temporary quarters at the Barge Office near Castle Garden until the new station, the rather Moorish brick building that still stands, was ready for occupancy on December 17, 1900.

Though federal authorities repeatedly tried to protect immigrants, newcomers were still at the mercy of hustlers and runners once they left Ellis Island and landed at the Battery. For that reason, the Mission and its sister institutions—the German St. Raphael Society's Leo Haus, for one—continued to provide protection to young immigrant girls beyond that which the federal authorities could offer. The Mission maintained a presence on Ellis Island. Their agent Patrick McCool interviewed girls as they arrived, furnished them with advice and accompanied all girls not settled by 4:30 p.m. to the Mission home.

A Mission milestone was its Silver Jubilee celebrated at the Mission Chapel on Rosary Sunday, October 8, 1908 and a month later at a Carnegie Hall concert. Statistics compiled for the jubilee give some sense of the degree to which the Mission had succeeded. Between 1883 and 1908, 307,823 Irish females aged 14–44 arrived at the Port of New York; their average age was 23. During that time the Mission served nearly one-third of those immigrant girls. They found jobs for 12,000. Possibly the best measure of the Mission's success was its support by the young women it served. Writing about the Mission's Silver Jubilee in an article in *The Catholic News*, Father Michael Henry, Mission rector in 1908, wrote:

> The Mission has received no financial aid from city, state or federal sources, no generous bequests from philanthropic millionaires. It has depended entirely for support on voluntary contribution and has been supported almost entirely by the dollar cheerfully given by the Irish working girl whom it was probably the first to befriend on her arrival in this country. She has been the mainstay of the Mission and to her credit must redound much of the great good which the Mission undoubtedly has been instrumental in doing.

The Mission's fortunes followed those of Ellis Island. After the great tide of European immigration between 1901–1914, numbers decreased during World War I. Post-war immigration was curtailed by the quota laws in 1921 and 1924. While Irish emigration was not seriously limited by these laws, there were changes in emigration procedure. Emigrants were examined at American consulates abroad and were able, as a result, to bypass Ellis Island. Still the Mission continued to open its doors to arriving Irish immigrant girls. When Father Patrick Temple arrived at the Mission on October 1, 1930 five ships with several hundred Irish girls aboard landed at the Port of New York; fifty went on to the Mission.

During the Depression, visas were restricted for fear immigrants would become a public charge. Immigration from Ireland to the United States dropped to 801 in 1931 while 3,407 Irish returned home to the Irish Free State in that year. With few immigrant girls arriving at 7 State Street, Father Temple kept up interest in the Mission with a quarterly called *Old Castle Garden* which ran to forty numbers between 1931–1940. Publishing articles on Irish Catholic culture and American history and culture, *Old Castle Garden* reflected the piety and patriotism that characterized Irish-Catholic sensibility of the day.

In addition to the articles documenting the Mission's history and offering sensible advice about education and employment, the quarterly offered the immigrant literature as a way to deal with loss. It published poems which articulated the Irish immigrant experience: Thomas Daly's "At Castle Garden," Patrick MacDonough's "A Hosting at Castle Garden," and James Reidy's "The American Wake."

By World War II, Ellis Island was no longer a reception center for immigrants but a detention and deportation depot, and changes in lower Manhattan reduced the parish population to about fifty families. While the Mission of Our Lady of the Rosary for the Protection of Irish Immigrant Girls never closed, the premises have become the Saint Elizabeth Seton Shrine. Unmarked at State Street, the Mission's monument is the grateful memories of the more than 100,000 Irish immigrants it served.

Maureen Murphy is Historiographer of the Society.

Section 3 — Politics

During the early decades of this century the American Irish Historical Society played a major role in securing United States recognition for an independent Ireland. The Cohalan and Devoy papers in our Archives document the critical contribution made by concerned, persistent and literate Americans in the struggle for Irish freedom.

During the last decade the injustices in Northern Ireland demanded American attention. Our Society once again assumed a leadership role in fashioning a political position based on careful analyses and historical facts.

The Quest for Peace in the North of Ireland

TERENCE CARDINAL COOKE

Recent discussion about the traditional Saint Patrick's Day Parade in New York City has focused public attention again on Ireland — on the division and the political, economic and social unrest existing there, on the injustice and the denial of human rights, the suffering and the violence which affect that land which has contributed so much through its people, its faith and its heritage to the United States and to the nations of the world.

Here in the New York metropolitan area, many of us who are Irish or of Irish descent have strong convictions and deep emotions about the situation in Ireland — specifically about the oppression, the injustice, the denial of human rights and equal opportunity which have existed in that nation for centuries and which tragically still exist in the North of Ireland.

As a son of Irish immigrants, whose parents and ancestors have experienced this suffering and oppression, I would like once again to share my own convictions and call on my fellow American citizens, especially those who are of Irish heritage, to take very definite steps which will help the cause of peace, justice, freedom and the restoration of basic human rights and equal opportunity in that troubled land.

The continuing situation of injustice, suffering and extremist terror in the North of Ireland is the primary issue facing us today, and it must be addressed with urgency.

The late President Eamon de Valera, who was born in New York one hundred years ago, spoke these words about Ireland: ". . . this small nation . . . has stood alone, not for a year or two, but for several hundred years, against aggression . . . has endured spoilations, famines, massacres in endless succession . . . was clubbed many times into insensibility . . . could never be got to accept defeat and had never surrendered her soul."

We are criticized for our long historical memory. "Can you Irish ever forget?" we are sometimes asked. The answer is no. We remember our past. We celebrate our glories. We try to eliminate our sins. We go on attempting to correct injustices, especially those which continue on into the present.

From generation to generation, in Ireland, there has been suffering, religious persecution, usurpation of land and property, lack of equal opportunity, and injustice. This is the tragic reality of the history of the Irish people. At times this has shattered their spirits and scattered their families all over the world. It cannot be denied or forgotten, and really there is no way of understanding the present situation without realizing what has happened over eight centuries. The denial of freedom, of religious, political and economic rights has had drastic effects on the people of Ireland and has caused suffering almost beyond human imagination. Indeed, in the nineteenth century, the economic oppression of the British Government and foreign landlords resulted in the families of agricultural Ireland being dependent on one crop for survival. When that single crop failed, the famine which occurred decimated the population of Ireland, ending the lives of millions of men, women and children in the most extreme, cruel fashion. At the same time, British landlords were forcing the exportation of more than enough crops to save these millions of lives. This monumental tragedy caused a migration which has had lasting effects on America and on this metropolitan area.

In these eight centuries, there have been armed struggles against the occupying and oppressive forces of England. However, what stands out most of all during this time has been the resiliency, the courage, the determination of the Irish to live in peace, in freedom with justice and to maintain their faith, their identity and their independence, — in the words of de Valera ". . . not to surrender their soul. . ." This spirit of the Irish people, not unlike that of their suffering brothers and sisters in other places and countries, has been an inspiration to the members of the human family. In the most trying of circumstances the Irish have been a people of good will who have tried — sometimes fruitlessly — to maintain a calmness of spirit and to seek solutions to the problems that face them.

What are the elements of the situation in the North of Ireland which have led to the continuing violence, death and destruction of the last fourteen years? We have spoken about this before, and they are many and complex. They are rooted in history; yet, they are very much part of the lives of individuals, families and communities in the present moment.

If we as Americans are to help them in finding solutions, we must try to understand some of the elements which constitute the problem.

- First, there is the division of a nation. Although it was perhaps intended as a compromise, this division was an unnatural and gerrymandered one. It did not separate out from Ireland the nine counties of the traditional Province of Ulster, but only six counties, in order to create a permanent political majority favorable to the Crown. This has never been accepted by the people of all of Ireland. As long as it exists, it will unfortunately continue to be a potential cause of conflict.

523

- Second, within the context of a divided Ireland, there is the ongoing tragedy in the North of Ireland of institutionalized injustice and denial of human rights, experienced from generation to generation, by a sizable minority of the population. This has to be seen and experienced to be believed. I have seen and experienced it and assure you it is true. This denial of human and civil rights is evidenced in employment, housing, education, and in the legal system of Northern Ireland.

In Catholic areas, widespread unemployment and underemployment persists at a shamefully high level. It is not unusual for three generations of the same family successively to face life without the prospect of the dignity of gainful work.

Thousands of families are crowded in deteriorating slums, at times built by the Government far removed from any possible places of employment for Catholics. They are idle and discouraged about the future. They live in fear and frustration, hoping against hope for an end to the bloodshed, the bombing and the violent tactics of extremists on both sides.

The failure of the educational system too has been part of the festering problem that touches the lives of hundreds of thousands of people. In some areas of Northern Ireland, where the Catholic minority lives, as many as fifty percent of the graduates of National Schools remain unemployed a year after graduation.

The current legal system in Northern Ireland permits detention without charge and the suspension of trial by jury of one's peers. This amounts to a denial of due process and of the basic civil liberties which we cherish so much and which are enshrined in the Bill of Rights of our country.

- Third, and closely related to the first two factors, are the cultural, social, economic and religious divisions of the people. These are part of the history of this section of Ireland. They do not manifest themselves as blending elements which make up a rich diversity. They are rather sources of tension, repression and conflict. To perceive the problem as being solely or even primarily religious, ignoring the political, cultural, social and economic aspects, is to deny the truth and the realities of the current situation.

- The fourth element in the Northern Ireland problem is the EXTREMIST VIOLENCE which has resulted from the division of the nation, the injustice and denial of human rights, and from the tensions existing among segments of the population.

The violence is seen in the continuing presence of the British Army which, to a sizable part of the population, is regarded as an occupying, foreign force.

The polarized deadly factions in Northern Ireland seize upon the use of any means, including indiscriminate violence and the killing of innocent people, as a way to achieve political and social effects. On one extreme, the violent forces, such as the Ulster Defense Association, the Ulster Volunteer Force and other similar organizations, seek continued identification with the Crown. On the other, the forces of violence, such as the Provisional Irish Republican Army, the Irish National Liberation Army and other similar organizations, claim as their goal the immediate withdrawal of the British presence, the reunification of Ireland and the elimination of injustice.

This indiscriminate violence, no matter what motivates it or to what goal it is directed, is both futile and immoral. It has hindered the cause of peace and the attainment of any kind of political solution. In the gerrymandered

Province of Ulster, with a population of one and a half million, more than two thousand have been killed since 1969. To understand the magnitude of the carnage, if these tragedies occurred here in the United States, the proportionate death toll would approach 300,000; 10,000 in New York City alone. Countless thousands are scarred in body and spirit. There is hardly a family which tragedy has not touched in one way or another.

During a trip to Ireland, I visited a parish in Belfast. While in that one small church, I spoke with a woman whose son had been killed the Monday before. When her husband heard the news, he collapsed and died of a heart attack. One of the curates had been ambushed and shot when he responded, in dead of night, to a spurious sick call. I met a young couple who were about to be married. The priest performing the cermony had lost a brother to death-by-violence a few months earlier. The happy bride of that morning, now the mother of a beautiful child, is also a window, her husband the victim of a senseless killing.

The tragedies of the people I met in that little church in Belfast are typical of so many communities in the North of Ireland. In another era of history, a martyred saint, Oliver Plunkett, who shed his blood for the cause of religious freedom and justice in Ireland, spoke out — over and over again — against the futility of violence.

In our time, another Apostle of Peace, Pope John Paul II, followed in the footsteps of Saint Patrick and went as a Pilgrim to Ireland. He pleaded for true peace, which he said "could not exist as long as injustice exists in any area that touches upon the dignity of the human person, be it in the political, social or economic field."

When he spoke of the violence afflicting Ireland, his words could not have been clearer. At an outdoor Prayer Service, near Drogheda in the Archdiocese of Armagh, overlooking the Valley of the Boyne, he spoke these words:

"Peace cannot be established by violence; peace can never flourish in a climate of terror, intimidation and death."

And in most dramatic words, the Holy Father cried out: "I appeal to you, in language of passionate pleading. On my knees I beg you to turn away from paths of violence and to return to the ways of peace. You may claim to seek justice. I too believe in justice and seek justice. But violence only delays the day of justice. Violence destroys the work of justice. Further violence in Ireland will only drag down to ruin the land you claim to cherish."

What, then, are the elements of the solution of the problem of the North of Ireland? How can peace be restored to that troubled land? Clearly, there has to be a recognition that indiscriminate violence only adds to the devastation and the senseless destruction of human life.

There must be a renewed spirit of hope and a realization that RECONCILIATION is possible among the vast majority of the people of the two communities in the North of Ireland. Ecumenical efforts among Protestants and Catholics, even though at times they are lost sight of because of attention given to terrorism, are making progress. Real fears, which members of the two communities have about each other, are removed when efforts are made for people to know and understand one another and to live together in peace. The people of violence on either extreme are in fact a small minority of the total population who must not be allowed to perpetuate their terror.

The absence of violence, though, and the presence of wholehearted efforts at reconciliation will not in themselves bring freedom and justice and unity to the people of Ireland. They will only be conditions for positive steps to be taken towards a solution of the complex and multi-faceted problem. There must be many elements to this solution.

- The injustice and continuing denial of basic human rights must be ended.

- New sustained initiatives for political, social and economic equity for all in the North of Ireland must be pursued with consistency and deliberate speed.

- The right to equal opportunity in housing and employment must be guaranteed and enforced.

- The right to peaceful and quiet enjoyment of homes and businesses must be a fact and not a dream.

- A political, constitutional process must be sought that will lead to a permanent solution and not to temporary compromises which can only postpone violence, or bring about an upsurge of violence.

- In this process, it will be necessary for the governments of Great Britain, the Republic of Ireland, the United States of America, the Common Market countries and the international community, to take an active role and to change intransigent positions that have resulted in a status-quo of persistent tension and conflict.

The crisis in the North of Ireland is not a hopeless situation. With the help of Almighty God, the God of Peace and Reconciliation, a troubled, divided nation can be whole again, and freedom, justice and equity can reign there.

We Americans can help the situation in many ways:

— through our prayers for peace;

— through assistance to families in need;

— through investment by our economic and industrial leaders in areas of vast Catholic unemployment and by substantial assistance to distressed areas;

— and through a positive involvement of our government and public officials in insisting that Great Britain move toward a permanent, peaceful solution, even with the thought of examining future relationships because of failure to act.

The one course of action which we cannot follow is to support — in any way, even by signs and symbols — the continuation of senseless, indiscriminate violence as a means to achieve political effects. This will only delay and perhaps destroy any chance for what is so close to the hearts of so many of us — peace and freedom, justice and unity in all of Ireland.

Healing Hands

KEVIN M. CAHILL, M.D.

For the past several years we have reprinted in the Recorder *articles which have had a significant impact on American-Irish affairs. The following article appeared in the Carnegie Foundation's publication,* Foreign Policy. *It offers positive proposals for a creative American-Irish endeavor.*

Ireland has always been a country of extremes. Religious wars, cultural antipathies, rural disorders, revolution, and famine have darkened its history, and their shadowy images still flash across the television screens; soldiers ambushed, royalty assassinated, stone-throwing youths in ancient streets. Today Northern Ireland remains a battleground. But it is not just a throwback to the emotions and divisions of the sixteenth century. The current tensions have more recent origins, for the six counties of Northern Ireland were ruled until the 1970's by a Protestant monopoly of economic and political power, compounding an inherited legacy of prejudice and bitterness. Now there is not even the pretense of democracy.

The government created in Ulster in 1920 has ceased to exist. Direct rule by Britain, symbolized by 35,000 policemen, deputies, and soldiers, keeps the geographic entity of the North alive, but the body politic is moribund. Britain and Ireland must begin to plan for some new political arrangement that recognizes that reality. Their role will, of course, be paramount, but the United States can also help to bring peace and reconciliation to Northern Ireland. Indeed, a new departure in official and private U.S. policy toward Northern Ireland is urgently needed.

It is unlikely that Americans will accept the fatalistic portents of those who regale innocent readers with the thesis that the "deep historic and cultural differences in Northern Ireland" make a solution to the strife impossible. They warn Americans away, stating that even their condemnations of violence will be "decoded" by terrorists as encouragement. These views are historically inaccurate and morally untenable, for on the contrary there are specific political, economic, and cultural steps America can take that would significantly contribute to peace in Northern Ireland.

American interest in Irish affairs dates back to the earliest days of the nation, and the flow of support has gone both ways across the Atlantic. America received the hungry, bruised bodies and the scarred, often hostile minds of Irish immigrants. James Joyce called the Atlantic "a bitter bowl of tears," and so it was to those who crossed it, mourning the loss of family and home, surviving the journey in steerage to the next parish to Ireland—America.

The concern of the new Catholic immigrants for the political destiny of their native land was strong. Since the great Diaspora of the 1840's, Irish history has been linked to the actions of the Irish in America. At first, the immigrants were a disorganized, disoriented mass of impoverished peasants who faced an uphill struggle against nativist resentment and economic and social dis-

531

crimination. Those experiences linked the new land with Mother Ireland. The self-image of the immigrants, their struggle in an Anglo-Protestant majority culture, moved them to consider Ireland's political humiliation a factor in their own fight for survival in America and their commitment to Irish self-government was a part of their American journey.

The abortive uprising in 1867 by the Fenians—a secret revolutionary organization founded almost simultaneously in Ireland and America—was a deceptively feeble demonstration of their support, and of their potential for making trouble. If nothing else, they succeeded in converting British Prime Minister William Gladstone to the idea that the Irish question now had an "American dimension" and that constructive measures must be taken to settle Irish grievances. And they made it clear that Irish-American money and support had become a powerful ally for Irish separatism. At the height of the home-rule agitation of the 1880's, Home Secretary Sir William Harcourt wrote:

> In former Irish rebellions the Irish were in Ireland. We could reach their forces, cut off their resources in men and money, and then to subjugate them was comparatively easy. Now there is an Irish nation in the United States, equally hostile, with plenty of money, absolutely beyond our reach.

Irish-American support was a critical component of Charles Steward Parnell's rise to the position of uncrowned king of Ireland in the late nineteenth century. In the summer of 1878, John Devoy, a Fenian convict and exile working as head of the foreign desk of the *New York Herald,* met with Michael Davitt, another Fenian exile, in New York City. There was born the "New Departure" in Irish politics, a movement that brought together revolutionary separatists, land reformers, and home rulers behind Parnell's leadership.

By 1910, the Clan-na-Gael, an American organization committed to Irish freedom, and the Irish Revolutionary Brotherhood were both approaching armed conflict with England in a movement that was largely funded and spiritually sustained by a passionate cadre of Irish-Americans. The struggle culminated in the Easter Rebellion of 1916, and that uprising and the subsequent executions of its leaders by the British began a new, intense wave of Irish-American interest and involvement.

The Irish-Americans were recognized as such an essential factor in the struggle for independence that Ireland's new national anthem paid tribute to those who helped "from the land across the sea." They fought fiercely to have Ireland's claim to self-determination accepted by the infant League of Nations. Woodrow Wilson's failure to appreciate the extent of the Irish-American commitment to recognition was a significant factor in the eventual rejection of the League in the United States.

The civil war in Ireland in the 1920's, the Great Depression of the 1930's, and Irish neutrality in World War II all contributed to a diminished identity between the next generation of Irish-Americans and their ancestral land. But an emotional resurgence followed the election of John F. Kennedy to the presidency, and then a new generation of American-Irish, secure in society but still aware of their origins, became intent on re-establishing ties with the land of their forebears. Tourism increased, and business links developed. Cultural programs flourished, and there was a new awakening to the wrongs that still existed in Northern Ireland.

But the recent concern for the problems of Northern Ireland is more than just a recrudescence of Fenianism. Irish-American pride or esteem is no longer at stake, and present attitudes arise from causes other than the memory of famines or exile. The experience in America of religious pluralism and of the Black civil rights movement has more to do with a commitment to seek peace and justice in the North of Ireland today than do dimly remembered legends. To dismiss the present American-Irish involvement as merely an atavistic attachment to a distant homeland is a mistake that is all too common in Britain. Instead of utilizing American-Irish interest and concern as a tool for peace, successive British governments still appear to view the American-Irish according to the nineteenth-century stereotype and still react to any suggestions from this side of the Atlantic as the utterances of an ill-informed, hostile monolith that should be silenced.

In 1975 four leading American-Irish politicians—Governor Hugh Carey and Senator Daniel Patrick Moynihan of New York, and Senator Edward Kennedy and House Speaker Thomas P. O'Neill of Massachusetts—issued a joint St. Patrick's Day statement, a thoughtful, cautious call for Americans to beware of contributing to the tragedy that was growing in Northern Ireland. It condemned the contributions of Americans who were supporting the Irish Republican Army

(IRA) and any forms of violence. This was no message of blarney and easy slogans, but a clear warning that Americans were playing a dangerous role in Northern Ireland.

These four leaders are not naive Americans willing to rush in where angels fear to tread. They have no desire to run the affairs of Westminster or Dublin or Belfast, but only a willingness to use their influence to put American moral prestige and resources behind any viable plan to make the past decade in Northern Ireland the last act in a tragedy that has been played out over 400 years.

In response to initiatives such as this, President Carter issued a statement on Northern Ireland in 1977, a call for peace, an end to violence, with an imprecise promise of American investment after the fighting was over. Inadequate though this statement appeared to some, it did represent the first acknowledgement by an American president that the tragedy of Northern Ireland was a legitimate concern of the U.S. government.

After Carter's statement, the then Irish Prime Minister, Jack Lynch, told an audience in New York that "the prospect of practical assistance of this kind is what is necessary and what will tell in the end." Yet Humphrey Atkins, Margaret Thatcher's Secretary of State for Northern Ireland, recently wrote in response to a proposed initiative by Carey that the problem of Northern Ireland was "a matter for negotiation between Her Majesty's Government, the Parliament at Westminster and the people of the Province." With one stroke, he dismissed not only the "American dimension" but, more importantly, the dimension of the Irish Republic.

During the first half of the 1970's, the economy

of the Republic boomed. Ireland's entry into the European Economic Community (EEC) opened new markets for its agricultural produce and eased its traditional dependence on England. An aggressive international campaign for external investment provided a new industrial base. The hemorrhage of emigration stopped. Ireland's gross national product and annual income skyrocketed; in fact, it enjoyed the fastest growing economy in Europe.

Simultaneously, the industrial base of the North—based largely on shipbuilding and textiles—collapsed; Ulster's economy could be sustained only by a massive infusion of British currency. The British subsidy in Ulster for 1978 was almost two billion dollars. Unemployment, almost a way of life for generations of Belfast and Derry families, increased.

Fortunately, during the past few years, rational men on both sides of the border have begun careful planning for cooperation and reconciliation as prerequisites for national unity. Under the leadership of the then Prime Minister Lynch the majority party began a series of studies on North-South joint projects, while Garret FitzGerald, leader of the opposition, issued a thoughtful white paper detailing the opportunities for common efforts in business, utilities, transportation, and social and cultural spheres. Both political leaders have been eloquent in their statements that national unity cannot be imposed but will succeed only with the consent of Northern Ireland's Protestant majority. Both have recognized that peace must accommodate the full richness and diversity of both traditions, the Republic's and Ulster's. Both have, however, been equally forceful in demanding that there be no return to the winner-take-all, majority-rule political system that for decades maintained the Protestants in total control of the North.

The emphasis of all three major parties of the Republic—Fianna Fail, Fine Gael, and the Labour party—and of the overwhelming proportion of the Irish people whom they represent is to persuade, not to coerce, the Protestant Northern majority to recognize that their interests coincide more frequently with those of the Republic of Ireland than with those of Britain, and that cultivation of these common Irish interests can make some form of national unity desirable. Whatever solution is ultimately reached in Northern Ireland must be based on a negotiated settlement by all the people of Ulster under agreements reached between the governments of Ireland and England. Whether that solution should be embodied in a strong federal government like that of the United States or in a looser confederation is almost irrelevant. What is important is that the killing stop now and that steps be taken toward economic and political justice for everyone.

Only then, it is conceded by all, will the paranoia of an embattled Protestant community in Ulster slowly lift in response to crossborder joint projects and programs. The Irish throughout the entire island recognize the overwhelming economic logic of regional ventures in agriculture and industry and are painfully aware of the escalating tax burden of maintaining the present state of near war within their land. In the Republic of Ireland the cost of border security alone is forty dollars a year for every man, woman, and child, higher even than the per capita contribution by the British for security on their side of the partition line.

Since Britain's imposition of a six-county Ulster enclave within the island of Ireland as the price for establishing the Free State in the remaining 26 counties in 1922, the policy of the Republic has been consistent. Its primary goal is—and always has been—to develop a nation where all Irish people could live in unity and peace. The 1937 constitution of Eire did not even recognize the partition and addressed itself to the entire Irish people; successive governments have sought a modus vivendi that would tend to unify the nation without causing civil war or precipitously forcing huge financial obligations on the relatively weak Irish economy. Yet, while Irish policy condemned violence, it did not offer a viable alternative. Demagogues—and terrorists—filled the vacuum, and Irish-American energies and money too often went to organizations that promised to win freedom by indulging in further conflict.

True leaders of the American-Irish community condemned violence as a solution and urged Americans not to contribute to further bloodshed. Carey, in a memorable Dublin speech in 1977, spoke of the futility of "the politics of death." But although forthright statements by the four leading American-Irish political figures succeeded in slowing the flow of money to the IRA, they failed to satisfy an aroused ethnic community that desired to contribute in some manner.

Recently, a series of articles in the *New York Daily News* proposed specific moves that the United States could make to foster peace. One of these articles was translated—virtually verbatim—into a unanimous resolution by the AFL-CIO

538

Labor Movement calling for American action to help secure peace and justice in Northern Ireland. Another article noted the broadening base of American concern for Northern Ireland among Jewish groups who can readily identify with a Catholic minority suffering religious discrimination and among Black civil rights veterans who share a knowledge of harsh police tactics and repeated violations of human rights.

A new departure is made possible today by international concern for protecting human rights and by international vehicles for conveying assistance to communities exposed to the ravages of discrimination. It would obviously require the personal involvement of President Carter, whose commitment would be the sine qua non of significant U.S. government participation. Since human rights is the self-imposed standard of the Carter foreign policy, it should not be difficult for the President to add his voice to those of Amnesty International and the European Court in calling for an end to the British military presence and for a prompt reestablishment—this time with effective guarantees of minority rights—of political institutions for self-rule. The president has used his position in the interest of peace in the Middle East. Now, he should heed the call of Ireland for help. Unfortunately, the 1977 presidential message has been followed by more than two years of silence and inaction.

There must be substance behind America's effort to restore peace in Northern Ireland. Calls for reconciliation are noble, but they do not produce jobs, and without jobs there can be no dignity and there will be no peace. Meanwhile, the likelihood that England will share in a new search for peace seems to be increasing. Recent British governments have depended on the ten swing votes of the Ulster Unionists to maintain a slim mandate. But Thatcher enjoys a forty-three member majority. And she has given evidence, in Rhodesia, of her ability to make bold moves to break an impasse.

Yet outsiders—friends of both Ireland and England—must keep the pressure on. Northern Ireland's Catholic minority remembers that in 1973–1974 another British government lacked the moral courage to stand up to militant Protestants who sabotaged agreements that their more moderate leaders had reached for sharing power between the two religious communities. Fearful of the link with the Republic that a proposed Council of Ireland would have established, Northern Protestants launched a general strike. Lasting a fortnight, the strike precipitated the collapse of the Northern Ireland executive government and the assumption of direct rule by London. Catholic leaders now insist that British rhetoric be backed by concrete actions that can persuade a suspicious people to believe and follow. Only then will the strident voices of violence finally yield to rational calls for reconciliation and will those who seek a solution with guns feel truly unwelcome in the mean back streets of Belfast and Derry.

In this effort, as in Rhodesia, Britain's will can be strengthened by American political pressure and by the promise of American financial aid. The EEC's special fund for depressed areas offers a fortuitous international mechanism through which American help can be channeled. Its use would avoid the politically difficult task of seeking direct congressional appropriations for either

England or Ireland. There is ample precedent for America's participation in a consortium with organizations such as the EEC. Similar programs through the World Bank or the United Nations Development Program have often been preferred American methods for involvement in overseas projects.

Dollar diplomacy cannot be a substitute for thoughtful action. No specific assistance program will be as important as an effort led by major political figures to arouse sensitivity to the situation in Northern Ireland so that it remains an issue that Americans cannot ignore. For the United States will respond in substance only when it appreciates the dangers Northern Ireland poses for Western society—the threat of unchecked terrorism, with the contending groups increasingly linked to other international anarchists such as the Palestine Liberation Organization (PLO) or the Italian Red Brigades; the pressure of prolonged political instability on the development of a strong European community; the moral wrong of flagrant discrimination accompanied by repeated violations of human rights. Promoting full political discussion of Northern Ireland in the United States is the only way to avoid the current extremes of either uninformed support for those who seek a simple solution through further terrorism and retribution, or empty hopelessness in the face of the problem's complexity.

Specific U.S. government programs should be coupled with the political response to assist in reconstructing an area that has suffered a decade of near civil war and a half century of neglect.

The United States should establish a matching fund with the EEC to develop cross-border projects. Such a multi-level approach has already been used to assist Turkey, through a consortium of nations under the Organization for Economic Co-operation and Development, and to aid Portugal jointly with thirteen other nations. (The American contribution to these ventures has been $248 million and $300 million, respectively.)

The U.S. should assist in the reconstruction of Northern Ireland communities that have been destroyed by civil war. Rebuilding the lives of those who have survived the devastation of Derry or central Belfast and securing political stability in Northern Ireland are surely as critical to American security as well as traditions, as is resettling the homeless of Cyprus, for whom the United States has provided over $100 million.

A major cultural exchange program should be established by the U.S. to help reduce the sense of isolation that feeds the paranoia of both communities in Northern Ireland. Funds need not be used merely to transfer American orchestras or art shows around the world but could also be applied to student exchange programs and travel grants for those in the labor movement, the churches, and academe so that these critical figures in Northern Ireland's life might be exposed to broader views in America or in international meetings. The success of cultural exchange programs in revitalizing—as well as reorienting— post World War II Italy, Germany, and Japan is a solid precedent.

The United States should allocate technical assistance funds through the Department of Housing and Urban Development to assist in the reconstruction of the working-class ghettos of Belfast and Derry. Decent housing will have to be relocated near factories if the industrial base of Northern Ireland is to be rebuilt. A major urban redevelopment program will be needed, along the lines of the Brazilian project in which the United States has recently participated, to break the cycle of poverty and ignorance that fuels the hatreds of its people.

The U.S. should also allocate technical assistance funds for mass transportation. A large-scale transportation program for Cairo has recently been part of America's contribution to the semi-settlement of a struggle almost as ancient as that of Northern Ireland—the Arab-Israeli conflict. This kind of project is central to the effort to end discrimination; today, public transportation in Northern Ireland is inadequate to permit minority workers to reach existing work sites.

Direct and prompt U.S. subsidies should be provided through the flexible Security Support Assistance programs. These funds have been effectively used in recent years in countries as diverse as Jordan and Israel, and federal financial support for the overwhelming burden of border security and law enforcement is desperately required both in the North and in the Republic of Ireland.

Finally, as part of the official government effort, Export-Import Bank credits should be established to promote American investment in and trade from Northern Ireland. This could be critical to the economic development of this depressed area. To facilitate rapid industrial growth in another isolated area, the administration has recently proposed a major new program of bank credits for development in the People's Republic of China. American investment in Northern Ireland should be encouraged along the same lines. It would be desirable, moreover, if British and Irish tax abatement inducements could be better correlated in order that new private-sector jobs be directed to the areas most in need.

In the private sector America can also make a major contribution towards peace. American private enterprise already plays a major role in Northern Ireland. Over twelve per cent of the industrial jobs in the province are in American-owned companies. British subsidies and tax abatement programs have recently attracted several large, American-directed firms to locate in Northern Ireland. If these ventures do not offer jobs in the minority community where the unemployment rate is often four to five times that in the Protestant areas, then America, through its firms, will be perpetuating the pattern of discrimination that lies at the heart of Northern Ireland's conflict. Decent housing, adequate transportation, and quality education are desirable goals, but breaking the cycle of unemployment is essential. American corporate leaders must be as aware of that responsibility as they are mindful of the need for profits.

The American labor movement has, as already noted, placed its power behind a resolution calling for presidential attention to Northern Ireland. The AFL-CIO has also authorized the longshoremen's union to refuse to handle cargo from England if there is no progress toward peace in Northern Ireland. Rather than employ this negative tactic, the American labor movement should supplement its political activity by contributing funds and talent to personnel retraining programs for the vast number of unemployed Ulster workers whose skills were honed for industries that no longer exist.

There has been only minimal involvement by American academic and voluntary organizations in the problems of Northern Ireland. No foundation has provided any substantial aid for projects in the North. The critical seed money necessary to initiate studies of the many unique sociological aspects of the present disaster in Ulster is missing. The opportunity to learn from the tragedy of the last decade and thereby to plan for the future is being lost. The children of Northern Ireland, the innocent victims of fear and hatred, are being fashioned into the terrorists of tomorrow by circumstances beyond their control. Neglect should not contribute to this process.

It seems appropriate to ask American Catholic and Protestant groups and their foundations to join in mutual human service projects, particularly in those geared to the needs of the young. What the American Jewish community does for Israel through its charitable organizations, the Christian descendants of Irish immigrants who flourished in America should do for Ireland.

The bitter legacy of history will not suddenly disappear from Northern Ireland. Ancient differences will not die, and old hatreds take a long time to fade. But tolerance, and the community of shared interests on which it is built, have been achieved in even more difficult situations.

We already know the harm done by inaction and neglect in Northern Ireland. The present policy of permitting a glacial resolution to its problems is merely a sentence of violent death for future generations of Irish children. It displays a fatalistic despair that Britain and America have rejected in every other domestic and international problem they have faced. There are historic reasons why a continued American dimension in Northern Ireland is inevitable, and for strong moral and pragmatic reasons that dimension is fully consistent with current U.S. foreign policy. There are ample precedents to justify—and indeed encourage—a strong American political and economic contribution to this struggle for peace and justice.

Dr. Cahill is President-General of the Society.

The Politics of Death

HUGH L. CAREY

This was a solemn day for Ireland, the day your Primate, Cardinal Conway, was buried. While I walked the strand at Portmarnock this morning, gale winds blew as if nature were speeding a soul to heaven. The gusts blew the mists away and Ireland's Eye was before me, guarding the entrance to Dublin, symbolizing the strength of this land in the face of adversity.

I am proud and grateful to have been invited to the Royal College of Surgeons in Ireland to deliver the Harry O'Flanagan Lecture. Proud because I am a citizen of the United States, and the first to be so honored. Grateful, because I love this College, the city in which it sits, and the Country of which Dublin is the heart.

The Royal College is a personal place to me.

The rooms and the corridors, this building's magnificent and pitted facade and the green place across the street—all bring back the pieces of conversation, the smiles and concerns of the last joyous visit I made here with my wife, Helen, before her young death.

And this is the place in Ireland where my children and I have chosen to memorialize her, for she loved it so, the people in it and their work.

So I am no stranger in the spirit to the Royal College—I am as comfortable in this building and in your presence as I am in the great halls of my own State Capitol across the sea.

I am grateful to you all for that, and I shall attempt in the thoughts I express today to be guided and inspired

547

by my deep personal affiliation with this institution.

We have other bonds as well, less distinct but no less strong; that bond of belief that in the healing process lies the greatest potential to show human love, and by so doing confound the voices of hate throughout the world.

As a young man, in the Congress of the United States, my closest friend and mentor was John Fogarty of Rhode Island—a man who created health systems and institutions through his use of the law-making process, a man who was blessed with the ability to bring dreams of adequate health care for all into being through sheer determination and the proper use of political powers. Throughout his active life, John and I worked together, and the product of our efforts can be seen in our Government's medical research institutes as well as in neighborhood health centers delivering care to the needy.

Disease knows no national boundaries, and the healing arts may well provide the mortar that will eventually bind the wounds of a troubled world. Prior to becoming Governor, I wrote and lectured on—and sponsored legislation—in my country that recognized the unique role of health as a vehicle for international peace. We sought to have America unequivocally identify our global goals with the well-being—rather than any particular political orientation—of people in developing lands. It is no accident that I have cited health as the top priority of my administration for I have known the impact of illness as well as the marvels of modern medicine. No field offers a greater challenge to the political leader seeking to have government truly serve the people.

Over 130 years ago, the first academic post in public health in the English speaking world was created at this very College. The title given the post was "Professorship in Political Medicine", and while I did not have the opportunity to take the course, I can only hope that by my life's work to date, I can be counted as a student in the field—thus furthering the ties I feel to the College of Surgeons.

To return to Ireland is always an experience that is uniquely moving to me—as it is to most of my countrymen of Irish descent. Those of you who have lived your lives here must understand and be patient with some of us—for we come back with our heads full of stories and myths acquired at the kitchen tables of our youth. We know the counties and the legends, the ballads and the poems. We know the tales of sacrifice and valor by heart. Those of us who are Roman Catholic were taught by the priests and nuns whom you sent. And we have family and civic traditions that reinforce all of these things—no matter how distorted by time, no matter how far from reality.

For we live in a country that is young, transient and too often impersonal—little wonder that we hope to find an Ireland that conforms to our view of what is stable and traditional in life.

But, there is no such Ireland of story and song. The Ireland I see and know is a mature and growing nation. A land no different from other Western countries struggling with the burdens of its past, straining to emerge into its promising future, and questioning the rules established by still cherished institutions. And I find an Ireland as vibrant in her new development as I did in the tales of her past.

Even one, however, who understands the difference between fable and fact is moved upon return to this country—for no matter how far removed by distance in space or time, the bond remains. When Ireland progresses, we share in her joy, when Ireland is suffering we suffer, and as a people there is the tie of common traits and quite similar emotional responses to the problems of life. When thinking of my own grandparents, I often

549

reflect that I do not owe them so much that they came to America, but that they were born in this place—allowing me to be a part of that segment of the human family called Irish.

Yet, on my trip here for this occasion, I know I owe them more—whatever courage they displayed in uprooting their lives and moving to an often hostile country, calls upon me to speak with candor, not only here, but in my own beloved City and State, on the questions that currently surround Ireland.

For me, a government leader, to be worthy of them and of you, I must follow my conscience. Therefore, I cannot stand here today and utter polite, meaningless words while children die in violence on this very soil.

I am here to fulfill my moral responsibility, my genetic commitment to the country to which I owe my tongue and my laugh and my tears, the country which I love very much.

I am not here as an outsider to interfere. I am here as the Governor of a state of the United States, a state of 18 million people, with a city of eight million people, a place containing more Irish than there are in all of Ireland. And it is a state, New York, which always embraced the great Irish leaders when they came to us for strength and refuge and support.

Wolfe Tone came to our City as did O'Donovan Rossa and Davis and Devoy and Parnell. And James Connolly and Pearse and DeValera and Patrick McCarten, a graduate of this College, who combined the worlds of medicine and politics at a critical juncture in your history.

They came to America, to the city that is the womb of my country, my city of New York. When they returned to Ireland they were no longer alone.

As Americans, we were proud to have participated in their struggles, and we shall not shrink from involvement now. The Iroquois Indians in New York State speaking of our Hudson River—which is to us what the Liffey is to you, the river of our Capital—called it "the stream that flows both ways." So it is in human affairs, and I come before you tonight confident in the tradition of mutual support that has sustained our people through so many centuries of travail.

I stand here as a political leader in the United States well aware of the torment in the North, well aware of the fact that children—both Catholic and Protestant—are called upon to die in Northern Ireland by those who debate and actively deal in the politics of death.

To be in a school of medicine and to speak of death as a political instrument may seem incongruous. To ask those who have contracted for a lifetime of work for life to listen to a man speak out against death seems a very proper request. Those fascinated by death as a political weapon are surely as sick as people can be, and I have a history of looking to people of medicine for their abilities to be employed far beyond their chosen careers. The fact that this College holds the distinction of being the most international medical school in the Western world, with students from over 35 newly independent and developing countries, bears out the point that in medicine and its development lies so much of our hope for future peace in the world. So I will speak to death—and its brother, violence—only to condemn it in my own land and yours.

One cannot have been in American political life since 1960 and not be a student of this subject. For myself, I was drawn to public life by the candidacy of John F. Kennedy. I worked long and hard for his success in achieving office. What sickness killed him, but the disease of another man's mind. His brother, Robert, was my political leader, friend, and indeed my neighbor. What disease did he die of but that contracted by a man who thought he had a cause—a holy cause stretching back to

551

the religious differences of the Middle East? I knew Martin Luther King and was inspired by his total commitment to non-violence and love among people who seek change through the political process. He died from fear and hate, from those who see no future if the past must submit to change. To men of medicine, I submit these are diseases and no less cancerous than those described in your texts.

And, during the sixties my nation went to war. We attempted, and we succeeded, at killing people who would not respond to our vision of an orderly and balanced world. It was a national disease spread by jingoism, a disease not treated because of apathy or the fear of speaking out. My children were raised in the presence of nightly news broadcasts that always began with the day's body-count in Southeast Asia. And in this setting, all protest tended to violence, for whatever the cause; all protest became more righteous than man could bear—and campuses closed, and some of our cities were put on fire, and people died.

To what end? To what end did all the violence and all of the deaths bring us? At the violent death of our President, commentators said that perhaps some good would flow for America—not so, we went on to war. When Martin Luther King died, it was hoped that the cause of civil rights would advance—not so, we still await the day for true equality for all races in America. When my friend Robert Kennedy died, we were told that American Presidential politics would forever be different—not so, for in his absence we had a Watergate and the first Presidential resignation in our history. And in the wake of Vietnam, that war filled with political but devoid of moral purpose, we have only a populace more distrustful of governmental acts abroad regardless of merit.

To what end then do the apostles of death and violence lead us? To no end, I say, worthy of human consideration. Is the assassin the best hope for positive political change? Is the bomber to be trusted to end economic or religious persecution? Is it human rights that flows from the barrel of a gun? Just what is this mad fascination with killing and maiming and burning?

This activity is, I would suggest, the politics of death.

The politics of death that allows gains to be made in the short run by those who call for it, who revel in it, who can easily judge others by their adherence to its use. It is my belief that whatever gains there are for those so stricken with this disease, it is only because our own fear or apathy allows them their moment, their moment, not in the sun, but in the mania of a fearful night. The criminal who kills for lust or money is frightening enough, but the political acts of indiscriminate killing are reflections of the deepest and darkest tendencies in mankind. Too often it is merely the wanton slaughter of the innocent, and no one can defend that. And the slightest indication that it is condoned by any member of any society is the encouragement upon which that tendency feeds. No matter how strong the argument to differentiate the cause, no matter what the history of the dispute, no matter how deep the frustrations that give rise to the act, the political killer is to be condemned! For literally thousands of years the best in mankind have sought to repress this darkest side of human behavior to little avail, and this rough beast, this politics of death, each time feeling "its hour come round at last, slouches toward Bethlehem to be born."

Is this to say that on no occasion may men of good will arm themselves, defend themselves and resort to force? Of course it is not, and to answer otherwise is to deny our own sophistication to detect a true peril to human life from one concocted in the sick and selfish interests of a few. I have no desire now to enter into a discourse on the "just war" or the ability of people to defend their lives and loved ones. I have been involved in war, I have been decorated in war, I have buried my friends in war—including my brothers from Britain, Ireland and Canada. I believe I know war and when its horror can be justified in a man's heart. Suffice it to say, therefore, that I believe most conflicts that arise in the human experience lend themselves to the politics of accommodation, compromise and ultimate peaceful settlement. Those that do not are readily apparent to the vast majority of informed opinion and call for different acts. But all of this is different from those who play at death and who seek to enhance themselves by these means in a society that has otherwise denied them respect and status. How easy it is to cry in terms of outrage and make violence seem righteous when you are far away. They, to me, are the leaders in the politics of death. They, to me, are the most reprehensible,—and they must be stopped.

I dwell upon my experiences from the United States because I am somewhat reluctant to speak as an expert on the difficulties in the North of Ireland. I have studied the problem, I know of the history, I have been to Belfast, and I have friends with strong opinions. Yet none of this makes me expert in the affairs of Ireland, except on the broadest philosophic level. I would appreciate the moment, however, to express some views that are strongly held.

On March 17th of this year, I signed a public statement along with Thomas P. O'Neill, Speaker of the House of Representatives, Senator Edward M. Kennedy of Massachusetts and Senator Daniel Patrick Moynihan of New York. This is the first time in my memory of the United States that four elected officials at the State and Federal level joined in a call for peace and reconciliation in Northern Ireland. The response to that statement was favorable among Americans of Irish descent. From all across the country, from every walk of life, I heard not only sentiments of concurrence, but received statements of active support for the stand that we took. Naturally, there were some letters of rebuke, threats of reprisals, and even the interruption of a public meeting that I was conducting. I have not responded to those communications, for I have determined that those who approve of violence and death will never, God willing, approve of me.

I recount this only to make the point that I am convinced that in the United States there is an overwhelming sentiment among Irish citizens that the havoc wreaked by the violence on both sides of the North must cease. There is a recognition that to whatever extent violations of human rights continue to exist, to whatever extent class economic discrimination prevails, to whatever extent denial of political involvement is prevalent, no further death will right the wrongs. There are no bombs nor guns available to mankind that will cause the creation of the new political institutions that are needed for a peace and future in the North. There has been enough bleeding by far, and too many children's lives destroyed or warped to be eager for any more.

Those, in the United States, who really love Ireland, love all of it, all of the people who live there, and only hope for its well being and the well being of its future generations. The people of the North—both Protestant and Catholic—should know that the vast majority of the Irish American community have no desire to intrude upon any future form of government democratically arrived at. We have full faith in the people of goodwill on both sides to create their own institutions and laws in the making of an equitable society. And the people of the North should know, as all people in Ireland should know, that we are sickened by the violence, the waste and the wrecking of human lives in a land that we all hold dear in our hearts.

We have no simple solutions to offer. We Americans now know the danger of that. We have hopes, however, that I must express as a friend who is mindful that he is a guest in your land.

Our hope for the North is not based on the quick or easy answer that lends itself to the slogan. We know that the repetition and replication of wrongs have built a dogma of distrust that has tragically become tradition. We know that many minds are frozen shut to the ordinary acts of compromise by which brothers usually settle their political differences. Our hope is that among the leaders of the Protestant community and among the Catholic leaders there will arise—in the best Irish tradition—those with the moral courage to make the first moves to end death and start a new political life. And we hope such people will be actively encouraged by the rest of Ireland and the leading voices of Church and State. In this hope I pledge that those men and women of both traditions who seek to find the way, who seek to create the new political institutions that will guide and govern the North of the future, will receive whatever assistance they should ask from the American Irish community.

If our goodwill and voice of support is enough—those with the courage to compromise have it now. If support is needed in organized world forums, those committed to the end of death in the North need only ask—and they will have it. If any peaceful material resource would be of assistance, or any direct moral or political suasion would assist—we pledge ourselves to it.

Are these the hollow words of an easy assurance? No! I know that jobs and the dignity of human labor are essential for any lasting peace, I have seen the despair that flows from economic discrimination and unemployment. And violence has too often been relied upon when there seems to be no hope. I know, too, that the inbred

556

evils of ignorance and bigotry flourish in the pockets of poverty that shame our lands.

So I speak of jobs and I speak of knowledge. Do you think that my great people will not respond to legitimate requests? I have seen what teaching and training can do for unskilled hands. Person-to-person, and job by job we can defeat despair and create a new day of decency and dignity for children.

Why? Because if we do not do so those very children will only live and learn to kill and die. And I will not let this happen—that is my pledge against the politics of death.

It is my personal pledge—that I will bend every effort in dealing with other leaders in American life to see that any request of assistance from men of peace and justice in the North shall never go unheeded. It is our view that the day is gone when those on either side who call for "ourselves alone" will be listened to—for now we in America hear the new voices, we are taken with the men of new courage—men of worth who say "without brotherhood we will have only soil. Without brotherhood, that Irish soil will form only our common Irish grave."

And for all of the people of this land we have our hopes. We hope for an Ireland that successfully seeks her economic future in the European community, an Ireland of growth and prosperity that finds her rightful industrial and technological place in the Western world of the future. Not simply the Ireland of the past that gave to the world by sending her sons and daughters to teach, heal and labor—but an Ireland that now receives, keeping her gifted children at home and welcoming those who wish to come to her and participate in the new day.

Finally, in keeping with this future, we hope for an Ireland that is sensitive to the demands of the new age.

The moderation of tradition is hard and we all seek change that does the least harm to long held values of the past. Too slow has been the emergence of women in America as equal partners in all social economic activities, but great and inspiring have been the results.

But ultimately, in my own land we have discovered that all human hope is in the mind of the child. While a painful process in the United States, we have fought to see the races educated in unison; we have fought against chaining the child to the wall of our own prejudices, be they religious, racial or regional. We believe our future demands no less and we are committed to it. We hope for the same here.

And so it is that while the Ireland of yore is in my heart, the Ireland of today and tomorrow is on my mind and lips. Between the past and this future, however, there is the dark creature of unreasoned hate and violence, of misguided righteousness and fear—that plague, that from time to time affects all mankind but in the modern Western world is peculiar and particular to the land of my family.

I pray for its removal, I speak to men of medicine to help seek its cure, I shall work and dedicate myself to those who pledge to speak against it. As a politician, I shall fight against the politics of death so that the people I love will live, finally freed of the curse of past religious differences that the true Christ had no hand in making.

I come from across the sea to the home of my forebears and hold out one single human hand to the others gathered here who hate death. And I ask that I be permitted to join in the true humane effort of our time. I want to be a part of that attempt in the sentiment of Yeats, in calling down the hawk from the air, and hooding or caging him until his yellow eye has grown mild.

And so I take you back to my morning's walk in the gusts of wind and hail near Ireland's Eye. And I ask that you share with me, through the mists, a vision of this island—one where the eyes of my country and your own will see only peace and love and beauty.

Governor Carey is a former Medalist of the Society.

America's Role in Northern Ireland

KEVIN M. CAHILL, M.D.
and
HUGH L. CAREY

A Life Before Death

Two years ago, President Carter became the first American President in memory to address the issue of Northern Ireland. There also have been annual statements by most American-Irish political leaders urging all concerned to end the stalemate and violence in Northern Ireland. Today, it is clear that annual statements are not enough. There is a need for action.

The impending British elections offer the opportunity to focus international attention on England's continued failure to solve its most terrible problem, the "damnable" Irish question.

Yet both the Labor and Conservative Parties are once again pandering for the votes of the Ulster Unionists, promising the implacable foes of a unified Ireland additional parliamentary seats and other inducements to preserve the status quo. This is wrong because peace and justice deserve a higher priority than votes.

Somehow the British must be given the will—prodded if necessary—to do what is right for all the tragic people of Ulster who have contributed so much to America's heritage. Something can be done to end their long suffering. And there are opportunities now that we must not lose.

There have been steady, significant changes in Ireland. The economy of the Republic is growing while the North is suffering a depression; the average English citizen is weary of the senseless expenditure of billions of dollars annually to sustain an anachronistic enclave in a post-colonial era, and certainly weary of the obscene annual loss of life from the conflict in the North. There also is a growing climate of conciliation in the Republic of Ireland, a willingness to change laws and customs and even the constitution to alleviate the fears of an insular Protestant community in Ulster that has legitimate concerns about life in an overwhelmingly Catholic Ireland.

Recently, Mr. Jack Lynch, prime minister of Ireland, held out a hand in friendship to the Ulster Unionists. "We cannot," he said, "force unity and should not wish to do so. Those in Northern Ireland whose aspirations are opposed to ours are entitled to our affection and understanding . . . Our ambition cannot be to remake others in our image but to welcome their tradition in an Ireland of which we are all citizens."

These are the voices of moderation and compromise that we must encourage and support. Those of good will in the North should not be forced to endure their present frustrations. They have already waited too long for fruit from the barren branch of patience.

The Irish tragedy is not just an internal affair of the British government but a moral affront to the entire world community. We have only to remind ourselves that the daily body count still goes on in

Northern Ireland and that reports of official brutality in the police interrogation centers in Ulster continue despite the British government's pledge to the European Court of Human Rights that such practices had been discontinued.

Only last month, two Northern Irish Protestant physicians resigned as police surgeons because of injuries inflicted on prisoners during interrogation. The British compounded the wrong by making a shameful effort to discredit the witnesses, giving us an insight into the tawdry and corrupt world the British have concealed even from their own people for so long.

We have only to remind ourselves that the political and social environment in Northern Ireland has led to what credible social scientists describe as a policy of psychological genocide for the innocent young of Belfast and Derry. This horror was most poignantly expressed in the tormented question put by an Ulster mother: "My God, what are we doing to our children?" What indeed? What is the effect when children are raised in a world where the gun, the bomb, the brickbat, the hood and the riot helmet replace reason, compromise and the rule of law, where loyalty is judged by the condition of one's kneecaps, where opportunity depends entirely upon an accident of birth, and where the weeds of fear and suspicion choke out the young seedlings of joy and innocence? How can a principled people remain uninvolved when a child in a bombed-out area of Belfast scrawls a terrible question on a wall: "Is there a life before death?"

The European Court's condemnation of Britain received such scant notice in American newspapers that many Americans view as logical Britain's contention that it can do nothing in Northern Ireland until the majority and minority factions there reach some sort of agreement. But this is neither logical nor honest. It is like removing a heart and then expressing surprise that there is no pulse.

Britain after all, forced the partition of Ireland in 1921. And in the more than 50 years since then, it has countenanced or even encouraged the continuing social and economic oppression of the Catholic minority. It has a responsibility; it could act to bring peace and justice to Ulster if it had the will.

The violence admittedly has ebbed to what the British government considers an "acceptable" level—755 shooting incidents, 455 explosions and 81 killings last year.

But senior British army officers and police officials in Ulster have reached the grim conclusion that, while they can contain the violence, they cannot effectively suppress it, nor prevent its spread to England and the continent. They now concede that the IRA can turn the violence on or off at will, in the streets of Belfast, the garage of the House of Commons, or in Dublin or Amsterdam.

All this bodes ominously for the future and belies the superficial calm and apathy that now prevail in the North and in Britain. And it highlights the futility of the British policy. For it is a futile hope to expect security measures alone to yield peace. They must be accompanied by parallel political action.

For if history holds one clear lesson for us it is that, when political leaders refuse to use constitutional means to achieve justice, revolutionaries will use violent means.

And conversely, if men of peace are allowed to pursue their goals, the man of violence would be given no quarter. The British government's present policy in Northern Ireland perverts this order and provides frustration to the peacemakers and incentives to the violent. Just as surely as there is fire in the belly of the flint, there is disaster within such a policy.

We must condemn violence as a solution, for it not only prolongs the agony in Ulster but diminishes each of us. Pope John Paul II recently warned that in condoning or tolerating terrorist violence "contemporary man is risking the death of his conscience."

The question then is not really why get involved in Northern Ireland's problems but, rather, how can we avoid doing so? Should our government's concern, and the pressure it can exert, be any less on behalf of an Irishman in British Ulster than it is for a Jew in Russia, or a Nicaraguan in Managua? America is burnishing its tarnished image as a moral leader in the world by helping to restore peace in the Middle East. We have in Ulster an equal opportunity to show real moral leadership, to act on principle and not for gain.

It is not easy to rebuke a friend like Britain. Yet it is not noble to ignore another friend, one in need. Our concern for human rights and human dignity must prevail.

Today there is a new awareness of injustice in Northern Ireland, a spirit of conciliation and compromise in the South. The British elections on May 3 offer Americans an opportunity that has not existed before. We must galvanize American opinion by publicizing the facts of life in modern Ulster. We must bring pressure on whichever party is elected in Britain to take steps toward ending the strife now and to provide the basis for a settlement that will bring peace and justice to all the people of Northern Ireland within a defined timetable. What can America do?

• The government and the people of the United States should lend their moral support to the voices of moderation and compromise in Ulster and in the Republic. Too often in the past American intervention has been misguided. American dollars have supported extremists on both sides of the conflict, thus prolonging the violence. There is now a growing consensus that a viable solution will have to steer a course somewhere between exclusive Protestant domination in the North and complete union of the North with the Republic. There will have to be a pluralistic approach in which the traditions of both sides will be respected.

• We should urge the British government to develop and announce a strong plan for political and physical withdrawal from Northern Ireland. In 1921 Eamon de Valera wrote to Lloyd George, "If your Government stands aside we can effect a complete reconciliation." Today, it is clear that the British presence in Ulster—which amounts to a guarantee of continued unilateral control by the Unionists—is more a part of the problem than a means to solution. But British withdrawal cannot be abdication without responsibility. It cannot be the exasperated abandonment of a lost cause. Withdrawal of British forces must obviously be preceded by the commitment to establish an equitable political system open to all the people of Northern Ireland. Surely it is better for England, proud of her history but aware of the interdependent world of today, to plan a departure with dignity and graciousness and charity, rather than eventually retreat in disgrace.

• The United States must also be willing to provide technical assistance and direct financial support through grants and loans to whatever viable form of government is arrived at in Northern Ireland. President Carter promised aid *after* peace was established, but that clearly will be too long to wait.

• In keeping with President Carter's 1977 pledge, the United States should work with other nations to encourage job-creating investment in Northern Ireland. The government should also urge American corporations, which have been investing in Northern Ireland under the stimulus of British subsidies, to channel job opportunities to the most severely depressed areas. We should not help continue a pattern of job discrimination which has produced 35% unemployment in Derry and 50% in the Catholic areas of Belfast.

• If political encouragement and financial incentives do not succeed in strengthening Britain's willingness to initiate moves towards peace, then the American Congress should seriously consider applying the same economic sanctions that are employed against Rhodesia, Russia and other nations for violations of human rights.

• The American press and media have an opportunity—and it seems to us, an unfulfilled responsibility—to educate our citizens on Northern Ireland. They can focus world attention not only on violations and offenses, but on the quiet courage and tenacity of so many in Northern Ireland who desperately seek peace.

The effort to heal the wound between North and South will require the deft but strong touch of master surgeons. It will require delicate instruments in sure hands, but the patient can wait no longer.

The flames of bigotry still burn and the drums of ignorance still sound on the hills of Ulster. Futile and self-destructive violence continues; there has been an obvious unwillingness in England to risk the votes of the past for peace in the future.

But the impending English elections and the positive movements by moderate leaders and a war-weary citizenry offer the hope for which so many have struggled and waited so long. We can help, by American corporate and official acts, to shape the framework for a decent life in Ulster. To stay uninvolved—to continue to view Northern Ireland as an internal British affair—is to participate in the further destruction of democracy and the death of freedom in part of an island that once nurtured our own nation with spirit, and poetry, and song, and, almost ironically, with the compassionate and concerned religions of Christ, both Protestant and Catholic.

A Perverse Silence

There was a time, eons ago, when the Celtic myths were new and the secrets of Irish life found expression in heroic figures. Cuchulainn and Finn McCool, Dierdre and Maeve and all the characters of *The Tain* were used in ancient times to capture the hard realities of life in a cold, rough island adrift off the west coast of Europe. The mysteries of love and combat and death were molded into tales that still thrive in Ireland. This survival is due, in part, to the Irish love of words and talk, but it also reflects the harsh fact that the past, particularly the violent sins of the past, still dominates the present in part of that lovely land.

The myths and symbols of the Druids and Bards are now misused to justify terrorism, as if a new generation of Irish had no other option than to repeat the primordial acts of bloodletting and human sacrifice. The hills of Ulster, which once thundered with the roar of Cuchulainn's battle chariot, today echo with the sounds of strife and bitterness, with the modern clamor of gunfire and plastic explosives. Such scenes, enchanting as they might be in ancient history or mythology, are a tragedy to those who live them and a shame to those who witness them in silence.

That is why, in a lengthy article (Daily News, April 22), we recently spoke out once again to draw American and international attention to Northern Ireland—a subdivision of Eire unknown to the ancient Celts and unworkable for the modern. We sought, with our own means, to identify with the innocent victims of Belfast fighting for "a life before death in Northern Ireland."

We called upon the United States to encourage Britain to plan conscientiously now for what seems inevitable to most observers—a future in which the island of Ireland will be governed only by the Irish. We suggested a series of specific acts that the United States could take to promote peace and justice in Northern Ireland now.

We called upon the American press and other media to educate our citizens about Northern Ireland, to show not only the horrible impact of continuous violence, but also to focus on the hope for peace that lies in the courage and tenacity of those political leaders who have worked so long to establish an equitable system of government.

British politicians reacted quickly and strongly to our statement, denouncing the impropriety of foreign intervention into what they claim is an internal matter. England has, since our article, had a national election, and a new party is now in power. But for Northern Ireland, nothing seems to change. A conspiracy of silence and perverse political neglect is the apparent policy of the day. In the queen's 30-minute address to the new Parliament, the topic of Northern Ireland rated 20 seconds. Our own government did not react officially at all. The American press carried our statement and the British reaction, but nothing has happened since, except a mindless continuation of the daily body count published in some obscure corner of the newspaper.

It is almost as though the subject is tabu. In the Irish myths, there is an element of primitive magic called the *geis*—an absolute prohibition from doing certain things. Somehow, in mythology, that can make sense. But in the reality of today it is difficult to imagine what *geis* has been applied that prevents our government and our press from being involved in, or even talking about, Northern Ireland.

There has been ample documentation of violations of human rights in Ulster, especially in its detention centers. The evidence has come not only from the oppressed themselves but from Amnesty International, the European Court of Human Rights, Protestant prison physicians, and even an official British government report.

The Catholic minority in the North exists under an historical burden of gross social and economic discriminations and still has no effective political power. The majority Unionist Party adamantly refuses to consider any suggestion of power-sharing. And the British government, using a remarkably circular logic, reasons that it can do nothing to bring about a political solution until the majority party in Northern Ireland, which it created, agrees.

Is it some sort of magic *geis* that strikes our government dumb in the face of this intolerable situation, when it is so willing to speak out strongly on Rhodesia, and Russia, and Nicaragua, and Ghana?

Or is Ireland somehow a victim of its own mythology and folklore? Are we doomed to believe that this "most distressful country" will ever be such; that Deirdre is doomed to destroy herself, that Kathleen ni Houlihan will never be released from the grip of sadness and tragedy? Certainly there is a fairly widespread notion in this country that nothing will ever change in Northern Ireland. People say: "It's been going on for 400 years and will probably go on for another 400." This sort of intellectual evasion springs, no doubt, from the complexity of Irish history, both ancient and modern, and a willingness to follow a mental course of least resistance. The problems in Ulster are complex. They are deeply rooted in political, religious and ethnic differences and will not yield to simplistic solutions. But that cannot be an excuse for inactivity.

Where would we be today if, in the early '60s, the lawmakers of our country had decided that racial discrimination had gone on for 200 years and would probably continue for another 200? We have not yet realized the ideal of equality embodied in our laws, but we have made a start.

That is what is needed today in Northern Ireland—to make a start, to break the stalemate. We contend, again, that our government has an obligation to use its influence in motivating Britain to begin to seek a resolution which will offer political equality to all of Ireland.

American intervention in other troubled areas of the world has too frequently been based on financing one faction or the other. Our record of success with this approach has certainly not been very good, and more and more Americans are realizing the cold immorality of contributing to bloodshed in a safely distant country.

Equally insidious, however, is our apparently

selective inactivity and the puzzling unwillingness of a great and powerful nation to condemn repetitive violations of basic human rights in Ireland. The failure to speak out unequivocally against these wrongs and to use our enormous influence to secure peace amounts to a condoning of injustice and hatred, to sharing in the waste of young, innocent lives and the imprisonment of the elderly in chains of fear.

There are no innocent bystanders when human rights are at stake. Those who are aware of the terrible wrongs in Northern Ireland and remain silent are guilty of prolonging the tragedy. Those who let themselves be daunted by the complexity are guilty of an intellectual timidity akin to moral cowardice. Those who could lead but choose to confine their efforts to their own problems and to ignore a brother in need are guilty, to say the least, of a lack of charity.

We do not pretend to have all the answers. We cannot, like Finn McCool, eat the salmon from the river Boyne and thereby gain all knowledge. Nor do we wish to impose any particular solution.

But this small—and in today's scale of value, globally insignificant—country has a call upon our conscience that we shall not neglect. Ireland has made a vast contribution to our country that we cannot forget. We will not dismiss the people of Northern Ireland, Protestant or Catholic, merely because their numbers are small or because their struggle is embarrassing to England, a nation for whom we have been a willing ally in wars and a desired friend in peace.

We will continue—as we have done for years—to condemn the futile, self-destructive terrorism of the IRA and to warn against any American sup-

572

port for those emissaries of violence with their politics of death. But, far more importantly, we shall continue to promote American economic incentives that offer hope for a decent life in Northern Ireland. We shall continue to support those positive efforts of elected representatives of Ireland, North and South, to fashion, with England, the basis for a lasting, viable peace. That will come, it seems to us, only when a real demand for true justice and basic human rights moves the United States government and our news media to become more involved in shaping a future for a land that is still caught in the web of her sad history and ancient myths.

We appeal to the decency and compassion of all who read this article—whether they be concerned American-Irish or not—to join us in convincing our national leaders that silence is not a solution to one of the great wrongs of the Western World.

Reconciliation in a Divided Community

GARRET FITZGERALD

The boundaries of men's loyalties are limited. They focus primarily on the family. They extend to the local community, and beyond that to a 'tribe' with whom a sense of kinship exists, whether based on blood relationships or on something more amorphous. The original 'tribe' was an extension of the family, and in nomadic societies it was a group unrelated to a fixed territory but held together by a sense of extended kinship.

With settlement came a new element—that of territory, complicating the old tribal relationship in several ways. First, loyalty to the tribe involved defense of its territory and an attachment to land as well as—in some cases eventually in place of—people. Moreover, as movements of peoples invaded the territory of others, the inhabitants of a territory became mixed, sometimes without any relationship or loyalty being developed between conquerors and conquered. In other cases, with what is called 'miscegenation,' the population itself became of mixed race, with eventually, in many instances, a merging of identities, or the loss of one identity in another.

In some cases, loyalties became centered on a priestly or ruling family, which might be able to solidify loyalties of peoples of mixed origins or even in some cases of different languages.

But thus far, at least, in human existence there have always been limits to the extension of loyalty—usually geographical limits. In recent centuries, these loyalties have extended from smaller communities to the level of nation-states, or more recently to superstates like the United States of America, created by settlement in areas distant from the homeland, where a need for the settlers, whatever their origins, to bond together in a common interest has come to be recognized, and to be carefully fostered.

We have yet to see an extension of loyalties beyond this level, however. In Europe, a conscious attempt has been made to create a wider focus of loyalty than the traditional nation-states of Western Europe, in the form of the European Community, but for most of the 260 million inhabitants of this new semi-superstate, the national loyalties remain strong, and are transcended only to a limited degree and for specific purposes, where a common interest is clearly seen in such an extension.

This long and complex process, over many centuries, which has led to the division of the world into over 160 organized political entities, many of them artificial in their origins and mixed in their racial and cultural composition, has created new tensions within many states that lack some elements of homogeneity. There are states which comprise regions, or in some parts of the world tribes, to which ancient loyalties remain—loyalties which in certain conditions can be revived even to the extent of endangering the stability of what may appear to have become for a time a stable political entity. We have seen this process at work in recent times in Canada, in Spain, in France, momentarily several years ago within Great Britain itself. We have also seen signs of it in African countries whose frontiers were artificially imposed by the colonizers, cutting across ancient tribal boundaries, but which have survived the colonization period because of the deep-seated fear that any attempt to modify them could lead to a general fragmentation of what are still political units with a weak sense of cohesion. In these states, there are divided loyalties—divided between the region or tribe and the state, although many people find it possible to accommodate both levels of loyalty simultaneously.

There are other states, however, where the population lacks cultural homogeneity because history has thrown together within a single, often well-defined, geographical space people of different traditions, perhaps different religions, different languages and different historical memories and myths.

Some of these cases involve the cohabitation of two or more quite distinct races within a particular territory, the racial differences being so well-defined, and representing such an obstacle to a fusion of cultures, that tensions between them can be very sharp indeed. South Africa is an obvious case in point, one, indeed, where the problem is so acute that many despair of a solution being found to it.

But the sense of identity of a people does not necessarily depend upon anything so striking as differences in color, or even of language. Where the same geographical area is inhabited by people who have two different historical senses of identity, and where these are kept alive by distinguishing features clear-cut enough to sustain these senses of identity over a prolonged period of time—such as religion—a problem of divided loyalties within the same geographical area can also arise. In such cases, the very similarities of race, of language, of culture and customs can even prove negative factors—seeming to threaten the sense of identity based on a cultural factor like religion. Paradoxically, the problem of divided loyalties can be most acute and can create the maximum tension where the actual differences are least marked—so long as they exist in some form clear-cut enough to maintain the two identities.

Northern Ireland is, perhaps, one of the most striking examples of this phenomenon. Here, differences of language—which, for a minority at least, existed until quite recent times—have disappeared with the extinction of the

576

Irish language in this region as a native tongue, so that the only tangible distinguishing mark between those who feel themselves to be descendants of the indigenous population of the pre-settlement period, and those who feel themselves to be descendants of the settlers of the 17th century and later, is religion. I say 'those who feel themselves to be descendants of' one or the other group because in fact many Protestants are descended from indigenous Irish people who for one reason or another have in the past assimilated with the settlers, and some Catholics are probably descended primarily from settlers who 'went native.' But it is what people feel they are that matters, rather than their actual biological origins and descent. There are other parts of the world where the coexistence of peoples of different origins in the same territory is a phenomenon that gives rise to great tensions, but in many such cases, language remains a distinguishing factor, as in Cyprus. Accordingly, we do not talk of tensions between Orthodox Christians and Muslims in that island—we talk of tensions between Greeks and Turks. In Lebanon, on the other hand, the people are Arabic-speaking, and the differentiation between various groups is religious—the principal groups being Muslims of the Sunnite and Shiite traditions, and Christians of the Roman Catholic and Greek Orthodox communions.

Neither in Lebanon nor in Northern Ireland is the principal source of dispute religious. Neither area, to tell the truth, has any great tradition of theological debate at any level of sophistication. In both areas, religion is simply the means by which different groups retain and distinguish their senses of identity.

I do not press the analogy between Northern Ireland and Lebanon very far; the problems on the ground are quite different in the two cases.

To a large degree, indeed, the Northern Ireland problem is *sui generis,* and analogies with Lebanon or Cyprus or

South Africa confuse more than they enlighten. Nevertheless, the problem in Northern Ireland has a basic similarity to that in such other areas in that it involves two people with separate senses of identity inhabiting the same geographical area.

These two peoples are barely if at all differentiated racially, because most of them are descended from ancestors many of whom, throughout the whole historical period of 12 centuries or more for which documentary records exist, were moving backwards and forwards across the narrow channel, only 12 or 14 miles wide at one point, that links northeast Ireland, with southwest Scotland, rather than dividing one from another.

The language, accent and dialects, customs, food preferences and music of the two sections of the community, Catholic and Protestant, are for all practical purposes identical, and they share several sports in which both identify themselves as Irish. Their separate senses of identity are, therefore, concentrated almost exclusively on religious identification, which for a majority amongst the Protestants and a growing minority amongst the Catholics does not even involve religious practice—and to that extent is tribal rather than theological.

They cannot therefore reasonably be described as distinct nations, although most Protestants feel that they belong to the British nation while in many cases asserting vigorously their simultaneous Irishness. The Northern Ireland Catholics feel unambiguously that they belong to the Irish nation, although holding themselves somewhat apart from, and often evincing a certain sense of superiority vis-a-vis, the rest of the Irish nation living in the Irish State across the border.

It should be added that the religious factor does have a certain genuine religious dimension, for on the part of the Protestant community there is a real fear of what they might describe as Roman Catholic triumphalism, and of

578

the possibility that were they to join in a single Irish State, their religious freedom would in some way be jeopardized. This fear is bolstered by the fact that within the independent Irish State, constitutional provisions, laws and administrative practices grew up over half a century which bear the marks of the influence of Roman Catholic thought. But none of these developments could fairly be described as discriminatory, and they were for the most part accepted without protest by Protestants in the Irish State, either because they found them unobjectionable at the time, or perhaps in some cases because their satisfaction at their general treatment in a state in which they formed a tiny minority of the population made them reluctant to make an issue of these matters.

A complicating factor in terms of the perceptions of Northern Protestants has been the fact that in the Republic, as distinct from Northern Ireland, the Protestant population is, except in border areas and parts of Dublin, very thinly spread, with the result that, despite social pressures against religious mixed marriages within their community—as within the Catholic community—about one-quarter of all Protestants have married Catholics.

Because of the stringency of the requirements of the Roman Catholic Church with respect to mixed marriages, more especially in the pre-Vatican II period, and because of the fidelity with which most Roman Catholics in Ireland observe the obligations entered into with respect to the religious upbringing of the children of such marriages, this ratio of mixed marriages was a major factor in the halving of the size of the Protestant community within the first half-century of Irish independence.

For historical reasons, Protestants in the Irish State have traditionally been economically advantaged, the Protestant 4% -5% of the population holding throughout most of the period of the existence of an independent Irish State between a fifth and a quarter of the higher professional and management posts, as well as, probably, a similar proportion of property. As a result, emigration amongst Protestants has actually been slightly lower than amongst Catholics, despite the closer ties of Protestants with Britain, which have led many of them to seek positions in the British administration or armed forces. Nevertheless, the rapid decline of the Protestant population, for reasons which have in fact been entirely demographic and primarily related to the mixed-marriage problem, has been widely misinterpreted in Northern Ireland as in some way reflecting a process by which Protestants were 'driven out' or forced to leave the Republic.

This image, however absurd, has naturally strengthened Northern Protestant fears of a closer relationship with the Republic, although such a closer relationship could not in the nature of things involve the extension to Northern Ireland of the decline in the Protestant population in the Irish State, the reasons for which are peculiar to the demography and population-spread in the Republic.

There are a number of *theoretically* possible solutions to the problem of the two identities in Northern Ireland. But against most of them, compelling arguments exist.

Thus, it would be theoretically possible to exchange populations between different parts of Northern Ireland, creating a homogeneously Protestant district in the east of the area, the remainder, rendered entirely Catholic in population by this process, to be merged with the Republic. This is open to several major objections, however.

First, such an exchange of populations, involving the movement of hundreds of thousands of people, a very large proportion of whom would either be moved from urban areas in the east out into the countryside of the west, or from the country areas of the west to the cities and towns of the east, would impose intolerable hardship on those involved, and would leave a massive residue of discontent amongst those uprooted and transferred to uncongenial surroundings in which most of them would not be equipped to earn their living.

Moreover, it would not resolve an important part of the underlying problem, which is the deep conviction of Irish Nationalists that the island of Ireland is a natural geographical area forming historically a single cultural and political unity—even if its political unity in recent centuries has been within the context of British colonial rule. Irredentist feelings would not be stilled by such a solution, and the 200,000 Catholics uprooted from the eastern areas and 'settled' in the west, away from familiar urban surroundings, could very readily become the displaced Palestinians of Northwest Europe. At the same time, Protestant farmers from the west would continue to hanker after their land as they languished in unfamiliar urban surroundings. And the resultant all-Protestant state in east Ulster would be an unstable anomaly in a modern European context with a 'siege mentality' even more acute than that which exists at present amongst many of the Protestant population of the present Northern Ireland.

A variant of this would be a simple border adjustment, designed to draw the frontier between North and South in a manner that would minimize the number of Nationalists or Unionists on the 'wrong' side of the line.

Such a solution is conceivable. The present boundary was deliberately drawn so as to incorporate the maximum amount of territory that would be compatible with an overall population ratio of about two to one in favor of Protestants, and it runs a good deal south and west of the line that would be optimal from the point of view of minimizing minorities in either area. But such a revision of the boundary would leave the basic problem unsolved; at best, it would leave almost half of the existing Nationalist population still within the boundaries of Northern Ireland, where they would, however, constitute a much smaller and more vulnerable minority than in the present situation. And the aspiration to Irish unity would remain, while the prospect of ever finding a majority in its favor amongst the people of the redefined Northern Ireland, even under very much changed conditions, would have been reduced virtually to zero.

It would also theoretically be possible for the one million Protestants of Northern Ireland, like the one million French of Algeria who returned to France in the early 1960s, to move to Britain. But these are people whose ancestors came to Northern Ireland at about the same time as the colonists came to North America, and it would be about as reasonable to propose this solution as to propose that the American white and black populations should go back to Europe and Africa, and return all of North America to the Indians.

A fourth possibility would be the abandonment by the Catholic Nationalist minority in Northern Ireland of their Irish identity, and the acceptance by the people of the Irish State of the permanence of the division of the island. But there is no means by which four million people can be persuaded to change their aspirations to an Ireland in which the two sections of the Irish community might live together, especially as all but a small minority amongst them accept that this aspiration can be fulfilled only peacefully and by the free consent of a majority in Northern Ireland.

A fifth possibility would be the forced unification of the island. This is impossible of achievement, as the Irish people reject the use of force, which the vast majority of them abhor, having seen at first hand the results of political violence. Moreover, the force required to implement such a policy, against the resistance of one million Protestant Unionists, does not exist and could not be created.

A sixth possibility would be the integration of Northern Ireland with Britain, incorporating Northern Ireland into

582

the administrative structure of that island in a permanent way. This would deprive the people of Northern Ireland of any possibility of having a say in their own government, and by denying the possibility of any expression ever being given to the Irish identity of the Catholic, Nationalist minority, it would ensure the continuation of violence there, but with the danger of a much greater degree of support from within that community in Northern Ireland, and from the people of the Irish State, than has hitherto ever been available to the IRA. It would be a recipe for bitter division between Ireland and Britain, and would be a source of permanent instability in that corner of Europe.

None of these theoretical answers would in fact resolve a problem that is clearly much too complex to be settled by any simplistic approach of the types outlined. Nor, in conclusion, would the restoration of the old form of government in the area, by a permanent Protestant majority, excluding the Catholic Nationalists indefinitely from any prospect of ever playing any part in the executive government of the area in which they lived—as they were excluded for over 50 years, from 1920 to 1972—be an acceptable solution so far as the minority is concerned. And after their experience of the consequences of this form of government, no British Administration is ever likely to revert to this system.

Clearly, then, the answer must lie in a process that recognizes the intractable elements in the existing situation and seeks to accommodate them in a balanced way that could conceivably command eventual acceptance by a majority in both sections of the community. Such an accommodation necessarily excludes the imposition of a North-South political solution against the wishes of a majority in Northern Ireland; equally, it requires that the identity of the Northern Nationalist minority be recognized in tangible ways that would place it on a footing of equality with that of the majority.

583

Such an accommodation must on the one hand recognize the aspiration of the Protestant Unionist majority to retain their British identity and to be safeguarded against the fear of absorption in an Irish State with what they see as a Gaelic, Catholic ethos. But on the other hand, it must recognize the aspiration of the Nationalist minority to recognition of the equal validity of their Irish identity.

This double accommodation also requires that the eventual political solution be not prejudiced or foreclosed, but be left open, to be determined by future generations of Northern Ireland people as their perceptions of their interests and ideals change with time. We are talking therefore necessarily of an open-ended process, but one which secures the majority against any imposed solutions with respect to the North-South relationship.

At the level of publicly stated political attitudes, the achievement of this kind of accommodation may appear impossible, for each section of the community publicly aspires to a system of government that is incompatible with the aspirations of the other. In order to see how an accommodation might be achieved, it is necessary therefore to look beneath the surface, with a view to identifying and understanding the motivation behind these publicly stated attitudes, for public attitudes reflect private fears.

On the Unionist side, the motivation for their attitudes lies in a fear of the loss of their identity as a community, which many of them define as a British identity, although it differs considerably from the idea of Britishness held by the average inhabitant of Great Britain itself. They see this identity threatened by what they regard as a much more powerful force, the nationalist identity shared by four million people in the island. And they see the Nationalists in Northern Ireland as some kind of fifth column, seeking to undermine their identity.

The defensive barriers they have thrown up against this threat include an identification with Britain as the original

584

source and inspiration of their Protestantism, a kind of geographically near but historically distant mother country.

They have little confidence in British Governments, which they see as having destroyed their polity by abolishing their majority-vote Parliament, by disbanding the Protestant auxiliary police force known as the B Specials, and by failing to defeat the IRA. But their lack of confidence in, and even at times contempt for, British Governments is combined with an almost mystical sense of being more British than the British themselves, and they find the symbol of their Britishness in the Crown.

The threat against which they are seeking to guard themselves is that of absorption in a culture which to them is alien: Roman Catholic and Gaelic. They see what they regard as their 'civil and religious liberties' as threatened by Catholicism in particular, justifying this belief not merely by reference to their version of history but also by reference to features of the present Irish State—the enshrinement of a ban on the dissolution of marriage in its constitution, the legal controls that still exist on contraception, and an educational system in which the Catholic Church plays a major role.

Finally, they are aware that the Protestant population in the Republic has been halved in the past 60 years. And many of them presume—without the slightest factual basis, as has been pointed out earlier—that this has come about through some form of discrimination against Protestants.

This is necessarily an incomplete catalogue of the fears which have led Protestants in Northern Ireland to reject the idea of a united Ireland. There are doubtless other motives, too, such as concern to retain the benefits of British subsidies which the Republic could not easily replace. But enough has been said to suggest some of the main parameters within which any solution must ultimately be found if it is ever to receive even grudging acceptance by Unionists.

joinder: "Shame on you—a young boy in Ireland would think he was king to set down to a meal like this!" Or, after I "became an American" and had the temerity to complain about a new pair of shoes: "I'll send them to your cousins, *they'll appreciate them.*"

Is it any wonder that even today an Irish-American can never close his wallet to an appeal from Ireland. I must tell you that when I finally visited Ireland and found the prosperous modern country in which my relatives shared, it was both a surprise and a sheer relief. But I must also admit my disappointment with "the West." Since my weekends in Brooklyn always seemed to be round of benefit dances for priests from Mayo, I half expected to find the whole country cluttered with churches on the scale of St. Patrick's Cathedral.

The arrival of TV in my home also sparked the flames of ambition. Although I hadn't thought much about my future, I had toyed with the idea of becoming a cowboy. This did not exactly excite my mother who tended to view myself and the other urban cowboys on 58th Street as descendants of "tinkers in the old country."

But I soon found a new passion: baseball, or its environmental child, stickball. Following the Dodgers on TV, I decided to replace Pee Wee Reese when I grew up. Since I was the smallest fellow on the block, I felt eminently qualified.

However, my mother was no more enthusiastic about baseball than she was about life on the range. Her chance came one rainy Saturday afternoon when our stickball game was washed out and warnings of a hurricane put the local Loews Alpine out of the question. She suggested I read a good book. I think she hoped that an interest in learning might bloom into a vocation: the desire of every Irish mother. I consented. The book was Dan Breen's *My Fight for Irish Freedom*. The style was simple and to the point. Dan Breen became my first hero.

However, the book was more inclined to inspire young men to overthrow colonial rule—as it did in Asia and Africa—than to enter the seminary.

But whatever orientation problems individuals like myself were facing it was nothing compared to the problems faced by those coming here. My sister and I knew something big was about to happen. After we were sent to bed, my father and mother held long and serious discussions in the kitchen. Finally, my mother told us: "Your father has decided to 'bring out' my youngest sister." My Aunt Bridget was soon "situated" with a family on Shore Road.

Her first culture shock came soon after. Arriving home from work, she found my father in bed at the astounding hour of 5 PM and myself crumpled on the living room floor bathed in tears. Fearing some family disaster, she rushed into the kitchen to find my mother quietly sipping tea. My mother shrugged, "In this country, they are mad about baseball. The Dodgers just lost the World Series." To see grown men driven to bed in the early afternoon and young children reduced to tears stimulated her curiosity. The following spring she became my chaperone to the world beyond: Ebbets Field. This face to face confrontation only increased her mystification. I thought I was educating her until I overheard her comment to my mother on the silliness of young adults fighting over a pillow in the middle of a field—a reference, I suspected, to a disputed steal of second base that afternoon.

Well, I better get down to business. I have not mentioned school until now for a good reason: I hated it. Next to my first day in basic training, my entrance into kindergarten was the most traumatic moment in my life. On that fateful day, we were escorted by our mothers to the door where we were placed in the charge of Sister Agnes Brendan. As we waited to take our seats, you could smell

683

whom they have a more limited acquaintance. But they would like to be able to play a role in the general government of the island.

To the extent that the above paragraphs correctly describe the principal fears and aspirations of the two communities—and there will be those on both sides who will say that the listing is incomplete or incorrect—they set parameters within which any solution, interim or definitive, must I believe ultimately can be found.

First, it seems evident that a Northern State with its own government is necessary to provide a sense of security to the Protestant Unionist population—and also that such a state is not necessarily, on certain conditions, excluded by most Catholics. Secondly, such a state would not necessarily have to be sovereign. It would, however, have to retain some link with Britain to reflect the British identity of the Unionists, while at the same time being linked to the remainder of Ireland also, by some political mechanism.

This suggests an Irish Confederation, within which each state would exercise control internally—subject to certain safeguards—but involving the sharing at confederal level of control in areas where the common interest and common sense suggest that such sharing would be beneficial to the people of both states.

Such areas would include security, which can be effectively dealt with only on an all-Ireland basis; foreign affairs, where the material interests of both parts of Ireland, especially within the EEC, are similar, and are often sharply differentiated from those of Britain; and perhaps certain economic matters. The Northern Ireland State in this Confederation could have a special relationship with Britain to reflect the British sense of identity of many amongst the Unionist population. Both states might perhaps have some form of international recognition in parallel with that accorded to the Confederal Government that handled foreign affairs. Thus, for example, diplomats could, were this thought helpful, be accredited to and by the heads of the two component states.

Safeguards for the minority within Northern Ireland could be provided by a Bill of Rights. The interests of the majority in Northern Ireland would be safeguarded by the fact that all matters except those delegated to Confederal level would remain within the competence of the Northern Ireland State. The inhabitants of each would have an entitlement formally recognized by both the British and the Irish Confederal Government to either or both Irish and British citizenship.

Recognition must also be given to the suspicions that exist in Northern Ireland about the influence of the Catholic Church on the Constitution and laws of the Republic, and the resentment of the Unionist community in the North at the inclusion in the present Constitution of the Irish State of articles claiming, while simultaneously abrogating, sovereignty over Northern Ireland for the Government and Parliament elected by the people of that state.

The creation of a climate in which progress might be made towards the kind of solution outlined above, which endeavors to accommodate the different aspirations and fears of the two sections of the community in Northern Ireland, requires action by the Irish State to make such changes as would be necessary to create a fully pluralist society within the territory of the State, and to remove the claim of sovereignty over Northern Ireland contained in the Constitution. A modification of the present application of the mixed-marriage code of the Roman Catholic Church in Ireland, if this could be secured in co-operation between the Roman Catholic hierarchy and the Holy See, would also help to still Northern Protestant resentments and fears.

This is no more than a brief outline of how an accommodation might eventually be secured between what

589

the English Parliament, 'We have lost America through the Irish.' "

That afternoon, we walked out of class thinking we were here before the Indians. And we quickly assumed our role as spokesmen and standard setters for "the foreigners"—those in the class who were not of Irish parents.

At home, "becoming an American" gave me a separate identity and solved the problem of whether I was from Cork or Waterford. However that announcement at the supper table did not dent my father's Cork-bred superiority. Henceforth, I was increasingly referred to as a "narrowback." And all subsequent indications of independent thought or action at the supper table were always met with an observation to my aunt, "He's a real American, isn't he?" Nor did education ever improve my status. Once, while helping my father in the cellar, a plasterboard fell on my head. He merely shrugged, "Got a college degree, and he can't even hammer a nail." My mother, on the other hand, expressed not only admiration but, I might say, wonder at my new-found identity.

By the seventh grade, my contemporaries and I were breaking family records for educational endurance, if not achievement. But the ultimate accolade came from my aunt who asked "the young American" to help her study for the citizenship test. Soon her girlfriend joined my class. I was a "teacher" at the age of twelve. My father, however, took care of the post-citizenship training with a single sentence, "When you go in, find the Democratic line and vote straight down."

Needless to say, it all went to my head. And, despite my mother's pleasure with my acculturation, it was she who provided my ultimate downfall on the morning of St. Patrick's Day in the 7B. In my growing intellectual curiosity, I had uncovered a remarkable fact: *St. Patrick's*

Day was not a Holy Day of Obligation in America, at least not in Brooklyn. This was mind-boggling. For not only did we have a day off from school, but mother's usual ritual of dressing us up to attend the 9 o'clock Mass at OLPH was totally unnecessary.

On the morning of the great day, I remained in bed smugly observing the family preparing for Mass. When my mother finally got around to telling me to hurry up, I condescendingly explained to her that I was an American and did not have to go to Mass since it was not a holy day of obligation. For a moment she paused. Then, to the envy of Cassius Clay, her arm shot across the covers to my pajama collar lifting me clear out of bed for a face to face confrontation. "As long as you are in this house, you will go to Mass on St. Patrick's Day."

The pastor himself, Father Alyward, delivered an impassioned sermon on the sacrifices of the Irish for the faith from the time of Cromwell to his own parents. And thanking our parents for their loyalty, he expressed the hope and prayer that their children would continue the tradition.

Needless to say, I was among those who heard that sermon.

Tim Driscoll is co-author of
An Album of The Irish Americans.

Northern Ireland and America's Responsibility

WILLIAM V. SHANNON

Northern Ireland is not a country in itself, but a small fragment torn from the living body of Ireland where now the last act of its long struggle for independence is being played out. Once more, as in the upheaval of fifty-five years ago when the rest of Ireland fought its way to freedom, familiar scenes are acted out. Once again, there is a Bloody Sunday, once again there is the shadow of the gunman and the crack of the sniper's rifle, once again Irish freedom fighters are interned in British prisons without a trial, once again terrorist gangs stalk the streets, and history is being written in the blood of the innocent. It is as if an old newsreel were being rerun but in slow motion. It was only seven years from the Easter Rebellion in Dublin in 1916 to the spring of 1923 when the military opposition to the Irish Free State collapsed and the Irish civil war ended. But it is already nearly seven years since the civil rights movement began its protests against political and economic injustice in Northern Ireland—a protest that has turned into a smouldering guerrilla war, and the end in Northern Ireland is nowhere in sight.

There is a critical difference between events in Ireland today and those of our fathers' time in 1916 to 1923. Then, Americans and particularly Americans of Irish heritage followed events with keen interest and by their protests, their propaganda, their political pressure, and their money played a significant part in influencing the final outcome. Today, Americans, even those of us of Irish background, are curiously silent and apathetic. There is quiet interest, some money is raised for Irish causes, there is an occasion flurry of political interest, but compared to the sustained outburst of feeling and concern of fifty-five years ago, it is almost nothing. We are spectators, not participants in the making of history.

This comparative silence is not unique to Boston and New York and Washington. It is no different in Cork or Dublin or London. Everywhere, the same three statements are repeated until they have hardened in clichés. First, everyone says, "The killing and the terrorism in Northern Ireland are terrible things." Secondly, everyone says, "The Protestants and the Catholics in Northern Ireland should work with the British Government to settle the matter peacefully because any decision has to be agreeable to both sides there." (One is reminded of the remark attributed to Warren Austin, an early American ambassador at the United Nations, who is alleged to have said, speaking of Palestine, "You Jews and Arabs should settle this in a Christian manner.") Finally, we *Americans* say, the Government in *Dublin* says, the Government in *London* says, "It is impossible to see what we can do about it all."

But these platitudes deploring violence, urging a settlement within Ulster's boundaries, and expressing bewilderment and hopelessness about the role of any outsider are the ABC of violence. They almost guarantee a disaster, an inexorable drift toward civil war. For let there be no mistake. The problems of Northern Ireland cannot be solved as long as they are left in the narrow, confining context of the Six Counties. Ulster's problems are Ireland's problems and they must be seen—and solved—in an all-Ireland context. Secondly, let there be no bland assumption that Britain is going to stay the course indefinitely in Northern Ireland. On the contrary, the British people are sick and tired of Northern Ireland's quarrels, sick

593

hour days. One morning he didn't wake up and at age 51 Mother was left with the three of us and a mortgaged house.

It was impossible to get a job. So she put her "thinking cap" on and came up with a solution. A sign, "Furnished rooms, Kitchen Privileges" was bought and tacked over the doorbell. The neighbors demurred. They didn't mind "Furnished rooms" but "kitchen privileges" stuck in their craw. Always agreeable, Mother snipped off the bottom half, thanking the Lord she hadn't wasted money on a metal sign that would have been impossible to alter.

And then began the parade of people who were to be woven into the fabric of our lives for the next five years.

There was Miss Mills, the grammar school teacher who tried valiantly to teach me the piano. I never got past "Drifting."

There were Mr. and Mrs. Fields who took the big, front bedroom for five dollars a week with the garage thrown in. They asked Mother if they could bring their dog, Buck. No dog lover, Mother asked doubtfully how big he was. Mrs. Fields made a little cupping move with her hands, a motion suitable to describe a toy poodle and reluctantly Mother agreed that their pet could join our establishment.

Buck was a wild-eyed boxer. He had the instincts of an attack dog and we huddled behind closed doors in the dining room when Eddy Fields brought him down for his airing. Eddy was a slight man and his feet never seemed to touch the floor as he came hurtling down the stairs behind Buck who by then was frenzied to relieve himself.

A twenty-one year old Phi Beta Kappa student in the WPA took over my room. He was so thin that Mother worried about him and often invited him to have dinner with us. This meant that Joseph, John and I had to

690

endure the dirgelike music he favored and played on the phonograph which he thoughtfully brought to the dining room table.

Before any new tenant came in, Mother gave what we called her "palace guard" speech. "Yes," she would say, "we're blessed with excellent police protection here. There's Officer Potters to the left and Officer Ahlis on the right. There's Sergeant Garrigan across the street and directly opposite him. . .", here she paused so the full weight of her piece de resistance could sink in. . . . "directly opposite him we have *Inspector* Whelan."

Mother had been going steady with a moving man when she was in her twenties and had somehow caught the virus that is the *sine qua non* of his profession. She *loved* to move furniture. We all got to recognize that speculative look in her eyes. "I was thinking if we put the piano at the window and the couch on the stair wall and. . . " No matter how loud and heartfelt our protests, Joe and John and I would find ourselves on the lighter end of the piece to be moved, lifting and hauling as she admonished, "Now don't strain yourself."

Her peccadillo led to the entrapment of her one and only paying guest failure who was two weeks behind in his rent and was trying to tiptoe out at dawn. Unfortunately for his scheme, we'd moved the furniture the night before and he tripped over a lamp that had been freshly placed on the landing at the bottom of the staircase. Mother rushed out from the dining room-turned-bedroom to find him sprawled on the floor, his feet entangled in the lamp cord.

She sighed. "If you didn't have the money to pay, all you had to do was to tell me," she said. "God knows I can understand that." When he left, he had two dollars pressed in his hand. He'd claimed he'd been promised a job in New Jersey. It would be nice to say that our departing roomer never forgot the kindness and re-

691

But so far, it has remained only a dream. Since Belfast began to be a sizable industrial city in the middle of the 19th century, it has attracted both Protestant and Catholic workers but at critical moments they have always broken apart along religious lines. The sectarian violence we read about now is nothing new. There were major Protestant-Catholic riots in Belfast in 1857, in 1866, and again in 1878, each time involving the loss of many lives. Since 1886, when Gladstone first proposed Home Rule for Ireland, there have been violent episodes in Belfast and Londonderry almost every year on the 12th of July, the traditional day of Protestant celebration. In 1921 and 1922, when unemployment was heavy in the Belfast shipyards, Protestant workers fought pitched battles with Catholic workers to prevent the rehiring of Catholics who had lost their jobs after the boom of the first World War. This economic discrimination in the North was of great concern to Arthur Griffith and Michael Collins when they were trying to organize the provisional Government of the Irish Free State in 1922, but the world's attention was distracted by the more dramatic scenes of British withdrawal from the South and the beginning of the Irish Civil war there.

More recently, when unemployment was again high in Belfast during the Great Depression, there were three days of religious rioting in 1935. In short, today's violence has deep historic roots. We experience it today with greater intensity because television brings the brutality and the bloodshed to every home screen and also because technology makes the instruments of violence—the guns and the easily-constructed bombs—more readily available to the participants. But violence in the North is not new. It is Ulster's way of life.

It cannot be said that the English ruling class in London or in Northern Ireland has given the Protestant poor much in the way of constructive leadership. On the contrary, their record runs the narrow gamut from demagogery to cowardice. In 1886, Sir Winston Churchill's father—Lord Randolph Churchill—saw that the Home Rule issue provided the Conservatives with an opportunity to drive Gladstone and the

Liberals out of office. This is what he called "playing the Orange card." He rushed over to Belfast and openly exploited the bigotry and ignorance of the Protestant poor. His slogan was: "Ulster will fight, Ulster will be right."

In 1914, when Prime Minister Asquith and another Liberal Government were again about to introduce Home Rule, another demagogue—Sir Edward Carson—rushed to the barricades. Carson, of course, was not an Ulster man at all. He was a Dublin lawyer who had hardly ever visited the North. His objective was to exploit Protestant feeling in and around Belfast in order to defeat Home Rule for the whole country. He was more interested in keeping Dublin and the South in the United Kingdom with England than he was in Ulster itself. Ulster was only to be a tool in achieving that larger objective. That was proved after 1920 when the British tried to compromise the Irish issue by partitioning the country and creating a semi-independent Northern Ireland that—at the time—nobody really wanted. Carson thereafter took a prestigious judgeship in London and turned his back on Ulster after he had done his damage.

His political heirs in the North—Sir James Craig, the first Prime Minister of Northern Ireland who held office for twenty years, Sir Basil Brooke, his successor who held the prime ministership for another twenty years, right down to their successors of today, the Chichester-Clarks, Brian Faulkner and the rest—created a genteel tyranny, a little make-believe state. At the beginning a few jobs were thrown to Catholics, but soon the lid was clamped down, and power became the monopoly of one party and one sect. The Protestants have an approximately two-to-one majority in the North and the small clique of ruling families, joined in recent years by lower-class demagogues, such as the Rev. Ian Paisley, have by their words and by their deeds made it unmistakably clear that to be regarded as a loyal citizen of Northern Ireland one has to be a Protestant and a Tory. Sir James Craig once described Stormont, the Northern Irish Parliament, as "a Protestant Parliament for a Protestant people." Speaking

597

and sees a possible Messiah. It's equally true that an Irish mother gazes at her firstborn son and sees the Christ-child. Joseph was a premature baby weighing only four pounds when he was born. She fed him with an eye-dropper that first year and never left him for an instant. I found a diary she kept and in it she wrote, "I was so afraid he'd slip away. He was such a beautiful baby. The other two had allergies."

Growing up, Joseph justified her pride in him. He won the General Excellence medal all eight years of grammar school. He won a scholarship to Fordham Prep. He was the Captain of every team, the lead in every school play. He had the newspaper route and every penny he earned he brought home to her, turning his pockets inside out to make sure he didn't forget a dime. Then they shared their own special treat, a half-pint of ice cream.

At thirteen, Joe contracted osteomyelitis. Mother was told that an operation to remove the hipbone was neces-sary to save his life. Widowed only a few months she made the stunning decision not to operate. She wouldn't make a cripple of Joseph and she knew God wouldn't take him from her. It was Christmas. He was on the critical list and the doctors held no hope for his recovery. Mother and John and I carried all his presents to the hospital. His main gift was a hockey stick. "You'll use it next year," she promised him. He did.

Joe graduated from high school in 1944. Mother could have claimed him as her sole support and kept him out of service. Instead she let him enlist in the navy with his friends. Six months later she took the only long trip of her life, a plane ride to California to be at Joe's deathbed in the Long Beach Naval Hospital. To the people who fumbled for words of sympathy she said, "It is God's will. I couldn't let Joseph go when he was sick the other time but now God wants him even more than I do."

That June when I graduated from Villa Maria Academy

Mother threw a party for me that held no hint of sadness. It was my day and nothing was going to spoil it. Johnny graduated from grammar school a few weeks later and he too had all the aunts and uncles and cousins and friends there to celebrate. She bought a black and white print dress to wear to both occasions. She felt her black mourning dress was out of place those two days.

Her pride in all of us was enormous. We were never simply doing well in school. We were "taking all the honors." I never had a job. I had "a big job." When John went to Notre Dame she must have written a dozen letters to long-forgotten cousins. The letters began, "My, what a busy summer, what with getting John ready for Notre Dame. . ." This kick-off would be followed by a careful explanation of why Notre Dame was the finest college in the world and therefore eminently qualified to educate her son.

After Warren and I were married, she never quite forgave us for moving to New Jersey. Warren urged her to live with us and avoid the endless bus trips back and forth, but even given *carte blanche* to come with all her beloved furniture there was never the faintest chance she'd move. You only had to drive her halfway across the George Washington Bridge to have her start sniffing the air and remarking on the heavenly breezes that originated in the Bronx.

She delighted in being a grandmother. She had a deep horror of my leaving the children with a young babysitter and thought nothing of taking the two-hour, three-bus trip to New Jersey to mind them.

From the time they could toddle half a block alone, Mother was whisking them on the Circle Line Tour, to the Central Park Zoo, to the Statue of Liberty, to parades and to beaches. She especially adored amusement parks. In 1939 she took my brothers and me to the World's Fair.

"In the name of God and of the dead generations from which she receives her old traditions of nationhood, Ireland, through us, summons her children to her flag and strikes for her freedom. . . .

"The Irish Republic is entitled to, and hereby claims, the allegiance of every Irishman and Irishwoman. The Republic guarantees religious and civil liberty, equal rights and equal opportunities to all its citizens, and declares its resolve to pursue the happiness and prosperity of the whole nation and of all its parts, cherishing all the children of the nation equally."

And the record of the Republic has made good the promise of those words. The accomplishments in high public office of Douglas Hyde and Erskine Childers, of William Warnock and Robert Briscoe, and of many other non-Catholic Irishmen are proof of the political civility and tolerance that have long prevailed in the Republic of Ireland.

Secondly, I cite the record on Northern Ireland because I draw a *different* political conclusion from that record than do the Governments of Great Britain and of Ireland. Thus, the April 12 issue of *British Record* (the official summary issued by the British Information Service) reiterates the same threadbare clichés about Northern Ireland. "The purpose of the [Northern Ireland Constitutional] Convention," the *Record* says, "will be to devise a form of government that will enable the Catholic minority both to share in the administration of the country and to maintain its long-term aspiration of unification with the Irish Republic, while at the same time reassuring the Protestant majority that the status of Northern Ireland as an integral part of the United Kingdom will not be broken unless and until they, the majority, so desire."

". . . Of prime importance to the British Government is that the solution, when it comes, shall be a Northern Ireland one, worked out by delegates representing all shades of opinion without outside interference."

To this I say there is no need for the Catholic minority in the North to "devise a form of government." One has already been devised that brilliantly expresses the genius of the Irish people and its name is the Republic of Ireland. Secondly, the status of Northern Ireland *ought* to be broken because the so-called "majority" is a *minority* of the Irish nation, a *minority* which has long since forfeited any political or moral claim to run its shell game in Belfast and call it a country. If there is ever to be a just solution, it cannot be simply "a Northern Ireland one." It will *have* to be achieved by the "outside interference" of the rest of Ireland, of Britain, and of the United States.

My viewpoint is not the viewpoint officially expressed by the Irish Government. Garret Fitzgerald, the Foreign Minister of Ireland in an address last September 19 to the American Irish Historical Society, reiterated a policy parallel to the position of the British Government. Now I want to preface my disagreement with Dr. Fitzgerald with an expression of my admiration for him. He is not only a man of wit, charm, and high intelligence but he is also, like myself, a journalist, and there are not so many of us journalists in high office that I disagree with one of them lightly.

"The Irish and British governments are continuing to work toward [a] solution," Dr. Fitzgerald said. "The solution we seek . . . is that of a power-sharing government in Northern Ireland operating in close cooperation with the Government in the Republic until such time as a majority in Northern Ireland may decide freely in favor of a closer political relationship between North and South."

I will interject my own opinion here and say that a man who believes any of that is going to happen this year or any other foreseeable year is a man who can believe in six impossible things before breakfast. And the fact that British and Irish statesmen go on solemnly repeating these impossible things to one another does not bring them any closer to being true.

How does Dr. Fitzgerald expect this Utopian state of affairs to arrive in the North? "The immediate objective of Irish policy, as indeed of British policy, must in these cir-

601

Paradoxically she may have sped her own end by electing to go into a nursing home for a few weeks rest. After all, she pointed out, she was spending three dollars a month for Medicare and getting nothing out of it. As soon as she began to take it easy everything in her body slowed up. Her heartbeat became more and more uncertain. I knew it would soon be over when one day, just coming out of a sleep, she said drowsily, "Mary, I had the children down to the beach and Carol wandered off. I couldn't find her. I just don't think I really can take care of them anymore." She could no longer take care of others and didn't want anyone to have to take care of her.

She had a total of seventeen hundred dollars in insurance from nickle and dime policies she'd paid on for years. They were tied together in an old brown envelope. There was a note to Johnny and me with them. It said, "Don't waste more than a thousand dollars on the funeral. Give one hundred dollars to each of my grandchildren." She didn't realize that she'd already given us all a priceless legacy, her ceaseless devotion and unfailing love.

And Mother is still part of us. "Remember when Nanny. . . ." is heard frequently in my home and after the story is told, there's bound to be laughter. Last fall, Patty, my youngest, was in the attic, apprehensively getting out suitcases to pack for her freshman year in college. She began rummaging and came down, wrapped in a pale pink terrycloth robe. "It still smells like Nanny," she said happily and surely it did. The faint scent of her talcum was there and the robe went off to college with Pat.

I have Mother's old black felt hat with the brief edging of black veiling in my closet. It's battered now and out of shape but over the years when things weren't going well, when the bills were piling up or one of the children was sick, I'd give it a quick rub and say, "Come on, Nora, do your stuff." I had no doubt that my first novel would be successful because it was dedicated to her. "I can just see Nora," a friend said laughing, "Dear Lord, not to bother you. . . .the paperback sale on the book was excellent but *how about the movie rights?*"

Time is slipping by so quickly. Months and seasons become years. My contemporaries and I ruefully discuss the fact that now *we* are the older generation. But when dawns the day that shall be my last, I'll have no fear. Because I am very sure that the first sound I hear when I enter eternity will be that well-loved voice anxiously asking, "Is that you, Mary?"

Ms. Clark is a well known authoress of books including Where are the Children *and* A Stranger is Watching.

be free to practice his religion and every landowner and investor knows his property will be safe if the Republic extends its authority throughout the North.

Secondly, since half of the people of the North live in Belfast and its suburbs within a twenty-five mile radius of the city and since resistance to political reunification of Ireland is centered in that region, I suggest that people in this enclave be given dual Irish and British citizenship with the right to appeal to British courts for enforcement of their rights if they feel that Irish courts have not rendered them justice. In effect, Belfast and its environs would become another city state like medieval Venice or modern Hong Kong or Singapore, but under a joint Irish-British condominium.

Thirdly, I am pessimistic about the Protestants and Catholics ever sharing power in Belfast itself in view of their generations of bitterness. But I know of no poems praising the beauty of Belfast—it is surely the ugliest city in the world. Therefore, I propose that an entire new city be built elsewhere in Ireland and that those of the Catholic population of Belfast who wish to do so be strongly induced by guaranteed jobs, by housing grants, and by quality schools to relocate there. British architects and city planners have created wholly new communities in Britain, the so-called "new towns," that are a model for the world. Building a new city or a series of new towns in a united Ireland would be a far better investment of British money and talent than subsidizing a sick, divided Northern Ireland and keeping a standing army there to prevent it from tearing itself apart. This would instead be a constructive enterprise in which American knowledge and American financial help might also be expected to participate.

Whatever family memories and ties of sentiment may hold Belfast Catholics to their present neighborhoods, they can hardly be stronger than those which millions of Irish men and women forsook in generations past to emigrate across the seas to America, to Canada, to distant Australia. In leaving the green-clad hills of Ballyvaughan and Tralee, or the mist-shrouded mountains of Kerry and Wicklow, or the rolling fields of Cork and Kildare, those earlier Irish emigrants sought a door marked hope through which they might enter and find a better life for themselves and, if not for themselves, then for their children. That is what the people of Belfast want as well. It would be a far lesser hardship for them to move thirty or fifty miles away to another community in Ireland once they know it existed and that they would be made welcome and assisted to begin a new life there.

It is in the name of the living that we must act. In 1916 the leaders of the Easter Rebellion consciously chose to risk their death. They wanted to throw their lives like gleaming stars into the dark heavens to serve as beacons for the Irish people. Pearse and his comrades thought that their blood was needed to nourish the tree of Irish freedom. In his lovely poem "The Rose Tree," Yeats expressed their feeling:

> "'O words are lightly spoken,'
> Said Pearse to Connolly,
> 'Maybe a breath of politic words
> Has withered our Rose Tree;
> Or maybe but a wind that blows
> Across the bitter sea.'
>
> 'It needs to be but watered,'
> James Connolly replied.
> 'To make the green come out again
> And spread on every side,
> And shake the blossom from the bud
> To be the garden's pride.'
>
> 'But where can we draw water,'
> said Pearse to Connolly,
> 'When all the wells are parched away?
> O plain as plain can be
> There's nothing but our own red blood
> Can make a right Rose Tree.'"

605

Thomas Addis Emmet was born in 1764—14 years before the birth of his youngest brother, Robert. He began his professional life as a physician and attained eminence in that field at a relatively young age. However, when his older brother Christopher, who was a lawyer, died, Thomas gave up medicine for his more favoured profession—the law. He passed the bar and became a distinguished barrister in Dublin.

When the Society of United Irishmen, which had been founded in 1792, was being reorganized in the face of further repression by the government, Tom Emmet became an important member of the directory of the Society. Although, prior to this time, it was known to only a few that he had any connection with the democratic movement, Emmet had, in fact, been actively engaged for several years organizing branch societies in different counties of Ireland while under the guise of travelling in the practice of his legal profession. Eventually, his relationship with the United Irishmen was discovered and, in March 1798, he and the other leaders were arrested as the result of information supplied by an informer who had infiltrated the Society. He and the others were then charged with treason and imprisoned in Kilmainham.

The government thereafter proclaimed martial law and an orgy of terrorism and bloodshed began. Those who were able to escape managed to reach the mountains and carry on guerrilla warfare which the British army was unable entirely to suppress. Frustrated by their inability to stamp out the movement, the authorities began negotiations with the imprisoned leaders, offering them amnesty and passage to emigrate if they would. use their influence with the guerillas to put down their arms. The English never lived up to their end of the agreement although the Irish did. In 1799, Thomas Emmet and the others were transferred to Fort George in Scotland where Thomas was again held in close confinement.

As a sidelight, you might be interested to know that his wife, Jane Patten, a strong-willed and cogent woman, finally persuaded the authorities to let her visit her husband. When she reached Fort George, she not only induced Governor Stuart, who was in charge of the prison, to let her stay with her husband during his confinement, but also to take the three Emmet children into his own household. It was at Fort George, in April 1802, that a daughter was born to the Emmets. Her name was Jane Erin Emmet.

Shortly thereafter, the British government finally agreed to release all the leaders of the movement who had been arrested in 1798 but kept in prison in violation of the amnesty agreement. Thomas Addis' name was omitted from the list to be discharged. Governor Stuart, on his own authority, released him with the others, as a consequence of which he lost his post.

Thomas Addis and his family went into exile in Brussels and made plans to emigrate to the United States. But before they were completed, he was asked by the directory of the Society of United Irishmen to represent them in Paris as Minister from the Provisional Irish Republic. It was expected, throughout this period, that Bonaparte and France would aid the Irish cause as part of the general French campaign against England. With hope that a French invasion of Ireland was imminent, the Emmets moved to Paris. Needless to say, a major French invasion of Ireland never materialized.

While in Paris, Thomas Addis received news of his brother's plans to mount a new insurrection in Ireland. Despite his renewed efforts to obtain a commitment from France for the necessary financial and military support, these were not forthcoming.

As we know, Robert Emmet and his small band of followers set out to capture Dublin Castle on July 23, 1803. Much of the promised support from counties outside Dublin faded at the crucial moment and the rebellion was quickly checked. Within days, Robert was captured. Within weeks, he was tried and, on September 20, 1803, executed. Thomas received the news stoically, and, a year later, when further prospects for a republic appeared hopeless, emigrated to New York.

He and the family arrived there in November 1804, bringing with him a number of letters of introduction, among them from which a man could provide a decent minimum for his family but generate little cash income. In the west of Ireland where the ancestors of so many of us in this room came from, it was still sadly said that the biggest export were the boys and girls of each high school graduating class—off to find jobs in the factories of England or to make the long transatlantic journey to start a new life in the United States.

But in 1955 change was already under way. The hydroelectric project on the Shannon River was bringing cheap electricity to the rural parts of western Ireland. Subsequently, the Irish Government began an intensive campaign of industrialization. In the last 20 years, more than 200 American corporations have started factories in Ireland. It has many natural advantages for industry—land available on which to build factories, abundant water, clean air, and a literate and intelligent workforce. Those advantages have all reinforced one another since Ireland joined the European Community in 1973. Ireland is now part of the vast European Common Market. A factory in Ireland has access to a market of 260 million customers. As a result, every year Ireland is setting new records in gross national product, in national income, and in economic growth. Last year, for example, Ireland had the highest economic growth and the biggest increase in exports of any country in western Europe.

Prosperity has meant better housing, more education, a higher standard of health care, and more leisure. With more and more jobs available in electronics, computers, data processing, medical technology, and chemicals, young Irish men and women no longer need to go abroad to find work.

608

Emigration has come to a halt. The census taken this year shows that population has increased in every county except one. And with industrial prosperity has come a new national psychology. Gone is the old conservatism, the old atmosphere of stagnation. Ireland has become a young man's—and a young woman's—country, striding confidently and energetically toward a better future.

Irish agriculture is sharing in this new prosperity. It used to be that the Irish farmer was tied to the English market where prices have traditionally been low. But since joining the Common Market, the Irish farmer sells his beef and butter and grain in the much larger and higher priced markets of continental Europe. The change has been like a blood transfusion to the Irish countryside. When I first knew Ireland, it was rare to see an automobile on a country road. A man who had a car automatically stopped to offer a lift to any pedestrian he passed because it seemed the neighborly thing to do. Now automobiles are commonplace in rural Ireland. And so are the aerials of color television sets, new threshers and harvesters, newly painted barns.

In agriculture as in industry, America has been a constructive influence. When the United States gave Ireland aid under the Marshall Plan 30 years ago, the money was wisely used to found an agricultural research institute at Moore Park outside Limerick. Today there are eight such research centers and it is exciting for me as your Ambassador to visit them and learn that so many of the scientists who are teaching Irish farmers how to increase their productivity received their own ad-

The Aran Islands and Me

DENNIS SMITH

THIS IS MY FIRST DAY ON THE ARAN ISLANDS. ON THE BIG
island. There are two smaller islands I will walk another day,
but for now I sit on the edges of a huge bed in a small room,
hunched over a night table pulled away from the wall. The
table and my writing pad are illumined by soft, flickering
candlelight, and I can hear the Atlantic waters crashing
against the rocks beyond the window, the inescapable, uncontrollable sound of Aran. It is a wonderful sound, a wonderful place.

The sky was dark this morning as I hoped it would be, and
as I walked to the Galway pier I could hear the wind's melody
passing through the town and across Galway Bay. It was a
brisk morning, chilled and wet-aired.

The boat is called the Naomh Eanna, Irish for St. Enda,
the fifth century son of a Druid chieftain who founded a
monastery at Killeany on the big island. It is old, its decks
of splintering wood, and is made for perhaps two hundred
people. It seemed to be full this morning, with Irish speakers,
islanders I thought, laden with cardboard boxes from Galway
shopping, and with tourists, Leicas hanging from their necks
as Olympic medals. And me, carrying one suitcase and a
canvas picnic bag filled with books and two writing pads. I
bought a ticket from a man in a ramshackle hut at the pier's
edge, and boarded. I would read from a biography of Synge

for the time of the trip, for it is because of him, after all, that I came here.

John Millington Synge (pronounced "sing") first went to the Aran Islands at W. B. Yeats's urging in 1898. He had been in Paris, unhappy and unproductive, and Yeats assured him of an awakening in the west of Ireland, amid the folkways of a people made poor by rocks, but rich in language by the hardships of isolation.

The three Aran Islands are thirty miles into the Atlantic, west of Galway city. The largest, Inishmore, where I now sit, is about nine miles long by two wide. It is sometimes called Aranmore, and it is the only one of the three accessible by large craft. The middle island, Inishman, is nearly round, about three and a half miles in diameter, and the small island, Inishere, is also round in appearance, and about two miles across.

These three rock ledges in Galway Bay are world famous, and it was Synge who brought them fame. Between 1898 and 1901 he visited the islands four times. His longest stay was for six weeks, but in these short periods he felt as if he were "beyond the dwelling place of man," in "a world of inarticulate power." He was a natural romantic, and as Byron found Greece, Synge found Aran, and from his experiences here he wrote a diary, *The Aran Islands,* and two plays, "Riders to the Sea" and "The Playboy of the Western World."

I love these works for they tell the story of a simple, natural, courageous people as distant from the sophisticated, electronic, competitive society we endure as Pluto from Mercury. I wondered if these islands were different today from the islands of Synge's time, and so I left my wife, Pat, and my sons, Brendan, Dennis, and Sean, in Athlone, safe on the inland banks of the Shannon River, and I came to see.

When Synge first boarded a steamer for the Aran Islands in 1898, the crossing was completed in three hours, and it was as long and as tiresome today as it was three quarters of a century past. There is an eight-passenger airplane to Aranmore each morning, at least during the tourist season, but I leged to watch all the preparations for the Pope's visit as they went on week by week. On the great day itself, more than 1,200,000 people streamed into the park, arranged themselves in perfect order and in complete good humor, and under a brilliant sky transformed the Pope's visit into a festival of joy. They came in family groups with parents and children and the very old and the very young. The vast crowd meant that about one-third of the whole Irish nation had come together in one place. There was no regimentation; order was kept and directions given by civilian volunteers wearing homemade armbands. In a time when many fear totalitarianism is the way of the future, it was a beautiful display of the self-discipline and moral authority of free men. The poet Emily Dickinson wrote: "The abdication of belief makes the behavior small." The Irish people have not abdicated their belief and, regardless of changing material circumstances, their moral behavior will be as dependable as their belief is large.

Ireland is a country where history comes forth to meet you. At every turning in the road, down every city street, through the mists across every lough and glen, one can see a place where history was made—the home of a fallen statesman, the flour mill and the post office where the heroes of 1916 raised the rebel flag, the ruined tower where a poet wrote, or the roofless abbey where half a millennium ago monks baked bread, kept bees, and illuminated missals and manuscripts that still excite our admiration today.

History can be seen in the burial ground at New Grange where 2,000 years before Christ a mysterious people little known to history worshipped the sun and built burial chambers with such an exact knowledge of astronomy that only on the morning of the winter solstice do the rays of the sun strike the innermost chamber.

History's evidence can be seen in the battle grounds of a river valley like the Boyne where successive invaders, Viking, Norman, and Tudor marched on their paths of conquest.

The most poignant history of all is the mute evidence of the humble and the obscure who left Ireland in centuries past. I think of the tumble-down walls of tiny cottages now open to wind and weather on virtually every hillside in Connemara. Each of these was once home to a farmer or a farm laborer. Here he returned after a long day in the fields. Here children played by the door and a granny sat by the fire. Each of these homes was abandoned when their occupants went in search of a better life in America.

It is no accident that those cottage walls have tumbled down, no accident that the towers are usually in ruins or the abbeys roofless or that the battlegrounds are scenes of famous defeats. Most of Ireland's history has been a dark history. But the Ireland of today is a new Ireland. It has become a land of hope and accomplishment. The energy, the aggressiveness, the imagination, the willingness to work hard that have brought the American Irish to success in so many fields in this country, those qualities have now been unleashed in Ireland itself. And is this not the fulfillment of the age-old dream of the Irish who came to America? Their ambition was not only to achieve a better life for themselves and their children but also—somehow and in some way—they could not be sure of the exact means—they wanted to con-

When Christ was born in Bethlehem, a fierce group of Belgic Celts were wrestling stones on the Aran Islands. It is historical speculation to say where they came from, for no record is written of them. It is sure though, that they were adventurers, and fish eaters, perhaps a beaten tribe searching for an impregnable shelter.

Unlike the Egyptians, they left us barren monuments like this Dun Aengus—just walls, mortarless, and in places more than twelve feet thick, built on the edge of a three hundred foot cliff, overlooking a sea that cannot rest.

I sat and remembered the monographs about the fortress a friend in Dublin had given me to read. The outer rampart contains an inner rampart and the fort on eighteen acres. The outer rampart is itself, in places, eighteen feet high, and outside of it is a broad range of sharp pillar stones, which is called a *chevaux de frise*. These stones are so placed that one could not survive a tripping unscathed. A thrown stone hitting its mark here would have done double its damage, and I am forced to wonder what blood must have stained these pillar-stones in battle.

A stone lying by itself might move a geologist's adrenalin, but for most of us the singular stone is unworthy, perhaps boring. When, though, stones are piled one on another, and given shape as walls or fortresses, they take on another meaning—for me a dark, toilsome, moribund reminder of the past, the survival battles of our ancestors.

Still, when they are shaped into dwellings, they become alive, immediate, and utilitarian. One monograph stated conclusively that Dun Aengus would hold two hundred cows, while another said over a thousand. In any case, I am reminded of jelly beans in a glass jar, a big jar. How many jelly beans, how many stones.

Each stone is a man's effort in lifting, carrying and placing. So many stones, so much lifting. The count is endless.

I will climb up to the fort tomorrow, but I decided then to go to a bar that is run by a man who seems to be famous for never smiling—a rare man, it was told, on this island.

There were perhaps thirty people seated around, and there were no seats left, so I and all who followed after me stood.

Nearly everyone there was a native and spoke Irish. In one corner was a group of young women, seventeen or eighteen who were dressed in a way that I mistook them for mainland girls, and city girls at that. It was only three years ago that girls began to frequent bars here. There were no older women, but many older men, who were treated with sincere deference by the young men who bought them drinks and spoke to them kindly, never avoiding them as we do in America. Old people are never patronized in the Aran Islands.

A man began to play the accordion, first reels and then more recent music like "Liverpool Lu," which the girls sang. A man sang in Irish that I thought would never end, long ballads being particularly disconcerting when the words are not understood. I noticed one girl who seemed shy in the first hour become overly loud with song after she had a few stouts. I sang "Johnny, I Hardly Knew Ye," and then the bar closed. It was 10:30.

I met two sisters, in their late thirties, who are also guests of Mrs. O'Flaherty. They remind me of Sean O'Faolain characters, academic, overly polite, but genuinely kind. We got into a van, picked up Mrs. O'Flaherty, and drove to a Ceili at the Island Hall.

The hall was filled with islanders and Irish was spoken everywhere around me. In Synge's time the language was declining, and I noticed turn of the century headstones inscribed in English on the roadside, but very little English is spoken now, and the contemporary road signs and headstones are only in Irish.

There was a drummer and an accordionist on stage, and they announced each dance, in Irish of course. I sat on the side of the hall and watched as the islanders, old and young alike, arranged themselves for a set dance. The music began, and a few of the younger men began to swing their partners madly, causing total disharmony to the set, but nobody seemed to care much, and enjoyed being knocked about by each other.

Now we ask—how did this come about? How did this man, of no great previous accomplishment, possessing no qualities of distinction (except for the sordidness of his past), suddenly stand a heart beat away from the presidency?

I find it unbelievable that there was not at least some public knowledge of the payments of graft he received in his Maryland days. Yet no one was shocked, or offended, or concerned: this is the way our system works. Put in other terms, "everybody does it." Because he not only was not stopped then, but prospered, he went on to hold the second highest office in the land, still a grafter.

It is the public, the average citizen, who is at fault. Graft and corruption will always be with us unless and until the people of this nation decide they want no more of it. Then and only then will it be halted.

Of course, it takes two to bribe, the briber and the bribed. The businessman decides he wants government action quickly, or desires that which he is not entitled to have. The officeholder lets him know that his vote—or his intercession—is available, for a price. The scene is set and the crime is committed.

As a federal prosecutor I have had the opportunity to see close-up (and to strike out at) the ugly face of political corruption. It is eroding our nation's vital force, the public confidence in our governmental institutions. It must be smashed. It can be smashed—as the following pages demonstrate.

It is good to keep in mind what Yeats said in "The Second Coming":

> Turning and turning in the widening gyre
> The falcon cannot hear the falconer;
> Things fall apart; the centre cannot hold;
> Mere anarchy is loosed upon the world,
> The blood-dimmed tide is loosed, and
>   everywhere
> The ceremony of innocence is drowned;

The best lack all conviction; while the
   worst
Are full of passionate intensity.

"Things fall apart; the centre cannot hold. . . ." An apt
description indeed—"Things fall apart." But is it also true
today—that "the centre cannot hold"? That I think is the
central question of our time.

Fundamental to that question are our current attitudes,
social and political, toward our governmental institutions.
We must first achieve a perspective. Tawney said

The state is an important instrument. . . . But it only an
instrument, and nothing more. Fools will use it, when
they can, for foolish ends, and criminals for criminal ends.
Sensible and decent men will use it for ends which are
sensible and decent, and will know how to keep fools and
criminals in their place.

Pope put it another way. "For forms of government let
fools contest; that which is best administered is best."

We are fond of saying—"Ours is a government of laws,
not of men." *But*—inescapably we must rely on men and
women. The human force.

Let's take New Jersey at the State level. Over the last
decade corruption has been manifest. The roll of the convicted officials in just the last four years is an imposing one:
two Secretaries of State and two Treasurers; the head of the
Garden State Parkway; officials in various counties; a Con-
gressman; virtually the entire municipal government in the
City of Newark; and this merely scratches the surface.
Why such massive corruption? How is this explained? Is
our form of government at fault?

Again Yeats' first stanza illumines the subject—
The last 3 lines bear repeating:

"The ceremony of innocence is drowned
"The best lack all conviction; while the worst
"Are full of passionate intensity."

617

That, on our political scene, is what breeds and always has bred corruption, the difference in commitment between the best and the worst.

John W. Gardner, in his book "No Easy Victories," puts it this way:

> You can if you wish tell yourself that society has fallen into the hands of unworthy people, and that virtuous, clear-eyed spirits such as yourself haven't a chance. You can suck that lollipop of self-deceit all your life long and die, secure in the belief, that the world would have been different had they turned it over to you.

Corruption eats away at the vitals of our political institutions. If unchecked "the centre cannot hold." Yet it can be checked. But the job is not one for spasmodic effort that waxes and wanes. Untiring integrity, unbending courage, commitment and dedication to preserving our fragile values, these are what are needed. This is so whether you are an office holder or a good citizen.

Of course there is the opportunity for hypocrisy. The candidate for public office who suddenly finds corruption an issue and vows to do something about it, after eschewing such a purpose his entire life, reminds me of the young worker who had been loafing for most of the past year, and approached an older man just before he was to be reviewed for a raise. "Do you think," he asked anxiously, "that if I really work hard for the next two weeks, I'll get a raise?"

"Son," the older worker replied, "you make me think of a thermometer in a cold room. You can make it register higher by holding your hand over it, but you won't be warming the room."

What we want, then, are people who want to "warm the room."

In September 1969 I assembled a staff to "warm the room." Before leaving private practice to become United States Attorney, I received from Senator Case who recommended my appointment not only absolute assurance of a

618

free hand but of utmost cooperation in whatever I sought to undertake. I hired eager and able people without regard to political affiliation.

Thus one recommendation springs forth: law enforcement, and particularly the prosecution arm, must be on a non-political basis.

Now—what did we do? We needed manpower. I had only 18 assistants. Today there are 54 assistants.

We needed accountants to review books and records of cities and counties, of companies doing business with governmental agencies. We got them primarily from Internal Revenue Service, with additional assistance from the Federal Bureau of Investigation.

Within 5 months we were well on our way. We had only one Grand Jury acting in September 1969. Soon we had three hearing evidence. The Newark indictments came in early December 1969; and in March 1970 I decided that, with what we had learned in our Newark investigation, we were now prepared to storm the mighty-ramparts of Hudson County and Jersey City. We had learned that it was not impossible to make a "breakthrough." Indeed, it is ludicrously easy to find in a company's accounting records the raising and outlay of large cash sums. One contractor, for example, was doing city work and received intermittent payment by check. Within ten days of receipt of such a check his books would reveal writing and cashing of checks to various members of his family for "expenses." These always added up to about 10% (the "standard") of the city's check received two weeks before.

Our detractors were many in the beginning. They sought to depict us as the equivalent of Gulliver's mad scientist who extracted sunbeams from cucumbers. The allegory is mine, not theirs. They were less literary and more pungent. But we struck again and again.

The City of Newark was corruptly run. Gangsterism and bossism were hand-in-hand as City Hall became a haven for thieves and plunderers. They were routed. The leaders are still behind bars. We moved into Hudson

County. There the stealing was even more wanton and reckless. Kenny had been embraced by an anaesthetized populace. Emboldened by their adulation, his avarice was unrestrained. We struck at the top. We subpoenaed before the Grand Jury Kenny himself, Whalen the Mayor, and other leaders. Soon their house was in disarray. They began returning cash to the victims of their extortion, as if that undoes the crime. And what did we find—that the fortress that political corruption seems to create, largely through the myth of invincibility it sells, was no more impenetrable a barrier than the Maginot Line had been three decades before. Thus, one engineering firm was called in and given back $25,000. We heard of this and sent out two agents with a subpoena *duces tecum* for the cash which was in a safe deposit box to be brought before the Grand Jury. We had 23 startled and wide eyed grand jurors that day as this cash was dropped on a table before them.

Another businessman for a nationally known corporation had been victimized into paying $10,000 in cash. The return was meant to be shrewd and sophisticated. Nine thousand dollars in cash was given to the Police Chief of Hudson County. County officials collaborated on a letter: "Dear Mr. X," it read, "when you were here recently you gave us $10,000 and asked us to reserve a table for you at our Democratic dinner. You must have misunderstood us and thought we said it was $1,000 a ticket instead of $100 which it is. You owe us only $1,000 and we are returning $9,000 to you." In a comic scene thereafter, the businessman, having heard of what was afoot, took a hastily arranged vacation. He really did not want his $9,000 returned to him.

As bad as Newark was, particularly because of the connection between political figures and leaders of organized crime, it was a model city when contrasted to what we found in Hudson County. Friends of mine who had known the Mayor of Jersey City when he was an executive of the New Jersey Bell Telephone Company told me that no matter what I found in Hudson County, their friend Tommy Whelan would be "clean." This is the man who, with Council President Flaherty, and their wives, had over $1,200,000 in a secret account in a Miami bank. A huge reservoir project was planned by Jersey City at a cost of $40,000,000. A contractor was told to add 7% "on the top" to his bid for a cash pay off to get the job. The project was dropped when our investigation developed these facts.

But there is nothing new about political corruption. "E'en grave divines submit to glittering gold," Dr. Wolcot wrote, "The best of consciences are bought and sold." And in Plato's Republic we find this dialog:

> But do you not admire, I said, the coolness and dexterity of these ready ministers of political corruption? Yes, he said, I do; but not all of them, for there are some whom the applause of the multitude has deluded into the belief that they are really statesmen, and these are not much to be admired.

In a later day there was Boss Tweed. Still more recently, and still dealing with the great city of New York, Jimmy Walker, he who said that a reformer was one who floated through a sewer in a glass-bottom boat. There is an obvious corollary to this—"Don't rock the boat."

And so ironically there is comfort in history. Corruption has long been with us because we are human beings. Strong though most of us may be, there are those crooked few who cannot abjure temptation.

And there are more examples.

You may recall the testimony of Detective Phillips before the Knapp Commission, as he described the dirty and sordid bribery of New York City policemen. How many recall that in 1894 a minister by the name of Charles H. Parkhurst inveighed against the police graft of Tammany, led by Boss Croker, and singlehandedly forced the New York State legislature to appoint a commission to investigate his charges.

That Commission, headed by Senator Lexow, and therefore called th Lexow Commission, called as a witness a certain Captain Schmittberger. Lincoln Steffens in his auto-biography describes what happened next, thus:

"They've got us," said Captain Schmittberger; and a few days later he went on the witness stand and told everything. Steffens continued:

"After Schmittberger's 'squeal,' other officers 'laid down,' too. [Chief of Police] Byrnes resigned; other 'higher-ups' confessed; and the defeat of Tammany was assured. Even the bad people, the poor and the mean, who always followed their leaders and voted the Tammany ticket—as solid as the Democratic solid South—even Tammany voters voted for reform."

And the reform Mayor appointed a new police commissioner to deal with this outrageous corruption. His name was Theodore Roosevelt.

The "Reformers" lasted only one term of course, and Tammany was back in business again.

Later Jimmy Walker met his Samuel Seabury. Tammany fell, only to rise again. Then Jimmy Hines was brought down by Thomas Dewey.

On the national scene—Teapot Dome, and then, the recent example of the tragic betrayal of a public trust, Spiro Agnew. He started as a grafter at the county level. He finished as a grafter in the nation's second highest office.

I mentioned Lincoln Steffens, the "muckraker," who wrote in the early part of this century. He linked corruption with the people who not only tolerated it, but who fed it and gave it strength. Who were and who are these people? They are our friends and neighbors. They are executives of corporations, they are the office clerks of corporations. They are the small shopkeeper. They are the industrial giant. What do they have in common, these people of such diverse backgrounds?

They all want certain special treatment. They in their own way lack confidence in our system. In my own experience I saw a company, owned by seven major oil companies, succumb to the criminal extortion of two miserable petty officials in Woodridge, New Jersey. The company wanted its building permits and variances for storage tanks immediately, rather than after hearings. The law, to it, was an impediment. Nor did it have confidence in law enforcement: it is unthinkable, they said, that we should report this extortion. And so they paid. I am pleased to say that now in New Jersey there is an office—the United States Attorney— where a businessman can go to report an attempt at extortion, and do so with the confidence that something will be done about it.

As a lawyer I lived through the most massive antitrust litigation this country has ever seen. My client sued the large electric equipment manufacturers. Their executives, some earning as much as $200,000 a year, went to jail. In later civil suits, hundreds of millions of dollars in damages were paid. I shall never forget one man, a vice president of one of the nation's largest companies, who was a Scout Leader, a Sunday School Superintendent, active in service organizations like Rotary and Kiwanis—this man, a pillar of community rectitude on his own time—a Dr. Jekyll, turned into a Mr. Hyde once the business day began. He lied, he filed false reports, he falsified his expense accounts. Indeed, to cover his presence in New York (where he actually was meeting with his counterparts in two competitor companies to rig bids on massive turbine-generators), he filed an expense account showing a round-trip from his Philadelphia office to Newark, and then took a credit for having as luncheon guests two executives of my client. Unfortunately for him, the two people were not in Newark that day. As we showed in court, one was at an industry meeting in Denver, the other was in the hospital.

I mince no words. You should not be shocked at cosmic corruption at the vice president's level if you are not equally shocked at corruption at the municipal, county and state level, or at crooked practices of businessmen.

The corruption of the vice-president began—according to the written explanation filed by the Justice Department at the time of his conviction—at the county level. It continued into the State House and finally carried forward with the man himself into the second highest office of the country.

The point is simple: People do not come into high office without first holding lesser ones; and ethics in government must start where most men in government begin—at the lowest local level.

If we, the people of a city, are not shocked by the bribe to the building inspector; if we the people of the county blink at the bribe for a zoning variance; if we the people of the State do not make war on graft and influence peddling for state contracts, then how can we, the people of America, honestly proclaim such shock and surprise when the corruption touches the governorship of Illinois or the vice presidency of the United States.

Which of course generates the question: do the people really want good decent government?

Seventy years ago Steffens asked the most important question about ethics in government:

> . . . Do the people want good government? Are they better than the politician? Isn't our corrupt government, after all, representative?

The answer he found was:

> . . . The corruption that shocks us in public affairs we practice ourselves in our private concerns. There is no essential difference between the pull that gets your wife into society or for your book a favorable review, and that which gets a heeler into office, or a thief out of jail.

> . . . It's all a moral weakness; a weakness right where we think we are strongest. Oh, we are good—on Sunday, and we are 'fearfully patriotic' on the Fourth of July. But the bribe we pay to the janitor to prefer our interests to the landlord's is the little brother of the bribe passed to the alderman to sell a city street. . . .

Who is it that Steffens says is at fault when government is not ethical?

. . . No one class is at fault, nor any one breed, nor any particular interest or group of interests. The misgovernment of the American people is misgovernment by the American people.

In modern terms that means that as long as we have a business community prepared to pay a bribe, we will have graft in government. It means, also, that for as long as we tolerate commercial bribery in private enterprise, we will encourage it in public enterprise.

The question today is the same as the question seventy years ago—do the people want good government?

The answer, too, is the same: Ethics in government must begin at a more basic level than even on the local borough level of government. It must be in the minds and the hearts of a people; a people prepared not merely to legislate morality, not even merely to demand it, but a people who are also prepared to live it themselves.

Every company big and small that sold bandages, pins, pencils, paper, automobiles, books, playground equipment to Jersey City or Hudson County; that paved streets or built buildings; that provided services of any kind, paid tribute. Meantime a city and county were dying. Yet for decades it went on, through the Hagues and Kennys. No one really fought it hard, if at all.

It is an inaccuracy to speak of public and private morality as if they are separate and distinct concepts. They are one and the same. They are indivisible.

Now, let me sound a hopeful note. As a United States Attorney, as a judge, and as a former law school teacher and practicing lawyer, I don't feel the situation is hopeless. To be sure, I don't believe corruption can ever be stamped out. To lift a phrase from the Federalist Papers, "If men were angels" we might end it; but men are not angels. Corruption, however, can be fought. We must first recognize not only its basic immorality, but the destructive threat it offers to our institutions. We can refuse to tolerate it. We can by our own lives demonstrate we have confidence in our system so that we are willing to be treated like the poorest among us, seeking no favor.

Is it hopeless? Of course not. Didn't we in New Jersey show that? Fuller said:

> If the wicked flourish, and thou suffer
> Be not discouraged.
> They are fatted for destruction
> Thou are dieted for health.

Federal Judge Lacey is a former United States Attorney, whose investigative techniques in New Jersey have had a profound impact on criminal prosecution throughout the country.

The Importance of
a Neighborhood

ANDREW M. GREELEY

The British poet Rupert Brooke, scribbling in the mud of the trenches during the Great War, wrote these words about his home:

> If I should die, think only this of me:
>   That there's some corner of a foreign field
> That is for ever England. There shall be
>   In that rich earth a richer dust concealed;
> A dust whom England bore, shaped, made aware,
>   Gave, once, her flowers to love, her ways to roam,
> A body of England's, breathing English air,
>   Washed by the rivers, blest by suns of home.
>
> And think, this heart, all evil shed away,
>   A pulse in the eternal mind, no less
>   Gives somewhere back the thoughts by England
>   given;
> Her sights and sounds; dreams happy as her day;
>   And laughter, learnt of friends; and gentleness,
>   In hearts at peace, under an English heaven.

Such longing for a place is unfashionable in our age of computers, television, jet airplanes, and alleged "future shock."

Modern man, we are told, does not need roots; he lives in a temporary society in which physical environment is no longer important. We have broken with our primitive pasts where we needed ground on which to stand, land of our own. Our savage tribal ancestors may have needed turf of their own, but all we need is a network of human relationships. The place where this network exists is nothing more than scenery.

That there are today men and women to whom place is not important is undeniable. University professors, journalists in the upper levels of the mass media, government bureaucrats, some corporation executives, military and diplomatic officers, either by choice or necessity, are prepared to move almost at a moment's notice to anywhere. It is worth noting, however, that wherever they go, they do not blend into the native scenery but rather create an American professional-class suburb. Like airports, these American enclaves are interchangeable and represent one of the few cultural constants all over the globe. The mobile Americans, the members of the temporary society, have solved the problem of place by taking their place, a standardized, mass-produced place, with them wherever they go. As a general rule of thumb, I would argue that anywhere you can get *The New York Times* within two days is a suburb of Manhattan, and any place where the pro football results can be known by Monday night is a part of American suburbia.

Man, then, is a creature of place. Indeed, as Paul Tillich, the theologian, points out, a man is a man precisely because he is in a place. Were he not in a place, he would no longer be a man but an angel or some other such marvelous creature. And while some of us may have greater need than others to be explicitly conscious of our place, or perhaps we have merely the wisdom to acknowledge our "placedness," still, by our very nature as physical creatures, we have profound longings for a place that is our own. People in the military, college students, even prisoners, do their best to impress a personality on the place where they are. The traveling businessman puts his shaving kit in the bathroom, his clothes on the hangers, and the picture of his wife and family on the dresser of his hotel room. Now it has become "his place," distinguishable from every other cubicle in the building.

In addition to place, each of us has a heritage, even if he is not conscious of it. Henry Ford once echoed the characteristic American attitude when he said, "History is bunk." Until very recently, most Americans paid little attention to the historical experiences that shaped their own particular attitudes and values. It is now clear that the hand of history lies heavy on all of us. Our basic world view, our definition of appropriate roles, particularly in intimate relationships, our goals, our aspirations, our values are all acquired very early in life and less by instruction than by imitation. The riches of past heritages—and their burdens too—are passed on even when those who are doing the passing are completely unaware of it. Although we may not be conscious of our heritages, we still know intuitively and instinctively that some others are "our kind of people" because they have shared certain important, fundamental experiences with us. Others, however admirable they may be, are just not our kind of people; their experiences are not the same as ours.

In many, if not most, American cities, a "neighborhood" is where place and heritage combine. It is not only our ground, our land; it is also a place inhabited by our kind of people. It is our turf not just physically but socially and psychologically; we become attached to the streets, the parks, the schools, churches, shops, all those unique and special characteristics beyond the people who live there that mark our neighborhood as distinct from others. That which threatens our neighborhood threatens us because the neighborhood has become an extension of our selfhood. Obviously, it is not as important to us as our families, but in a very fundamental and primordial sense the neighborhood is a continuation of the family.

The neighborhood is, from another perspective, the peasant village of Europe recreated within American cities. It is not, I think, merely an ethnic phenomenon, though obviously eth-

629

nicity reinforces the sense of neighborhood. Even in cities where there are no substantial ethnic populations, neighborhoods still come into being, and in some European cities at least, there are neighborhoods. One thinks, for example, of London or Berlin. Even now, refugees of Hitler's persecution are capable of speaking with some fondness of the neighborhood in Berlin from which they came. It would be an exaggeration to say that all urban men live in neighborhoods; clearly some do not, and many who do not have no interest in doing so. Nevertheless, the neighborhood persists as a facet of American urban life.

Many of those who shape elite American culture and, to some extent, the culture of the mass media, do not understand neighborhoods. They have never lived in them, and they tend to believe that neighborhoods are "irrational" or "tribal." I am always fascinated when a denizen of the skyscrapers of midtown Manhattan assures me that there are no neighborhoods in New York City. What he means, of course, is that he and his friends are not aware of any. But the bulldozers have not eliminated all the ethnic neighborhoods even from the island of Manhattan. And one need only cross the Brooklyn Bridge or the Queensborough Bridge, for that matter, to know that Flatbush and Astoria are alive and well; indeed, they contain many people who rarely if ever venture to the maelstrom of Manhattan.

Until "experts," administrators, professional doers-of-good, journalists, radical reformers, foundation staff members, and scholarly pontificators (many of whom seem to think they can rearrange the population of a metropolis with the same ease they move pins around a map) become sophisticated enough to recognize that they are dealing with neighborhoods as well as people, their elegantly contrived schemes are likely to be frustrated. Do not misunderstand me. I am not against urban planning. Neither am I against social reform nor the solution of certain problems by sophisticated techniques of population dispersion. All I am saying is that planning and reform simply will not be successful until the profound sentiment and affection which tie many urban men to a particular place that is their own turf are clearly understood.

This approach to urban life has come under severe criticism recently. Naomi Bliven has called it "primitive and un-American" in *The New Yorker*. Sidney Callahan, in *The National Catholic Reporter*, has called it "bankrupt and a fraud." Both writers seem to believe that only in a city where heritages are ignored and a sense of place is unimportant can there be unity. Unity, in other words, is created by uniformity. One solves problems not by integrating diversity but by eliminating it. The particularistic is second-rate, Naomi Bliven tells us, and nothing important has ever really come out of such a parochial viewpoint. It is the universal, that which embraces the whole human condition, regardless of time and place, that is fully human. The tribal, the ethnic, the particularistic, the local is inferior and deficient.

All of this sounds enlightened, rational, civilized until one stops to think about it for a few moments. Ms. Bliven cites Jesus of Nazareth as the classic example of a man who has such a universalist world viewpoint. But Jesus was a Galilean Jew who only a few times in his life crossed the boundaries of his home country. He never visited Rome; he probably did not speak or read Greek; there is no evidence that he was familiar with the great Athenian philosophical tradition; his religious imagery was entirely Semitic; he wept over the capital of his country and was incensed over the profanation of its chief shrine. He died with a Hebrew prayer on his lips. Jesus, in other words, did indeed preach a world vision that would penetrate to the ends of the earth down through human history, but he did so not by denying and repressing his own particularistic heritage, not by fleeing from his own particular piece of turf but by profoundly understanding his heritage and by being deeply committed to his own nation. The great man does not deny his heritage or his place; he rather transcends them both. Shakespeare was not an Anglo-Saxon or an Englishman so much as he was a Londoner. And Dante and his successors were not Mediterraneans or Latins or even

Italians; they were Florentines, and they were convinced that the little town straddling the muddy waters of the Arno was the epicenter of their universe. For a while, it almost was. Indeed, one is hard put to think of any great work of ideas or art which was not firmly rooted in a particular time and a particular place.

I am arguing that one's own place and one's own heritage and, for many of us, one's own neighborhood are transcended not by repressing them but by understanding them. The neighborhood is a ground on which to stand, a base from which to operate, a home from which to venture forth and to which to return. It is surely not the end of our world, unless we are dreadfully narrow; it is the beginning of our world, and, until we understand our beginnings, we are not likely to go very far. He who does not start from *somewhere* will be unable to go any place else.

I would therefore argue that an appropriate goal for urban life is not to eliminate neighborhoods but to understand them, not to repress our own heritage but to transcend it, not to homogenize the population, but to integrate its diversity. The facile, shallow, glib liberalism that writes off neighborhoods as a residue of a tribal past merely displays its own uncultured ignorance.

There are two extremes to be avoided in our approach to neighborhoods.

Many of the children, grandchildren and great-grandchildren of the immigrants *reject* their neighborhoods. They want to break out of its rigidities and restrictions; they have nothing but contempt for its narrowness and superstition, nothing but ridicule for those who remain behind. Their heritage and place are worthless, and they swear that they will never return. But many of those self-proclaimed rebels go on to seek other neighborhoods which are every bit as narrow and rigid as the old ones. There is nothing more oppressive than a commune, and there is no neighborhood in the city more parochial and provincial than Hyde Park—a different kind of provincialism, perhaps, than one would find in Beverly or

Morgan Park, but provincial it is, despite the fact that its residents are convinced that they are the only non-provincial people in the world.

The other extreme is *uncritical acceptance*. Large numbers of Americans, particularly if they be of immigrant stock, are not socially or economically secure enough to be able to look at their neighborhoods objectively. The neighborhood is an extension of their own selfhoods, and must as it is risky and threatening to attempt to examine oneself objectively, so it is frightening to take a critical look at one's turf. Uncritical acceptance of one's neighborhood pretends to represent great and strong loyalty. In fact, it is a manifestation of fear and insecurity. If one really loved his community, one would be able to criticize it because he would know that criticism does not destroy love or loyalty. It is only the person who, deep in his soul, is uncertain about his loyalty who is incapable of critical examination. True love is not blind. On the contrary, it sees much more acutely; it does not have to align itself with inadequacy. Rather, it can proclaim its commitment despite inadequacy and also its intention to reduce inadequacy. Uncritical acceptance precludes progress. I would contend that in the present state of our cities and our nation, the combination of sympathetic acceptance and critical understanding is absolutely essential. We will be able to live with others in the city and to balance concern for the neighborhood with concern for the metropolis only when we can face the strong points and the weaknesses, the assets and the liabilities, the riches and the inadequacies of our place, our heritage, and our neighborhood.

Our neighborhoods need to be understood by us whether we live in them now or not. This understanding will come neither from the extremes of rejection nor sloppy, shallow, sometimes blubbering, uncritical acceptance. There are great riches in our communities, riches that deserve to be shared with the rest of the world; but they cannot be shared until the people in them are strong enough and convinced enough to be able to view themselves and their communities with a critical eye, and a warm and affectionate eye as well.

I like to think occasionally that my own neighborhood is about the size of Florence at the time of Dante, that Longwood Drive winds its way through my neighborhood something like the Arno River; and I lament the fact that there is no one to celebrate the glories of this community or to mourn its tragedies. Such celebrants and mourners have long been missed.

Father Greeley is the Director of the Center for the Study of American Pluralism at the University of Chicago's National Opinion Research Center.

The Celtic Flaw

ROBERT COULSON

With the climactic surrender of Vercingetorix on the ramparts of Alesia in 52 B.C., aspirations for Celtic glory faded. Even in the green valleys of Ireland and Wales, the Celts exhibited their renowned genius for controversy.

One Irish hero after another fought his way to power, then fell under the jealous assault of his rivals. "It is better to be quarrelsome than to be lonesome," the saying goes.

Mighty battles were recorded between friendly Irish heroes. Cuchulainn fought his friend Ferdiad for four consecutive days, finally killing him:

> "What is there to rise for now that he has
> fallen by my hand?"

Finn mac Cumhaill and Goll mac Morna bickered and slaughtered away their lives, according to the flickering light of the great Irish legends. Irish blood and Celtic eloquence was wasted on the cold flagstones of Tara.

Long after the Druids were driven away from their gore-flecked altars, the last great King of Ireland was excommunicated by Bishop Ruadan for snatching a murderer from the sanctuary of a chapel: "Desolate be Tara, forever and ever."

Even the eloquence of Daniel O'Connell before a crowd of more than one million Irishmen, standing on the ruins of Tara in 1843 could no longer call forth Celtic unity. When the Irish Free State was established in 1922, the ancient legal tradition had faded away. The Celtic Brehon law was forgotten, gone forever.

Why did our ancient stock fall so inevitably to the harsh vengeance of history? What is the Celtic flaw? Do the Irish, the Welsh, the Scots and the Bretons still carry the Curse of Tara into the Twentieth Century?

Ancient legal systems reflect the culture of the societies they serve. Perhaps the quarrelsomeness of the Irish can be understood by raking the cold embers of Druid justice: a harsh and brutal system indeed.

The Druid fraternity combined the functions of priest, historian and judge. They were the masters of the early Celts, controlling the fighting chiefs. Excommunication and death were the not so mystic weapons of this ancient power elite. Their solemn curse was the greatest punishment of all, imposing living death upon the victim.

Then, after the Roman heel crushed the bloody Druids, Christian missionaries crept into the void left behind in the Celtic soul. The Curse of Tara by Bishop Ruadan was nothing new: the fighting Irish seem to crave the certainty of mystic rule.

In short, the Celtic flaw rests upon an inability to unite under stable yet flexible leadership. The Irish seem to hunger for factionalism, still to be seen in North Ireland and in the privileged rooms of American Politics.

Is it that the Irish are unable to detach themselves from faith-held certainties? Surely, the strength of institutions is to be found in their ability to change with the times. The Druids could not change: they were exterminated. The Brehons could not change: the Celtic law was brushed aside by British jurists. Are there contemporary Irish institutions that still hang frozen in the winds of time?

Perhaps the Curse of Tara will not be broken until the remnants of the Celtic tribes fight their way free from ancient prejudices. Our fast-shrinking planet demands an end to clannishness. Imaginative and eloquent leaders are needed to direct the world community towards peace.

The resolution of political and economic controversy requires a deeper understanding of the dispute settlement process. Ireland has produced its fair share of negotiators and mediators. But, in general, it is fair to say that the Irish are not known for their willingness to compromise, particularly as to matters of ideology. Would it not be useful to propagate a mutation in the Irish personality, seeking that delicate detachment of mind which facilitates man's ability to submit disputes to impartial determination? In the end, the demands of modern life will humble the stubborn Celtic stance; but can we not introduce such change voluntarily, by sweet submission to the imperatives of Man?

On the Plain of Carnac, three thousand mysterious stone dolmens still stand, but the Celtic race is scattered around the globe. Once the bloody magic of the Druids is lifted from our spirits, the deep devoted loyalty of the Celts can be dedicated to resolving the current problems of all mankind.

Mr. Coulson is President of the American Arbitration Association.

Section 4 — Personal

Congressional Record, 97th Congress

Through the kindness of Senator Daniel Patrick Moynihan, the speeches given by President Reagan and myself at last year's annual banquet were entered into the Congressional Record. They are reprinted here in our own Recorder to preserve a memorable day in the Society's history.

Dreams, Reality, Tradition

KEVIN M. CAHILL, M.D.

Mr. President, Your Eminence Cardinal Cooke, as a personal representative of the Prime Minister of Ireland we have with us Special Advisor to the Government, Mr. Alexis Fitzgerald and Mrs. Fitzgerald; representing our sister cultural societies in Ireland, Sir John and Lady Galvin, Frank and Eily Patterson of whom you shall hear shortly, previous Medalists and Presidents of our Society, Fellow members and your guests, Ladies and Gentlemen.

Eighty five years ago a group of immigrant realists gathered, unheralded, in a cold Boston hotel room, and dreamed, not of the ancient past, but of a better future—for America and Ireland, and they began the tradition that we experience once again this evening.

Out of steerage and fear and poverty they determined that the annual meeting of this Society should be held at a banquet, much like the Pilgrims celebrated their arrival in America—and their survival in a strange new land—with a feast of Thanksgiving. So, if we are able to dine tonight on five gourmet courses we do so as the descendants of those who taught us to share our bounty and enjoy—with food and drink—the land that is ours.

Our Founders were obviously dreamers, and I suspect they would not be surprised to find us here on this great night. The Irish immigrant worked hard to see his dreams become reality—there are few ditches in this city he didn't dig and the train tracks and canals that opened this nation were lubricated with American-Irish sweat and determination. But those men and women left behind—even in the throes of their poverty—dreamlike cathedrals so the rest of the community would know of their faith and their heritage. From the dreams of the frightened hordes that fled the Irish potato famine in 1845 came that great Irish expression of trust and confidence that epitomizes New York, the church of our beloved Cardinal, St. Patrick's Cathedral.

Today our dreams continue. I once courted my wife with the lovely lines of Yeats:

> Had I the heavens' embroidered cloths,
> Enwrought with the golden and silver light,
> The blue and the dim and the dark cloths
> Of night and light and the half light,
> I would spread the cloths under your feet:
> But I, being poor, have only my dreams;
> I have spread my dreams under your feet;
> Tread softly because you tread on my dreams.

We still dream—as did our immigrant ancestors—of an even better life for our children, of an

America that fulfills her potential for all, particularly for the poor and oppressed who bear the burden our fathers and mothers fought against. We dream of an Ireland in peace and prosperity, as American descendants of those who dreamed and worked so hard we have a tradition, and indeed an obligation to help end the pain and suffering that now scars a land the Founders of this Society asked us not to forget.

I have spoken briefly of dreams, reality and tradition. I have fulfilled my mandate to deliver once again, the required address by the President-General to this Society's annual banquet.

I suspect that I have inherited some of the well-known Celtic need to communicate, and if you feel I have rambled on a bit may I remind you that the records of our Society contain annual reports by my predecessors that clearly lived up to the highest expectations of an oral culture, for at least one speech I know went on for several hours. But I equally suspect you came not to hear further details of our activities, and besides I have tried to summarize these in the Introduction to our annual book, the *Recorder*.

You came to join me in honoring an American of Irish extraction who holds the highest office in our land. My version of his biography is in your *Recorder*, and need not be repeated now, but the Ballyporeen origins, and the rise from a humble home in Tampico to the White House is both the dream and the reality this Society celebrates.

It is a privilege to bestow on Ronald Wilson Reagan, President of the United States of America, our highest award, the Medal of the American Irish Historical Society.

Address at the 84th Annual Banquet of the Society

PRESIDENT RONALD REAGAN

Thank you. Thank you very much.

Dr. Cahill, I thank you and all those who are responsible for this great honor. And I want to say that I happen to know that there is one among us here who has known also today the same joy and even greater, if possible, that I could feel, and that is Dr. Cahill himself who this morning was presented by Cardinal Cooke on behalf of the Pope, the Grand Cross Pro Merito Melitensi. He is the first American to ever receive this award.

Your Eminence, the other clergy here at the head table, the other distinguished guests, and one in particular that I might pick out and mention, Teddy Gleason of the International Longshoremen's Association. And I mention him because on Sunday he is going to celebrate the 42nd anniversary of his 39th birthday.

Teddy, I have found that for some time it makes it much easier to greet each one of these annual occasions.

But I do thank you very much. There is the legend in Ireland of the happy Colleen of Ballisodare who lived among the wee people, the tiny people for seven years and then when she came home discovered that she had no toes. She had danced them off. I feel happy enough when I get home tonight I am going to count mine.

Nancy is sorry that she could not be here, and so am I. She sends her warm regards and her regrets. Unfortunately, the last trip into town she picked up the bug.

Now, I am happy to say that is not a situation for me like the two sons of Ireland who were in the pub one evening and one asked the other about his wife. And he said, "Oh, she's terribly sick." He said, "She's terribly ill." And the other one says, "Oh, I'm sorry to hear that." But he said, "Is there any danger?" But he said, "No, she's too weak to be dangerous anymore."

A writer for the Irish press who was based in Washington, a correspondent for the press there, stated to me the other day—or stated the other day about me that I have only recently developed a pride in my Irish heritage or background and that up till now I have had an apathy about it. Well, let me correct the record. That is not so. I have been troubled until fairly recently about a lack of knowledge about my father's history.

My father was orphaned at age six. He knew very little about his family history. And so I grew up knowing nothing more beyond him than an old photograph, a single photo that he had of his mother and father and no knowledge of that family history. But somehow a funny thing happened to me on the way to Washington. When I changed my line of work about a year ago, it seemed that I became of certain interest to people in Ireland who very kindly began to fill me in. And so I have learned that my great grandfather took off from the village of Bally Poreen in County Tipperary to come to America. And that isn't the limit to all that I have learned about that.

Some years ago when I was just beginning in

Hollywood in the motion picture business, I had been sentenced for the few years I'd been there to movies that the studio didn't want good, it wanted them Thursday.

And then came that opportunity that every actor asks for or hopes for and that was a picture that was going to be made on the biography of the late Knute Rockne, the great immortal coach of Notre Dame. Pat O'Brien was to play Rockne. And there was a part in there that from my own experience as a sports announcer I had long dreamed of, the part of George Gip. And generously Pat O'Brien, who was then a star at the studio, held out his hand to a young aspiring actor, and I played Gip. Pat playing Rockne, he himself will say, was the high point of his theatrical career. My playing the Gip opened the door to stardom and a better kind of picture.

I've been asked at times what's it like to see yourself in the old movies, the re-runs on T.V.? It's like looking at a son you never knew you had. But I found out in learning about my own heritage, going back to Bally Poreen, that believe it or not what a small world it is. Pat O'Brien's family came from Bally Poreen.

But, I've been filled in much more since. An historian has informed me that our family was one of the four tribes of Tara and from the year 200 until about 900 A.D., they defended the only pass through the Slieve Bloom Mountains, they held it for all those centuries and adopted the motto, "The Hills forever." And that too is strange because for the better part of nine months now, I've been saying much the same thing, only in the singular. "The Hill forever." Capitol Hill, that is.

I do remember my father telling me once when

646

I was a boy, and with great pride he said to me, "The Irish are the only people in the country in America that built the jails and then filled them." I was a little perturbed even then at that tender age because at the sound of pride in his voice and from the way I had been raised, I couldn't quite understand why that was something to be proud of until I then later learned, which he had never explained to me, that he was referring to the fact that the overwhelming majority of men wearing the blue of the police department in America were of Irish descent.

You know, those weren't the only jobs that were open to the Irish. Back in the high day of Vaudeville, long before sound pictures drove it out, there were, very popular in this country, comedians who would reach great stardom in Vaudeville with a broad German accent. German comedians coming on "Ach and himmel Sie der."

What is little known in show business is that almost without exception, they were Irish. Their wit and humor that made them comedians they came by naturally and honestly. I was on a mission to England for our government some ten years ago. I should say to Europe to several countries and finally wound up and the last country was Ireland.

On the last day in Ireland I was taken to Cashell Rock. I didn't know at that time that it is only 25 miles from Bally Poreen. But I do know that the young Irish guide who was showing us around the ruins of the ancient cathedral there on the rock finally took us to the little cemetery. We walked with great interest and looked at those ancient tombstones and the inscriptions.

And then, we came to one and the inscription

said: "Remember me as you pass by, for as you are, so once was I. But as I am, you too will be, so be content to follow me." That was too much for the Irish wit and humor of someone who came after because underneath was scratched: "To follow you I am content. I wish I knew which way you went."

But the Irish, like many, a great many of the people and like my grandfather, great-grand-father, were driven to the new world by famine and by tragedies of other kinds. The Irish, they built the railroads, they opened the West wearing the blue and gold of the United States cavalry. There was John L. Sullivan, the heavyweight champion of the world, writers like Eugene O'Neill, clergy like Cardinal Cooke, and even physicians to the Pope like Dr. Cahill.

And it goes all the way back in our history. George Washington said, "When our friendless standard was first unfurled, who were the strangers who first mustered around our staff, and when it reeled in the fight who more brilliantly sustained it than Erin's generous sons?"

And a century and a half later, who else than George M. Cohan would write of the Grand Old Flag, the Stars and Stripes and Yankee Doodle Dandy, with the line, "I'm a real live nephew of my Uncle Sam." There must have been a divine plan that brought to this blessed land people from every corner of the earth and here, those people kept their love for the land of their origin at the same time that they pledged their love and loyalty to this new land, this great melting pot. They worked for it, they fought for it, and yes, they died for it. And none more bravely than Erin's generous sons.

Tragedy, as I've said, very often was the impetus that sent many to America. Today, as it's been said here already tonight, there is tragedy again in the Emerald Isle. The Cardinal prayed and His Holiness pleaded for peace when he visited Ireland. I think we all should pray that responsible leaders on both sides and the governments of the United Kingdom and the Republic of Ireland can bring peace to that beautiful Isle once again.

Once again, we can join John Locke in saying, "Oh, Ireland isn't it grand you look like a bride in her rich adornment. And with all the penned up love in my heart, I bid you top of the morning."

No, I have no apathy, no feeling at all. I am just so grateful that among the other things that happened when I was allowed to move into public housing—I had a chance finally to learn of the very rich heritage that my father had left me. And I can only say once again, with heartfelt thanks, I wear this and take it home, with a feeling of great honor, and say something that I know to all of you is as familiar as "top of the morning" or anything else. That is, "May the road rise beneath your feet, the sun shine warm upon your face, and the wind be always at your back. And may God, until we meet again, hold you in the hollow of his hand."

Thank you.

A Painter's Notes on His Irishness

LOUIS LE BROCQUY

Mon imagination c'est mon mémoire
—Jules Renard

Although I was born in Dublin in the year of the Rebellion and brought up entirely in Ireland, I do not remember being conscious of being particularly Irish. I remember being acutely aware of being *human*, for as a child it seemed to me that I might just as well have been born a goat or a hedgehog—an animal for which I had an early sympathy.

Besides, my immediate paternal forbears were of Belgian stock. My great-grandfather was supposed to have been involved as a boy in the Belgian war of independence of 1830 capturing riderless Dutch horses for the rebels. Afterwards, on maneuvers with a battery of field artillery, he was thrown from his horse under a gun carriage, injuring his leg. Unable to ride thereafter, he maintained his love and extraordinary judgment of that animal, which eventually led him via Chelsea, London, to his last home at Newgrove, Raheny, Dublin, where he married a Kilkenny girl named Anne Walsh and passed a good-humored and expansive life buying strings of Irish horses for the Belgian remount.

My mother's people included earlier foreigners—Normans, Cromwellians—who somehow managed to remain Catholic along with the yet earlier Celto-Iberian stocks with which they inter-married.

When I was a young man (with the derisory term *West British* in mind) I occasionally referred to myself ironically as "a West Belgian." No one seemed to me less manifestly Irish than that small family whose name I bore. Then, one day in my twenty-first year, I precipitously sailed from Dublin into a new life as a painter studying in the museums of London, Paris, Venice and Geneva (temporarily the home of the Prado collection). Alone among the great artists of the past, in these strange related cities, I became vividly aware for the first time of my Irish identity to which I have remained attached all my life.

Yet within this vital inner discovery lay the exclusive peril of self-consciousness. Art begets art, however, and my imagination was full of the paintings of Rembrandt, of Manet, of the great Spaniards—each simultaneously himself, his race and *universal*. From the very beginning their transcendent universality helped protect this incipient painter from self-consciousness—from self-conscious nationalism for instance, inducing picturesque images perhaps of Irish country folk dressed in the clothes of a preceding generation, or of thatched cottages arranged like dominoes under convenient hills; images no more respectable in themselves than the sterile Nazi *kultur*, or indeed the ordained Marxist aesthetic of "social" irreality with its own insistence on compulsively happy peasants.

Peasants perhaps; but those humbly and critically approached or obliquely overheard by a John Millington Synge, or by a Federico Garcia Lorca, whose whole being gave form and utterance to their stifled cry. For art is neither an instrument nor a convenience, but a secret logic of the imagination. It is another way of seeing, the whole sense and value of which lies in its autonomy, its distance from actuality, its *otherness*.

I believe that true art is a form of intelligence nine-tenths of which, like the iceberg, lie below the surface. It is as artificial and as natural as riding a bicycle. Indeed you may say that sham art is quite simply self-conscious art and, since we are all more or less self-conscious, every artist is in some danger of manipulating his art. Art does not survive being used or manipulated. Essentially autonomous, it is the leafing, the flowering of our imagination nourished by roots hidden in our native soil.

Every artist faces that self-conscious danger, I think, and the recurrent fear of it throughout his life. As a child my favorite nursery rhyme was not strictly a nursery rhyme at all, as I remember it:

> The Centipede was happy quite
> until the toad in fun
> asked him which leg came after which.
> This set his mind to such a pitch
> that he lay distracted in a ditch
> considering how to run.

I think all art is essentially as unconscious, as complex, as simple and as mysterious as the Centipede of my childhood. I have always done my best to steer clear of the Toad.

Louis LeBrocquy is Ireland's premier artist. His work is currently the subject of a major retrospective show at the New York State Museum.

A Kerry Homecoming

ROBERT EMMET MURPHY

He came into our view, a frail figure in the
doorway, as we climbed the boreen from the
paved Cromane road. I remembered the place
now: the squat, somber old house at the top of
the narrow road, the wide, grassy yard opening
before it. I remembered a house with little light
and no soft furnishings, with an open kitchen
fireplace, still common then in that part of Kerry,
and one of those uncovered cement kitchen floors
that, to an American boy first arriving in Ireland,
bespoke an unimagined crudity of life. I remembered it as a house without a woman.

The summer I was turning nine Dan Shea's son
was my companion. Donal was thirteen, very
much older than I for those years, but he showed
no condescension towards me.

There seemed, in fact, to be a bigger gap between Donal and his brother, Michael, just a year
or two older, than between Donal and me. Certainly between me and Michael, tall and manly in
my eyes, there was a great gap. Michael was after
girls, and Donal hadn't got past thinking about
them. He and I walked and cycled about that
country place with the freer motives of boyhood.
He took me through his father's fields and introduced me to a donkey foal. Once I was careless
following his steps and fell calf-deep into a bog-
hole. My uncles were amused by that.

I have a photograph of Donal somewhere. He

was small for his age and wore knee pants. That helps to explain, I see now, how we could ignore the differences in our ages. His face was broad and handsome, its native ruddiness set off by a heap of sandy hair. He was a demure, polite, generous boy. One day outside Florrie McCarthy's shop he put a threepenny bit in my hand just because he wanted me to have it. It was an English octagonal threepenny bit, and he must have sensed that its novelty appealed to me.

Four years later when I revisited Kerry, Donal called for me to take me to a pub. He still didn't see the difference in our ages, but it was clear to me that we couldn't be that summer the mates we had been before.

Donal's mother was dead, had been dead, I had heard, since he was very young. I have in mind's eye a dim picture of her being carried by night in an ambulance to Killarney, 20 miles distant, and dying along the way. It may not have been exactly like that, but some such story is part of the sad lore of the locality. She died, anyway, and left Dan Shea, known as Dan Junior, with two sons to raise, in a gloomy house without a female voice.

As we got nearer the house now, I remembered the first time we had approached him in his doorway. He was then a handsome, healthy man in his forties, a bit contentious, yet warm-natured, after all, quick-witted and a capable dancer. He was fit and able for a wife, but Irishmen seldom marry twice, and he'd remain all his days amid the hard furnishings.

The Sheas lived two doors from my grandmother and uncles, the Sullivans, whose house was a cheerful, active place where, at that time, before the first pub had been built in the district or the first television installed, neighbors gathered every night. Someone might play a tin whistle or a squeeze box or offer a song; if not, there was always talk, always company. Dan was there most nights.

During the weeks that my mother and sister and I stayed in that house, Dan grew familiar to us and, in a subtle, understated Irish way, grew quite attached to us. He became attached, I think, more than he or we realized and, in the Irish way, more than he was likely to express, and I think this attachment had to do with the aura of newness, of differentness, we brought with us, as Christy Mahon brought it to the Western World of Mayo. We had none of us killed our Da, but we had come to that provincial place from a vast, strange, faroff land. Nearly every Irishman has thought of going to that land, and many, confined in the narrow round of rural life, have wondered at those who did, especially if, like Dan Shea, fate had cheated them.

American visitors, intoxicated with Ireland's beauty, with the gentleness and wit of its people, with the drink and the song and the cows in the road, are inclined to overlook the meanness and sadness of much of Irish life. They arrive in the summer, when the sun is in the sky past ten o'clock, and forget there is a countervailing winter darkness. If they have good weather, they don't think, as all the Irish do, that there is plenty of bad weather coming. And they are not as keenly aware as their Irish hosts that their visit, like any stretch of sunny days, will soon be over. My parents' generation was still post-famine Ireland, the Ireland of emigration, of loss. But a legacy of loss had not benumbed them; they embraced

655

the hardship of attachment to what's passing, of caring unto painfulness. They inject in each visit a measure of their archetypal sense of loss, and in parting from them one feels that loss—and the experience can be almost unbearable.

I found at nine years old that I had fallen in love with Ireland on the day in September that I had to leave it, when I hid behind the house as the car came that would bring us to Shannon. Then, when I had been flushed out, Dan Shea disappeared behind the same house, took a slow walk around it, because he was not ready to say goodbye. I remember how he finally came forward, before the front door, his hand pushed quickly at me, his words choked, his face pulling away to one side because there were tears in it he did not want me to see. How remarkable that was to me, how unbelievably sad the whole scene. Was it then or later that I realized that my sobs had been added to the terrible moan of goodbye lowing throughout Ireland for more than a hundred years?

Three summers later my Aunt Nora went back, for the first time, with a teenage son and a daughter, Mary, in her twenties. There are hints that with Mary Kelly Dan Junior had some kind of romance. Perhaps it wasn't much. Maybe they held hands once or danced a polka or two or took a few evening walks down the boreen past Dan's house to the salmon-crowded inlet the locals call "the say"—perhaps no more than that, perhaps more, but men winked around there and mentioned Dan Junior for years afterward when her name came up.

That had been 18 years ago. The local talk about Dan Junior now took a different, more dire direction. Even in the ten years since I had last seen him, much had changed. I had heard that he was in a bad way, wasted by arthritis. "He's not able to lift the bottle of porter in his hand, the poor man," one of my uncles told me.

Donal and Michael had long since gone to England and left their father for a time quite alone with his house and farm. But Michael had come home, with an English wife and the beginnings of a family and, for whatever reason, the wife's mother and father, also native English. With skills he had learned abroad and the father-in-law's help Michael built two houses down the hill from his father and resettled the land while the wives planted flowers in the dooryards.

Michael was the son I didn't know, the one my memory, imperfect or prejudiced as it may be, records as having been cold, even haughty. I have thought this in part because Donal was the opposite, yet was there something about Donal I missed? Was there distance between him and his father? They seldom made their visits side-by-side to the Sullivan house. Michael seemed independent, but was Donal independent without seeming so, his sensitivity breeding withdrawal from his family? It was, in any case, Michael who came back, and gave more than comfort to his father in his fast-declining years—gave him a sort of life. Donal, after the first few years following his going, never came back, not even to visit. No one outside the family, if anyone within it, knew where Donal was.

And his father was an old, dying man. We walked up to him.

"Do you remember this lad?" my uncle Eugene asked.

"I do, give me a minute," Dan said. He was shrunken and bent, grey and wan in an old shirt and soiled pajama bottoms and slippers.

"Robert Murphy from New York," Euge said.

"Ah, yes, I heard you were over, boy."

I extended my hand, thinking of that mournful valediction two decades past.

"Oh, I'm not able to take your hand," he protested, "I'm not able to take it."

It was a reddish, almost purple, thing, at once withered and swollen, almost useless and surely painful.

"I'm barely able to hold a fag in that hand," he said.

Behind us in the fine afternoon the daughter-in-law, an ample young woman in dungarees, rubbed wash in a basin; a round, ruddy child of ten or twelve months played in a pram beside her. Euge called hello to her, and I waved.

"Will ye take a drop of porter?" Dan asked.

"We won't say no," said Euge—a stock answer.

We followed him inside, stepping onto the same hard floor I remembered, sat on a wooden bench and watched with concern his attempt to produce and open three bottles of Guinness. He proved able to get them out of the press and to bring an opener for us to finish the job. He was able, too, to lift the bottle in his hand. My uncle's report was not accurate.

He pointed out to us how he could handle the bottle. "If I grab it like this, you see," he explained, pinching the neck in the crook of his thumb, "I can manage it all right."

We drank. "How is your mother?" he asked me.

I told him that she was good, that she stayed much the same.

"And your sister that was here—last year, was it?"

"Kitty. Yes, that was last year. She's fine, thanks, plenty busy with a large family."

"Do you remember Mona?" I asked him. That was the sister I was there with the first time.

"I do, of course. Didn't she marry that ginger-haired fella—what's that his name is?—Gerard?"

"She did. They have two beautiful children, both redheads."

"They would be," he said, nodding in his way of first raising, then dropping his head.

He sat bent toward the floor, his face turning to me to ask these things. He turned once more.

"And Mary Kelly? How is Mary Kelly?"

"Mary Kelly?" I repeated. What could I say about Mary Kelly? She was a sweet, nervous woman whom I sometimes met in the laundromat or the supermarket back home and guiltily promised to go up and visit her and her mother and invalid sister. I thought of what was most significant to me about Mary Kelly.

"She never married, you know," I said.

He knew. "No, she didn't. 'Tis a pity."

The chorus of an Irish song, usually rendered with deceptive jollity, came to me: "Give me any man atall who will take me out of pity./ Oh, dear me,/ How would it be/ If I died an old maid in the garret?"

Euge looked out the door. "Isn't it a grand view from here?" he said. In durable sunshine that had been rare this summer the road dipped toward a wide brown bog where men were cutting turf for the winter. Behind them rose the dappled green Kerry mountains.

"It certainly is," I said.

659

Dan, as they say there, "took no notice" of this interchange. The view was not a topic to him. He asked about Paddy Harry, whom I knew in America, and talked about the circumstances under which he left Ireland and a wife and two sons half a century ago. When the wife died, it had been 20 years since Paddy had seen her. It was nearly nine years now since he'd seen the one son still living.

"You don't see Donal any more?" I asked Dan.

"No, boy, we don't see Donal atall."

I didn't ask, but it was said that Michael had set aside land for his brother, should he return. I wondered if Donal were in jail.

We had other visits to make while the weather was fine, so we drained our stout and took leave. I said I hoped to come back before I went home, but I knew that wasn't likely, and I never did.

Nor, in the end, could I have. A week later, Eugene watched an ambulance pass and re-marked, "That's going for Dan Junior, now, I'm sure of it." I pictured again the ambulance taking his wife to Killarney, during the night, long before I knew him.

"It's a good job you saw him when you did," Euge said.

Robert Murphy, a native of Brooklyn, is a freelance writer.

The Future Revisited

THOMAS M. QUINN

"Parochialism is universal," wrote the poet
Patrick Kavanagh, "it deals with fundamentals."
With that in mind, I returned one Sunday to hear
mass in a South Bronx neighborhood that had
been at the center of an Irish-American world I
once expected to inherit. My mother had been
born there in a tenement that still stands—abandoned and roofless now. My father's first law office, a few blocks away, was a shattered pile of
bricks. For three generations these streets and
playgrounds and bars and churches had comprised my family's share of America. Yet we had
left hardly a trace.

The neighborhood itself seemed to be disap-
pearing, as if the clock was now running backwards and history occurring in reverse. Old pos-
ters, advertising breweries and stores long
defunct, reappeared on the sides of buildings, the
adjoining structures now demolished; a single
tenement, robbed of its neighbors, stood in an
open lot, much as it must have appeared sixty or
seventy years ago; a row of old brownstones re-
claimed their nineteenth-century setting, the
taller buildings that once surrounded them reduced to great heaps of rubble.

Foremost in this stark rearrangement were the
churches, which took on a new prominence in the
opening spaces. Some appeared almost medieval
in the way they dominated the area around them;

others seemed like beached whales, grey and forlorn. Yet they were all still in use, the last point of functional contact between the people who built them and the people who used them. And if the Irish were no longer physically present, their names remained in the stained glass and brass plates that announced the generosity of the O'Hanlons, the Conroys, the McMahons, et al.

This Sunday morning the congregation half filled the church, a shadow of what I remembered from my childhood, when it took five or six masses to contain the parishioners of a parish like this. Outside, the periodic advance and retreat of sirens occasionally drowned out the priest, his Spanish so reminiscent of the old Latin rite. The celebrant was an Irish-American, like myself a product of the pre-Vatican II Church. His sermon was far above the usual Sunday rehash: brief, impassioned, close to the Gospel.

I wandered back after mass to talk to him, and to ask him how, and if, he had weathered the passage from the old cultural matrix into this world.

Thirty years ago, in the heyday of the Bronx, he would have been part of one of the nation's great ecclesiastical establishments. The Bronx's 70 parishes, 72 Catholic schools, 12 Catholic high schools, two Catholic colleges and a Catholic university were all prospering, and the president of Fordham University, Robert I. Gannon, S.J., could remark (only half in jest) that the Jesuits need never fear for the location of their school, since "we could predict with moral certainty that the neighborhood would always be, exclusively, in fact, Irish."

Behind that impressive ecclesiastical machine

was an equally impressive political one. Ed Flynn and his successor, Charlie Buckley, ran the most powerful Democratic organization in the state, perhaps in the country, and stood as benevolent secular allies to their church. Now, however, the power and the glory were gone. The South Bronx was less a place than the name of a disease that was rotting away vast sections of America's older cities.

I imagined our talk would be a private sharing of the past in which we two psychic refugees would discuss the loss of that unity of culture and religion that had formed us. But he was baffled from the start. I sat there with my theories and histories and realized I was an interloper. He belonged where he was. His voice resonated with the particular stresses and rhythms of Puerto Rican English. He had the vaguest memories of twenty years ago, when he began as a curate in a Bronx-Irish parish. Since then he had been here, in this culture, and he was at home. He could share neither my doubts nor my detached observations.

I was depressed at first. This was not the priest of my fantasies, neither an Irish prophet among the new poor nor a stranger struggling to adjust to an alien environment. He was quiet, reserved, polite but distant, a bit bemused, I think, with my presence. This was where he lived, and he was totally caught up in the day-to-day drama of the people's lives he shared.

In the weeks that followed I visited several other parishes in the area and was left with the same impression: a clergy still mostly Irish was working patiently and hard to preach the Gospel and create a sense that this was not just a neighborhood in extremis, of interest only to social scientists, but a place where people lived and worked and planned a better future.

In its passing, the old Irish-Catholic monolith, stripped of its civil and religious trappings, was experiencing its finest hour. These Irish-American priests and sisters and brothers, like their predecessors of a millennium before, the Irish monks who bridged two cultures and planted the seeds of a new moral order in Northern Europe, were shedding their cultural identity to help leaven the faith of those with whom they lived and worshipped.

I have come to believe that their road, in one form or another, must be travelled by the generation of Irish-American Catholics that is leaving behind forever the ethnic enclaves that supported and nourished their Catholicism. We are travelling away from the ties of a distinct, self-contained tradition into a countryside of suburbs and subdivisions, where Catholicism is no longer the center nor even a part of a separate cultural identity.

Our past is ceasing to matter. White ethnic Catholics are no longer suspect to the rest of America, and this loss of separateness might provide us with the opportunity of the priests and nuns working in the South Bronx. Finally entering the American mainstream, where the established religion seems to be that of the Free Market (a faith based on Malthus and Darwin), where conscience often seems identical with self-interest, we will decide the legacy of the immigrant Church.

Perhaps we can speak with a voice that incorporates the best of that past, that makes, say, the stubborn spirituality of the Irish a part of our collective identity, refusing to accept quietly a system of values where life and the environment are consumed and discarded, like the Bronx—no deposit, no return.

Thomas M. Quinn, a native of the Bronx, is a freelance writer.

Irish I

SHAUN O'CONNELL

WHEN HE FINALLY TRIED TO LEAVE HOME, SO THE FAMILY
story goes, my father was called back to the house. Though
that was half a century ago, I can still see him standing there,
on a walk outside the family home, like a supplicant before a
station of the cross—his mother on the step above him, looking
down on her Scott Fitzgerald-like groomed and doomed
youngest going off into the wider world to be a chauffeur for
"high-ups." His leather bags would have been propped, erect
and waiting; the creases in his trousers (white duck, perhaps)
a sharp, unbroken line; the high-ups' sleek car humming, while
my father came back and bowed his head, his center-parted
hair fixed, like his rigid jaw. His mother sprinkled him with
holy water and, through her own holy tears, said "God bless
and keep you."

I suppose he didn't cry then, proud and stiff as he was,
though I can tell you he learned to cry later. But then he
would have been embarrassed, anxious to be off, perhaps
secretly afraid that if he didn't leave at just that moment he
would never leave at all. As it turned out, God didn't bless
and keep him so well as did his Irish family. I think now that
it was all so real to him—his mother, his family, the holy water
—that no matter how far he went, he never really left home.

Elizabeth Savage's fine novel about Irish-American life, *A*

Good Confession, is about a time, my father's time, when "people used to belong." But things fall apart: "in our time families are spun apart as by centrifuge." Gone are the days of that novel, that time, all the *nevermore* implied when Savage's narrator says "we used to be a big family, rife with feuds and brief indignations and very long on love."

They shared that then, my father, his three older brothers and two older sisters; they moved through dooms of love—ties that bound them in but also made them safe in themselves—that I can only guess at, hear about, read about. Fragments of family history through archeological reconstruction, through literary divination.

Like characters in *A Good Confession*, they shared a common language, a communion cup from which they all drank and tasted each other. Little pitchers indeed have big ears: I heard all I could. "Nobody says 'thanks be to God' unless they are one of us." But that's dying too, that muffled yet lyrical talk. As they would say, it's as scarce as hen's teeth. Over a Navy Grog in the bar of "Trader Vic's," my mind wandering away from a friend's monologue on the latest form of infidelity, I wonder: what else did they say?

Seamus Heaney reads his poetry at Boston University; chunky and graceful, precise and lyrical, he chants of bogs in the back of beyond. Ulsterman, on his way back from Berkeley to his new home in the Irish Republic in the Wicklow hills, Heaney reads of Irish excavations into the underworld in "Digging": "Between my finger and my thumb/The squat pen rests; snug as a gun." Under his window, his father spades in real ground, after the fashion of *his* father who "cut more turf in a day/Than any other man on Toner's bog." Heaney, the poet, will not dig in the old Irish ways.

> Between my finger and my thumb
> The squat pen rests.
> I'll dig with it.

We each dig with what implements we have: perhaps even a typewriter can loosen chips and bits of lost times, father and grandfather times, gone times, Irish times.

After the reading, Heaney's reception was hosted by Helen Hennessy Vendler, astute and gracious scholar of all things poetic: her "Hennessy" side gave us *Yeat's Vision and the Later Plays*. She introduces me to Heaney and, in a sometime Irish way, overgenerously praises my critical prose. Heaney, more intrigued by my name, says "Sean O'Connell is a grand Derry cornerback." I understand, tell him my father borrowed my name—down to its phonetical, Anglicized spelling—from a Harvard half-back of the '20's. My father's grandfather, like Heaney's, may have dug turf, but when it came time to name his son, my father reached beyond his grasp, like Fitzgerald's Gatsby, for elusive, classy glory—a Harvard half-back.

My grandfather couldn't read. In his last years, when I knew him, he *heard* of the wider world as he sat beside a Philco radio shaped like a Norman church. My father, in his last years, spent some time in a dreary flat amidst the smelly clutter of yellowing white shirts, smoking Luckies, reading hundreds of mysteries and Westerns, drinking straight rye. After four years of perfecting my skill at straight pool and billiards, I read all the right books and, eventually, went to Harvard. By then my father was dead, so he was spared vicarious pride and ultimate disillusionment. For the half-back and his shimmering nimbus were gone and I hated that invidious institution. But that is another story.

Heaney and I talked about all this as best we could amidst the boozy bluster of a cocktail party. Clearly there was more to say between this displaced Ulsterman poet and this third generation Irish-American; we would talk again in the Wicklow hills.

Years ago, when I first crossed the sea to Ireland, it seemed a magically elusive country, but, after a time, I came to understand that it was solid enough, a hard place which could draw blood. Scudding, wind-maddened clouds above—"days of dappled seaborne clouds," says Joyce—and harsh, jutting rocks lining fields and roads below. First we were in flux, sprung free from American ritual—all blessedly behind. In Ireland we drove on the left, from one unknown to another. In that state of nearly purposeless motion—heightened by the heady sensation of having lifted aloft through a blank, sleepless night— we came upon Yeat's tower (between Shannon and Galway, just outside Gort), set deep in the midst of almost tropical foliage, dead quiet and eerie.

> Under my window-ledge the waters race,
> Otters below and moor-hens on the top,
> Run for a mile undimmed in Heaven's face
> Then darkening through 'dark' Raftery's 'cellar'drop,
> Run underground, rise in a rocky place
> In Coole demesne, and there to finish up
> Spread to a lake and drop into a hole.
> What's water but the generated soul?

So said Yeats, describing the ways in which moving things dissolve and vanish before your touch in this land where, as Richard Weber (another poet) said, "reality doesn't exist."

After we left Ballylee, we went to Coole Park, where, of course, Lady Gregory's manor had long since dissolved into ruins. No memorial for the gracious lady who helped Yeats and so many other Irish writers, who helped establish the Abbey Theater, who thanked "God that she has been able to work so long, and above all that anything she has done that is worth the doing has been in Ireland and through Ireland and for Ireland's sake." Amidst the wind-swirled greenery we tried to find "the brimming water among the stones" from which Yeats saw nine-and-fifty wild swans ascend, but, as we were told by the whimsical Irishman (who was painting tar upon a tree), the pond "comes and goes," was nowhere to be found at that time of year.

Of course, Yeats wrote of this flux from the heavy solidity of a 700 year old tower—what was he walling out?—a thick, angular fortification. Stairs wind up and up, ever narrowing; the cold, rough walls close in upon you as you ascend, almost squeezing you back from the roof which, however, gives you a misty view of the surrounding countryside: more wind-whipped greenery. Later we would go to that other writer's fortification, Joyce's tower in Sandycove, just south of Dublin, only to find that it was closed for repairs. McGrail, my friend, and I climbed the six-foot wall surrounding the tower, managed to get up the outer stairway where we found the key missing, the door locked, just as Stephen found it at one point in *Ulysses*.

Later we went to Howth, where we could see it all—from Ireland's Eye in the north, down the coast to Bray Head in the south, over to the Wicklow hills in the southwest, down onto dear dirty Dublin. In simultaneous flux: clouds rolling, dappling the light, wind making us feel we were about to topple over the high cliffs onto the rocks below, gulls wheeling and reeling *beneath* us, between us and the choppy sea which scaled from white through snot-green to royal blue, all the way to purple-black. From there—what Joyce called the breast of Ireland, where Molly and Bloom made love—we could look across the bay to Dun Laoghaire, on down to Sandycove, to the rocky "40 feet" (the place where men come to swim naked at all hours of the day and night), to Joyce's tower, where McGrail and I had talked late, drank beer and wondered about the meaning of many things. It's that kind of land: fact dissolves into symbol. What's water but the generated soul? A place where imagination and reality cohere.

When I was invited to speak before the Friendly Sons of Saint Patrick on Irish-American fiction, I broke out with hives of ambivalence. As an Irish-American and an Associate Professor of English at the University of Massachusetts in Boston, specializing in the novel, my credentials were in order and, after fifteen years of lecturing on fiction before variously sized and composed groups, I was hardly seized with the anxieties of the *ingénue*. Still, I was ambivalent. Perhaps I took too seriously a young, Irish lawyer's warning: most would come to hear me praise my subject, not bury it. But that would be their problem; my problem was that I was not personally inclined to do a Bing Crosby before this group of genial but, I suspected, overly-pious Irish-Americans: I just could not bring off the lecturing equivalent of "Galway Bay." Nor did I think there was that much to sing about; my "song," such as it would be, had to be cheaper, more tawdry. That is, I had to note that something had gone wrong during the passage from Ireland to America to strike so many eloquent Irishmen literarily dumb in their new world.

Committed to this perverse course of disappointing my kind hosts—I still feel guilty about it—I noted, in my opening remarks, that the greatest Irish-American novelist, Henry James, wholly suppressed his Irish lineage; in 1881, writing from London's Reform Club, James told his mother this about "the abominable Irish": "there are surely bad races and good races, just as there are bad people and good people, and the Irish belong to the category of impossible." So much for ethnic loyalty! James, who finally became a British subject, was recently plaqued in Westminster Abbey! Of course, there were Scott Fitzgerald, John O'Hara and James Farrell, those writers William Shannon makes great claims for in *The American Irish;* however, I suggested, even were we to grant the justice of Shannon's chauvinistic claims for these writers' high individual achievements, these few hardly constitute an impressive ethnic contribution in comparison, say, with the qualitative proliferation of Jewish-American fiction. Some audience uneasiness at that!

But, finally, the audience was more generous than I; here and there they cocked an eye—what's this lad up to?—but after I had given them the back o' me hand in my talk, they held out to me their own open, forgiving hands. Prodigal sons, apostates, hand-biters—these are nothing new to the Irish.

Of course, the young lawyer and his friends loved what I said. Like me, third generation institutional hustlers and professionals, they had had it up to here with all that did-your-

671

mother-come-from-Ireland guff and blarney. They eased me out of the prim lecture room of the Women's City Club of Boston—a neatly ironic setting for the celebration-damnation of the Irish-American literary experience—and trotted me off to a proper bar: the (compounding ironies) "Library Lounge" of the Parker House, where the Irish elite meet to eat and drink in Boston. These young lawyers, politicos, architects and promoters were furious at the club's old guard pushing for Pat O'Brien as recipient of their man of the year award; these young turks, or micks, had proposed a Harvard Irish scholar, but had been rejected. So my speech, to the extent that it ticked off a few old-time shamrockers, was simply grand.

We are told now that the Irish, as an ethnic group, do quite well by themselves in America; only the Jews outdistance the Irish in money and status. At the third round of drinks I could believe it. There we were: a former Kennedy aide, a water-front property entrepreneur, a prize-winning architect—doctorates and other degrees galore. We'd come a long way from our grandfather's Tipperary, or Mayo, or Galway, or Cork. The days of forelock tugging, of "Irish Need Not Apply," of potted Paddys—those days were over and done with. Begod, we were successful Americans!

Only, I wondered as we moved into the fifth round of drinks, how come we all had those thick-mick names, passed them along to our own children and took such savage joy in being together? How come, if we were so free of our heritage, we took such ethnically characteristic delight in backstabbing absent Irishmen? How come, if we were all so damn successful, so free of old-time stereotypes, so enlightened—how come we were booming it up in a dark Irish bar, drinking ourselves silly in the middle of a week-day afternoon? Answer me that one, I asked myself.

When I visited McGrail at the drunk farm in New Hampshire, he was woozy from thorazine and Alcoholics Anonymous rhetoric. Slumping, drifting, out of focus and phase, he beckoned me out into the drizzle and wet grass. He lapsed into his Aer Lingus brogue. "A soft day," he said. We walked down to a lake and stared into the tired, grey water and looked across to the humped hills. "Galway," he said. "You remember?" I remembered, but that, as they say, was in another country, before my friend, my brother of sorts, went round the bend on booze and women, putting at risk his career, his marriage, his children, his friends' loyalties. But I remembered. Fitzgerald said "life is a state of occasionally relieved unhappiness," an Irishman's metaphysic. Now that my friend was so unhappy, I remembered the rare occasions on which he found relief. For this relief, as Hamlet said, much thanks.

I remember, too, my father asleep on the lawn, the morning after a boozy bout. After my mother died, he left me with his older sister and her Yankee husband, then he went to Ireland to find work and forgetfulness. On his way home the Germans sank his boat. Finally home, he enlisted for the "duration." In the Fiji Islands as a Seabee, he was shot-up with specific diseases and obscure intensities. In his rare visits he was full of fear and trembling—holding me and crying, telling me not to practice "White Christmas" on the piano because Tokyo Rose played it all the time, begging me to remember my mother whom I had forgotten. He would splurge, taking me to Red Sox games and movies; but, to get himself through these days, he would nip off for a shot or two from time to time; then he would take me home to my aunt, duck out to the Cozy Cafe where he would drink himself numb and get sent "home" in a cab. Often he would sleep it off on the lawn.

I once interviewed a famous Southern novelist at his summer home on Martha's Vineyard, gathering material for an essay. Courtly and gracious, we talked all day and far into the night. Toward dawn, drinking gin and looking out across his blue Vineyard Haven lawn, I think we talked about the last page of *The Great Gatsby*, Fitzgerald's morose, Irish lyricism. "He had come a long way to this blue lawn, and his dream must have seemed so close that he could hardly fail to grasp it.

He did not know that it was already behind him . . ." I *think* that's what we talked about, but I might be imagining that that was what we *should* have talked about. The next morning, hung over and trying to get down some coffee, I found I had no notes, no clear recollection of what was said and not said. What's liquor but the degenerated soul?

This is Catholic:

> "Holy Mary, Mother of God, pray for us sinners, now and at the hour of our death," is the prayer of Notre Dame. Now and at the hour of our death are seen as one. The fruit of the Virgin's womb, even in the womb, hangs already *sub specie aeternitatis* upon the cross. We who are living are already, in God's eyes, dead; and so the most perfect deeds we are to achieve in life may already, like an aging athlete's, be behind us.
>
> —from Michael Noval's *The Joy of Sports*

This in Irish:

> If you've been reared to believe in the Mother of Mercy and stop to think about how many things require her mercy, you learn to steady your coffee cup with your thumb so it won't rattle.
>
> —from Elizabeth Savage's *A Good Confession*

My Irishness is elliptical, tangential, fragmentary. I hear only hints of a richly-interwoven family history; at family funerals I wonder at what I've missed. Again and again, I have gone back to the old country, but my eye is too dazzled by surface; I miss substance. Mostly I apprehend my Irishness in a way which would have mystified my grandfather: I *read* about it.

In *The Irish* Thomas J. O'Hanlon—an Irishman transformed into a *Fortune* editor—sees Innisfail (Island of Destiny) stuck between a stone and a hard place. Irishmen stone one another in Ulster, get stoned on drugs and stout to relieve the anxieties of sexual and religious repression, abandon their stone-framed fields and emigrate. "The Irish personality," says O'Hanlon,

674

"is mercurial, moving from serene optimism to extreme pessimism like a cloud passing over the sun." Irish mist and staying stoned.

When I reviewed John McGahern's novel, *The Leavetaking*, for *The Boston Globe*, I was attacked in a Letter to the Editor by a South-Boston, Irish M.D. I had noted that the Irish Republic is still a land of systematic literary repression. Though once-banned writers (Joyce, O'Casey) are now celebrated in Ireland—now that they are safely dead and gone —troublesome young writers, like McGahern, are throttled in the hands of church and state. The good doctor defended literary suppression as a means of protecting citizens from awareness of all things illegal and immoral. Of course, I, like most Irishmen, never avoid a haggle; here is the conclusion to my *Globe* reply to the doctor:

> In heavy irony, Dr. Donovan hopes that Ireland will join global perversity, will reach a stage of "appreciation for the mental processes of true liberals, such as Shaun—not Sean is it?—O'Connell, John McGahern and *The Boston Globe*." I know he means nothing of the kind, but I hope Dr. Donovan reads McGahern's novel, continues to read me in the *Globe* and senses the sympathetic intention of this letter, though I could never go so far as to hope that two Irishmen could ever agree about anything. Note to Dr. Donovan: it is Shaun (not Sean)—a perfectly decent Irish name.

The Boston Globe, already out of favor with the Boston Irish community over its support of court-ordered busing to achieve school integration, did not print my rebuttal!

However, my favorite recent work on Irishness took a different tack into the wind. In *I Am Of Ireland*, Richard Howard Brown tells how he *chose* to be Irish. Sick of American reality—the predictable pattern of growing family, mortgaged home, dull work—he elected to identify himself with that patchy, poxed land 3000 miles away. He knew he was "slightly foolish," seeking an Irish grail at a time when, as Yeats said, "romantic Ireland's dead and gone," but he did it;

he became involved in the Trouble; he (again Yeats) "resigned his part in the casual comedy" and became "transformed utterly." He knows that his Ireland may not be the Ireland of others and he realizes "that a native land can exist in the mind, be an idea, a fantasy," but his insistent involvement makes the "fantasy" real. He becomes that on which he meditates—Irish.

My aunt Ann and uncle Bill were being feted at a tacky suburban restaurant; it was their 50th wedding anniversary. A fairly small group, eight or ten tables clustered at one end of a ballroom. Immediate family at the head table, golden grandchildren at another, old friends at another, extended family scattered randomly at the rest. A four-piece group mysteriously played Polish polkas.

I was on the extreme pessimism swing of O'Hanlon's mercurial Irish personality range. Suffering from a heavy spring cold, I fumbled with tissues and drank gin to clear my head. One cousin at my table talked about the good old days when there was real discipline, when she was a stern matron at a girls' reformatory. A pilot passed around lurid photos of a plane crash; his wife, another cousin, talked about hating to be alone, how she drank and kept pet squirrels and lizards. I got another drink.

At the cutting of the cake, my uncle Bill, enfeebled and befuddled by age and illness, had a lovely moment of clarification: suddenly he knew where he was and what was expected of him. He fed his wife a piece of cake, pulled her into his arms and did three turns around the floor. Magically, the Polish polka group managed a version of "When Irish Eyes Are Smiling." Uncle Bill whooped, did a bit of a jig, and reeled us into his joy.

Late in the party I talked with Kay. This itself was something, for I had spent many years avoiding any talk with Kay. I first met her just after WWII; she lived down the hall from my father during his yellowing shirts, Luckies, rye and Westerns phase. Clearly there was something between them;

676

I, a moral lad, disapproved. Later they married; then he killed himself. Somehow I always associated her with that sadness, so, for more than twenty years, I had not talked much with Kay.

But here I now was, a head full of spring cold and gin, about the same age my father had been when he appeared to take me off to Red Sox games, to later get drunk and sleep it off on my aunt's lawn. Here was Kay, full of years, small prides—she was good, she said, at finding money on the side-walk—and long loyalties. She had, after all, like me, loved my father. Even for Irishmen, I belatedly realized, there must be a statute of limitations on ill-founded grudges!

She talked of my father as a young man, how handsome and courtly he was. This did not surprise me, for even I could remember the ways my father generated affection from men and love from women. The men with whom he played golf, shot pool, told stories, drank. The women: his sainted mother, of course; my mother; Kathleen—an Irish maid who never forgot him, who never married, who always loved me, after whom I named by daughter—and, last, Kay. But I was stunned that Kay had known my father as a young man, for I had assumed that she had gathered him into herself only when he was busted-up and broken down after WWII.

"Oh, yes. When I came from Buffalo to Boston in the '20's, we were great together," Kay said.

Then she said *it*. Jesuit-trained James Joyce would call it an *epiphany*. That thing said, that still moment in time when mist lifts and you can see what had been obscured, when it all hangs together before you—sole and whole—when, once heard or seen, you are not what you were before.

"In 1926.we wanted to get married, but your father asked me to wait. He couldn't bring himself to marry while his mother was alive."

There it was. The old high way of Irish love, Irish families, Irish repressions, Irish secrets. I kissed Kay, finally, promised to see her again, soon and often. For at that point I too had chosen to resist no longer. I was, after all the fragmentation and ambivalence, as Irish as Paddy's pig; the map of Ireland, as they say, is written on my face. Like others, I too was of Ireland, maybe especially in my roundabout approach, my efforts to fight it off. That, I then saw, was what it had all been about—my father, my Irish poets, my books, my lectures, my flying visits to Erin, my blood-brother Irish friends. "Thanks be to God, we finally got together," Kay added. I understood and did some thanking of my own.

Professor O'Connell is self-characterized.

The Awakening

TIMOTHY DRISCOLL

I think I was ten or eleven before I realized I was living in America. But thanks to Sister Agnes Wilfred, the sixth grade teacher at Our Lady of Petpetual Help Grammar School in the Bay Ridge section of Brooklyn, my awakening was pleasant. She also provided the solution to my first identity crisis. But more about that later.

I am the child of a "mixed marriage"—my father came from Cork and my mother from the adjoining county, Waterford. The root cause of my identity problem was my father's total lack of modesty on the subject of his origins. After supper, he would often wax eloquent on "the glories of Cork" or the greatness of Mike Quill and the TWU. With Christy Ring, the barefooted "Babe Ruth of Irish Hurling," and Tom Barry, West Cork's legendary IRA leader, it seemed that Cork had won every all-Ireland Hurling Championship since the beginning of time. Moreover, to hear him tell it, "Rebel Cork" had singlehandedly defeated the Black and Tans with little or no assistance from the rest of Ireland.

Now my mother usually held her peace until the conclusion when my father, with a wink, would draw his uncomprehending brood into his confidence, "You know, your mother made quite a step up in the world when she married a man from Cork." This would invariably elicit a rhetorical question-statement from my

679

mother, "If Cork people are so great; you'll notice they never marry *one of their own.*" My mother would often add that Waterford people were quiet and civilized unlike Corkonians—a not-so-subtle reference to rowdy elements on the Driscoll side.

Although my father was the ultimate power—and the disciplinarian of last resort—mother was the day to day reality of power. There was a general acceptance of the view that the nurturing of children, like pregnancy, was beyond the comprehension of the male. So my sister and I retained a studious neutrality on the subject of origin.

At the age of eight, I received permission to "play in the street." This was also my first indication that I was not living in Ireland. For permission was granted with a stern warning, "Don't get into trouble because they'll blame it on the foreigners." I didn't know what foreigners meant but I knew who "they" were: *the Sullivan family*. Since they were the only parents on the block born in America, they had acquired all the qualities of a Brahmin class. Their son and my contemporary, John Barry Sullivan, also seemed to be a cut above the rest of us. He knew his way not only around the block but beyond. Besides, young Sullivan had a "girlfriend." This struck me as strange since he seemed normal in every other way. I soon found out the reason for this aberration.

Soon after my arrival on the street scene, John invited me to "saddle up" and meet in his areaway at 7 the following Thursday evening. Using altar boy practice as an excuse, I galloped down the street that night to my rendezvous. There was John Sullivan and several of the gang. At a signal from John we mounted "our horses" and sped down to the end of the block. We arrived at the backdoor of *Pop's Bar and Grill*. Pop was not only the father of John's girlfriend but the owner of the only TV on 58th Street. For the next half hour we gave our undivided attention to the exploits of the Lone Ranger and Tonto.

This ritual continued for several months until one evening Father McCann passed by to make his annual collection from the owner for the Holy Name Society. That Sunday, at the Holy Name Communion Breakfast, he gently suggested to Mr. Sullivan that it was but a short step from the backroom to the bar.

When our parents found out about the "altar boy practice," they were in a rage. With "typical American ingenuity" Mr. Sullivan decided to go out and buy a TV for his family. We were soon spending more free time at John's house than at home. Our parents were mortified—and determined not to be outdone by the likes of the Sullivans. And despite what any other historian of the period will tell you, that is how TV came to 58th Street.

My interest in TV was westerns but its main impact on me was a certain cultural shock. Take, for example, the question of food. With shock I watched a TV mother punish her child by sending him to bed without supper. Mother of God. In my family, food in the refrigerator and whiskey in the closet were veritable status symbols. Social psychologists might call it "the Post Famine Syndrome" but the one thing you did not do in my house was *not eat*. In fact, the only avenue of protest my sister and I had was to threaten a hunger strike at supper. This produced total disbelief and consternation among our elders. And one time, when it looked as if our determination would overcome our hunger pangs, my mother felt compelled to force feed us. Eating was no joke.

The food issue also dramatically changed my perceptions of Ireland. For "Ireland" was increasingly becoming a cudgel, a form of social control. The refusal to eat or a complaint about food would bring the following re-

681

joinder: "Shame on you—a young boy in Ireland would think he was king to set down to a meal like this!" Or, after I "became an American" and had the temerity to complain about a new pair of shoes: "I'll send them to your cousins, *they'll appreciate them.*"

Is it any wonder that even today an Irish-American can never close his wallet to an appeal from Ireland. I must tell you that when I finally visited Ireland and found the prosperous modern country in which my relatives shared, it was both a surprise and a sheer relief. But I must also admit my disappointment with "the West." Since my weekends in Brooklyn always seemed to be round of benefit dances for priests from Mayo, I half expected to find the whole country cluttered with churches on the scale of St. Patrick's Cathedral.

The arrival of TV in my home also sparked the flames of ambition. Although I hadn't thought much about my future, I had toyed with the idea of becoming a cowboy. This did not exactly excite my mother who tended to view myself and the other urban cowboys on 58th Street as descendants of "tinkers in the old country."

But I soon found a new passion: baseball, or its environmental child, stickball. Following the Dodgers on TV, I decided to replace Pee Wee Reese when I grew up. Since I was the smallest fellow on the block, I felt eminently qualified.

However, my mother was no more enthusiastic about baseball than she was about life on the range. Her chance came one rainy Saturday afternoon when our stickball game was washed out and warnings of a hurricane put the local Loews Alpine out of the question. She suggested I read a good book. I think she hoped that an interest in learning might bloom into a vocation: the desire of every Irish mother. I consented. The book was Dan Breen's *My Fight for Irish Freedom*. The style was simple and to the point. Dan Breen became my first hero.

However, the book was more inclined to inspire young men to overthrow colonial rule—as it did in Asia and Africa—than to enter the seminary.

But whatever orientation problems individuals like myself were facing it was nothing compared to the problems faced by those coming here. My sister and I knew something big was about to happen. After we were sent to bed, my father and mother held long and serious discussions in the kitchen. Finally, my mother told us: "Your father has decided to 'bring out' my youngest sister." My Aunt Bridget was soon "situated" with a family on Shore Road.

Her first culture shock came soon after. Arriving home from work, she found my father in bed at the astounding hour of 5 PM and myself crumpled on the living room floor bathed in tears. Fearing some family disaster, she rushed into the kitchen to find my mother quietly sipping tea. My mother shrugged, "In this country, they are mad about baseball. The Dodgers just lost the World Series." To see grown men driven to bed in the early afternoon and young children reduced to tears stimulated her curiosity. The following spring she became my chaperone to the world beyond: Ebbets Field. This face to face confrontation only increased her mystification. I thought I was educating her until I overheard her comment to my mother on the silliness of young adults fighting over a pillow in the middle of a field—a reference, I suspected, to a disputed steal of second base that afternoon.

Well, I better get down to business. I have not mentioned school until now for a good reason: I hated it. Next to my first day in basic training, my entrance into kindergarten was the most traumatic moment in my life. On that fateful day, we were escorted by our mothers to the door where we were placed in the charge of Sister Agnes Brendan. As we waited to take our seats, you could smell the fear in the silence. Suddenly, Bernie Walsh, in tears, bolted for the door and freedom. Sister Agnes Brendan was soon in hot pursuit screaming at the mothers in the entrance to stop him. Some minutes later Bernie was dragged across the floor by his belt to Sister's desk. A rope was procured and Bernie was lashed to his seat for the rest of the day. I knew then there was no escape. Nor could I run to my mother for comfort. It seems Sister Agnes came from County Sligo. My mother had a sister in Sligo. I was told that I had to be an especially good boy—or Sister might write to my aunt in Sligo.

In the fourth grade, my father joined the conspiracy. Somewhat taken back by "one of those American parents" disagreeing with the sister's low estimation of her son, he volunteered the following advice on Parent-Teachers day, "Feel free to give him (me) a good kick anytime, Sister."

The sixth grade did not start auspiciously either. Realizing that she was dealing with a group of "potential Studs Lonigans," Sister Agnes Wilfred pointed out that although she had a withered right arm, God had transferred all its strength to her left and she would be more than happy to knock any of us clear across the room, out the window, and on to the sidewalk two stories down. Moreover, she pointed out that the superior had picked her to teach us because of an interesting item on her resumé—she had been a policewoman before she joined the convent.

Having established her authority, she proceeded to teach American History, among other subjects. Today there are many sophisticated names for what she did but the nuns had turned educating the children of immigrants into an art form long before educational theorists even started writing about the process.

We were indeed an ethnic mix. Sister seized the common denominator: our Catholicism. It was quite obvious "we " were all over the New World—French Catholics in Canada, Spanish Catholics in South America, Florida, and California. Of course, there was a small settlement of English in Plymouth, Massachusetts—for whom, I must confess, I had a secret admiration. After what the Indians did to the Jesuits, those Puritans had a lot of courage to invite them to Thanksgiving Day dinner.

But for us Irish, the early discovery of America was not exactly our finest hour. In fact, it was humiliating. Through explorations—often dangerous—of other blocks, we had learned that we were Irish. This was thanks to the Italians who were rapidly replacing the English as the national enemy. Now we had to bear the knowledge that Christopher Columbus had discovered the place where we lived.

However, our moment was at hand. As Sister pointed out, those early Americans suffered under the tyranny of English Rule. The stories of the Black and Tans cemented into our memories, we were immediately sympathetic. However, in those days there were a lot of English in the country. So, one-third of the people were against the revolution, one-third neutral, and one-third for. We knew immediately with which third the Irish were.

Sister did not disappoint us. Jeremiah O'Brien, Commodore Barry, the father of the American Navy, and General Sullivan were right up there with Washington. Not to leave the other kids out, she also noted that Washington had called upon Kosciusko from Poland and Steuben from Germany to help. Of course, Catholic France and Spain were with us. And it was also implied that the Pope, an Italian, was a secret supporter.

At the end of the lecture, I found out another amazing fact: Mountjoy was not only a place but a person. Until then, my mother, on more than one occasion, predicted that my ultimate destination might be "Mountjoy"—the Irish Sing-Sing. But Sister called upon the devil himself to verify our achievement, "As Lord Mountjoy said in the English Parliament, 'We have lost America through the Irish.' "

That afternoon, we walked out of class thinking we were here before the Indians. And we quickly assumed our role as spokesmen and standard setters for "the foreigners"—those in the class who were not of Irish parents.

At home, "becoming an American" gave me a separate identity and solved the problem of whether I was from Cork or Waterford. However that announcement at the supper table did not dent my father's Cork-bred superiority. Henceforth, I was increasingly referred to as a "narrowback." And all subsequent indications of independent thought or action at the supper table were always met with an observation to my aunt, "He's a real American, isn't he?" Nor did education ever improve my status. Once, while helping my father in the cellar, a plasterboard fell on my head. He merely shrugged, "Got a college degree, and he can't even hammer a nail." My mother, on the other hand, expressed not only admiration but, I might say, wonder at my new-found identity.

By the seventh grade, my contemporaries and I were breaking family records for educational endurance,if not achievement. But the ultimate accolade came from my aunt who asked "the young American" to help her study for the citizenship test. Soon her girlfriend joined my class. I was a "teacher" at the age of twelve. My father, however, took care of the post-citizenship training with a single sentence, "When you go in, find the Democratic line and vote straight down."

Needless to say, it all went to my head. And, despite my mother's pleasure with my acculturation, it was she who provided my ultimate downfall on the morning of St. Patrick's Day in the 7B. In my growing intellectual curiosity, I had uncovered a remarkable fact: *St. Patrick's*

Day was not a Holy Day of Obligation in America, at least not in Brooklyn. This was mind-boggling. For not only did we have a day off from school, but mother's usual ritual of dressing us up to attend the 9 o'clock Mass at OLPH was totally unnecessary.

On the morning of the great day, I remained in bed smugly observing the family preparing for Mass. When my mother finally got around to telling me to hurry up, I condescendingly explained to her that I was an American and did not have to go to Mass since it was not a holy day of obligation. For a moment she paused. Then, to the envy of Cassius Clay, her arm shot across the covers to my pajama collar lifting me clear out of bed for a face to face confrontation. "As long as you are in this house, you will go to Mass on St. Patrick's Day."

The pastor himself, Father Alyward, delivered an impassioned sermon on the sacrifices of the Irish for the faith from the time of Cromwell to his own parents. And thanking our parents for their loyalty, he expressed the hope and prayer that their children would continue the tradition.

Needless to say, I was among those who heard that sermon.

Tim Driscoll is co-author of
An Album of The Irish Americans.

My Wild Irish Mother

MARY HIGGINS CLARK

In 1967 when she was eighty, I tossed a birthday party for Mother. There were over seventy people present; my generation and hers; friends and cousins; our children; cronies from way-back years. The party started at three in the afternoon because I was sure that Mother and the other old girls would get tired early. I should have known better. Twelve hours later, I and my contemporaries sat limply in the den while Mother and her peers stood around the piano lustily singing "Sweet Molly Malone."

That night I marveled at Mother. Wearing her best beige lace dress, her silver hair framing her almost unlined face and bright blue eyes, she was obviously having the time of her life. Before that party finally ended, she had cast her cane aside, locked arms with the remaining "Bungalow Girls"—Rockaway Beach circa 1912—and led a spirited rendition of an Irish polka.

My mother, Nora, the first-generation of her family to be American born, was the second child of Bridget Kennedy Durkin and Thomas Durkin, a pair of youngsters newly arrived from County Sligo. All her life she was to personify the best of her Irish heritage—a warm and generous heart, undauntable faith in her God, unswerving allegiance to the Democratic party, heroic resiliency in trouble and always, always, an unquenchable sense of humor.

By the time Nora was thirteen, seven more children had arrived to fill the parlor-floor-and-basement apartment on East 79th Street and she went off to work. Her first job at McCreery's paid three dollars for a 48-hour week. She walked the two miles back and forth each day to save the nickel carfare and at nights went to high school and Hunter College. She worked her way up from messenger girl at McCreery's to buyer at Altman's.

She was determined that when she married she would be able to give her children everything and would have enough money saved for lifelong security. Hers was a typical Irish courtship. She and my father "kept company" for seven years and were nearly forty when they exchanged vows.

She promptly produced three children. The firstborn was Joseph. I, Mary, was next. When my younger brother arrived a few years later the doctor came into her room, looked at the baby nestled in her arms and the rosary entwined in her fingers and sighed, "I assume this one is Jesus."

He was half-serious. Mother was a devout Catholic with a pipeline to Heaven. For seventy years she received Holy Communion every First Friday. The one break in the chain occurred when she went to the hospital to have her third child. Forever after she fretted that she really had had time to make Church. After all, she'd been in the hospital a good twenty minutes before John was born. She was then 45 years old.

All her life, Mother had dreamt of owning a home of her own and she and my father bought one a few years after they were married. To Mother, Buckingham Palace, the Taj Mahal and Shangri-La were all wrapped up in that six room, brick, semi-detached dwelling in the Pelham Parkway section of the Bronx. But then the depression years set in. My father's once-flourishing Irish Pub began to lose money. Their stocks were lost in the crash; their savings dwindled to nothing. My father let one of the bartenders go and began working twenty-hour days. One morning he didn't wake up and at age 51 Mother was left with the three of us and a mortgaged house.

It was impossible to get a job. So she put her "thinking cap" on and came up with a solution. A sign, "Furnished rooms, Kitchen Privileges" was bought and tacked over the doorbell. The neighbors demurred. They didn't mind "Furnished rooms" but "kitchen privileges" stuck in their craw. Always agreeable, Mother snipped off the bottom half, thanking the Lord she hadn't wasted money on a metal sign that would have been impossible to alter.

And then began the parade of people who were to be woven into the fabric of our lives for the next five years.

There was Miss Mills, the grammar school teacher who tried valiantly to teach me the piano. I never got past "Drifting."

There were Mr. and Mrs. Fields who took the big, front bedroom for five dollars a week with the garage thrown in. They asked Mother if they could bring their dog, Buck. No dog lover, Mother asked doubtfully how big he was. Mrs. Fields made a little cupping move with her hands, a motion suitable to describe a toy poodle and reluctantly Mother agreed that their pet could join our establishment.

Buck was a wild-eyed boxer. He had the instincts of an attack dog and we huddled behind closed doors in the dining room when Eddy Fields brought him down for his airing. Eddy was a slight man and his feet never seemed to touch the floor as he came hurtling down the stairs behind Buck who by then was frenzied to relieve himself.

A twenty-one year old Phi Beta Kappa student in the WPA took over my room. He was so thin that Mother worried about him and often invited him to have dinner with us. This meant that Joseph, John and I had to

690

endure the dirgelike music he favored and played on the phonograph which he thoughtfully brought to the dining room table.

Before any new tenant came in, Mother gave what we called her "palace guard" speech. "Yes," she would say, "we're blessed with excellent police protection here. There's Officer Potters to the left and Officer Ahlis on the right. There's Sergeant Garrigan across the street and directly opposite him. . .", here she paused so the full weight of her piece de resistance could sink in. . . . "directly opposite him we have *Inspector* Whelan."

Mother had been going steady with a moving man when she was in her twenties and had somehow caught the virus that is the *sine qua non* of his profession. She *loved* to move furniture. We all got to recognize that speculative look in her eyes. "I was thinking if we put the piano at the window and the couch on the stair wall and. . . " No matter how loud and heartfelt our protests, Joe and John and I would find ourselves on the lighter end of the piece to be moved, lifting and hauling as she admonished, "Now don't strain yourself."

Her peccadillo led to the entrapment of her one and only paying guest failure who was two weeks behind in his rent and was trying to tiptoe out at dawn. Unfortunately for his scheme, we'd moved the furniture the night before and he tripped over a lamp that had been freshly placed on the landing at the bottom of the staircase. Mother rushed out from the dining room-turned-bedroom to find him sprawled on the floor, his feet entangled in the lamp cord.

She sighed. "If you didn't have the money to pay, all you had to do was to tell me," she said. "God knows I can understand that." When he left, he had two dollars pressed in his hand. He'd claimed he'd been promised a job in New Jersey. It would be nice to say that our departing roomer never forgot the kindness and re-

691

turned the gift a thousandfold but unfortunately that was not the case. He was a deadbeat.

In spite of all our concerted efforts, the roomers who came and went, our babysitting jobs and Joe's newspaper route, Mother couldn't keep up the mortgage payments and lost the house. She was urged to take Joseph out of school and put him to work but she refused. "Education is more important than any house," she said firmly. "Joseph will get his diploma." Our next stop was a three room apartment near the trolley line and into it she moved the full contents of the six rooms, sure that someday our fortunes would change and we'd get the house back. We never did, and whenever she returned from visiting the old neighborhood, here eyes would shine with unshed tears as she remarked how beautifully her roses had grown.

As the only girl, she guarded me with the vigor of a dragon-slaying St. George. She felt it was her duty to my dead father to see that I came unscathed through the dating years. I called her Barbara Fritchie because whenever I came up the block with a date, no matter what the hour, she would be at the window. Shoot if you must this old gray head, I'd groan inwardly and wait for the familiar call, "Is that you, Mary?" I'd want to reply "no, it's Gunga Din." But her methods were effective. No date ever got "fresh" with that alert sentry dangling twenty feet above his head.

Her prayer was that I'd marry an Irish Catholic with a Government Job so that someday I'd have a pension. She had a mortal fear that I'd marry outside the faith and if I ever went out with a non-believer, she began a flying novena to St. Jude that the romance would cool.

When at twenty-one I began dating Warren Clark, she was delighted. So good looking, so bright, half the girls in the parish had set their caps for him. How had he ever stayed single for twenty-nine years? And a more respected family could not be found. His mother, Alma Claire Clark, was the national head of the Companions of the Forest of America. For the first time Mother withdrew from her window perch and went to bed early because I was safe with Mrs. Clark's son. When I remarked that dating Mrs. Clark's son was not precisely the same as dating Mrs. Clark, the insinuation sailed completely over her head and she continued to slumber blissfully away while in between kissing him goodnight, I would hiss, "Warren, you know better than that!"

Mother was a Democrat to the marrow of her bones. A Captain in her district she took her duties seriously and no matter how insignificant the election, she'd ring the bell of every voter in her area and urge one and all to go to the polls. To her the Democratic Party understood the needs of the working man and took care of its own. The one thing she couldn't forgive Warren was that he took me to register for my first vote and "turned me into a Republican."

The two of them relished many a political discussion and Warr spent the remainder of his life trying to wring from her the admission that just maybe, occasionally, the Republican candidate was better qualified than his Democratic opponent.

Finally he thought he had her. "Mrs. Higgins," he inquired, "if the Party put up Joseph Stalin for President, *would you vote for him?*"

It was a lady or tiger question. . . her Catholicism and her devotion to the Democrats were on the line but Mother skirted the issue neatly. She replied that if the *Party* put up Stalin she'd surely vote for him, because they'd have a good reason for putting him up. "Warren, mark my words, they always know what they are doing."

Her occupation and hobby, vocation and avocation was Motherhood. A Jewish mother looks into the cradle and sees a possible Messiah. It's equally true that an Irish mother gazes at her firstborn son and sees the Christ-child. Joseph was a premature baby weighing only four pounds when he was born. She fed him with an eye-dropper that first year and never left him for an instant. I found a diary she kept and in it she wrote, "I was so afraid he'd slip away. He was such a beautiful baby. The other two had allergies."

Growing up, Joseph justified her pride in him. He won the General Excellence medal all eight years of grammar school. He won a scholarship to Fordham Prep. He was the Captain of every team, the lead in every school play. He had the newspaper route and every penny he earned he brought home to her, turning his pockets inside out to make sure he didn't forget a dime. Then they shared their own special treat, a half-pint of ice cream.

At thirteen, Joe contracted osteomyelitis. Mother was told that an operation to remove the hipbone was necessary to save his life. Widowed only a few months she made the stunning decision not to operate. She wouldn't make a cripple of Joseph and she knew God wouldn't take him from her. It was Christmas. He was on the critical list and the doctors held no hope for his recovery. Mother and John and I carried all his presents to the hospital. His main gift was a hockey stick. "You'll use it next year," she promised him. He did.

Joe graduated from high school in 1944. Mother could have claimed him as her sole support and kept him out of service. Instead she let him enlist in the navy with his friends. Six months later she took the only long trip of her life, a plane ride to California to be at Joe's deathbed in the Long Beach Naval Hospital. To the people who fumbled for words of sympathy she said, "It is God's will. I couldn't let Joseph go when he was sick the other time but now God wants him even more than I do."

That June when I graduated from Villa Maria Academy

Mother threw a party for me that held no hint of sadness. It was my day and nothing was going to spoil it. Johnny graduated from grammar school a few weeks later and he too had all the aunts and uncles and cousins and friends there to celebrate. She bought a black and white print dress to wear to both occasions. She felt her black mourning dress was out of place those two days.

Her pride in all of us was enormous. We were never simply doing well in school. We were "taking all the honors." I never had a job. I had "a big job." When John went to Notre Dame she must have written a dozen letters to long-forgotten cousins. The letters began, "My, what a busy summer, what with getting John ready for Notre Dame. . ." This kick-off would be followed by a careful explanation of why Notre Dame was the finest college in the world and therefore eminently qualified to educate her son.

After Warren and I were married, she never quite forgave us for moving to New Jersey. Warren urged her to live with us and avoid the endless bus trips back and forth, but even given *carte blanche* to come with all her beloved furniture there was never the faintest chance she'd move. You only had to drive her halfway across the George Washington Bridge to have her start sniffing the air and remarking on the heavenly breezes that originated in the Bronx.

She delighted in being a grandmother. She had a deep horror of my leaving the children with a young babysitter and thought nothing of taking the two-hour, three-bus trip to New Jersey to mind them.

From the time they could toddle half a block alone, Mother was whisking them on the Circle Line Tour, to the Central Park Zoo, to the Statue of Liberty, to parades and to beaches. She especially adored amusement parks. In 1939 she took my brothers and me to the World's Fair.

It was the summer Daddy died and I can still see her, the long mourning veil trailing wraith-like behind her as we plunged down on the parachute jump. A quarter of a century later, when she was 76, she was taking my five offspring on the steeplechase at Coney Island.

Long years of making one dollar do the work of ten couldn't be unlearned and if the kids had any complaint, it was that Nanny made them share a soda or divide a sandwich in the Automat. She once promised my then five-year old that she'd take him up to the top of the Empire State Building. Upon realizing that she had to pay for the tickets to the Observation Tower, she whisked him up on the business elevator to the 86th floor, stood him at a window and said brightly, "Here we are at the top. Isn't this fun?"

Her caring for the children encompassed Warren and me. She adored Warr and to her "himself" was the grandest husband any girl could have. "The disposition of a saint," she'd sigh, "I hope you know how lucky you are, Mary." The only time she wavered in her devotion to him was during my pregnancies when, totally unconsciously, and to our huge amusement Mother would speak of Warren as "that fellow."

But even then she'd be fussing over him, making his tea just the way he liked it, worrying over his habit of never wearing a hat even in the coldest weather. One night I awoke to find Mother tucking the covers around him. "Mother in God's name what are you doing in here," I groaned. "Mary, he'll catch his death of cold," she sighed. After that whenever she stayed over, I locked the door of the master bedroom and she darkly murmured something to the effect of "you two barricading yourselves in there when your children might need you."

We'd been married ten years when Warren began having chest pains and we learned that incredibly, this

696

handsome, vibrant man who excelled in every sport had the arteries of an eighty year old. In the next four years he had two heart attacks. He'd just come home from the hospital when a third attack took him from us.

"God's will but oh it is so hard sometimes," Mother said and I made myself remember that she'd never taken her grief out on us and I wouldn't take mine out on my children. It was because of Mother that I was able to go out to work but of course she didn't think she was minding only five youngsters. She immediately resumed her role as guardian of a young girl. . . .me.

A week after Warren's death, the funeral director came in with some papers for me to sign. Mother herded the boys upstairs. In five minutes my visitor was gone and Marilyn, my high school freshman turned on her French language records. For the next thirty minutes, a suave masculine voice asked such questions as "Voulez vous aller au bibliothèque avec moi?" When the record was finished, Mother rushed down the stairs, indignation etched in every line of her face. "Mary, what was that fellow doing talking French to you?" she demanded.

Another evening I came home at midnight to find her waiting in the living room. "Mary, what will the neighbors think of a girl your age coming home at this hour of the night?" she demanded. I was then thirty-six.

Mother began having arthritis when she was twenty. It was in keeping with her whole approach to life that she caught it dancing barefoot in the snow in Central Park. As she aged it spread into her knees and legs, her feet and hands and back. Her feet were the worst and she literally walked to heaven on those painful appendages, so swollen and sore, she could hardly endure her weight on them. She probably would have been confined to a wheelchair except that her need to do for other people was so great that she kept pushing herself, forcing activity on those tired limbs, literally willing them to function.

Paradoxically she may have sped her own end by electing to go into a nursing home for a few weeks rest. After all, she pointed out, she was spending three dollars a month for Medicare and getting nothing out of it. As soon as she began to take it easy everything in her body slowed up. Her heartbeat became more and more uncertain. I knew it would soon be over when one day, just coming out of a sleep, she said drowsily, "Mary, I had the children down to the beach and Carol wandered off. I couldn't find her. I just don't think I really can take care of them anymore." She could no longer take care of others and didn't want anyone to have to take care of her.

She had a total of seventeen hundred dollars in insurance from nickle and dime policies she'd paid on for years. They were tied together in an old brown envelope. There was a note to Johnny and me with them. It said, "Don't waste more than a thousand dollars on the funeral. Give one hundred dollars to each of my grandchildren." She didn't realize that she'd already given us all a priceless legacy, her ceaseless devotion and unfailing love.

And Mother is still part of us. "Remember when Nanny. . . ." is heard frequently in my home and after the story is told, there's bound to be laughter. Last fall, Patty, my youngest, was in the attic, apprehensively getting out suitcases to pack for her freshman year in college. She began rummaging and came down, wrapped in a pale pink terrycloth robe. "It still smells like Nanny," she said happily and surely it did. The faint scent of her talcum was there and the robe went off to college with Pat.

I have Mother's old black felt hat with the brief edging of black veiling in my closet. It's battered now and out of shape but over the years when things weren't going well, when the bills were piling up or one of the children was sick, I'd give it a quick rub and say, "Come on, Nora, do your stuff." I had no doubt that my first novel would be successful because it was dedicated to her. "I can just see Nora," a friend said laughing, "Dear Lord, not to bother you. . . .the paperback sale on the book was excellent but *how about the movie rights?"*

Time is slipping by so quickly. Months and seasons become years. My contemporaries and I ruefully discuss the fact that now *we* are the older generation. But when dawns the day that shall be my last, I'll have no fear. Because I am very sure that the first sound I hear when I enter eternity will be that well-loved voice anxiously asking, "Is that you, Mary?"

Ms. Clark is a well known authoress of books including Where are the Children *and* A Stranger is Watching.

My Ancestors

GRENVILLE T. EMMET III

I FIRST BECAME AWARE OF WHAT "EMMET" MEANS TO IRISH-men from a story told me by my father. Shortly after he was graduated from college, he and several friends made a trip around Europe. They spent the first month in Ireland. While there, they arrived one weekend in a small town which was holding its annual fair. Being a shy man, my father made no effort to attract attention to himself. His friends, however, had no such diffidence, and made it known to one and all in a local pub that they were with a *bona fide* Emmet. With that my father was swept up, treated regally, and the entire group was unable to pay for anything during the festivities. I think my father was pleased with his sudden star status, even though he claims to have been embarrassed. His friends, with youthful college exuberance, had no such hang-ups. They were delighted to reap the full benefits of their association with a descendant of "Bold Robert."

My wife and I had a similar personal experience several years ago when we stayed with friends in Ireland. They had hired for the summer a Dublin school teacher. Our hostess explained on our arrival that things were rather chaotic, and they had yet to have even a satisfactory breakfast. The next morning we all approached the table with some wariness. As it turned out, we had a feast fit for the Gods. Our hostess was incredulous. She sped to the kitchen to find out what had accounted for the miracle. She emerged to explain that the teacher had learned I was descended from Robert Emmet. Thereafter, our children and we could do no wrong in her eyes.

Such recognition of the Emmet name today is heartening for those of us who have inherited it. The fact it has such an emotional significance to so many Irishmen is a reflection of the deep-seated passion and longing this great people has always felt for the causes of liberty and justice.

Unsuccessful as his efforts were at the time to free the Irish people from a foreign tyranny which had preserved itself for centuries, Robert Emmet, through his martyrdom, symbolized the hopes of the great mass of Irish people and their deeply held nationalism.

Less remembered today, but far better known at the time was Thomas Addis Emmet, Robert's older brother. A contemporary of Wolfe Tone, Edmund Fitzgerald, Napper Tandy and others, Thomas Addis Emmet was a leader in the Society of United Irishmen. Like the others, he spent years in prison and was exiled. During this exile, he lived first in Brussels and then moved to Paris to represent the provisional government of Ireland as Minister. Then, after his brother's abortive insurrection, he emigrated to the United States where he had an illustrious career.

Since he is the founding father of the American branch of the Emmet family, and the one from whom I am directly descended, the reader might be interested in a few observations about his life and career. Dr. Robert Emmet, who was State Physician of Ireland, had three sons: Christopher, Thomas and Robert. The family was Protestant, well to do, and firmly part of the Establishment. This is significant because it helps explain why the reactionary colonial regime in Dublin Castle felt that the Society of United Irishmen was so pernicious. It was the first time that Protestant members of the Establishment had joined together with the dispossessed Catholic population to espouse democratic reform. The administration at Dublin Castle referred to this movement as "The Society of Associated Scoundrels."

Thomas Addis Emmet was born in 1764—14 years before the birth of his youngest brother, Robert. He began his professional life as a physician and attained eminence in that field at a relatively young age. However, when his older brother Christopher, who was a lawyer, died, Thomas gave up medicine for his more favoured profession—the law. He passed the bar and became a distinguished barrister in Dublin.

When the Society of United Irishmen, which had been founded in 1792, was being reorganized in the face of further repression by the government, Tom Emmet became an important member of the directory of the Society. Although, prior to this time, it was known to only a few that he had any connection with the democratic movement, Emmet had, in fact, been actively engaged for several years organizing branch societies in different counties of Ireland while under the guise of travelling in the practice of his legal profession. Eventually, his relationship with the United Irishmen was discovered and, in March 1798, he and the other leaders were arrested as the result of information supplied by an informer who had infiltrated the Society. He and the others were then charged with treason and imprisoned in Kilmainham.

The government thereafter proclaimed martial law and an orgy of terrorism and bloodshed began. Those who were able to escape managed to reach the mountains and carry on guerrilla warfare which the British army was unable entirely to suppress. Frustrated by their inability to stamp out the movement, the authorities began negotiations with the imprisoned leaders, offering them amnesty and passage to emigrate if they would use their influence with the guerillas to put down their arms. The English never lived up to their end of the agreement although the Irish did. In 1799, Thomas Emmet and the others were transferred to Fort George in Scotland where Thomas was again held in close confinement.

As a sidelight, you might be interested to know that his wife, Jane Patten, a strong-willed and cogent woman, finally persuaded the authorities to let her visit her husband. When she reached Fort George, she not only induced Governor Stuart, who was in charge of the prison, to let her stay with

702

her husband during his confinement, but also to take the three Emmet children into his own household. It was at Fort George, in April 1802, that a daughter was born to the Emmets. Her name was Jane Erin Emmet.

Shortly thereafter, the British government finally agreed to release all the leaders of the movement who had been arrested in 1798 but kept in prison in violation of the amnesty agreement. Thomas Addis' name was omitted from the list to be discharged. Governor Stuart, on his own authority, released him with the others, as a consequence of which he lost his post.

Thomas Addis and his family went into exile in Brussels and made plans to emigrate to the United States. But before they were completed, he was asked by the directory of the Society of United Irishmen to represent them in Paris as Minister from the Provisional Irish Republic. It was expected, throughout this period, that Bonaparte and France would aid the Irish cause as part of the general French campaign against England. With hope that a French invasion of Ireland was imminent, the Emmets moved to Paris. Needless to say, a major French invasion of Ireland never materialized.

While in Paris, Thomas Addis received news of his brother's plans to mount a new insurrection in Ireland. Despite his renewed efforts to obtain a commitment from France for the necessary financial and military support, these were not forthcoming.

As we know, Robert Emmet and his small band of followers set out to capture Dublin Castle on July 23, 1803. Much of the promised support from counties outside Dublin faded at the crucial moment and the rebellion was quickly checked. Within days, Robert was captured. Within weeks, he was tried and, on September 20, 1803, executed. Thomas received the news stoically, and, a year later, when further prospects for a republic appeared hopeless, emigrated to New York.

He and the family arrived there in November 1804, bringing with him a number of letters of introduction, among them

703

one from Lafayette, the French general and statesman who had fought in the American Revolution, and others addressed to Governor Clinton of New York and Daniel Tompkins, who later became Vice President under President Monroe. With their assistance, a special act was passed by the New York legislature admitting him to the vacancy at the Bar resulting from the recent death of Alexander Hamilton.

By 1811, Thomas Addis had become an important figure on the New York scene and, in 1812, was elected Attorney General of the State. Also, in keeping with his medical background, he became Counsellor to the Medical Society of the County of New York. And, during the war of 1812, he commanded an Irish reserve regiment when an attack against New York City was threatened by the British.

Thomas was a great friend of Robert Fulton, the inventor of the steamboat, whom he had known well in Paris. A diary which Thomas kept in Paris indicates, as an interesting historical sidelight, that Fulton had hoped to join the French expedition to Ireland for the purpose of testing his recently invented torpedo against the English. Regrettably, their friendship had an unhappy ending. Within the Emmet family it is said that Fulton accompanied Thomas on his return to New York from trying a case for Fulton in Trenton, New Jersey. Unable to cross the Hudson by ferry because the river was iced over, they attempted to cross on foot. Thomas had reached portly proportions by this time, and the ice could not support his weight. In his efforts to save Emmet, Fulton contracted a severe cold. Without waiting to recover, he went out in foul weather the following day and died three days later.

Thomas Emmet never actively engaged in American politics though, in 1807, he did have satisfaction of significantly contributing to the defeat of Rufus King, who was the candidate of the Federalist Party for Governor of New York State. King had been the United States Minister to the Court of St. James when Emmet was jailed in 1798. It was he who had blocked Emmet and the other imprisoned leaders from

704

emigrating to the United States when the English government first proposed amnesty, thus giving the British an excuse for prolonging their imprisonment. None of this was widely known in New York, but, with a large Irish American electorate in the state, Emmet was determined to make sure the voters were aware of the rôle King had played on behalf of the English against the Irish patriots. He wrote two letters to King which were published, detailing the latter's obstruction of justice in the cause of Irish independence. As a direct result King was overwhelmingly defeated and never sought elective office again.

Thomas Emmet died as dramatically as he had lived. He had taken a case for charity, which acquired much notoriety. Known as the "Sailors' Snug Harbor" case, it involved the contest of a will and went as far as the Supreme Court of the United States. In the midst of his argument to the court, he suffered a stroke and died without regaining consciousness.

Since Thomas Addis Emmet emigrated to America 172 years ago, the Emmet family in the United States has produced several well-known personalities in the family: Robert Emmet Sherwood, the playwright; Lydia Emmet, an esteemed artist in her day; as well as my grandfather, who was Franklin Roosevelt's law partner, and minister to Holland and Austria in the 1930's. Whether celebrated or not, however, the members of the family have steadfastly remained true to the traditions of Robert and Thomas Addis Emmet in their dedication to every man's right to justice and liberty.

Mr. Emmet is a banker and sportsman.

705

The Aran Islands and Me

DENNIS SMITH

THIS IS MY FIRST DAY ON THE ARAN ISLANDS. ON THE BIG island. There are two smaller islands I will walk another day, but for now I sit on the edges of a huge bed in a small room, hunched over a night table pulled away from the wall. The table and my writing pad are illumined by soft, flickering candlelight, and I can hear the Atlantic waters crashing against the rocks beyond the window, the inescapable, uncontrollable sound of Aran. It is a wonderful sound, a wonderful place.

The sky was dark this morning as I hoped it would be, and as I walked to the Galway pier I could hear the wind's melody passing through the town and across Galway Bay. It was a brisk morning, chilled and wet-aired.

The boat is called the Naomh Eanna, Irish for St. Enda, the fifth century son of a Druid chieftain who founded a monastery at Killeany on the big island. It is old, its decks of splintering wood, and is made for perhaps two hundred people. It seemed to be full this morning, with Irish speakers, islanders I thought, laden with cardboard boxes from Galway shopping, and with tourists, Leicas hanging from their necks as Olympic medals. And me, carrying one suitcase and a canvas picnic bag filled with books and two writing pads. I bought a ticket from a man in a ramshackle hut at the pier's edge, and boarded. I would read from a biography of Synge

706

for the time of the trip, for it is because of him, after all, that I came here.

John Millington Synge (pronounced "sing") first went to the Aran Islands at W. B. Yeats's urging in 1898. He had been in Paris, unhappy and unproductive, and Yeats assured him of an awakening in the west of Ireland, amid the folkways of a people made poor by rocks, but rich in language by the hardships of isolation.

The three Aran Islands are thirty miles into the Atlantic, west of Galway city. The largest, Inishmore, where I now sit, is about nine miles long by two wide. It is sometimes called Aranmore, and it is the only one of the three accessible by large craft. The middle island, Inishman, is nearly round, about three and a half miles in diameter, and the small island, Inishere, is also round in appearance, and about two miles across.

These three rock ledges in Galway Bay are world famous, and it was Synge who brought them fame. Between 1898 and 1901 he visited the islands four times. His longest stay was for six weeks, but in these short periods he felt as if he were "beyond the dwelling place of man," in "a world of inarticulate power." He was a natural romantic, and as Byron found Greece, Synge found Aran, and from his experiences here he wrote a diary, *The Aran Islands,* and two plays, "Riders to the Sea" and "The Playboy of the Western World."

I love these works for they tell the story of a simple, natural, courageous people as distant from the sophisticated, electronic, competitive society we endure as Pluto from Mercury. I wondered if these islands were different today from the islands of Synge's time, and so I left my wife, Pat, and my sons, Brendan, Dennis, and Sean, in Athlone, safe on the inland banks of the Shannon River, and I came to see.

When Synge first boarded a steamer for the Aran Islands in 1898, the crossing was completed in three hours, and it was as long and as tiresome today as it was three quarters of a century past. There is an eight-passenger airplane to Aranmore each morning, at least during the tourist season, but I

707

determined to travel as Synge did, a determination I would little advise to others.

After an hour out to sea, beneath the black, racing clouds, we began to roll and pitch as, it seemed, a plastic toy on the surface of a whirlpool bath. Many of the passengers, experienced islanders as well, became ill, and hung over the side as war-wounded, bewailing each wave. I was sitting aft on a coil of thick tie rope, drinking tea from a paper cup, trying to hold flat the windblown pages of my book. I read just a little, and then giving it up, moved to the front of the boat and awaited the islands. The full pushing of the wind against me felt cleansing, and I was happy there, though cold and wet.

The islands finally appeared, first as vague outlines through the mist, as a Seurat painting, and then clearer and clearer as the boat rushed on. In full view the islands seemed to sit as three proud rocks in bold defiance of their isolation. How far they are from the world, I thought. We stopped first at Inishere, the small east island, anchoring a hundred yards from shore, and canvas-covered curraghs (pronounced "curracks") came towards us as swimming beetles. The small crafts were steadied in the splashing water by weather-worn young men pulling on strange oars called modjee raw, oars that are the same width, about four inches, at both ends. A crowd of islanders stood on the shore, either waiting for parcels, or, more simply, for the small entertainment of the diversion. We anchored next off Inishman, the middle island, where, besides the supply boxes, there were also two passengers who left the boat, speaking in their native language. There seemed to be no space between their words and the intonation range is greater than any language I've heard, more a vocalese than songful.

The boat docked at Kilronen, the pier town of the large island, but there were surprisingly few villagers waiting as on the smaller islands. There were twenty or so horse-pulled carts, their drivers hawking an hour's sightseeing ride to the tourists who had come out just for the day. It reminded me of the pony ride for children in Central Park. Aren't all tourists like children? I asked one if he would take me to Mrs. O'Flaherty's house in Oat Quarter, and I climbed into the back of the cart. I did not speak, for I became immediately preoccupied, nearly hypnotized by the unending irregularity of the design of the rock walls all about me. As there are stars in the sky, there is silver-gray stone on Aranmore.

After four miles of progressive climbing the horse finally stopped in front of Aras Bhrid (Bridget's House), the O'Flaherty house. I paid the driver. Mrs. O'Flaherty, a woman of 55 or 60 perhaps, keen-eyed, smiling, wiping her hands on an apron, welcomed me.

"Is it Dennis Smith?," she asked.

It was, I told her.

"You were due here yesterday," she said in soft reprimand. "Come in now and I'll give you some tongue."

I thought she meant a meal, and I was disinclined to eat. I followed her into the two-story, concrete washed house, thinking of an apology to refuse the food, until she sat me down, whereupon I realized it was a tongue lashing she meant.

"I have a telephone you know," she said. I should have called her from Galway, I regretted that I did not, and I told her so without explaining that I was not picked up in Athlone as promised, and therefore arrived a day late. She is a kind woman, and I have the feeling she will want to kiss me as I leave.

In the house I found the O'Flaherty's speak Irish in conversation. Mrs. O'Flaherty explained that English was her second language and she apologized for any mistakes she might make. I said, "I'd bet you can't remember the last time you made a mistake in English." It seemed to please her.

I asked if there was someone available to teach me practical Irish phrases, and she said that she would speak to her son about it tomorrow, and that if he had time he would make a good job of it. I was shown to my room where I sat for a while reading, and afterwards I took a walk down the road.

I walked for more than a mile, until I could see, on a high hill, Dun Aengus, an ancient fortress.

When Christ was born in Bethlehem, a fierce group of Belgic Celts were wrestling stones on the Aran Islands. It is historical speculation to say where they came from, for no record is written of them. It is sure though, that they were adventurers, and fish eaters, perhaps a beaten tribe searching for an impregnable shelter.

Unlike the Egyptians, they left us barren monuments like this Dun Aengus—just walls, mortarless, and in places more than twelve feet thick, built on the edge of a three hundred foot cliff, overlooking a sea that cannot rest.

I sat and remembered the monographs about the fortress a friend in Dublin had given me to read. The outer rampart contains an inner rampart and the fort on eighteen acres. The outer rampart is itself, in places, eighteen feet high, and outside of it is a broad range of sharp pillar stones, which is called a *chevaux de frise*. These stones are so placed that one could not survive a tripping unscathed. A thrown stone hitting its mark here would have done double its damage, and I am forced to wonder what blood must have stained these pillar-stones in battle.

A stone lying by itself might move a geologist's adrenalin, but for most of us the singular stone is unworthy, perhaps boring. When, though, stones are piled one on another, and given shape as walls or fortresses, they take on another meaning—for me a dark, toilsome, moribund reminder of the past, the survival battles of our ancestors.

Still, when they are shaped into dwellings, they become alive, immediate, and utilitarian. One monograph stated conclusively that Dun Aengus would hold two hundred cows, while another said over a thousand. In any case, I am reminded of jelly beans in a glass jar, a big jar. How many jelly beans, how many stones.

Each stone is a man's effort in lifting, carrying and placing. So many stones, so much lifting. The count is endless.

I will climb up to the fort tomorrow, but I decided then to go to a bar that is run by a man who seems to be famous for never smiling—a rare man, it was told, on this island.

There were perhaps thirty people seated around, and there were no seats left, so I and all who followed after me stood.

Nearly everyone there was a native and spoke Irish. In one corner was a group of young women, seventeen or eighteen who were dressed in a way that I mistook them for mainland girls, and city girls at that. It was only three years ago that girls began to frequent bars here. There were no older women, but many older men, who were treated with sincere deference by the young men who bought them drinks and spoke to them kindly, never avoiding them as we do in America. Old people are never patronized in the Aran Islands.

A man began to play the accordion, first reels and then more recent music like "Liverpool Lu," which the girls sang. A man sang in Irish that I thought would never end, long ballads being particularly disconcerting when the words are not understood. I noticed one girl who seemed shy in the first hour become overly loud with song after she had a few stouts. I sang "Johnny, I Hardly Knew Ye," and then the bar closed. It was 10:30.

I met two sisters, in their late thirties, who are also guests of Mrs. O'Flaherty. They remind me of Sean O'Faolain characters, academic, overly polite, but genuinely kind. We got into a van, picked up Mrs. O'Flaherty, and drove to a Ceili at the Island Hall.

The hall was filled with islanders and Irish was spoken everywhere around me. In Synge's time the language was declining, and I noticed turn of the century headstones inscribed in English on the roadside, but very little English is spoken now, and the contemporary road signs and headstones are only in Irish.

There was a drummer and an accordionist on stage, and they announced each dance, in Irish of course. I sat on the side of the hall and watched as the islanders, old and young alike, arranged themselves for a set dance. The music began, and a few of the younger men began to swing their partners madly, causing total disharmony to the set, but nobody seemed to care much, and enjoyed being knocked about by each other.

It could have been a dance in a suburb of Sacramento, but with different music. There was no traditional dress to be seen, no strange footwear called *pampooties*, no flannel shirts, no black shawls. The men were in flared pants, checked or striped, and knit shirts. Some girls were in blue jeans, or long dresses, but most were in short, loose dresses that flew high up as they turned, exposing their underwear. But the men paid them no heed at all, for they are very free here, unrepressed, both in their self-perception and their perception of others. It would have been titillating or shameful to the American Irish.

On the mainland I found the men to be generally more good looking than the women, but here they are equally handsome, and equally spirited, too. The hall was bursting with energy, and reckless dancing and spinning. Even the youngest, the 11- and 12-year-olds would not yield to the older and wilder 17- and 18-year-olds, and they, boys and girls too, braced their shoulders and danced directly into any gyrating couple that happened by.

The Seige of Venice and the Stack of Barley were played, two dances that I know how to perform, and although I felt compelled to ask a girl to join me, my regard for physical safety dissuaded me. I found myself grimacing in anxious expectation as the couples rammed into one another. I would rather be in a fire, I thought, than to dance in my moccasins on that floor.

In a corner of my eye I saw Mrs. O'Flaherty swinging with three others, their hands joined around the backs. Suddenly that group was bounced into, and the four fell to the floor. I was very concerned for my hostess, but she seemed to care not at all, but they did sit down after that. I decided then to have one dance for the evening, and Mrs. O'Flaherty and I did a Stack of Barley.

I have never before seen people enjoy themselves with such innocent abandon, and as the "Soldiers Song" was played, I hoped that Synge was looking down from the great Where at all this happiness on the place he loved so much.

We arrived back at the house at 2:00 in the morning, and I met the other house guests, a priest from Galway and his niece named Colette, a natural wild beauty. I was wearing an Aran sweater which was remarked on, and over tea Mrs. O'Flaherty told this story:

> "It was about tirty years ago, there were only three wimen on this island that could knit those sweaters, and my mother was one 'a them. Then one day she took sick, and I decided then to learn to do the job myself. And I did learn to do it, and I used to knit sweaters for the men here whose wimen didn't know how to do it themselves. Then we got together, and kind of taught each other how to do it. You know. And there was a man from Dublin used to come here by the name of Farrell, and he used to pay us to make those sweaters. Then he got one woman to copy out the stitches on a piece of paper, and now all the world knows how to do it, and they call them Aran sweaters whether they are made here or no."
> "Ahh," said the priest, "if only they could have patented the name of Aran."

The priest's niece is a wild beauty of about twenty, quite smart, and we talked about books, and about the film "Man of Aran" made by Robert Flaherty. Mrs. O'Flaherty told me that Maggie Dirrine, the woman who was featured in the film, was during her youth her next door neighbor, and that she is still living just a mile or so north of here. I will try to meet her. Mrs. O'Flaherty saw the film, and I asked her opinion of it. "I thought good of it," she said, "up until the part where he grabbed her by the hair. Do you remember? Well, if that was his own woman, his own wife, he would not have grabbed her so rough, and I didn't like that at all." I remembered that the film's featured man and woman were not married, but brought together by Flaherty for the parts. Still, it is an honest documentary of life on the Aran Islands as it was.

Mrs. O'Flaherty, who is related to the writer Liam O'Flaherty is a natural story teller, although she does not think of herself as one. She doesn't flower her words, and gets right to the point, and like many Irish people I've met, she could earn a living as a writer if the opportunity came.

There is no electricity here, and my eyes cannot any longer withstand the wavering candlelight. I will close my eyes then and try to discern the sounds of the wind and the waves, sounds that now seem one. There are another twenty tomorrows for me on these islands.

Mr. Smith is a well-known author.

The Travelling People

ELIZABETH SHANNON

Every visitor to Ireland has seen the sites of the Travelling People, strung out along roadsides at the edge of cities and towns. Their laundry dries on hedgerows beside their tents and caravans. Used car parts, junk, and smouldering fires litter the sites. By no stretch of a romantic imagination does a Travelling site conjure up scenes of gay gypsy nomad life. Rather, it is a sad, forlorn picture of Ireland's subculture. They used to be called Tinkers. Some people call them gypsies, which they are not. Social workers call them Itinerants. They prefer to be called Travelling People.

Since Pre-Christian times in Ireland, there has been a tradition of a travelling population. They were "whitesmiths" in earliest times, working in gold, bronze and silver. By the 12th Century, the word "Tinkler" appeared as both a trade and a name.

Throughout the Middle Ages, they went from village to village, doing jobs that were not self-sustaining in just one village, such as tin smithing, chimney cleaning and horse-trading, the latter a skill at which they were extremely proficient. They were called Tinkers, which the American Heritage Dictionary defines as "A travelling mender of metal household utensils," or "a person who enjoys repairing and experimenting with machine parts." They were not Romany gypsies, like so many other itinerants throughout Europe. They were Irish.

The eviction of tenant farmers during and after the potato famines of the 1830's put thousands more homeless Irish on the road. By 1840, there were over two million itinerants without a settled home in Ireland. Many of them were displaced farm laborers, and they became "spalpeens" or migratory farm workers. They walked the countryside, never travelling the whole of Ireland but circulating in a small geographic area. Before the 19th Century, they slept in hedges or outbuildings, and they walked from village to village. By the 19th Century, they had colorful barrel-shaped carts, very much like the ones now used by the Irish tourist's horse-drawn caravans. Modern trailers or tents have displaced the horse-drawn carts now.

The Travellers developed a language of their own. It has no roots in the Romany language, but is derived from the Irish, using words which have been altered or disguised. Some scholars believe that the language, which is called "Shelta" or "Gammon" came from the secret language spoken in Irish monasteries.

The Travelling People in Ireland are criticized bitterly by settled people for being lazy and shiftless, dishonest and "on the dole." But contemporary life has done away with their traditional sources of income. Gas and oil heat have eliminated the need for chimney sweeps. Machines have replaced horses and the need for farm laborers. The plastics industry has done away with tin smithing. So they are in an age of transition, trying to develop new skills and trades in an industrial society. They deal now in scrap metal, buying and selling used car parts and other scrap. Their campsites are often used as their "showroom" which accounts for their unsightly appearance.

Women and children Travellers often beg on city streets. The men would never lower themselves to that extent, but a man is considered lucky if he has a wife who is a "good" beggar. One of the myths surrounding the Travellers is that they have large sums of money stashed away, and could easily "buy out" their poor, hardworking, settled neighbors. But the fact is that the vast majority of them are desperately poor, ill-fed, illiterate, and often incapable of dealing with the complexities of modern life.

There are about 1700 Travelling families in Ireland today. Of those, 1100 families have been settled. Of those remaining, about 300 families have no desire to settle and prefer their life on the road. They would like to see campsites which had facilities for them to use, such as running water, toilets, showers, etc. But they prefer the freedom of the road and the chance to move on to other sites. The families who would like to be settled and be assimilated into the mainstream of Irish life find it hard going. Their childhood on the road has deprived them of continuity of schooling, so they are not well enough educated to do anything but the most menial tasks. (There are 6103 school age children today, but only 3002 of them attend school regularly.) And because of their reputation for thieving, laziness, and irresponsibility, many employers would not dream of hiring a Traveller.

Mr. Victor Bewley, who is the honorary secretary for the Dublin Committee for Travelling People, and also the owner of a chain of restaurants, has done more for the Travellers than almost anyone else in Ireland. He has, for many years, employed them in his businesses, and has always found them satisfactory, both in their honesty, their industry and their relationships with their fellow employees. "Many of them will only stay with me for a short while, and then, for a variety of reasons, move on. But while they are with me, I have never had trouble with them, and I find that after explaining to my other employees that a Traveller may begin working, they are open and friendly in their reception."

But Victor Bewley is an exception.

I first became acquainted with Travelling families while visiting Galway City last November. I met Sister Brigid of the Little Sisters of the Assumption, who is a social worker and is involved with the Travelling Families of Galway. When I expressed an interest in them, she invited me to visit one of their campsites, and then her Fairgreen Training Center, for teenaged girls.

Galway has the largest population of Travelling People, next to Dublin. They are strung out along the main roads leading into Galway, and scattered around empty lots throughout the city. The site I visited was a small one, with just a half a dozen caravans, and a few tents propped up in an incredibly muddy, litter-strewn smelly lot. A horde of bright-eyed, dirty, rosy-cheeked children surrounded our car as we pulled into the site, and women came out of their tents and caravans, staring sullenly and suspiciously at us, until they recognized Sister Brigid in the car. Then their hostility turned into eager, welcoming smiles, and as we got out of the car, the children engulfed Sister with their hugs.

I was introduced to the children, all pre-schoolers, and to their mothers, then led into a tent. To my astonishment, the inside of the tent was immaculate. The dirt floor was swept clean, the crib and one double bed made up neatly, the dishes washed and sitting on the shelves of a small cupboard. Those three items were the only pieces of furniture in the tent. The parents slept in the double bed with the youngest infant between them. The next three children slept together in the crib. The rest of the 8 children slept on pallets on the dirt floor.

The mother of the family was a handsome woman, articulate and bitter. She said: "Welcome into my lovely home. Wouldn't you like to live here?" She went on to explain how many times and for how many years the family had applied for public housing but had been turned down. That was a familiar refrain around the site. A few months earlier, a family had been settled in a local housing estate and the other residents protested bitterly against their coming. The Travelling People have a reputation of being bad tenants and neighbors. Settled people are loathe to have them move in next door. Sister Brigid has housed 34 families in Galway over the past five years, but she has met much hostility and prejudice on the part of the settled community. In a city as small as Galway, everyone knows who the Travellers are, and it is very difficult for them to be accepted by the settled community, even after many years. "Put a Traveller in a street of houses, and twenty years later they will still be called Travellers," Sis-

719

ter Brigid said. They are accused of bringing in numerous members of the families to live with them, of having late nights, noisy parties, drinking too much, fighting, and sleeping all day. Sometimes it is true; often it is not.

After we left the site, we went to the Fairgreen Center, and had tea with the teenagers there. There are five training centers in Ireland for the Travelling teenagers; Bray, Ennis, Limerick, and Newcastle West also have Centers. The boys are taught metal work, wood work, mechanical skills, and welding. The girls are taught industrial machine work, crafts, cookery, dressmaking, and childcare. They are all taught hygiene and literacy. The students are paid an allowance while they attend the Centers. Although their sporadic elementary school attendance has left them without reading and writing skills, many of them are becoming proficient seamstresses and cooks, mechanics and carpenters. And yet, Sister Brigid says that many of the boys and girls in the Centers are immature and not ready to take up work in the settled community.

All the girls I met at Fairgreen were warm and hospitable to me. They gave me a tea which they had prepared, and showed me the sewing projects they were involved with. They were all attractive, poised girls who clearly showed the results of their training and involvement with the Center.

We had a good time together and soon established a warm and easy relationship. When it was time to go, and I was telling them good-bye I had a sudden urge to see them again and to return their hospitality, so I invited them back to my house in Dublin for a tea party. They were stunned into silence. One of them finally said: "I've never been invited to anyone's house for tea in my life." Another said: "We couldn't go to Dublin. We couldn't afford the bus fare."

I promised them, not knowing how I would keep the promise, that I would arrange for their transportation. As I walked from the door to the car, they all shouted over and over again, "Don't forget. Don't forget."

After the Christmas holidays, Sister Brigid wrote to say the girls were talking about nothing else but their trip to Dublin. I contacted Mr. Joe Malone of the Irish Tourist Board, who found a very generous donor of a bus to take the girls back and forth from Galway. And so on January 26, a bitterly cold and windy winter day, the girls from Galway arrived. Since the bus was large, they had brought the boys from their brother training school with them, but the boys opted out of the tea party.

Our Embassy staff notified the media about the party, as they routinely do with every large gathering we have at the Embassy. Usually the coverage is slight. The girls from Galway brought out the press and television cameras en masse. They walked into our front hall in the glare of T.V. lights and popping flash bulbs. People in Ireland don't generally invite Itinerants to tea, especially Ambassadors' wives. It was a big story, from the Press' point of view.

The girls were lovely guests, enthusiastic and receptive, full of wonder and delight at seeing such a big, beautiful house, but at the same time, they were dignified and not overawed. We had sandwiches and cakes, and I introduced them to the delights of chocolate chip cookies, and tea. I gave them a tour of the house and told them a bit about its history, which did not interest them. They are much more interested in people than in places or dates, and they were much more fascinated with me and with my family than they were with the house. They had made a beautiful embroidered pillow for me, which I treasure. My son David used the pillow as a kneeler when he made his First Communion here in the house this spring.

After tea, we played the piano and sang, and visited. All the journalists stayed throughout the party, and chatted with the girls. I think they went home with a somewhat changed view of Travelling People. Their stories the next day were very sensitive and perceptive.

They drove back to Galway at the end of the afternoon, and I think they had had a very good time. It was, in a symbolic sense, a breaking down of barriers for them, and I think that gave them a good feeling about themselves. A tea party is, of course, just a gesture; Sister Brigid and her colleagues are the ones doing the slow, difficult and sometimes unrewarding work of bringing the boys and girls into the mainstream of society. I was very proud to be a part of their work for one day, to open the Embassy doors to them and to make them feel welcome here. Now it's their turn, and I'm waiting for my return invitation to Galway!

Elizabeth Shannon, wife of the American Ambassador to Ireland, is a writer.

A Journey to the Edge

TERENCE CARDINAL COOKE

Both by nature and grace, the Celt is a traveler. There are few nations in the history of the world whose people have traveled as far, into such different corners of the world, on so many and varied a journey, as the Irish. Even the early legends of the Irish race, the hagiographical tales of the Irish saints, are so often focused on their journeyings. The travels of St. Patrick in his evangelization of the Emerald Isle are a rich part of this history. St. Brendan is said to have reached the New World in his journeys. Other saints have been hailed as wanderers and pilgrims and workers of miraculous forms of locomotion in their quest for justice and honor, and the spread of the kingdom of God on the earth.

We know that the early Irish monks, venturing forth from their great stone monasteries, were the apostles not only of the Christian Faith but also of the stored-up knowledge and culture of the Western World during the closing years of the Dark Ages. By ship, by mule, and by foot, they made their way from the Isle of Saints and Scholars into central Europe, and even into Italy to bring back the light which had been lost by the ravages of the barbarians and the petty squabbles of the early feudal lords. Saint Gall in Switzerland is named for the Irish monk, St. Galen, and the Irish monasticism reached one of its greatest glories in the Abbey of Bobbio on the Italian peninsula.

In more recent times, the flight of the wild geese figuratively portrays the scattering to the four winds of the pride of Irish manhood who left Ireland to journey to the Continent and to the New World to serve in the armies of foreign lands while their own beloved country was occupied often by strangers. The generals of the armies of liberation of so much of Latin America proudly bore Irish surnames, a testimony to the travels and the qualities of leadership of the Irish.

The last one hundred and fifty years have seen the Irish move in great multitudes around the world to settle new nations, such as America, Canada and Australia, and to find work and livelihood in far-off places in Africa, Oceania and Asia. In the story of the Irish immigrants of the nineteenth and twentieth centuries, we see once again the saga of the Irishman as traveler, filled with the joy of the road even as he undertakes to bear its burden, eager to turn the next corner, enthusiastic at the challenge it holds.

No wonder then that your President-General, when he asked that I contribute this article, suggested that a tale of one of my own travels might be of interest. As the son of Irish immigrants to the United States, and in my present rôle which requires a great deal of journeying, I can be true to my own heritage and write of a journey which I recently made.

The journey began in Rome. Attending there a month-long theological seminar for American bishops, we spoke frequently about the terrible poverty and the near-starvation of so many people throughout the world. Our attention was focused on the problem of hunger in western and central Africa in particular, since both the organs of the United Nations headquartered in Rome and the missionary organizations serving those areas of Africa had made it a point to describe the situation in great detail. Since the major arm of the American Catholic Church's thrust in this field, the Catholic Relief Services, has its headquarters in New York, and because of my deep interest in its work, I was encouraged by its officials to visit these countries.

724

The object of the journey was two-fold: witnessing at first hand the extent of starvation and general malnutrition, and observing and encouraging the work of our own relief efforts, in addition to the opportunity of visiting with the local churches.

"Sahel" means an edge, a fringe, or a border. The lands of the Sahel are those which stretch along the edge of the Sahara, lying almost as if situated on the shore of a great body of water. As in the erosion of land through the action of a tireless sea, the countries in this belt of central Africa are washed by the Sahara's sands. For the past several years, the great desert has been creeping south several miles each year, and, in its path, oases, towns, farms and pastures are inundated by the flowing burning sands. As the people retreat south each year, not only do they become a burden on the limited economy of the areas into which they are forced to migrate, but their former sources of the food supply disappear as less land is available for farming and pasture.

It is the lack of rain which draws the desert down so many miles each year. When rain does not come, the water table falls, vegetation cannot survive, and the land turns to desert. If this lack of rainfall persists over a number of years, livestock perishes and arable land can no longer produce a sufficient yield. Each year much of this green country turns to desert as the land is parched by the heat of the tropical sun. The rains, if they eventually come in sufficiency, can make the land again fertile for a while and one or two crops can be harvested. If they come too late or stay too short a time, the millet—which is the staple grain of these regions—can be harvested only once. And that is not enough to feed the people, and far from enough for export purposes to generate foreign exchange to enable them to purchase goods so sorely needed from other lands.

The plans for our visit to this area were carefully made and conducted by both the central headquarters of the Catholic Relief Services in New York and its local offices in western and central Africa. While in Rome, contact was made with Cardinal Zoungrana, the Archbishop of Ouagadougou in Upper Volta, which was to be our first stop. Additionally, contact was almost made with the Bishop of Dakar and the new Bishop of Nouakchott in Mauretania.

Upper Volta is located in Central Africa and is land-locked with few water resources. It had been hard hit by the long-lasting drought and, because of its poverty, was suffering great need. Because of the tightness of our schedule, our anticipated visit to this country was unfortunately not made. An airline problem in Paris, where we had to make flight connections, left us stranded overnight and made our stop in Ouagadougou impossible. It was a good lesson at the start of the trip. To those accustomed to the variety of airline schedules in the United States, and to the ease of changing one plane for another in case difficulties arise, the problem of finding air transportation between Paris and Central Africa was a sobering reminder of the different world to which we were to travel. To many of the cities in that region, plane transportation is available only once or twice a week, and if one's schedule cannot adjust to fewer options, he had best make up his mind not to try the journey at all.

After several frustrating hours at the de Gaulle Airport, our party, consisting of Monsignors Theodore McCarrick, William McCormack and myself, was rescheduled for a direct flight to Dakar in Senegal. Situated on the point of land farthest to the West on the African continent, Dakar was for centuries a leading city, both to the early African empires and later to the colonizing nations which found its climate refreshing and its harbor inviting. Parts of Dakar make it seem like a city of France. Its architecture and boulevards reflect the centuries of French influence. French is still spoken by much of the population, and the influence of French culture is readily apparent.

When we arrived there, we were joined by several of the local officials of the Catholic Relief Services and a photographic team who were to accompany us and record the work of the relief operations so that the impact of American generosity could be relayed graphically to our people at home. In places supervised by the Catholic Relief Services, we were to see supplies of grain, cereals, and fertilizer sent as a gift of the people of the United States to help their African brothers to eke out a meager existence to tide them over this period of crisis. We were to visit the dispensaries, the old colonial hospitals, and the new neighborhood health centers which were always filled to capacity with long lines of primarily children outside. And the common complaint, the common denominator of all this suffering was hunger, and the handicap which hunger imposes on the basic ability of human beings to survive, much less to develop. The Catholic Relief Services, the Catholic Medical Mission Board, and many other Church-related, as well as non-sectarian, agencies from many countries of the world were helping. It was much, but in the context of the totality of the need, it was a small measure.

The projects to provide relief for the hungry and to fight the drought were found on the outskirts of great metropolitan centers like Dakar, in the poorest sections of a new tent city on the outskirts of Nouakchott, and near the hamlets which ring the fast-flowing Senegal river, which divides Senegal and Mauretania.

One of the most novel of these projects was one which is being undertaken close to Dakar. It involves the principle of drip irrigation: since there is water enough only for the nourishment of seeds, and insufficient for spreading over an entire field, the water is directed exactly to the location of the seed. The drip irrigation project feeds water through a long series of plastic tubes fed from an elevated barrel of water, which, in turn, must be replenished from a nearby well. One barrel of precious water can theoretically serve the moisture needs of a whole field. I use the word "theoretically" to describe the effect of the process, since both nature and man can interfere with its success. Animals and insects can chew on the tubing and render it useless, and

727

often the native farmer will unwittingly try to enlarge the minute holes through which the drops of water pass.

The well-drilling operations are intriguing. Some wells must go down several hundred feet, and as the level of the water table descends owing to the continual encroachment of the desert, many previously useful wells become dry and must be deepened. Accordingly, the well-digger plays a crucial rôle in these communities. It is he who, with a simple flashlight and suspended on a rope chair, must cut away the earth and rock hundreds of feet below the surface. The physical exertions required by this work are great; the psychological strain is enormous. Dangers lurk in these deep caverns, too, in terms of sudden rock slides and exposure to toxic gases. He is the hero of this land of drought since a working well may save the people of his village a trek of ten miles or more twice a day.

Water control and large irrigation projects are possible in the area of the Senegal river, and there an attempt is being made to produce crops to support less blessed regions. But even this river, mighty in the days of the rainy season, is transformed to a small channel during the terrible season of dryness when the sky is never touched by a single rain cloud.

After Senegal, we travelled to Mauretania, which lies in the desert in the north. Although it is an Islamic nation, the Catholic Relief Services are working closely with the staff of the Red Crescent Society. The latter organization is parallel to the Red Cross in its activities and has the strong support of the local governmental officials. We found its workers most gracious, efficient, and enthusiastic. Our common concern for the hungry was a bond that united us during our short visit.

The medical profession in both Senegal and Mauretania impressed us by their dedication, and by their frustration in the face of staggering odds. For instance, a para-medical technician, whose "office" was in an airless and dark hut on the edge of a tent city near the desert, seemed to pass most of his working hours in giving vaccine to babies. One problem here, he told us sadly, was that families are so fearful of plague and other formidable diseases that they brought children back day after day for still another inoculation. Correcting this practice was an uphill struggle.

The old hospital of St. Louis in Senegal is still staffed by sisters from France, and, from these good women, we learned the extent of epidemics which follow in the wake of malnutrition. A little baby died while we were there. It never had the chance to live because there was just not enough food to nuture it. One doctor explained the paradox of the African mother who is determined to keep her baby alive and who therefore continues to breast-feed the child long after this manner of nourishment ceases to provide sufficient sustenance for growth and development. The child does not survive, because the mother in her loving ignorance is unaware that what she is doing is counterproductive to her baby's life!

The haggard faces and intense eyes of these African doctors and the European nuns as they spoke so earnestly of their people and the diseases they were fighting gave eloquent testimony of the magnanimity of so many in the midst of tragedy. It was here that we learned of the continuing deadly presence of malaria, not knowing at the time that some of us would shortly be feeling its effects.

Our conversations with leaders of governments and other religious faiths provided insights that could not be perceived without face-to-face contact. One of the more noteworthy moments while in Senegal was our visit with President Senghor, who is not only a successful man of public affairs, but a poet and a philosopher as well. He has been guiding his nation since the early days of independence from France, and has played a major rôle in the efforts of Black Africa to unite in a common crusade against famine and for multinational development.

The leaders of the Moslem community whom we met were no less impressive and thoughtful men. Representatives of the head of the Grand Mosque of Dakar led us through that great edifice and told us, with great fervor and conviction, not only about it but about the way of life of Islam. A visit to Touba's magnificent mosque and a conversation with the Grand Khalifa was memorable if only to see the vast throngs of the faithful who gathered to pray and to listen to the holy man's words. Dressed simply in a plain robe with a woolen cap on his head—a most common headpiece in this desert land, surprisingly enough—he never spoke above a whisper and one of his aides conveyed his thoughts to us and the rest of the audience.

We had made the journey in the holy month of Ramadan when the faithful Moslem fasts from sunrise to sunset. The fast is a total one and includes abstaining from all liquids, even water. To do this at any time is difficult, but to observe such mortification in heat which often rises to 115 degrees Fahrenheit, and while continuing to perform all of one's ordinary duties, must be close to heroism! These men who accompanied us—whether occupying high government posts or employed at menial tasks—gave striking examples of faith in God and prayerfulness. Several times each day, they excused themselves and moved off to a quiet spot to kneel and pray. God surely will hear their prayers for themselves and their unfortunate lands.

* * * * *

Our journey to the Sahel was rich in observations like these. We were face-to-face with hunger and poverty on a vast scale and became more convinced than ever that food is a sacred trust. Our horizons were broadened as we saw the rich cultures of both Black and Islamic Africa and sensed the cultural and spiritual treasures that each holds. We were reminded that, in the journey of life, we all come from God and return to God—not alone, but as members of His human family.

Our Irish ancestors deepened their understanding of God's world by their journeyings around it. May it be that we have

730

learned more about the interdependence, the wonder, and the rich variety of His human family through this voyage along the Sahel—the desert's edge.

Cardinal Cooke is Archbishop of New York.

Working Among the Irish of Africa

KEVIN M. CAHILL, M.D.

Although I have worked in many of the most remote areas of Africa - and in various and sundry parts of Asia and Latin America - Somalia holds a special and soft place in my heart. Possibly the genes of my Kerry forebears—who survived on bare rocky hills far from the lush green fields of Eire—influenced this selection. As we all know, Irish genes are most unusual, and if the attraction to Somalia was purely hereditary, that alone might explain why I found and held firm to this isolated and forgotten part of East Africa.

Yet, as I have gone back over and over again - on twelve trips in fifteen years - and traversed all Somaliland, working among the sick, carrying on medical research, rejoicing with my Somali friends as their own new nation evolved - and while relishing every hot, dirty, lonely moment - I've found it is the people, more than the land, that captured me, for here are "The Irish of Africa."

When Sir Richard Burton - not the colorful Celtic thespian of today but the explorer and linguist who discovered one of the sources of the Nile, mapped much of Africa and was the first non-Moslem to visit Mecca and survive - left Aden in 1854 he traveled across the Gulf into an unknown land. Five months later, with a Somali spear having pierced his jaw and with one of his companions dead on the beach at Berbera, he returned to "civilization." He had visited the holy city of Harar, had recorded the customs and language of the Somalis and described the people as "a fierce race of Republicans, the Irish of Africa" in his classic *First Footsteps in East Africa.*

In addition to their possessive love of the land the Somalis had other typical Celtic qualities of great respect for poetry, religion, song, democracy and age; they loved to talk and had a highly developed sense of humor. They were brave but reckless; as Burton noted, they had "an unquestioned - if not occasionally injudicious - war-like manner." Above all they had a fanatic pride in Somalia and the Somalis. Burton wrote "they are full of curiosity and travel the world accepting almost any job without feeling a sense of inferiority, perhaps because they believe that they are superior to everyone else." Surely that is a rather typical Irish trait.

It is not irrelevant that Burton's ancestral background included a grandfather who was the Protestant pastor of Tuam in Galway, and whose father "was a thorough Irishman." To justify that statement on his paternity Burton noted his father constantly spent the family fortune "on the wildest speculations," and on two separate occasions, after wounding an adversary in a duel over a minor matter, he devotedly nursed his opponents back to health. Clearly Burton was suited by heredity to initiate Western contact with the Somalis and open the area for exploration.

The Eastern Horn of Africa is the land of the Somalis. Its coastline, the largest in Africa, runs from the Red Sea and the Gulf of Aden down the Indian Ocean for 1600 miles. The strategic significance of that vast expanse of shoreline and particularly its critical position across the oil lanes from Arabia and at the entry to the Red Sea has not been missed by the superpowers of today. In the Southern part of the country two fertile strips of arable land surround the Juba and Scebelli rivers that run from the Ethiopian highlands towards the Indian Ocean. But the rest of the Horn is harsh and arid.

The Somalis are primarily a nomadic people who migrate endlessly with their herds of camel, goat and cattle over the dry savannah and semi-desert plains that cover 80 percent of Somaliland. In the dry season it is almost incredibly hot, with temperatures regularly exceeding 110° F., but with relatively cool evenings. Scrub bush and occasional acacia thorn trees dot the lanscape and life revolves around an endless quest for water. The culture reflects an existence geared to a constant struggle for survival, and the success or failure of the semi-annual rains is the subject of poems and song and virtually continuous conversation.

I have traveled the bush for weeks on end with the nomads, slept under the sky with the Southern Cross shining, and shared their meals, while tracking their diseases. I have come away with an enormous respect—almost approaching an awe and certainly reflecting a love that can only be forged in hardship—for their strength, their kindness to and concern for the stranger, their silent wisdom, their knowledge of nature and their remarkable ability to read the stars and the hot winds.

The physician has a unique opportunity to communicate with even the proudest people from totally different cultures. Healing wounds and preventing epidemic diseases and caring for sick babies are entrees to isolated societies afforded few others. In Somalia the common ground of concern for health bound us closely.

When I first went to Somalia in 1962 the nation had just become independent. There were no Somali physicians and, in fact, few health facilities and even fewer personnel. The health system was a chaotic amalgam of the British and Italian colonial medical services, such as they were. During the first 40 years of this century the Italians ruled the southern part of Somaliland while the English controlled the area along the Gulf of Aden and inland to the Ethiopian highlands. Medical programs for the indigenous population were not a main feature of colonial governments at that time. The vagaries of international politics since the mid-1930s made this early neglect in native welfare programs almost appear positive.

Mussolini launched his transient dream for an Italian East African empire from Somaliland. The pressures of initial military conquest quickly followed by retreat and surrender left little energy or enthusiasm for attention to local health problems. When the English army assumed control of all Somaliland in 1941 they did so only as a holding operation and the continuity of planning and administration necessary for social programs was wanting. Even during the period of UN trusteeship from 1950-1960 higher priorities were - possibly for justifiable reasons - given to the construction of roads, internal security, the establishment of a police and army, and the development of a bare economy rather than to health or education.

One of the most mind-boggling obstacles was the fact that the Somali language had no script, and all writing - including even rather basic documents - a constitution, laws and regulations - had to be promulgated in the foreign tongues of English, Italian and Arabic. The common mode of recording history, for example, was by reciting epic poems. Many the night I lay by a fireside under the open sky at some remote nameless well listening to an elder recite. My translator would render his lilting words as I tried to discover whether smallpox or malarious fever or the bloody cough of tuberculosis had plagued that particular tribe. Such were the methods for defining the epidemiology of disease on the Horn of Africa. In 1972 an acceptable script was finally devised and now an entire nation is embarked on the difficult journey from a totally vocal culture into one where literacy in a brand new written language is expected for young and old alike. Only with the spirit of self-reliance that marks the revolutionary government of Jalle Siad could all educated teen-agers be assigned to the bush for a 6 months' crash teaching program in order that their nomad brethren also be able to read and write. These are the heroic - and humbling - efforts of emerging Africa.

My own studies in Somalia have been recorded in some 20 odd technical research papers and a book, *Health on the Horn of Africa.* When those studies began Somalia held the unenviable record of having no data available for 22 of 24 diseases surveyed in Africa. There had been virtually no medical studies emanating from the Horn for several decades, and the essential statistics for rational planning of health programs were simply non-existent.

Although my book on health in Somalia must hold the record for the least-selling volume in publishing history, I have, nevertheless, the inordinate satisfaction that that slim book still serves as the basis for the Somali medical services. To have been afforded the privilege of setting up a new nation's health system must be akin to the joy a lawyer might experience if asked to write a new constitution. That joy is rare and treasured. As I write this article for *The Recorder* in Mogadiscio in June 1977 the roots of Kerry are deep in the soil of Africa. I'm received as - and feel - a part of the people.

I can hear the chant of the muezzin calling the faithful of Islam to evening prayer. There can be few more beautiful or melodious sounds. One fellow African traveler described my reaction as one of having the unreasonable feeling that I have discovered what I have been searching for without really defining what it is. I only know I fall asleep feeling once more at home among the Irish of Africa.

Dr. Cahill is the President-General of the Society.

736

I am of Ireland

RICHARD HOWARD BROWN

I only knew my grandfather when he was old, gray, and bald, a large quiet man with glasses and a closely trimmed white stubble moustache. He was a steel man and on those visits to his home when I was little, I'd have breakfast with him at the kitchen table before he would go to work at the mill. It was a special treat to have that early morning time set aside for me to eat shredded wheat with Grandpa and have him prepare an orange in quarters for me, making small boats by cutting off the sinewy white core along the top edge and then separating the fruit from the pointed ends of the peel.

He drank his coffee black from a cup so large that it seemed to me a bowl. Sometimes on those mornings he would draw pictures for me, just a few quick easy lines on a piece of paper, and there, surprisingly, would be a deer or a funny man in a big hat. I learned how to draw from him and as I grew older, and became something of a schoolboy artist, my mother would set aside the good things that I did to take with us on the next visit to her parents.

To me, who saw him only with the eyes of a child or a teen-ager impatient with the binds of family, my grandfather was a private person. That is my idea of him, though I don't believe we were together more than two dozen times in my life, and I was too young, even at the end, to talk with him seriously about anything. I do remember telling him apologetically that I didn't want to be a steel man; that I wanted to read books and see the world. He was sitting on a bench in front of the summer cottage he had on Lake Skaneateles and I was a twelve-year-old skimming flat stones out on the water, looking away from him, sorry that I'd said what I did. His way was quiet. He just told me that no one expected me to be a steel man, but that a man had to be responsible, and that he had also wanted to read books and go to college and travel, but there had been no choice for him when he was fifteen, and that he'd gone to work instead.

He'd been a good football player when he was young and followed the game all of his life, and when I was eight years old, he showed me how to throw a forward pass. Of the pictures that I have of him, the one that is my favorite is a cracked sepia photo from the mid-1890s mounted on cardboard that shows him as captain of a team, perhaps from the steel mill back in Canton, Ohio, where he was raised: a young man with tousled wavy hair and a big moustache in a long-sleeved striped jersey open at the neck, a melon-shaped ball held in the crook of his arm, his teammates posed casually about him.

He was Richard Sebastian Read. Both his parents were dead when that picture was taken. At twenty-one he'd been appointed superintendent of the open hearth at the Canton Steel Company, the position his father had held before his death. "Do you think you can do the job, Rich?" the head of the mill had asked. "If I can't, sir, you'll be the first to know."

He was already courting my grandmother, who was Katherine Price. Because he was responsible for raising six younger brothers and sisters, the courtship lasted almost four years and there were times when she thought it might be better to marry a man people did not think of as already a widower with a large family to support.

My grandmother was a small, finely featured woman then, with deep-set blue eyes, sentimental and highly strung. Throughout her life she alternated the spelling of her name as the mood struck her, changing the "K" to "C," the "I" to a

"Y," and sometimes concluding with an "E," and sometimes not. She had a beautiful parlor voice and an independent spirit and persuaded her father to send her to Boston to study singing at the conservatory of music there, an adventurous undertaking for a young woman to embark upon alone in the 1890s and one that saddened my grandfather, who was afraid she'd meet some bachelor with no responsibilities.

He wrote to her often during her stay in Boston, sometimes illustrating the envelopes or the top margin of the writing paper with the same sort of little drawings that years later he drew for me, commenting on what he was doing and indicating, in a funny way, how much he missed her.

Much of what I know about my mother's family I associate with half-heard stories and random anecdotes told through the years at the dinner table at my grandparents' home in Syracuse. I remember where I always sat, at the lower end near the pantry door. Some things were said for my benefit alone, in a "Remember this, this is very interesting" sort of way, which meant it was a story that would provide additional evidence of the good stock from which I came, but much of it was just grown-up talk and reminiscences that bored me and sometimes the voices had that disconnected background sound you hear before falling off to sleep.

Many of those bits of stories and references to people long dead stayed with me and helped to create an image of the old-time Ohio world they came from, where all those relatives and family friends they spoke of existed in my mind as figures in some period piece of Americana set against white clapboard houses and streets lined with big elm trees. The women all wore long dresses with puffed sleeves and thick hair piled on top of their heads. They baked raisin bread and johnnycakes, made sweet boiled hams and potato salads, and everyone drank root beer and lemonade. The men were oldtime rollers and melters and puddlers from the steel mill, all sons of Irish and German immigrants in summer straw hats and white shirtsleeves and stiff collars, who on Sunday outings pitched horseshoes and smoked cigars. Someone played a concertina and my grandmother sang "The Harp That Once Thru' Tara's Halls" and my grandfather listened proudly but appeared to be indifferent.

My grandmother's father, Edward Price, was an Irishman from Sligo. He knew McKinley well, and before his own marriage had aspired to the hand of the girl who was to be McKinley's wife. A prominent baker's daughter named Ida Saxton, she courteously rebuffed his attentions by "giving him the mitten," a kindly ritual of rejection favored by well-bred Ohio ladies of that day.

Sometimes I'd let my mind play with the idea that as McKinley's friend, he could well have been Vice-President, and then upon McKinley's death, the President. Or because he was a machinist and part-time inventor of various locks and mechanisms for which he never troubled to take out patents, and the designer of a simple collapsible fence that he sold for a modest sum to a man who passed his yard and foresaw the larger possibilities of what was to become the playpen, I'd speculate on what might have been and imagine that we were rich and living in a big house with servants.

* * *

I'm Irish because of these people, a tenuous connection perhaps, but one that matters to me. In addition to my grandmother's father from Sligo, who came out during the Great Famine and served in the Civil War with an Ohio militia unit called "The Squirrel Hunters," and afterward married Catherine Kiley from Limerick, there was another great-grandfather, a Dubliner who was a merchant seaman with three voyages to his credit by the time he was nineteen. With the passing of years, it has turned out that he was the one who mattered to me most.

But it was the Sligo man, Edward Price, whom I was told of first, and that because of the Civil War and my interest in it and in soldiers, when I was in the eighth grade at St. Catharine's parochial school and studying American history. I didn't care anything about Ireland then, or about the Famine or the coffin ships that brought the Irish here in hordes, or that Edward Price had been among them, a five-year-old boy who left Ireland with his uncle in 1848.

What the family circumstances were that prompted their departure, or whether his parents were still alive or already among those dead of typhus, I don't know. His father played the violin and was a teacher, so his people were of modest means, or had been once, and not peasants evicted from some hut and left to wander destitute on the roads or die in ditches. But the distinction probably mattered little then, as those were years of terrible hunger and disease in Ireland. Sligo, in the western province of Connaught, was among the counties that suffered most and poverty touched everyone.

The saving and preparation for their trip took almost a year because few of the ship owners trafficking in emigrants provided food or sleeping quarters. Transporting the Irish to the New World in the time of the Famine was a speculative business, which meant that owners invested as little as possible and moved as many as they could crowd onto a ship. Travelers provided their own bedding and provisions and payment for the trip covered passage only and a supply of water, which on the ship my great-grandfather sailed on was down to a cup a day per person within a month because most of the casks leaked and two had previously contained vinegar and the contents were undrinkable.

There were only two stoves on deck and the cooking lines were long. When winter storms kept everyone down below, the food was eaten raw. The supplies of some of the passengers ran out early in the voyage, either through miscalculation or because portions that had been gnawed by rats had been thrown overboard to feed the fish. Some families shared what they had with others but still there were fights for the food that remained and two men were killed, and the fastidiousness of the first weeks was forgotten when some of those same people who had thrown food away tried to catch the rats so they could eat them.

741

The ship landed in Quebec one day short of seven weeks after leaving Sligo Bay. Most of those who disembarked were weak and sickly, a sorrier lot by far than when they started. Of the four hundred who set out from Ireland with my great-grandfather, sixteen never survived to see the fabled New World that was going to change their lives. Except for the few killed in fights for food, they died of dysentery and typhus and were thrown overboard as soon as they were dead.

* * *

This part of my family's background didn't concern me at thirteen, and if I thought about it at all, I'm sure I found the poverty and passive suffering distasteful. It means something to me now because I've lived through years that have seen millions die in concentration camps. Flying to Ireland when it was early morning and we were still an hour away from land, I looked down through the cotton bars of clouds to the flat blue of the ocean. I was drinking coffee and eating pastry and some men were standing near me in the aisle singing Irish songs, and I realized that Edward Price had already been a week at sea to reach that area of blue that I could see from thirty-seven thousand feet.

At thirteen, though, it was the idea of a great-grandfather who'd been a soldier in the Civil War that I liked, though the designation "Squirrel Hunters" for the minutemen who in the fall of 1861 protected Ohio's southern border from invasion by "secheschers" hardly created an image of prowess in my mind. Not that saving Ohio mattered to me. My father's people were mostly Southern and a great-granduncle and several distant cousins had served in the Army of Tennessee on the side of the Confederacy, and they were part of history too. Being able to claim family service on both sides of my country's most traumatic conflict appealed to me. A kind of historical snobbishness was involved.

However, to have Civil War veterans in one's ancestry, including one who was Irish, was a rather esoteric claim in those years. The fathers of most of the boys I knew had been in what was still called the World War, and on rainy days we would scavenge through basement and attic trunks looking for helmets, bayonets, kit bags, and other souvenirs of what up to then had been the great American military adventure of this century. With Pearl Harbor, though, the reality of a new war dominated the newspapers and movie newsreels, providing fodder for such easily roused imaginations as ours, and past wars were forgotten.

*   *   *

My grandfather's father, Richard Joseph Read, was not a soldier but a merchant sailor. Because he died so young, only forty-five and unknown even to my grandmother, he was never part of the nineteenth-century Ohio world I created out of all the family conversations I heard while growing up.

There are no anecdotes about him that I know, except the story of my grandfather's elevation to his job after his death. Yet though he was remote, I was always aware of his presence as father to my grandfather. Through my grandfather, I bear his name. I wore his ring—a dark green, red-flecked bloodstone—from the time of my grandfather's death when I was eighteen until only a few years ago, when the gold became too worn around the edge to hold the stone.

It may be that in some irrational way, the two are one to me, and the romantic idea of the young Dublin seafarer complements the image of the young football player who was my grandfather and counterbalances all the sober responsibility and industriousness that characterized his life.

Or maybe it is simply because his past can be precisely placed in a house on Rathgar Avenue in Dublin that I have chosen him to justify my own desire to be Irish.

Though little was said about him when I was growing up, I know him differently from the way I do the others. Still surviving today are four letters written to him by his mother in the 1870s when he was a young man making a start in life in this new country, the certificates of discharge that record the teen-age years he spent as a seaman on the merchant ships *Nonpareil* and *Countess of Minto*, and the Dublin house he finally left forever when he came to America in 1869.

I've known about that house since I was in high school and even daydreamed that I would some day buy it. It had been called Eagle Lodge in his time and when I heard it spoken of in my boyhood, the name made me think it was an inn or a saloon. "We used to own this bar in Ireland," is the way I'd account for my Irish ancestry to friends then. It sounded loose and carefree. I was descended from a long line of whiskey drinkers, and what could be more Irish, I thought. Respectability is no great virtue to a teen-ager.

I was not aware then of the letters my great-grandfather received from his mother in Ireland when he first came over, the letters I have now, that cautioned him to be always frugal and industrious, to be careful in his decisions, to attend Mass regularly, and above all things, to avoid strong drink. There is no evidence that he lived contrary to those standards and, to the best of my knowledge, they were passed on to his children, particularly to his oldest son, my grandfather, who never in his life drank whiskey in a public bar.

* * *

I visited that home in Dublin my great-grandfather left more than a hundred years ago, and sat talking in front of an electric heater with the present owners in the musty-smelling upstairs living room. It was late on a Saturday afternoon and turning cool, and coming up Rathgar Avenue in a cab, I recognized the house immediately from my memory of an old photograph my grandfather had. It was stark square stucco and had large rectangular windows of unpaned glass and center steps with iron railings leading to a second-floor entry. In front there was a forecourt of dirt and gravel, and walls extended from either side of the main box-like structure of the house to block the rear property from view. There was a time, and that old photograph showed it, when decorative eagles molded in concrete were centered on top of both those walls to give the house its name, but the eagles have long been lost to time and weather.

Rathgar is in the Dublin outskirts, not wholly suburban, not really city. A comfortable area for the most part, old middle class from a day when middle class meant modestly successful merchants and soliciters, responsible-sounding titles in the British Civil Service, men in banks with good positions: a smaller and thus more distinctive social grouping than it is today. These are not the red brick structures of Dublin's Georgian period that went to slum and have been renovated into smart flats and townhouses. The Rathgar homes seem all dark sand and gray—the colors of stucco, stone, and mortar —with small front gardens, forecourts, and walls; all cozy gray respectability from the mid-Victorian years.

A professor at University College Dublin, a big-bodied man named Hanley, his graying hair worn long, lives with his wife and three small children in that Rathgar house today. They were courteous and hospitable, in part because I was American, a visitor to their country, an exception to the familiar routine of daily life, but also because their attachment to the past was far more deeply grounded than my own. The house had belonged to their family for almost fifty years and they were truly interested in all that had to do with its history before their time.

They showed me through the old high-ceilinged rooms, all casual disorder, with books and picture frames and mirrors stacked against the walls, and told me of the Earl of Beauchamp, who built it as a hunting lodge when Rathgar was only fields and meadows. We went downstairs and out and through the back, past an overhanging roof and over flagstones, where two big dogs were barking, then past a gardening shed with wood and long-handled tools piled against it, to a deep stretch of lawn and bushes, and beyond the trees there was a house that James Joyce had lived in as a boy.

Inside again, and upstairs in the musty living room, they brought out a sheaf of heavy documents and bills of sale for me to see, papers that accounted for the various owners of the house back to the Earl of Beauchamp. One of those large handwritten sheets, creased with the folds of a hundred and fifteen years, and, in accordance with the legal fashion and requirements of the day, detailing the various relationships of my great-grandfather's family background into the eighteenth century, was signed by *his* father, my great-*great*-grandfather, also named Richard.

I ran the side of my thumb across the signature to touch with my flesh the paper where his flesh had rested. It was remarkable that I held this document in my hands and that I was sitting in the room where men and women, some of whose names I had never heard of until that afternoon, and yet who were of my blood, had preceded me in a traceable line of life and consciousness, had sat in the gaslit evenings of another century; that finally, after all the talk about someday doing it, after all the big city streets and office buildings in another country, all the places and people I had known and things I had done that were so far removed from this house in Dublin, I was there.

We talked about our families and the past; about America and their wish to visit it; about Dublin life and academic meetings in London, where professors kidded Hanley because he was Irish, as if he lived with savages in the wilds somewhere; and about the IRA, to which no one in Ireland was indifferent.

Afterward, walking down the steps and across the gravel forecourt, I was smiling. I didn't even mind that there was a Texaco station diagonally across the street to spoil the tacky mid-Victorian gentility of the setting. A gas station across the street from the onetime hunting lodge of the Earl of Beauchamp, from the house where my great-grandfather was a boy! Walking down the street to the bus stop I kept looking back to fix the image of it in my mind: the way it was set in the gray of early evening against the trees and other houses, the sense that I had been there, because it confirmed whatever claim I had to care about this land, to identify with these Irish people.

My great-grandfather had walked those streets. He had done chores in that house behind me, played in that deep back garden, studied by gas lamp in those now-musty rooms. I pictured him reading books about sailing ships and dreaming of the sea. Why else would he have gone to it, a middle-class boy not yet seventeen? His time was not the Famine. He was born when it was over. Was he an indifferent student, then, unsure of what he wanted out of life? Those were Fenian years in Ireland, when he first shipped out in 1866. The men who dreamed of insurrection then were not the violent rustics of the agrarian secret societies, but city workers, office clerks, and shop boys. Walking to the bus, I let myself think that he had been among them, and that when the rebellion came to naught, crushed before it started because of informers, that he had run away to sea. Was it possible that young Richie Read had been a rebel on the run, a sailor for two and a half years and then a revolutionary exile to America for the rest of his life? From this respectable neighborhood? So sober and hard-working all his life in America and an oathbound Fenian rebel at seventeen?

When I was seventeen I would sit staring like a detective at those seaman's papers of his, the three certificates of discharge that accounted for thirty months of sailing to ports of call around the world. I'd read all the official small print, the brief formalities scratched in the blank spaces with the quick smudged script of a ship's master signing off a crew; and my great-grandfather's hand, quick too, and smudged, acknowl-edging receipt of his pay. Year of birth: 1850. Place of birth: Dublin. How many dozens of forms have I filled in like that, hardly thinking, providing simple answers to simple questions, and yet those few simple answers in his own hand are almost all that's left of him.

If only because those papers survived, that time must have mattered to him. He must have saved them in a drawer or in a box back on some closet shelf, and maybe he came upon them over the years of his marriage, the way I do pictures from the Army or old letters from girls who were once away at college, and sat down on a high-posted bed on a Sunday, with flowered feminine patterns all around him, and read them and remembered when he was a young man, sailing to faraway places and not working in a Canton steel mill every day and raising a family of seven children in America.

I'd try to picture the ships he sailed on: *Countess of Minto* and *Nonpareil*. What did they carry? What was it like to live and work on them then? And most of all, where did they go? What were the places that he saw?

When I was seventeen, I wanted to see the world that I imagined out of books and movies, and one summer night drinking beer with a high school friend, we made a pact and swore we'd meet in Singapore in four years' time. We never did.

* * *

I thought of these things riding the double-decker bus back through the Dublin outskirts, past the high walls that line those roads, the mortar fallen away in patches from old bricks and stones; past small shops and pubs and churches; and those ordinary structures different because this was Ireland. I wished I could ask Grandpa about the man whose home I had just left, and in that chill gray early evening, looking down from the upper deck at those commonplace Irish streets that were so foreign to me, I thought of my grandfather as living still and not twenty-five years dead.

My grandparents died two months apart. My grandmother was first to go. The Saturday that she was dying, my aunts and mother persuaded my grandfather, who was seventy-two and not really well himself, to stay home and not keep any vigil by her bed or in the hospital waiting room. My mother stayed with him, trying to seem busy in the kitchen and the den, crossing through the hall occasionally to go upstairs, but really to look in on her father in the living room.

It was the late fall of 1946 and the great undefeated Army team of Davis and Blanchard was playing its last game against the Navy on the radio. My grandfather would listen for a

748

while and then turn the game off and sit there with his arms across his knees, his hands clasped in front of him, looking at the rug. He was rarely casual in his manner or attire and that day he was wearing the dark trousers to one of his business suits and a white shirt and tie and brown sweater-jacket. My mother came in during one of those times when the room was silent and encouraged him to turn the game back on, telling him there was no way he could help by worrying, and didn't he know how much my grandmother had enjoyed his liking football through the years.

The Navy quarterback was "Ribs" Baysinger and his father, who had also been a football player called "Ribs," used to date my mother in college and many times had stood there in that living room where my grandfather was sitting while my grandmother was dying in the hospital. My mother asked him if he remembered how the older "Ribs" had come over to the house on Saturday nights after a game to take her to some dance with his nose scraped or his lip puffed out. My grandfather nodded and stared through the window and across the street. My mother turned on the radio again and he tried to care that "Ribs" Baysinger's son was taking Navy down the field in a wild finish that almost beat the great undefeated Army team.

* * *

My grandfather was well thought of by steel men, particularly for a remark he had made many times in his career: "The company makes the good steel; I make the bad." He worked until the day before he died and while they were waiting for the ambulance the night he was taken to the hospital, he asked my aunt to be sure to call the mill in the morning to check on a melting formula.

He was dead before that new steel was made. I came up from college for his funeral and it was after we returned from the cemetery that I was given his ring, the one that had been his father's. Because I was only eighteen, I was made to promise that I wouldn't give it away to some girl as a token of affection during a two-month romance. I never did, but I never thought that much about the ring either, and it was not until more than twenty years later that it began to have any meaning to me.

When my grandparents died, it was a simple fact of life: everybody dies and their time had come. I wasn't touched by it, because they were old and I was young. I was quiet and serious and tried to say the right things around my mother and aunts, but their deaths didn't involve me then. I never knew them, really. They were old and I was young.

It is still a simple fact that everybody dies, but looking back I see them differently. I sense now their reality as persons other than the grandpa and grandma I visited once or twice a year and counted on to give me money for Christmas and my birthday. They are father and mother to my mother and my aunts, children to immigrant parents back in Canton, who in turn had been children too. I didn't know then that when I became a parent and talked with teen-age sons about school and sports, that I would be still a son myself: or that as a grown man, I would regret that my grandfather had been a stranger to me. At eighteen, I didn't realize that something of me would remain that age, fixed inside my head for always.

* * *

Those are my Irish forebears. The Ireland of the IRA is not a part of the heritage they provide. For all my romantic speculation on that Rathgar street, there are no Fenians among them, no rebels on the run to America, no great orators pleading for Ireland's freedom. These people who preceded me were not extraordinary. Respectable "lace-curtain Irish" in the old Ohio years, true to their Catholic faith all the days of their lives, they were indeed the good stock that my aunts and mother were so proud to be descended from.

Perhaps it is because I know nothing of the things that must have troubled them; have no sense of wild dreams or deeply held commitments that were unreasonable, other than their faith, which I'm sure to them seemed almost rational; was never told of any flaws of character or bad behavior, that the adolescent part of me is unimpressed by their virtue and dependability, their hard work and responsible self-sacrifice. That is the part which now regrets the passing of my grandfather, whom I never really knew, and daydreams sometimes of that other man before him, the young Dubliner, Richie Read, sailing out of Liverpool abroad the *Nonpareil* and bound for strange-sounding ports of call across the seas.

Mr. Brown is a business executive and author of a recent book published by Harper & Row, which bears the same title as the above article.

Seeing the World Through Irish-American Eyes

EDWARD WAKIN

The first day my parents moved into an Irish-Catholic neighborhood in Brooklyn the Doyle boys next door beat me up. It involved an argument over baseball cards (Ebbets Field and the Brooklyn Dodgers were not far away) and I came home in tears. I was in the second grade, and though getting beat up in those days meant only a push and a shove, it was enough to arouse my father's quick temper. Also to remind my parents that we were in Irish territory.

Not surprisingly, the Doyle and Wakin families soon became very close. We used their phone and they borrowed our catsup—continuously. They were eating meat with catsup all over it and we were eating Lebanese things like stuffed grape leaves. I still remember the shaking of the clothes line across the air well separating their apartment and ours. It was a signal to open the window and exchange messages, which time and again meant that the Doyles were out of catsup. So I would go to the window which was next to theirs and pass the red stuff.

No one around the neighborhood used such phrases as "melting pot" or ethnicity, but we were nonetheless living the immigrant story one or two generations removed. We were preparing "to make it" in America. For

752

me it meant growing up surrounded by the Irish and experiencing the world through Irish eyes.

There was the world of Irish-Catholic parochial school, Irish-Catholic parish, and Irish-Catholic schoolyard (when it wasn't stickball, stoopball, or punchball in the street). Later, it was Irish girls at parish dances and priests and professors on an Irish-dominated college campus. The whole world seemed Irish. I never paid attention to the historical experiences that had shaped my Irish friends next door and all around. I took them as they were—both defensive and aggressive, great friends to have on your side, strong on conformity and loyalty, quick with the cutting word, and fun to be with. I still remember Mr. Doyle's way of putting someone down: "He speaks with his mouth."

I had no sense of historical overtones, of famines, Fenians, and "No Irish Need Apply" signs. The connections between past experiences and present behavior became clear later, but never clearer than in writing *Enter the Irish-Americans*, my own presumptuous account of how Irish-Americans became what they are.

I remember distinctly that my family referred to the Irish as the *Americans*. In fact, the Irish are still called the *Americans* by other ethnic groups.

"Remember Georgie over on Prospect Park West? He married an American girl."

"Who was that?"

"You know, that Irish girl he was going out with."

In the 19th century, Irish immigrants would have laughed to be called *Americans*. That's the last thing they were being called. In 1851, an Irishman wrote home to Ireland that the position of his countrymen was "one of shame and poverty" and that he heard a black man complain that his master was "a great tyrant" who treated him as badly as if he were "a common Irishman." In 1868, the *Chicago Post* described "Paddy O'Flaherty" as a "born savage" with "hair on his teeth," adding:

"Scratch a convict or a pauper, and the chances are that you tickle the skin of an Irish Catholic."

A haughty New York lawyer wrote in his diary in the 1860s that England was right about the lower class of Irish: "They are brutal, base, cruel cowards, and as insolent as base. . . .My own theory is that St. Patrick's campaign against the snakes is a popish delusion. They perished of biting the Irish people." He called the Irish as remote from native Americans "in temperament and constitution as the Chinese."

Then how did the Irish come to be regarded as the *Americans* by later immigrants from Eastern Europe and the Mediterranean countries? It's because the Irish, who were here as the first large group of immigrants, had "joined the force." Not only as the policeman on the corner, but as firefighter, city worker, city hall functionary, local judge, and ward leader. On arriving, later immigrants were introduced to America by Irish guards and immigration officials at Ellis Island. Probably a busy Irishman decided how I am spelling my last name. No doubt the line was long on Ellis Island and there was not time for a careful phonetic rendition of the Arabic name for the biblical Joachim.

One of the colorful turn-of-the-century Tammany politicians, George Washington Plunkitt, "explained" Irish gratitude to New York City and their prominent place in city jobs. While an Irishman is still in the old country, Plunkitt noted, "his friends here often have a good place in one of the city departments picked out for him," adding: "Is it any wonder that he has a tender spot in his heart for old New York when he is on its salary list the mornin' after he lands?"

My favorite story of how the Irish "Americanized" later immigrants was told by Jewish humorist Harry Golden about his father. In 1910, Golden's father appeared before "a sober, dignified, white-haired Irish

754

judge" and after answering the appropriate questions was sworn in as a U.S. citizen. The judge said, "Now you are all American citizens." Then, lowering his voice, he added: "And don't forget to vote the straight Democratic ticket." Golden adds that his father told this story "for the rest of his life and he always said that he was not only made a citizen that day but completely Americanized."

Growing up Catholic I was never really able to separate what was Irish from what was Catholic. We thought of a "good Catholic" and we saw red hair and heard a brogue.

At our parish church, not only were priests and nuns militantly Irish, so was the housekeeper at the rectory (where they probably used plenty of catsup, too). I particularly remember the retreats that scared the hell out of us, almost always delivered by a stern-faced Irish priest.

There was the time one retreat master held us in his grip. St. Teresa's Church was filled to capacity and over on the side aisle, a row of us kids was hearing what hell was like and how fast you could go there. "So be prepared, live as if it is your last day," etc. For example, the priest told us, there was a young man he knew who had cut his hand, thought it was nothing at all, and all of a sudden he was dead!

It happened that Connie, who had a deadeye set shot in schoolyard basketball, had cut his hand the previous day. He sat there stunned, drained of all color, looking at his hand. He sweated, and all of us in merry-macabre Irish style doubled over to control our laughter at the expression on his face.

Of course, in the history of the Catholic Church in America, the Irish stand out. As Sir Shane Leslie noted in the *Dublin Review* of August 1918: "The Germans are a pillar of the Church in America, but the Irish have always held the rooftop." In 1886, of the 69 bishops in the United States 35 were Irish; the Germans were a distant second with only 15. Between 1789 and 1935, 268 of the 464 U.S. bishops were born in Ireland or were sons of Irish immigrants. (The total does not even include third-generation Irish bishops.)

An Irish family, which has always felt blessed by a son in the priesthood or daughter in religious habit, was very happy to see an altar boy in the brood when I was growing up. That was my younger brother, not me. Elderly Irish women used to stop my mother on the street and describe how they saw my brother Tom walking along the street early in the morning, cassock and surplice on his arm. He had the 6 o'clock Mass weekdays. They told my mother how wonderful it was to see him on the way to serve Mass. They no doubt thought they saw a priest in the making. They were wrong.

The piety of such Irish women has always been hailed by observers. Back in the 1860s when Irish journalist John Francis Maguire visited America, he described them as "naturally religious" and filled with "devotional enthusiasm." Growing up at about that time was Boston's William Cardinal O'Connell, who recalled that the day began with prayer at his mother's knee, continued "with constant reminders of God's care and love and providence" and ended in the evening with recitation of the Rosary—"which all children, no matter what their age, were bound to attend."

The memorable thing about the Irish was the certainty of their faith. Way back in the 1820s, when the fighting archbishop of New York, John Hughes, was a young man he wrote an obscure but characteristic story about *The Conversion and Edifying Death of Andrew Dunn*. The "edifying" came from Dunn's conversion after his Catholic friend advised him that "the Catholic religion is the safest to die in" and assured him that no lifetime Catholic was "ever known to wish to die a Protestant." Late in the same century, the eloquent Irish-Catholic

756

journalist, John Boyle O'Reilly, was writing in the *Atlantic Monthly* that "a great, loving, generous heart will never find peace and comfort" except in the Catholic Church. . . . "There is no other church; they are all just way stations." By the time I was in college, I was hearing—as were my classmates—an updated campus version of this certainty delivered by a Jesuit (believe it or not, with a noticeable brogue): "*They* have all the questions, but *we* have all the answers."

Growing up with the Irish meant being confronted always by their militancy—without realizing how their history of oppression had shaped them. England's treatment of Ireland was not only historically stupid; it was shamefully cruel. Quite simply, the English tyrannized the Irish in a manner summarized in a quotation cited by English historian Cecil Woodham-Smith: "The moment the very name Ireland is mentioned, the English seem to bid adieu to common feeling, common prudence, and common sense, and to act with the barbarity of tyrants and the fatuity of idiots."

Coming to America to escape the famine, the tyranny, and the poverty, the Irish found no rest. They arrived poor and unskilled and were promptly blamed for that, too. The Irish, as would the later immigrants, had to fight for an American foothold. Given their prior experience, their sense of the mythic, and their fervor, the Irish were probably the most militant of all immigrant groups.

My childhood friends were never more militant than on St. Patrick's Day, and I never questioned the Wearing of the Green—for me, too. I took it for granted that I went to school on March 17 wearing a green tie. Mine wasn't one of those glaring green ties; it was a dark green, but green it was. I still am amazed to walk up New York's Fifth Avenue and see Orientals, Africans, Italians, Spaniards, whomever, wearing green on March 17. It's an impressive accomplishment. No other immigrant group has succeeded in converting the entire country, including all the other ethnic and racial groups, to celebration of *their* holiday. Actually, this is nothing new. St. Patrick's Day was being celebrated by the Irish in America as early as 1737. During the American Revolution, Washington singled out St. Patrick's Day for special recognition in official orders for a day that was "enthusiastically observed in the American army," according to one Irish-American chronicler. I particularly remember the description of New York's Mayor Oakley Hall on St. Patrick's Day, 1870. He not only wore a shamrock, but his tie, kid gloves, and coat were green!

Any day, though, was a day to defend Ireland and proclaim her glories: such as the time I argued with Jimmy W. about the island of saints and scholars. I scoffed at the scholar part and wouldn't accept my Irish opponent's assertions. We went on to other things and finally went home for the day. Then, just before dinner, my doorbell rang. There was my friend standing with a volume of the *Britannica* in his hands to prove his point.

I don't know where Jimmy is today, but he would have relished one characteristic meeting of academics and others interested in Irish studies. They bemoaned the neglect of the Irish in academia, in the now-fashionable ethnic studies, and in media treatment of immigrant groups. The Irish were being left out. Amid the academic atmosphere of that all-Irish group (with one exception), the familiar militancy was coming out.

I thought to myself: "Isn't the reason that the Irish as a group are not up in arms about their neglect on campus and on TV the fact that they have largely made it, that they really feel like 'Americans,' that they are now coping with America without leaning on ethnic heritage. Sure it's true that the study of Irish-Americans tells a great deal not only about them, but about the entire story

758

of immigration. But is it realistic to talk of mobilizing the Irish on behalf of their Irishness? Someone at this seminar mentioned the question of defining an Irish-American. Someone answered that it refers to those who regard themselves as Irish and to anyone whom others define as Irish. Why not leave it at that, and concentrate on what can be learned about Irish-Americans—without raising a battle cry?''

But I didn't say any of this. I kept quiet. After all, I did learn something from that first time I confronted the Doyle brothers.

Edward Wakin is the author of Enter the Irish-American.

A. M. D. G.

EDWARD R. F. SHEEHAN

I have led an odd life. I was born into a religious, Irish-Catholic family, but I say that with some diffidence. My father was Irish on both sides, the son of immigrants; my mother was (still is) half French and half Yankee. What matters is that my family was of the Boston-Irish upper *bourgeoisie* that settled in Newton, and that the values of Boston-Irish culture dominated my childhood and my education. I was educated by the Sisters of St. Joseph, then by Jesuits in high school and university. On Sundays, and on weekdays before school, I served the Mass of the Auxiliary Bishop, before he became Richard Cardinal Cushing. Even now, as I scribble these words, I can hear his voice droning out the *Confiteor*, the *Gloria* and the Creed; I could recite the entire Ordinary of the Mass by heart before I was twelve. I was raised on a regimen of sensual repression, religious mystery, ecclesiastical pageantry.

The nuns taught me to spell; the Jesuits taught me to read and write Latin and Greek. In university (Boston College) I was an indifferent student, but I applied myself at Boston College High School (located then in the South End, the most disreputable of the Boston slums) and by the time I was seventeen or so I had learned (without realizing it) a great deal of pagan mythology. I could, I remember, translate Homer and Horace into creditable English, and perhaps I could even render English into something which resembled Homeric or Horatian verse. (My Greek has vanished, save for some sediment that clings to corners of my mind, but I can still grope my way through a Latin text.) The Jesuits—the Church at large—taught me something else. They made me revere myth—the basis of poetry, of all literature—and from pagan myth and historical Christianity I learned the ineluctable lesson of accountability: that personal actions invariably have consequences, that the evil one does will inevitably be punished, and the good—I am less certain of this, but I remain hopeful—will somehow, some way, some day, be rewarded, if not on this earth then ultimately in paradise.

In retrospect that seems a large lesson, but it was not sufficient for me when I was twenty. I had many times heard the truism that the Irish do best beyond their own environment, and I was determined to escape from mine. No sooner out of the university and military service but I fled to Europe, commissioned by *The Boston Globe* and other New England newspapers (for pittance wages) as a foreign correspondent. I traveled Europe from one end to the other, doing what foreign correspondents are supposed to do—witnessing riots and rebellions, interviewing cabinet ministers, and (catering to my Boston audience) reporting on the health of the Pope. I was in Madrid one month, Belgrade the next, Bad Godesberg the next. I spent a weekend as Evelyn Waugh's guest in Gloucestershire, where he made sport of my American innocence. In my spare time I haunted museums and concert halls; I adored Perugia and Salzburg; Waugh was right—I was groggy with cultural shock. I spent a summer in Ireland, visiting my father's kin in Kerry, loving the poetry of the spoken word, dismayed by the constant rain and the dismal towns. As the years progressed I could never involve myself in Ireland or its problems, and even today I am not impassioned by the events of Ulster. Ireland was too wet, too cold, too sunless, too gray, too remote and northern for me. It was the Mediterranean I loved, and its problems that enchanted me.

In the spring of 1955 I went to Morocco. This was my first

glimpse of the Arab labyrinth, and it happened during the dying moment there of French imperialism, before independence, when Morocco was still a protectorate. With dazzled eyes I penetrated Moorish palaces to meet such legendary and barbarous potentates as the Pasha of Marrakesh, then with schoolboyish glee I ran races with the French secret police as I darted down twisted alleys for midnight interviews with Mehdi Ben Barka, the "Lenin of Morocco" who at that time was intriguing for his nation's independence and who later was assassinated in Paris at the behest of the (independent) Moroccan Government.

I was "hooked." The following spring I went to Egypt, Lebanon, Syria, Jordan, Israel—it was the eve of the Suez war. I sailed up the Suez Canal, attended a reception at the Soviet Embassy in Cairo where I met President Gamal Abdel Nasser and another amiable, brown man who impressed me less—Anwar Sadat. Araby was in the throes of Nasser's passion, feeding on the fantasies of his speeches, flexing muscles it did not yet possess, living on illusions that did not vanish till, eleven years later, it was crushed by Israel in the war of 1967. I fled from the fantasies and the rhetoric to camp in Jordan with Bedouin tribes, acquiring for a time the T. E. Lawrence syndrome, the notion that the "savage" is somehow nobler than the rest of us, then descended on the cradle of Christianity in Jerusalem and the rest of Palestine.

I returned to America penniless, badly in need of a decent job. I was only slightly less callow than I had been in Gloucestershire, but the United States Government mistook me for an expert on the Middle East and dispatched me back to Cairo as press officer at the American Embassy. Now I had a palatial home near the Nile, a pair of Nubian servants, and the excitement of being spied upon by the Egyptian secret police. My work at the Embassy was less rewarding. I was part of the United States Information Service staff; our task was to dispense implausible propaganda to a population whose government was deliriously attacking America every day in

762

the newspapers and on the radio. The irrelevance of the American propaganda I was instructed to convey in my daily news bulletin was ludicrous enough; the contortions of my colleagues in this exotic country made me a player in a theater of the absurd. As a roving correspondent I had consorted with princes, prime ministers and kings; as an attaché I was confined to functionaries in the Foreign Office, flunkies from the Ministry of Information, the nonentities of Egyptian journalism. As time passed I embarked upon secret contacts for the Embassy with the Algerian and black African revolutionaries who had sought asylum in Cairo, and with the chief of Soviet intelligence in Egypt, but generally I remained unhappy. In retrospect it was all marvelous, and a few years later I put it all in a novel, *Kingdom of Illusion*, which was praised in *The New Yorker* but which, alas, did not sell so well as I expected.

I was transferred eventually to the American Embassy in Beirut, where (again in retrospect) my main accomplishment was my friendship with another Soviet spy, the notorious Kim Philby. I did not, of course, know at the time that he was the chief undercover Soviet agent in the Middle East. Kim was correspondent for *The Observer* and *The Economist*, and he called on me from time to time at the Embassy to engage in chitchat; I never had the feeling that he was pumping me. He was a shy man, even when he was drinking, and he spoke with a stutter, even when he was not. He was handsome, in a melancholy way, and he had charm to burn. Men liked him. Women wanted to mother him. At cocktail parties, into a room crammed with chattering diplomats, foreign correspondents and Arab intellectuals he would appear hesitantly, tentatively, like a crumpled letter delivered to the wrong address. As he squeezed past me mumbling "Ch-cheers, old b-boy," I could catch the clove and peppermint on his breath, and wonder at what hour of the day he had mixed his first drink. He defected to Moscow in 1963, but even when I wrote a major article about him after that for the old *Saturday Eve-*

ning Post, I could not persuade myself that a man so often so drunk as he could have been truly useful to the Russians or to anybody in the Middle East.

Such were the flotsam and jetsam of my existence as a young journalist and diplomat; my life-style was established, and before I was thirty I must have perceived that from this life, at least, there was no escape. But I escaped from government service, resigning when I was thirty to resume my quest of the tenebrous corners of the earth, as though intent to parody Joseph Conrad and Graham Greene, and, like them, "to write novels." I had been already beyond the Hindu Kush, to the temples of the Ganges and Nepal, to the pagodas that gaze upon the China Sea. Now I went to Africa—to observe Tanganyika and Kenya and Uganda and Zanzibar upon the eve of independence, as anxious as I had been in Morocco to be present in that twilight that divides the old order from the (often more cruel) new order that ensues. And so it was for the next decade of my life. Back and forth, back and forth, from Africa to Boston to the Middle East to Paris (to set up a flat, full of books, and to write another novel, this one about the ignoble savagery of Boston politics) and to Africa again. In 1966, I realized my fantasy of Conrad, and sailed up the River Congo for *The New York Times*. Going up that river was, just as Conrad said, "like traveling back to the earliest beginnings of the world, when vegetation rioted on the earth and the big trees were kings. An empty stream, a great silence, an impenetrable forest. . . ."

At Mbandaka, the somnolent capital of Equatorial Province, I alighted at the Mission of Iyonda, a large leprosarium overlooking the river, run by the Fathers of the Sacred Heart. There was an old nun there, deaf and almost blind, so fond of her profession of dressing lepers' wounds that she refused to return to Belgium to die in indolence. The Mission was divided from the lepers' village by a marsh. In my mosquito net at night I could hear the fluting of Lukulakoko birds and the tom-toms of the lepers on the other side of the swamp.

Memories; impressions; nostalgia. Two summers later, I

went to Nigeria and Biafra for *The Saturday Evening Post* to cover the Biafran war. I was nearly killed once or twice. In Biafra, the children were starving. They had the wrinkled faces and the haunted staring eyes, the apathy of aged men and women. Some looked like witchcraft dolls, their heads tufted with halos of white or reddish hair, their huge eyes popping out from hunger. On the Nigerian side, approaching the front in a Land Rover, I fell asleep from exhaustion, awoke with a jolt and then, in an hallucinatory scene, perceived the bodies of headless men littered along the read. I was too tired to be horrified; I receded into sleep.

In 1970, I returned to the Middle East for *The New York Times Magazine*, and I have kept hastening back there from Paris and from Harvard ever since. In September of 1970, in Amman, I witnessed the civil war between the Palestinian commandos and the King of Jordan. As in Nigeria fatigued from the bombardments of the nights before, I went to my hotel room one afternoon to take a nap. As I lay there, a bullet pierced my windowpane and came to rest in the reading lamp an inch from my face, splashing glass all over me and the bed. I took my pillow into the bathroom, lay down in the bathtub, and continued my snooze. Night fell; all over Amman electricity was cut. I groped my way to the basement, glanced out at Amman, and glimpsed the marvel of tracer bullets and mortar fire illumining the black town. All of mankind, it seems to me, is a little like that: mostly groping in the dark, illumined now and then by the pyrotechnics of its own misdeeds.

Later I went to Libya to interview Colonel Moamer Qadhafi, who received me at midnight in his barracks during Ramadan and did his utmost to convert me to Islam; then back to Egypt to be present during the Arab-Israeli war of October, 1973. I stayed awake during that war. I crossed the Suez Canal again, this time with Egyptian soldiers in a Russian jeep. We descended a bank, spurted forward in a sandy tempest, and came presently to Qantara, whose bougainvillaea and mud-brick buildings, mellow mosques and lanquid coffee-houses had been everywhere profaned by bullets and by bombs. The bodies had been buried, but there lingered the stench of death and the idea of death became a commonplace as we proceeded deeper into the desert. We passed through graveyards of blackened Israeli Patton tanks and dismembered Skyhawk bombers, and then gazed upward. An Israeli plane streaked across the cloudy sky; the Egyptians fired their SAM missiles—and missed.

But the Arabs did much better in that war. Their leaders, freed of the fantasies of Nasser, had grown up, learned how the world is run, established limited military objectives to maximize their political gain. In fact, the Arabs did not win the war militarily, but neither did they suffer another humiliating defeat, and politically they were the victors. President Sadat was no longer the amiable nonentity I had met in 1956; shrewdly he used the war to disengage the United States from total support of Israel the better that the U.S. might mediate a peace palatable to the Arabs. American policy in the Middle East became more balanced, and Sadat has progressively linked the destiny of Egypt to the gymnastics of Henry Kissinger's diplomacy. Whether Dr. Kissinger will in the end be able to deliver to the Arabs the territory seized by Israel in 1967 is quite another question, but it is comforting that the Egyptians—so wary of the Russians after years of hard experience—are still exhorting him to try.

The changes in American policy, such as they are, were imposed by a fact that few foresaw before 1973—the Arabs have become a world power. The dimensions of that power dawned on me when, soon after the October war, I visited Saudi Arabia and the other oil sheikhdoms of the Persian Gulf. The power of the oil princes is not from arms but from the fabulous reserves of cash they have acquired by raising the price of petroleum. Saudi Arabia alone earned nearly $30 billion last year; Kuwait has established the most opulent welfare state on earth; Abu Dhabi, with its miniscule population, enjoys a per capita income of between $30,000 and $100,000, depending on whether you count alien laborers as well as indigenous Abu Dhabians. Abu Dhabi must be seen to be believed. It was a desert a decade ago, its capital a backwater of palm-frond houses and tin-roofed shops on squeezed and twisting streets, but now doctoral dissertations and heroic rhyme should be composed about it as a paradigm of instant development. Abu Dhabi town has become a vast construction site—boulevards of Parisian scope and a *corniche* that rivals Alexandria's crisscross sand as white as moonlight; cranes and scaffolds are more numerous than trees. Here is a salt flat, there a city dump; blink and see a bank, a school, a hospital, a Hilton hotel. The Guest Palace on the periphery has golden ceilings and marble coffee tables, and when it is filled with soldiers with silver daggers and notables in their robes, it resembles the evenings of Scheherazade.

Already the Gulf has emerged as a major source of world capital, just as its wealth has attracted a host of African and Asian paupers and avaricious merchants from the West. That migration already resembles the California gold rush. Moreover, the Arabian peninsula's subsoil teems with other riches that have hardly been tapped—natural gas, tin, copper, zinc, aluminum, iron ore, silver, gold and uranium. What desert soothsayer at the dawn of this century, what callow journalist from Boston in 1956 or omniscient New York pundit on the morrow of Araby's ignominious defeat by Israel only eight years ago, would have dared to prophesy such ironies?

Not that wealth buys happiness. The richest man I ever met, and the saddest it seemed to me, was Saudi Arabia's King Faisal. He received me at the Royal Palace in Riyadh, in an immense room with a yellow carpet and painted green walls. The room was thronged with retainers, petitioners, soldiers; but when the King motioned me into an armchair beside his own, all of that entourage, in a magical exodus of whispering robes, vanished from our presence, leaving only an aide and a servant who served us glasses of sweet tea. As I sipped, I regarded the hawkish profile of the King, his draped head surmounted by a band of woven gold, his shoulders hunched and his body bent, his nails picking compulsively at the lint on his cloak. He exuded an exquisite melancholy. His hands were mottled, his face ravaged from years of pain produced by stomach ulcers. Most remarkable was his mouth, frozen as though with permanent disdain for the burden of his Kingdom's fortune and the follies of the human race. His voice, on Israel or whatever subject, was a lamentation. Perhaps, amongst his other preoccupations, he sensed his eventual end.

These are fragments of my experience, glimpses of a life that may enchant few, but I have a point. Now I am at Harvard, still venturing from there to Washington and Europe and the Middle East, but with sufficient leisure halfway through life to look back and wonder what I have done. I doubt I could have digested Harvard when I was twenty, but now I am forty-five it is simply another experience. I am happy here, intellectually challenged, vastly amused from time to time, and also slightly ill at ease. The priests were wrong when they said it was a sin to go to Harvard (they would never say that now) but they were right when they warned against its secularism. Harvard, once a seminary for divines, is today a de-christianized place, and I can never be comfortable with that.

For I am nostalgic, not for the repression of the system that raised me, but for the positive mystery and pageantry that went with it. I care little for my purely Irish heritage—I never really did—but in many ways I mourn for the Church of my youth, and for its passing. Not for the obscurantism and abuse of authority, but for the sense of awe and order that the Church inspired and now so seldom does. Like many Roman Catholics of my generation, I rejoiced when the Second Vatican Council was proclaimed, but I have been disillusioned by its results. I have had enough of gum-chewing nuns in mini-skirts, guitar-strumming priests in blue denim, and Masses in the vernacular. I long for the Latin mass, for a little of the pomp and circumstance of frankincense and cardinal's crimson that is vanishing so rapidly in the Roman Church and being expropriated—for it fulfills a deep human need—by the Anglicans. In Holland not long ago I met a

Marxist Jesuit who said, "Jesus Christ was a saint—like Che Guevara." That is not the sort of mystery I was raised on, and there is no room for it in the Church I cherish, but today I wonder if that Church exists.

I am exaggerating, of course. The Church as always will prevail, even over its present confusion. I am a victim of satiety, a shipwreck who has seen too many cultures and too much chaos in the world, who yearns for some pattern to give it meaning. The pattern, I suppose, must be perforce the one I learned in youth, for all the others I have found wanting. I have not seen all of the world, but I have seen enough to know that the other systems are not better than the one to which I happened to be born. And thus, after Salzburg and the Congo and the sunsets of the Nile, do I thrash about, at a loss for any meaning save for the meaning I began with. Scott Fitzgerald summed it up: "So we beat on, boats against the current, borne back ceaselessly into the past."

Mr. Sheehan is at present a Fellow at Harvard's Center for International Affairs. Among various citations, he has received the Overseas Press Club Award for his interpretation of foreign affairs.

Points of View

JAMES N. McHUGH

"To the crab," says the Japanese proverb, "all humans move sideways." This traditional saying has considerable significance in underlining how humans are essentially conditioned by their individual environment and upbringing.

Inevitably our assessment of other peoples and of their beliefs is bounded by the limited field of vision of our own distorting lens and evaluated against the standards and principles inherent in our environment and preached by our elders, clerical or lay. The impact of the unexpected is consequently something of a shock. It tends to produce disorientated defensive reaction and a forceful denial of its validity and value.

There is an old classical example of the Greek Senator addressing the Senate and enquiring as to what could induce any one of the Senators to eat the body of his dead father. To this appalling suggestion they indignantly responded that nothing could induce any of them to perform such a hideous act as they were accustomed to burn the dead.

The Senator then produced a group of Africans and to them he put the question as to what inducement he could offer them to burn the bodies of their dead fathers. They were equally horrified as their custom was to devour them.

A similar reaction may be obtained in Northern Ireland by taking a typical Ulsterman to the massive North of Ireland Parliament Building, Stormont, to see the huge painting of the triumphant King William III of Orange defeating the Catholic King James II at the famous Battle of the Boyne in 1690. The picture dominates the Assembly.

All goes well until it is pointed out that the clerical figure clearly visible in the clouds and obviously regarding King James' defeat with amiable approval is none other than His Holiness the Pope.

This produces a satisfactory disorientation in the observer's reaction irrespective of whether he be Protestant Unionist or Catholic Nationalist, for few are aware that Pope Innocent XI, who is depicted in the vast background, was at the time in deep dispute with King Louis XIV of France, the ally of the defeated King James. The cause at issue was the fiat of King Louis that the State was omnipotent and the temporal sovereignty of the French Kings completely independent of the Pope. This was the reason why Pope Innocent favoured William's victory.

It may well be practicable to obtain an equally satisfactory reaction from a selected class of educated New Yorkers by suggesting that the "Communist" Karl Marx and his friend Engels in their time wrote a great many of the leading articles on Asia in the *New York Daily Tribune*. In fact they did and their very professional contributions were published as leading articles in the latter half of the nineteenth century without naming or crediting the authors.

It is with very considerable surprise that the average citizen of a Western European country can be persuaded to admit the obvious geographical fact that Europe, in perspective, is a compara-

771

tively small peninsula of the vast land mass of Asia in which lives about half of the world's population. As a minute island off its western perimeter, Ireland's early contacts with the Middle, or the Far East, are unexpected. Yet in the valley of the Boyne River, no more than thirty miles north of Dublin's fair city, may be seen one of Europe's most spectacular groups of prehistoric monuments—the mighty megalithic tombs at Newgrange, Knowth and Dowth.

These massive stone graves and tumuli dominate the mounds and stone monuments of a large prehistoric cemetery and are dated by radio-carbon to 4,500 years ago.

They were very probably constructed by colonists who migrated originally from the Middle East via the Mediterranean to Spain, Portugal and thence to Brittany and to Ireland. Similar tombs are found along the route of their migration and those in Brittany are older than 5,000 years.

Many of the great stones are decorated with curious patterns of which such counterparts as the "double spiral" are to be found incised on megaliths across the Middle East, in India, Japan and South-East Asia.

Every year about the time of the Winter solstice the early light of the rising sun for a short period shines through a narrow rectangular stone frame over the entrance lintel of the great megalithic tomb at Newgrange. Its pale rays pass along the long passage under the hill and briefly illumine the dark interior of the tomb's main chamber.

Little is known of the Neolithic agricultural settlers who built the giant tombs, but their existence in the Boyne valley and also elsewhere in the Irish Republic used to be advanced by local ancients as convincing evidence of the former existence of a race of giants in Ireland.

I was reminded of this by hearing a young Malay boy ask his father, who like myself was viewing some prehistoric standing stones at the edge of the jungle in West Malaysia, whether it was indeed true that they had been erected by *gergasi* (giants).

One is so prepared for sharp contrasts between East and West—e.g., white as the Oriental mourning colour instead of the traditional European black—that the sudden coincidence of beliefs can be surprising.

When I first went to South-East Asia as a young Civil Engineer and was studying for the Government examinations in the Malay language I engaged a young Malay civil servant as my teacher. He had been educated at the local Christian Brothers' English School and as a result not only had received an excellent English language education but also, through some of the Irish Brothers, had acquired an interest in Ireland.

So I lent him an English translation of a book, *Twenty Years a-growing*, which had been originally transcribed from the spoken Irish of the Blasket Islands. He enjoyed it greatly and used to read it aloud to his elderly mother in the evenings. She had been a teacher in a local Malay vernacular school and did not know English. Accordingly Zainal Aibidin read it to her in Malay, translating the English text as he read.

Apart from such enquiries as to what was "porter"—the islanders' drink—or what *gliog-gliag*—the Irish for the sound of wavelets in the seaweed—only one difficulty arose. This was that his mother steadfastly refused to believe that the book was originally based on an Irish islander's life but was convinced that it was derived from life in a Malay fishing village on the east coast of Malaya. She had grown up in such an environment and insisted that such was the case.

There was of course the sea and all its problems and phases, the fishing and its hazards and storms, the cultivation of poor soil. There was the description of the visit of a European official to the village and the difficulty of not laughing at the strange harsh sound of spoken English heard for the first time, the prospect of boys going off to a town for training as young policemen and so on.

It was not until I lived near a small Malay fishing village on the coast of the China Sea some years later that I fully appreciated her viewpoint. There too I first learned something of the invisible world of spirits and demons which was an essential factor in the daily lives of the villagers.

Thus, on a sunny tropical evening I stood on the beach by invitation for the basic ceremony of the re-opening of the fishing season after the floods, gales and pounding seas of the monsoon season had passed. The fishing boats, which were all sailing craft, were lined up on the brown sand of the steeply sloping beach. The coloured sarongs of the fishermen and their families were vivid against the dark background of the jungle trees. Among those present was the local Muslim religious official as well as the local *bomoh*, or negotiator with the spirit world.

An exotic little scene, but oddly enough there was an unexpected dominant feature which at once carried my mind back to Killorglin in County Kerry and the three traditional days of Puck Fair: the Day of the Gathering on August

10th, the Fair Day on the 11th and the Day of the Scattering on Old Lammas Day.

Tethered to a wooden platform on top of a specially erected pole and gazing down with sharp dark eyes on the assembly below was a large male goat. He had been made up for the big occasion with gilded horns and coloured streamers adorned his post. He was as they say "the dead spit" of the goat who from his elevated platform annually superciliously regards the milling crowd at the Killorglin Fair. Both of these horned fertility symbols are from the pagan mists of the past, but the Malaysian one was the less fortunate in that he was destined to be sacrificed, albeit in the prescribed Muslim religious style. Various parts of his anatomy were then offered to the invisible elemental Powers of the Wind and the Sea in a number of specially prepared bamboo sacrificial trays. The trays were incensed by the religious official before being disposed at strategic points. The remainder of the animal provided the basis of a good meal at the celebration which followed.

It all made a fine spectacle and I was reminded of Synge's comment that "these people (the Aran Islanders) make no distinction between the natural and the supernatural," presumably because of their matter-of-fact way of dealing with either order in a traditional way.

The Celts who had dominated most of Europe and sacked Rome in 390 B.C. had vanquished the megalithic tomb builders and established themselves in Ireland by about the middle of the second century before Christ. It is of interest that when St. Paul addressed himself to the Galatians in Asia Minor he was addressing a Celtic people, whose kinsmen were well settled in Ireland and whose art had found expression there in the design of beautifully ornamented artifacts in gold and other metals.

Language helps to illustrate the ancient connections between countries widely separated and to indicate the roots and origins of peoples. The language of the Celts was a branch of the Indo-European group which includes such tongues as Sanskrit, Greek and Persian among others, and Gaelic is derived from it.

The social structure of the Celts with their nobles, brehons, bards and their sagas has much in common with Aryan India. Early Celtic law has been described by eminent historians as finding its closest parallel with traditional Indian law and Grenville Cole terms Ireland "the last outpost of Eurasia." The reasons for this are evident from the survival in its folklore, in the Gaelic language, of elements of the Indo-European world. The descriptions of the Celtic chariot-riding heroes and their behaviour in the Irish sagas are similar to those of the nobles and warriors in the epic Sanskrit poem, the Mahabharata, composed in Northern India several centuries before Christ.

The famous shadow plays of Java and Malaysia, which are still immensely popular in rural areas of South-East Asia, continue to the present time to perform plots based on ancient tales from the Mahabharata as their main attraction.

Fortunately we know a good deal about our ancestors the Celts, who conquered the megalithic builders on the Boyne valley. This is not only due to descriptions of them and of their customs by Roman historians in Europe, but also because the old Celtic sagas in the Gaelic tongue endured in Ireland in the mouths of storytellers and bards. In

776

the epic poems, sagas and legends, which were recorded in writing by Christian scribes, from about the eighth century, emerges the mythology of the Irish race.

It comprises legendary accounts in Gaelic of people and of places, of political and genealogical tradition, of Gods, heroes and battles long ago, of magic weapons and of invulnerability, of demons and hags, witchcraft and spells, giants and fairies. These have influenced the customs and the superstitions of the Irish people despite the vigorous efforts of the English colonists in the past to eradicate the Irish language—and indeed, at times, the people who spoke it.

Irish folklore is the surviving record of an extremely ancient way of thinking and of living. Its links in Ireland stretch back to prehistoric times and preserve elements from the remote period of animistic beliefs.

Although Christianity was opposed to most of the superstitions of the old myths it very sensibly tidied the infinity of evil spirits into the single general realm of the Devil and postulated effective procedures for dealing with them. The Church retitled with the names of Christian saints such established rural focal points for pilgrim piety as peaks of mountains and many shrines, springs and wells.

This was a practice similar to that effectively followed by the Buddhist missionaries in the East, who readily transformed fearsome figures of the Hindu religion into energetic guardians of their new Buddhist faith.

Islam is the major religion of South-East Asia today where the majority of the people are peasants and fisher folk. Their lives, still in harmony with the rhythms of the planting seasons and the tides, are spent not far from the jungle or the sea. The jungle still sprawls across some two-thirds of the land and related to it there survive in the folk beliefs, particularly among the aborigines, a considerable number of formidable *Hantu* (a generic name for elementals and spirits). The hazards are considerable and vary from the sharp spear of the Spectre Huntsman, or the talons of the Vampire, to the equally dangerous summons of the Ghost Princess calling men away to the depths of the gloomy jungle never more to return.

One could readily produce an impressive list of living Asian superstitions—from the choice of lucky and unlucky days for journeys or enterprises, to the type of herb for an infusion or a love charm, or related to birth, death, planting and reaping—which can be mirrored in rural Irish beliefs in the extensive records of the Department of Folklore of University College Dublin.

However, one major belief in South-East Asia will suffice to illustrate the common ground of humans of our times. The Malays and Indonesians alike share an ancient belief that all that exists in the contemporaneous world, in whatever form, shares a common entity, termed *semangat*. All living things have a semangat, which must be respected and not misused, but so too have all inanimate things, minerals, metals, food, clothes, boats, machines and other objects. The term is difficult to define in English. It is not a soul, nor a spirit, but has been described as a vital force, or essence. Like the Western physicists' nuclei it cannot be observed directly, but may only be assessed by its traces and by the effect it produces on its surroundings. Humans essentially must be aware of this entity because they share it with all creation and all creation exists through and in God (Allah). This belief encourages the neat, gentle approach rather than that of the bulldozer and makes for tolerance in dealing with humans and Hantus alike.

There is reference in Frazer's *Golden Bough* to a similar belief among certain American Indians: "The Indians of Guiana do not see any sharp line of distinction between one kind of animal and another, or between animals—man included—and inanimate objects. On the contrary, to the Indian, all matter animate and inanimate, seem exactly of the same nature except that they differ in the accident of bodily form."

In this nuclear age the educated world accepts the scientists' conclusions that matter has lost its solidity and substantiality and has become, as Russell put it, "a mere ghost haunting the scene of its former splendours." The comforting solidity of the pre-atomic world has dissolved into a frightening unreality where the composition of all existing matter, which formerly appeared reassuringly solid and stable, is dissolved into abstractions. Even worse, the sacred spell $E = MC^2$ is the now familiar code governing the release of the Demon of nuclear energy.

It is curious how the ultra-modern and the primitive should now become bed-fellows and that East and West should share a common fear of the unseen power inherent in their varying environments and the inevitable annihilation which could follow its release. "Stretch a bow to the fullest extent," says the Taoist philosopher's book of the fourth century B.C. "and you will wish you had stopped in time."

It is indeed a fearsome and an extremely difficult prospect to face up to. One needs the common sense of a young Donegal woman, which shines through in the following true account of an incident there, as related by her mother.

After a sing-song in a house in a rural area of Donegal one winter evening, the girl was walking in the moonlight along the narrow country road which led to her home about half a mile away on the hill. A young man of the house she had just left thought it would be a good idea to give her "a bit of a fright." He accordingly took a sheet from the house and took to the fields. He arrived at a hedge alongside a turn in the road.

As soon as she reached the hedge he groaned and moved the draped sheet to and fro, but was disappointed to have her merely utter the words "Good night" and hurry past along the road.

He repeated the performance after darting across muddy fields to another turn in the road, but met with a similar response. Finally, he had a third try and although he was muddy and out of breath she was again confronted by a ghostly figure in the hedge groaning and moaning with increased intensity. This time she halted. "I said good night to ye twice already," she said firmly. "Is it prayers ye want or what?"

Combining as it does tolerance, sympathy and an offer of constructive aid, this seems an essential and a very reasonable attitude for our times, if either humans or crabs are to continue to move at all and to avoid oblivion.

James McHugh, Chairman of the Asia Association of Ireland and a Trustee of the Chester Beatty Library in Dublin, has spent most of his professional life in the Far East.

The Irish Host at
the Castle Gate

MARY MACDONOUGH PHILLIPS

On page nine hundred and sixty-five of *The Modern Book of Home Verse*, this poem appears:

Via Longa

It's far I must be going,
  Some night or morning gray,
Beyond the oceans' flowing,
  Beyond the rim of day;
And sure it's not the going,
  But that I find the way.

PATRICK MACDONOUGH

Turning to the index of authors, one is disappointed to find under his name, "No biographical data available."
Who is Patrick MacDonough?
In the words of a former president of Notre Dame:

"Pat is a beautiful soul, and one of the old boys of whom we are most proud. He gave up prospects of a brilliant career in order to work for the poor Irish immigrants. He is probably one of the most talented men who ever received a degree from Notre Dame."

Pat was born in Sligo in 1871. He attended local elementary and intermediate schools. He shipped from Sligo Town, and after some wandering and delay, came to New York.

He worked his way through Notre Dame and was graduated in 1903. During his years there, he worked as sportswriter for *The Chicago Tribune*, edited *The Notre Dame Scholastic*, and welcomed his countryman, W. B. Yeats, to the university. He later studied at Fordham and Columbia. After two years of law at Columbia, he gave up the study "for what I regarded as a better opportunity to serve my faith and race. This occurred when I accepted the position of landing agent for the Mission of the Rosary and the Irish Emigrant Society." He remained in this field of immigrant welfare work—at Ellis Island, on the piers and on shipboard for fifty years. Irish immigrant girls were guests at the Mission at the rate of 4,000 a year in the great exodus from Ireland, and he personally met more than 100,000 of them. They stayed until relatives claimed them, or until they got jobs.

In March 1931 the first issue of *Old Castle Garden* appeared. It was started by the Rev. Patrick Temple and the other priests and workers of the Mission with a view to perpetuating the memory of the immigrants—particularly the Irish—and the Mission's indelible imprint on their lives. It built a special identity for itself because as MacDonough, its literary editor, wrote in the first issue:

"Castle Garden—what memories the name conjures up! From 1855 to 1890 it was the great landing depot for immigrants arriving in New York. It is safe to say during this period and for long after no other place on the American continent was so well known throughout Europe. Certainly this is true in regard to Ireland. 'Landed at Castle Garden'—a phrase which conveyed the eagerly awaited and consoling news that loved ones had completed the voyage, which in those days was fraught with privation and danger. Of the 8,000,000 which passed through Castle Garden, at least 1,750,000 came from Ireland. Many of these Irish immigrants are still living, thank God, and not a few are numbered among the parents and grandparents of our readers. Because of its association with so many of our kith and kin, its proximity to the Mission, and the work in which we are engaged in behalf of the Irish immigrant, we have selected *Old Castle Garden* as the title of this little publication."

It was the editor's avowed aim, often by the poet's pen, to cultivate interest in the history of old New York—a story that never loses interest, particularly for the Irish who played such a part in its building.

The Streets of Old Manhattan

The streets of Old Manhattan,
  They wander up and down,
And east and west and crosswise
  They span the little town,
That in the days long vanished
  Was fief of Holland's crown.

Who was it thus that planned them,
  A-winding here and there?
'Twas *kinderen* from Holland
  Without a fret or care;
They led through brake and bracken
  When summer days were fair.

And anxious mothers followed,
  And so the trampled clay
Became the path and roadbed,
  The streets we tread today;
The haunted ways and splendid
  That lure from far away.

The streets of Old Manhattan,
  I know them ev'ry one;
They're silver in the moonlight
  And golden in the sun;
And o'er them at the dawning
  A veil of dreams is spun—

783

The dreams that youth brought over
   Across the crested main;
The purple dreams of glory,
   The gilded dreams of gain;
And fairest—those of lovers
   Whose love was all in vain.

Dear streets of Old Manhattan,
   Lie north, south, east or west;
Though fine be foreign highways
   That royal feet have pressed;
Though aimless seem your courses,
   I love you still the best.

Battery Park

What garden fair is all the world
   Is half so fair to me;
Thy walks with loveliness apparel'd,
   Beloved Battery.

The city lifts a thousand towers
   Above thy verdant lea;
In none the charm of thy bowers,
   O friendly Battery.

Beside thy marge the stately ships
   Sail proudly home from sea;
Fair freight with fingers to the lips
   Salute thee, Battery.

And Argive Helen never died,
   Each day at noon comes she,
For one brief hour, immortal bride,
   To walk the Battery.

How New York needs this kind of poetry today!
Remsen Crawford wrote of Pat in *The New York Sun* in
July 1931:

"Patrick MacDonough is literary editor of *Old Castle
Garden.* For years upon years the workers on Ellis Island

784

have known Pat MacDonough as a kindly, sympathetic welfare worker representing the Irish Society. He would meet the sons and daughters of Erin when they used to come by thousands, would buy their railroad tickets, put them on trains and minister generally to their comfort on landing and on leaving for their destination wherever it might be in the United States. It now appears Mr. Mac-Donough was a poet all the time he was playing the rôle of immigrant escort. A poem by him called 'A Hosting at the Castle Gate' indicates what was on his mind when Ellis Islanders would see him tenderly pushing little immigrant children and babies from Erin onto railroad trains.

> When the witching-hour comes down the sky,
>   When the wind is cold and the moon rides low,
> And the tide comes in with a sob and sigh,
>   Like a mother burdened with care and woe;
> Oh, then, as in days of the long ago,
>   When clipper and brig brought over freight,
> They troop again in a ghostly show,
>   The Irish host at the Castle Gate."

He is represented in several anthologies of American and Irish verse. One of his more memorable poems appeared in 1939 when his lifelong friend, W. B. Yeats, died:

Bring Home the Poet

> *If I die here, bury me up there*
> *on the mountain [the mountain cemetery,*
> *Rocquebrune, France] and then after a*
> *year or so dig me up and bring me pri-*
> *vately to Sligo. William Butler Yeats.*

> Bring home the poet, laurel-crowned,
> Lay him to rest in Irish ground;
> Make him a grave near Sligo Bay,
> At fair Drumcliffe or Knocknarea,
> For near his mother's kindred dwelt,
> And at Drumcliffe his fathers knelt,
> And all about in beauty's haze,

The print of proud, heroic days,
With wind and wave in druid hymn
To chant for aye his requiem.
And he'll have mourners at his bier,
The fairy hosts who hold him dear,
And Father Gilligan, he'll be there,
The martial Maeve and Deirdre fair,
And lads he knew in town and glen,
The fisher folk and sailor men;
The Dooney fiddler and the throng
He made immortal with his song;
And proud in grief his rightful queen,
Ni Houlihan, the brave Kathleen.
Bring home the poet, let him rest
In the old land he loved the best.

One of the Irish girls Pat met upon her arrival in 1908 was Helen Healy. He married her a year later. She was his most valued editor. He never published prose or verse without her approval, and if she suggested a word or idea he would happily include it.

Because he was such a true scholar, Pat MacDonough enjoyed the challenge Regis High School offered his two less scholarly sons, Edward and Brian. Not only could he outrun them to catch the elusive Fifth Avenue bus but he never lost his love for Latin and Greek, and was amused by their complaints of the difficult Regis curriculum.

Never a gregarious character, he had many friendships with outstanding literary figures and countrymen. John Butler Yeats, the artist and father of the poet, was indeed a close friend. He would visit him in his room above the old Petti Pas restaurant and there sketched him in 1908. Oliver St. John Gogarty, John Quinn, Lindsay Crawford, Joseph and Henry Gavin, Michael O'Brien, and Francis Donnelly of the Society of Jesus were all his friends and contributors to *Old Castle Garden*.

His pen lost its creative touch after the death of his wife in 1939. He began working over the poems he had written earlier and putting them in order. He dedicated them to "The Irish Immigrant Girl," and, on some future day, they will appear in book form.

After his death in July 1960, Monsignor John Halpin, who knew him from the days of the Mission, remarked:

> "Pat was a poet and idealist but above all a spiritual and dedicated man from the Irish people. He spent his 89 years well and never lost his faith and glory in the genuine Irish character. He was a gentleman that anyone with Irish blood in his being can well be proud of, and gave us reason to live our lives for such ideals and never sell short the heritage that is ours. Pat once said that a dreamer lived forever and a toiler dies in a day. He meant that ideals never die and the ideal of this Irishman will never die in the memory of those who knew him. If you ever wished to meet one who was everything that an Irishman should embody, you should have met Pat MacDonough."

I am lucky—I am his daughter—

Mrs. Phillips is Marketing Director of Harper's Bazaar *magazine.*

Irish Roots, American Soil

JAMES PATRICK GANNON

The year 1977 will be remembered as the year of "Roots." Alex Haley's prize-winning novel, which was turned into a remarkable, eight-day television happening, managed to touch some latent yearning within millions of Americans. The experience tells us something important about America in the late twentieth century, decades after the great migration waves brought most of our ancestors to these shores.

For Black Americans, "Roots" had a special meaning and impact, bridging the great void that exists between that distant, misty existence as free men in Africa and the modern present, with the era of slavery in between. But "Roots" obviously stirred intense interest among white Americans, too, because its message is universal: to know yourself, you must know your heritage, that long chain of people and events which links you to some past and connects you to your offspring and the future.

Perhaps each of us comes away from a cultural event like "Roots" with a different meaning. For me, Alex Haley's work reinforced a belief that has grown gradually as I have searched for my own roots: that a man's sense of self—a sense of belonging and being somebody—is tied closely to some *place*, some corner of God's good earth, however big or small, which is home. Roots thrive only in the soil, and a man's sense of having roots is strongest and most comforting when there is a continuing connection with the soil, some piece of land that silently speaks the word "home."

As I muse upon my own roots, two scenes stand out in my memory.

The dark and brooding ruins of a Norman castle look down upon the village of Trim, in Ireland's County Meath. Crows circle its ancient tower, still standing tall after more than 750 years, as cows graze incongruously within the castle's walls. High in the rugged stone walls, two large windows peer open like eyes; they have seen my people, ages ago.

Thousands of miles away, in the valley of the Minnesota River, the rich black soil is carpeted by summer's green wealth of corn. The land rolls away from a big white farmhouse in waves of green, cut into neat squares by gravel country roads. It is an inexhaustibly rich land, inviting man's plow each spring and rewarding his labor each autumn with a recurring bounty that is more reliable and predictable than life itself.

The link between the two places is a man who came to know each as his home. The Norman castle was already 600 years old when Lawrence Gannon, my great-grandfather, was a boy in Trim. Perhaps he played within those walls, on that soil where I stood two years ago, watching the crows circle overhead. The scene in 1825 may not have been much different from what it was in 1975; such ancient ruins mock our sense of time, and mark 150 years as we might mark 15.

What drove the boy from Trim I do not know, nor what he left behind. The sketchy family records only show that he left Ireland around 1850, when the great outmigration caused by the potato famine was filling ships bound for America with thousands and thousands like him. Chances are, he left little behind. In those overpopulated days of Ireland's direst poverty, the common folk scratched out a grim subsistence on tiny plots of land, more often rented than owned.

Overpopulation and unemployment in Ireland at that time bred a national disaster. "Unless an Irish laborer could get hold of a patch of land and grow potatoes on which to feed himself and his children, the family starved," historian Cecil Woodham-Smith wrote in *The Great Hunger*, her masterful epic of the Irish famine of 1845-49. As she explained: "The consequence was the doom of Ireland. The land was divided and sub-divided, again and again, and holdings were split into smaller and still smaller fragments, until families were attempting to exist on plots of less than an acre, in some cases half-an-acre....as the population increased and the demand for a portion of ground grew more frantic, land became like gold in Ireland....the possession of a piece of land was literally the difference between life and death."

From this background of famine and land-hunger, Lawrence Gannon joined the stream of destitute Irish flowing to that vast promised land of America with its endless horizons of frontier territory, waiting to be populated. He landed in New York City and stayed for a time, but unlike the thousands of Irish immigrants who settled into urban poverty, the land-hunger stayed with him, and drove him West.

He had reached Ohio, according to family accounts, when he learned that land could be obtained from the Government in Minnesota for free, merely by settling there and staking a claim. An Irishman's impossible dream: free land. The year was 1855, this place called Minnesota wasn't even yet a state, and was said to be full of savage Indians. But free land! It was enough to lure many immigrants, not only Irish but Germans and Scandinavians too, despite the distance and the hardship. Lawrence Gannon, his wife Bridget and their New

York-born son John, aged four, headed for Minnesota.

The Minnesota River was a main highway to the west from St. Paul in those days, and it brought my great-grandfather to a village called Belle Plaine, Minnesota. A French trader had first established an outpost there in 1852, and within a few years, many Irish immigrants were settling in the area. Lawrence Gannon followed his countrymen and became one of the log-cabin pioneers in an area then known as "the big woods." With their sweat and their axes, those immigrants turned the big woods into open, fertile fields.

In the summer of 1976, I made my own journey down the Minnesota River—but on a four-lane highway that now runs parallel to it. With my twelve-year-old son, Michael, sharing my roots-search, I stopped to dig into old land records in the county courthouse at Shakopee. There, in musty deed-books that date back to pioneer days, Lawrence Gannon's impossible dream is recorded in the elegant script penmanship of that age.

The message fairly leapt out of the page at me: The United States of America grants unto Lawrence Gannon a tract of 160 Acres. "In testimony whereof, I, Abraham Lincoln, president of the United States, have caused these letters to be made patent, and the seal of the General Land Office to be hereunto affixed." The paper is dated June 1, 1861.

The decree is so official, so final. "Now know ye, that there is therefore granted by the United States unto the said Lawrence Gannon and to his heirs, the tract of land above described: to have and to hold the said tract of land with the appurtenances thereof, unto the said Lawrence Gannon and to his heirs and assigns, forever."

Forever.

It is a compelling word, one rarely used any more. In the mobile, transient, throw-away society which we live in, forever is a word that's becoming obsolete. No longer do marriages last forever; nor do jobs, nor friends, nor beliefs. Our culture encourages us to trade them all in, periodically, on a new model: a new job, a new wife, a new home town. The past is disposable; the future is prefabricated. Nothing lasts forever.

Yet there it was, in black and white, in the official records: Lawrence Gannon and his heirs were granted this land, forever. But it was not to be.

Just six months after Abraham Lincoln was assassinated, as the nation began to bind up its Civil War wounds, Lawrence Gannon died. The year was 1865, and each of his two young sons, John, and Christopher, who was my grandfather, inherited half a dream: 80 acres each. But Christopher's life was cut short; in 1890, at the age of 33, he contracted typhoid fever and died, leaving his widow Mary and two babies, including a one-year-old boy named Lawrence Patrick, my father.

I think the saddest family record I own is a folded, yellowed handbill, carefully preserved through the years by my father's sister Agnes. The handbill reads as follows:

PUBLIC SALE!

The Subscriber Will Sell At Auction on
Thursday, Oct. 23d, 1890,
At her Residence, 6 Miles South-east of the Borough
of Belle Plaine, Commencing at 10 O'Clock A.M.
The Following Described Property:

"One pair of working horses, two colts, 5 calves, four milch cows, one 2-year old Heifer, one yearling bull, a lot of spring pigs, a new McCormick binder, a new two-seated buggy, two wagons, one drag, one seeder, one hay rake, one cultivator, one corn plow, and numerous other articles. J.B. Fitzsimmons, Auctioneer."

At the bottom of the handbill is the name of Mrs. Chris. Gannon, my grandmother.

The harvest was in; the Irish immigrant's son was buried; the impossible dream was dead. Forever was over.

The widow left the land, taking her two babies to the town of Belle Plaine, then later moving to the city of Minneapolis. Under law, the land passed to the two children, but it couldn't be sold legally until they became adults. Life had to go on, however, and two children cannot run a farm, so it was rented by their mother until it could be sold. The old volumes in the County Courthouse yield the last chapter: a deed dated Dec. 31, 1910, recording the sale of the Gannon land to one Joseph Koenig, for the sum of $5,500.

I wondered what had happened to that farm in the 65 years since that deed was recorded, so I drove down that dusty gravel road, six miles southeast of the village of Belle Plaine, just as that 1890 handbill had advised. The sun was shining, the July corn was tall, and the green countryside was heavy with the promise of another full harvest.

I found a mailbox bearing the name Koenig, and drove up the driveway to a large white farmhouse shaded by old, sheltering trees. Lawrence Koenig, a husky farmer in his mid-forties, greeted me with the wariness that strangers wandering in the countryside expect and deserve. But his suspicion turned to hospitality after I displayed a copy of the 1910 deed, showing the land passing from my family to his.

"Joseph Koenig—that was my grandfather," he said.

"Mary Gannon—that was my grandmother," I replied.

He welcomed me into his kitchen. We exchanged family stories, and Mr. Koenig hauled out a big tin safebox containing a wealth of old documents about the farm, some of which passed with the land from my family to his. Among the papers was a probate court's final decree in the estate of Christopher Gannon, dated Oct. 2, 1891. It showed that the Irish immigrant's son left his heirs the grand sum of $684.83 in cash. The money was divided three ways, among the two children and widow, with each granted $228.27.

Lawrence Koenig, the third generation of his family to farm my great-grandfather's homestead, introduced me to his four sons. He is sure they will carry on for another generation. I wished them well and left, departing with some envy for that land, but with satisfaction that a family has its roots firmly in that soil first tilled by the man from County Meath.

And I understand now, though I did not understand in my youth, why my father felt an attachment to that Minnesota River valley. He visited there often, sometimes tending to the graves of his grandfather Lawrence and his father Christopher, whom he never knew.

All his life, my father had in his blood that Irish land-hunger. As a Minneapolis grain merchant, he spent most of his working life traveling the rural backwaters of Minnesota and the Dakotas, drumming up business for his grain firm from country elevators and farmers. He bought some farm land in South Dakota, raised cattle as an absentee gentleman farmer, and made some money. It was an outlet for his land-hunger, but more a business deal than a permanent attachment. Family roots do not grow in commercial soil.

That is all past now, and a third-generation Irish-American like myself can ponder the irony of our times: that land ownership once again has become an impossible dream for most of us. Victims of inflation, captives of urban living, slaves to America's mobile culture, we are land-poor again. Despite America's vast open spaces, the land where we live and work—in our major urban centers—has been divided and subdivided into tiny plots. We are not potato-famine poor, but our plastic credit-card wealth is as disconnected from the land as was the evicted tenant farmer.

And that is why I believe Alex Haley's story of "Roots" struck into our hearts. We know we are rootless descendants of immigrants who hungered for America's land and sacrificed mightily to settle it. We have left the land and huddled together in sprawling cities like so many newly-arrived immigrants. This strange reversal of history's tide has left us, I believe, with a void where our sense of roots should be.

I am enough of an Irish dreamer to conjure up visions of a day when my family will be reconnected to the land. It is perhaps a romantic notion, but then the Irish have thrived on such always. It could happen. And it could last. Forever.

Mr. Gannon is a reporter in the Washington Bureau of The Wall Street Journal.

N. Y. S. P.

WILLIAM G. CONNELIE

The law which established a state police force in New York prohibits the use of troopers "within the limits of any city to suppress rioting and disorder except by the direction of the Governor or upon the request of the Mayor of the city with the approval of the Governor."

On March 17th, 1976, there were no riots nor any disorders of great consequence in New York City when a grey-clad contingent of troopers formed into ranks at 45th Street in Manhattan. They had come from every section of the state not to enforce the law but to represent the New York State Police—for the first time in its sixty-year history—in the St. Patrick's Day Parade.

When the group swung out onto Fifth Avenue to begin their proud march up to 86th Street, the crowd of spectators reacted warmly to their military appearance and bearing. All along the parade route, the children and adults lining the avenue seemed to catch the spirit of these men and women—a pride in self and pride of organization which was particularly evident that day as they marched behind their color guard.

As the contingent passed the home of the American Irish Historical Society, the leader of the group saluted the members of the Society who were reviewing the parade from the balcony. Few spectators were aware of the special bond that exists between these two great organizations.

How could they know that this organization, the Division of New York State Police, like so many other famous law enforcement agencies, had its roots in Ireland?

Local government in Ireland was the traditional preserve of the landlords whose economic power was reinforced by their positions as justices of the peace. The administration of justice varied greatly, and the police powers of the local authorities were often abused. In some areas the rule of "Captain Moonlight" or some other embodiment of the ubiquitous secret societies held sway, while in others the landlord ruled with absolute authority. In the aftermath of an upheaval such as the Rising of '98, the local authorities could use their powers to exact a terrible revenge, designed to intimidate the peasantry.

Under the Chief Secretaryship of Robert Peel the first steps were taken to provide Ireland with an effective central government. Peel was no friend of Irish national aspirations but neither was he a puppet of the Protestant Ascendancy. He tried to make the government of Ireland efficient, honest and, if not representative, at least impartial. One important step in this direction was the creation of the Royal Irish Constabulary in 1819.

Based on a quasi-military model, using military discipline and organization, the R. I. C. was a national police force that executed the law apart from, purely local interests. Its members wore military type uniforms and bore arms, an innovation for police forces. The "Peelers", as they were popularly known, gave Ireland a measure of honest police administration it had not formerly known. They were the model for the London Metropolitan Police, "the Bobbies," also nicknamed after Peel, formed while he was the Home Secretary in 1829.

During the formation of the Canadian Confederation, faced with the problems of frontier life and a disturbed political situation, the cental government was painfully aware of the need for a disciplined and cohesive police force. The authorities turned to the successful model of the Royal Irish Constabulary, and in 1873 the Royal Canadian Mounted Police were brought into existence. Patrolling an immense territory—in many cases as practically the sole representative of the King's Law—they adapted the basic structure of the R. I. C. to their own situation.

Shortly thereafter, the similar requirements of the Texas Territory brought Sir Robert's principles to the United States. The Texas Rangers, like the Mounties, adapted the structure of the R. I. C. to their own special needs and played a famous role in bringing law and order west of the Pecos.

Some thirty years passed before the first orthodox State Police organization was formed. About this time, in Pennsylvania's anthracite region, the "Molly Maguires," a secret society with roots in Ireland, exerted its power. This organization, composed mostly of Irish immigrants, was formed to combat a double menace: the exploitation of the miners by the coal barons and the discrimination against the Irish on the part of the earlier settlers in the region—the Welsh and English— who sought to exclude the later arriving immigrants from the right to earn a living in the mines. The "Mollies" resented their economic lot and were particularly determined to undermine the power of the coal companies and their bosses. Unfortunately, their tactics included intimidation, terror and sometimes murder. Their power was so absolute and pervasive in some regions that local police forces were rendered powerless. An agency not subject to local pressures was needed to combat this organization and the Pennsylvania State Police was born. Its charter, providing for the appointment of a Superintendent responsible only to the Governor, was the model for all future State Police organizations. Its first Superintendent went to Ireland, studied the organization and procedures of the Royal Irish Constabulary and incorporated many of them into this new organization.

In New York, the coming of the automotive age and the improvement of roads at the beginning of this century made previously remote areas more accessible. It also left them vulnerable to increased criminal attacks which local authorities were often ill-equipped to handle.

While the growing public agitation for a State Police organization would have made its formation inevitable in time, the catalyst for its creation was the murder of Sam Howell on a Saturday morning in 1913 and the effect it had on two women, the Misses M. Moyca Newell and Katherine Mayo.

Howell, foreman of the construction crew building a home for Miss Newell at Bedford Hills in Westchester County, was ambushed by four men as he approached the property on motorcycle with the payroll for the carpenters. Riddled by bullets, he nevertheless continued to the construction site, delivered the payroll and, before he lost consciousness, identified two of the gunmen as men he had hired. Three days later he died.

The two women were witnesses to the inertia of the local sheriff and of the village constable who was called to the scene from his grocery store in Katonah. The four assailants had retired to an islet of woods, surrounded by open fields, practically on the scene of the crime, but no attempt was made to arrest them or to bar their escape. None of the bandits was ever captured.

Resolved to do something about this deplorable lack of law enforcement, the women launched a campaign for a State constabulary that would bring to rural areas police protection equal to that afforded city dwellers. Their efforts led to the formation of the "Committee for a State Police," an alliance of farmers and suburbanites which carried the fight to the Legislature. Miss Mayo, meanwhile, had journeyed to Pennsylvania to study the State Police there and set down her findings in a book, "Justice for All," which became a valuable propaganda weapon.

On April 11th, 1917, Governor Whitman, a former New York County District Attorney, signed into law a bill establishing the New York State Police as a rural police force. George Chandler, a physician and military man, was named by the Governor as its first Superintendent. Chandler, following the tradition of the Royal Irish Constabulary, recruited his first candidates from the military. He personally supervised the selection process as described in his book, "Dawn Days of the State Police":

> We held the first examination in the Assembly Chamber in the Capitol. About two thousand applicants appeared and nearly swamped us. We gave those that were examined a practical examination: Stripped them, looked them over well for physical defects; had them write a 200 word letter about their trip to Albany—or about some important happening in their

800

lives, so that I could ascertain whether they could write legibly, were able to express themselves, and had some imagination; following this, a three minute psychological test—on a printed sheet of paper; then a memory test, where thirty different objects were placed upon a table . . . and after a three minute study, if any of the candidates could not write down twenty of these objects, he was out. A few practical questions about a horse and his care concluded the examination.

The new recruits were formed into troops— hence, the designation Troopers. Inspector Cornelius Calhane of the New York City Police Department was chosen to supervise their training. From the beginning Chandler himself provided any necessary medical care for the men.

Obviously, some of these early methods are now outmoded, but Chandler's personal view of the trooper's role, expressed in his Bulletin No. 1, is as valid today as then:

A physician aims to save life and cure disease; a lawyer helps people out of trouble; a clergyman tries to make people better; a soldier fights for his country in time of war. These are fine professions, all of them. They are professions of service. The service a state trooper renders to his community is an auxiliary to all of these and his duty in a measure embraces the work of these four great professions. . . . Go about with the idea of helpfulness and a friendliness that wins the confidence of the people. Never permit a child to be afraid of you. Never hesitate to render assistance of any kind. . . . Remember that you represent the authority of the Governor, that you are an executive officer and a state official. Be proud of it, live up to it.

Since that first Superintendent, until the present, six other men have espoused that philosophy in commanding the State Police. They bore the names Warner, Gaffney, McGarvey, Johnson, Cornelius and Kirwan, all of whom, like the organization they commanded, had roots in Ireland.

The scope of State Police activities has grown dramatically over the years. Today, its sphere stretches from the most isolated farm road to the inner structure of organized crime. Many New York City residents, who are used to seeing Troopers only on the Thruway—and, for the last four years in their St. Patrick's Day Parade—are unaware of the many other facets of their work.

The State Police still supply patrol to the rural areas of the state but, in addition, their expertise as one of the finest detective organizations in the world is offered to those areas of the state capable of patrol but not of sustained sophisticated investigations. The Division is also responsible for administering the communication links that tie together all law enforcement agencies in the state and the nation through a computerized teletype system. Forensic laboratory services for both police and medical examiners are offered to all but a few major cities in the state. The work of Troopers in issuing over one-half million summonses in 1977 not only helped in saving 472 lives otherwise lost in traffic deaths but succeeded in having our state declared number one in the nation in compliance with the 55 m.p.h. law by the National Highway Safety Administration.

Despite their deserved reputation for courteous service to the public, State Policemen effected over 40,000 criminal law arrests this past year, thus performing the ultimate service to the community by bringing before the bar of justice those who would disrupt the peace and tranquility of the community by violating its standards.

Over sixty years of devoted service by a dedicated procession of men and women has written a brilliant chapter in the history of our state and assures a glowing future on behalf of its citizens.

If the spectators that lined the route of march realized their accomplishments, they would understand why these men and women in grey are such a proud group and why they radiate that pride in self and in organization. They know what their roots are, they know what is expected of them: nothing less than their best effort; and what their mandate is: supplying courteous, efficient service to the public. They have a reason to march proudly.

Bill Connelie is the Superintendent of the New York State Police.

The Descendants
of the High Kings
# of Ireland

*This final selection is an excerpt from an address by the
President-General at our Annual Banquet.*

KEVIN M. CAHILL, M.D.

When I was a young boy, my father filled the house with tales
of Irish heroes. Since the Cahills are direct descendants of the
High Kings of Ireland, there was, naturally enough, a modest
emphasis on our own genetic strain. In all fairness, I should
note that the land of our forebears was blessed with an inordinate number of High Kings; the rest of the population
were saints, scholars, poets, and patriots, although there was
constant argument as to who belonged in the latter group.

After a series of reverses, the Court of the Cahill royal line
moved from some misty mound in Ireland to a picturesque
area just off Fordham Road in the Bronx. There, in cold
water apartments, affectionately known as the Kerry flats,
were the heroes we were taught to admire. There was nothing mythical about them—they were Irish immigrants.

I could never quite distinguish between the blood relatives
and the boat relatives, those who had shared the common
bond of surviving together the trail to Ellis Island. To a

youngster, these heroes were sometimes overwhelming—they certainly, on occasion, drank too much and fought—mostly with words—and struggled, usually unsuccessfully, to shed the past too quickly. But far more impressive was how deeply they loved the clan, and they were loyal almost to a fault. There was nothing subtle about their dreams—they had come to this land so that their children could enjoy a better life. These American-Irish heroes did not leave the soft, gentle Ireland celebrated in song. The wealthy land-owner and the city gentleman did not leave—our ancestors were the survivors of oppression and famine, those desperate enough to seek refuge in steerage. But when their spirit burst forth upon this great land of the United States, they and the nation prospered.

They gave a strength to America that still nourishes her. The broad backs of the Irish laborers opened this nation's frontiers, built her railroads, dug her tunnels, and policed her streets. They were hod carriers and longshoremen, plumbers, painters, and policemen.

The ability to compromise was not a quality of the Irish immigrant woman. If she started as a domestic servant, it took only a generation to find Irish beauty in the front parlor, and, by God, anyone who knows the Irish woman knows she made it there on her own terms. With few publicized exceptions, the journey from poverty to security was not linked with lace curtains but with hard work, humor, a deep faith, and an almost unreasonable optimism in the future of the United States.

Yes, we have known loneliness and coldness and rejection, and those scars are just beneath the surface of most of us. The genes of our immigrant ancestors have left us a sensitive lot, easily moved to joy and sadness, maybe too easily hurt—too often by our own—but with a resiliency that permits us to overcome almost any obstacle, or at least adapt it to our own ends.

Dr. Cahill is President-General of the Society.

INDEX OF AUTHORS